THE CJ SOLUTION

Every 4LTR Press solution includes:

Heading Numbers Connect Print & eBook

Visually Engaging Textbook

Online Study Tools

Tear-out Review Cards

Interactive eBook

STUDENT RESOURCES:

- Interactive eBook
- Auto-Graded Quizzes
- Flashcards
- Beat the Clock
- Animations
- Learning Modules
- Review Cards

Students sign in at **www.cengagebrain.com**

INSTRUCTOR RESOURCES:

- All Student Resources
- Engagement Tracker
- First Day of Class Instructions
- LMS Integration
- Instructor's Manual
- Online Lesson Plans
- Test Bank
- PowerPoint® Slides
- Instructor Prep Cards

Instructors sign in at **www.cengage.com/login**

"Like a good recipe, you simply can't alter things that are already great. Love this layout and the study tools provided online are fantastic!"

– **Amanda Brenek**, Student, *The University of Texas at San Antonio*

JULY 2010

4LTR Press adds eBooks in response to a 10% uptick in digital learning preferences.

Engagement Tracker launches, giving faculty a window into student usage of digital tools.

1 out of every 3 (1,400) schools has adopted a 4LTR Press solution.

AUGUST 2010

750,000 students are IN.

NOVEMBER 2010

Third party research confirms that 4LTR Press digital solutions improve retention and outcomes.

 **CourseMate**
Students access the 4LTR Press website at 4x's the industry average.

60 unique solutions across multiple course areas validate the 4LTR Press concept.

IN 2011

1 out of every 2 (2,000) schools has a 4LTR Press adoption.

APRIL 2011

2,000

IN 2011

Over 1 million students are IN.

We're always evolving. Join the 4LTR Press In-Crowd on Facebook at www.facebook.com/4ltrpress

AUGUST 2011

2013 AND BEYOND

CENGAGE
Learning®

CJ3
Larry K. Gaines and **Roger LeRoy Miller**

Senior Vice President, Global Product Management Higher Education: Jack W. Calhoun

Vice President and General Manager, Social Sciences & Qualitative Business: Erin Joyner

Product Director, 4LTR Press: Steve Joos

Senior Product Manager: Carolyn Henderson Meier

Product Assistant: Audrey Espey

Content Coordinator: Casey Lozier

Media Developer: Andy Yap

Sr. Content Digitization Project Manager: Lezlie Light

Senior Marketing Manager: Kara Kindstrom

Market Development Manager: Angeline Low

Production Manager: Brenda Ginty

Manufacturing Planner: Judy Inouye

Sr. Content Project Manager: Ann Borman

Rights Acquisition Specialist: Dean Dauphinais

Sr. Rights Acquisition Director: Robert Kauser

Art Director, Interior and Cover Design: Brenda Carmichael, PreMedia Global

Copyeditor: Jeanne Yost

Proofreader: Pat Lewis

Indexer: Terry Casey

Compositor: Parkwood Composition Service

Cover Images: justice statue: ER_09/Shutterstock; judge: Fuse/Getty Images; bailiff: Fuse/Getty Images; female CSI: Anthony Ladd/Getty Images; police officer: Luiz Fellipe Castro/Getty Images

Design image credits: Torn paper: stockcam/Getty Images; CJ & Tech background: Alila Medical Media/Shutterstock; Social media icon: Natchapon L./Shutterstock

For product information and technology assistance, contact us at
Cengage Learning Customer & Sales Support
1-800-354-9706
For permission to use material from this text or product,
submit all requests online at
www.cengage.com/permissions.
Further permissions questions can be e-mailed to
permissionrequest@cengage.com.

Library of Congress Control Number: 2013949592

ISBN-13: 978-1-285-46048-2

Cengage Learning
200 First Stamford Place, 4th Floor
Stamford, CT 06902
USA

Cengage Learning is a leading provider of customized learning solutions with office locations around the globe, including Singapore, the United Kingdom, Australia, Mexico, Brazil, and Japan. Locate your local office at: **www.cengage.com/global**.

Cengage Learning products are represented in Canada by Nelson Education, Ltd.

To learn more about Cengage Learning, visit **www.cengage.com**.

Purchase any of our products at your local college store or at our preferred online store **www.cengagebrain.com**.

Printed in the United States of America
3 4 5 6 7 17 16 15 14

Mandel Ngan/AFP/Getty Images

PART TWO
THE POLICE AND LAW ENFORCEMENT

4
LAW ENFORCEMENT TODAY 72
What's Going On? 73

5
PROBLEMS AND SOLUTIONS IN MODERN POLICING 94
Justified? 95

6
POLICE AND THE CONSTITUTION: THE RULES OF LAW ENFORCEMENT 116

What's That Smell? 117

PART THREE
CRIMINAL COURTS

7
COURTS AND THE QUEST FOR JUSTICE 138

Dark Honeymoon 139

AP Photo/Lawrence Jackson, File

AP Photo/Virginia Department of Corrections

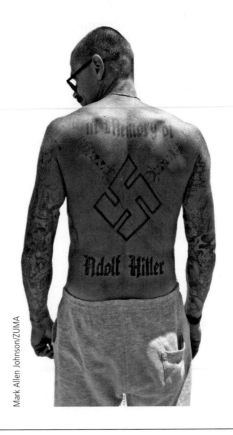

Mark Allen Johnson/ZUMA

PART FIVE
SPECIAL ISSUES

13
THE JUVENILE JUSTICE SYSTEM 278

Bloody Sunday 279

AP Photo/Mark Duncan

14
TODAY'S CHALLENGES IN CRIMINAL JUSTICE 302

Bad Day at Sandy Hook 303

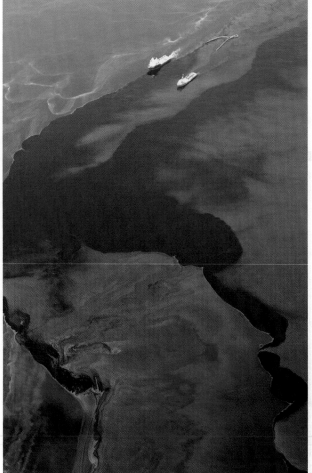

Ted Jackson/*The Times-Picayune*/Landov

SKILL PREP

A STUDY SKILLS MODULE

what's inside

After reading through and practicing the material in this study skills module, you will be better prepared to . . .

- **Make good choices**
  (Life Prep, p. xiii)

- **Manage your time**
  (Time Prep, p. xv)

- **Be engaged in your studies**
  (Study Prep, p. xvii)

- **Study for quizzes and exams**
  (Test Prep, p. xxi)

- **Read your textbook for learning**
  (Read Prep, p. xxiii)

- **Write your papers**
  (Write Prep, p. xxv)

René Mansi/iStockphoto.com

WELCOME!

With this course and this text- book, you've begun what we hope will be a fun, stimulating, and thought- provoking journey into the world of criminal justice. In this course, you will lean all the basics about crime, law enforcement, the court system, corrections, and other special issues like justice for juveniles, homeland security, and cyber crime. Knowledge of these basics will get you well on your way for a great future in criminal justice.

To help you get the most from this course, and this textbook, we have developed this study skills module. Perhaps you're a recent high school graduate now moving on to college. Maybe you're a working professional continuing your education. Maybe you've been away from school for a few years and you're making your way back to the classroom. **Whatever type of student you are, what you want most when you study is RESULTS.** You want to understand the issues and ideas presented in the textbook, to talk about them intelligently during class and discussions, and to remember them as you prepare for exams and papers.

This study skills module is designed to help you develop the skills and habits you'll need to get the results that you want from this course. With tips on lifestyle decisions, how to manage your time more effectively, how to be more engaged when you study, how to get the most out of your textbook, how to prepare for quizzes and exams, and how to write papers, this guide will help you develop the skills you need to be the best learner you can be!

life PREP

It takes several things to succeed in a class—hard work, concentration, and commitment to your studies. In order to work hard, concentrate, and demonstrate commitment, you need energy. When you are full of energy, time seems to pass quickly, and it is easier to get things done. When you don't have energy, time feels as if it is standing still, and even your favorite activities can feel like a burden. To have the energy you need to be a great learner, it is important to make good lifestyle choices. You need to get enough sleep, eat well, take care of yourself, and maintain good relationships. An important part of being a successful student is to pay attention to what goes on in your life so that you have all the ingredients you need to maintain your focus and energy.

Here are some suggestions that you can use to keep up your energy so that you can succeed in everything you do.

- **Take care of your health.** It is crucial that you eat a balanced diet, exercise regularly, and get enough sleep. If you don't take care of your physical well-being, other areas of your life will inevitably suffer.

- **Become a good listener.** Hearing is not the same thing as listening. We often hear what we want to hear as we filter information through our own experiences and interests. When talking with friends, instructors, or family members, focus carefully on what they say—it may reveal something unexpected.

MOST PEOPLE WHO **succeed** HAVE A **plan**.

- **Be very careful about what you tweet or post on the Internet.** A good rule of thumb is "Don't post anything that you wouldn't want the world to know." Many employers search the Internet for information concerning potential employees, and one embarrassing photo or tweet can have long-term damaging consequences.

- **Make a plan for success.** Do you have a life plan? If not, you can start by making a list of your lifetime goals, even though they may change later on. You can also create a career plan that includes a list of skills you will need to succeed. Then, choose classes and extracurricular activities that will help you develop these skills.

- **Learn to welcome feedback.** When we start doing something new, whether in school or in other areas of life, we usually aren't very good at it. We need feedback from those who are good in that area—such as instructors—to improve and succeed. Therefore, you should welcome feedback, and if it isn't given, you should ask for it.

- **Exercise for your body and your mind.** A study at Naperville Central High School, in Naperville, Illinois, showed that students who participated in a morning gym class performed significantly better on math and reading standardized tests than those who did not. So take a little time to exercise each day—it'll help you feel great and it'll make you a better learner. (Vanessa Richardson, "A Fit Body Means a Fit Mind," *Edutopia,* May 27, 2009, www.edutopia.org/exercise-fitness-brain-benefits-learning).

- **Become a better writer.** Your college or university probably has a writing center with resources to help you with your writing assignments. If not, find a tutor who will help you figure out what you are trying to communicate and how to put it effectively on paper.

- **Organize your finances.** First, label file folders for different categories of income, such as paycheck stubs, bank statements, and miscellaneous. Then, do the same for expenses, such as clothes, food, and entertainment. If you find you need another category, just set up a new folder.

- **Become a better public speaker.** Consider using your campus's audiovisual resources to develop this difficult but rewarding skill. Record yourself speaking and then critique your performance. Join a school organization such as a debate or drama club to gain confidence in front of a live audience.

- **Nurture your independence.** For example, learn how to cook for yourself. Get a job that does not interfere (too much) with your schoolwork. Save money and pay your own bills. Rent your own living space. Most important, have confidence in yourself.

- **Learn to be flexible.** More often than not, in school and life, things do not go as planned. When this happens, you need to be flexible. Don't focus on your disappointment. Instead, try to accept the situation as it is, and deal with it by looking at the future rather than dwelling on the past.

- **Be thankful for the people who care about you.** Your family and good friends are a precious resource. When you have problems, don't try to solve them by yourself. Talk to the people in your life who want you to succeed and be happy, and listen to their advice.

- **Don't jump to conclusions.** Critical thinking is a crucial skill that only gets better with practice. Whether you are considering a friend's argument, a test question, a major purchase, or a personal problem, carefully weigh the evidence, balance strengths and weaknesses, and make a reasoned decision.

- **Trust yourself.** Rather than constantly seeking approval from others, try to seek approval from the person who matters the most—yourself. If you have good values, then your conscience will tell you when you are doing the right thing. Don't let worries about what others think run, or ruin, your life.

If you don't take care of your **physical well-being**, other areas of your life will inevitably suffer.

"Twenty years from now you will be more disappointed by the things that you didn't do than by the ones you did. So throw off the bowlines. Sail away from the safe harbor. Catch the trade winds in your sails. Explore. Dream. Discover."

Mark Twain
(American author, 1835–1910)

time PREP

Skip Odonnell/iStockphoto.com

Taking a college-level course involves a lot of work. You have to go to class, read the textbook, pay attention to lectures, take notes, complete homework assignments, write papers, and take exams. On top of that, there are other areas of your life that call for your time and attention. You have to take care of where you live, run daily errands, take care of family, spend time with friends, work a full- or part-time job, and find time to unwind. With all that you're involved in, knowing how to manage your time is critical if you want to succeed as a learner.

The key to managing your time is to know how much time you have and to use it well. At the beginning of every term, you should evaluate how you use your time. Keep a record of what you do hour by hour for a full week. Once you see where all your time goes, you can decide which activities you might modify in order to have "more" time.

To manage your time well, you need to know where it is going.

Here are some other helpful tips on how to make the most of your time.

- **Plan your study schedule in advance.** At the beginning of each week, allocate time for each subject that you need to study. If it helps, put your schedule down on paper or use one of the many calendar apps for efficient daily planning.

- **Don't be late for classes, meetings with professors, and other appointments.** If you find that you have trouble being on time, adjust your planning to arrive fifteen minutes early to all engagements. That way, even if you are "late," in most cases you will still be on time.

- **Avoid Internet time-wasters.** When doing research online, start with a clear idea of your task.

Paul IJsendoorn/iStockphoto.com

Use a trusted search engine and focus only on that subject. Do not allow yourself to be sidetracked by other activities such as checking e-mail or social networking.

- **Stay on track.** Set aside a little time each day to assess whether you are going to meet the deadlines for all of your classes—quizzes, papers, and exams. It is critical to ensure that deadlines don't "sneak up" on you. Use a calendar program or app, which can help you keep track of target dates and even give you friendly reminders.

- **Save often and back up all of your important files periodically.** Nothing wastes more time—or is more aggravating—than having to redo schoolwork that was somehow lost on your computer. You can copy files onto an external drive or use one of the many cloud storage options.

Concentrate on doing **one thing** at a time.

- **Do one thing at a time.** Multitasking is often a trap that leads you to do several things quickly but poorly. When you are studying, don't carry on a text conversation with a friend or have one eye on the Internet at the same time.

- **Set deadlines for yourself,** not only with schoolwork but also with responsibilities in other areas of your life. If you tell yourself, "I will have this task done by Monday at noon and that other task finished before dinner on Wednesday," you will find it much easier to balance the many demands on your time.

- **Ignore your phone.** Constantly checking texts and tweets not only interrupts the task at hand, but also is an easy excuse for procrastination. Set aside specific times of the day to check and answer messages, and, when necessary, make sure that your cell phone is off or out of reach.

- **Break down large tasks.** A large assignment due several weeks away can seem overwelming, making it easy to put off. Instead of procrastinating, break it into a series of small tasks. Then, make a list of the tasks, and as you finish each one, give yourself the satisfaction of crossing it off.

- **Study during your peak times.** Many of us have a particular time of day when we are most alert—early morning, afternoon, or night. Plan to do schoolwork during that time, when you will be most efficient, and set aside other times of the day for activities that do not require such serious concentration.

- **Learn to say "no."** We may have a hard time refusing when others ask for favors that take up our time. Sometimes, though, unless the person is experiencing a real emergency, you have to put your schoolwork or job first.

- **Slow down.** You may think that you are getting more work done by rushing, but haste inevitably leads to poor decisions, mistakes, and errors of judgment, all of which waste time. Work well, not quickly, and you will wind up saving time.

- **If you can, outsource!** Give someone else some of your responsibilities. If you can afford to, hire someone to clean your house. Send your dirty clothes to a laundry. If money is tight, split chores with friends or housemates so that you can better manage your work-life responsibilities.

- **Bundle activities.** In marketing, *to bundle* means to combine several products in one. In time management, it means combining two activities to free up some time. For example, if you need to exercise and want to socialize, bundle the two activities by going on a jog with your friends. Take along some schoolwork when you head to the laundromat—you can get a lot done while you're waiting for the spin cycle. Or, you can record class lectures (ask the professor for permission) so that you can review class material while you're out running errands.

Paul Ijsendoorn/iStockphoto.com

- **Set time limits for tasks, both in and out of school.** You will find that with a time limit in mind, you will waste less time and work more efficiently.

- **Use reminders.** Even the best time management and organization can be waylaid by forgetfulness. Many free calendar apps will send alerts to your phone or desktop calendar to remind you of assignments, tests, and other important dates.

- **Take the first step.** A Chinese adage goes, "The longest journey starts with a single step." If you are having trouble getting started on a project or assignment, identify the first task that needs to be done. Then do it! This helps avoid time-wasting procrastination.

Bundling, or combining two activities, will help you save time.

Rubberball/iStockphoto.com

study PREP

What does it take to be a successful student? Like many people, you may think that success depends on how naturally smart you are, that some people are just better at school than others. But in reality, successful students aren't born, they're made. What this means is that even if you don't consider yourself naturally "book smart," you can do well in this course by developing study skills that will help you understand, remember, and apply key concepts.

There are five things you can do to develop good study habits:

> be engaged
> ask questions
> take notes
> make an outline
> mark your text

BE ENGAGED

If you've ever heard elevator music, you know what easy listening is like—it stays in the background. You know it's there, but you're not really paying attention to it, and you probably won't remember it after a few minutes. That is not what you should be doing in class. You have to be engaged. Being engaged means listening to discover (and remember) something. In other words, listening is more than just hearing. Not only do you have to hear what the professor is saying in class, you have to pay attention to it. And as you listen with attention, you will hear what your instructor believes is important. One way to make sure that you are listening attentively is to take notes. Doing so will help you focus on the professor's words and will help you identify the most important parts of the lecture.

ASK QUESTIONS

If you are really engaged in your criminal justice course, you will ask a question or two whenever you do not understand something. You can also ask a question to get your instructor to share her or his opinion on a subject. However you do it, true engagement requires you to be a participant in your class. The more you participate, the more you will learn (and the more your instructor will know who you are!).

TAKE NOTES

Note-taking has a value in and of itself, just as outlining does. The physical act of writing makes you a more efficient learner. In addition, your notes provide a guide to what your instructor thinks is important. That means you will have a better idea of what to study before the next exam if you have a set of notes that you took during class.

MAKE AN OUTLINE

As you read through each chapter of your textbook, you might want to make an outline—a simple method for organizing information. You can create an outline as part of your reading or at the end of your reading. Or you can make an outline when you reread a section before moving on to the next. The act of physically writing an outline for a chapter will help you retain the material in this text and master it, thereby obtaining a higher grade in class. Even if you make an outline that is no more than the headings in this text, you will be studying more efficiently than you would be otherwise.

To make an effective outline, you have to be selective. Outlines that contain all the information in the text are not very useful. Your objectives in outlining are, first, to identify the main concepts and, then, to add the details that support those main concepts.

Your outline should consist of several levels written in a standard format. The most important concepts are assigned Roman numerals; the second most important, capital letters; the third most important, numbers; and the fourth

SV-Art/iStockphoto.com

iStockphoto.com

most important, lowercase letters. Here is a quick example:

> I. What Is The Criminal Justice System?
>   A. The Purpose of the Criminal Justice System
>   1. Controlling and Preventing Crime
>   2. Maintaining Justice
>   B. The Structure of the Criminal Justice System
>   1. Law Enforcement
>   a. Local and County Law Enforcement
>   b. State Law Enforcement
>   c. Federal Law Enforcement
>   2. The Courts
>   3. Corrections
>   C. The Criminal Justice Process
>   1. The Assembly Line
>   2. The Formal Criminal Justice Process
>   3. The Informal Criminal Justice Process
>   a. Discretionary Basics
>   b. Discretionary Values
>   c. The "Wedding Cake" Model of Criminal Justice

MARK YOUR TEXT

Now that you own your own textbook for this course, you can greatly improve your learning by marking your text. By doing so, you will identify the most important concepts of each chapter, and at the same time, you'll be making a handy study guide for reviewing material at a later time.

Different Ways of Marking The most commonly used form of marking is to underline important points. The second most commonly used method is to use a felt-tipped highlighter, or marker, in yellow or some other transparent color. Marking also includes circling, numbering, using arrows, jotting brief notes, or any other method that allows you to remember things when you go back to skim the pages in your textbook prior to an exam.

IMPORTANT

Why Marking Is Important Marking is important for the same reason that outlining is—it helps you to organize the information in the text. It allows you to become an active participant in the mastery of the material. Researchers have shown that the physical act of marking, just like the physical acts of note-taking during class and outlining, helps you better retain the material. The better the material is organized in your mind, the more you'll remember. There are two types of readers—passive and active. The active reader outlines or marks. Active readers typically do better on exams. Perhaps one of the reasons that active readers retain more than passive readers is because the physical act of outlining and/or marking requires greater concentration. It is through greater concentration that more is remembered.

Two Points to Remember When Marking

Read one section at a time before you do any extensive marking. You can't mark a section until you know what is important, and you can't know what is important until you read the whole section.

Don't overmark. Just as an outline cannot contain everything that is in a text (or, with respect to note-taking, in a lecture), marking can't be of the whole book. Don't fool yourself into thinking that you have done a good job just because each page is filled up with arrows, asterisks, circles, and underlines. If you do mark the whole book, when you go back to review the material, your markings will not help you remember what was important.

Take a look at the two paragraphs below:

Parole, a conditional release, is the most common form of prison release. About two-thirds of all inmates who leave incarceration do so under the supervision of a parole officer. The remaining one-third are subject to various other release mechanisms. Prisoners receive an unconditional release when they have completed the terms of their sentence and no longer require incarceration or supervision. One form of unconditional release is mandatory release (also known as "maxing out"), which occurs when an inmate has served the maximum amount of time on the initial sentence, minus reductions for good-time credits.

Parole, a conditional release, is the most common form of prison release. About two-thirds of all inmates who leave incarceration do so under the supervision of a parole officer. The remaining one-third are subject to various other release mechanisms. Prisoners receive an unconditional release when they have completed the terms of their sentence and no longer require incarceration or supervision. One form of unconditional release is mandatory release (also known as "maxing out"), which occurs when an inmate has served the maximum amount of time on the initial sentence, minus reductions for good-time credits.

The second paragraph, with all of the different markings, is hard to read and understand because there is so much going on. There are arrows and underlines and highlights all over the place, and it is difficult to identify the most important parts of the paragraph. The first paragraph, by contrast, has highlights only on a few important words, making it much easier to identify quickly the important elements of the paragraph. The key to marking is *selective* activity. Mark each page in a way that allows you to see the most important points at a glance. You can follow up your marking by writing out more in your subject outline.

With these skills in hand, you will be well on your way to becoming a great student.

We study **best** when we are **free from distractions**.

Here are a few more hints that will help you develop effective study skills.

- **Read textbook chapters actively!** Underline the most important topics. Put a check mark next to material that you do not understand. After you have completed the entire chapter, take a break. Then, work on better comprehension of the check-marked material.

- **As a rule, do school work as soon as possible when you get home after class.** The longer you wait, the more likely you will be distracted by television, video games, phone calls from friends, or social networking.

- **Take notes by hand.** Many students are tempted to take class notes on a laptop computer. This is a bad idea for two reasons. First, it is hard to copy diagrams or take other "artistic" notes on a computer. Second, it is easy to get distracted by checking e-mail or surfing the Web.

- **Study free from distractions** such as the Internet, cell phones, and friends. That's why your school library is often the best place to work. Set aside several hours a week of "library time" to study in peace and quiet.

- **Reward yourself for studying!** From time to time, allow yourself a short break for surfing the Internet, going for a jog, or doing something else that you enjoy. These interludes will refresh your mind and enable you to study longer and more efficiently.

- **When writing papers, never turn in a first draft.** Allow yourself time to revise and polish your final draft. Good writing takes time—you may need to revise a paper several times before it's ready to be handed in.

- **A neat study space is important.** Staying neat forces you to stay organized. The only work items that should be on your desk are those that you are working on that day.

- **Often, studying involves pure memorization.** To help with this task, create flash (or note) cards. On one side of the card, write the question or term. On the other side, write the answer or definition. Then, use the cards to test yourself on the material.

- **Use mnemonic (ne-mon-ik) devices**—tricks that increase our ability to memorize. A well-known mnemonic device is the phrase ROY G BIV, which helps people remember the colors of the rainbow—Red, Orange, Yellow, Green, Blue, Indigo, Violet. Of course, you don't have to use mnemonics that other people made. You can create your own for whatever you need to memorize. The more fun you have coming up with mnemonics for yourself, the more useful they will be.

- **Take notes twice.** First, take notes in class. Then, when you get back home, rewrite your notes. The rewrite will act as a study session by forcing you to think about the material. It will also, invariably, lead to questions that are crucial to the study process.

- **Turn headings into questions.** Notice that each major section heading in this textbook has been written in the form of a question. By turning headings or subheadings in all of your textbooks into questions—and then answering them—you will increase your understanding of the material.

- **Multitasking while studying is generally a bad idea**. You may think that you can review your notes and watch television at the same time, but your ability to study will almost certainly suffer.

= BAD IDEA!

Paul Ijsendoorn/iStockphoto.com

Troels Graugaard/iStockphoto.com

test PREP

You have worked hard throughout the term, reading the book, paying close attention in class, and taking good notes. Now it's test time, when all that hard work pays off. To do well on an exam, of course, it is important that you learn the concepts in each chapter as thoroughly as possible; however, there are additional strategies for taking exams. You should know which reading materials and lectures will be covered. You should also know in advance what type of exam you are going to take—essay or objective or both. (Objective exams usually include true/false, fill-in-the-blank, matching, and multiple-choice questions.) Finally, you should know how much time will be allowed for the exam. By taking these steps, you will reduce any anxiety you feel as you begin the exam, and you'll be better prepared to work through the entire exam.

Petek ARICI/iStockphoto.com

FOLLOW DIRECTIONS

Students are often in a hurry to start an exam, so they take little time to read the instructions. The instructions can be critical, however. In a multiple-choice exam, for example, if there is no indication that there is a penalty for guessing, then you should never leave a question unanswered. Even if only a few minutes are left at the end of an exam, you should guess on the questions that you remain uncertain about.

Additionally, you need to know the weight given to each section of an exam. In a typical multiple-choice exam, all questions have equal weight. In other types of exams, particularly those with essay questions, different parts of the exam carry different weights. You should use these weights to apportion your time accordingly. If the essay portion of an exam accounts for 20 percent of the total points on the exam, you should not spend 60 percent of your time on the essay.

Finally, you need to make sure you are marking the answers correctly. Some exams require a No. 2 pencil to fill in the dots on a machine-graded answer sheet. Other exams require underlining or circling. In short, you have to read and follow the instructions carefully.

Jesus Jauregui/iStockphoto.com

OBJECTIVE EXAMS

An objective exam consists of multiple-choice, true/false, fill-in-the-blank, or matching questions that have only one correct answer. Students usually commit one of two errors when they read objective-exam questions: (1) they read things into the questions that do not exist, or (2) they skip over words or phrases. Most test questions include key words such as:

- all
- never
- always
- only

If you miss any of these key words, you may answer the question wrong even if you know the information. Consider the following example:

> *True or False?*
> *All cases in which one person kills another person are considered murder.*

In this instance, you may be tempted to answer "True," but the correct answer is "False," because the charge of murder is only brought in cases in which one person *intentionally* killed another. In cases in which a person unintentionally killed another, the charge is manslaughter.

Whenever the answer to an objective question is not obvious, start with the process of elimination. Throw out the answers that are clearly incorrect. Typically, the easiest way to eliminate incorrect answers is to look for those that are meaningless, illogical, or inconsistent. Often test authors put in choices that make perfect sense and are indeed true, but they are not the answer to the question under study.

If you follow the above tips, you will be well on your way to becoming an

efficient, results-oriented student. Here are a few more that will help you get there.

- **Take notes in class.** Instructors usually lecture on subjects they think are important, so those same subjects are also likely to be on the exam. Review your class notes thoroughly as part of your exam preparation.

- **Create a study schedule for midterms and finals.** Make a list of each study topic and the amount of time needed to prepare for that topic. Then, create a study schedule to reduce stress and give yourself the best chance for success.

- **Join or form a study group** (with two or three other students). Discussing a topic out loud can improve your understanding of that topic and will help you remember the key points that often come up on exams.

- If the test requires you to read a passage and then answer questions about that passage, **read the questions first.** This way, you will know what to look for as you read.

- **When you first receive your exam, look it over quickly to make sure that you have all the pages.** If you are uncertain, ask your professor or exam proctor. This initial scan may uncover other problems as well, such as illegible print or unclear instructions.

- **Keep exams in perspective.** If you do poorly on one test, it's not the end of the world. Rather, it should motivate you to do better on the next one.

- **Review your lecture notes immediately after each class,** when the material is still fresh in your mind. Then, review each subject once a week, giving yourself an hour to go back over what you have learned. Reviews make tests easier because you will feel comfortable with the material.

- **Use old exams as study tools.** Some professors make old exams available, either by posting them online or putting them on file in the library. Old tests can give

Grades aren't a matter of **life and death,** and worrying about them can have a **negative effect** on your performance.

you an idea of the kinds of questions the professor likes to ask.

- **With essay questions, look for key words such as "compare," "contrast," and "explain."** These will guide your answer. If you have time, make a quick outline. Most important, get to the point quickly without wasting your time (or your professor's) with statements such as "There are many possible reasons for . . ."

- **Cramming just before the exam is a dangerous proposition.** Cramming tires the brain unnecessarily and adds to stress, which can severely hamper your testing performance. If you've studied wisely, have confidence that the information will be available to you when you need it.

- **Review your answers.** When you finish a test early, your first instinct may be to hand it in and get out of the classroom as quickly as possible. It is always a good idea, however, to look over your answers. You may find a mistake or an area where some extra writing will improve your grade.

- **Be prepared.** Make a list of everything you will need for the exam, such as a pen or pencil, watch, and calculator. Arrive at the exam early to avoid having to rush, which will only add to your stress.

- **Be sure to eat before taking a test.** Having food in your stomach will give you the energy you need to concentrate. Don't go overboard, however. Too much food or heavy foods will make you sleepy during the exam.

Cramming just before the exam is a **dangerous** proposition.

read PREP

This textbook is the foundation for your introduction to criminal justice. It contains key concepts and terms that are important to your understanding of what criminal justice is all about. This knowledge will be important not only for you to succeed in this course, but for your future as you pursue a career in criminal justice. For this reason, it is essential that you develop good reading skills so that you can make the most out of this textbook.

Of course, all students know how to read, but reading for a college-level course goes beyond being able to recognize words on a page. As a student, you must read to learn. You have to be able to read a chapter with the goal of understanding its key points and how it relates to other chapters. In other words, you have to be able to read your textbook and be able to explain what it is all about. To do this, you need to develop good reading habits and reading skills.

READING FOR LEARNING REQUIRES FOCUS

Reading (and learning from) a textbook is not like reading a newspaper or a magazine or even a novel. The point of reading for learning isn't to get through the material as fast as you can or to skip parts to get to the stuff you're interested in. A textbook is a source of information about a subject, and the goal of reading a textbook is to learn as much of that information as you can. This kind of reading requires attention. When you read to learn, you have to make an effort to focus on the book and tune out other distractions so that you can understand and remember the information it presents.

READING FOR LEARNING TAKES TIME

When reading your textbook, you need to go slow. The most important part of reading for learning is not how many pages you get through or how fast you get through them. Instead, the goal is to learn the key concepts of criminal justice that are presented in each chapter. To do that, you need to read slowly, carefully, and with great attention.

READING FOR LEARNING TAKES REPETITION

Even the most well-read scholar will tell you that it's difficult to learn from a textbook just by reading through it once. To read for learning, you have to read your textbook a number of times. This doesn't mean, though, that you just sit and read the same section three or four times. Instead, you should follow a preview-read-review process. Here's a good guide to follow:

The First Time The first time you read a section of the book, you should preview it. During the preview, pay attention to how the chapter is formatted. Look over the title of the chapter, the section headings, and highlighted or bolded words. This will give you a good preview of the important ideas in the chapter. You should also pay close attention to any graphs, pictures, illustrations, or figures that are used in the chapter, since these provide a visual illustration of important concepts. You should also pay special attention to the first and last sentence of each paragraph. First sentences usually introduce the main point of the paragraph, while last sentences usually sum up what was presented in each paragraph.

The goal of previewing the section is to answer the question "What is the main idea?" Of course, you may not be able to come up with a detailed answer yet, but that's not the point of previewing. Instead, the point is to develop some general ideas about what the section is about so that when you do read it in full, you can have a guide for what to look for.

The Second Time After the preview, you'll want to read through the passage in detail. During this phase, it is important to read with a few questions in mind: What is the main point of this paragraph?

Andrzej Tokarski/iStockphoto.com

What does the author want me to learn from this? How does this relate to what I read before? Keeping these questions in mind will help you to be an attentive reader who is actively focusing on the main ideas of the passage.

It is helpful to take notes while reading in detail. There are several different methods of doing this—you can write notes in the margin, highlight important words and phrases, or write an outline. Whatever method you prefer, taking notes will help you read actively, identify important concepts, and remember them. Then when it comes time to review for the exam, the notes you've made will make your studying more efficient. Instead of reading through the entire chapter again, you can focus your studying energy on the areas that you've identified as most important.

After you have completed a detailed read of the chapter, take a break so that you can rest your mind (and your eyes). Then you should write up a summary or paraphrase of what you just read. You don't need to produce a detailed, lengthy summary of the whole chapter. Instead, try to produce a brief paraphrase that covers the most important ideas of the chapter. This paraphrase will help you remember the main points of the chapter, check the accuracy of your reading, and provide a good guide for later review.

The Third Time (and Beyond) After you've finished a detailed reading of the chapter, you should take the time to review the chapter (at least once, but maybe even two, three, or more times). During this step, you should review each paragraph and the notes you made, asking this question: "What was this paragraph about?" At this point, you'll want to answer the question in some detail; that is, you should develop a fairly good idea of the important points of what you read before.

A reading group is a great way to review the chapter. After completing the reading individually, group members should meet and take turns sharing what they learned from their reading. Sharing what you learned from reading and explaining it to others will

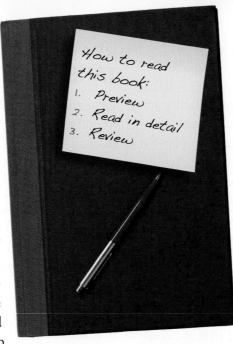

reinforce and clarify what you already know. It also provides an opportunity to learn from others. Getting a different perspective on a passage will increase your knowledge, since different people will find different things important during a reading.

Whether you're reading your textbook for the first time or reviewing it for the final exam, here are a couple of tips that will help you be an attentive and attuned reader.

Set aside time and space.

To read effectively, you need to be focused and attentive, and that won't happen if your phone is ringing every two minutes, if the TV is on in the background, if you're updating Twitter, or if you're surrounded by friends or family. Similarly, you won't be able to focus on your book if you're trying to read in a room that is too hot or too cold, or sitting in an uncomfortable chair. So when you read, find a quiet, comfortable place that is free from distractions where you can focus on one thing—learning from the book.

Take frequent breaks.

Reading your textbook shouldn't be a test of endurance. Rest your eyes and your mind by taking a short break every twenty to thirty minutes. The concentration you need to read attentively requires lots of energy, and you won't have enough energy if you don't take frequent breaks.

Keep reading.

Effective reading is like playing sports or a musical instrument—practice makes perfect. The more time that you spend reading, the better you will be at learning from your textbook. Your vocabulary will grow, and you'll have an easier time learning and remembering information you find in textbooks.

write PREP

A key part of succeeding as a student is learning how to write well. Whether writing papers, presentations, essays, or even e-mails to your instructor, you have to be able to put your thoughts into words and do so with force, clarity, and precision. In this section, we outline a three-phase process that you can use to write virtually anything.

1. Getting ready to write
2. Writing a first draft
3. Revising your draft

PHASE 1: GETTING READY TO WRITE

First, make a list. Divide the ultimate goal—a finished paper—into smaller steps that you can tackle right away. Estimate how long it will take to complete each step. Start with the date your paper is due and work backwards to the present: For example, if the due date is December 1, and you have about three months to write the paper, give yourself a cushion and schedule November 20 as your targeted completion date. Plan what you want to get done by November 1, and then list what you want to get done by October 1.

Pick a Topic To generate ideas for a topic, any of the following approaches work well:

- **Brainstorm with a group.** There is no need to create in isolation. You can harness the energy and the natural creative power of a group to assist you.

- **Speak it.** To get ideas flowing, start talking. Admit your confusion or lack of clear ideas. Then just speak. By putting your thoughts into words, you'll start thinking more clearly.

- **Use free writing.** Free writing, a technique championed by writing teacher Peter Elbow, is also very effective when trying to come up with a topic. There's only one rule in free writing: Write without stopping. Set a time limit—say, ten

minutes—and keep your fingers dancing across the keyboard the whole time. Ignore the urge to stop and rewrite. There is no need to worry about spelling, punctuation, or grammar during this process.

Refine Your Idea After you've come up with some initial ideas, it's time to refine them:

- **Select a topic and working title.** Using your instructor's guidelines for the paper or speech, write down a list of topics that interest you. Write down all of the ideas you think of in two minutes. Then choose one topic. The most common pitfall is selecting a topic that is too broad. "Terrorism" is probably not a useful topic for your paper. Instead, consider "The Financing of Terrorist Activities."

- **Write a thesis statement**. Clarify what you want to say by summarizing it in one concise sentence. This sentence, called a *thesis statement,* refines your working title. A thesis is the main point of the paper; it is a declaration of some sort. You might write a thesis statement such as "Drug trafficking and other criminal activities are often used to finance terrorism."

Set Goals Effective writing flows from a purpose. Think about how you'd like your reader or listener to respond after considering your ideas.

- If you want someone to think differently, make your writing clear and logical. Support your assertions with evidence.

- If your purpose is to move the reader into action, explain exactly what steps to take and offer solid benefits for doing so.

To clarify your purpose, state it in one sentence—for example, "The purpose of this paper is to discuss and analyze the various explanations for the nation's decreasing crime rate."

Begin Research At the initial stage, the objective of your research is not to uncover specific facts about your topic. That comes later. First, you want to gain an overview of the subject. Say that you want to persuade the reader to vote against the death penalty in your state. You must first learn enough about the death penalty to summarize for your reader its history, application, effectiveness as a deterrent, and so on.

Make an Outline An outline is a kind of map. When you follow a map, you avoid getting lost. Likewise, an outline keeps you from wandering off topic. To create your outline, follow these steps:

1. Review your thesis statement and identify the three to five main points you need to address in your paper to support or prove your thesis.

2. Next, look closely at those three to five major points or categories and think about what minor points or subcategories you want to cover in your paper. Your major points are your big ideas; your minor points are the details you need to fill in under each of those ideas.

3. Ask for feedback. Have your instructor or a classmate review your outline and offer suggestions for improvement. Did you choose the right categories and subcategories? Do you need more detail anywhere? Does the flow from idea to idea make sense?

Do In-Depth Research Three-by-five-inch index cards are an old-fashioned but invaluable tool for in-depth research. Simply write down one idea or piece of information per card. This makes it easy to organize—and reorganize—your ideas and information. Organizing research cards as you create them saves time. Use rubber bands to keep *source cards* (cards that include the bibliographical information for a source) separate from *information cards* (cards that include nuggets of information from a source) and to maintain general categories.

When creating your cards, be sure to:

- Copy all of the information correctly.

- Always include the source and page number on information cards.

- Be neat and organized. Write legibly, using the same format for all of your cards.

In addition to source cards and information cards, generate *idea cards*. If you have a thought while you are researching, write it down on a card. Label these cards clearly as containing your own ideas.

PHASE 2: WRITING A FIRST DRAFT

To create your draft, gather your index cards and confirm that they are arranged to follow your outline. Then write about the ideas in your notes. It's that simple. Look at your cards and start writing. Write in paragraphs, with one idea per paragraph. As you complete this task, keep the following suggestions in mind:

- **Remember that the first draft is not for keeps.** You can worry about quality later; your goal at this point is simply to generate lots of words and lots of ideas.

- **Write freely.** Many writers prefer to get their first draft down quickly and would advise you to keep writing, much as in free writing. Of course, you may pause to glance at your cards and outline. The idea is to avoid stopping to edit your work.

stuartbur/iStockphoto.com

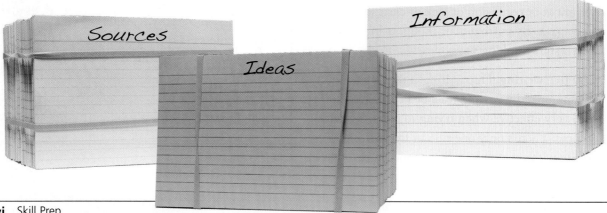

- **Be yourself.** Let go of the urge to sound "official" or "scholarly" and avoid using unnecessarily big words or phrases. Instead, write in a natural voice. Address your thoughts not to the teacher but to an intelligent student or someone you care about. Visualize this person, and choose the three or four most important things you'd say to her about the topic.

- **Make writing a habit.** Don't wait for inspiration to strike. Make a habit of writing at a certain time each day.

- **Get physical.** While working on the first draft, take breaks. Go for a walk. Speak or sing your ideas out loud. From time to time, practice relaxation techniques and breathe deeply.

- **Hide it in your drawer for a while.** Schedule time for rewrites before you begin, and schedule at least one day between revisions so that you can let the material sit. The brain needs that much time to disengage itself from the project.

PHASE 3: REVISING YOUR DRAFT

During this phase, keep in mind the saying "Write in haste; revise at leisure." When you are working on your first draft, the goal is to produce ideas and write them down. During the revision phase, however, you need to slow down and take a close look at your work. One guideline is to allow 50 percent of writing time for planning, researching, and writing the first draft. Then use the remaining 50 percent for revising.

There are a number of especially good ways to revise your paper:

1. Read it out loud.

The combination of voice and ears forces us to pay attention to the details. Is the thesis statement clear and supported by enough evidence? Does the introduction tell your reader what's coming? Do you end with a strong conclusion that expands on what's in your introduction rather than just restating it?

Izabela Habur/iStockphoto.com

2. Have a friend look over your paper.

This is never a substitute for your own review, but a friend can often see mistakes you miss. Remember, when other people criticize or review your work, they are not attacking you. They're just commenting on your paper. With a little practice, you will learn to welcome feedback because it is one of the fastest ways to approach the revision process.

3. Cut.

Look for excess baggage. Avoid at all costs and at all times the really, really terrible mistake of using way too many unnecessary words, a mistake that student writers often make when they sit down to write papers for the various courses in which they participate at the fine institutions of higher learning that they are fortunate enough to attend. (Example: The previous sentence could be edited to "Avoid unnecessary words.") Also, look for places where two (or more) sentences could be rewritten as one. Resist the temptation to think that by cutting text you are losing something. You are actually gaining—a clearer, more polished product. For maximum efficiency, make the larger cuts first—sections, chapters, pages. Then go for the smaller cuts—paragraphs, sentences, phrases, words.

4. Paste.

In deleting both larger and smaller passages in your first draft, you've probably removed some of the original transitions and connecting ideas. The next task is to rearrange what's left of your paper or speech so that it flows logically. Look for consistency within paragraphs and for transitions from paragraph to paragraph and section to section.

5. Fix.

Now it's time to look at individual words and phrases. Define any terms that the reader might not know, putting them in plain English whenever you can. In general, focus on nouns and verbs. Using too many adjectives and adverbs weakens your message and adds unnecessary bulk to your writing. Write about the details, and be specific. Also, check your writing to ensure that you are:

- Using the active voice. Write *"The research team began the project"* rather than (passively) *"A project was initiated."*

- Writing concisely. Instead of *"After making a timely arrival and perspicaciously observing the unfolding events, I emerged totally and gloriously victorious,"* be concise with *"I came, I saw, I conquered."*

- Communicating clearly. Instead of *"The speaker made effective use of the television medium, asking in no uncertain terms that we change our belief systems,"* you can write specifically, *"The reformed criminal stared straight into the television camera and shouted, 'Take a good look at what you're doing! Will it get you what you really want?'"*

6. Prepare.

In a sense, any paper is a sales effort. If you hand in a paper that is neat and presentable, your instructor is more likely to buy it. Format your paper following accepted standards for margin widths, endnotes, title pages, and other details. Ask your instructor for specific instructions on how to cite the sources used in writing your paper. You can find useful guidelines in the *MLA Handbook for Writers of Research Papers,* a book from the Modern Language Association. If you cut and paste material from a Web page directly into your paper, be sure to place that material in quotation marks and cite the source. Before referencing an e-mail message, verify the sender's identity. Remember that anyone sending e-mail can pretend to be someone else. Use quality paper for the final version of your paper. For an even more professional appearance, bind your paper with a plastic or paper cover.

7. Proof.

As you ease down the home stretch, read your revised paper one more time. This time, go for the big picture and look for the following:

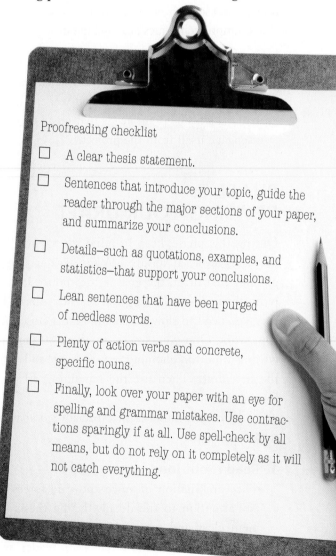

Feng Yu/iStockphoto.com

Proofreading checklist

☐ A clear thesis statement.

☐ Sentences that introduce your topic, guide the reader through the major sections of your paper, and summarize your conclusions.

☐ Details—such as quotations, examples, and statistics—that support your conclusions.

☐ Lean sentences that have been purged of needless words.

☐ Plenty of action verbs and concrete, specific nouns.

☐ Finally, look over your paper with an eye for spelling and grammar mistakes. Use contractions sparingly if at all. Use spell-check by all means, but do not rely on it completely as it will not catch everything.

When you are through proofreading, take a minute to savor the result. You've just witnessed something of a miracle—the mind attaining clarity and resolution. That's the *aha!* in writing.

ACADEMIC INTEGRITY: AVOIDING PLAGIARISM

Using another person's words, images, or other original creations without giving proper credit is called *plagiarism*. Plagiarism amounts to taking someone else's work and presenting it as your own—the equivalent of cheating on a test. The consequences of plagiarism can range from a failing grade to expulsion from school. Plagiarism can be unintentional. Some students don't understand the research process. Sometimes they leave writing until the last minute and don't take the time to organize their sources of information. Also, some people are raised in cultures where identity is based on group membership rather than individual achievement. These students may find it hard to understand how creative work can be owned by an individual.

To avoid plagiarism, ask an instructor where you can find your school's written policy on this issue. Don't assume that you can resubmit a paper you wrote for another class for a current class; many schools will regard this as plagiarism even though you wrote the paper. The basic guidelines for preventing plagiarism are to cite a source for each phrase, sequence of ideas, or visual image created by another person. While ideas cannot be copyrighted, the specific way that an idea is *expressed* can be. You also need to list a source for any idea that is closely identified with a particular person. The goal is to clearly distinguish your own work from the work of others. There are several ways to ensure that you do this consistently:

- **Identify direct quotes.** If you use a direct quote from another writer or speaker, put that person's words in quotation marks. If you do research online, you might find yourself copying sentences or paragraphs from a Web page and pasting them directly into your notes. This is the same as taking direct quotes from your source. To avoid plagiarism, identify such passages in an obvious way.

- **Paraphrase carefully.** Paraphrasing means restating the original passage in your own words, usually making it shorter and simpler. Students who copy a passage word for word and then just rearrange or delete a few phrases are running a serious risk of plagiarism. Remember to cite a source for paraphrases, just as you do for direct quotes. When you use the same sequence of ideas as one of your sources—even if you have not paraphrased or directly quoted—cite that source.

- **Note details about each source.** For books, details about each source include the author, title, publisher, publication date, location of publisher, and page number. For articles from serial print sources, record the article title and the name of the magazine or journal as well. If you found the article in an academic or technical journal, also record the volume and issue number of the publication. A librarian can help identify these details. If your source is a Web page, record as many identifying details as you can find—author, title, sponsoring organization, URL, publication date, and revision date. In addition, list the date that you accessed the page. Be careful when using Web resources, as not all Web sites are considered legitimate sources. Wikipedia, for instance, is not regarded as a legitimate source; the National Institute of Justice's Web site, however, is.

- **Cite your sources as endnotes or footnotes to your paper.** Ask your instructor for examples of the format to use. You do not need to credit wording that is wholly your own. Nor do you need to credit general ideas, such as the suggestion that people use a to-do list to plan their time. When you use your own words to describe such an idea, there's no need to credit a source. But if you borrow someone else's words or images to explain the idea, do give credit.

Dedication

This book is dedicated to my good friend
and colleague, Lawrence Walsh, of the
Lexington, Kentucky Police Department.
When I was a rookie, he taught me about
policing. When I became a researcher,
he taught me about the practical
applications of knowledge. He is truly an
inspiring professional in our field.

L.K.G.

To My Students,

You certainly know how
to challenge me.

R.L.M.

Learning OUTCOMES *After studying this chapter, you will be able to . . .*

1 Define crime and identify the different types of crime.

2 Outline the three levels of law enforcement.

3 List the essential elements of the corrections system.

4 Define ethics, and describe the role that it plays in discretionary decision making.

5 Contrast the crime control and due process models.

CRIMINAL JUSTICE TODAY

Do-It-Yourself Terror

Samir Khan's advice for his fellow Islamic *jihadists* was simple and straightforward: think small. Khan, an American who moved to the Middle East to start the online magazine *Inspire,* thought that terrorist actions on the scale of the September 11, 2001, attacks against the United States were no longer feasible. Instead, he wrote, solo, under-the-radar operations have a better chance of success. "The effect is much greater, it always embarrasses the enemy, and these types of individual decision-making attacks are nearly impossible for [anti-terrorism efforts] to contain," Khan counseled.

Khan was killed by an American drone strike in Yemen in 2011, but his words echoed loudly on April 15, 2013. That day, Tamerlan Tsarnaev, 26, and his younger brother Dzhokhar, 19, detonated two bombs near the finish line of the Boston Marathon, killing three and wounding more than 260. The Tsarnaevs fashioned the bombs by packing pressure cookers with nails, ball bearings, and black powder taken from fireworks. The devices were triggered by simple egg timers. Following his capture, Dzokhar admitted that that the pressure-cooker explosives were created using instructions found in *Inspire,* which frequently published Web articles with titles such as "Make a Bomb in the Kitchen of Your Mom."

Dzhokhar also told authorities that he and his brother, who was killed in a shootout with police, were motivated by religious fervor but had not received any help from international terrorist organizations. In 2012, Tamerlan did spend several months in Dagestan, a republic of Russia that is marked by violence committed by and against Islamic separatists. On his return, he made a YouTube playlist that indicated a growing interest in Islamic radicalism. Even so, the brothers—who had lived in the Boston area for about ten years—were fully assimilated in American culture and proved skillful at hiding their plans from close acquaintances. When surveillance images of the as-yet-unidentified bombers showed up on the Internet, one of Dzhokhar's friends noted his resemblance to the suspect. "Lol," Dzhokhar replied. "You better not text me."

Law enforcement used surveillance videos to identify Boston Marathon bombing suspects Dzhokhar Tsarnaev, left, and his brother Tamerlan, right.

AP Photo/FBI

3

1-1
what IS CRIME?

The carnage caused by Tamerlan and Dzhokhar Tsarnaev's improvised explosive devices was extensive. Eyewitnesses sounded like reporters from a war zone. "These runners just finished and they don't have legs now," said Roupen Bastajian, a former Marine, from the scene of the blasts. "There are so many people without legs. It's all blood. There's blood everywhere."[1] (**CAREER TIP:** *Forensic nurses* are healthcare professionals who are trained not only to attend to victims in emergency circumstances such as the Boston Marathon bombings, but also to collect evidence and act as liaisons with the criminal justice system.)

Indeed, as we shall see in Chapter 14, some politicians wanted the U.S. government to treat Dzhokhar as a captive of war, therefore denying him those protections afforded criminal defendants in this country.[2] Instead, Dzhokhar was charged with the *crime* of using a weapon of mass destruction, therefore setting in motion a chain of events that will act as the backbone of this textbook. In general, a **crime** can be defined as a wrong against society proclaimed by law and, if committed under certain circumstances, punished by society. One problem with this definition, however, is that it obscures the complex nature of societies. A society is not static—it evolves and changes, and its concept of criminality evolves and changes as well. Different societies can have vastly different ideas of what constitutes a crime. In 2012, for example police in West Sumatra, Indonesia, arrested Alexander Aan for writing "God is not great" on Facebook. An Indonesian court sentenced Aan to two and a half years in prison for violating a criminal prohibition against "inciting religious hatred." Such legislation would not be allowed in the United States because of our country's long traditions of freedom of speech and religion.

To more fully understand the concept of crime,

Crime An act that violates criminal law and is punishable by criminal sanctions.

Consensus Model A criminal justice model in which the majority of citizens in a society share the same values and beliefs. Criminal acts are acts that conflict with these values and beliefs and that are deemed harmful to society.

Morals Principles of right and wrong behavior, as practiced by individuals or by society.

Conflict Model A criminal justice model in which the content of criminal law is determined by the groups that hold economic, political, and social power in a community.

it will help to examine the two most common models of how society "decides" which acts are criminal: the consensus model and the conflict model.

1-1a
The Consensus Model

The term *consensus* refers to general agreement among the majority of any particular group. Thus, the **consensus model** rests on the assumption that as people gather together to form a society, its members will naturally come to a basic agreement with regard to shared norms and values. Those individuals whose actions deviate from the established norms and values are considered to pose a threat to the well-being of society as a whole and must be sanctioned (punished). The society passes laws to control and prevent unacceptable behavior, thereby setting the boundaries for acceptable behavior within the group.[3]

The consensus model, to a certain extent, assumes that a diverse group of people can have similar **morals.** In other words, they share an ideal of what is "right" and "wrong." Consequently, as public attitudes toward morality change, so do laws. In seventeenth-century America, a person found guilty of *adultery* (having sexual relations with someone other than one's spouse) could expect to be publicly whipped, branded, or even executed. Furthermore, a century ago, one could walk into a pharmacy and purchase heroin. Today, social attitudes have shifted to consider adultery a personal issue, beyond the reach of the state, and to consider the sale of heroin a criminal act.

1-1b
The Conflict Model

Some people reject the consensus model on the ground that moral attitudes are not constant or even consistent. In large, democratic societies such as the United States, different groups of citizens have widely varying opinions on controversial issues of morality and criminality such as abortion, the war on drugs, immigration, and assisted suicide. These groups and their elected representatives are constantly coming into conflict with one another. According to the **conflict model,** then, the most politically powerful segments of society—based on class, income, age, and race—have the most influence on criminal laws and are therefore able to impose their values on the rest of the community.

Consequently, what is deemed criminal activity is determined by whichever group happens to be holding power at any given time. Because certain groups do not have access to political power, their interests are not served by the criminal justice system. To give one example, with the exception of Oregon and Washington State, physician-assisted suicide for the terminally ill is illegal in the United States. Although opinion polls show that the general public is evenly divided on the issue,[4] several highly motivated interest groups have been able to convince lawmakers that the practice goes against America's shared moral and religious values.

1-1c
An Integrated Definition of Crime

LO 1 Considering both the consensus and conflict models, we can construct a definition of crime that will be useful throughout this textbook. For our purposes, crime is an action or activity that is:

1. Punishable under criminal law, as determined by the majority or, in some instances, by a powerful minority.

2. Considered an *offense against society as a whole* and prosecuted by public officials, not by victims and their relatives or friends.

3. Punishable by sanctions based on laws that bring about the loss of personal freedom or life.

At this point, it is important to understand the difference between crime and **deviance,** or behavior that does not conform to the norms of a given community or society. Deviance is a subjective concept. For example, some segments of society may think that smoking marijuana or killing animals for clothing and food is deviant behavior. Deviant acts become crimes only when society as a whole, through its legislatures, determines that those acts should be punished—as is the situation today in the United States with using illegal drugs but not with eating meat. Furthermore, not all crimes are considered particularly deviant—little social disapprobation is attached to those who fail to follow the letter of parking laws. In essence, criminal law

> **Deviance** Behavior that is considered to go against the norms established by society.

Several years ago, the federal government and several state governments banned the sale of Four Loko, here being enjoyed by college students in Fort Collins, Colorado. The drink, known as "blackout in a can," combines the alcohol content of nearly six beers with a strong dose of caffeine. Why might society demand that the sale of this product be made a criminal offense?

Matthew Staer/Landov

reflects those acts that we, as a society, agree are so unacceptable that steps must be taken to prevent them from occurring.

1-1d
Types of Crime

The manner in which crimes are classified depends on their seriousness. Federal, state, and local legislation has provided for the classification and punishment of hundreds of thousands of different criminal acts, ranging from jaywalking to first degree murder. For general purposes, we can group criminal behavior into six categories: violent crime, property crime, public order crime, white-collar crime, organized crime, and high-tech crime.

VIOLENT CRIME Crimes against persons, or *violent crimes*, have come to dominate our perspectives on crime. There are four major categories of violent crime:

- **Murder,** or the unlawful killing of a human being.
- **Sexual assault,** or *rape*, which refers to coerced actions of a sexual nature against an unwilling participant.
- **Assault** and **battery,** two separate acts that cover situations in which one person physically attacks another (battery) or, through threats, intentionally leads another to believe that he or she will be physically harmed (assault).
- **Robbery,** or the taking of funds, personal property, or any other article of value from a person by means of force or fear.

As you will see in Chapter 3, these violent crimes are further classified by *degree*, depending on the circumstances surrounding the criminal act. These circumstances include the intent of the person committing the crime, whether a weapon was used, and (in cases other than murder) the level of pain and suffering experienced by the victim.

PROPERTY CRIME The most common form of criminal activity is *property crime*, or those crimes in which the goal of the offender is some form of economic gain or the damaging of property. Pocket picking, shoplifting, and the stealing of any property that is not accomplished by force are covered by laws against **larceny,** also known as *theft*. **Burglary** refers

Murder The unlawful killing of one human being by another.

Sexual Assault Forced or coerced sexual intercourse (or other sexual acts).

Assault A threat or an attempt to do violence to another person that causes that person to fear immediate physical harm.

Battery The act of physically contacting another person with the intent to do harm, even if the resulting injury is insubstantial.

Robbery The act of taking property from another person through force, threat of force, or intimidation.

Larceny The act of taking property from another person without the use of force with the intent of keeping that property.

Burglary The act of breaking into or entering a structure (such as a home or office) without permission for the purpose of committing a felony.

to the unlawful entry of a structure with the intention of committing a serious crime such as theft. *Motor vehicle theft* describes the theft or attempted theft of a motor vehicle, including all cases in which automobiles are taken by persons not having lawful access to them. *Arson* is also a property crime. It involves the willful and malicious burning of a home, automobile, commercial building, or any other construction.

PUBLIC ORDER CRIME The concept of **public order crimes** is linked to the consensus model discussed earlier. Historically, societies have always outlawed activities that are considered contrary to public values and morals. Today, the most common public order crimes include public drunkenness, prostitution, gambling, and illicit drug use. These crimes are sometimes referred to as *victimless crimes* because they often harm only the offender. As you will see throughout this textbook, however, that term is rather misleading. Public order crimes may create an environment that gives rise to property and violent crimes.

WHITE-COLLAR CRIME Business-related crimes are popularly referred to as **white-collar crimes.** The term *white-collar crime* is broadly used to describe an illegal act or series of acts committed by an individual or business entity using some nonviolent means to obtain a personal or business advantage. As you will see in Chapter 14, when we consider the topic in much greater detail, certain property crimes fall into this category when committed in a business context. Although the extent of this criminal activity is difficult to determine with any certainty, the Association of Certified Fraud Examiners estimates that white-collar crime costs businesses worldwide as much as $3.5 trillion a year.[5]

ORGANIZED CRIME White-collar crime involves the use of legal business facilities and employees to commit illegal acts. For example, a bank teller can't embezzle unless he or she is first hired as a legal employee of the bank. In contrast, **organized crime** describes illegal acts by illegal organizations, usually geared toward satisfying the public's demand for unlawful goods and services. Organized crime broadly implies a conspiratorial and illegal relationship among any number of persons engaged in unlawful acts. More specifically, groups engaged in organized crime employ criminal tactics such as violence, corruption, and intimidation for economic gain.

The hierarchical structure of organized crime operations often mirrors that of legitimate businesses, and, like any corporation, these groups attempt to capture a sufficient percentage of any given market to make a profit. For organized crime, the traditional preferred markets are gambling, prostitution, illegal narcotics, and loan sharking (lending funds at higher-than-legal interest rates), along with more recent ventures into counterfeiting and credit-card scams.

HIGH-TECH CRIME The newest variation on crime is directly related to the increased presence of computers in everyday life. The Internet, with approximately 2.5 billion users worldwide, is the site of numerous *cyber crimes,* such as selling pornographic materials, soliciting minors, and defrauding consumers through bogus financial investments. The dependence of businesses on computer operations has left corporations vulnerable to sabotage, fraud, embezzlement, and theft of proprietary data. We will address this particular criminal activity in much greater detail in Chapter 14.

1-2 what IS THE PURPOSE OF CRIMINAL JUSTICE?

Defining which actions are to be labeled "crimes" is only the first step in safeguarding society from criminal behavior. Institutions must be created to apprehend alleged wrongdoers, to determine whether these

Public Order Crime Behavior that has been labeled criminal because it is contrary to shared social values, customs, and norms.

White-Collar Crime Nonviolent crimes committed by business entities or individuals to gain a personal or business advantage.

Organized Crime Illegal acts carried out by illegal organizations engaged in the market for illegal goods or services, such as illicit drugs or firearms.

persons have indeed committed crimes, and to punish those who are found guilty according to society's wishes. These institutions combine to form the **criminal justice system.** As we begin our examination of the American criminal justice system in this introductory chapter, it is important to have an idea of its purpose.

1-2a
Maintaining Justice

As its name implies, the explicit goal of the criminal justice system is to provide *justice* to all members of society. Because **justice** is a difficult concept to define, this goal can be challenging, if not impossible, to meet. Broadly stated, justice means that all individuals are equal before the law and that they are free from arbitrary arrest or seizure as defined by the law. In other words, the idea of justice is linked with the idea of fairness. Above all, we want our laws and the means by which they are carried out to be fair.

Justice and fairness are subjective terms, which is to say that people may have different concepts of what is just and fair. If a woman who has been beaten by her husband retaliates by killing him, what is her just punishment? Reasonable persons could disagree, with some thinking that the homicide was justified and that she should be treated leniently. Others might insist that she should not have taken the law into her own hands. Police officers,

Review the four goals of the criminal justice system listed on this page. Which of the goals would be met by rehabilitating James Holmes, shown here in a Colorado court, and returning him to society? Which would be met by putting him in prison for life?

RJ Sangosti-Pool/Getty Images

judges, prosecutors, prison administrators, and other employees of the criminal justice system must decide what is "fair." Sometimes, their course of action is obvious, but often, as we shall see, it is not.

1-2b
Protecting Society

Within the broad mandate of "maintaining justice," Megan Kurlychek of the University at Albany, New York, has identified four specific goals of our criminal justice system:

1. To protect society from potential future crimes of the most dangerous or "risky" offenders.

2. To determine when an offense has been committed and provide the appropriate punishment for that offense.

3. To rehabilitate those offenders who have been punished so that it is safe to return them to the community.

4. To support crime victims and, to the extent possible, return them to their pre-crime status.[6]

Again, though these goals may seem straightforward, they are fraught with difficulty. Take the example of James Holmes, who was charged with twenty-four counts of murder and 116 counts of attempted murder by law enforcement officials on July 30, 2012. Ten days earlier, Holmes—armed with an assault rifle and three other guns—had apparently opened fire on the audience at a late-night screening of a Batman movie in Aurora, Colorado. Following the incident, authorities at the University of Colorado, where Holmes had been a

Criminal Justice System The interlocking network of law enforcement agencies, courts, and corrections institutions designed to enforce criminal laws and protect society from criminal behavior.

Justice The quality of fairness that must exist in the processes designed to determine whether individuals are guilty of criminal wrongdoing.

graduate student, came under heavy criticism for not reacting more forcefully to staff concerns about his behavior. Next chapter, we will revisit Holmes's behavior as part of a discussion on the challenges of predicting criminality.

A month after the attack, Holmes's defense attorneys told a district judge that their client was mentally ill, causing many in Aurora and throughout the country to worry that he would never receive an appropriate punishment for his actions (see the photo on the facing page). In Chapter 3, you will learn how insanity can be used as a defense to criminal wrong-doing. Furthermore, regardless of his mental state, should Holmes ever be set free? In Chapters 9 and 12, we will discuss the concept of rehabilitation and the role that victims play in the eventual return of offenders to the community. Throughout this text-book, you will come to better understand the criminal justice system by exposure to differing opinions on these topics and many others. (The feature *You Be the Legislator—Banning Distracted Walking* below examines just how far criminal law should stretch to protect citizens from harm.)

1-3 how DOES CRIMINAL JUSTICE WORK?

To understand the structure of the criminal justice system, you must understand the concept of **federalism,** which means that government powers are shared by the national (federal) government and the states. The framers of the U.S. Constitution, fearful of tyranny and a too-powerful central government, chose the system of federalism as a compromise.

The appeal of federalism was that it established a strong national government capable of handling large-scale problems while allowing for state powers and local traditions. For example, earlier in the chapter we noted that physician-assisted suicide, though banned in most of the country, is legal in Oregon and Washington State. Several years ago, the federal government challenged the decision made

Federalism A form of government in which a written constitution provides for a division of powers between a central government and several regional governments.

YOU BE THE LEGISLATOR

BANNING DISTRACTED WALKING

THE SITUATION A twenty-four-year-old woman walks into a telephone pole while texting. A twelve-year-old boy, his attention focused on a handheld video game, is struck by a pickup truck as he crosses the street. Over a period of six years, according to a University of Maryland study, 116 pedestrians have been killed or seriously injured while wearing headphones. These are examples of the dangers of "distracted walking," which—by some measures—has become a national safety concern. Although driver traffic fatalities in the United States are dropping, pedestrian traffic fatalities and injuries are increasing. Young people seem particularly vulnerable. One special interest group found that the number of teens injured in pedestrian accidents rose 25 percent from 2006 to 2010. Many observers explain these figures by pointing to an epidemic of distracted walking.

THE LAW At present, no state has passed a criminal law banning any form of distracted walking. (By

contrast, thirty-nine states ban texting while driving, and ten states prohibit all drivers from using handheld cell phones.)

YOUR DECISION Suppose that you are a member of your state legislature. One of your colleagues puts forth a bill prohibiting the act of walking while using an electronic device such as a smartphone. In supporting this potential legislation, your colleague cites a University of Washington study showing that distracted walking is as risky for a pedestrian as drunk driving is for a driver. Would you favor such legislation? Why or why not? Under what circumstances do you believe the criminal justice system has a responsibility to protect citizens from their own risky behavior?

[To see how several state legislatures have responded to the idea of banning distracted walking, go to Example 1.1 in Appendix A.]

Gina Sanders/Shutterstock

by voters in these two states to allow the practice. The United States Supreme Court sided with the states, ruling that the principle of federalism supported their freedom to differ from the majority viewpoint in this instance.[7]

The Constitution gave the national government certain express powers, such as the power to coin money, raise an army, and regulate interstate commerce. All other powers were left to the states, including police power, which allows the states to enact whatever laws are necessary to protect the health, morals, safety, and welfare of their citizens. As the American criminal justice system has evolved, the ideals of federalism have ebbed somewhat. Specifically, the powers of the national government have expanded significantly. Crime is still primarily a local concern, however, and the majority of all employees in the criminal justice system work for local government (see Figure 1.1 on the facing page).

1-3a
Law Enforcement

The ideals of federalism can be clearly seen in the local, state, and federal levels of law enforcement. Though agencies from the different levels cooperate if the need arises, they have their own organizational structures and tend to operate independently of one another. We briefly introduce each level of law enforcement here and cover them in more detail in Chapters 4, 5, and 6.

LOCAL LAW ENFORCEMENT On the local level, the duties of law enforcement agencies are split between counties and municipalities. The chief law enforcement officer of most counties is the county sheriff. The sheriff is usually an elected post, with a two- or four-year term. In some areas, where city and county governments have merged, there is a county police force, headed by a chief of police. The bulk of all police officers in the United States are employed on a local level. The majority of these work

CAREERPREP

LOCAL POLICE OFFICER

JOB DESCRIPTION:

- Protect the lives and property of citizens in the community.
- Maintain order, catch those who break the law, and strive to prevent crimes.
- Testify at trials and hearings.

WHAT KIND OF TRAINING IS REQUIRED?

- Almost every police department requires that applicants be high school graduates, and an increasing number of departments expect a college degree.
- Minimum height, weight, eyesight, and hearing requirements, as well as the passage of physical examinations and background checks.
- Graduation from a police academy.

ANNUAL SALARY RANGE?

- $30,000–$80,000

Photodisc/Getty Images

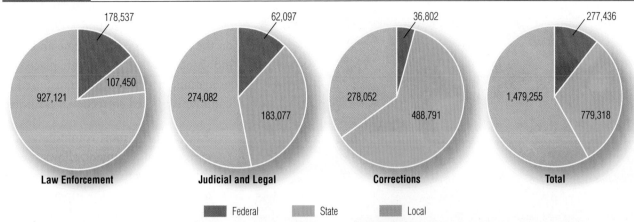

Source: Bureau of Justice Statistics, *Justice Expenditure and Employment in the United States, 2009* (Washington, D.C.: U.S. Department of Justice, May 2012), Table 2.

in departments that consist of fewer than 10 officers, though a large city such as New York may have a police force of about 36,000.

Local police are responsible for the "nuts and bolts" of law enforcement work. They investigate most crimes and attempt to deter crime through patrol activities. They apprehend criminals and participate in trial proceedings, if necessary. Local police are also charged with "keeping the peace," a broad set of duties that includes crowd and traffic control and the resolution of minor conflicts between citizens. In many areas, local police have the added obligation of providing social services such as dealing with domestic violence and child abuse.

STATE LAW ENFORCEMENT Hawaii is the only state that does not have a state law enforcement agency. Generally, there are two types of state law enforcement agencies, those designated simply as "state police" and those designated as "highway patrols." State highway patrols concern themselves mainly with infractions on public highways and freeways. Other state law enforcers include fire marshals, who investigate suspicious fires and educate the public on fire prevention; and fish, game, and watercraft wardens, who police a state's natural resources and often oversee its firearms laws. (**CAREER TIP:** Eighteen state governments completely or partially control the sale of alcoholic beverages. These states rely on *alcoholic beverage control officers* to enforce regulations on beer, wine, and distilled spirits within their borders.)

FEDERAL LAW ENFORCEMENT The enactment of new national anti-terrorism, gun, drug, and vio-

lent crime laws over the past forty years has led to an expansion in the size and scope of the federal government's participation in the criminal justice system. The Department of Homeland Security, which we will examine in detail in Chapter 4, combines the police powers of twenty-four federal agencies to protect the United States from terrorist attacks. Other federal agencies with police powers include the Federal Bureau of Investigation (FBI), the Drug Enforcement Administration (DEA), the U.S. Secret Service, and the Bureau of Alcohol, Tobacco, Firearms and Explosives (ATF). In fact, almost every federal agency, including the postal and forest services, has some kind of police power.

Unlike their local and state counterparts, federal law enforcement agencies operate throughout the United States. In May 2012, for example, the FBI conducted a nationwide sweep targeting health-care fraud, arresting more than one hundred doctors, nurses, and other medical professionals in seven cities ranging from Los Angeles to Chicago to Miami. Federal agencies are also able to provide support for local police departments, as happened several years ago when agents from the ATF joined forces with the Tulsa (Oklahoma) Police Department to combat a string of armed robberies that had plagued the city for nearly six months.

1-3b

The Courts

The United States has a *dual court system*, which means that we have two independent judicial systems, one at the federal level and one at the state level. In practice,

At midyear 2012, America's jails held approximately 744,000 inmates, including these residents of the Orange County jail in Santa Ana, California. What are the basic differences between jails and prisons?

Lucy Nicholson/Reuters/Landov

this translates into fifty-two different court systems: one federal court system and fifty different state court systems, plus that of the District of Columbia. As allowed under the rules of federalism, the U.S. (federal) criminal code lists about 4,500 crimes, and each state has its own criminal statutes that determine illegal acts under state law. In general, those defendants charged with violating federal criminal law will face trial in federal court, while those defendants charged with violating state law will appear in state court.

The *criminal court* and its work group—the judge, prosecutors, and defense attorneys—are charged with the weighty responsibility of determining the innocence or guilt of criminal suspects. We will cover these important participants, their roles in the criminal trial, and the court system as a whole in Chapters 7, 8, and 9.

1-3c
Corrections

LO **3** Once the court system convicts and sentences an offender, she or he is relegated to the corrections system. (Those convicted in a state court will be under the control of that state's corrections system,

and those convicted of a federal crime will find themselves under the control of the federal corrections system.) Depending on the seriousness of the crime and their individual needs, offenders are placed on probation, incarcerated, or transferred to community-based correctional facilities.

- *Probation,* the most common correctional treatment, allows the offender to return to the community and remain under the supervision of an agent of the court known as a probation officer. While on probation, the offender must follow certain rules of conduct. When probationers fail to follow these rules, they may be incarcerated.
- If the offender's sentence includes a period of incarceration, he or she will be remanded to a correctional facility for a certain amount of time. *Jails* hold those convicted of minor crimes with relatively short sentences, as well as those awaiting trial or involved in certain court proceedings. *Prisons* house those convicted of more serious crimes with longer sentences. Generally speaking, counties and municipalities administer jails, while prisons are the domain of federal and state governments.
- *Community-based corrections* have increased in popularity as jails and prisons have been plagued with problems of funding and overcrowding. Community-based correctional facilities include halfway houses, residential centers, and work-release centers. They operate on the assumption that all convicts do not need, and are not benefited by, incarceration in jail or prison.

The majority of those inmates released from incarceration are not finished with the corrections system. The most frequent type of release from a jail or prison is *parole,* in which an inmate, after serving part of his or her sentence in a correctional facility, is allowed to serve the rest of the term in the community. Like someone on probation, a parolee must conform to certain conditions of freedom, with the same consequences if these conditions are not followed. Issues of probation, incarceration, community-based corrections, and parole will be covered in Chapters 10, 11, and 12.

1-3d
The Criminal Justice Process

In its 1967 report, the President's Commission on Law Enforcement and Administration of Justice asserted that the criminal justice system

> is not a hodgepodge of random actions. It is rather a continuum—an orderly progression of events—some of which, like arrest and trial, are highly visible and some of which, though of great importance, occur out of public view.[8]

The commission's assertion that the criminal justice system is a "continuum" is one that many observers would challenge.[9] Some liken the criminal justice system to a sports team, which is the sum of an indeterminable number of decisions, relationships, conflicts, and adjustments.[10] Such a volatile mix is not what we generally associate with a "system." For most, the word **system** indicates a certain degree of order and discipline. That we refer to our law enforcement agencies, courts, and correctional facilities as part of a "system" may reflect our hopes rather than reality. Still, it will be helpful to familiarize yourself with the basic steps of the *criminal justice process,* or the procedures through which the criminal justice system meets the expectations of society. These basic steps are provided in Figure 1.2 on the following page.

In his classic study of the criminal justice system, Herbert Packer, a professor at Stanford University, compared the ideal criminal justice process to an assembly line "down which moves an endless stream of cases, never stopping."[11] In Packer's image of assembly-line justice, each step of the **formal criminal justice process** involves a series of "routinized operations" with the end goal of getting the criminal defendant from point A (his or her arrest by law enforcement) to point B

CAREER TIP: For those interested in both a military and a law enforcement career, the U.S. Army's *Criminal Investigation Command* is responsible for investigating crimes involving military personnel.

(the criminal trial) to point C (if guilty, her or his punishment).[12] As Packer himself was wont to point out, the daily operations of criminal justice rarely operate so smoothly. In this textbook, the criminal justice process will be examined as the end product of many different decisions made by many different criminal justice professionals in law enforcement, the courts, and corrections.

1-4
how DO CRIMINAL JUSTICE PROFESSIONALS MAKE DECISIONS?

Practically, the formal criminal justice process suffers from a serious drawback: it is unrealistic. Law enforcement agencies do not have the staff or funds to investigate *every* crime, so they must decide where to direct their limited resources. Increasing caseloads and a limited amount of time in which to dispose of them constrict many of our nation's courts. Overcrowding in prisons and jails affects both law enforcement agencies and the courts—there is simply not enough room for all convicts.

The criminal justice system relies on *discretion* to alleviate these pressures. By **discretion,** we mean the authority to choose between and among alternative courses of action, based on individual judgment and conscience. Collectively, the discretionary decisions

System A set of interacting parts that, when functioning properly, achieve a desired result.

Formal Criminal Justice Process The model of the criminal justice process in which participants follow formal rules to create a smoothly functioning disposition of cases from arrest to punishment.

Discretion The ability of individuals in the criminal justice system to make operational decisions based on personal judgment instead of formal rules or official information.

FIGURE 1.2 The Criminal Justice Process

This diagram provides a simplified overview of the basic steps of the criminal justice process, from criminal act to release from incarceration. Next to each step, you will find the chapter of this textbook in which the event is covered.

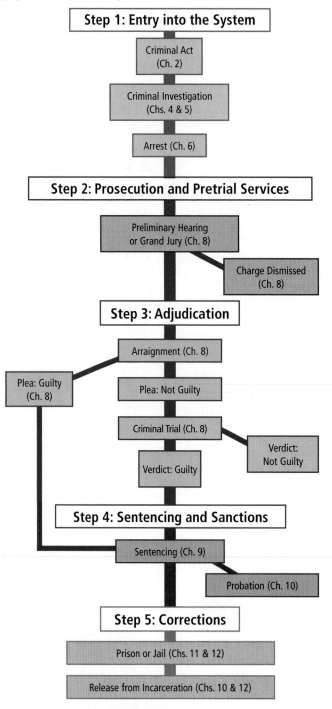

Step 1: Entry into the System

Criminal Act (Ch. 2)

Criminal Investigation (Chs. 4 & 5)

Arrest (Ch. 6)

Step 2: Prosecution and Pretrial Services

Preliminary Hearing or Grand Jury (Ch. 8)

Charge Dismissed (Ch. 8)

Step 3: Adjudication

Arraignment (Ch. 8)

Plea: Guilty (Ch. 8)

Plea: Not Guilty

Criminal Trial (Ch. 8)

Verdict: Not Guilty

Verdict: Guilty

Step 4: Sentencing and Sanctions

Sentencing (Ch. 9)

Probation (Ch. 10)

Step 5: Corrections

Prison or Jail (Chs. 11 & 12)

Release from Incarceration (Chs. 10 & 12)

Informal Criminal Justice Process A model of the criminal justice system that recognizes the informal authority exercised by individuals at each step of the criminal justice process.

made by criminal justice professionals are said to produce an **informal criminal justice process** that does not operate within the rigid confines of formal rules and laws.

1-4a

Informal Decision Making

By its nature, the informal criminal justice system relies on the discretion of individuals to offset the rigidity of criminal statutes and procedural rules. For example, even if a prosecutor believes that a suspect is guilty, she or he may decide not to bring charges against the suspect if the case is weak or the police erred during the investigative process. In many instances, prosecutors will not squander the scarce resource of court time on a case they might not win. Some argue that the informal process has made our system more just. Given the immense pressure of limited resources, the argument goes, only rarely will an innocent person end up before a judge and jury.[13]

DISCRETION IN ACTION Law enforcement also uses discretion to best allocate its scarce resources. For example, in the *You Be the Legislator* feature earlier in the chapter, we mentioned the proliferation of state laws banning texting while driving. Georgia's ban took effect in July 2010, yet over the next two years fewer than fifty people a month in the entire state were convicted of that offense.[14] Apparently, police officers in Georgia are using their discretion to loosely enforce the texting-while-driving law, given what we know to be the prevalence of such behavior.

There are several reasons for this use of discretion. First, it is difficult for police officers to prove that a person has been texting and driving. In court, the suspect will often claim that he or she was simply accessing a GPS navigation system or using his or her hands for some other legal activity. If a judge believes this argument, as is often the case, the police officer has wasted his or her time.[15] Second, police officers may not consider enforcement of texting-while-driving laws to be the best use of their limited time. From July 2010 to September 2012, Georgia law enforcement officers were able to secure about 22,500 convictions for drunk driving compared to 1,281 convictions for texting while driving.[16] Despite evidence that the two behaviors are comparably dangerous, Georgia police obviously give higher priority to getting drunk drivers off state roadways.

In Chapters 4, 5, and 6, we will examine many other circumstances that call for discretionary decision making by law enforcement officers. (See Figure 1.3 below for a description of some of the important discretionary decisions that make up the informal criminal justice process.)

THE PITFALLS OF DISCRETION Unfortunately, the informal criminal justice system does not always benefit from measured, rational decision making. Individual judgment can be tainted by personal bias, erroneous or irrational thinking, and plain ill will. When this occurs, discretion becomes "the power to *get away* with alternative decisions (emphasis added)."[17] Indeed, many of the rules of the formal criminal justice process are designed to keep its employees from substituting their own judgment for that of the general public, as expressed by the law.

Regarding the texting-while-driving bans discussed above, many observers worry that such laws will exacerbate the incidence of racial profiling in the United States.[18] As you will learn in Chapter 6, racial profiling is the police practice of improperly targeting members of minority groups based on personal characteristics such as race or ethnicity. Furthermore, associate Supreme Court justice Antonin Scalia has criticized discretion in the courts for its tendency to cause discriminatory and disparate criminal sentences, a subject we will discuss in Chapter 9. According to Scalia, the need for fairness and certainty in the criminal justice system outweighs the practical benefits of widespread and unpredictable discretionary decision making.[19]

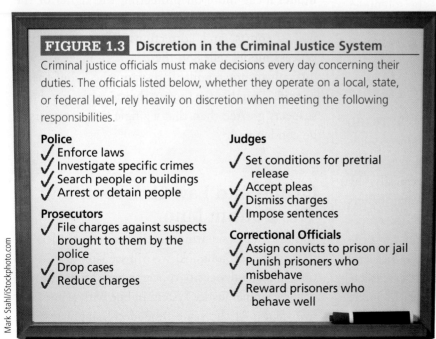

FIGURE 1.3 Discretion in the Criminal Justice System

Criminal justice officials must make decisions every day concerning their duties. The officials listed below, whether they operate on a local, state, or federal level, rely heavily on discretion when meeting the following responsibilities.

Police
- ✓ Enforce laws
- ✓ Investigate specific crimes
- ✓ Search people or buildings
- ✓ Arrest or detain people

Prosecutors
- ✓ File charges against suspects brought to them by the police
- ✓ Drop cases
- ✓ Reduce charges

Judges
- ✓ Set conditions for pretrial release
- ✓ Accept pleas
- ✓ Dismiss charges
- ✓ Impose sentences

Correctional Officials
- ✓ Assign convicts to prison or jail
- ✓ Punish prisoners who misbehave
- ✓ Reward prisoners who behave well

Mark Stahl/iStockphoto.com

1-4b
Ethics and Justice

LO 4 How can we reconcile the need for some sort of discretion in criminal justice with the ever-present potential for abuse? Part of the answer lies in our initial definition of discretion, which mentions not only individual judgment but also *conscience*. Ideally, actors in the criminal justice system will make moral choices about what is right and wrong based on the norms that have been established by society. In other words, they will behave *ethically*.

Ethics in criminal justice is closely related to the concept of justice. Because criminal justice professionals are representatives of the state, they have the power to determine whether the state is treating its citizens fairly. If some law enforcement officers in fact make the decision to pull over a texting driver based on that driver's race, then they are not only acting unethically but also unjustly.

ETHICS AND THE LAW The line between ethics and justice is often difficult to discern, as ethical standards are usually not written into criminal statutes. Consequently, individuals must often "fill in" the ethical blanks. To make this point, ethics expert John Kleinig uses the real-life example of a police officer who refused to arrest a homeless person for sleeping in a private parking garage. A local ordinance clearly prohibited such behavior. The officer, however, felt it would be unethical to arrest a homeless person under those circumstances unless he or she was acting in a disorderly manner. The officer's supervisors were unsympathetic to this ethical stance, and he was suspended from duty without pay.[20]

ETHICS AND CRITICAL THINKING Did the police officer in the above example behave ethically by inserting his own beliefs into the letter of the criminal law? Would an officer who arrested peaceful homeless trespassers be acting unethically? In some cases, the ethical decision will be *intuitive*, reflecting an automatic response determined by a person's background and experiences. In other cases, however, intuition is not enough. *Critical thinking* is needed for an ethical response.[21] Throughout this textbook, we will use the principle of critical thinking—which involves developing analytical skills and reasoning—to address the many ethical challenges inherent in the criminal justice system.

1-5
what's HAPPENING IN CRIMINAL JUSTICE TODAY?

LO 5 In describing the general direction of the criminal justice system as a whole, many observers point to two models introduced by Professor Herbert Packer: the *crime control model* and the *due process model*.[22] The underlying value of the **crime control model** is that the most important function of the criminal justice process is to punish and repress criminal conduct. The system must be quick and efficient, placing as few restrictions as possible on the ability of law enforcement officers to make discretionary decisions in apprehending criminals.

Although not in direct conflict with crime control, the underlying values of the **due process model** focus more on protecting the rights of the accused through formal, legal restraints on the police, courts, and corrections. That is, the due process model relies on the courts to make it more difficult to prove guilt. It rests on the belief that it is more desirable for society that ninety-nine guilty suspects go free than that a single innocent person be condemned.[23]

1-5a
Crime and Law Enforcement: The Bottom Line

It is difficult to say which of Packer's two models has the upper hand today. As we will see later in this section, homeland security concerns have brought much of the criminal justice system in line with crime control values. At the same time, decreasing arrest and imprisonment rates suggest that due process values

Ethics The moral principles that govern a person's perception of right and wrong.

Crime Control Model A criminal justice model that places primary emphasis on the right of society to be protected from crime and violent criminals.

Due Process Model A criminal justice model that places primacy on the right of the individual to be protected from the power of the government.

BIOMETRICS

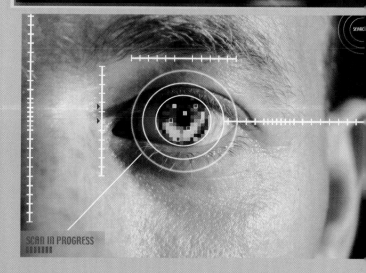

SCAN IN PROGRESS

THE science of biometrics involves identifying a person through her or his unique physical characteristics. In the criminal justice context, the term *biometrics* refers to the various technological devices that read these characteristics and report the identity of the subject to the authorities. The use of biometrics is becoming more common in law enforcement. Public cameras equipped with facial recognition software can now scan crowds and pick out criminals by matching their features against those stored in a database.

Furthermore, several years ago law enforcement agents in about forty counties began using the Mobile Offender Recognition and Identification System (MORIS). With the device, which weighs about twelve ounces and attaches to a smartphone, the police officer takes a photograph of a suspect's face from five feet away, or of the suspect's eyes from a distance of six inches. The app is then engaged to search for a facial or iris match from a national database to determine if the suspect has a previous record. Without MORIS, a police officer must take the suspect back to the station house,

take her or his fingerprints, and then wait up to a week to hear if the FBI was able to produce a match. With MORIS, the digital search is completed within seconds.

THINKING ABOUT BIOMETRICS

Does law enforcement's increased use of biometrics better fit the crime control model or the due process model? Explain your answer.

shutterstock.com

---

are strong, as well. Indeed, despite that fact that most Americans believe our crime problem to be worsening,[24] the number of violent crimes in the United States is presently at its lowest level in four decades. Furthermore, property crimes have been declining every year for the past decade.[25]

As we will discuss in Chapter 2, such trends contradict conventional wisdom, which holds that when people are out of work and need money, they turn to crime as a last resort. Despite the economic downturn that has gripped the county for the past several years, the expected higher levels of criminality have not occurred. Juvenile crime rates are also declining, a subject we will address in Chapter 13. Alfred Blumstein of Carnegie Mellon University in Pittsburgh has called all this good news "striking," because it comes "at a time when everyone anticipated [crime rates] could be going up because of the recession."[26]

1-5b
Homeland Security and Domestic Terrorism

Without question, the attacks of September 11, 2001—when terrorists hijacked four commercial airlines and used them to kill nearly three thousand people in New York City, northern Virginia, and rural Pennsylvania—were the most significant events of the first decade of the 2000s as far as crime fighting is concerned. As we will see throughout this textbook, the resulting **homeland security** movement has touched nearly every aspect of criminal justice. This movement has the ultimate goal of protecting America from **terrorism,** which can be broadly defined as the

Homeland Security
A concerted national effort to prevent terrorist attacks within the United States and reduce the country's vulnerability to terrorism.

Terrorism The use or threat of violence to achieve political objectives.

random use of staged violence to achieve political goals.

THE PATRIOT ACT The need to respond to the terrorist threat led American politicians and police officials to turn sharply toward crime control principles, discussed on page 16. In particular, the Patriot Act,[27] passed six weeks after the 9/11 attacks, strengthened the ability of federal law enforcement agents to investigate and incarcerate suspects. The 342-page piece of legislation is difficult to summarize, but some of its key provisions include the following:

- An expansion of the definition of what it means to "engage in terrorist activity" to include providing "material support" through such activities as fund-raising or operating Web sites for suspected terrorist organizations.
- Greater leeway for law enforcement agents to track Internet use, access private financial records, and wiretap those suspected of terrorist activity.
- A reduction in the amount of evidence law enforcement agents need to gather before taking a terrorist suspect into custody.

HOMELAND SECURITY AND CIVIL LIBERTIES In a recent poll, 34 percent of those questioned about the Patriot Act felt that the law "goes too far and poses a threat to *civil liberties*." Another 42 percent considered the legislation "a necessary tool that helps the government find terrorists."[28] The term **civil liberties** refers to the personal freedoms guaranteed to all Americans by the U.S. Constitution, particularly the first ten amendments, known as the Bill of Rights. (**CAREER TIP:** If you are interested in ensuring that all Americans are treated equally by federal, state, and local governments, you should consider becoming a *civil liberties lawyer*.)

Concerns about balancing personal freedoms and personal safety permeate our criminal justice system. In fact, an entire chapter of this textbook—Chapter 6—is needed to discuss the rules that law enforcement must follow to protect the civil liberties of crime suspects. Many of the issues that we will address in that chapter are

Civil Liberties The basic rights and freedoms for American citizens guaranteed by the U.S. Constitution, particularly in the Bill of Rights.

particularly relevant to counterterrorism efforts. For example:

1. The First Amendment to the U.S. Constitution states that the government shall not interfere with citizens' "freedom of speech." Does this mean that individuals should be allowed to support terrorist causes on the Internet?

2. The Fourth Amendment protects against "unreasonable searches and seizures." Does this mean that law enforcement agents should be able to seize the computer of a terrorist subject without any actual proof of wrongdoing?

3. The Sixth Amendment guarantees a trial by jury to a person accused of a crime. Does this mean that the U.S. military can find a suspect guilty of terrorist actions without providing a jury trial?

Critics of counterterrorism measures, including intercepting suspected terrorists' e-mails and increasing security at airports, believe that the government has overstepped its bounds. Supporters of these and other tactics point out that such efforts succeeded in protecting Americans from another large-scale terrorist attack until the bombings at the Boston Marathon on April 15, 2013.

1-5c
Inmate Population Trends

The proposition seems logical: if more criminals spend more time behind bars, crime rates will decline. Rising incarceration rates cannot be conclusively linked to the recent crime decline, however. For the first time in four decades, incarceration rates are not rising. After increasing by 500 percent from 1980 to 2008, the inmate population in the United States has leveled off and, as you can see in Figure 1.4 on the facing page, has even decreased slightly over the past several years. Certainly, these decreases have been small, and the American corrections system remains immense. More than 2.2 million offenders are in prison or jail in this country, and another 4.8 million are under community supervision.[29] Still, the new trend reflects a series of crucial changes in the American criminal justice system.

For many years, the growing prison population was fed by a number of "get tough on crime" laws

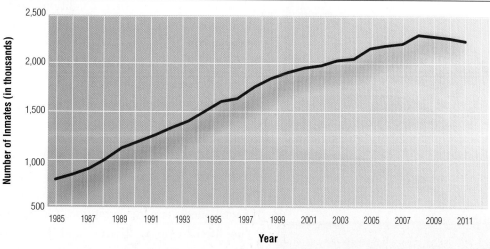

FIGURE 1.4 Prison and Jail Populations in the United States, 1985–2011

Sources: Bureau of Justice Statistics, *Correctional Populations in the United States, 1995* (Washington, D.C.: U.S. Department of Justice, June 1997), Table 1.1, page 12; and Bureau of Justice Statistics, *Correctional Populations in the United States, 2011* (Washington, D.C.: U.S. Department of Justice, November 2012), Table 2, page 3.

escape punishment for the death of Martin, an unarmed African American teenager. (Zimmerman, eventually acquitted of second degree murder, successfully claimed he was acting in self-defense, a subject we will cover in Chapter 3.)

Levels of national anger were certainly fueled by the wide availability and use of *social media*, the popular tem for Internet-based technologies that allow users to interact with each other and with the larger community of users. The most popular outlets are social networking sites such as Facebook and Google+, through which users can create and share personal profiles, and microblogs such as Twitter, where they can post short comments for public consumption. The protests following Zimmerman's acquittal were an outgrowth of countless Facebook postings on the subject, and opinions on Twitter captured the mood of the national debate.

passed by politicians in response to the crime wave of the late 1980s and early 1990s. These sentencing laws—discussed in Chapter 9—made it more likely that a person arrested for a crime would wind up behind bars and that, once there, he or she would not be back in the community for a long while. The recent reversal of this pattern does not mean that the due process model, which favors rehabilitation over incarceration, is beginning to dominate the American criminal justice system. Rather, as Ram Cnaan, a professor at the University of Pennsylvania, notes, it reflects a painful truth about prison and jail inmates: "They simply cost too much."[30] Each year, federal and state governments spend more than $57 billion on corrections.

1-5d
The Social Media Revolution

SOCIAL MEDIA AND CJ

Many cities and counties in the United States offer **"crime stopper" Facebook pages** to keep the local community informed on relevant criminal justice topics. Go to Facebook and search for "Crimestoppers" plus the name of your city, county, or state.

Not long after Trayvon Martin was shot and killed by George Zimmerman on February 26, 2012, in Sanford, Florida, angry protests erupted throughout the country. The demonstrations were spurred by the perception among many that Zimmerman, a Hispanic neighborhood watch volunteer, would

TECHNOLOGICAL STRATEGIES Social media's impact on the criminal justice system goes well beyond increasing public interest in high-profile murder cases. Criminal justice professionals are increasingly adapting the technology to their specific endeavors. Leading up to George Zimmerman's 2013 trial, his defense attorney Mark O'Meara set up a Twitter page and a Facebook account on behalf of his client. O'Meara consistently used these social media sites to deliver updates to the public about his strategy, avoiding journalists and other representatives of traditional news outlets. Prosecutors have also begun to mine social media, scouring sites for relevant information on defendants and witnesses.

As we will discuss in Chapter 4, law enforcement agents are benefiting from social media as an investigative tool. Departmental Facebook pages have proved to be a popular thoroughfare for anonymous

Local police patrol the grounds of the Ladue Middle School in Ladue, Missouri, on January 17, 2013. That day, school officials received a threatening post on Instagram. What particular challenges do threats delivered on social media pose to law enforcement agencies?

UPI/Bill Greenblatt /LANDOV

that allows residents to receive instant alerts about dangerous weather conditions, road closures, and "hot spots" of criminal activity. (**CAREER TIP:** A number of law enforcement agencies are now hiring *social media strategists* to develop and maintain systems for using this technology to communicate with the public.)

TECHNOLOGICAL OFFENSES As a rule, technology that helps law enforcement provides new outlets for criminals as well. Social media are no exception. Groups of shoplifters employ Twitter and Facebook to organize "flash-robs," in which a certain establishment is targeted and raided within minutes. Street gangs go to the Internet to recruit new members and organize criminal enterprises, as do homegrown terrorists. After the FBI arrested four Southern California men in November 2012 for planning to kill U.S. soldiers overseas, the federal agents revealed that the aspiring terrorists had "liked" each others' anti-American sentiments on Facebook.[32]

crime tips, and police officers can develop important leads on suspects without leaving their desks. Several years ago, Houston police solved a bank robbery thanks to an incriminating trail of Facebook posts—including "Got $$$" and "Wipe my teeth with hundreds"—left by the perpetrators.[31] Law enforcement agencies are also using social media to provide information. The Hillsborough (New Jersey) Police Department, for example, has created a Twitter feed

Because of the anonymity they provide, social media are also natural outlets for stalking, bullying, and harassment, topics we address in Chapter 14's section on cyber crime. "The fascinating thing about technology is that once we open the door, it's going to move in ways that we can't always predict and are slow to control," says Scott Decker, a criminal justice professor at Arizona State University.[33]

REVIEW

✔️ **Review what you've read with the quiz below.**

Rip out the Chapter Review card at the back of this book, which includes:
- Chapter Summary and Learning Outcomes
- Key Terms

Or you can go online to CourseMate at www.cengagebrain.com to:
- Complete Practice Quizzes to prepare for tests.
- Review Key Terms Flash Cards (online or print).
- Play games to master concepts.

quiz

1. Murder, assault, and robbery are labeled _____ crimes because they are committed against persons.

2. The category of crime that includes larceny, motor vehicle theft, and arson is called _____ crime.

3. To protect against a too-powerful central government, the framers of the U.S. Constitution relied on the principle of _____ to balance power between the national government and the states.

4. The United States has a dual court system, with parallel court systems at the federal level and at the _____ level.

5. At every level, the criminal justice system relies on the _____ of its employees to keep it from being bogged down by formal rules.

6. Ideally, criminal justice professionals rely on a strong sense of _____ to make moral and just decision as part of their daily routines.

7. The _____ _____ model of criminal justice places great importance on high rates of apprehension and conviction of criminal suspects.

8. The _____ _____ model emphasizes the rights of individual criminal defendants over the powers of the government.

9. Despite predictions to the contrary, crime rates in the United States have steadily _____ over the past several years.

10. America's homeland security system has been designed to protect the country from violent acts committed to further political goals, otherwise known as _____.

Answers can be found on the Chapter 1 Review card at the end of the book.

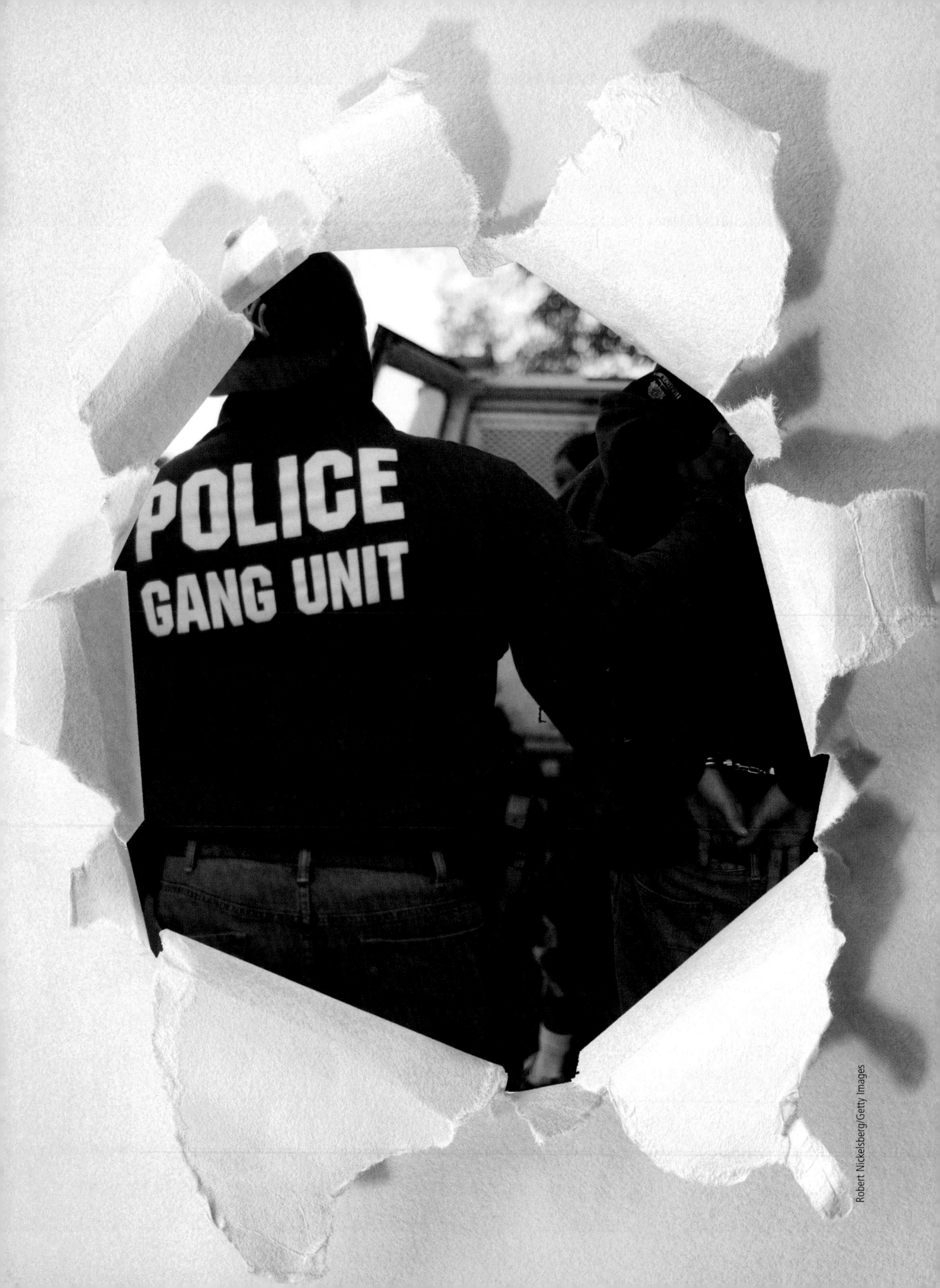

Robert Nickelsberg/Getty Images

Learning OUTCOMES
After studying this chapter, you will be able to . . .

1 Discuss the difference between a hypothesis and a theory in the context of criminology.

2 Contrast the medical model of addiction with the criminal model of addiction.

3 Distinguish between the National Crime Victimization Survey (NCVS) and self-reported surveys.

4 Describe the three ways that victims' rights legislation increases the ability of crime victims to participate in the criminal justice system.

5 Identify the three factors most often used by criminologists to explain changes in the nation's crime rate.

THE CRIME PICTURE: THEORIES AND TRENDS

Loner Gunman

In their continuing efforts to make college campuses safer places, crime experts have tried to come up with a method to identify potential sources of violence. These efforts have led to the development of a "profile" of school shooters. According to this profile, such offenders are almost always male and often are older graduate students. They also tend to be socially awkward and isolated, and in many instances have experienced a "significant disruption" in their lives just prior to an eruption of violent behavior.

James Holmes did not open fire on a college campus. Instead, his attack occurred in a movie theater in Aurora, Colorado, on July 20, 2012. In a number of other ways, however, Holmes does fit the profile of a school shooter. He was a twenty-four-year-old graduate student, having spent a year at the University of Colorado's Center for Neuroscience. About a month before his shooting spree, in which he killed

twelve moviegoers and wounded fifty-eight others, Holmes abruptly quit the program after performing poorly on an oral exam. Following the incident, one fellow graduate student remarked that Holmes was a silent loner who "always seemed to be off in his own world, which did not involve other people."

In retrospect, there were other hints that Holmes might pose a danger to the community. Six weeks before the shootings, a University of Colorado psychiatrist who had been treating Holmes expressed concerns about his mental

well-being to the school's threat assessment team. Furthermore, Holmes himself planned the attack with "calculation and deliberation," stockpiling an arsenal of guns and ammunition over the course of several months. He also booby trapped his apartment with explosives on the day of the shootings and purchased his movie ticket twelve days in advance. For many, this showed that Holmes's behavior could only be explained one way. "He's not crazy," said Tom Teves, whose son had been killed during Holmes's rampage. "He's evil."

With this memorial, community members show their support for the victims of James Holmes's July 2012 shooting spree in Aurora, Colorado.

AP Photo/*The Denver Post*, Hyoung Chang

2-1 what IS A THEORY?

The study of crime, or **criminology,** is rich with different reasons as to why people commit crimes. However, *criminologists,* or those who study the causes of crime, warn against using models or profiles to predict violent behavior. After all, not every socially awkward, male graduate student who suddenly drops out of school should be treated as a future mass murderer. To make such a judgment, researchers Michael L. Sulkowski and Philip J. Lazarus point out, would lead to a "gross overidentification of potential threats."[1]

Still, in the case of James Holmes, there did seem to be some connection between his characteristics and his violent outburst, particularly when one considers that he may have been suffering from mental illness. That is, there may have been a *correlation* between his behavior and his crimes, a concept that is crucial to criminology.

2-1a Correlation and Cause

Correlation between two variables means that they tend to vary together. **Causation,** in contrast, means that one variable is responsible for the change in the other. As we will see later in the chapter, there is a correlation between drug abuse and criminal behavior: statistically, many criminals are also drug abusers. But drug abuse does not cause crime: not everyone who abuses drugs is a criminal.

To give another example, the states with the strictest gun laws, such as Hawaii and Massachusetts, generally have low gun death rates. The states with the most lenient gun laws, such as Alabama and Alaska, generally have high gun death rates.[2] Nevertheless, few criminologists would assert that gun laws *cause* gun deaths, though many might argue that such laws are a contributing factor. Many more elements must be taken into account to get a full picture of the root causes of firearm homicides in any particular geographical area.

So, correlation does not equal cause. Such is the quandary for criminologists. We can say that there is a correlation between many factors and criminal behavior, but it is quite difficult to prove that the factors directly cause criminal behavior. Consequently, the question that is the underpinning of criminology—What causes crime?—has yet to be definitively answered.

2-1b The Role of Theory

Criminologists have, however, uncovered a wealth of information concerning a different, and more practically applicable, inquiry: Given a certain set of circumstances, why do individuals commit criminal acts? This information has allowed criminologists to develop a number of *theories* concerning the causes of crime. Most of us tend to think of a *theory* as some sort of guess or a statement that is lacking in credibility. In the academic world, and therefore for our purposes, a **theory** is an explanation of a happening or circumstance that is based on observation, experimentation, and reasoning. Scientific and academic researchers observe facts and their consequences to develop *hypotheses* about what will occur when a similar fact pattern is present in the future. A **hypothesis** is a proposition that can be tested by researchers or observers to determine if it is valid. If enough authorities do find the hypothesis valid, it will be accepted as a theory. See Figure 2.1 on the facing page for an example of this process, known as the *scientific method,* in action.

1 LO

2-2 which THEORIES OF CRIME ARE MOST WIDELY ACCEPTED?

As you read this chapter, keep in mind that theories are not the same as facts, and most, if not all, of the criminological theories described in these pages have their detractors. Over the past century, however, a

---

Criminology The scientific study of crime and the causes of criminal behavior.

Correlation The relationship between two measurements or behaviors that tend to move in the same direction.

Causation The relationship in which a change in one measurement or behavior creates a recognizable change in another measurement or behavior.

Theory An explanation of a happening or circumstance that is based on observation, experimentation, and reasoning.

Hypothesis A possible explanation for an observed occurrence that can be tested by further investigation.

FIGURE 2.1 The Scientific Method

The scientific method is a process through which researchers test the accuracy of a hypothesis. This simple example should provide an idea of how the scientific method works.

 Observation: I left my home at 7:00 this morning, and I was on time for class.

 Hypothesis: If I leave home at 7:00 every morning, then I will never be late for class.
(Hypotheses are often presented in this "If . . . , then . . ." format.)

 Test: For three straight weeks, I left home at 7:00 every morning. Not one time was I late for class.

 Verification: Four of my neighbors have the same morning class. They agree that they are never late if they leave by 7:00 A.M.

 Theory: As long as I leave home at 7:00 A.M., I don't have to worry about being late for class.

 Prediction: Tomorrow morning I'll leave at 7:00, and I will be on time for my class.

Note that even a sound theory supported by the scientific method such as this one does not *prove* that the prediction will be correct. Other factors not accounted for in the test and verification stages, such as an unexpected traffic accident, may disprove the theory. Predictions based on complex theories such as the criminological ones we will be discussing in this chapter are often challenged in such a manner.

---

number of theories of crime have gained wide, if not total, acceptance. We now turn our attention to these theories, starting with those that focus on the psychological and physical aspects of criminal behavior.

2-2a

The Brain and the Body

Perhaps the most basic answer to the question of why a person commits a crime is that he or she makes a willful decision to do so. This is the underpinning of the **rational choice theory** of crime, summed up by criminologist James Q. Wilson (1931–2012) as follows:

> At any given moment, a person can choose between committing a crime and not committing it. The consequences of committing a crime consist of rewards (what psychologists call "reinforcers") and punishments; the consequences of not committing the crime also entail gains and losses. The larger the ratio of the net rewards of crime to the net rewards of [not committing a crime], the greater the tendency to commit a crime.[3]

In other words, a person, before committing a crime, acts as if she or he is weighing the benefits (which may be money, in the case of a robbery) against the costs (the possibility of being caught and going to prison or jail). If the perceived benefits are greater than the potential costs, the person is more likely to commit the crime.

"THRILL OFFENDERS" Expanding on rational choice theory, sociologist Jack Katz has stated that the "rewards" of crime may be sensual as well as financial. The inherent danger of criminal activity, according to Katz, increases the "rush" a criminal experiences on successfully committing a crime. Katz labels the rewards of this "rush" the *seduction of crime*.[4] For example, the National Coalition for the Homeless documented nearly 900 unprovoked attacks against the homeless in the decade that ended in 2010, including 244 fatalities.[5] In most of these incidents, the assailants were "thrill offenders" who kicked, punched, or set on fire homeless persons for the sport of it. Katz believes that such seemingly "senseless" crimes can be explained by rational choice theory only if the intrinsic (inner) reward of the crime itself is considered.

RATIONAL CHOICE THEORY AND PUNISHMENT
The theory that wrongdoers choose to commit crimes is a cornerstone of the American criminal justice system. Because crime is seen as the end result of a series of rational choices, policymakers have reasoned that severe punishment can deter criminal activity by adding another variable to the decision-making process. Supporters of the death penalty—now used by thirty-two states and the federal government—emphasize its deterrent effects, and legislators have used harsh mandatory sentences to control illegal drug use and trafficking.

TRAIT THEORIES OF CRIME If society is willing to punish crimes that are the result of a rational decision-making process, what should be its response to criminal behavior that is irrational or even unintentional? What if, for example, a schoolteacher who made sexual advances to young

Rational Choice Theory A school of criminology that holds that wrongdoers act as if they weigh the possible benefits of criminal or delinquent activity against the expected costs of being apprehended.

CAREERPREP | CRIMINOLOGIST

zhang bo/iStockphoto

girls, including his stepdaughter, could prove that his wrongdoing was actually caused by an egg-sized tumor in his brain? Somewhat in contrast to rational choice theory, *trait theories* suggest that certain *biological* or *psychological* traits in individuals could incline them toward criminal behavior given a certain set of circumstances. **Biology** is a very broad term that refers to the scientific study of living organisms, while **psychology** pertains more specifically to the study of the mind and its processes. "All behavior is biological," pointed out geneticist David C. Rowe. "All behavior is represented in the brain, in its biochemistry, electrical activity, structure, and growth and decline."[6]

Biology The science of living organisms, including their structure, function, growth, and origin.

Psychology The scientific study of mental processes and behavior.

Hormone A chemical substance, produced in tissue and conveyed in the bloodstream, that controls certain cellular and body functions such as growth and reproduction.

Testosterone The hormone primarily responsible for the production of sperm and the development of male secondary sex characteristics such as the growth of facial and pubic hair and the change of voice pitch.

Hormones and Aggression One trait theory holds that *biochemistry*, or the chemistry of living matter, can influence criminal behavior. For example, chemical messengers known as **hormones** have also been the subject of much criminological study. Criminal activity in males has been linked to elevated levels of hormones—specifically, **testosterone**, which controls secondary sex characteristics and has been associated with traits of aggression. Testing of inmate populations shows that those incarcerated for violent crimes exhibit higher testosterone levels than other prisoners.[7] Elevated testosterone levels have also been used to explain the age-crime relationship, as the average testosterone level of men under the age of twenty-eight is double that of men between thirty-one and sixty-six years old.[8]

A very specific form of female violent behavior is believed to stem from hormones. In 2012, Rasesh Patel of Lakeland, Florida, told investigators that his wife Neha was suffering from *postpartum psychosis* when she drowned their one-year-old son in a bathtub. This temporary illness, believed to be caused

TODAY, technology has made it relatively easy (if not always inexpensive) for scientists (and defense attorneys) to show brain irregularities such as schizophrenia. Computer axial tomography (CAT) scans combine X-ray technology with computer technology to provide an exact three-dimensional image of the brain. Magnetic resonance imaging (MRI) technology uses a very powerful magnet to create a magnetic field, which is then bombarded with radio waves. These waves can provide a very detailed image of brain tissue, allowing doctors to determine whether the tissue is damaged or diseased. Functional magnetic resonance imaging (fMRI) permits researchers to study the function of the brain as well as its structure. This technique determines which areas of the brain are in use by measuring blood flow patterns. When a brain area is active, it consumes more oxygen and therefore requires increased amounts of blood.

Yakobchuk Vasyl/Shutterstock.com

THINKING ABOUT BRAIN-SCANNING DEVICES

The technologies discussed above allow scientists to discover and measure brain malfunctions that are associated with various neurological disorders such as schizophrenia. Given the correlation between schizophrenia and violent behavior, how could brain scanners be used to prevent crime? What would be some of the problems with using these devices to identify potential criminals before they had in fact committed any crimes?

---

partly by the hormonal changes that women experience after childbirth, triggers abnormal behavior in a small percentage of new mothers.[9]

The Brain and Crime The study of brain activity, or *neurophysiology,* has also found a place in criminology. Cells in the brain known as neurons communicate with each other by releasing chemicals called **neurotransmitters.** Criminologists have isolated three neurotransmitters that seem to be particularly related to aggressive behavior:

1. Serotonin, which regulates moods, appetite, and memory.

2. Norepinephrine, which regulates sleep-wake cycles and controls how we respond to anxiety, fear, and stress.

3. Dopamine, which regulates perceptions of pleasure and reward.[10]

Researchers have established that, under certain circumstances, low levels of serotonin and high levels of norepinephrine are correlated with aggressive behavior.[11] Dopamine plays a crucial role in drug addiction, as we shall see later in the chapter.

According to the federal government, more than half of all prison and jail inmates have mental health problems, with smaller percentages suffering from severe brain disorders.[12] After fatally shooting six people and wounding fourteen others on January 8, 2011, in Tucson, Arizona, Jared Loughner was diagnosed with *schizophrenia,* a

Neurotransmitter A chemical that transmits nerve impulses between nerve cells and from nerve cells to the brain.

On May 1, 2012, police struggle to control anticapitalism protesters in Seattle, Washington. How does social psychology help explain acts of violence or disorder by large groups of people?

Stuart Isett/Bloomberg via Getty Images

chronic brain disorder that can lead to erratic, uncontrollable behavior. Persons suffering from this disease are at an unusually high risk for committing suicide or harming others. Psychiatrist E. Fuller Torrey estimates that schizophrenics commit about a thousand homicides each year.[13]

Further research shows that even moderate use of alcohol or drugs increases the chances that a schizophrenic will behave violently.[14] Still, it is important to note that about 2.4 million Americans—1 percent of the adult population—have been diagnosed with schizophrenia, and the vast majority of them will never become criminal offenders. That is, there may be a correlation between schizophrenia and violence, but the brain disorder cannot be said to cause violence.

PSYCHOLOGY AND CRIME Like biological theories of crime, psychological theories of crime operate under the assumption that individuals have traits that make them more or less predisposed to criminal activity. To a certain extent, however, psychology rests more heavily on abstract ideas than does biology. Even Sigmund Freud (1856–1939), perhaps the most influential of all psychologists, considered the operations of the mind to be, like an iceberg, mostly hidden.

One influential branch of psychology—*social psychology*—focuses on human behavior in the context of how human beings relate to and influence one another. Social psychology rests on the assumption that the way we view ourselves is shaped to a large degree by how we think others view us. Generally, we act in the same manner as those we like or admire because we want them to like or admire us. Thus, to a certain extent, social psychology tries to explain the influence of crowds on individual behavior.

About three decades ago, psychologist Philip Zimbardo highlighted the power of group behavior in dramatic fashion. Zimbardo randomly selected some Stanford University undergraduate students to act as "guards" and other students to act as "inmates" in an artificial prison environment. Before long, the students began to act as if these designations were real, with the "guards" physically mistreating the "inmates," who rebelled with equal violence. Within six days, Zimbardo was forced to discontinue the experiment out of fear for its participants' safety.[15] One of the basic assumptions of social psychology is that people are able to justify improper or even criminal behavior by convincing themselves that it is actually acceptable behavior. This delusion, researchers have found, is much easier to accomplish with the support of others behaving in the same manner.[16] (**CAREER TIP:** *Psychologists* study how a person's mental functions cause him or her to think or act in certain ways. Many psychologists, such as Philip Zimbardo, apply their knowledge to the mysteries of criminal behavior.)

2-2b

Bad Neighborhoods and Other Economic Disadvantages

While America's current economic problems have not, as yet, resulted in national crime increases, the same cannot be said for local trouble spots. The city of Chicago, for example, experienced 506 homicides in 2012, a 16 percent increase over the previous year. The vast majority of these murders (more than 80 percent) took place in neighborhoods on the south and west sides of the city.[17] These areas are marked by long-term financial hardship, unemployment, abandoned buildings, and high levels of gang activity. Indeed, for decades, criminologists focusing on **sociology** have argued that neighborhood conditions are perhaps the most important variable in predicting criminal behavior. (**CAREER TIP:** A *sociologist* is someone who studies human social behavior. Because crime is such an important—and interesting—facet of human behavior, sociologists often study criminality.)

SOCIAL DISORGANIZATION THEORY In the early twentieth century, juvenile crime researchers Clifford Shaw and Henry McKay popularized sociological explanations for crime with their **social disorganization theory.** Shaw and McKay studied various high-crime neighborhoods in Chicago and discovered certain "zones" that exhibited high rates of crime. These zones were characterized by "disorganization," or a breakdown of the traditional institutions of social control such as family, school systems, and local businesses. In contrast, in the city's "organized" communities, residents had developed certain agreements about fundamental values and norms.

Shaw and McKay found that residents in high-crime neighborhoods had to a large degree abandoned these fundamental values and norms. Also, a lack of social controls had led to increased levels of antisocial, or criminal, behavior.[18] According to social disorganization theory, factors that lead to crime in these neighborhoods are perpetuated by continued elevated levels of high school dropouts, unemployment, deteriorating infrastructures, and single-parent families. (See Figure 2.2 below to better understand social disorganization theory.)

STRAIN THEORY Another self-perpetuating aspect of disorganized neighborhoods is that once residents gain the financial means to leave a high-crime

> **Sociology** The study of the development and functioning of groups of people who live together within a society.
>
> **Social Disorganization Theory** The theory that deviant behavior is more likely in communities where social institutions such as the family, schools, and the criminal justice system fail to exert control over the population.

FIGURE 2.2 The Stages of Social Disorganization Theory

Social disorganization theory holds that crime is related to the environmental pressures that exist in certain communities or neighborhoods. These areas are marked by the desire of many of their inhabitants to "get out" at the first possible opportunity. Consequently, residents tend to ignore the important institutions in the community, such as businesses and education, causing further erosion and an increase in the conditions that lead to crime.

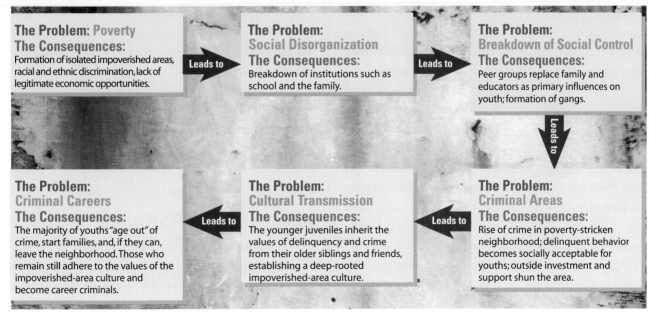

The Problem: Poverty
The Consequences: Formation of isolated impoverished areas, racial and ethnic discrimination, lack of legitimate economic opportunities.

Leads to

The Problem: Social Disorganization
The Consequences: Breakdown of institutions such as school and the family.

Leads to

The Problem: Breakdown of Social Control
The Consequences: Peer groups replace family and educators as primary influences on youth; formation of gangs.

Leads to

The Problem: Criminal Areas
The Consequences: Rise of crime in poverty-stricken neighborhood; delinquent behavior becomes socially acceptable for youths; outside investment and support shun the area.

Leads to

The Problem: Cultural Transmission
The Consequences: The younger juveniles inherit the values of delinquency and crime from their older siblings and friends, establishing a deep-rooted impoverished-area culture.

Leads to

The Problem: Criminal Careers
The Consequences: The majority of youths "age out" of crime, start families, and, if they can, leave the neighborhood. Those who remain still adhere to the values of the impoverished-area culture and become career criminals.

Source: Adapted from Larry J. Siegel, *Criminology,* 10th ed. (Belmont, CA: Thomson/Wadsworth, 2009), 180.

Two law enforcement officers investigate a murder in the Desire neighborhood of New Orleans. How would a criminologist who advocates social conflict theories of criminal behavior explain high crime rates in low-income neighborhoods such as Desire?

Michael DeMocker/*The Times-Picayune*/Landov

community, they usually do so. This desire to escape the inner city is related to a second theory based in sociology: **strain theory.** Most Americans have similar life goals, which include gaining a certain measure of wealth and financial freedom. The means of attaining these goals, however, are not universally available. Many citizens do not have access to the education or training necessary for financial success. This often results in frustration and anger, or *strain*.

Strain theory has its roots in the works of French sociologist Emile Durkheim (1858–1917) and his concept of **anomie** (derived from the Greek word for "without norms"). Durkheim believed that *anomie* resulted when social change threw behavioral norms into a flux, leading to a weakening of social controls and an increase in deviant behavior.[19] Another sociologist, American Robert K. Merton, expanded on Durkheim's ideas in his own theory of strain. Merton believed that *anomie* was caused by a social structure in which all citizens have similar goals without equal means to achieve them.[20] One way to alleviate this strain is to gain wealth by the means that are available to the residents of disorga-

nized communities: drug trafficking, burglary, and other criminal activities.

SOCIAL CONFLICT THEORIES
Strain theory and the concept of *anomie* seem to suggest that the unequal structure of our society is, in part, to blame for criminal behavior. This argument forms the bedrock of **social conflict theories** of crime. These theories, which entered mainstream criminology in the 1960s, hold capitalism responsible for high levels of violence and crime because of the disparity of income that it encourages.

According to social conflict theory, the poor commit property crimes for reasons of need and because, as members of a capitalist society, they desire the same financial rewards as everybody else. They commit violent crimes because of the frustration and rage they feel when these rewards seem unattainable. Laws, instead of reflecting the values of society as a whole, reflect only the values of the segment of society that has achieved power and is willing to use the criminal justice system as a tool to keep that power.[21] Thus, the harsh penalties for "lower-class" crimes such as burglary can be seen as a means of protecting the privileges of the "haves" from the aspirations of the "have-nots."

2-2c
Life Lessons and Criminal Behavior

Some criminologists find class theories of crime overly narrow. Surveys that ask people directly about their criminal behavior have shown that the criminal instinct is pervasive in middle- and upper-class communities, even if it is expressed differently. Anybody,

Strain Theory The assumption that crime is the result of frustration felt by individuals who cannot reach their financial and personal goals through legitimate means.

Anomie A condition in which the individual feels a disconnect from society due to the breakdown or absence of social norms.

Social Conflict Theories A school of criminology that views criminal behavior as the result of class conflict.

these criminologists argue, has the potential to act out criminal behavior, regardless of class, race, or gender.

THE ABANDONED CAR EXPERIMENT Philip Zimbardo conducted a well-known, if rather unscientific, experiment to show the broad potential for misbehavior. The psychologist placed an abandoned automobile with its hood up on the campus of Stanford University. The car remained in place, untouched, for a week. Then, Zimbardo smashed the car's window with a sledgehammer. Within minutes, passersby had joined in the destruction of the automobile, eventually stripping its valuable parts.[22] **Social process theories** function on the same basis as Zimbardo's "interdependence of decisions experiment": the potential for criminal behavior exists in everyone and will be realized depending on an individual's interaction with various institutions and processes of society. Two major branches of social process theory are (1) learning theory and (2) control theory.

LEARNING THEORY Popularized by Edwin Sutherland in the 1940s, **learning theory** contends that criminal activity is a learned behavior. In other words, a criminal is taught both the practical methods of crime (such as how to pick a lock) and the psychological aspects of crime (how to deal with the guilt of wrongdoing). Sutherland's *theory of differential association* held that individuals are exposed to the values of family and peers such as school friends or co-workers. If the dominant values one is exposed to favor criminal behavior, then that person is more likely to mimic such behavior.[23] Sutherland concentrated particularly on familial relations, believing that a child was more likely to commit crimes if she or he saw an older sibling or a parent doing so.

More recently, learning theory has been expanded to include the growing influence of the media. In the latest in a long series of studies, psychologists at the University of Michigan's Institute for Social Research released data in 2003 showing that exposure to high levels of televised violence increases aggressive behavior among young children.[24] Such findings have spurred a number of legislative attempts to curb violence on television.[25] James Holmes, whose crimes were described at the beginning of this chapter, was a devoted player of "hack and slash" video games such as Diablo III and World of Warcraft.

CONTROL THEORY Criminologist Travis Hirschi focuses on the reasons why individuals do not engage in criminal acts, rather than why they do. According to Hirschi, social bonds promote conformity to social norms. The stronger these social bonds—which include attachment to, commitment to, involvement with, and belief in societal values—the less likely that any individual will commit a crime.[26] **Control theory** holds that although we all have the potential to commit crimes, most of us are dissuaded from doing so because we care about the opinions of our family and peers.

James Q. Wilson and George Kelling described control theory in terms of the "broken windows" effect. Neighborhoods in poor condition are filled with cues of lack of social control (for example, broken windows) that invite further vandalism and other deviant behavior.[27] If these cues are removed, according to Wilson and Kelling, so is the implied acceptance of crime within a community.

LIFE COURSE THEORIES OF CRIME If crime is indeed learned behavior, some criminologists are asking, shouldn't we be focusing on early childhood—the time when humans do the most learning? Many of the other theories we have studied in this chapter tend to attribute criminal behavior to factors—such as unemployment or poor educational performance—that take place long after an individual's personality has been established. Practitioners of **life course criminology** believe that lying, stealing, bullying, and other conduct problems that occur in childhood are the strongest predictors of future criminal

Social Process Theories A school of criminology that considers criminal behavior to be the predictable result of a person's interaction with his or her environment.

Learning Theory The hypothesis that delinquents and criminals must be taught both the practical and the emotional skills necessary to participate in illegal activity.

Control Theory A series of theories that assume that all individuals have the potential for criminal behavior, but are restrained by the damage that such actions would do to their relationships with family, friends, and members of the community.

Life Course Criminology The study of crime based on the belief that behavioral patterns developed in childhood can predict delinquent and criminal behavior later in life.

behavior and have been seriously undervalued in the examination of why crime occurs.[28]

Self-Control Theory Focusing on childhood behavior raises the question of whether conduct problems established at a young age can be changed over time. Michael Gottfredson and Travis Hirschi, whose 1990 publication *A General Theory of Crime* is one of the foundations of life course criminology, think not.[29] Gottfredson and Hirschi believe that criminal behavior is linked to "low self-control," a personality trait that is formed before a child reaches the age of ten and can usually be attributed to poor parenting.[30]

Someone with low self-control is generally impulsive, thrill seeking, and likely to solve problems with violence rather than his or her intellect. Gottfredson and Hirschi think that once low self-control has been established, it will persist. In other words, childhood behavioral problems are not "solved" by positive developments later in life, such as healthy personal relationships or a good job.[31] Thus, these two criminologists ascribe to what has been called the *continuity theory of crime,* which essentially says that once negative behavior patterns have been established, they cannot be changed.

The Possibility of Change Not all of those who practice life course criminology follow the continuity theory. Terrie Moffitt, for example, notes that youthful offenders can be divided into two groups. The first group are life-course-persistent offenders: they are biting playmates at age five, skipping school at ten, stealing cars at sixteen, committing violent crimes at twenty, and perpetrating fraud and child abuse at thirty.[32] The second group are adolescent-limited offenders: as the name suggests, their "life of crime" is limited to the teenage years.[33] So, according to Moffitt, change is possible, if not for the life-course-persistent offenders (who are saddled with psychological problems that lead to continued social failure and misconduct), then for the adolescent-limited offenders.

Drug Any substance that modifies biological, psychological, or social behavior; in particular, an illegal substance with those properties.

Psychoactive Drug A chemical that affects the brain, causing changes in emotions, perceptions, and behavior.

2-3
what IS THE CONNECTION BETWEEN DRUG USE AND CRIME?

Criminologists have long studied the link between crime and drugs. In general, offenders who use greater amounts of alcohol and illegal drugs have significantly higher crime rates than those who are less involved with these substances. Actually, alcohol falls under the broadest possible definition of a drug, which is any substance that modifies biological, psychological, or social behavior. In popular usage, however, the word **drug** has a more specific connotation. When people speak of the drug problem, or the war on drugs, or drug abuse, they are referring specifically to illegal **psychoactive drugs,** which affect the brain and alter consciousness or perception. Almost all of the drugs that we will be discussing in this textbook, such as marijuana, cocaine, heroin, and amphetamines, are illegal and psychoactive.

About 22.5 million Americans regularly use illegal drugs such as marijuana and cocaine, with another 200 million using legal drugs such as alcohol and nicotine. For criminologists, these data raise two questions. First, why do people use drugs? Second, what are the consequences for the criminal justice system?

2-3a
The Criminology of Drug Use

At first glance, the reason people use drugs, including legal drugs such as alcohol, is obvious: such drugs give the user pleasure and provide a temporary escape for those who may feel tension or anxiety. Ultimately, though, such explanations are unsatisfactory because they fail to explain why some people use drugs while others do not.

THEORIES OF DRUG USE Several of the theories we discussed earlier in the chapter have been used by experts to explain drug use. *Social disorganization theory* holds that rapid social change can cause people to become disaffiliated from mainstream society, causing them to turn to drugs. *Control theory* suggests that a lack of social control, as provided by entities such as the family or school, can lead to antisocial behavior.

DRUGS AND THE "LEARNING PROCESS" Focusing on the question of why first-time drug users become habitual users, sociologist Howard Becker sees three factors in the "learning process." He believes first-time users:

1. Learn the techniques of drug use.
2. Learn to perceive the pleasurable effects of drug use.
3. Learn to enjoy the social experience of drug use.[34]

Becker's assumptions are evident in the widespread belief that positive images of drug use in popular culture "teach" adolescents that such behavior is not only acceptable but desirable. The entertainment industry, in particular, has been criticized for glamorizing various forms of drug use. (**CAREER TIP:** Teen drug abuse is a significant problem in the United States, and you can work toward alleviating it by becoming a *substance abuse counselor*.)

DRUG USE AND DRUG ABUSE Another theory rests on the assumption that some people possess overly sensitive drug receptors in their brains and are therefore biologically disposed toward drug use.[35] Though there is little conclusive evidence that biological factors can explain initial drug experimentation, scientific research has provided a great deal of insight into patterns of long-term drug use.

In particular, science has aided in understanding the difference between drug use and drug *abuse*. **Drug abuse** can be defined as the use of any drug—licit or illicit—that causes either psychological or bodily harm to the abuser or to third parties. Just as most people who drink beer or wine avoid abusing alcohol, most users of illegal substances are not abusers. For most drugs except nicotine, only between 7 and 20 percent of all users suffer from compulsive abuse.[36]

Despite their relatively small numbers, drug abusers have a disparate impact on the drug market. The 20 percent of Americans, for example, who drink the most consume more than 80 percent of all alcoholic beverages sold in the United States. The data are similar for illicit substance abusers, leading to the conclusion that, to a large extent, abusers and addicts sustain the market for illegal drugs. As Figure 2.3 below shows, alcohol is, by a large margin, the most frequently abused drug in the United States.

2-3b
The Drug-Crime Relationship

Of course, because many drugs are illegal, anybody who sells, uses, or in any way promotes the use of these drugs is, under most circumstances, breaking the law. The drug-crime relationship goes beyond the

---

FIGURE 2.3 Drug Abuse and Dependency in the United States

In 2011, about 20.6 million Americans were classified as being addicted to or abusing drugs. As this figure shows, the majority of this substance abuse involves alcohol, with marijuana being the most abused illicit drug.

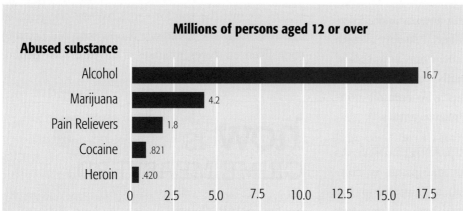

Source: Substance Abuse and Mental Health Services Administration, *Results from the 2011 National Survey on Drug Use and Health: Summary of National Findings* (Washington, D.C.: National Institute on Drug Abuse, 2012), 74–75.

Drug Abuse The use of drugs that results in physical or psychological problems for the user, as well as disruption of personal relationships and employment.

Do you think that drug abusers, such as this man injecting heroin into his arm, should be treated as criminals to be punished or as ill people in need of treatment? Explain your answer.

language of criminal drug statutes, however. About 37 percent of state prisoners and 33 percent of jail inmates incarcerated for a violent crime were under the influence of alcohol at the time of their arrest.[37] Similarly, according to one recent study, about two-thirds of all arrestees in ten major American cities tested positive for illicit drugs when apprehended.[38] As we will see throughout this textbook, the prosecution of illegal drug users and suppliers has been one of the primary factors in the enormous growth of the American correctional industry.

MODELS OF ADDICTION Is criminal conviction and incarceration the best way for society to deal with addicts? Those who follow the **medical model of addiction** believe that addicts are not criminals, but mentally or physically ill individuals who are forced into acts of petty crime to "feed their habit." Those who believe in the *enslavement theory of addiction* advocate treating addiction as a disease and hold that society should not punish addicts but rather attempt to rehabilitate them, as would be done for any other unhealthy person.[39]

LO **2**

Although a number of organizations, including the American Medical Association, recognize alcoholism and other forms of drug dependence as diseases, the criminal justice system tends to favor the **criminal model of addiction** over the medical model. The criminal model holds that illegal drug abusers and addicts endanger society with their behavior and should be punished the same as persons who commit non-drug-related crimes.[40]

MARIJUANA TRENDS As far as marijuana is concerned, a third trend has emerged over the past two decades, based on the loosening of absolute prohibition. Eighteen states and the District of Columbia allow for the medical use of the drug to alleviate pain. Eight states have *decriminalized* marijuana, meaning that possession of small amounts of pot is treated as an infraction, like a traffic ticket, rather than a crime. Six states treat marijuana possession as a fine-only misdemeanor offense, with no prison or jail time.[41]

Then, in November 2012, Colorado and Washington became the first two states to *legalize* the possession and sale of marijuana for personal use. In both states, possession of up to an ounce is no longer against the law for those twenty-one years of age and older. The substance is now sold and taxed in state-licensed stores, much as is the case with alcohol and tobacco.

Medical Model of Addiction An approach to drug addiction that treats drug abuse as a mental illness and focuses on treating and rehabilitating offenders rather than punishing them.

Criminal Model of Addiction An approach to drug abuse that holds that drug offenders harm society by their actions to the same extent as other criminals and should face the same punitive sanctions.

2-4
how IS CRIME MEASURED ?

So far in this chapter, you have been exposed to numerous studies relating to criminal behavior. For the most part, these analyses have dealt with narrow topics such as the relationship between states' gun laws and their gun death rates, the possible violent tendencies of schizophrenics, and the neighborhood distribution of crime in Chicago. The best-known annual survey of criminal behavior, however, tries to answer the broadest of questions: How much crime is there in the United States?

2-4a
The Uniform Crime Report

Suppose that a firefighter dies while fighting a fire at an office building. Later, police discover that the building manager intentionally set the fire. All of the elements of the crime of arson have certainly been met, but can the manager be charged with murder? In some jurisdictions, the act might be considered a form of murder, but according to the U.S. Department of Justice, arson-related deaths and injuries of police officers and firefighters due to the "hazardous natures of their professions" are not murders.[42]

The distinction is important because the Department of Justice provides us with the most far-reaching and oft-cited set of national crime statistics. Each year, the department releases the **Uniform Crime Report (UCR).** Since its inception in 1930, the UCR has attempted to measure the overall rate of crime in the United States by organizing "offenses known to law enforcement."[43] To produce the UCR, the Federal Bureau of Investigation (FBI) relies on the voluntary participation of local law enforcement agencies. These agencies—approximately 18,200 in total, covering 95 percent of the population—base their information on three measurements:

1. The number of persons arrested.
2. The number of crimes reported by victims, witnesses, or the police themselves.
3. Police employee data.[44]

Once this information has been sent to the FBI, the agency presents the crime data in two important ways:

1. As a *rate* per 100,000 people. So, for example, suppose the crime rate in a given year is 3,500. This means that, for every 100,000 inhabitants of the United States, 3,500 *Part I offenses* (explained in the next column) were reported to the FBI by local police departments. The crime rate is often cited by media sources when

discussing the level of crime in the United States.

2. As a *percentage* change from the previous year or other time periods. From 2000 to 2010, there was a 20.2 percent decrease in violent crime and an 18.7 percent decrease in property crime. Thus, according to the UCR, the first decade of the twenty-first century saw a significant reduction in criminal behavior in the United States.[45]

The Department of Justice publishes its data annually in *Crime in the United States.* Along with the basic statistics, this publication offers an exhaustive array of crime information, including breakdowns of crimes committed by city, county, and other geographic designations and by the demographics (gender, race, age) of the individuals who have been arrested for crimes. (**CAREER TIP:** With their expert knowledge of statistics and their ability to organize numerical data, *statisticians* are crucial employees for the FBI and other federal and state law enforcement agencies that regularly publish crime reports.)

2-4b
Part I Offenses

The UCR divides the criminal offenses it measures into two major categories: Part I and Part II offenses. **Part I offenses** are those crimes that, due to their seriousness and frequency, are recorded by the FBI to give a general idea of the "crime picture" in the United States in any given year. For a description of the seven Part I offenses, see Figure 2.4 on the next page.

Part I violent offenses are those most likely to be covered by the media and, consequently, inspire the most fear of crime in the population. These crimes have come to dominate crime coverage to such an extent that, for most Americans, the first image that comes to mind at the mention of "crime" is one person physically attacking another person or a robbery taking place with the use or threat of force.[46] Furthermore, in the stereotypical crime, the offender and the victim usually do not know each other.

Uniform Crime Report (UCR) An annual report compiled by the FBI to give an indication of criminal activity in the United States.

Part I Offenses Crimes reported annually by the FBI in its Uniform Crime Report. Part I offenses include murder, rape, robbery, aggravated assault, burglary, larceny, and motor vehicle theft.

FIGURE 2.4 | Part I Offenses

Every month local law enforcement agencies voluntarily provide information on serious offenses in their jurisdiction to the FBI. These serious offenses, known as Part I offenses, are defined here. (Arson is not included in the national crime report data, but it is sometimes considered a Part I offense nonetheless, so its definition is included here.) As the graph shows, most Part I offenses reported by local police departments in any given year are property crimes.

Murder. The willful (nonnegligent) killing of one human being by another.

Forcible rape. The carnal knowledge of a female forcibly and against her will.*

Robbery. The taking or attempting to take of anything of value from the care, custody, or control of a person or persons by force or threat of force or violence and/or by putting the victim in fear.

Aggravated assault. An unlawful attack by one person on another for the purpose of inflicting severe or aggravated bodily injury. This type of assault is usually accompanied by the use of a weapon or by means likely to produce death or great bodily harm.

Burglary—breaking or entering. The unlawful entry of a structure to commit a felony or a theft. Attempted forcible entry is included.

Larceny/theft (except motor vehicle theft). The unlawful taking, carrying, leading, or riding away of property from the possession or constructive possession of another.

Motor vehicle theft. The theft or attempted theft of a motor vehicle.

Arson. Any willful or malicious burning or attempt to burn, with or without intent to defraud, a dwelling house, public building, motor vehicle or aircraft, personal property of another, and the like.

Pie chart labels: Murder 0.1%; Forcible Rape 0.8%; Robbery 3.5%; Aggravated Assault 7.3%; Motor Vehicle Theft 7%; Larceny/Theft 60%; Burglary 21.3%

*A new definition of rape was adopted by the Department of Justice in 2012, and thus had not yet gone into effect for these data.

Sources: Federal Bureau of Investigation, *Crime in the United States, 2011* (Washington, D.C.: U.S. Department of Justice, 2012), at **www.fbi.gov/about-us/cjis/ucr/crime-in-the-u.s/2011/crime-in-the-u.s.-2011/offense-definitions** and **www.fbi.gov/about-us/cjis/ucr/crime-in-the-u.s/2011/crime-in-the-u.s.-2011/tables/table-1**.

Given the trauma of violent crimes, this perception is understandable, but it is not accurate. According to UCR statistics, a relative or other acquaintance of the victim commits at least 44 percent of the homicides in the United States.[47] Furthermore, as is evident from Figure 2.4, the majority of Part I offenses committed are property crimes. Notice that 60 percent of all reported Part I offenses are larceny/thefts, and another 21 percent are burglaries.[48]

2-4c
Part II Offenses

Not only do violent crimes represent the minority of Part I offenses, but Part I offenses are far outweighed by **Part II offenses,** which include all crimes recorded by the FBI that do not fall into the category of Part I offenses. While Part I offenses are almost always felonies, Part II offenses include criminal behavior that is often classified as a misdemeanor. Of the nineteen categories that make up Part II offenses, the most common are drug abuse violations, simple assaults (in which no weapons are used and no serious harm is done to the victim), driving under the influence, and disorderly conduct.[49]

Information gathered on Part I offenses reflects those offenses "known," or reported to the FBI by local agencies. Part II offenses, in contrast, are measured only by arrest data. In 2011, the FBI recorded about 2.1 million arrests for Part I offenses in the United States. That same year, about 10.2 million arrests for Part II offenses took place.[50] In other words, a Part II offense was five times more common than a Part I offense. Such statistics have prompted Marcus Felson, a professor at Rutgers University School of Criminal Justice, to comment that "most crime is very ordinary."[51]

Part II Offenses All crimes recorded by the FBI that do not fall into the category of Part I offenses. These crimes include both misdemeanors and felonies.

2-4d

The National Incident-Based Reporting System

In the 1980s, the Department of Justice began seeking ways to revise its data-collecting system. The result was the National Incident-Based Reporting System (NIBRS). In the NIBRS, local agencies collect data on each single crime occurrence within twenty-two offense categories made up of forty-six specific crimes called Group A offenses. These data are recorded on computerized record systems provided—though not completely financed—by the federal government.

The NIBRS became available to local agencies in 1989. Twenty-four years later, thirty-six states have been NIBRS certified, with about 40 percent of the agencies in those states using the updated system.[52] Even in its limited form, however, criminologists have responded enthusiastically to the NIBRS because the system provides information about four "data sets"—offenses, victims, offenders, and arrestees—unavailable through the UCR. The NIBRS also presents a more complete picture of crime by monitoring all criminal "incidents" reported to the police, not just those that lead to an arrest.[53] Furthermore, because jurisdictions involved with the NIBRS must identify bias motivations of offenders, the procedure is very useful in studying hate crimes, a topic we will address in the next chapter.

2-4e

Victim Surveys

One alternative method of data collecting attempts to avoid the distorting influence of the "intermediary," or the local police agencies. In **victim surveys,** criminologists or other researchers ask the victims of crime directly about their experiences, using techniques such as interviews or e-mail and phone surveys. The first large-scale victim survey took place in 1966, when members of 10,000 households answered questionnaires as part of the President's Commission on Law Enforcement and the Administration of Justice. The results indicated a much higher victimization rate than had been previously expected, and researchers felt the process gave them a better understanding of the **dark figure of crime,** or the actual amount of crime that occurs in the country.

Criminologists were so encouraged by the results of the 1966 experiment that the federal government decided to institute an ongoing victim survey. The result was the National Crime Victimization Survey (NCVS), which started in 1972. Conducted by the U.S. Bureau of the Census in cooperation with the Bureau of Justice Statistics of the Justice Department, the NCVS conducts an annual survey of nearly 80,000 households with about 143,000 occupants over twelve years of age. Participants are interviewed twice a year concerning their experiences with crimes in the prior six months. As you can see in Figure 2.5 on the next page, questions are quite detailed in determining the experiences of crime victims.

2-4f

Self-Reported Surveys

Based on many of the same principles as victim surveys, but focusing instead on offenders, **self-reported surveys** are a third source of data for criminologists. In this form of data collection, persons are asked directly—through personal interviews or questionnaires, or over the telephone—about specific criminal activity to which they may have been a party. Self-reported surveys are most useful in situations in which the group to be studied is already gathered in an institutional setting, such as a juvenile facility or a prison. One of the most widespread self-reported surveys in the United States, the Drug Use Forecasting Program, collects information on narcotics use from arrestees who have been brought into booking facilities.

Because there is no penalty for admitting to criminal activity in a self-reported survey, subjects tend to be more forthcoming in discussing their behavior. Researchers interviewing a group of male students at a state university, for example, found that a significant number of them admitted to committing minor crimes for which they had never been arrested.[54] This fact points to the most striking finding

Victim Surveys A method of gathering crime data that directly surveys participants to determine their experiences as victims of crime.

Dark Figure of Crime A term used to describe the actual amount of crime that takes place. The "figure" is "dark," or impossible to detect, because a great number of crimes are never reported to the police.

Self-Reported Surveys A method of gathering crime data that relies on participants to reveal and detail their own criminal or delinquent behavior.

31a. What were the injuries you suffered, if any?
a. None
b. Raped
c. Attempted rape
d. Sexual assault other than rape or attempted rape
e. Knife or stab wounds
f. Gun shot, bullet wounds
g. Broken bones or teeth knocked out
h. Internal injuries
i. Knocked unconscious
j. Bruises, black eye, cuts, scratches, swelling, chipped teeth

37. Still thinking about your distress associated with being a victim of this crime, did you feel any of the following ways for A MONTH OR MORE?
a. Worried or anxious?
b. Angry?
c. Sad or depressed?
d. Vulnerable?
e. Violated?
f. Like you couldn't trust people?
g. Unsafe?

78a. Were any of the offenders a member of a street gang?
a. Yes.
b. No.
c. Don't know.

78b. Were any of the offenders drinking or on drugs?
a. Yes
b. No.
c. Don't know.

104b. What was the value of the PROPERTY that was taken?
a. $ _____.

© www.imagesource.com

Source: Adapted from U.S. Department of Justice, *National Crime Victimization Survey 2009* (Washington, D.C.: Bureau of Justice Statistics, 2011).

of self-reported surveys: the dark figure of crime, referred to earlier as the *actual* amount of crime that takes place, appears to be much larger than the UCR or NCVS would suggest.

2-5
what ROLE DO VICTIMS PLAY IN CRIMINAL JUSTICE?

It is no coincidence that the U.S. Department of Justice launched the first version of the National Crime Victimization Survey in the 1970s. The previous decade had seen a dramatic increase in the rights afforded to criminal defendants. To offset what they saw as a growing imbalance in the American criminal justice system, advocates began to argue that **crime victims** also needed greater protection under the law. Initially, the victims' rights movement focused on specific areas of crime, such as

Crime Victim Any person who suffers physical, emotional, or financial harm as the result of a criminal act.

domestic violence, sexual assault, and, through the efforts of Mothers Against Drunk Driving, vehicular homicide.[55] Today, an emphasis on the rights of all crime victims has a profound impact on the workings of law enforcement, courts, and corrections in the United States.

2-5a
Legal Rights of Crime Victims

Thirty years ago, a presidential task force invited federal and state legislatures to "address the needs of the millions of Americans and their families who are victimized by crime every year and who often carry its scars into the years to come."[56] This call to action was, in large part, a consequence of the rather peculiar position of victims in our criminal justice system. That is, once a crime has occurred, the victim is relegated to a single role: being a witness against the suspect in court. Legally, he or she has no say in the prosecution of the offender, or even whether such a prosecution is to take place. Such powerlessness can be extremely frustrating, particularly in the wake of a traumatic, life-changing event.

In May 2012, family members of murder victim Martin Caballero address a criminal court in Mays Landing, New Jersey. Should crime victims and their families have the "right" to participate in the criminal justice system? Why or why not?

AP Photo/*Press of Atlantic City*, Danny Drake

One victim of child pornography has collected restitution totaling $1.6 million from more than 150 men who viewed or sold her image illegally.[59]

LEGISLATIVE ACTION To remedy this situation, all states have passed legislation creating certain rights for victims. On a federal level, such protections are encoded in the Crime Victims' Rights Act of 2004 (CVRA), which gives victims "the right to participate in the system."[57] This participation primarily focuses on three categories of rights:

LO 4

1. The right to be *informed*. This includes receiving information about victims' rights in general, as well as specific information such as the dates and time of court proceedings relating to the relevant crime.

2. The right to be *present*. This includes the right to be present at those court hearings involving the case at hand, as long as the victim's presence does not interfere with the rights of the accused.

3. The right to be *heard*. This includes the ability to consult with prosecutorial officials before the criminal trial (addressed in Chapter 8), to speak during the sentencing phase of the trial (Chapter 9), and to offer an opinion when the offender is scheduled to be released from incarceration (Chapter 10).[58]

Some jurisdictions also provide victims with the right of law enforcement protection from the offender during the time period before a criminal trial. In addition, most states require *restitution*, or monetary payment, from offenders to help victims repay any costs associated with the crime and rebuild their lives.

VICTIM SERVICES Crime victims suffer a number of serious consequences. Many feel some degree of anger, guilt, shame, and grief as a result of their victimization. In particular, victims of violent crimes are at a high risk of post-traumatic stress disorder (PTSD), a condition that burdens sufferers with extreme anxiety and flashbacks relating to the traumatic event. Crime victims also experience higher-than-normal levels of depression, drug abuse, and suicidal tendencies.[60]

SOCIAL MEDIA AND CJ

The National Center for Victims of Crime supports victims' rights and provides training for victim advocates. To learn more, go to their Web page and click on the Facebook icon.

In addition to the emotional support of family and friends, a number of victim services exist to help with these symptoms of victimization. Hundreds of *crisis intervention* centers operate around the country, providing a wide range of aid. For example, the Donald W. Reynolds Crisis Intervention Center in Fort Smith, Arkansas, offers counseling, shelter, and relocation guidance to victims of domestic violence and sexual assault. These centers also allow for contact with *victim advocates,* or individuals that help victims gain access to public benefits, health care, employment and educational assistance, and numerous other services. The impact of such programs is, however, somewhat limited. Only about 9 percent of victims of violent crimes avail themselves of victim service agencies.[61]

2-5b

The Risks of Victimization

Anybody can be a victim of crime. This does not mean, however, that everybody is at an equal risk of being victimized. For example, residents of neighborhoods with heavy concentrations of payday lending businesses are targeted by criminals at unusually high rates.[62] To better explain the circumstances surrounding this type of victimization, criminologists Larry Cohen and Marcus Felson devised the *routine activities theory*. According to Cohen and Felson, most criminal acts require the following:

1. A likely offender.

2. A suitable target (a person or an object).

3. The absence of a capable guardian—that is, any person (not necessarily a law enforcement agent) whose presence or proximity prevents a crime from happening.[63]

When these three factors are present, the likelihood of crime rises. Cohen and Felson cite routine activities theory in explaining the link between payday lenders and crime. People who use payday lenders often leave those establishments with large sums of cash, late at night or during weekends when there is less street traffic. Consequently, they act as suitable targets, attracting likely offenders to neighborhoods where the payday lenders are located.[64]

REPEAT VICTIMIZATION Cohen and Felson also hypothesize that offenders attach "values" to suitable targets. The higher the value, the more likely that target is going to be the subject of a crime.[65] A gold watch, for example, would obviously have a higher value for a thief than a plastic watch and therefore is more likely to be stolen. Similarly, people who are perceived to be weak or unprotected can have high value for criminals. Law enforcement officials in southern Florida, for

CAREERPREP

NATIONAL VICTIM ADVOCATE

JOB DESCRIPTION:

- Provide direct support, advocacy, and short-term crisis counseling to crime victims.

- Act as a liaison between victims or witnesses and district attorneys or law enforcement, and provide court support for victims.

WHAT KIND OF TRAINING IS REQUIRED?

- A bachelor's degree in criminal justice, social work/ psychology, or a related field.

- A minimum of two years' experience in the criminal justice system, one year of which should have involved direct services with victims.

ANNUAL SALARY RANGE?

- $29,000–$44,000

SOCIAL MEDIA CAREER TIP

Social media technologies are about connecting and sharing information—which means privacy is an important issue. Make sure you understand who can see the material you post and how you can control it. Facebook has numerous privacy settings, for example, as does Google+.

Aldo Murillo/iStockphoto.com

example, believe that undocumented immigrants in the area have high victimization rates because criminals know they are afraid to report crimes to authorities for fear of being removed from the country.

Resources such as the National Crime Victimization Survey provide criminologists with an important tool for determining which types of people are most valued as potential victims. Statistics clearly show that a relatively small number of victims are involved in a disproportionate number of crimes. These findings support an approach to crime analysis known as **repeat victimization.** This theory is based on the premise that certain populations—mostly low-income resident of urban areas—are more likely to be victims of crimes than others and, therefore, past victimization is a strong predictor of future victimization.[66]

THE VICTIM-OFFENDER CONNECTION Not only does past victimization seem to increase the risk of future victimization, but so does past criminal behavior. In New Orleans, for example, 64 percent of homicide victims have previously been arrested for a felony. In Milwaukee, the number is even higher, at 75 percent.[67] "The notion that [violent crimes] are random bolts of lightning, which is the commonly held image, is not the reality at all," says David Kennedy, a professor at New York's John Jay College of Criminal Justice.[68]

Kennedy's point is further made by Figure 2.6 below, which identifies young African American males from urban neighborhoods as the most common victims of crimes. This demographic, as will become clear later in the chapter, is also at the highest risk for criminal behavior. Increasingly, law enforcement agencies are applying the lessons of repeat victimization and other victim studies to concentrate their attention on "hot spots" of crime, a strategy we address in Chapter 5.

FIGURE 2.6 Crime Victims in the United States

According to the U.S. Department of Justice, African Americans, residents of urban areas, and people between the ages of eighteen and twenty-four are most likely to be victims of violent crime in this country.

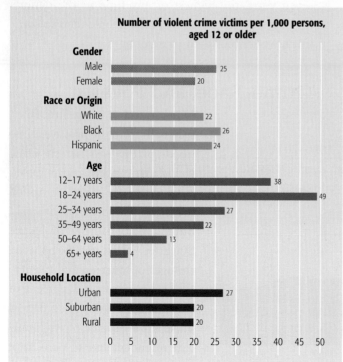

Source: Bureau of Justice Statistics, *Criminal Victimization, 2011* (Washington, D.C.: U.S. Department of Justice, October 2012), 5, 6.

2-6 what IS THE STATE OF CRIME IN THE UNITED STATES?

The UCR, NCVS, and other statistical measures we have discussed so far in this chapter, though important, represent only the tip of the iceberg of crime data. Thanks to the efforts of government law enforcement agencies, educational institutions, and private individuals, more information on crime is available today than at any time in the nation's history. When interpreting and predicting general crime trends, experts tend to rely on what University of California at Berkeley law professor Franklin Zimring calls the three "usual suspects" of crime fluctuation:

5 LO

1. *Imprisonment,* based on the principle that (a) an offender in prison or jail is unable to commit a crime on the street, and (b) a potential offender on the street will not commit a crime because he or she does not want to wind up behind bars.

Repeat Victimization
The theory that certain people and places are more likely to be subject to repeated criminal activity and that past victimization is a strong indicator of future victimization.

2. *Youth populations,* because offenders commit fewer crimes as they grow older.

3. The *economy,* because when legitimate opportunities to earn income become scarce, some people will turn to illegitimate methods such as crime.[69]

Pure statistics do not always tell the whole story, however, and crime rates often fail to behave in the ways that the experts predict.

2-6a
Looking Good: Crime in the 1990s and 2000s

In 1995, eminent crime expert James Q. Wilson, noting that the number of young males was set to increase dramatically over the next decade, predicted that "30,000 more young muggers, killers, and thieves" would be on the streets by 2000. "Get ready," he warned.[70] Fortunately for the country, Wilson was wrong. As is evident from Figure 2.7 below, starting in 1994 the United States experienced a steep crime decline that we are still enjoying today.

THE GREAT CRIME DECLINE The crime statistics of the 1990s are startling. Even with the upswing at the beginning of the decade, from 1990 to 2000 the homicide rate dropped 39 percent, the robbery rate 44 percent, the burglary rate 41 percent, and the auto theft rate 37 percent. By most measures, this decline was the longest and deepest of the twentieth century.[71] In retrospect, the 1990s seem to have encompassed a "golden era" for the leading indicators of low crime rates. The economy was robust. The incarceration rate was skyrocketing. Plus, despite the misgivings of James Q. Wilson and many of his colleagues, the percentage of the population in the high-risk age bracket in 1995 was actually lower than it had been in 1980.[72]

CONTINUING DECREASES In the early years of the 2000s, the nation's crime rate flattened for a time before resuming its downward trend. By 2011, property crime rates had dropped for the eighth straight year, and violent crime rates had shrunk to their lowest levels since the early 1970s. Given that, in recent years, the economy has been mired in a recession, with unemployment running at unusually high levels, the positive crime figures have come as something of a surprise.

Gary LaFree, a criminology professor at the University of Maryland, calls this trend "fascinating," because "we'd normally expect crime to go up when we are in an economic downturn."[73] Again, as in the 1990s, law enforcement is receiving much of the credit for the good news, particularly information-based policing techniques that use computer programs to focus crime prevention tactics on "hot spots" of criminal activity. In addition, LaFree points out, the median age in the United States is around thirty-seven years, the highest of any time in the nation's history.[74] As noted earlier, older people tend to commit fewer crimes than younger ones.

2-6b
Crime, Race, and Poverty

One group has noticeably failed to benefit from the positive crime trends of the past fifteen years: young African American males. According to data compiled by Alexia Cooper and Erica L. Smith of the Bureau of Justice Statistics, black males between the ages of fourteen and twenty-four, who represent 1 percent of the country's total population, make up a quarter of its homicide offenders and 16 percent of its homicide victims.[75] Overall, since 2000, while the total num-

---

FIGURE 2.7 **Violent Crime in the United States, 1990–2011**

According to statistics gathered each year by the FBI, American violent crime rates dropped steadily in the second half of the 1990s, leveled off for several years, and now have begun to decrease anew.

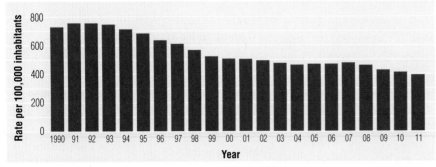

Source: Federal Bureau of Investigation.

What is your opinion of the theory that economic disadvantage, rather than skin color, accounts for the disproportionate number of African Americans in U.S. prisons, such as these inmates at Florida's Dade County Correctional Facility?

Joe Sohm/Visions of America/Newscom

ber of murders in the United States has dropped by 5 percent, the number of male black victims has increased by more than 10 percent.[76] In cities with rising murder rates, a large part of the violence is taking place within the African American community—nationwide, most murder victims are killed by someone of the same race (93 percent for blacks, 85 percent for whites).[77]

RACE AND CRIME Homicide rates are not the only area in which there is a divergence in crime trends between the races. Official crime data seem to indicate a strong correlation between minority status and crime: African Americans—who make up 13 percent of the population—constitute 38 percent of those arrested for violent crimes and 30 percent of those arrested for property crimes.[78] A black man is almost twelve times more likely than a white man to be sent to prison for a drug-related conviction, while black women are about five times more likely than white women to be incarcerated for a drug offense.[79] Furthermore, a black juvenile in the United States is nearly three times more likely than a white juvenile to wind up in delinquency court.[80]

CLASS AND CRIME The racial differences in the crime rate are one of the most controversial areas of the criminal justice system. At first glance, crime statistics seem to support the idea that the subculture

of African Americans in the United States is disposed toward criminal behavior.

Not all of the data, however, support that assertion. A recent research project led by sociologist Ruth D. Peterson of Ohio State University gathered information on nearly 150 neighborhoods in Columbus, Ohio. Peterson and her colleagues separated the neighborhoods based on race and on levels of disadvantage such as poverty, joblessness, lack of college graduates, and high levels of female-headed families. She found that whether the neighborhoods were predominantly white or predominantly black had little impact on violent crime rates. Those neighborhoods with higher levels of disadvantage, however, had uniformly higher violent crime rates.[81]

Peterson's research suggests that, regardless of race, a person is at a much higher risk of violent offending or being a victim of violence if he or she lives in a disadvantaged neighborhood. Given that African Americans are two times more likely than whites to live in poverty and hold low-wage-earning jobs, they are, as a group, more susceptible to the factors that contribute to criminality.[82] Indeed, a wealth of information suggests that income level is more important than skin color when it comes to crime trends. A study conducted by William A. Pridemore of Indiana University found a "positive and significant association" between poverty and homicide.[83] Lack of education, another handicap most often faced by low-income citizens, also seems to correlate with criminal behavior. Forty-one percent of all inmates in state and federal prisons failed to obtain a high school education, compared with 18 percent of the population at large.[84]

2-6c
Women and Crime

To put it bluntly, crime is an overwhelmingly male activity. More than 68 percent of all murders involve a male victim and a male perpetrator, and in only 2.2 percent of homicides are both the offender and the victim female.[85] Only 13 percent of the national jail population and 7 percent of the national prison population are female, and in 2011 only 26 percent of all arrests involved women.[86]

These statistics fail to convey the startling rate at which the female presence in the criminal justice system has been increasing. Between 1991 and 2011, the number of men arrested each year declined by approximately 90,000. Over that time period, annual arrests for women increased by almost 700,000.[87] In 1970, there were about 6,000 women in federal and state prisons, but today, there are more than 111,000.[88] There are two possible explanations for these increases. Either (1) the life circumstances and behavior of women have changed dramatically in the past forty years, or (2) the criminal justice system's attitude toward women has changed over that time period.[89]

In the 1970s, when female crime rates started surging upward, many observers accepted the former explanation. "You can't get involved in a bar fight if you're not allowed in the bar," said feminist theorist Freda Adler in 1975.[90] It has become clear, however, that a significant percentage of women arrested are involved in a narrow band of wrongdoing, mostly drug- and alcohol-related offenses or property crimes.[91] Research shows that as recently as the 1980s, many of the women now in prison would not have been arrested or would have received lighter sentences for their crimes.[92] Consequently, more scholars are convinced that rising female criminality is the result of a criminal justice system that is "more willing to incarcerate women."[93]

CAREER TIP: When a mother becomes involved with the criminal justice system, the state can decide to place her sons or daughters in a foster home. The professionals who oversee this process and look out for the best interests of the children, and their families, are called *foster care case workers*.

AP Photo/*The Independent*, Kevin Goldy

2-6d
Mental Illness and Crime

In the context of the criminal justice system, the term *mental illness* covers a wide variety of symptoms, ranging from reoccurring depression and anger to hallucinations and schizophrenia. It also indicates recent treatment from a mental health care practitioner. Government research indicates that, using this description, about 11 percent of Americans over the age of eighteen suffer from some form of mental illness.[94] Does this mean that 26 million adults in this country are at a high risk for violent behavior? Not necessarily.

After Adam Lanza killed twenty children and six adults at an elementary school in Newtown, Connecticut, on December 14, 2012, many observers called for stricter laws to keep guns out of the hands of the mentally ill. Although Lanza had never been diagnosed with any specific mental illness, at least half a dozen states moved to revise their mental health laws to that effect. Today, forty-four states regulate the sale of firearms to the mentally ill, and the federal government bars such sales to any person who is a "mental defective."[95]

Critics say that the emphasis on the mentally ill with regard to violent crime is unfair and inaccurate. Of the tens of thousand of gun deaths that occur in this country, few are caused by people with mental illness.[96] Furthermore, a 2006 study published in the *American Journal of Psychiatry* claimed that only 4 percent of violent crime in the United States can be attributed to people with a mental illness.[97] Although the possibility of violent behavior increases for those with serious conditions such as schizophrenia or bipolar disorder,[98] the most significant risk factor for the mentally ill is substance abuse. Between 80 and 90 percent of all mentally ill inmates in American prisons and jails are abusers of alcohol or other drugs.[99]

REVIEW

✓ **Review what you've read with the quiz below.**

Rip out the Chapter Review card at the back of this book, which includes:
- Chapter Summary and Learning Outcomes
- Key Terms

Or you can go online to CourseMate at www.cengagebrain.com to:
- Complete Practice Quizzes to prepare for tests.
- Review Key Terms Flash Cards (online or print).
- Play games to master concepts.

quiz

1. Researchers who study the causes of crime are called _____.

2. If a hypothesis proves valid, it can be used to support a _____ that explains a possible cause of crime.

3. _____ _____ theory holds that criminals make a deliberate decision to commit a crime after weighing the possible rewards or punishments involved.

4. Social _____ focuses on how individuals justify their own antisocial or criminal behavior by patterning it after similar behavior by others.

5. Social _____ theory examines living conditions to explain the crime rate in any given neighborhood or community.

6. Among social process theories, _____ theory could be used to explain why the younger sibling of a gang member would be at a particular risk to join a gang him- or herself.

7. Drug _____ is defined as the use of any drug that causes harm to the user or a third party.

8. To produce its annual _____ _____ _____ , the Federal Bureau of Investigation relies on the cooperation of local law enforcement agencies.

9. _____ surveys rely on those who have been the subject of criminal activity to discuss the incidents with researchers.

10. _____-_____ surveys ask participants to detail their own criminal behavior.

Answers can be found on the Chapter 2 Review card at the end of the book.

Learning OUTCOMES | *After studying this chapter, you will be able to . . .*

1 List the four written sources of American law.

2 Explain the differences between crimes *mala in se* and *mala prohibita.*

3 List and briefly define the most important excuse defenses for crimes.

4 Describe the four most important justification criminal defenses.

5 Distinguish between substantive and procedural criminal law.

INSIDE CRIMINAL LAW

3

Murder or a Heart Attack?

According to police investigators, Rickie Lee Fowler was angry about being thrown out of a family member's house in California's San Bernardino Mountains. As retaliation, Fowler started one of the largest wildfires in state history. Known as the Old Fire, the 91,000-acre blaze lasted nine days, destroyed 1,003 homes, and caused the deaths of five men. Fowler was eventually convicted on two counts of arson and five counts of murder. In January 2013, a jury sentenced him to be executed. "You're not going to find a better case than this for the death penalty," said San Bernardino County deputy district attorney Robert Bullock.

Not everybody in the legal community agreed. "I've never heard of a case like this," said Loyola (Los Angeles) Law School professor Stan Goldman. The legal definition of murder requires the offender to have some prior intent to harm the victim. Though Fowler intentionally started the Old Fire, there was

no indication that he intended to hurt any people. Furthermore, the five victims did not die of smoke inhalation or burn injuries. Rather, they all died of heart attacks brought about by stress experienced due to the fire. One of the victims, who lost his house and his business to the flames, did not suffer his fatal heart attack until a week after the event.

Fowler's attorneys claimed that their client obviously never intended to kill anyone, and that it was ludicrous to blame him for the heart attacks.

Professor Goldman believes that the "real question is whether we should be executing people when the [murders] were not an easily foreseeable consequence of the criminal act." Local law enforcement officials, however, insist that criminal law must be flexible enough to punish behavior that is not marked by obvious intent yet still poses a threat to society. "The fact of the matter is that these lives were directly lost as a result of Rickie Fowler's actions," observed deputy district attorney Bullock.

Rickie Lee Fowler, right, was convicted of two counts of arson and five counts of murder for the damage he caused by starting the Old Fire in California's San Bernardino Mountains.

AP Photo/*The Sun,* LaFonzo Carter

what ARE THE WRITTEN SOURCES OF AMERICAN CRIMINAL LAW?

LO **1** Originally, common law was *uncodified.* That is, it relied primarily on judges following precedents, and the body of the law was not written down in any single place. Uncodified law, however, presents a number of drawbacks. For one, if the law is not recorded in a manner or a place in which the citizenry has access to it, then it is difficult, if not impossible, for people to know exactly which acts are legal and which acts are illegal. Furthermore, citizens have no way of determining or understanding the procedures that must be followed to establish innocence or guilt. Consequently, U.S. history has seen the development of several written sources of American criminal law, also known as "substantive" criminal law. These sources include:

1. The U.S. Constitution and the constitutions of the various states.

2. Statutes, or laws, passed by Congress and by state legislatures, plus local ordinances.

3. Regulations, created by regulatory agencies, such as the federal Food and Drug Administration.

4. Case law (court decisions).

We describe each of these important written sources of law in the following pages. (For a preview, see Figure 3.1 on the facing page.)

3-1a
Constitutional Law

The federal government and the states have separate written constitutions that set forth the general organization and powers of, and the limits on, their respective governments. **Constitutional law** is the law as expressed in these constitutions.

Constitutional Law Law based on the U.S. Constitution and the constitutions of the various states.

Statutory Law The body of law enacted by legislative bodies.

The U.S. Constitution is the supreme law of the land. As such, it is the basis of all law in the United States. Any law that violates the Constitution, as ultimately determined by the United States Supreme Court, will be declared unconstitutional and will not be enforced. The Tenth Amendment, which defines the powers and limitations of the federal government, reserves to the states all powers not granted to the federal government. Under our system of federalism (see Chapter 1), each state also has its own constitution. Unless they conflict with the U.S. Constitution or a federal law, state constitutions are supreme within their respective borders. (You will learn more about how constitutional law applies to our criminal justice system throughout this textbook.)

3-1b
Statutory Law

Statutes enacted by legislative bodies at any level of government make up another source of law, which is generally referred to as **statutory law.** *Federal statutes* are laws that are enacted by the U.S. Congress. *State statutes* are laws enacted by state legislatures, and statutory law also includes the ordinances passed by cities and counties. A federal statute, of course, applies to all states. A state statute, in contrast, applies only

George Washington, standing at right, presided over the constitutional convention of 1787, which resulted in the U.S. Constitution. Why is this document considered the supreme law of the United States?

Bettmann/Corbis

FIGURE 3.1 Sources of American Law

Constitutional law	**Definition:** The law as expressed in the U.S. Constitution and the various state constitutions.	**Example:** The Fifth Amendment to the U.S. Constitution states that no person shall "be compelled in any criminal case to be a witness" against himself or herself.
Statutory law	**Definition:** Laws or *ordinances* created by federal, state, and local legislatures and governing bodies.	**Example:** Texas state law considers the theft of cattle, horses, or exotic livestock or fowl a felony.
Administrative law	**Definition:** The rules, orders, and decisions of federal or state government administrative agencies.	**Example:** The federal Environmental Protection Agency's rules criminalize the use of lead-based paint in a manner that causes health risks to the community.
Case law	**Definition:** Judge-made law, including judicial interpretations of the other three sources of law.	**Example:** A federal judge overturns a Nebraska state law making it a crime for sex offenders to use social networking sites on the ground that the statute violated the constitutional right of freedom of speech.

within that state's borders. City or county ordinances (statutes) apply only to those jurisdictions where they are enacted.

LEGAL SUPREMACY It is important to keep in mind that there are essentially fifty-two different criminal codes in this country—one for each state, the District of Columbia, and the federal government. Originally, the federal criminal code was quite small. The U.S. Constitution mentions only three federal crimes: treason, piracy, and counterfeiting. Today, according to a recent study, federal law includes about 4,500 offenses that carry criminal penalties.[1] Inevitably, these federal criminal statutes are bound to overlap or even contradict state statutes. In such cases, thanks to the **supremacy clause** of the Constitution, federal law will almost always prevail. Simply put, the supremacy clause holds that federal law is the "supreme law of the land."

So, in 2012, U.S. district judge Donald Molloy ruled that federal law enforcement agents were justified in arresting Montana residents for possessing medical marijuana, even though use of the drug for medicinal purposes is legal under the criminal laws of that state. Federal drug law does not allow for medical marijuana use, however, and, as Judge Molloy stated, "we are all bound by federal law, like it or not."[2] Along the same lines, any statutory law—federal or state—that violates the Constitution will be

overturned. In the late 1980s, for example, the United States Supreme Court ruled that any state laws banning the burning of the American flag were unconstitutional because they impinged on the individual's right to freedom of expression.[3]

BALLOT INITIATIVES On a state and local level, voters can write or rewrite criminal statutes through a form of direct democracy known as the **ballot initiative.** In this process, a group of citizens draft a proposed law and then gather a certain number of signatures to get the proposal on that year's ballot. If a majority of the voters approve the measure, it is enacted into law. Currently, twenty-four states and the District of Columbia accept ballot initiatives, and these special elections have played a crucial role in shaping criminal law in those jurisdictions.

In the mid-1990s, for example, California voters approved a "three-strikes" measure (discussed in Chapter 9) that increased penalties for third-time felons, transforming the state's criminal justice system in the process. In 2012, when Colorado and Washington decided to legalize the sale and possession of small amounts of marijuana, voters

Supremacy Clause A clause in the U.S. Constitution establishing that federal law is the "supreme law of the land" and shall prevail when in conflict with state constitutions or statutes.

Ballot Initiative A procedure in which the citizens of a state, by collecting enough signatures, can force a public vote on a proposed change to state law.

Smoking marijuana in this Denver park no longer carries a high risk of arrest by state and local police. What method did Colorado voters use to legalize the possession of small amounts of marijuana in 2012? What are some of the pros and cons of this method of creating new criminal laws?

AP Photo/Brennan Linsley

in those states approved this dramatic legal change through ballot initiatives. As we just noted, however, ballot initiatives do not supplant federal law, and marijuana sellers and users in these states are still subject to arrest under federal drug laws.

3-1c

Administrative Law

A third source of American criminal law consists of **administrative law**—the rules, orders, and decisions of *regulatory agencies*. A regulatory agency is a federal, state, or local government agency established to perform a specific function. The Occupational Safety and Health Administration (OSHA), for example, oversees the safety and health of American workers. The Environmental Protection Agency (EPA) is concerned with protecting the natural environment, and the Food and Drug Administration (FDA) regulates food and drugs produced in the United States. (**CAREER TIP:** The federal government employs law enforcement agents called *consumer safety officers* to investigate reports of injury, illness, or death caused by certain consumer products.)

Administrative Law The body of law created by administrative agencies (in the form of rules, regulations, orders, and decisions) in order to carry out their duties and responsibilities.

Precedent A court decision that furnishes an example of authority for deciding subsequent cases involving similar facts.

Case Law The rules of law announced in court decisions.

Disregarding certain laws created by regulatory agencies can be a criminal violation. Federal statutes, such as the Clean Water Act, authorize a specific regulatory agency, such as the EPA, to enforce regulations to which criminal sanctions are attached.[4] So, in 2012, following a criminal investigation led by the EPA, a North Carolina hog farm was found guilty of discharging waste into the Waccamaw River watershed. As punishment, a federal judge sentenced the company to pay $1.5 million in fines and sent its president to prison for six months.

3-1d

Case Law

Another basic source of American law consists of the rules of law announced in court decisions, or **precedents.** These rules of law include interpretations of constitutional provisions, of statutes enacted by legislatures, and of regulations created by administrative agencies. Today, this body of law is referred to variously as the common law, judge-made law, or **case law.**

Case law relies to a certain extent on how courts interpret a particular statute. If you wanted to learn about the coverage and applicability of a particular statute, for example, you would need to locate the statute and study it. You would also need to see how the courts in your jurisdiction have interpreted the statute—in other words, what precedents have been established in regard to that statute. The use of precedent means that judge-made law varies from jurisdiction to jurisdiction.

3-2
why DO SOCIETIES NEED LAWS?

Many criminologists believe that criminal law has two basic functions: one relates to the legal requirements of a society, and the other pertains to the society's need to maintain and promote social values.

3-2a
Protect and Punish: The Legal Function of the Law

The primary legal function of the law is to maintain social order by protecting citizens from *criminal harm*. This term refers to a variety of harms that can be generalized to fit into two categories:

1. Harms to individual citizens' physical safety and property, such as the harm caused by murder, theft, or arson.

2. Harms to society's interests collectively, such as the harm caused by unsafe foods or consumer products, a polluted environment, or poorly constructed buildings.[5]

The first category is self-evident, although even murder, as you shall soon see, has different *degrees,* or grades, of offense to which different punishments are assigned. The second category, however, has proved more problematic, for it is difficult to measure society's "collective" interests.

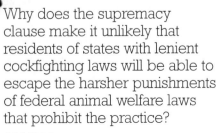

3-2b
Maintain and Teach: The Social Function of the Law

If criminal laws against acts that cause harm or injury to others are almost universally accepted, the same cannot be said for laws that criminalize "morally" wrongful activities that may do no obvious, physical harm outside the families of those involved. Why criminalize gambling or prostitution if the participants are consenting?

SOCIAL MEDIA AND CJ

Criminal Law@CrimLaw provides a constant stream of tweets concerning criminal law topics and other crime news and stories of interest. To access it, search for Criminal Law@crimlaw.

EXPRESSING PUBLIC MORALITY The answer lies in the social function of criminal law. Many observers believe that the main purpose of criminal law is to reflect the values and norms of society, or at least of those segments of society that hold power. Legal scholar Henry Hart has stated that the only justification for criminal law and punishment is "the judgment of community condemnation."[6]

Take, for example, the misdemeanor of bigamy, which occurs when someone knowingly marries a second person without terminating her or his marriage to an original husband or wife. Apart from moral considerations, there would appear to be no victims in a bigamous relationship, and indeed many societies have allowed and continue to allow bigamy to exist. In the American social tradition, however, as John L. Diamond of the University of California's Hastings College of the Law points out:

Why does the supremacy clause make it unlikely that residents of states with lenient cockfighting laws will be able to escape the harsher punishments of federal animal welfare laws that prohibit the practice?

Al Bello/Getty Images

Marriage is an institution encouraged and supported by society. The structural importance of the integrity of the family and a monogamous marriage requires unflinching enforcement of the criminal laws against bigamy. The immorality is not in choosing to do wrong, but in transgressing, even innocently, a fundamental social boundary that lies at the core of social order.[7]

Of course, public morals are not uniform across the entire nation, and a state's criminal code often reflects the values of its residents. Illinois and the District of Columbia, for example, are the only parts of the United States where people cannot, under any circumstances, carry a concealed weapon in public. Sometimes, local values and federal law will conflict with one another. In South Carolina, operating a cockfighting operation is a misdemeanor, and violators are often let off with a fine. Under federal animal welfare laws, however, the same activity carries a potential five-year prison term.[8] In 2012, five South Carolinians arrested by federal agents for cockfighting claimed—unsuccessfully—in court that their convictions were illegitimate because the federal government has no authority to regulate the "sport" within state borders.[9] **(CAREER TIP:** *Animal control officers* are instrumental in breaking up illegal cockfighting rings. These government employees also work to protect stray, injured, abused, and unwanted animals.)

TEACHING SOCIETAL BOUNDARIES Some scholars believe that criminal laws not only express the expectations of society, but "teach" them as well. Professor Lawrence M. Friedman of Stanford University thinks that just as parents teach children behavioral norms through punishment, criminal justice "'teaches a lesson' to the people it punishes, and to society at large." Making burglary a crime, arresting burglars, putting them in jail—each step in the criminal justice process reinforces the idea that burglary is unacceptable and is deserving of punishment.[10]

This teaching function can also be seen in traffic laws. There is nothing "natural" about most traffic laws: Americans drive on the right side of the street, the British on the left side, with no obvious difference in the results. These laws, such as stopping at intersections, using headlights at night, and following speed limits, do lead to a more orderly flow of traffic and fewer accidents—certainly socially desirable goals. The laws can also be updated when needed. Over the past few years, several states have banned the use of handheld cell phones while driving because of the safety hazards associated with that behavior. Various forms of punishment for breaking traffic laws teach drivers the social order of the road.

3-3 what IS THE DIFFERENCE BETWEEN CIVIL AND CRIMINAL LAW?

All law can be divided into two categories: civil law and criminal law. As U.S. criminal law has evolved, it has diverged from U.S. civil law. These two categories of law are distinguished by their primary goals. The criminal justice system is concerned with protecting society from harm by preventing and prosecuting crimes. A crime is an act so reprehensible that it is considered a wrong against society as a whole, as well as against the individual victim. Therefore, the state prosecutes a person who commits a criminal act. If the state is able to prove that a person is guilty of a crime, the government will punish her or him with imprisonment or fines, or both.

Civil law, which includes all types of law other than criminal law, is concerned with disputes between private individuals and between entities. Proceedings in civil lawsuits are normally initiated by an individual or a corporation (in contrast to criminal proceedings, which are initiated by public prosecutors). Such disputes may involve, for example, the terms of a contract, the ownership of property, or an automobile accident. Under civil law, the government provides a forum for the resolution of *torts*—or private wrongs—in which the injured party, called the **plaintiff,** tries to prove that a wrong has been committed by the accused party, or the **defendant.** (Note

Civil Law The branch of law dealing with the definition and enforcement of all private or public rights, as opposed to criminal matters.

Plaintiff The person or institution that initiates a lawsuit in civil court proceedings by filing a complaint.

Defendant In a civil court, the person or institution against whom an action is brought. In a criminal court, the person or entity who has been formally accused of violating a criminal law.

that the accused party in both criminal and civil cases is known as the *defendant*.)

3-3a

Guilt and Responsibility

A criminal court is convened to determine whether the defendant is *guilty*—that is, whether the defendant has, in fact, committed the offense charged. In contrast, civil law is concerned with responsibility, a much more flexible concept. For example, when baby Sofia Blunt developed cerebral palsy soon after her birth, a civil court in San Louis Obispo, California, blamed Kurt Haupt, the presiding doctor. Apparently, Haupt failed to take proper steps to increase blood flow to Sofia's brain during delivery. Even though Haupt was never charged with any crime, the civil court decided that he was **liable,** or legally responsible, for Sofia's condition because of his carelessness.

Most civil cases involve a request for monetary damages to compensate for the wrong that has been committed. Thus, in 2012, the civil court had Kurt Haupt's insurance company pay $74 million to Sofia Blunt's parents to cover the medical costs they will incur over their daughter's lifetime.

3-3b

The Burden of Proof

Although criminal law proceedings are completely separate from civil law proceedings in the modern legal system, the two systems do have some similarities. Both attempt to control behavior by imposing sanctions on those who violate society's definition of acceptable behavior. Furthermore, criminal and civil law often supplement each other. In certain instances, a victim may file a civil suit against an individual who is also the target of a criminal prosecution by the government.

Because the burden of proof is much greater in criminal trials than civil ones, it is almost always easier to win monetary damages than a criminal conviction. Several years ago, for example, store manager Richard Moore was found not guilty of sexually abusing an employee in O'Fallon, Illinois, because investigators could not match his DNA to physical evidence found near the alleged incident. A separate civil court, however, ruled that Moore had sexually abused the woman and ordered his employer, the furniture chain Aaron's, to pay her $41 million in damages. During the criminal trial, the court did not find enough evidence to prove **beyond a reasonable doubt** (the burden of proof in criminal cases) that Moore was guilty of any crime. Nevertheless, the civil trial established by a **preponderance of the evidence** (the burden of proof in civil cases) that Moore had thrown the employee to the floor and sexually abused her. (See Figure 3.2 below for a comparison of civil and criminal law.)

Liability In a civil court, legal responsibility for one's own or another's actions.

Beyond a Reasonable Doubt The degree of proof required to find the defendant in a criminal trial guilty of committing the crime. The defendant's guilt must be the only reasonable explanation for the criminal act before the court.

Preponderance of the Evidence The degree of proof required to decide in favor of one side or the other in a civil case. In general, this requirement is met when a plaintiff proves that a fact more likely than not is true.

FIGURE 3.2 Civil Law versus Criminal Law

ISSUE	CIVIL LAW	CRIMINAL LAW
Area of concern	Rights and duties between individuals	Offenses against society as a whole
Wrongful act	Harm to a person or business entity	Violation of a statute that prohibits some type of activity
Party who brings suit	Person who suffered harm (plaintiff)	The state (prosecutor)
Party who responds	Person who supposedly caused harm (defendant)	Person who allegedly committed a crime (defendant)
Standard of proof	Preponderance of the evidence	Beyond a reasonable doubt
Remedy	Damages to compensate for the harm	Punishment (fine or incarceration)

what ARE THE DIFFERENT CATEGORIES OF CRIME?

Depending on their degree of seriousness, crimes are classified as *felonies* or *misdemeanors*. **Felonies** are crimes punishable by death or by imprisonment in a federal or state penitentiary for one year or longer (though some states, such as North Carolina, consider felonies to be punishable by at least two years' incarceration). The Model Penal Code, a general guide for criminal law, provides for four degrees of felony:

1. Capital offenses, for which the maximum penalty is death.
2. First degree felonies, punishable by a maximum penalty of life imprisonment.
3. Second degree felonies, punishable by a maximum of ten years' imprisonment.
4. Third degree felonies, punishable by a maximum of five years' imprisonment.[11]

For the most part, felonies involve crimes of violence such as armed robbery or sexual assault, or other "serious" crimes such as stealing a large amount of money or selling illegal drugs.

A police officer writes a citation after making a traffic stop in Mount Pocono, Pennsylvania. What is the difference between an infraction, such as a speeding violation, and a crime? Why does it make sense that infractions do not appear on a person's criminal record?

AP Photo/*Pocono Record*, Keith R. Stevenson

3-4a
Types of Misdemeanors

Under federal law and in most states, any crime that is not a felony is considered a **misdemeanor.** Misdemeanors are crimes punishable by a fine or by confinement for up to a year. If imprisoned, the guilty party goes to a local jail instead of a penitentiary. Disorderly conduct and trespassing are common misdemeanors. Most states distinguish between *gross misdemeanors,* which are offenses punishable by thirty days to a year in jail, and *petty misdemeanors,* or offenses punishable by fewer than thirty days

in jail. Probation and community service are often imposed on those who commit misdemeanors, especially juveniles. As you will see in Chapter 7, whether a crime is a felony or misdemeanor can also determine in which criminal court the case will be tried.

3-4b
Infractions

The least serious form of wrongdoing is often called an **infraction** and is punishable only by a small fine. Even though infractions such as parking tickets or traffic violations technically represent illegal activity, they generally are not considered "crimes." Therefore, infractions rarely lead to jury trials and are deemed to be so minor that they do not appear on the offender's criminal record. In some jurisdictions, the terms *infraction* and *petty offense* are interchangeable. In others, however, they are different. Under federal guidelines, for example, an infraction can be punished by up to five days of jail time, while a petty offender is only liable for a fine. Finally, those who string together a series of infractions (or fail to pay the fines that come with such offenses) are in danger of being

Felony A serious crime, usually punishable by death or imprisonment for a year or longer.

Misdemeanor A criminal offense that is not a felony; usually punishable by a fine and/or a jail term of less than one year.

Infraction In most jurisdictions, a noncriminal offense for which the penalty is a fine rather than incarceration.

criminally charged. In Illinois, having three or more speeding violations in one year is considered criminal behavior.[12]

3-4c

Mala in Se and Mala Prohibita

Criminologists often express the social function of criminal law in terms of *mala in se* or *mala prohibita* crimes. A criminal act is referred to as **mala in se** if it would be considered wrong even if there were no law prohibiting it. *Mala in se* crimes are said to go against "natural laws"—that is, against the "natural, moral, and public" principles of a society. Murder, rape, and

LO 2 theft are examples of *mala in se* crimes. These crimes are generally the same from country to country or culture to culture.

In contrast, the term **mala prohibita** refers to acts that are considered crimes only because they have been codified as such through statute—"human-made" laws. A *mala prohibita* crime is considered wrong only because it has been prohibited. It is not inherently wrong, though it may reflect the moral standards of a society at a given time. Thus, the definition of a *mala prohibita* crime can vary from country to country and even from state to state. Bigamy, or the offense of having two legal spouses, could be considered a *mala prohibita* crime.

Some observers question the distinction between *mala in se* and *mala prohibita*. In many instances, it is difficult to define a "pure" *mala in se* crime. That is, it is difficult to separate a crime from the culture that has deemed it a crime.[13] Even murder, under certain cultural circumstances, is not considered a criminal act. In a number of poor, traditional areas of the Middle East and Asia, the law excuses "honor killings" in which men kill female family members suspected of sexual indiscretion. Our own legal system excuses homicide in extreme situations, such as self-defense or when a law enforcement agent kills in the course of upholding the law. Therefore, "natural" laws can be seen as culturally specific. Similar difficulties occur in trying to define a "pure" *mala prohibita* crime. More than 150 countries, including most members of the European Union, have legalized prostitution. With the exception of seven rural counties of Nevada, prostitution is illegal in the United States.

what ARE THE ELEMENTS OF A CRIME?

In fictional accounts of police work, the admission of guilt is often portrayed as the crucial element of a criminal investigation. Although an admission is certainly useful to police and prosecutors, it alone cannot establish the innocence or guilt of a suspect. Criminal law normally requires that the **corpus delicti,** a Latin phrase for "the body of the crime," be proved before a person can be convicted of wrongdoing.[14] *Corpus delicti* can be defined as "proof that a specific crime has actually been committed by someone."[15] It consists of the basic elements of any crime, which include (1) *actus reus,* or a guilty act; (2) *mens rea,* or a guilty intent; (3) concurrence, or the coming together of the criminal act and the guilty mind; (4) a link between the act and the legal definition of the crime; (5) any attendant circumstances; and (6) the harm done, or result of the criminal act.

3-5a

Criminal Act: *Actus Reus*

Suppose Mr. Smith walks into a police department and announces that he just killed his wife. In and of itself, the confession is insufficient for conviction unless the police find Mrs. Smith's corpse, for example, with a bullet in her brain and establish through evidence that Mr. Smith fired the gun. (This does not mean that an actual dead body has to be found in every homicide case. Rather, it is the fact of the death that must be established in such cases.)

Most crimes require an act of *commission*, meaning that a person must do something in order to be accused of a crime. The prohibited act is referred to as the **actus reus,** or guilty act. Furthermore, the act of commission must be voluntary. For example, if Mr. Smith had an epileptic seizure while holding a

Mala in Se A descriptive term for acts that are inherently wrong, regardless of whether they are prohibited by law.

Mala Prohibita A descriptive term for acts that are made illegal by criminal statute and are not necessarily wrong in and of themselves.

Corpus Delicti The body of circumstances that must exist for a criminal act to have occurred.

Actus Reus (pronounced *ak*-tus *ray*-uhs). A guilty (prohibited) act.

hunting rifle and accidentally shot his wife, he normally would not be held criminally liable for her death. (To better understand this principle, see the feature *You Be the Judge—A Voluntary Act?* below.)

A LEGAL DUTY In some cases, an act of *omission* can be a crime, but only when a person has a legal duty to perform the omitted act. One such legal duty is assumed to exist based on a "special relationship" between two parties, such as a parent and child, adult children and their aged parents, and spouses.[16] Those persons involved in contractual relationships with others, such as physicians and lifeguards, must also perform legal duties to avoid criminal penalty. Hawaii, Minnesota, Rhode Island, Vermont, and Wisconsin have even passed "duty to aid" statutes requiring their citizens to report criminal conduct and help victims of such conduct if possible.[17] Another example of a criminal act of omission is failure to file a federal income tax return when required by law to do so.

A PLAN OR ATTEMPT The guilty act requirement is based on one of the premises of criminal law— that a person is punished for harm done to society. Planning to kill someone or to steal a car may be wrong, but the thoughts do no harm and are therefore not criminal until they are translated into action. Of course, a person can be punished for *attempting* murder or robbery, but normally only if he or she took substantial steps toward the criminal objective and the prosecution can prove that the desire to commit the crime was present. Furthermore, the punishment for an **attempt** normally is less severe than if the act had succeeded.

3-5b
Mental State: *Mens Rea*

A wrongful mental state—**mens rea**—is usually as necessary as a wrongful act in determining guilt. The mental state, or requisite *intent*, required to establish guilt of a crime is indicated in the applicable statute or law. For theft, the wrongful act is the taking of another person's property, and the required mental state involves both the awareness that the property belongs to another and the desire to deprive the owner of it.

THE CATEGORIES OF *MENS REA* A guilty mental state includes elements of purpose, knowledge, negligence, and recklessness. A defendant is said to have *purposefully* committed a criminal act when he or she desires to engage in certain criminal conduct or to cause a certain criminal result. For a defendant to have *knowingly* committed an illegal act, he or she must be aware of the illegality, must believe that the

Attempt The act of taking substantial steps toward committing a crime while having the ability and the intent to commit the crime, even if the crime never takes place.

Mens Rea (pronounced mehns ray-uh). Mental state, or intent. A wrongful mental state is usually as necessary as a wrongful act to establish criminal liability.

YOU BE THE JUDGE

A VOLUNTARY ACT?

THE FACTS On a bright, sunny afternoon, Emil was driving on Delaware Avenue in Buffalo, New York. As he was making a turn, Emil suffered an epileptic seizure and lost control of his automobile. The car careened onto the sidewalk and struck a group of six schoolgirls, killing four of them. Emil knew that he was subject to epileptic attacks that rendered him likely to lose consciousness.

THE LAW An "act" committed while one is unconscious is in reality not an act at all. It is merely a physical event or occurrence over which the defendant has no control—that is, such an act is involuntary. If the defendant voluntarily causes the loss of consciousness by, for example, using drugs or alcohol, however, then he or she will usually be held criminally responsible for any consequences.

YOUR DECISION Emil was charged in the deaths of the four girls. He asked the court to dismiss the charges, as he was unconscious at the time of the accident and therefore had not committed a voluntary act. In your opinion, is there an *actus reus* in this situation, or should the charges against Emil be dismissed?

[To see how the appellate court in New York ruled in this case, go to Example 3.1 in Appendix A.]

illegality exists, or must correctly suspect that the illegality exists but fail to do anything to dispel (or confirm) his or her belief.

Negligence Criminal **negligence** involves the mental state in which the defendant grossly deviates from the standard of care that a reasonable person would use under the same circumstances. The defendant is accused of taking an unjustified, substantial, and foreseeable risk that resulted in harm. In 2012, for example, a San Diego County, California, man named Richard Fox killed his girlfriend by accidentally shooting her with a homemade cannon. The fireworks enthusiast obviously did not intend for his girlfriend to die. At the same time, there is certainly a foreseeable risk inherent in operating homemade cannons around other people. Eventually, Fox was arrested for negligently discharging an explosive instead of murder.

Recklessness A defendant who commits an act recklessly is more blameworthy than one who is criminally negligent. The Model Penal Code defines criminal **recklessness** as "consciously disregard[ing] a substantial and unjustifiable risk."[18] So, in 2012, a Waldo County, Maine, jury found Luke Bryant guilty of criminal recklessness in the death of his friend Tyler Seaney. Bryant killed Seaney while the two were playing a game that involved pointing unloaded shotguns at each other and pulling the trigger. Even though Bryant was unaware that the gun was actually loaded in this instance, the risk of harm associated with this game was so great that the jury felt he should have taken greater safety measures. (As you can see, the difference between negligence and recklessness is not always clear. One could certainly argue that Richard Fox's behavior in causing the death of his girlfriend, described above, rose to the level of recklessness.)

DEGREES OF CRIME Crimes are graded by degree. Generally speaking, the degree of a crime is a reflection of the seriousness of that crime, and is used to determine the severity of any subsequent punishment.

With many crimes, degree is a function of the criminal act itself, as determined by statute. For example, most criminal codes consider a burglary that involves a nighttime forced entry into a home to be a burglary in the first degree. If the same act takes place during the day and involves a nonresidential building, then it is burglary in the second degree. As you might expect, burglary in the first degree carries a harsher penalty than burglary in the second degree.

Willful Murder With murder, the degree of the crime is, to a large extent, determined by the mental state of the offender. Murder is generally defined as the willful killing of a human being. It is important to emphasize the word *willful*, as it precludes homicides caused by accident or negligence. A death that results from negligence or accident generally is considered a private wrong and therefore a matter for civil law.

In addition, criminal law punishes those who plan and intend to do harm more harshly than it does those who act wrongfully because of strong emotions or other extreme circumstances. First degree murder—usually punishable by life in prison or the death penalty—occurs under two circumstances:

1. When the crime is premeditated, or contemplated beforehand by the offender, instead of being a spontaneous act of violence.

2. When the crime is deliberate, meaning that it was planned and decided on after a process of decision making. Deliberation does not require a lengthy planning process. A person can be found guilty of first degree murder even if she or he made the decision to kill only seconds before committing the crime.

Second degree murder, usually punishable by a minimum of fifteen to twenty-five years in prison, occurs when no premeditation or deliberation was present, but the offender did have *malice aforethought* toward the victim. In other words, the offender acted with wanton disregard for the consequences of his or her actions. (*Malice* means "wrongful intention" or "the desire to do evil.")

The difference between first and second degree murder is illustrated in a case involving a California man who beat a neighbor to death with a partially full brandy bottle. The crime took place after Ricky

Negligence A failure to exercise the standard of care that a reasonable person would exercise in similar circumstances.

Recklessness The state of being aware that a risk does or will exist and nevertheless acting in a way that consciously disregards this risk.

JOB DESCRIPTION:

- Assist lawyers in many aspects of legal work, including preparing for trial, researching legal documents, drafting contracts, and investigating cases.

- In addition to criminal law, work includes civil law, corporate law, intellectual property, bankruptcy, immigration, family law, and real estate.

WHAT KIND OF TRAINING IS REQUIRED?

- A community college–level paralegal program that leads to an associate degree.

- For those who already have a college degree, a certificate in paralegal studies.

ANNUAL SALARY RANGE?

- $30,000–$75,000

SOCIAL MEDIA CAREER TIP

Find groups on Facebook and LinkedIn in which people are discussing the criminal justice career or careers that interest you. Participate in the discussions to get information and build contacts.

©Andresr/iStockphoto

McDonald, the victim, complained to Kazi Cooksey, the offender, about the noise coming from a late-night barbecue Cooksey and his friends were holding. The jury could not find sufficient evidence that Cooksey's actions were premeditated, but he certainly acted with wanton disregard for his victim's safety. Therefore, the jury convicted Cooksey of second degree murder rather than first degree murder.

Types of Manslaughter A homicide committed without malice toward the victim is known as *manslaughter* and is commonly punishable by up to fifteen years in prison. Voluntary manslaughter occurs when the intent to kill may be present, but malice is lacking. **Voluntary manslaughter** covers crimes of passion, in which the emotion of an argument between two friends may lead to a homicide. Voluntary manslaugh-

Voluntary Manslaughter
A homicide in which the intent to kill was present in the mind of the offender, but malice was lacking.

Involuntary Manslaughter A homicide in which the offender had no intent to kill her or his victim.

Strict Liability Crimes
Certain crimes, such as traffic violations, in which the defendant is guilty regardless of her or his state of mind at the time of the act.

ter can also occur when the victim provoked the offender to act violently.

Involuntary manslaughter covers incidents in which the offender's acts may have been careless, but he or she had no intent to kill. Several years ago, for example, Dr. Conrad Murray was convicted of involuntary manslaughter for his role in the death of pop star Michael Jackson. Murray had provided Jackson with a powerful anesthetic to help Jackson sleep, and the dosage proved fatal. Although Murray had certainly not intended for Jackson to die, he was held criminally responsible for the singer's death and sentenced to four years in prison.

STRICT LIABILITY For certain crimes, criminal law holds the defendant to be guilty even if intent to commit the offense is lacking. These acts are known as **strict liability crimes** and generally involve endangering the public welfare in some way. Drug-control statutes, health and safety regulations, and traffic laws are all strict liability laws.

To a certain extent, the concept of strict liability is inconsistent with the traditional principles of criminal law, which hold that *mens rea* is required for an act to be criminal. The goal of strict liability laws is to protect the public by eliminating the possibility that wrongdoers could claim ignorance or mistake to absolve themselves of criminal responsibility.[19] Thus, a person caught dumping waste in a protected pond or driving 70 miles per hour in a 55 miles-per-hour zone cannot plead a lack of intent in his or her defense.

One of the most controversial strict liability crimes is **statutory rape,** in which an adult engages in a sexual relationship with a minor. In most states, even if the minor consents to the sexual act, the crime still exists because, being underage, he or she is considered incapable of making a rational decision on the matter.[20] Therefore, statutory rape has been committed even if the adult was unaware of the minor's age or was misled to believe that the minor was older.

ACCOMPLICE LIABILITY Under certain circumstances, a person can be charged with and convicted of a crime that he or she did not actually commit. This occurs when the suspect has acted as an accomplice, helping another person commit the crime. Generally, to be found guilty as an *accomplice,* a person must have the "dual intent" (1) to aid the person who committed the crime and (2) that such aid would lead to the commission of the crime.[21] As for the *actus reus,* the accomplice must have helped the primary actor in either a physical sense (for example, by providing the getaway car) or a psychological sense (for example, by encouraging her or him to commit the crime).[22]

In some states, a person can be convicted as an accomplice even without intent if the crime was a "natural and probable consequence" of his or her actions.[23] This principle has led to a proliferation of **felony-murder** legislation. Felony-murder is a form of first degree murder that applies when a person participates in any of a list of serious felonies that results in the death of a human being. Under felony-murder law, if two men rob a bank, and the first man intentionally kills a security guard, the second man can be convicted of first degree murder as an accomplice to the bank robbery, even if he had no intent to hurt anyone. Along these same lines, if a security guard

Statutory Rape A strict liability crime in which an adult engages in a sexual act with a minor.

Felony-Murder An unlawful homicide that occurs during the attempted commission of a felony.

CAREERPREP

CRIMINAL COURT JUDGE

JOB DESCRIPTION:

- Preside over trials and hearings in federal, state, and local courts. Ensure that all proceedings are fair and protect the legal rights of everyone involved.
- Rule on admissibility of evidence, monitor the testimony of witnesses, and settle disputes between prosecutors and defense attorneys.

WHAT KIND OF TRAINING IS REQUIRED?

- A law degree and several years of legal experience.
- Depending on the jurisdiction, judges are either appointed or elected.

ANNUAL SALARY RANGE?

- $93,000–$162,000

Frances Twitty/Getty Images

accidentally shoots and kills a customer during a bank robbery, the bank robbers can be charged with first degree murder because they committed the underlying felony.

In the case that opened this chapter, authorities were able to charge Rickie Lee Fowler under California's felony-murder law. Even though Fowler, at worst, intended to commit arson, that particular crime is a felony, and the wildfire was found to have caused the five fatal heart attacks. (**CAREER TIP:** *Certified arson investigators* are trained to read the clues left by suspicious fires and determine their causes. In the words of one arson specialist, "Fire does not destroy evidence—it creates it.") These kinds of laws have come under criticism because they punish individuals for unintended acts or acts committed by others. Nevertheless, the criminal codes of more than thirty states include some form of the felony-murder rule.[24]

3-5c
Concurrence

According to criminal law, there must be *concurrence* between the guilty act and the guilty intent. In other words, the guilty act and the guilty intent must occur together.[25] Suppose, for example, that a woman intends to murder her husband with poison in order to collect his life insurance. Every evening, this woman drives her husband home from work. On the night she plans to poison him, however, she swerves to avoid a cat crossing the road and runs into a tree. She survives the accident, but her husband is killed. Even though her intent was realized, the incident would be considered an accidental death because she had not planned to kill him by driving the car into a tree.

3-5d
Causation

Criminal law also requires that the criminal act cause the harm suffered. In 1989, for example, nineteen-year-old Mike Wells shook his two-year-old daughter, Christina, so violently that she suffered brain damage. Soon after the incident,

Attendant Circumstances The facts surrounding a criminal event that must be proved to convict the defendant of the underlying crime.

Hate Crime Law A statute that provides for greater sanctions against those who commit crimes motivated by bias against an individual or a group based on race, ethnicity, religion, gender, sexual orientation, disability, or age.

Wells served prison time for aggravated child abuse. Seventeen years later, in 2006, Christina died. When a coroner ruled that the cause of death was the earlier brain injury, Pasco County (Florida) authorities decided that, despite the passage of time, Wells was criminally responsible for his daughter's death. In 2010, Wells pleaded guilty to second degree murder and received a fifteen-year prison sentence. (**CAREER TIP:** In court proceedings, children such as Christina who are harmed by their parents are often represented by trained community volunteers called *child advocates*.)

3-5e
Attendant Circumstances

In certain crimes, **attendant circumstances**—also known as accompanying circumstances—are relevant to the *corpus delicti*. Most states, for example, differentiate between simple assault and the more serious offense of aggravated assault depending on the attendant circumstance of whether the defendant used a weapon such as a gun or a knife while committing the crime. Criminal law also classifies degrees of property crimes based on the attendant circumstance of the amount stolen. According to federal statutes, the theft of less than $1,000 from a bank is a misdemeanor, while the theft of any amount over $1,000 is a felony.[26] (To get a better understanding of the role of attendant circumstances in criminal statutes, see Figure 3.3 on the facing page.)

In most cases, a person's motive for committing a crime is irrelevant—a court will not try to read the accused's mind. Over the past few decades, however, nearly every state and the federal government have passed *hate crime laws* that make the suspect's motive an important attendant circumstance to his or her criminal act. In general, **hate crime laws** provide for greater sanctions against those who commit crimes motivated by bias against a person based on race, ethnicity, religion, gender, sexual orientation, disability, or age. On December 29, 2012, for example, Erika Mendez pushed Sunando Sen onto the tracks of an elevated subway station in Queens, New York.

Sen, born in India, was immediately killed by an oncoming train. Mendez told the police that she chose Sen, whom she believed to be a Muslim, "because I hate Hindus and Muslims ever since 2001 when they put down the twin towers I've been beating them up

FIGURE 3.3 Attendant Circumstances in Criminal Law

Most criminal statutes incorporate three of the elements we have discussed in this section: the act (*actus reus*), the intent (*mens rea*), and attendant circumstances. This diagram of the federal false imprisonment statute should give you an idea of how these elements combine to create the totality of a crime.

Intent	Act	Attendant Circumstances

Whoever intentionally confines, restrains, or detains another against that person's will is guilty of felony false imprisonment.

[sic]."[27] New York officials charged Mendez with second degree murder as a hate crime, meaning that, if convicted, she faces a minimum prison sentence of twenty years instead of fifteen years.

3-5f
Harm

For most crimes to occur, some harm must have been done to a person or to property. A certain number of crimes are actually categorized depending on the harm done to the victim, regardless of the intent behind the criminal act. Take two offenses, both of which involve one person hitting another in the back of the head with a tire iron. In the first instance, the victim dies, and the offender is charged with murder. In the second, the victim is only knocked unconscious, and the offender is charged with battery. Because the harm in the second instance was less severe, so was the crime with which the offender was charged, even though the act was exactly the same. Furthermore, most states have different degrees of battery depending on the extent of the injuries suffered by the victim.

Many acts are deemed criminal if they could do harm that the laws try to prevent. Such acts are called **inchoate offenses.** They exist when only an attempt at a criminal act was made. If Jenkins solicits Peterson to murder Jenkins's business partner, this is an inchoate offense on the part of Jenkins, even though Peterson fails to carry out the act. Threats and *conspiracies* also fall into the category of inchoate offenses. In 2012, a Cedar Lake, Indiana, man was arrested on charges of felony intimidation for threatening to set his wife on fire and "kill as many people as possible" at the school where she worked. The United States Supreme Court has ruled that a person could be convicted of criminal **conspiracy** even though police intervention made the completion of the illegal plan impossible.[28]

3-6
which DEFENSES ARE AVAILABLE UNDER CRIMINAL LAW?

According to prosecutors, Derrick Francois fatally shot Chandrick Harris in the head as part of a family feud that had gotten out of control in Gretna, Louisiana. On January 7, 2013, however, the day before Francois's murder trial was to begin, his defense attorneys presented pay stubs backing Francois's claim that he was working in Pascagoula, Mississippi, at the time of Harris's killing in Gretna. That is, they raised an **alibi** defense, saying that their client could not possibly have committed this murder because he was somewhere else when it occurred. Along with presenting an alibi, defendants can raise a number of other defenses for wrongdoing in our criminal courts. These defenses generally rely on one of two arguments: (1) the defendant is not responsible for the crime, or (2) the defendant was justified in committing the crime.

3-6a
Criminal Responsibility and the Law

The idea of responsibility plays a significant role in criminal law. In certain circumstances, the law recognizes that even though an act is inherently criminal, society will not punish the actor because he or she does not have the requisite

Inchoate Offenses Conduct deemed criminal without actual harm being done, provided that the harm that would have occurred is one the law tries to prevent.

Conspiracy A plot by two or more people to carry out an illegal or harmful act.

Alibi A defense offered by a person accused of a crime showing that she or he was elsewhere at the time the crime took place.

mental condition. In other words, the law "excuses" the person for his or her behavior. Insanity, intoxication, and mistake are the most important excuse defenses today, but we start our discussion of the subject with one of the first such defenses recognized by American law: infancy.

INFANCY Under the earliest state criminal codes of the United States, children younger than seven years of age could never be held legally accountable for crimes. Those between seven and fourteen years old were presumed to lack the capacity for criminal behavior, while anyone over the age of fourteen was tried as an adult. Thus, early American criminal law recognized **infancy** as a defense in which the accused's wrongdoing is excused because he or she is too young to fully understand the consequences of his or her actions.

With the creation of the juvenile justice system in the early 1900s, the infancy defense became redundant, as youthful delinquents were automatically treated differently from adult offenders. Today, most states either designate an age (eighteen or under) under which wrongdoers are sent to juvenile court or allow prosecutors to decide whether a minor will be charged as an adult on a case-by-case basis. We will explore the concept of infancy as it applies to the modern American juvenile justice system in much greater detail in Chapter 13.

Infancy A condition that, under early American law, excused young wrongdoers of criminal behavior because presumably they could not understand the consequences of their actions.

Insanity A defense for criminal liability that asserts a lack of criminal responsibility due to mental instability

M'Naghten Rule A common law test of criminal responsibility, derived from M'Naghten's Case in 1843, that relies on the defendant's inability to distinguish right from wrong.

Substantial-Capacity Test (ALI/MPC Test) A test for the insanity defense that states that a person is not responsible for criminal behavior when he or she "lacks substantial capacity" to understand that the behavior is wrong or to know how to behave properly.

INSANITY After Leo Kwaska killed and decapitated Shirley Meeks, his downstairs neighbor, he told psychiatrists that Meeks was a demon and that he needed to kill her to avert the end of the world. In 2012, a Jackson County, Mississippi, judge found that Kwaska's severe mental illness kept him from knowing that his actions were wrong. As a result, Kwaska was sent to a psychiatric hospital rather than prison. Thus, **insanity** may be a defense to a criminal charge when the defendant's state of mind is such that she or he cannot claim legal responsibility for her or his actions.

Measuring Sanity The general principle of the insanity defense is that a person is excused for his or her criminal wrongdoing if, as a result of a mental disease or defect, he or she

- Does not perceive the physical nature or consequences of his or her conduct;
- Does not know that his or her conduct is wrong or criminal; or
- Is not sufficiently able to control his or her conduct so as to be held accountable for it.[29]

Although criminal law has traditionally accepted the idea that an insane person cannot be held responsible for criminal acts, society has long debated what standards should be used to measure sanity for the purposes of a criminal trial. This lack of consensus is reflected in the diverse tests employed by different American jurisdictions to determine insanity. The tests include the following:

1. *The* M'Naghten *rule.* Derived from an 1843 British murder case, the **M'Naghten rule** states that a person is legally insane and therefore not criminally responsible if, at the time of the offense, he or she was not able to distinguish between right and wrong.[30] As Figure 3.4 on the facing page shows, half of the states still use a version of the *M'Naghten* rule. One state, New Hampshire, uses a slightly different version of this rule called the "product test." Under this standard, a defendant is not guilty if the unlawful act was the product of a mental disease or defect.

2. *The ALI/MPC test.* In the early 1960s, the American Law Institute (ALI) included an insanity standard in its Model Penal Code (MPC), mentioned earlier in the chapter. Also known as the **substantial-capacity test,** the **ALI/MPC test** requires that the defendant lack "substantial capacity" to either "appreciate the wrongfulness" of his or her conduct or to conform that conduct "to the requirements of the law."[31]

FIGURE 3.4 Insanity Defense

M'Naghten: "Didn't know what he was doing or didn't know it was wrong."

M'Naghten plus Irresistible Impulse: "Could not control his conduct."

ALI/MPC: "Lacks substantial capacity to appreciate the wrongfulness of his conduct or to control it."

Product test: "No criminal responsibility if the unlawful act is the product of a mental disease or defect."

No insanity defense established by state legislature.

3. *The irresistible-impulse test.* Under the **irresistible-impulse test,** a person may be found insane even if he or she was aware that a criminal act was "wrong," provided that some "irresistible impulse" resulting from a mental deficiency drove him or her to commit the crime.[32]

The ALI/MPC test is considered the easiest standard of the three for a defendant to meet because the defendant needs only to show a lack of "substantial capacity" to be released from criminal responsibility. Defense attorneys generally consider it more difficult to prove that the defendant could not distinguish "right" from "wrong" or that he or she was driven by an irresistible impulse.

Determining Competency Whatever the standard, the insanity defense is rarely entered and is even less likely to result in an acquittal, as it is difficult to prove.[33] Psychiatry is far more commonly used in the courtroom to determine the "competency" of a defendant to stand trial. If a judge believes that the defendant is unable to understand the nature of the proceedings or to assist in his or her own defense, the trial will not take place.

When **competency hearings** (which may also take place after the initial arrest and before sentencing) reveal that the defendant is in fact incompetent, criminal proceedings come to a halt. For example, in January 2013, an Alameda County (California) judge ruled that because One L. Goh suffered from paranoid schizophrenia, he was not fit to stand trial. Goh had been charged with seven counts of murder resulting from a shooting rampage on the campus of Oikos University in Oakland. As a result of the judge's decision, Goh would receive psychiatric treatment to restore his competency. When this goal was achieved, the criminal proceedings would continue.

INTOXICATION The law recognizes two types of **intoxication,** whether from drugs or from alcohol: *voluntary* and *involuntary*. Involuntary intoxication occurs when a person is physically forced to ingest or is injected with an intoxicating substance, or is unaware that a substance contains drugs or alcohol. Involuntary intoxication is a viable defense to a crime if the substance leaves the person unable to form the mental state necessary to understand that the act committed while under the

Irresistible-Impulse Test A test for the insanity defense under which a defendant who knew his or her action was wrong may still be found insane if he or she was unable, as a result of a mental deficiency, to control the urge to complete the act.

Competency Hearing A court proceeding to determine whether the defendant is mentally well enough to understand the charges filed against him or her and cooperate with a lawyer in presenting a defense.

Intoxication A defense for criminal liability in which the defendant claims that the taking of intoxicants rendered him or her unable to form the requisite intent to commit a criminal act.

According to prosecutors, seventeen-year-old Tyler Hadley beat his parents to death with a hammer in Port St. Lucie, Florida. Hadley claims that he took three pills of the psychoactive drug ecstasy before the homicides. How could Hadley's defense attorneys use this information in defending their client against first degree murder charges?

(AP Photo/St. Lucie County Sheriff's office)

influence was wrong.[34] In Colorado, for example, the murder conviction of a man who shot a neighbor was overturned on the basis that the jury in the initial trial was not informed of the possibility of involuntary intoxication. At the time of the crime, the man had been taking a prescription decongestant that contained phenylpropanolamine, which has been known to cause psychotic episodes.

Voluntary drug or alcohol intoxication is also used to excuse a defendant's actions, though it is not a defense in itself. Rather, it is used when the defense attorney wants to show that the defendant was so intoxicated that *mens rea* was negated. In other words, the defendant could not possibly have had the state of mind that a crime requires. Many courts are reluctant to allow voluntary intoxication arguments to be presented to juries, however. After all, the defendant, by definition, voluntarily chose to enter an intoxicated state. Twelve states have eliminated voluntary intoxication as a possible defense, a step that has been criticized by many legal scholars but was upheld by the United States Supreme Court in *Montana v. Egelhoff* (1996).[35]

MISTAKE Everyone has heard the saying, "Ignorance of the law is no excuse." Ordinarily, ignorance of the law or a *mistaken idea* about what the law requires is not a valid defense.[36] For example, several years ago retired science teacher Eddie Leroy Anderson and his son dug for arrowheads near their favorite campground site in Idaho, unaware that the land was a federally protected archaeological site. Facing two years in prison for this mistake, they pleaded guilty and were given a year's probation and a $1,500 fine each. "Folks need to pay attention to where they are," said U.S. attorney Wendy Olson.[37]

Mistake of Law As the above example suggests, strict liability crimes specifically preclude the *mistake of law* defense, because the offender's intent is irrelevant. For practical reasons, the mistake of law defense is rarely allowed under any circumstances. If "I didn't know" was a valid defense, the courts would be clogged with defendants claiming ignorance of all aspects of criminal law. In some rare instances, however, people who claim that they honestly did not know that they were breaking a law may have a valid defense if (1) the law was not published or reasonably known to the public or (2) the person relied on an official statement of the law that was erroneous.[38]

Mistake of Fact A *mistake of fact*, as opposed to a *mistake of law*, operates as a defense if it negates the mental state necessary to commit a crime. If, for example, Oliver mistakenly walks off with Julie's briefcase because he thinks it is his, there is no theft. Theft requires knowledge that the property belongs to another. The mistake of fact defense has proved very controversial in rape and sexual assault cases, in which the accused claims a mistaken belief that the sex was consensual, while the victim insists that he or she was coerced.

3-6b

Justification Criminal Defenses and the Law

In certain instances, a defendant will accept **4** LO responsibility for committing an illegal act, but contend that—given the circumstances—the act was justified. In other words, even though the guilty act and the guilty intent are present, the particulars of the case relieve the defendant of criminal liability. In 2011, for example, there were 653 "justified" killings of those who were in the process of committing a felony: 393 were killed by law enforcement officers and 260 by private citizens.[39] Four of the most important justification defenses are duress, self-defense, necessity, and entrapment.

DURESS **Duress** exists when the *wrongful* threat of one person induces another person to perform an act that she or he would otherwise not perform. In such a situation, duress is said to negate the *mens rea* necessary to commit a crime. For duress to qualify as a defense, the following requirements must be met:

1. The threat must be of serious bodily harm or death.
2. The harm threatened must be greater than the harm caused by the crime.
3. The threat must be immediate and inescapable.
4. The defendant must have become involved in the situation through no fault of his or her own.[40]

Note that some scholars consider duress to be an excuse defense, because the threat of bodily harm negates any guilty intent on the part of the defendant.[41]

When ruling on the duress defense, courts often examine whether the defendant had the opportunity to avoid the threat in question. In one case, the defendant claimed that an associate threatened to kill him and his wife unless he participated in a marijuana deal. Although this contention was proved true during the course of the trial, the court rejected the duress defense because the defendant made no apparent effort to escape, nor did he report his dilemma to the police. In sum, the drug deal was avoidable—the defendant could have made an effort to extricate (remove) himself, but he did not, thereby giving up the protection of the duress defense.

JUSTIFIABLE USE OF FORCE—SELF-DEFENSE

A person who believes he or she is in danger of being harmed by another is justified in defending himself or herself with the use of force, and any criminal act committed in such circumstances can be justified as **self-defense.** Other situations that also justify the use of force include the defense of another person, the defense of one's dwelling or other property, and the prevention of a crime. In all these situations, it is important to distinguish between deadly and nondeadly force. Deadly force is likely to result in death or serious bodily harm.

The Amount of Force Generally speaking, people can use the amount of nondeadly force that seems necessary to protect themselves, their dwellings, or other property or to prevent the commission of a crime. Deadly force can be used in self-defense if there is a *reasonable belief* that imminent death or bodily harm will otherwise result, if the attacker is using unlawful force (an example of lawful force is that exerted by a police officer), if the defender has not initiated or provoked the attack, and if there is no other possible response or alternative way out of the life-threatening situation.[42]

Deadly force normally can be used to defend a dwelling only if the unlawful entry is violent and the person believes deadly force is necessary to prevent imminent death or great bodily harm. In some jurisdictions, it is also a viable defense if the person believes deadly force is necessary to prevent the commission of a felony (such as arson) in the dwelling.

The Duty to Retreat When a person is outside the home or in a public space, the rules for self-defense change somewhat. Until relatively recently, almost all jurisdictions required someone who is attacked under these circumstances to "retreat to the wall" before fighting back. In other words, under this **duty to retreat** one who is being assaulted may not resort to deadly force if she or he has a reasonable opportunity to "run away" and thus avoid the conflict. Only when this person has run into a "wall," literally or otherwise, may deadly force be used in self-defense.

Recently, however, several states have changed their laws to eliminate this duty to retreat. For example, a Florida law did away with the duty to retreat outside the home, stating that citizens have "the right to stand [their] ground and meet force with force, including deadly force," if they "reasonably" fear for their safety.[43] The Florida law also allows a person to use deadly force against someone who unlawfully intrudes into her or his house (or vehicle), even if that person does not fear for her or his safety.[44]

The George Zimmerman Case At least twenty-five states have broadened their

Duress Unlawful pressure brought to bear on a person, causing the person to perform an act that he or she would not otherwise perform.

Self-Defense The legally recognized privilege to protect one's self or property from injury by another.

Duty to Retreat The requirement that a person claiming self-defense prove that she or he first took reasonable steps to avoid the conflict that resulted in the use of deadly force.

George Zimmerman, shown here in a Seminole County (Florida) courthouse, insisted that his voice could be heard screaming for help on a 911 recording of his deadly encounter with Trayvon Martin. How might this piece of evidence have helped Zimmerman's self-defense claims?

Stephen M. Dowell-Pool/Getty Images

self-defense laws to include a version of Florida's "stand your ground" statute. These laws became a topic of much debate when George Zimmerman shot and killed unarmed seventeen-year-old Trayvon Martin in Sanford, Florida, on February 26, 2012. Zimmerman told police that he had encountered Martin during his rounds as a neighborhood watchman, and that he had pulled the trigger only after being attacked by the younger man. Initially, Florida authorities accepted this version of events and did not arrest Zimmerman, who appeared to have acted within the limits of the state's "stand your ground" law.

This decision was met with a national outcry. Much of the anger focused on aspects of the incident that seemed to indicate racial bias. (Zimmerman is Hispanic, while Martin was African American.) Furthermore, critics worry that the proliferation of "stand your ground" laws has created a "nation where disputes are settled by guns instead of gavels, and where suspects are shot by civilians instead of arrested by police."[45] A special prosecutor eventually charged Zimmerman with second degree murder. In July 2013, a jury acquitted Zimmerman. The jurors, apparently influenced by photos of the defendant's bloodied head taken by police after the incident, agreed that he could have acted reasonably in defending himself against great bodily harm or death.[46]

Necessity A defense against criminal liability in which the defendant asserts that circumstances required her or him to commit an illegal act.

Entrapment A defense in which the defendant claims that he or she was induced by a public official—usually an undercover agent or police officer—to commit a crime that he or she would otherwise not have committed.

NECESSITY The **necessity** defense requires courts to weigh the harm caused by the crime actually committed against the harm that would have been caused by the criminal act avoided. If the avoided harm is greater than the committed harm, then the defense has a chance of succeeding. Several years ago, for example, a San Francisco jury acquitted a defendant of illegally carrying a concealed weapon because he was avoiding the "greater evil" of getting shot himself. The defendant had testified that he needed the gun for protection while entering a high-crime neighborhood to buy baby food and diapers for his crying niece. Murder is the one crime for which the necessity defense is not applicable under any circumstances.

ENTRAPMENT **Entrapment** is a justification defense that criminal law allows when a police officer or government agent deceives a defendant into wrongdoing. Although law enforcement agents can legitimately use various forms of subterfuge—such as informants or undercover agents—to gain information or apprehend a suspect in a criminal act, the law places limits on these strategies. Police cannot persuade an innocent person to commit a crime, nor can they coerce a suspect into doing so, even if they are certain she or he is a criminal.

According to the United States Supreme Court, entrapment occurs if a defendant who is not predisposed to commit a crime is enticed to do so by an agent of the government.[47] In a 1992 case, for example, over a two-year period agents from the U.S. Postal Investigation Service sent the defendant seven letters inquiring about his sexual preference, two sex catalogues, and two sexual-attitude surveys, all from fictitious organizations. (**CAREER TIP:** The *U.S. Postal Investigation Service,* made up of about 650 uniformed agents, is the law enforcement arm of the U.S. Postal Service.) Eventually, the defendant ordered a publication called *Boys Who Love Boys* and was arrested and convicted for breaking child pornography laws. The Supreme Court overturned the conviction, ruling that entrapment had taken place because the defendant had showed no predisposition to order the illicit publication in the absence of the government's efforts.[48]

how DO CRIMINAL PROCEDURES PROTECT OUR CONSTITUTIONAL RIGHTS

LO 5 To this point, we have focused on **substantive criminal law,** which defines the acts that the government will punish. We will now turn our attention to **procedural criminal law.** (The section that follows will provide only a short overview of criminal procedure. In later chapters, many other constitutional issues will be examined in more detail.) Criminal law brings the force of the state, with all its resources, to bear against the individual.

Criminal procedures, drawn from the ideals stated in the Bill of Rights, are designed to protect the constitutional rights of individuals and to prevent the arbitrary use of power by the government.

3-7a
The Bill of Rights

For various reasons, proposals related to the rights of individuals were rejected during the framing of the U.S. Constitution in 1787. The need for a written declaration of rights of individuals eventually caused the first Congress to draft twelve amendments to the Constitution and submit them for approval by the states. Ten of these amend-

ments, commonly known as the **Bill of Rights,** were adopted in 1791. Since then, seventeen more amendments have been added.

The Bill of Rights, as interpreted by the United States Supreme Court, has served as the basis for procedural safeguards of the accused in this country. These safeguards include the following:

1. The Fourth Amendment protection from unreasonable searches and seizures.

2. The Fourth Amendment requirement that no warrants for a search or an arrest can be issued without probable cause.

3. The Fifth Amendment requirement that no one can be deprived of life, liberty, or property without "due process" of law.

Substantive Criminal Law Law that defines the rights and duties of individuals with respect to one another.

Procedural Criminal Law Rules that define the manner in which the rights and duties of individuals may be enforced.

Bill of Rights The first ten amendments to the U.S. Constitution.

Why do most Americans accept certain precautions taken by the federal government—such as full body scans at airports—that restrict our individual freedom or compromise our privacy?

John Moore/Getty Images

4. The Fifth Amendment prohibition against *double jeopardy* (trying someone twice for the same criminal offense).

5. The Fifth Amendment guarantee that no person can be required to be a witness against (incriminate) himself or herself.

6. The Sixth Amendment guarantees of a speedy trial, a trial by jury, a public trial, the right to confront witnesses, and the right to a lawyer at various stages of criminal proceedings.

7. The Eighth Amendment prohibitions against excessive bails and fines and cruel and unusual punishments. (For the full text of the Bill of Rights, see Appendix A.)

The Bill of Rights initially offered citizens protection only against the federal government. Over the years, however, the procedural safeguards of most of the provisions of the Bill of Rights have been applied to the actions of state governments through the Fourteenth Amendment.[49] Furthermore, the states, under certain circumstances, have the option to grant even more protections than are required by the federal Constitution. As these protections are crucial to criminal justice procedures in the United States, they will be afforded much more attention in Chapter 6, with regard to police action, and in Chapter 8, with regard to the criminal trial.

CJ TECHNOLOGY

DUE PROCESS AND PREDATOR DRONES

BETWEEN 2008 and 2013, American Predator drones—remote controlled, unmanned aircraft armed with missiles—killed upwards of 3,000 suspected terrorists in Afghanistan, Pakistan, and Yemen. Although that tally includes an unknown number of innocent civilians, the most controversial target has been Islamist cleric Anwar al-Awlaki, who failed to survive a drone strike in Yemen on September 30, 2011.

Through his online sermons in English, Awlaki had been linked to more than a dozen terrorist operations, including a plot to blow up cargo airplanes bound for the United States. He was also a United States citizen. Because of Awlaki's citizenship, critics argued that his death by drone attack was illegal, given that the U.S. Constitution forbids the execution of American citizens without due process of law. Legal expert Glenn Greenwald noted that there had been no effort to charge Awlaki with committing any crime, and he had not been afforded a trial to prove his innocence. "[Awlaki] was simply ordered killed by the president: his judge, jury and executioner," Greenwald said.

Oleg Yarko/Shutterstock

THINKING ABOUT DUE PROCESS AND PREDATOR DRONES

In 2013, President Barack Obama's administration justified targeted assassinations of suspected terrorists—including U.S. citizens—as "lawful acts of self-defense." After reviewing our discussion of self-defense earlier in the chapter, what is your opinion of this argument?

Due Process

Both the Fifth and Fourteenth Amendments provide that no person should be deprived of "life, liberty, or property without due process of law." This **due process clause** basically requires that the government not act unfairly or arbitrarily. In other words, the government cannot rely on individual judgment and impulse when making decisions, but must stay within the boundaries of reason and the law. Of course, disagreements as to the meaning of these provisions have plagued courts, politicians, and citizens since this nation was founded, and will undoubtedly continue to do so.

To understand due process, it is important to consider its two types: procedural due process and substantive due process.

PROCEDURAL DUE PROCESS According to **procedural due process,** the law must be carried out by a *method* that is fair and orderly. It requires that certain procedures be followed in administering and executing a law so that an individual's basic freedoms are not violated.

The American criminal justice system's adherence to due process principles is evident in its treatment of the death penalty. To ensure that the process is fair, as we will see in Chapter 9, a number of procedural safeguards have been built into capital punishment. Much to the dismay of many victims' groups, these procedures make the process expensive and lengthy. In California, for example, the average time between conviction for a capital crime and execution is twenty-five years.[50]

SUBSTANTIVE DUE PROCESS Fair procedures would obviously be of little use if they were used to administer unfair laws. For example, suppose a law requires everyone to wear a red shirt on Mondays. You wear a blue shirt on Monday, and you are arrested, convicted, and sentenced to one year in prison. The fact that all proper procedures were followed and your rights were given their proper protections would mean very little because the law that you broke was unfair and arbitrary.

Thus, **substantive due process** requires that the laws themselves be reasonable. The idea is that if a law is unfair or arbitrary, even if properly passed by a legislature, it must be declared unconstitutional. In the 1930s, for example, Oklahoma instituted the Habitual Criminal Sterilization Act. Under this statute, a person who had been convicted of three felonies could be "rendered sexually sterile" by the state (that is, the person would no longer be able to produce children). The United States Supreme Court held that the law was unconstitutional, as there are "limits to the extent which a legislatively represented majority may conduct biological experiments at the expense of the dignity and personality and natural powers of a minority."[51]

Due Process Clause The provisions of the Fifth and Fourteenth Amendments to the Constitution that guarantee that no person shall be deprived of life, liberty, or property without due process of law.

Procedural Due Process A provision in the Constitution that states that the law must be carried out in a fair and orderly manner.

Substantive Due Process The constitutional requirement that laws used in accusing and convicting persons of crimes must be fair.

Spectators line up to enter the U.S. Supreme Court building in Washington, D.C. The Court recently upheld a federal law broadening the government's power to eavesdrop on international e-mails and phone calls. Why might the Court tend to defer to the federal government where questions of national security are concerned?

Mark Wilson/Getty Images

REVIEW

✓ **Review what you've read with the quiz below.**

Rip out the Chapter Review card at the back of this book, which includes:
- Chapter Summary and Learning Outcomes
- Key Terms

Or you can go online to CourseMate at www.cengagebrain.com to:
- Complete Practice Quizzes to prepare for tests.
- Review Key Terms Flash Cards (online or print).
- Play games to master concepts.

quiz

1. The U.S. _____ is the supreme law of the United States.

2. The body of law created by judicial decisions is known as _____ law.

3. Apart from criminal law, _____ law is concerned with disputes between private individuals and other entities.

4. A _____ is a serious crime punishable by more than a year in prison or the death penalty.

5. A person found guilty of a _____ will usually spend less than a year in jail or pay a fine.

6. With strict liability crimes, the law determines that a defendant is guilty even if he or she lacked the _____ to perform a criminal act.

7. Criminal law recognizes that a defendant may not be responsible for a criminal act if her or his mental state was impaired by _____, or mental instability.

8. Defendants may claim that they were justified in committing a crime because they were acting in _____ - _____ to protect themselves or others from serious bodily harm.

9. _____ occurs when a government agent deceives a defendant into committing a crime.

10. The United States _____ _____ ultimately decides whether the government has violated an individual's substantive or procedural due process rights.

Answers can be found on the Chapter 3 Review card at the end of the book.

Wilfred Y. Wong/Getty Images

LAW ENFORCEMENT TODAY

4

What's Going On?

Like the rest of American society, law enforcement has been swept up by the tide of social media. Over the past few years, most local police departments have taken advantage of Facebook and Twitter to improve their ability to communicate with the public. None have gone as far as the Seattle Police Department (SPD), however, and its new "Tweets-by-beat" initiative. Residents in fifty-one Seattle neighborhoods can now receive constant updates of nearby criminal activity directly from the police. Over the course of a single Sunday, for example, people living on Olive Way near downtown Seattle would have been notified of an "intoxicated person" on their street, along with two burglaries and several reports of "suspicious vehicles," accident investigations, and noise complaints.

"More and more people want to know what's going on on their piece of the rock," says Seattle police chief John Diaz. "This is just a different way we could put out as much information as possible as quickly as possible." Are the Seattle police providing the public with too much information? Eugene O'Donnell, a professor at John Jay College of Criminal Justice in New York City, worries that a greater awareness of local crime could lead to a greater, and unwarranted, fear of becoming a victim. Such awareness might also give residents the impression that the police are not doing their jobs effectively.

Furthermore, as highlighted by an incident in New Jersey, social media can be notoriously difficult to control. In January 2013, two West Orange police officers apparently joined a Facebook discussion concerning the shooting death of Raymar Lecky outside a Newark nightclub. One of the officers claimed that Lecky was a gang member and posted his criminal record. The other then wrote, "Live by the gun die by the gun BOOM" and added, referring to Lecky and his killer, "two birds with one stone. One dead and one will eventually go to jail." Amid the resulting outcry, Lecky's mother demanded that the two officers be "terminated—no less."

Neighborhood Twitter accounts allow the Seattle Police Department to keep community members up to date on local crime information, such as the status of this suspicious white van investigated by a patrol officer.

Michael Hanson/New York Times

4-1
what DO THE POLICE DO?

Police officers are the most visible representatives of our criminal justice system. Indeed, they symbolize the system for many Americans who may never see the inside of a courtroom or a prison cell. Still, the general perception of a "cop's life" is often shaped by television dramas such as the *CSI* series and *Hawaii Five-O.* Another stated goal of the Seattle Police Department's "Tweets-by-beat" project is to counteract this perception by giving the public a better understanding of the day-to-day work of law enforcement.[1] In reality, police spend a great deal of time on such mundane tasks as responding to noise complaints, confiscating firecrackers, and poring over paperwork.

Sociologist Egon Bittner warned against the tendency to see the police primarily as agents of law enforcement and crime control. A more inclusive accounting of "what the police do," Bittner believed, would recognize that they provide "situationally justified force in society."[2] In other words, the function of the police is to solve any problem that may *possibly,* though not *necessarily,* require the use of force.

Within Bittner's rather broad definition of "what the police do," we can pinpoint four basic responsibilities of the police:

LO **1**

1. To enforce laws.
2. To provide services.
3. To prevent crime.
4. To preserve the peace.

As will become evident over the next two chapters, there is a great deal of debate among legal and other scholars and law enforcement officers over which responsibilities deserve the most police attention and what methods should be employed by the police in meeting those responsibilities.

4-1a
Enforce Laws

In the public mind, the primary role of the police is to enforce society's laws—hence, the term *law enforcement officer.* In their role as "crime fighters," police officers have a clear mandate to seek out and apprehend those who have violated the law. The crime-fighting responsibility is so dominant that all police activity—from the purchase of new automobiles to a plan to hire more minority officers—must often be justified in terms of its law enforcement value.[3]

Police officers also see themselves primarily as crime fighters, or "crook catchers," a perception that often leads people into what they believe will be an exciting career in law enforcement. Although the job certainly offers challenges unlike any other, police officers normally do not spend the majority of their time in law enforcement duties. After surveying a year's worth of dispatch data from the Wilmington (Delaware) Police Department, researchers Jack Greene and Carl Klockars found that officers spent only about half of their time enforcing the law or dealing with crimes. The rest of their time was spent on order maintenance, service provision, traffic patrol, and medical assistance.[4]

Furthermore, information provided by the Uniform Crime Report shows that most arrests are made for "crimes of disorder" or public annoyances rather than violent or property crimes.[5] In 2011, for example, police made about 10.2 million arrests for drunkenness, liquor law violations, disorderly conduct, vagrancy, loitering, and other minor offenses, but only about 535,000 arrests for violent crimes.[6]

4-1b
Provide Services

The popular emphasis on crime fighting and law enforcement tends to overshadow the fact that a great deal of a police officer's time is spent providing services for the community. The motto "To Serve and Protect" has been adopted by thousands of local police departments, and the *Law Enforcement Code of Ethics* recognizes the duty "to serve the community" in its first sentence.[7] The services that police provide are numerous—a partial list would include directing traffic, performing emergency medical procedures, counseling those involved in domestic disputes, providing directions to tourists, and finding lost children.

Along with firefighters, police officers are among the first public servants called to conduct search and rescue operations. This particular duty adds con-

A Los Angeles police officer oversees community efforts to clean up trash and graffiti. What are the benefits and drawbacks of having law enforcement agents provide services that do not directly involve preventing and solving crimes?

Monica Almeida/*New York Times*/Redux Pictures

siderably to the dangers faced by law enforcement agents (discussed in more detail in Chapter 5). As we will see in the next chapter, a majority of police departments have adopted a strategy called community policing that requires officers to provide assistance in areas that are not, at first glance, directly related to law enforcement. In many ways, law enforcement agents are on the front lines when it comes to national health issues such as mental illness and substance abuse. Of all contacts that police officers have with members of the public, an estimated 20 percent involve those who are mentally ill or intoxicated.[8]

4-1c
Prevent Crime

Perhaps the most controversial responsibility of the police is to *prevent* crime, terrorist related or otherwise. According to Jerome Skolnick, co-director of the Center for Research in Crime and Justice at the New York University School of Law, there are two predictable public responses when crime rates begin to rise in a community. The first is to punish convicted criminals with stricter laws and more severe penalties. The second is to demand that the police "do something" to prevent crimes from occurring in the first place. Is it, in fact, possible for the police to "prevent" crimes? The strongest response that Professor Skolnick is willing to give to this question is "maybe."[9]

On a limited basis, police can certainly prevent some crimes. If a rapist is dissuaded from attacking a solitary woman because a patrol car is cruising the area, then the police officer behind the wheel has prevented a crime. Furthermore, exemplary police work can have a measurable effect. "Quite simply,

cops count," says William Bratton, who has directed police departments in Boston, Los Angeles, and New York. "[T]he quickest way to impact crime is with a well-led, managed, and appropriately resourced police force."[10] In Chapter 5, we will study a number of policing strategies that have been credited, by some, for decreasing crime rates in the United States.

In general, however, the deterrent effects of police presence are unclear. Carl Klockars has written that the "war on crime" is a war that the police cannot win because they cannot control the factors—such as unemployment, poverty, immorality, inequality, political change, and lack of educational opportunities—that contribute to criminal behavior in the first place.[11]

4-1d
Preserve the Peace

To a certain extent, the fourth responsibility of the police, that of preserving the peace, is related to preventing crime. Police have the legal authority to use the power of arrest, or even force, in situations in which no crime has yet occurred, but might occur in the immediate future.

In the words of James Q. Wilson, the police's peacekeeping role (which Wilson believed to be the most important role of law enforcement officers) often takes on a pattern of simply "handling the situation."[12] For example, when police officers arrive on the scene of a loud late-night house party, they may feel the need to disperse the party and even arrest some of the partygoers for disorderly conduct. By their actions, the officers have lessened the chances of serious and violent crimes taking place later in the evening. The same principle is often used when dealing with domestic disputes, which, if escalated, can lead to homicide. Such situations are in need of, to use Wilson's terminology again, "fixing up," and police can use the power of arrest, or threat, or coercion, or sympathy, to do just that.

4-1e

Policing Trends Today

Even as the four basic responsibilities of the police just discussed have remained fairly stable, the manner in which these duties are carried out is constantly changing. American law enforcement today faces challenges that would have been unfamiliar even fifteen years ago, and it has had to develop new areas of expertise to meet these challenges effectively. In particular, the process of collecting, analyzing, and mapping crime data has become a hallmark of policing in the twenty-first century.

INTELLIGENCE-LED POLICING

"Humans are not nearly as random as we think," says Jeff Brantingham, an anthropologist at the University of California, Los Angeles. "Crime is a physical process, and if you can explain how offenders move and how they mix with victims, you can understand an incredible amount."[13] Relying on this basic principle, Brantingham and several colleagues developed Predpol, a software program that strives to predict when and where crimes are most likely to occur. The software relies on a basic truism of criminal behavior: most crime is local. That is, offenders tend to commit crimes close to home, and they tend to victimize the same people and neighborhoods repeatedly.[14] (Remember, from Chapter 2, the concept of repeat victimization.)

The Predpol approach is known as predictive policing, or **intelligence-led policing** (IPL), because it relies on data—or intelligence—concerning past crime patterns to predict future crime patterns. In theory, IPL is relatively simple. Just as commercial fishers are most successful when they concentrate on the areas of the ocean where the fish are, law enforcement does well to focus its scarce resources on the areas where the most crime occurs. With programs such as Predpol and other "hot spot" technologies that we will discuss in the next chapter, police administrators are able to deploy small forces to specific locations, rather than blanketing an entire city with random patrols. Doing "more with less" in this manner is a particularly important consideration as police budgets shrink around the country.[15]

THE CHALLENGES OF COUNTERTERRORISM

If the importance of intelligence-based policing was not evident before September 11, 2001, the tragic events of that day made it clear that the nation's law enforcement agencies could not simply react to the crime of terrorism. With such a high toll in human lives, such attacks needed to be prevented. "Intelligence used to be a dirty word" for local police departments, according to David Carter, a professor of criminal justice at Michigan State University.[16] Today, however, financial support from the federal government has helped create more than one hundred local and state police intelligence units, with at least one in each state.[17] The New York Police Department, in a class by itself, has more than one thousand personnel assigned to homeland security and has stationed agents in six foreign countries. (**CAREER TIP:** *Transit officers,* who police transportation systems in many American cities, play a crucial role in anti-terrorism efforts. In the Washington, D.C., area, for example, Metro Transit Police officers use bomb-sniffing dogs to search for possible explosive devices on local commuter trains.)

Indeed, all police officers in the country are now expected to prepare for a terrorist attack in their communities, and counterterrorism has become part of the day-to-day law enforcement routine. This transition has not always been smooth. Many local police departments have had to shift personnel from traditional crime units, such as antigang or white-collar crime, to counterterrorism. Limited funds are also an issue. Raymond Kelly, police commissioner of New York, has testified to the "huge expenses" of counterterrorism and intelligence strategies.[18] Although the federal govern-

Intelligence-Led Policing
An approach that measures the risk of criminal behavior associated with certain individuals or locations so as to predict when and where such criminal behavior is most likely to occur in the future.

ment provided $31 billion in grants to state and local governments for homeland security between 2003 and 2010, many law enforcement agencies continue to rely on already-stretched-thin city budgets to cover the extra costs of anti-terrorism responsibilities.[19]

LAW ENFORCEMENT 2.0 Fortunately, just as more intelligence has become crucial to police work, the means available to gather such intelligence have also increased greatly. Nearly every successful anti-terrorism investigation has relied on information gathered from the Internet. More and more often, tra-ditional criminals are also getting caught on the Web. Police in South Charleston, West Virginia, arrested six young men who photographed themselves destroying a local hotel room and then posted the incriminating pictures on various Twitter accounts. Utah police discovered material on a convicted sex offender's MySpace account that proved forbidden contact with two youths. Memphis detectives were able to apprehend two burglars who had stolen alcohol from a restaurant when one of them wrote on Facebook, "I'd like to collect some of the booty we liberated Sunday, if there's any left." According to a recent poll, more than

CJ AND TECHNOLOGY — HIGH-TECH COP CARS

WHEN patrol cars came into common use by police departments in the 1930s, they changed the face of American policing. Nine decades later, the technology associated with patrol cars continues to evolve. Today, approximately 80 percent of all police cars in the United States are equipped with on-board computers. Specialized software for these computers allows law enforcement agents to turn cars into mobile offices. So, for example, if a patrol officer receives a call concerning an incident involving a known suspect, he or she can use the in-car computer to immediately access the suspect's criminal files. In Tampa, Florida, patrol officers have access to NC4 Safecop software, which allows them to analyze neighborhood crime data from the driver's seat.

Other recent innovations include Automatic License Plate Recognition, a three-camera computer-operated system that performs a "20-millisecond" background check on every license plate it sees, and the StarChase launcher, a small, laser-guided cannon that shoots a small, sticky radio transmitter at a fleeing vehicle. Once the offending car has been "tagged" with this device, police can track the fugi-

Michael Hanson/New York Times

tive at a safe distance without the need for a dangerous, high-speed pursuit.

THINKING ABOUT POLICE AUTOMOBILE TECHNOLOGY

One criminal justice expert has suggested that all police car computers be equipped with voice-to-text software, which would allow an officer's spoken words to be digitized immediately onto department databases. What would be some of the benefits of this technological upgrade?

80 percent of local police departments also use social media as a form of outreach to the public, as we saw at the beginning of this chapter.[20]

As the leaders of the reform movement envisioned, technology also continues to improve the capabilities of officers in the field. Using special applications on smartphones or tablet computers, police can instantly access the addresses of wanted persons, registered sex offenders, gang members, and recent crime locations. As we saw earlier in this section, the modern police car is quickly evolving into a command center on wheels, and police officers also enjoy the use of mobile fingerprint readers, less lethal weapons such as laser beams, and dozens of other technological innovations.

Some law enforcement veterans are concerned that the "art" of policing is being lost in an era of intelligence-led policing and increased reliance on technology. "If it becomes all about the science," says Los Angeles Police Department Deputy Chief Michael Downing, "I worry we'll lose the important nuances."[21] As the remainder of this chapter and the two that follow show, however, the human element continues to dominate all aspects of policing in America.

Recruitment The process by which law enforcement agencies develop a pool of qualified applicants from which to select new members.

4-2
how DOES SOMEONE BECOME A POLICE OFFICER?

In 1961, police expert James H. Chenoweth commented that the methods used to hire police officers had changed little since 1829 when the Metropolitan Police of London was created.[22] The past half-century, however, has seen a number of improvements in the way that police administrators handle the task of **recruitment,** or the development of a pool of qualified applicants from which to select new officers. Efforts have been made to diversify police rolls, and recruits in most police departments undergo a substantial array of tests and screens—discussed below—to determine their aptitude. Furthermore, annual starting salaries that can exceed $70,000, along with the opportunities offered by an interesting profession in the public service field, have attracted a wide variety of applicants to police work. (To learn what a police officer can expect to earn in his or her first year on the job, see Figure 4.1 below.)

FIGURE 4.1 Average Annual Salary for Entry-Level Officers by Size of Population Served

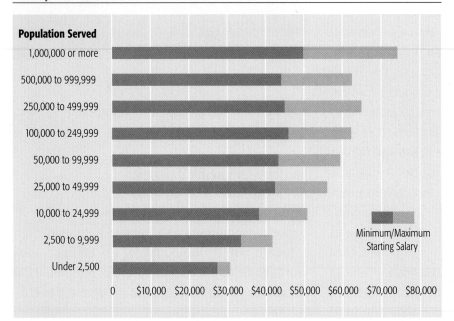

Source: Bureau of Justice Statistics, *Local Police Departments, 2007* (Washington, D.C.: U.S. Department of Justice, December 2010), Table 7, page 12.

4-2a
Basic Requirements

The selection process involves a number of steps, and each police department has a different method of choosing candidates. Most agencies, however, require at a minimum that a police officer:

- Be a U.S. citizen.
- Not have been convicted of a felony.
- Have or be eligible to have a driver's license in the state where the department is located.
- Be at least twenty-one years of age.
- Meet weight and eyesight requirements.

In addition, few departments will accept candidates older than forty-five years of age.

BACKGROUND CHECKS AND TESTS Beyond these minimum requirements, police departments usually engage in extensive background checks, including drug tests; a review of the applicant's educational, military, and driving records; credit checks; interviews with spouses, acquaintances, and previous employers; and a background search to determine whether the applicant has been convicted of any criminal acts. Police agencies generally require certain physical attributes in applicants: normally, they must be able to pass a physical agility or fitness test. (For an example of one such test, see Figure 4.2 below.)

In some departments, particularly those that serve large metropolitan areas, the applicant must take a psychological screening test to determine if he or she is suited to law enforcement work. Generally, such suitability tests measure the applicant's ability to handle stress, follow rules, use good judgment, and avoid off-duty behavior that would reflect negatively on the department.[23] Along these same lines, according to the International Association of Chiefs of Police, more than one-third of American police agencies now review an applicant's social media activity on sources such as Facebook, MySpace, and Twitter.[24] In one instance, the Middletown (New Jersey) Police Department rejected an applicant because he had posted photos of himself with "scantily clad women" online.

EDUCATIONAL REQUIREMENTS One of the most dramatic differences between today's police recruits and those of several generations ago is their level of education. In the 1920s, when August Vollmer began promoting the need for higher education in police officers, few had attended college. Today, 82 percent of all local police departments require at least a high school diploma, and 9 percent require a degree from a two-year college.[25] Although a four-year degree is necessary for certain elite law enforcement positions such as Federal Bureau of Investigation special agent, only about 5 percent of large local police departments have such a requirement.[26] Those officers with four-year degrees do, however, generally enjoy an advantage in hiring and promotion, and often receive higher salaries than their less educated co-employees.

Not all police observers believe that education is a necessity for police officers, however. In the words of one police officer, "effective street cops learn their skills on the job, not in a classroom."[27] By emphasizing a college degree, say some, police departments discourage those who would make solid officers but lack the education necessary to apply for positions in law enforcement.

4-2b
Training

If an applicant successfully navigates the application process, he or she will be hired on a

---

FIGURE 4.2 Physical Agility Exam for the Henrico County (Virginia) Division of Police

Those applying for the position of police officer must finish this physical agility exam within 3 minutes, 30 seconds. During the test, applicants are required to wear the equipment (with a total weight of between 9 and 13 pounds) worn by patrol officers, which includes the police uniform, leather gun belt, firearm, baton, portable radio, and ballistics vest.

1. Applicant begins test seated in a police vehicle, door closed, seat belt fastened.
2. Applicant must exit vehicle and jump or climb a six-foot barrier.
3. Applicant then completes a one-quarter mile run or walk, making various turns along the way, to simulate a pursuit run.
4. Applicant must jump a simulated five-foot culvert/ditch.
5. Applicant must drag a "human simulator" (dummy) weighing 175 pounds a distance of 50 feet (to simulate a situation in which an officer is required to pull or carry an injured person to safety).
6. Applicant must draw his or her weapon and fire five rounds with the strong hand and five rounds with the weak hand.

A recruit performs pushups under duress at the Cleveland Police Academy. Why are police academies an important part of the learning process for a potential police officer?

Marvin Fong/*Cleveland Plain Dealer*/Landov

Nine in ten police academies also provide terrorism-related training to teach recruits how to respond to terrorist incidents, including those involving weapons of mass destruction.[29] Academy instructors evaluate the recruits' performance and send intermittent progress reports to police administrators. (**CAREER TIP:** *Police academy instructors are often experienced in a wide variety of law enforcement areas, from sex crimes to crowd control to traffic investigation. Many continue to work in policing in addition to their instructor duties.*)

probationary basis. During this **probationary period,** which can last from six to eighteen months depending on the department, the recruit is in jeopardy of being fired without cause if he or she proves inadequate to the challenges of police work. Almost every state requires that police recruits pass through a training period while on probation. During this time, they are taught the basics of police work and are under constant supervision by superiors. The training period usually has two components: the police academy and field training. On average, local police departments serving populations of 250,000 or more require 1,648 hours of training—972 hours in the classroom and 676 hours in the field.[28]

ACADEMY TRAINING The *police academy,* run by either the state or a police agency, provides recruits with a controlled, militarized environment in which they receive their introduction to the world of the police officer. They are taught the laws of search, seizure, arrest, and interrogation; how and when to use weapons; the procedures of securing a crime scene and interviewing witnesses; first aid; self-defense; and other essentials of police work.

IN THE FIELD **Field training** takes place outside the confines of the police academy. A recruit is paired with an experienced police officer known as a field training officer (FTO). The goal of field training is to help rookies apply the concepts they have learned in the academy "to the streets," with the FTO playing a supervisory role to make sure that nothing goes awry. According to many, the academy introduces recruits to the formal rules of police work, but field training gives the rookies their first taste of the informal rules. In fact, the initial advice to recruits from some FTOs is often along the lines of "O.K., kid. Forget everything you learned in the classroom. You're in the real world now." Nonetheless, the academy is a critical component in the learning process, as it provides rookies with a road map to the job.

4-3

what IS THE STATUS OF WOMEN AND MINORITIES IN POLICING

For many years, the typical American police officer was white and male. As recently as 1968, African

Probationary Period A period of time at the beginning of a police officer's career during which she or he may be fired without cause.

Field Training The segment of a police recruit's training in which he or she is removed from the classroom and placed on the beat, under the supervision of a senior officer.

Americans represented only 5 percent of all sworn officers in the United States, and the percentage of "women in blue" was even lower.[30] Only within the past thirty years has this situation been addressed, and only within the past twenty years have many police departments actively tried to recruit women, African Americans, Hispanics, Asian Americans, and members of other minority groups. The result, as you will see, has been a steady though not spectacular increase in the diversity of the nation's police forces. When it comes to issues of gender, race, and ethnicity, however, mere statistics rarely tell the entire story.

4-3a
Working Women: Gender and Law Enforcement

In 1987, about 7.6 percent of all local police officers were women. Twenty years later, that percentage had risen to almost 12 percent.[31] That increase seems less impressive, however, when one considers that women make up more than half of the population of the United States, meaning that they are severely underrepresented in law enforcement.

LO 3 **ADDED SCRUTINY** There are several reasons for the low levels of women serving as police officers. First, relatively few women hold leadership positions in American policing. More than half of this country's large police departments have no women in their highest ranks,[32] and fewer than 1 percent of the police chiefs in the United States are women.[33] Consequently, female police officers have few superiors who might be able to mentor them in what can be a hostile work environment. In addition to the dangers and pressures facing all law enforcement agents, which we will discuss in the next chapter, women must deal with an added layer of scrutiny. Many male police officers feel that their female counterparts are mentally soft, physically weak, and generally unsuited for the rigors of the job. At the same time, male officers often try to protect female officers by keeping them out of hazardous situations, thereby denying the women the opportunity to prove themselves.[34]

Women in law enforcement also face the problem of tokenism, or the belief that they have been hired or promoted to fulfill diversity requirements and have not earned their positions. Tokenism cre-

Do you believe that female law enforcement agents such as this Miami (Florida) police officer, can be just as effective as their male counterparts? Why or why not?

Joe Raedle/Getty Images

ates pressure to prove the stereotypes wrong. As one female officer told researcher Teresa Lynn Wertsch:

> The guys can view you as a sex object instead of a professional. It makes me try harder to put up more fronts and play more of the macho, boy role rather than accept that I am a female.... You can't be meek or mild, too quiet. You can't be too loud or boisterous because then you would be a dike, too masculine. I wish it didn't have to be this way, but you're either a bitch, a dike, or a slut.[35]

In fact, most of the negative attitudes toward women police officers are based on prejudice rather than actual experience. A number of studies have shown that there is very little difference between the performances of men and women in uniform.[36]

SEXUAL HARASSMENT The female officer quoted above observed that male officers see her as a "sex object." Anecdotal evidence suggests that this attitude is commonplace in police departments and often leads to **sexual harassment** of female police officers. Sexual harassment refers

Sexual Harassment A repeated pattern of unwelcome sexual advances and/or obscene remarks in the workplace. Under certain circumstances, sexual harassment is illegal and can be the basis for a civil lawsuit.

to a pattern of behavior that is sexual in nature, such as inappropriate touching or lewd jokes, and is unwelcome by its target.[37] Over a nine-month period in 2010, the National Police Misconduct Statistics and Reporting Project confirmed eighty-six incidents of sexual harassment in police departments nationwide.[38] Self-reported surveys, however, suggest that the actual incidence is much higher, with most incidents going unreported.[39]

Despite having to deal with problems such as sexual harassment, outdated stereotypes, and tokenism, female police officers have generally shown that they are capable law enforcement officers, willing to take great risks if necessary to do their job. The names of nearly three hundred women are included on the National Law Enforcement Memorial in Washington, D.C.

4-3b
Minority Report: Race and Ethnicity in Law Enforcement

As Figure 4.3 below shows, like women, members of minority groups have been slowly increasing their presence in local police departments since the late 1980s. Specifically, in 2007, African American officers comprised about 12 percent of the nation's police officers, Hispanic officers, about 10 percent, and other minority groups such as Asians, American Indians, and Pacific Islanders, about 3 percent.[40] By some measures, members of minority groups are better represented than women in policing. Cities such as Detroit and Washington have local police departments that closely match their civilian populations in terms of diversity, and in recent years, a majority of police recruits in New York City have been members of minority groups. On other measures, such as promotion, minorities in law enforcement continue to seek parity.[41]

DOUBLE MARGINALITY According to Peter C. Moskos, a professor at the John Jay College of Criminal Justice in New York, "black and white police officers remain two distinct shades of blue, with distinct attitudes toward each other and the communities they serve."[42] While that may be true, minority officers generally report that they have good relationships with their white fellow officers.[43] Often, though, members of minority groups in law enforcement—particularly African Americans and Hispanics—do face the problem of **double marginality.** This term refers to a situation in which minority officers are viewed with suspicion by both sides:

1. White police officers believe that minority officers will give members of their own race or ethnicity better treatment on the streets.

2. Those same minority officers face hostility from members of their own community who are

Double Marginality The double suspicion that minority law enforcement officers face from their white colleagues and from members of the minority community to which they belong.

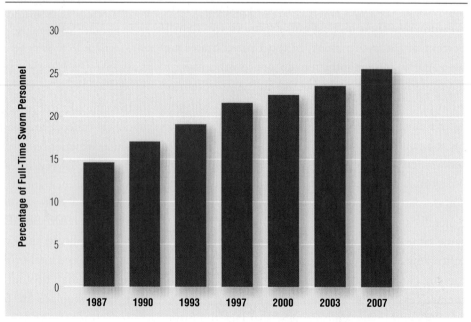

FIGURE 4.3 **Members of Minority Groups in Local Law Enforcement, 1987–2007**

Note: Includes blacks or African Americans, Hispanics or Latinos, Asians, Native Hawaiians or other Pacific Islanders, American Indians, Alaska Natives, and persons identifying two or more races.

Source: Bureau of Justice Statistics, *Local Police Departments, 2007* (Washington, D.C.: U.S. Department of Justice, December 2010), Figure 9, page 14.

under the impression that black and Hispanic officers are traitors to their race or ethnicity.

In response, minority officers may feel the need to act more harshly toward minority offenders to prove that they are not biased in favor of their own racial or ethnic group.[44]

THE BENEFITS OF A DIVERSE POLICE FORCE

In 1986, Supreme Court justice John Paul Stevens spoke for many in the criminal justice system when he observed that "an integrated police force could develop a better relationship [with a racially diverse citizenry] and therefore do a more effective job of maintaining law and order than a force composed of white officers."[45] Indeed, despite the effects of double marginality, African American officers may have more credibility in a predominantly black neighborhood than white police officers, leading to better community-police relations and a greater ability to solve and prevent crimes. Certainly, in the Mexican American communities typical of border states such as Arizona, Texas, and California, many Hispanic officers are able to gather information that would be very difficult for non-Spanish-speaking officers to collect. Finally, however, the best argument for a diverse police force is that members of minority groups represent a broad source of talent in this country, and such talent can only enhance the overall effectiveness of American law enforcement.

4-4
what ARE THE DIFFERENT KINDS OF LAW ENFORCEMENT AGENCIES?

On February 12, 2013, during a shootout with the police, Christopher Dorner took his own life inside a mountain cabin near Big Bear, California. The suicide ended a ten-day manhunt for Dorner, who was a suspect in three murders, including the ambush killing of a Riverside (California) police officer. Thousands of law enforcement agents took part in the intense search for Dorner, including members of the Federal Bureau of Investigation, U.S. Customs and Border Protection, the California Department of Fish and Wildlife, the San Bernardino County Sheriff's Department, and the Las Vegas and Los Angeles Police Departments.

As the effort to capture Dorner, which stretched across the southwest United States and into Mexico, shows, Americans are served by a multitude of police organizations. Overall, there are about 18,000 law enforcement agencies in the United States, employing about 880,000 officers.[46] For the most part, these agencies operate on three different levels: local, state, and federal. Each level has its own set of responsibilities, which we shall discuss starting with local police departments.

4-4a
Municipal Law Enforcement Agencies

According to federal statistics, there is one local or state police officer for every 400 residents of the United States.[47] About two-thirds of all *sworn officers,* or those officers with arrest powers, work in small- and medium-sized police departments serving cities with populations from 10,000 to one million.[48] While the New York City Police Department employs about 36,000 police personnel, 50 percent of all local police departments have ten or fewer law enforcement officers.[49]

Of the three levels of law enforcement, municipal agencies have the broadest authority to apprehend criminal suspects, maintain order, and provide services to the community. Whether the local officer is part of a large force or the only law enforcement officer in the community, he or she is usually responsible for a wide spectrum of duties, from responding to noise complaints to investigating homicides.

Larger police departments will often assign officers to specialized task forces or units that deal with a particular crime or area of concern. For example, in Washington, D.C., the police department features a Gay and Lesbian Liaison Unit that deals with anti-homosexual crimes in the city. The Knoxville (Tennessee) Police Department has a squad devoted to combating Internet crimes against children, while the three hundred officers assigned to the New York City Police Department's Emergency Services Unit are trained in suicide rescue, hostage negotiation, and SCUBA operations.

Lane County (Oregon) sheriff's deputies take part in an "active shooter" training exercise to protect local grade schools students. Why do sheriffs' departments and municipal police agencies often find themselves policing the same geographical areas?

AP Photo/*The Register-Guard*, Brian Davies

4-4b
Sheriffs and County Law Enforcement

The **sheriff** is a very important figure in American law enforcement. Almost every one of the more than three thousand counties in the United States (except those in Alaska) has a sheriff. In every state except Rhode Island and Hawaii, sheriffs are elected by members of the community for two- or four-year terms and are paid a salary set by the state legislature or county board.

As elected officials who do not necessarily need a background in law enforcement, modern sheriffs often must respond to pressures that have little to do with criminal justice. Simply stated, the sheriff is also a politician. When a new sheriff is elected, she or he will sometimes repay political debts by appointing new deputies or promoting those who have given her or him support.

SIZE AND RESPONSIBILITY OF SHERIFFS' DEPARTMENTS Like municipal police forces, sheriffs' departments vary in size. The largest is the Los Angeles County Sheriff's Department, with more than 9,400 deputies. Of the 3,063 sheriffs' departments in the country, thir-

Sheriff The primary law enforcement officer in a county, usually elected to the post by a popular vote.

teen employ more than 1,000 officers, while forty-five have only one.[50]

Keep in mind that cities, which are served by municipal police departments, often exist within counties, which are served by sheriffs' departments. Therefore, police officers and sheriffs' deputies often find themselves policing the same geographical areas. Police departments, however, are generally governed by a local political entity such as a mayor's office, while most sheriffs' departments are assigned their duties by state law. About 80 percent of all sheriffs' departments have the primary responsibility for investigating violent crimes in their jurisdictions. Other common responsibilities of a sheriff's department include:

- Investigating drug crimes.
- Maintaining the county jail.
- Carrying out civil and criminal processes within county lines, such as serving eviction notices and court summonses.
- Keeping order in the county courthouse.
- Collecting taxes.
- Enforcing orders of the court, such as overseeing the isolation of a jury during a trial.[51]

It is easy to confuse sheriffs' departments and local police departments. Both law enforcement agencies are responsible for many of the same tasks, including crime investigation and routine patrol. There are differences, however. Sheriffs' departments are more likely to be involved in county court and jail operations and to perform certain services such as search and rescue. Local police departments, for their part, are more likely to perform traffic-related functions than are sheriffs' departments.[52]

THE COUNTY CORONER Another elected official on the county level is the **coroner,** or medical examiner. Duties vary from county to county, but the coroner has a general mandate to investigate "all sudden, unexplained, unnatural, or suspicious deaths" reported to the office. The coroner is ultimately responsible for determining the cause of death in these cases. Coroners also perform autopsies and assist other law enforcement agencies in homicide investigations. (**CAREER TIP:** Some counties or districts employ *medical examiners* instead of coroners. Although they perform many of the same duties, medical examiners are licensed physicians, unlike coroners, and are usually appointed rather than elected.)

4-4c

State Police and Highway Patrols

The most visible state law enforcement agency is the state police or highway patrol agency. Historically, state police agencies were created for three reasons:

1. To assist local police agencies, which often did not have adequate resources or training to handle their law enforcement tasks.

2. To investigate criminal activities that crossed jurisdictional boundaries (such as when bank robbers committed a crime in one county and then fled to another part of the state).

3. To provide law enforcement in rural and other areas that did not have local or county police agencies.

Today, there are twenty-three state police agencies and twenty-six highway patrols in the United States. State police agencies have statewide jurisdiction and are authorized to perform a wide variety of law enforcement tasks. Thus, they provide the same services as city or county police departments and are restricted only by the boundaries of the state. In contrast, highway patrols have limited authority. Their duties are generally defined either by their jurisdiction or by the specific types of offenses they have the authority to control. As their name suggests, most highway patrols concentrate primarily on regulating traffic. Specifically, they enforce traffic laws and investigate traffic accidents. Furthermore, they usually limit their activity to patrolling state and federal highways.

Trying to determine what state agency has which duties can be confusing. The Washington State Highway Patrol, despite its name, also has state police powers. In addition, thirty-five states have investigative agencies that are independent of the state police or highway patrol. Such agencies are usually found in states with highway patrols, and they have the primary responsibility of investigating criminal activities. For example, in addition to its highway patrol, Oklahoma runs a State Bureau of Investigation and a State Bureau of Narcotics and Dangerous Drugs. Each state has its own methods of determining the jurisdictions of these various organizations.

4-4d

Federal Law Enforcement Agencies

Statistically, employees of federal agencies do not make up a large part of the nation's law enforcement

Coroner The medical examiner of a county, usually elected by popular vote.

A Connecticut State Police officer provides advice for a motorist stuck in a snowstorm on Interstate 84 in East Hartford. In what ways do state law enforcement officers supplement the efforts of local police officers?

AP Photo/Jessica Hill

force. In fact, the New York City Police Department has about one-third as many employees as all of the federal law enforcement agencies combined. Nevertheless, the influence of these federal agencies is substantial.

Unlike local police departments, which must deal with all forms of crime, federal agencies have been authorized, usually by Congress, to enforce specific laws or attend to specific situations. The U.S. Coast Guard, for example, patrols the nation's waterways, while U.S. Postal Inspectors investigate and prosecute crimes perpetrated through the use of the U.S. mails. In this section, you will learn the elements and duties of the most important federal law enforcement agencies, which are grouped according to the federal department or bureau to which they report. (See Figure 4.4 on the facing page for the current federal law enforcement "lineup.")

THE DEPARTMENT OF HOMELAND SECURITY

Comprising twenty-two federal agencies, the Department of Homeland Security (DHS) coordinates national efforts to protect the United States against international and domestic terrorism. While most of the agencies under DHS control are not specifically linked with the criminal justice system, the department does oversee three agencies that play an important role in counterterrorism and fighting crime: U.S. Customs and Border Protection, U.S. Immigration and Customs Enforcement, and the U.S. Secret Service.

U.S. Customs and Border Protection (CBP) In 2012, the federal government spent nearly $18 billion on enforcing immigration law.[53] A large chunk of these funds went to **U.S. Customs and Border Protection (CBP),** which polices the flow of goods and people across the United States' international borders. In general terms, this means that the agency has two primary goals: (1) to keep undocumented immigrants, illegal drugs, and drug traffickers from crossing our borders, and (2) to facilitate the smooth flow of legal trade and travel. Consequently, CBP officers are stationed at every port of entry and exit to the United States. The officers have widespread authority to investigate and search all international passengers, whether they arrive on airplanes, ships, or other forms of transportation.

The U.S. Border Patrol, a branch of the CBP, has the burden of policing both the Mexican and Canadian borders between official ports of entry. Its primary focus has been on the Mexican border, which is patrolled by nearly 21,500 agents, more than double the number of a decade ago. This increase in personnel seems to have had a deterrent effect. In 2011, about 325,000 illegal crossers were apprehended on that border. A decade earlier, that number was close to 1.6 million.[54] (The recent economic downturn in the United States, which has removed some of the economic incentives for illegal crossing, has probably also affected these figures.) Border Patrol agents also keep a significant amount of illegal drugs from entering the country—5 million pounds in 2011.[55]

Which federal law enforcement agency is responsible for apprehending those who attempt to illegally smuggle marijuana across the U.S. border from Mexico?

Joshua Lott/*New York Times*/Redux Pictures

U.S. Customs and Border Protection (CBP) The federal agency responsible for protecting U.S. borders and facilitating legal trade and travel across those borders.

FIGURE 4.4 Federal Law Enforcement Agencies

A number of federal agencies employ law enforcement officers who are authorized to carry firearms and make arrests. The most prominent ones are under the control of the U.S. Department of Homeland Security, the U.S. Department of Justice, or the U.S. Department of the Treasury.

DEPARTMENT OF HOMELAND SECURITY

Department Name	Approximate Number of Officers	Main Responsibilities
U.S. Customs and Border Protection (CBP)	37,000	• (1) Prevent the illegal flow of people and goods across America's international borders; (2) facilitate legal trade and travel
U.S. Immigration and Customs Enforcement (ICE)	12,500	• Uphold public safety and homeland security by enforcing the nation's immigration and customs laws
U.S. Secret Service	5,000	• (1) Protect the president, the president's family, former presidents and their families, and other high-ranking politicians; (2) combat currency counterfeiters

DEPARTMENT OF JUSTICE

Department Name	Approximate Number of Officers	Main Responsibilities
Federal Bureau of Investigation (FBI)	13,000	• (1) Protect national security by fighting international and domestic terrorism; (2) enforce federal criminal laws such as those dealing with cyber crime, public corruption, and civil rights violations
Drug Enforcement Administration (DEA)	4,500	• Enforce the nation's laws regulating the sale and use of drugs
Bureau of Alcohol, Tobacco, Firearms and Explosives (ATF)	2,500	• (1) Combat the illegal use and trafficking of firearms and explosives; (2) investigate the illegal diversion of alcohol and tobacco products
U.S. Marshals Service	3,500	• (1) Provide security at federal courts; (2) protect government witnesses; (3) apprehend fugitives from the federal court or corrections system

DEPARTMENT OF THE TREASURY

Department Name	Approximate Number of Officers	Main Responsibilities
Internal Revenue Service (IRS)	2,500	• Investigate potential criminal violations of the nation's tax code

Source: Bureau of Justice Statistics, *Federal Law Enforcement Officers, 2008* (Washington, D.C.: U.S. Department of Justice, June 2012), Table 1, page 2.

U.S. Immigration and Customs Enforcement (ICE) The CBP shares responsibility for locating and apprehending those persons illegally in the United States with special agents from **U.S. Immigration and Customs Enforcement (ICE).** While the CBP focuses almost exclusively on the nation's borders, ICE has a broader mandate to investigate and to enforce our

U.S. Immigration and Customs Enforcement (ICE) The federal agency that enforces the nation's immigration and customs laws.

country's immigration and customs laws. Simply stated, the CBP covers the borders, and ICE covers everything else. The latter agency's duties include detaining undocumented aliens and deporting (removing) them from the United States, ensuring that those without permission do not work or gain other benefits in this country, and disrupting human trafficking operations.

The U.S. Secret Service When it was created in 1865, the **U.S. Secret Service** was primarily responsible for combating currency counterfeiters. In 1901, the agency was given the added responsibility of protecting the president of the United States, the president's family, the vice president, the president-elect, and former presidents. These duties have remained the cornerstone of the agency, with several expansions. After a number of threats against presidential candidates in the 1960s and early 1970s, including the shootings of Robert Kennedy of New York and Governor George Wallace of Alabama, in 1976 Secret Service agents became responsible for protecting those political figures as well.

In addition to its special plainclothes agents, the agency also directs two uniformed groups of law enforcement officers. The Secret Service Uniformed Division protects the grounds of the White House and its inhabitants, and the Treasury Police Force polices the Treasury Building in Washington, D.C. This responsibility includes investigating threats against presidents and those running for presidential office. To aid its battle against counterfeiters and forgers of government bonds, the agency has the use of a laboratory at the Bureau of Engraving and Printing in the nation's capital.

Additional DHS Agencies Besides the three already discussed—CBP, ICE, and the U.S. Secret Service—three other DHS agencies play a central role in preventing and responding to crime and terrorist-related activity:

- The *U.S. Coast Guard* defends the nation's coasts, ports, and inland waterways. It also combats illegal drug shipping and enforces immigration law at sea.
- The *Transportation Security Administration* is responsible for the safe operation of our airline, rail, bus, and ferry services. It also operates the Federal Air Marshals program that places undercover federal agents on commercial flights.
- The *Federal Emergency Management Agency* holds a position as the lead federal agency in preparing for and responding to disasters such as hurricanes, floods, terrorist attacks, and *infrastructure* concerns. Our national **infrastructure** includes all of the facilities and systems that provide the daily necessities of modern life, such as electric power, food, water, transportation, and telecommunications.

THE DEPARTMENT OF JUSTICE The U.S. Department of Justice, created in 1870, is still the primary federal law enforcement agency in the country. With the responsibility of enforcing criminal law and supervising the federal prisons, the Justice Department plays a leading role in the American criminal justice system. To carry out its responsibilities to prevent and control crime, the department has a number of law enforcement agencies, including the Federal Bureau of Investigation, the federal Drug Enforcement Administration, the Bureau of Alcohol, Tobacco, Firearms and Explosives, and the U.S. Marshals Service.

The Federal Bureau of Investigation (FBI) Initially created in 1908 as the Bureau of Investigation, this agency was renamed the **Federal Bureau of Investigation (FBI)** in 1935. One of the primary investigative agencies of the federal government, the FBI has jurisdiction over nearly two hundred federal crimes, including white-collar crimes, espionage (spying), kidnapping, extortion, interstate transportation of stolen property, bank robbery, interstate gambling, and civil rights violations. With its network of agents across the country and the globe, the FBI is also uniquely positioned to combat worldwide criminal activity such as terrorism and drug trafficking. In fact, since 2001, the agency has shifted its focus from traditional crime to national

U.S. Secret Service A federal law enforcement organization with the primary responsibility of protecting the president, the president's family, the vice president, and other important political figures.

Infrastructure The services and facilities that support the day-to-day needs of modern life, such as electricity, food, transportation, and water.

Federal Bureau of Investigation (FBI) The branch of the Department of Justice responsible for investigating violations of federal law.

FEDERAL BUREAU OF INVESTIGATION (FBI) AGENT

JOB DESCRIPTION:

- Primary role is to oversee intelligence and investigate federal crimes. Agents might track the movement of stolen goods across state lines, examine accounting and business records, listen to legal wiretaps, and conduct undercover investigations.

- Special agent careers are divided into five paths: intelligence, counterintelligence, counterterrorism, criminal, and cyber crime.

WHAT KIND OF TRAINING IS REQUIRED?

- A bachelor's and/or master's degree, plus three years of work experience, along with a written and oral examination, medical and physical examinations, a psychological assessment, and an exhaustive background investigation.

- Critical skills required in one or more of the following areas: accounting, finance, computer science/information technology, engineering, foreign language(s), law, law enforcement, intelligence, military, and/or physical sciences.

ANNUAL SALARY RANGE?

- $61,100–$69,900

Courtesy Federal Bureau of Investigation/Department of Justice

SOCIAL MEDIA CAREER TIP

Don't forget about your phone! Every week, call at least three people from your social media networks and talk with them about your career interests. This kind of personal contact can be far more useful than an exchange of posts.

security. Over a recent two-year period, more than half of all FBI investigations have focused on groups or individuals suspected of terrorist activity as opposed to "ordinary" crimes.[56]

The FBI is also committed to providing valuable support for local and state law enforcement agencies. Its Identification Division maintains a large database of fingerprint information and offers assistance in finding missing persons and identifying the victims of fires, airplane crashes, and other disfiguring disasters. The services of the FBI Laboratory, the largest crime laboratory in the world, are available at no cost to other agencies. Finally, the FBI's National Crime Information Center (NCIC) provides lists of stolen vehicles and firearms, missing license plates, vehicles used to commit crimes, and other information to local and state law enforcement officers.

The Drug Enforcement Administration (DEA)

The mission of the **Drug Enforcement Administration (DEA)** is to enforce domestic drug laws and regulations and to assist other federal and foreign agencies in combating illegal drug manufacture and trade on an international level. The agency also enforces the provisions of the Controlled Substances Act, which governs the manufacture, distribution, and dispensing of legal drugs, such as prescription drugs.

DEA agents often work in conjunction with local and state authorities to prevent illicit drugs from reaching communities. The agency also conducts extensive operations with law enforcement entities in

Drug Enforcement Administration (DEA) The federal agency responsible for enforcing the nation's laws and regulations regarding narcotics and other controlled substances.

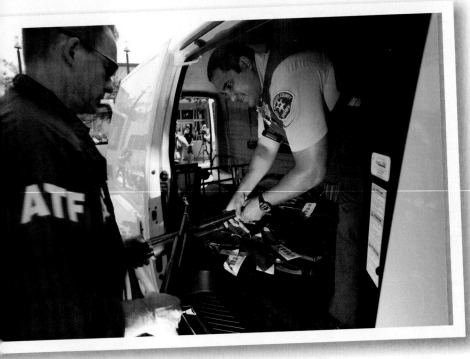

A sheriff's deputy transfers confiscated firearms to an ATF agent in Los Angeles. What are the primary duties of the ATF?

David McNew/Getty Images

other drug-producing countries. (**CAREER TIP:** Illegal drug manufacturers often try to outwit the DEA by creating new psychoactive substances that are not yet illegal under federal law. Consequently, the agency employs *forensic chemists* to identify these new illegal drugs and support their investigation by DEA special agents.)

The Bureau of Alcohol, Tobacco, Firearms and Explosives (ATF) As its name suggests, the Bureau of Alcohol, Tobacco, Firearms and Explosives (ATF) is primarily concerned with the illegal sale, possession, and use of firearms and the control of untaxed tobacco and liquor products. The Firearms Division of the agency has the responsibility of enforcing the Gun Control Act of 1968, which sets the circumstances under which firearms may be sold and used in this country. The bureau also regulates all gun trade between the United States and foreign nations and collects taxes on all firearm importers, manufacturers, and dealers. In keeping with these duties, the ATF is also responsible for policing the illegal use and possession of explosives. Furthermore, the ATF is charged with enforcing federal gambling laws.

Because it has jurisdiction over such a wide variety of crimes, especially those involving firearms and explosives, the ATF is a constant presence in federal criminal investigations. So, following Adam Lanza's December 2012 shooting rampage in Newtown, Connecticut, ATF agents raided a Hartford gun shop where Lanza's mother had purchased one of the guns used by her son in the attack. Furthermore, the ATF is engaged in an ongoing and crucial operation to keep American firearms out of the hands of Mexican drug cartels. The ATF has also formed multijurisdictional antigang task forces with other federal and local law enforcement agencies to investigate gang-related crimes involving firearms.

The U.S. Marshals Service The oldest federal law enforcement agency is the U.S. Marshals Service. In 1789, President George Washington assigned thirteen U.S. Marshals to protect his attorney general. That same year, Congress created the office of the U.S. Marshals and Deputy Marshals. Originally, the U.S. Marshals acted as the main law enforcement officers in the western territories. Following the Civil War (1861–1865), when most of these territories had become states, these agents were assigned to work for the U.S. district courts, where federal crimes are tried. The relationship between the U.S. Marshals Service and the federal courts continues today and forms the basis for the officers' main duties, which include:

SOCIAL MEDIA AND CJ

The **ATF Press Office** operates a Twitter page that doubles as a newsroom for the federal crime-fighting agency. To find this page, enter "ATF" and "Twitter" in your search engine.

1. Providing security at federal courts for judges, jurors, and other courtroom participants.

2. Controlling property that has been ordered seized by federal courts.

3. Protecting government witnesses who put themselves in danger by testifying against

the targets of federal criminal investigations. This protection is sometimes accomplished by relocating the witnesses and providing them with different identities.

4. Transporting federal prisoners to detention institutions.

5. Investigating violations of federal fugitive laws.[57]

THE DEPARTMENT OF THE TREASURY The Department of the Treasury, formed in 1789, is mainly responsible for all financial matters of the federal government. It pays all the federal government's bills, borrows funds, collects taxes, mints coins, and prints paper currency. The largest bureau of the Treasury Department, the Internal Revenue Service (IRS), is concerned with violations of tax laws and regulations. The bureau has three divisions, only one of which is involved in criminal investigations. The examination branch of the IRS audits the tax returns of corporations and individuals. The collection division attempts to collect taxes from corporations or citizens who have failed to pay the taxes they owe. Finally, the criminal investigation division investigates cases of tax evasion and tax fraud. Criminal investigation agents can make arrests.

The IRS has long played a role in policing criminal activities such as gambling and selling drugs for one simple reason: those who engage in such activities almost never report any illegally gained income on their tax returns. Therefore, the IRS is able to apprehend them for tax evasion. The most famous example took place in the early 1930s, when the IRS finally arrested famed crime boss Al Capone—responsible for numerous violent crimes—for not paying his taxes.

4-4e
Private Security

Even with increasing numbers of local, state, and federal law enforcement officers, the police do not have the ability to prevent every crime. Recognizing this, many businesses and citizens have decided to hire private guards for their properties and homes. In fact,

5 LO

CAREERPREP

U.S. MARSHAL

JOB DESCRIPTION:

- Provide security at federal courts, control property that has been ordered seized by federal courts, and protect government witnesses who put themselves in danger by testifying against the targets of federal criminal investigations.

- Transport federal prisoners to detention institutions and hunt and capture fugitives from federal law.

WHAT KIND OF TRAINING IS REQUIRED?

- A bachelor's degree or three years of qualifying experience, which includes work in law enforcement, correctional supervision, and volunteer teaching or counseling.

- A rigorous seventeen-and-a-half-week basic training program at the U.S Marshals Service Training Academy in Glynco, Georgia.

ANNUAL SALARY RANGE?

- $37,000–$47,000

Stephen Mulcahey/iStockphoto.com

A private security guard makes the rounds near the Food Court at Landmark Mall in Alexandria, Virginia. Why is being visible such an important aspect of many private security jobs?

Newhouse News Service/Landov

personnel to drive marked cars through their neighborhoods, making them a less attractive target for burglaries, robberies, vandalism, and other crimes.

CONTINUED HEALTH OF THE INDUSTRY

Indicators point to continued growth for the private security industry. The *Hallcrest Report II,* a far-reaching overview of private security trends funded by the National Institute of Justice, identifies four factors driving this growth:

according to the Freedonia Group, an industry-research firm, demand for **private security** generates revenues of nearly $50 billion a year.[58] More than 10,000 firms employing around 1.1 million people provide private security services in this country, compared with about 880,000 public law enforcement agents.

PRIVATIZING LAW ENFORCEMENT As there are no federal regulations regarding private security, each state has its own rules for this form of employment. In several states, including California and Florida, prospective security guards must have at least forty hours of training. Ideally, a security guard—lacking the extensive training of a law enforcement agent—should only observe and report criminal activity unless use of force is needed to prevent a felony.[59]

As a rule, private security is not designed to replace law enforcement. It is intended to deter crime rather than stop it.[60] A uniformed security guard patrolling a shopping mall parking lot or a bank lobby has one primary function—to convince a potential criminal to search out a shopping mall or bank that does not have private security. For the same reason, many citizens hire security

Private Security The practice of private corporations or individuals offering services traditionally performed by police officers.

1. An increase in fear on the part of the public triggered by media coverage of crime.

2. The problem of crime in the workplace. According to the University of Florida's National Retail Security Survey, American retailers lose about $34 billion a year because of shoplifting and employee theft. (**CAREER TIP:** *Loss prevention* is a catchall phrase used by retail companies to describe their efforts to reduce shoplifting and cash theft in their stores. Retailers need *loss prevention security officers* to keep an eye on suspicious shoppers and *loss prevention detectives* to investigate shoplifting and employee theft.)

3. Budget cuts in states and municipalities that have forced reductions in the number of public police, thereby raising the demand for private ones.

4. A rising awareness of private security products (such as home burglar alarms) and service as cost-effective protective measures.[61]

Another reason for the industry's continued health is terrorism. Private security is responsible for protecting more than three-fourths of the nation's likely terrorist targets such as power plants, financial centers, dams, malls, oil refineries, and transportation hubs.

REVIEW

✔ **Review what you've read with the quiz below.**

Rip out the Chapter Review card at the back of this book, which includes:
- Chapter Summary and Learning Outcomes
- Key Terms

Or you can go online to CourseMate at **www.cengagebrain.com** to:
- Complete Practice Quizzes to prepare for tests.
- Review Key Terms Flash Cards (online or print).
- Play games to master concepts.

quiz

1. In the opinion of many civilians and law enforcement officers, the primary duty of the police is to _____ criminal law.

2. In reality, police officers spend a great deal of their time providing _____ such as directing traffic and providing emergency medical aid.

3. _____-led policing is an umbrella term referring to the law enforcement practice of relying on data concerning past crime patterns to predict future crimes.

4. During the _____ period, which can last as long as eighteen months, police recruits attend a police academy to learn the rules of police work.

5. Minority law enforcement officers often face the problem of _____ marginality, in which they are viewed with suspicion by both white colleagues and members of their home communities.

6. Municipal police departments and _____ departments are both considered "local" organizations and have many of the same responsibilities.

7. On the state level, the authority of the _____ patrol is usually limited to enforcing traffic laws.

8. Nationally, agents from the _____ have the authority to investigate and make arrests regarding all federal crimes.

9. A federal law enforcement agency called the _____ regulates the sale and possession of guns in the United States.

10. Private security is designed to _____ crime rather than stop it.

Answers can be found on the Chapter 4 Review card at the end of the book.

Jared Wickerham/Getty Images

Learning **OUTCOMES** | *After studying this chapter, you will be able to . . .*

1 Explain why police officers are allowed discretionary powers.

2 List the three primary purposes of police patrol.

3 Describe how forensic experts use DNA fingerprinting to solve crimes.

4 Determine when police officers are justified in using deadly force.

5 Explain what an ethical dilemma is and name four categories of ethical dilemmas that a police officer typically may face.

PROBLEMS AND SOLUTIONS IN MODERN POLICING

Justified?

One morning in January 2012, thirteen-year-old Jaime Gonzalez walked into a first-period class at Cummings Middle School in Brownsville, Texas, and, for no apparent reason, punched another student in the face. As school administrators tried to calm an agitated Gonzalez in the hallway, their puzzlement turned to alarm—the eighth grader had a gun tucked into his pants. Within minutes, the school was in lockdown, and two local police officers had arrived on the scene. They shouted at Gonzalez to "Put the gun down! Put it on the floor!" Disregarding these orders, Gonzalez raised his weapon. The officers fired three times and hit the teenager twice, once in the chest and once in the abdomen. "Subject shot," one of the officers said as he called for emergency medical aid.

After Gonzalez died from his wounds in a local hospital, an already-shaken community learned one more piece of disturbing news. Although the weapon Gonzalez had been brandishing looked like a black Glock semiautomatic pistol, it was actually a relatively harmless .177-caliber BB gun, available on the Internet for $60. As might be expected, this development opened the Brownsville police to a great deal of criticism. "Why was so much excess force used on a minor?" asked Gonzalez's father, Jaime Sr. "What happened was an injustice," insisted Noralva, the boy's mother.

Brownsville interim police chief Orlando Rodriguez defended his officers' decision making. He stressed that, as far as the two men knew, they were dealing with an armed suspect who posed a serious threat to more than seven hundred students and about seventy-five staff members. "When I looked at that gun, there is no doubt [that] from a distance it's absolutely real," agreed school official Carl A. Montoya. "I think the officers responded, obviously, from their training. From that perspective, it was a real gun."

Noralva and Jaime Gonzalez embrace at the funeral of their son, who was fatally shot by Brownsville, Texas, police after brandishing what appeared to be a handgun at his school.

AP Photo/*Brownsville Herald*, Yvette Vela

how DO LAW ENFORCEMENT AGENTS USE DISCRETION ?

Certainly, the Brownsville police officers just discussed would have preferred not to have shot and killed Jaime Gonzalez, whether the boy was wielding a real gun or not. Their decisions were made in a split second, under stressful circumstances, and without the benefit of the evidence that came to light following the shooting. That is, the officers relied on their discretion, a concept you were introduced to in Chapter 1. Not all police discretion involves situations as serious as the one that led to Gonzalez's death, but it is a crucial aspect of all areas of law enforcement.

5-1a
Justification for Police Discretion

Despite the possibility of mistakes, courts generally have upheld the patrol officer's freedom to decide "what law to enforce, how much to enforce it, against whom, and on what occasions."[1] This judicial support of police discretion is based on the following factors:

LO 1

- Police officers are considered trustworthy and are therefore assumed to make honest decisions, regardless of contradictory testimony by a suspect.
- Experience and training give officers the ability to determine whether certain activity poses a threat to society, and to take any reasonable action necessary to investigate or prevent such activity.
- Due to the nature of their jobs, police officers are extremely knowledgeable in human, and by extension criminal, behavior.
- Police officers may find themselves in danger of personal, physical harm and must be allowed to take reasonable and necessary steps to protect themselves.[2]

Dr. Anthony J. Pinizzotto, a psychologist with the Federal Bureau of Investigation (FBI), and Charles E. Miller, an instructor in the bureau's Criminal Justice Information Services Division, take the justification for discretion one step further. These two experts argue that many police officers have a "sixth sense" that helps them handle on-the-job challenges. Pinizzotto and Miller believe that although "intuitive policing" is often difficult to explain to those outside law enforcement, it is a crucial part of policing and should not be discouraged by civilian administrators.[3]

5-1b
Factors of Police Discretion

There is no doubt that subjective factors influence police discretion. The officer's beliefs, values, personality, and background all enter into his or her decisions. To a large extent, however, a law enforcement agent's actions are determined by the rules of policing set down in the U.S. Constitution and enforced by the courts. These rules are of paramount importance and will be discussed in great detail in Chapter 6.

ELEMENTS OF DISCRETION Assuming that most police officers stay on the right side of the Constitution in most instances, four other factors generally enter the discretion equation in any particular situation. First, and most important, is the nature of the criminal act. The less serious a crime, the more likely a police officer is to ignore it. A person driving 60 miles per hour in a 55-miles-per-hour zone, for example, is much less likely to be ticketed than someone doing 80 miles per hour.

A second element often considered is the attitude of the wrongdoer toward the officer. A motorist who is belligerent toward a highway patrol officer is much more likely to be ticketed than one who is contrite and apologetic. Third, the relationship between the victim and the offender can influence the outcome. If the parties are in a familial or other close relationship, police officers may see the incident as a personal matter and be hesitant to make an arrest.

LIMITING POLICE DISCRETION The fourth factor of the discretion equation is departmental policy.[4] A **policy** is a set of guiding principles that law enforcement agents must adhere to in stated situations.

For example, about 35 percent of all police automobile pursuits of fleeing suspects end in car crashes,

Policy A set of guiding principles designed to influence the behavior and decision making of police officers.

causing around 350 fatalities each year. One-third of the victims are third parties—drivers or passengers in other cars or pedestrian bystanders.[5]

To limit the discretion that can result in these kinds of tragedies, 94 percent of the nation's local police departments have implemented police pursuit policies, with 61 percent restricting the discretion of officers to engage in a high-speed chase.[6] The success of such policies can be seen in the results from Los Angeles, which features more high-speed chases than any other city in the country by a wide margin. In 2003, Los Angeles police officers were ordered to conduct dangerous pursuits only if the fleeing driver was suspected of a serious crime. Within a year, the number of high-speed pursuits decreased by 62 percent, and injuries to third parties dropped by 58 percent.[7]

Furthermore, police discretion often is limited with regard to **domestic violence,** or physical abuse directed toward a spouse or other live-in partner. Evidence suggests that law enforcement officers, not wanting to get involved in family disputes, sometimes are reluctant to make an arrest in a domestic violence situation, even when the officer has strong evidence of an assault.[8] In light of this apparent reluctance, in the 1970s jurisdictions began passing legislation that severely limits police discretion in domestic violence cases. Today, twenty-one states have **mandatory arrest laws** that require a police officer to arrest a person who has abused someone related by blood or marriage.[9]

The theory behind mandatory arrest policies is relatively straightforward: they act as a deterrent to criminal behavior. Costs are imposed on the person who is arrested. He or she must go to court and face the possibility of time in jail. Statistically, these laws appear to have met their goals. Researchers have found significantly higher arrest rates for domestic violence offenders in states with mandatory arrest laws than in states without them.[10] (**CAREER TIP:** Many cities have shelters that provide therapeutic and practical services for both victims and perpetrators of domestic violence. These organizations rely on *domestic violence counselors* to provide such services.)

5-2
how DO POLICE OFFICERS FIGHT CRIME?

Brownsville police administrators placed the two officers involved in Jaime Gonzalez's death, discussed at the beginning of this chapter, on *administrative leave* pending an investigation into the incident. In other words, the officers were temporarily relieved of their duties, with pay. This step does not imply that they were suspected of any wrongdoing. Most law enforcement agencies react similarly when a firearm is

Domestic Violence The act of willful neglect or physical violence that occurs within a familial or other intimate relationship.

Mandatory Arrest Law Requires a police officer to detain a person for committing a certain type of crime as long as there is probable cause that he or she committed the crime.

fired in the line of duty, both to allow for a full investigation of the event and to give the officer a chance to recover from what can be a traumatic experience.

Administrative leave is a *bureaucratic* response to an officer-involved shooting. In a **bureaucracy,** formal rules govern an individual's actions and relationships with co-employees. The ultimate goal of any bureaucracy is to reach its maximum efficiency—in the case of a police department, to provide the best service for the community within the confines of its limited resources such as staff and budget. Although some police departments are experimenting with alternative structures based on a partnership between management and the officers in the field, most continue to rely on the hierarchical structure described below.

5-2a

The Structure of the Police Department

Each police department is organized according to its environment: the size of its jurisdiction, the type of crimes it must deal with,

Bureaucracy A hierarchically structured administrative organization that carries out specific functions.

and the demographics of the population it must police. A police department in a racially diverse city often faces different challenges than a department in a homogeneous one. Geographic location also influences police organization. The makeup of the police department in Miami, Florida, for example, is partially determined by the fact that the city is a gateway for illegal drugs smuggled from Central and South America. Consequently, the department directs a high percentage of its resources to special drug-fighting units. It has also formed cooperative partnerships with federal agencies such as the FBI and U.S. Customs and Border Protection in an effort to stop the flow of narcotics and weapons into the South Florida area.

CHAIN OF COMMAND Whatever the size or location of a police department, it needs a clear rank structure and strict accountability to function properly.[11] One of the goals of the police reformers, especially beginning in the 1950s, was to lessen the corrupting influence of politicians. The result was a move toward a militaristic organization of police.[12] As you can see in Figure 5.1 on the facing page, a typical police department is based on a "top-down"

FIGURE 5.1 A Typical Police Department Chain of Command

Most American police departments follow this model of the chain of command, though smaller departments with fewer employees often eliminate several of these categories.

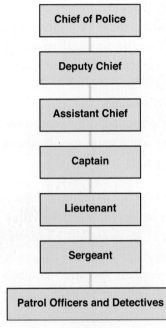

chain of command that leads from the police chief down to detectives and patrol officers. In this formalized structure, all persons are aware of their place in the chain and of their duties and responsibilities within the organization.

Delegation of authority is a critical component of the chain of command, especially in larger departments. The chief of police delegates authority to division chiefs, who delegate authority to commanders, and on down through the organization. This structure creates a situation in which nearly every member of a police department is directly accountable to a superior. As was the original goal of police reformers, these links encourage discipline and control and lessen the possibility that any individual police employee will have the unsupervised freedom to abuse her or his position.[13] Furthermore, experts suggest that no single supervisor should be responsible for too many employees. The ideal number of subordinates for a police sergeant, for example, is eight to ten patrol officers. This number is often referred to as the span of control. If the span of control rises above fifteen, then it is assumed that the superior officer will not be able to effectively manage his or her team.[14]

LAW ENFORCEMENT IN THE FIELD To a large extent, the main goal of any police department is the most efficient organization of its *field services.* Also known as "operations" or "line services," field services include patrol activities, investigations, and

special operations. According to Henry M. Wrobleski and Karen M. Hess, most police departments are "generalists." Thus, police officers are assigned to general areas and perform all field service functions within the boundaries of their beats. Larger departments may be more specialized, with personnel assigned to specific types of crime, such as illegal drugs or white-collar crime, rather than geographic locations. Smaller departments, which make up the bulk of local law enforcement agencies, rely almost exclusively on random patrol.[15]

5-2b
Police on Patrol: The Backbone of the Department

Every police department has a patrol unit, and patrol is usually the largest division in the department. More than two-thirds of the sworn officers, or those officers authorized to make arrests and use force, in local police departments in the United States have patrol duties.[16]

"Life on the street" is not easy. Patrol officers must be able to handle any number of difficult situations, and experience is often the best and, despite training programs, the only teacher. As one patrol officer commented:

> You never stop learning. You never get your street degree. The person who says . . . they've learned it all is the person that's going to wind up dead or in a very compromising position. They've closed their minds.[17]

It may take a patrol officer years to learn when a gang is "false flagging" (trying to trick rival gang members into the open) or what to look for in a suspect's eyes to sense if he or she is concealing a weapon. This learning process is the backdrop to a number of different general functions that a patrol officer must perform on a daily basis.

THE PURPOSE OF PATROL In general, patrol officers do not spend most of their shifts chasing, catching, and handcuffing suspected criminals. The vast majority of patrol shifts are completed without a single arrest.[18] Officers

 2 LO

Delegation of Authority
The principles of command on which most police departments are based, in which personnel take orders from and are responsible to those in positions of power directly above them.

Given that most patrol shifts end without an officer making a single arrest, what activities take up most of a patrol officer's time?

Rod Lamkey Jr/AFP/Getty Images

should be allowed to dominate patrol officers' duties. The question, however, remains: If the police do not handle these problems, who will? Few cities have the financial resources to hire public servants to deal specifically with, for example, finding shelter for homeless persons. Furthermore, the police are the only public servants on call twenty-four hours a day, seven days a week, making them uniquely accessible to citizen needs.

PATROL ACTIVITIES To recap, the purposes of police patrols are to prevent and deter crime and also to provide social services. How can the police best accomplish these goals? Of course, each department has its own methods and strategies, but William Gay, Theodore Schell, and Stephen Schack are able to divide routine patrol activity into four general categories:

1. *Preventive patrol.* By maintaining a presence in a community, either in a car or on foot, patrol officers attempt to prevent crime from occurring. This strategy, which O. W. Wilson called "omnipresence," was a cornerstone of early policing philosophy and still takes up roughly 40 percent of patrol time.

2. *Calls for service.* Patrol officers spend nearly a quarter of their time responding to 911 calls for emergency service or other citizen problems and complaints.

3. *Administrative duties.* Paperwork takes up nearly 20 percent of patrol time.

4. *Officer-initiated activities.* Incidents in which the patrol officer initiates contact with citizens, such as stopping motorists and pedestrians and questioning them, account for 15 percent of patrol time.[21]

The category estimates made by Gay, Schell, and Schack are not universally accepted. Professor of law

spend a great deal of time meeting with other officers, completing paperwork, and patrolling with the goal of preventing crime in general rather than focusing on any specific crime or criminal activity.

As police accountability expert Samuel Walker has noted, the basic purposes of the police patrol have changed very little since 1829, when Sir Robert Peel founded the modern police department. These purposes include:

1. The deterrence of crime by maintaining a visible police presence.

2. The maintenance of public order and a sense of security in the community.

3. The twenty-four-hour provision of services that are not crime related.[19]

The first two goals—deterring crime and keeping order—are generally accepted as legitimate police functions. The third, however, has been more controversial.

COMMUNITY CONCERNS The extent to which noncrime incidents dominate patrol officers' time is evident in the Police Services Study, a survey of 26,000 calls to police in sixty different neighborhoods. The study found that only one out of every five calls involved the report of criminal activity.[20] There is some debate over whether community services enforcement Gary W. Cordner argues that administrative duties account for the largest percentage of patrol officers' time. According to Cordner, when officers are not consumed with paperwork and meetings, they are either answering calls for service (which takes up 67 percent of the officers' time on the street) or initiating activities themselves (the remaining 33 percent).[22]

"NOISE, BOOZE, AND VIOLENCE" Indeed, there are dozens of academic studies that purport to answer the question of how patrol officers spend their days and nights. Perhaps it is only fair, then, to give a police officer the chance to describe the duties patrol officers perform. In the words of Anthony Bouza, a former police chief:

> [Patrol officers] hurry from call to call, bound to their crackling radios, which offer no relief—especially on summer weekend nights. . . . The cops jump from crisis to crisis, rarely having time to do more than tamp one down sufficiently and leave for the next. Gaps of boredom and inactivity fill the interims, although there aren't many of these in the hot months. Periods of boredom get increasingly longer as the nights wear on and the weather gets colder.[23]

Bouza paints a picture of a routine beat as filled with "noise, booze, violence, drugs, illness, blaring TVs, and human misery." This may describe the situation in high-crime neighborhoods, but it certainly does not represent the reality for the majority of patrol officers in the United States. Duties that all patrol officers have in common, whether they work in Bouza's rather nightmarish city streets or in the quieter environment of rural America, include controlling traffic, conducting preliminary investigations, making arrests, and patrolling public events.

5-2c
Detective Investigations

Investigation is the second main function of police, along with patrol. Whereas patrol is primarily preventive, investigation is reactive. After a crime has been committed and the patrol officer has gathered the preliminary information from the crime scene, the responsibility of finding "who dunnit" is delegated to the investigator, generally known as the **detective.**

The most common way for someone to become a detective is to be promoted from patrol officer. Detectives have not been the focus of nearly as much reform attention as their patrol counterparts, mainly because the scope of the detective's job is limited to law enforcement, with less emphasis given to social services or order maintenance.

5-2d
Aggressive Investigation Strategies

Detective bureaus also have the option of implementing aggressive strategies. For example, if detectives suspect that a person was involved in the robbery of a Mercedes-Benz parts warehouse, one of them might pose as a "fence"—or purchaser of stolen goods. In what is known as a "sting" operation, the suspect is deceived into thinking that the detective (fence) wants to buy stolen car parts. After the transaction takes place, the suspect can be arrested.

UNDERCOVER OPERATIONS Perhaps the most dangerous and controversial operation a law enforcement agent can undertake is to go *undercover,* or to assume a false identity in

Detective The primary police investigator of crimes.

Why might some police administrators seek to limit the amount of time law enforcement officers, such as this drug force operative, would be allowed to spend undercover?

Beatrice de Gea/*The New York Times*

order to obtain information concerning illegal activities. Though each department has its own guidelines on when undercover operations are necessary, all that is generally required is the suspicion that illegal activity is taking place. Today, undercover officers are commonly used to infiltrate large-scale narcotics operations or those run by organized crime.

In some situations, a detective bureau may not want to take the risk of exposing an officer to undercover work or may believe that an outsider cannot infiltrate an organized crime network. When the police need access and information, they have the option of turning to a **confidential informant (CI).** A CI is a person who is involved in criminal activity and gives information about that activity and those who engage in it to the police. As many as 80 percent of all illegal drug cases in the United States involve confidential informants. "They can get us into places we can't go," says one police administrator. "Without them, narcotics cases would practically cease to function."[24]

FIGHTING DOMESTIC TERRORISM Aggressive investigative strategies also play a crucial role in the federal government's efforts to combat **domestic terrorism.** As opposed to *international terrorism,* domestic terrorism involves terrorist acts that are carried out within one's own country with little or no direct foreign involvement. Because would-be domestic terrorists often need help to procure the weaponry necessary for their schemes, they are natural targets for well-placed informants and undercover agents. According to the Center on Law and Security at New York University, about two-thirds of the federal government's major terrorism prosecutions have relied on evidence provided by informants.[25]

Domestic Threat? On February 17, 2012, a Moroccan immigrant named Amine El Khalifi was arrested near the U.S. Capitol Building in Washington, D.C. El Khalifi, who had bragged that he "would be happy killing thirty people," was carrying an automatic weapon and wearing a suicide vest packed with what he thought were explosives.[26]

In Chapter 3, we saw that criminal law generally requires intent and action. A person must have both intended to commit a crime and taken some steps toward doing so. In most cases, criminal law also requires that a harm has been done and that the criminal act caused that harm. According to federal officials, however, El Khalifi never managed to contact an established terrorist group. His gun was inoperable, and his explosives were inert. Both had been provided by an FBI undercover agent acting as an al Qaeda operative. Indeed, El Khalifi had been under FBI surveillance for more than a year.

Preventive Policing The case of Amine El Khalifi provides a clear example of *preventive policing.* With preventive policing, the goal is not to solve the crime after it has occurred, but rather to prevent it from happening in the first place. Even though El Khalifi posed no immediate threat to the public, federal authorities were not willing to take the risk that he might eventually develop into a dangerous terrorist. Although some observers claim that law enforcement officials are exaggerating the threat posed by many of these accused plotters, the government points to a record of successes to justify this new approach. From the beginning of 2009 to 2012, preventive policing tactics aided in the arrests of nearly forty domestic terrorism suspects similar to El Khalifi.[27]

5-2e
Clearance Rates and Cold Cases

The ultimate goal of all law enforcement activity is to *clear* a crime, or secure the arrest and prosecution of the offender. Even a cursory glance at **clearance rates,** which show the percentage of reported crimes that have been cleared, reveals that investigations succeed only part of the time. In 2011, just 65 percent of homicides and 48 percent of total violent crimes were solved, while police cleared only 19 percent of property crimes.[28] For the most part, the different clearance rates for different crimes reflect the resources that a law enforcement agency expends on each type of crime. The police generally investigate a murder or a rape more vigorously than the theft of an automobile or a computer.

Confidential Informant (CI) A human source for police who provides information concerning illegal activity in which he or she is involved.

Domestic Terrorism Acts of terrorism that take place within the territorial jurisdiction of the United States without direct foreign involvement.

Clearance Rate A comparison of the number of crimes cleared by arrest and prosecution with the number of crimes reported during any given time period.

As a result of low clearance rates, police departments are saddled with an increasing number of **cold cases,** or criminal investigations that are not cleared after a certain amount of time. (The length of time before a case becomes "cold" varies from department to department. In general, a cold case must be "somewhat old" but not "so old that there can be no hope of ever solving it".[29]) Even using various technologies we will explore below, cold case investigations are usually unsuccessful. A recent RAND study found that only about one in twenty cold cases results in an arrest, and only about one in a hundred results in a conviction.[30]

5-2f
Forensic Investigations and DNA

Although the crime scene typically offers a wealth of evidence, some of it is incomprehensible to a patrol officer or detective without assistance. For that aid, law enforcement officers rely on experts in **forensics,** or the practice of using science and technology to investigate crimes. Forensic experts apply their knowledge to items found at the crime scene to determine crucial facts such as:

- The cause of death or injury.
- The time of death or injury.
- The type of weapon or weapons used.
- The identity of the crime victim, if that information is unavailable.
- The identity of the offender (in the best-case scenario).[31]

To assist forensic experts, many police departments operate or are affiliated with approximately 400 publicly funded crime laboratories in the United States. As we noted in the previous chapter, the FBI also offers the services of its crime lab to agencies with limited resources. The FBI's aid in this area is crucial, given that the nation's crime labs are burdened with a backlog of nearly one million requests for forensic services.[32]

CRIME SCENE FORENSICS The first law enforcement agent to reach a crime scene has the important task of protecting any **trace evidence** from contamination. Trace evidence is generally very small—often invisible to the naked human eye—and often requires technological aid for detection. Hairs, fibers, blood, fingerprints, broken glass, and footprints are all examples of trace evidence. A study released by the National Institute of Justice in 2010 confirmed that when police are able to link such evidence to a suspect, the likelihood of a conviction rises dramatically.[33] (**CAREER TIP:** A *bloodstain pattern analyst* can learn a great deal about a violent crime by examining where blood landed at the scene, the size and consistency of the drops, and the pattern of the blood spatter.)

Police will also search a crime scene for bullets and spent cartridge casings. These items can provide clues as to how far the shooter was from the target. They can also be compared with information stored in national firearms databases to determine, under some circumstances, the gun used and its most recent owner. The study of firearms and its application to solving crimes go under the general term **ballistics.** Comparing shell casings found at three different crime scenes, New York City police ballistics experts were able to determine that the same .22-caliber pistol was used to kill three Brooklyn-area merchants over a five-month period in 2012.

For more than a century, the most important piece of trace evidence has been the human fingerprint. Because no two fingerprints are alike, they are considered reliable sources of identification. Forensic scientists compare a fingerprint lifted from a crime scene with that of a suspect and declare a match if there are between eight and sixteen "points of similarity." This method of identification is not infallible, however. It is often difficult to lift a suitable print from a crime scene, and researchers have uncovered numerous cases in which innocent persons were convicted based on evidence obtained through faulty fingerprinting procedures.[34]

THE DNA REVOLUTION The technique of **DNA fingerprinting,** or using a suspect's DNA to match

Cold Case A criminal investigation that has not been solved after a certain amount of time.

Forensics The application of science to establish facts and evidence during the investigation of crimes.

Trace Evidence Evidence such as a fingerprint, blood, or hair found in small amounts at a crime scene.

Ballistics The study of firearms, including the firing of the weapon and the flight of the bullet.

DNA Fingerprinting The identification of a person based on a sample of her or his DNA, the genetic material found in the cells of all living things.

JOB DESCRIPTION:

- Examine, test, and analyze tissue samples, chemical substances, physical materials, and ballistics evidence collected at a crime scene.
- Testify as an expert witness on evidence or laboratory techniques in criminal trials.

WHAT KIND OF TRAINING IS REQUIRED?

- A bachelor's degree in science, particularly chemistry, biology, biochemistry, or physics.
- Certification programs (usually two years' additional study) can help prospective applicants specialize as forensic consultants, fingerprint technicians, forensic investigators, and laboratory technicians.

ANNUAL SALARY RANGE?

- $25,100–$65,000

SOCIAL MEDIA CAREER TIP

When people search for your name, they generally won't click past the first page. Regularly check to see where your online material appears and whether you want this material to be on the Internet.

Nancy Catherine Walker/iStockphoto.com

the suspect to a crime, emerged in the mid-1990s and has now all but replaced fingerprint evidence in many types of criminal investigations. The shift has been a boon to crime fighters: one law enforcement agent likened DNA fingerprinting to "the finger of God pointing down" at a guilty suspect.[35]

 DNA, which is the same in each cell of a person's body, provides a "genetic blueprint" or "code" for every living organism. DNA fingerprinting is useful in criminal investigations because no two people, save for identical twins, have the same genetic code. Therefore, lab technicians can compare the DNA sample of a suspect to the evidence found at the crime scene. If the match is negative, it is certain that the two samples did not come from the same source. If the match is positive, the lab will determine the odds that the DNA sample could have come from someone other than the suspect. Those odds are so high—sometimes reaching 30 billion to one—that a match is practically conclusive.[36]

The initial use of DNA to establish criminal guilt took place in Britain in 1986. The FBI used it for the first time in the United States two years later.

The process begins when forensic technicians gather blood, semen, skin, saliva, or hair from the scene of a crime. Blood cells and sperm are rich in DNA, making them particularly useful in murder and rape cases, but DNA has also been extracted from sweat on dirty laundry, skin cells on eyeglasses, and saliva on used envelope seals. Once a suspect is identified, her or his DNA can be used to determine whether she or he can be placed at the crime scene. Several years ago, for example, investigators connected Aaron Thomas, the "East Coast Rapist," to a series of sexual assaults that took place from Rhode Island to Virginia by obtaining Thomas's DNA sample from a discarded cigarette.

DNA IN ACTION The ability to "dust" for genetic information on such a wide variety of evidence, as well as that evidence's longevity and accuracy, greatly increases the chances that a crime will be solved. Indeed, police no longer need a witness or even a suspect in custody to solve crimes. What they do need is a piece of evidence and a database.

In 1985, for example, Saba Girmai was found strangled to death in a dumpster in Mountain

View, California. For nearly three decades, police were unable to establish any useful leads concerning Girmai's murderer. This changed when technicians at the Santa Clara County District Attorney's Crime Laboratory developed a DNA profile of the suspect using evidence found underneath Girmai's fingerprints. Checking these results against the state's crime database, the technicians found a match with Daniel Garcia, who had been previously convicted of a different crime. Twenty-eight years after the fact, in 2013, Garcia finally was arrested in connection with Girmai's death.

Databases and Cold Hits The identification of Daniel Garcia is an example of what police call a **cold hit,** which occurs when law enforcement finds a suspect "out of nowhere" by comparing DNA evidence from a crime scene against the contents of a database. The largest and most important database is the National Combined DNA Index System (CODIS). Operated by the FBI since 1998, CODIS gives local and state law enforcement agencies access to the DNA profiles of those who have been convicted of various crimes. CODIS contains DNA records of over 10 million people, and as of January 2013, the database had produced 200,300 cold hits nationwide.[37]

DNA Collections and Arrests Privacy and civil rights advocates protest that DNA collection has gone too far. Specifically, authorities in many states now collect samples from those who have been convicted of nonviolent crimes and, in some instances, from those who have merely been arrested for a crime but not convicted. In 2013, the U.S. Supreme Court upheld the practice of taking DNA samples from arrestees, as practiced in twenty-eight states and by the federal government.[38] Although the Court reasoned that such procedures are necessary to identify the suspect, its ruling will have the practical effect of greatly increasing DNA profiles stored in CODIS and other law enforcement databases.

5-2g
Police Strategies

Even though law enforcement officers do not like to think of themselves as being at the beck and call of citizens, that is the operational basis of much police work. All police departments practice **incident-driven policing,** in which calls for service are the primary instigators of action. Between 40 and 60 percent of police activity is the result of 911 calls or other citizen requests, which means that police officers in the field initiate only about half of such activity.[39]

Recognizing that the majority of emergency calls for service now involve mobile phones or VoIP (voice-over-Internet-protocol) technology, law enforcement is making the slow transition to Next Generation 911. This new system will rely on the Internet and will make it possible for officers to receive text messages, videos, photos, and

Cold Hit The establishment of a connection between a suspect and a crime, often through the use of DNA evidence, in the absence of an ongoing criminal investigation.

Incident-Driven Policing A reactive approach to policing that emphasizes a speedy response to calls for service.

Mark Randall/MTC/Landov

CAREER TIP: Although they are responsible for a crucial aspect of policing, *911 dispatchers* generally are not sworn police officers and do not need any law enforcement experience. Rather, they receive special training in dealing with emergency calls.

location data about crime incidents. For example, a store clerk who has just been robbed at gunpoint will be able to take a photo of the offender's getaway car and send that photo to police along with the emergency call for service.[40]

RANDOM AND DIRECTED PATROL Of course, officers to do not sit at the station waiting for incident calls. Earlier in this chapter, we noted that the majority of police officers are assigned to patrol duties. Most of these officers work **random patrol,** making the rounds of a specific area with the general goal of detecting and preventing crime. Every police department in the United States randomly patrols its jurisdiction using automobiles. In addition, 53 percent utilize foot patrols, 32 percent bicycle patrols, 16 percent motorcycle patrols, 4 percent boat patrols, and 1 percent horse patrols.[41] (**CAREER TIP:** *Mounted police officers* are often considered to have the most enjoyable patrol assignments, as they work on horseback. In most mounted divisions, however, officers must complete a grueling training regimen and care for their animals in addition to performing their regular police duties.)

In contrast to random patrols, **directed patrols** target specific areas of a city and often attempt to prevent a specific type of crime. Directed patrols have found favor among law enforcement experts as being a more efficient use of police resources than random patrols, as indicated by the recent Philadelphia Foot Patrol Experiment. During this experiment, extra foot patrols were utilized in sixty Philadelphia locations plagued by high levels of violent crime. During three months of directed patrols, arrests increased by 13 percent in the targeted areas, and violent crime decreased by 23 percent. In addition, an estimated fifty-three violent crimes were prevented over the three-month period.[42]

"HOT SPOTS" AND CRIME MAPPING The target areas for directed patrols are often called **hot spots** because they contain greater numbers of criminals and have higher-than-average levels of victimization. Needless to say, police administrators do not simply stick pins in maps to determine where hot spots exist. Rather, police departments are using **crime mapping** technology to locate and identify hot spots and "cool" them down. Crime mapping uses geographic information systems (GIS) to track criminal acts as they occur in time and space. Once sufficient information has been gathered, it is analyzed to predict future crime patterns.

Computerized crime mapping was popularized when the New York City Police Department launched CompStat in the mid-1990s. Still in use, CompStat starts with police officers reporting the exact location of crime and other crime-related information to department officials. These reports are then fed into a computer, which prepares grids of a particular city or neighborhood and highlights areas with a high incidence of serious offenses. (See Figure 5.2 on the facing page for an example of a GIS crime map.)

In New York and many other cities, the police department holds "Crime Control Strategy Meetings" during which precinct commanders are held accountable for CompStat's data-based reports in their districts. In theory, this system provides the police with accurate information about patterns of crime and gives them the ability to "flood" hot spots with officers at short notice. About two-thirds of large departments now employ some form of computerized crime mapping,[43] and Wesley Skogan, a criminologist at Northwestern University, believes that CompStat and similar technologies are the most likely cause of recent declines in big-city crime.[44]

5-2h
Arrest Strategies

Like patrol strategies, arrest strategies can be broken into two categories that reflect the intent of police administrators. **Reactive arrests** are those arrests made by police officers, usually on random patrol,

Random Patrol A patrol strategy that relies on police officers monitoring a certain area with the goal of detecting crimes in progress or preventing crime due to their presence. Also known as general or preventive patrol.

Directed Patrol A patrol strategy that is designed to focus on a specific type of criminal activity at a specific time.

Hot Spots Concentrated areas of high criminal activity that draw a directed police response.

Crime Mapping Technology that allows crime analysts to identify trends and patterns of criminal behavior within a given area.

Reactive Arrests Arrests that come about as part of the ordinary routine of police patrol and responses to calls for service.

FIGURE 5.2 A GIS Crime Map for a Neighborhood in New Orleans

This crime map shows the incidence of various crimes during a two-week period in a neighborhood near downtown New Orleans.

The Omega Group/crimemapping.com

Thus, the **broken windows theory** is based on "order maintenance" of neighborhoods by cracking down on "quality-of-life" crimes such as panhandling, public drinking and urinating, loitering, and graffiti painting. Only by encouraging directed arrest strategies with regard to these quality-of-life crimes, the two professors argued, could American cities be rescued from rising crime rates.

5-2i
Community Policing and Problem Solving

In "Broken Windows," Wilson and Kelling insisted that, to reduce fear and crime in high-risk neighborhoods, police had to rely on the cooperation of citizens. Today, a majority of police departments rely on a broad strategy known as **community policing** to improve relations with citizens and fight crime at the same time.

Community policing can be defined as an approach that promotes community-police partnerships, proactive problem solving, and community engagement to address issues such as fear of crime and the causes of such fear in a particular area. Neighborhood watch programs, in which police officers and citizens work together to prevent local crime and disorder, are a popular version of a community policing initiative.

Under community policing, patrol officers have the freedom to improvise. They are expected to develop personal relationships with residents and to encourage those residents to become involved in making the community a safer place. As part of Operation Heat Wave, for instance, Dallas

who observe a criminal act or respond to a call for service. **Proactive arrests** occur when the police take the initiative to target a particular type of criminal or behavior. Proactive arrests are often associated with directed patrols of hot spots, and thus are believed by many experts to have a greater influence on an area's crime rates.[45]

To a certain extent, the popularity of proactive theories was solidified by a magazine article that James Q. Wilson and George L. Kelling wrote in 1982.[46] In their piece, entitled "Broken Windows," Wilson and Kelling argued that policing strategies were focusing on violent crime to the detriment of the vital police role of promoting the quality of life in neighborhoods. As a result, many communities, particularly in large cities, had fallen into a state of disorder and disrepute, with two very important consequences. First, these neighborhoods—with their broken windows, dilapidated buildings, and lawless behavior by residents—send out "signals" that criminal activity is tolerated. Second, this disorder spreads fear among law-abiding citizens, dissuading them from leaving their homes or attempting to improve their surroundings.

Proactive Arrests Arrests that occur because of concerted efforts by law enforcement agencies to respond to a particular type of criminal or criminal behavior.

Broken Windows Theory Wilson and Kelling's theory that law enforcement should crack down on quality-of-life crimes to reduce overall crime.

Community Policing A policing philosophy that emphasizes community support for and cooperation with the police in preventing crime.

Two Washington, D.C., police officers offer suggestions to a six-year-old during the annual "Shop with a Cop" event in the nation's capital. How can establishing friendly relations with citizens help law enforcement agencies reduce crime?

Andrew Harnik/*Washington Times*/Landov

detectives go door-to-door in neighborhoods plagued by burglary and auto theft. During these face-to-face meetings, the detectives are able to gather information concerning recent victimizations and encourage attendance at community crime-watch meetings.[47] A 2011 survey of more than 1,200 officers in eleven police departments found that between 60 and 95 percent agreed with the idea that "police officers should try to solve non-crime problems on their beat."[48] A majority of the officers also reported having positive relations with members of the public, who they felt generally appreciated community policing efforts.[49]

Community policing has been criticized—not least by police officials—as having more to do with public relations than with actual crime fighting.[50] Having law enforcement establish a cooperative presence in the community, however, is a crucial part of another strategy that does focus on long-term crime prevention.

5-2j
Solving Problems

Introduced by Herman Goldstein of the Police Executive Research Forum in the 1970s, **problem-oriented policing** is based on the premise that police departments devote too many of their resources to reacting to calls for service

Problem-Oriented Policing A policing philosophy that requires police to identify potential criminal activity and develop strategies to prevent or respond to that activity.

and too few to "acting on their own initiative to prevent or reduce community problems."[51] To rectify this situation, problem-oriented policing moves beyond simply responding to incidents and attempts instead to control or even solve the root causes of criminal behavior.

Goldstein's theory encourages police officers to stop looking at their work as a day-to-day proposition. Rather, they should try to shift the patterns of criminal behavior in a positive direction. For example, instead of responding to a 911 call concerning illegal drug use by simply arresting the offender—a short-term response—the patrol officers should also look at the long-term implications of the situation. They should analyze the pattern of similar arrests in the area and interview the arrestee to determine the reasons, if any, that the site was selected for drug activity.[52] Then additional police action should be taken to prevent further drug sales at the identified location.

5-3
what ARE THE CHALLENGES OF BEING A POLICE OFFICER

The night after two police officers shot and killed Jaime Gonzalez, described in the opening to this chapter, the Brownsville police received several death threats. Apparently, some members of the community were unconvinced by the argument that the officers' actions were justified because Gonzalez appeared to be in possession of an actual handgun. Indeed, there seems to be a public perception, fueled by heavy coverage of police shootings, that American law enforcement agents are "trigger happy" when it comes to using their weaponry. The reality is that such fatal shootings are quite rare.[53] According to one estimate, the average New York City police officer would have to work 694 years to shoot and kill someone, and the likelihood is more remote in most other cities.[54]

The question of when to use lethal force is one of many on-the-job issues that make law enforcement such a challenging and often dangerous career. When faced with a scenario such as the one in the halls of Brownsville's Cummings Middle School, sometimes police officers make the right decisions, and sometimes they make the wrong ones. Often, it is difficult to tell the two apart.

5-3a
Police Subculture

As a rule, police officers do not appreciate being second-guessed when it comes to their split-second shooting decisions. To officers, it often seems that civilians believe that suspects with weapons should be given a "free shot" before being fired at by law enforcement.[55] Feelings of frustration and mistrust toward civilians are hallmarks of **police subculture,** a broad term used to describe the basic assumptions and values that permeate law enforcement agencies and are taught to new members of a law enforcement agency as the proper way to think, perceive, and act. Every organization has a subculture, with values shaped by the particular aspects and pressures of that organization. In the police subculture, those values are formed in an environment characterized by danger, stress, boredom, and violence.

From the first day on the job, rookies begin the process of **socialization,** in which they are taught the values and rules of police work. This process is aided by a number of rituals that are common to the law enforcement experience. Police theorist Harry J. Mullins believes that the following rituals are critical to the police officer's acceptance, and even embrace, of police subculture:

- Attending a police academy.
- Working with a senior officer, who passes on the "lessons" of police work and life to the younger officer.

- Making the initial felony arrest.
- Using force to make an arrest for the first time.
- Using or witnessing deadly force for the first time.
- Witnessing major traumatic incidents for the first time.[56]

Each of these rituals makes it clear to the police officer that this is not a "normal" job. The only other people who can understand the stresses of police work are fellow officers, and consequently law enforcement officers tend to insulate themselves from civilians. Eventually, the insulation breeds mistrust, and the police officer develops an "us versus them" outlook toward those outside the force. In turn, this outlook creates what sociologist William Westly called the **blue curtain,** also known as the "blue wall of silence" or simply "the code."[57] This curtain separates the police from the civilians they are meant to protect.

SOCIAL MEDIA AND CJ

Officer.com advertises itself as the "leading news and information source for the police and law enforcement community." To access its very active Twitter feed, go to **www.officer.com** and click on the Twitter icon.

5-3b
The Physical Dangers of Police Work

Police officers learn early in their careers that nothing about their job is "routine"—they face the threat of physical harm every day. According to the Officer Down Memorial Page, from January 2012 through May 2013, 169 law enforcement agents lost their lives in the line of duty.[58] In addition, about 55,000 assaults were committed against police officers in 2011, with 27 percent of these assaults resulting in an injury.[59] These numbers are hardly surprising. As police experts John S. Dempsey and Linda S. Forst point out, police "deal constantly with what may be the most dangerous species on this planet—the human being."[60]

Despite perceptions to the contrary, a high percentage of deaths and

Police Subculture The values and perceptions that are shared by law enforcement agents.

Socialization The process through which a police officer is taught the values and expected behavior of the police subculture.

Blue Curtain A metaphorical term used to refer to the value placed on secrecy and the general mistrust of the outside world shared by many police officers.

A fellow officer pays his respects during the funeral of Chattahoochee Hills, Georgia, police officer Mike Vogt, who was shot and killed while on patrol. Besides physical violence, what are some of the other occupational threats that police officers face on a daily basis?

AP Photo/Brant Sanderlin

injuries suffered by police officers are not the result of assaults by criminal suspects. Generally speaking, half of all law enforcement officer injuries are due to accidents, and about two-thirds of those injuries occur when officers are doing something other than making an arrest.[61] In particular, traffic accidents cause as many line-of-duty deaths as do firearms.[62] One reason for the fatalities is that a number of law enforcement officers do not take simple precautions when behind the wheel. A recent study conducted by the National Highway Traffic Safety Administration found that 42 percent of police officers killed in vehicle crashes were not wearing seat belts.[63]

5-3c
Stress and the Mental Dangers of Police Work

In addition to physical dangers, police work entails considerable mental pressure and stress. The conditions that cause stress—such as worries over finances or relationships—are known as **stressors.** Each profession has its own set of stressors, but police

Stressors The aspects of police work and life that lead to feelings of stress.

Burnout A mental state that occurs when a person suffers from exhaustion and has difficulty functioning normally as a result of overwork and stress.

are particularly vulnerable to occupational pressures and stress factors such as the following:

- The constant fear of being a victim of violent crime.
- Exposure to violent crime and its victims.
- The need to comply with the law in nearly every job action.
- Lack of community support.
- Negative media coverage.

Police face a number of internal pressures as well, including limited opportunities for career advancement, excessive paperwork, and low wages and benefits.[64] The unconventional hours of shift work can also interfere with an officer's private life and contribute to lack of sleep. Each of these is a primary stressor associated with police work.[65]

Police stress can manifest itself in different ways. A University at Buffalo study found that the stresses of law enforcement often lead to high blood pressure and heart problems.[66] Other research shows that police officers are three times more likely to suffer from alcoholism than the average American.[67] If stress becomes overwhelming, an officer may suffer from **burnout,** becoming listless and ineffective as a result of mental and physical exhaustion. Though some studies suggest that police officers have higher rates of suicide than the general population, it appears that most develop an extraordinary ability to handle the difficulties of the profession and persevere.[68]

5-3d

Authority and the Use of Force

If the police subculture is shaped by the dangers of the job, it often finds expression through authority. The various symbols of authority that decorate a police officer—including the uniform, badge, nightstick, and firearm—establish the power she or he holds over civilians. For better or for worse, both police officers and civilians tend to equate terms such as *authority* and *respect* with the ability to use force.

In general, the use of physical force by law enforcement personnel is very rare, occurring in only about 1.4 percent of the 40 million police-public encounters that occur annually. Still, the Department of Justice estimates that law enforcement officers threaten to use force or use force in encounters with 770,000 civilians a year, and nearly 14 percent of those incidents result in an injury.[69] Federal authorities also report that about 690 deaths occur in the process of an arrest on an annual basis.[70] Of course, police officers are often justified in using force to protect themselves and other citizens. As we noted earlier, they are the targets of tens of thousands of assaults each year. Law enforcement agents are also usually justified in using force to make an arrest, to prevent suspects from escaping, to restrain suspects or other individuals for their own safety, or to protect property.[71]

At the same time, few observers would be naïve enough to believe that the police are *always* justified in the use of force. A 2009 survey of emergency room physicians found that 98 percent believed that they had treated patients who were victims of excessive police force.[72] How, then, is "misuse" of force to be defined? To provide guidance for officers in this tricky area, nearly every law enforcement agency designs a *use of force matrix*. As the example in Figure 5.3 above shows, such a matrix presents officers with the proper force options for different levels of contact with a civilian.

TYPES OF FORCE To comply with the various, and not always consistent, laws concerning the use of force, a police officer must understand that there are two kinds of force: *nondeadly force* and *deadly force*. Most force used by law enforcement is nondeadly force. In most states, the use of nondeadly force is regulated by the concept of **reasonable force,** which allows the use of nondeadly force when a reasonable person would assume that such force was necessary. In contrast, **deadly force** is force that an objective police officer

FIGURE 5.3 The Orlando (Florida) Police Department's Use of Force Matrix

Like most local law enforcement agencies, the Orlando Police Department has a policy to guide its officers' use of force. These policies instruct an officer on how to react to an escalating series of confrontations with a civilian and are often expressed visually, as shown here.

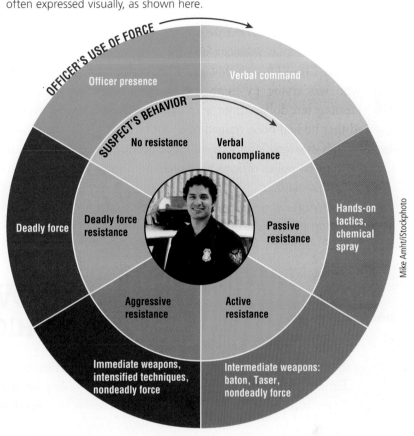

Source: Michael E. Miller, "Taser Use and the Use-of-Force Continuum," *Police Chief* (September 2010), 72.

Reasonable Force The degree of force that is appropriate to protect the police officer or other citizens and is not excessive.

Deadly Force Force applied by a police officer that is likely or intended to cause death.

realizes will place the subject in direct threat of serious injury or death.

THE UNITED STATES SUPREME COURT AND USE OF FORCE The United States Supreme Court set the limits for the use of deadly force by law enforcement officers in *Tennessee v. Garner* (1985).[73] The case involved an incident in which Memphis police officer Elton Hymon shot and killed a suspect

LO **4** who was trying to climb over a fence after stealing ten dollars from a residence. Hymon testified that he had been trained to shoot to keep a suspect from escaping, and indeed Tennessee law at the time allowed police officers to apprehend fleeing suspects in this manner.

In reviewing the case, the Supreme Court focused not on Hymon's action but on the Tennessee statute itself, ultimately finding it unconstitutional:

> When the suspect poses no immediate threat to the officer and no threat to others, the use of deadly force is unjustified. . . . It is not better that all felony suspects die than that they escape.[74]

The Court's decision forced twenty-three states to change their fleeing felon rules, but it did not completely eliminate police discretion in such situations. Police officers still may use deadly force if they have probable cause to believe that the fleeing suspect poses a threat of serious injury or death to the officers or others. (We will discuss the concept of probable cause in the next chapter.)

In essence, the Court recognized that police officers must be able to make split-second decisions without worrying about the legal ramifications. Four years after the *Garner* case, the Court tried to clarify this concept in *Graham v. Connor* (1989), stating that the use of any force should be judged by the "reasonableness of the moment."[75] In 2004, the Court modified this rule by suggesting that an officer's use of force could be "reasonable" even if, by objective measures, the force was not needed to protect the officer or ot7hers in the area.[76] (See the feature *You Be the Sheriff's Deputy—Threat Level* below.)

5-4

how IMPORTANT IS ETHICS IN POLICING?

If excessive force is a "strong" misuse of authority by law enforcement, then "soft" misuse of this authority manifests itself in *police corruption*. For general

---

YOU BE THE SHERIFF'S DEPUTY

THREAT LEVEL

THE SITUATION You receive a call from dispatch telling you that Lee Dylan, a mentally unstable man, has just escaped from a local jail where he was being held on suspicion of committing a nonviolent felony. Driving toward the jail, you see a man matching Dylan's description running down a back alley. Jumping out of your car, you and your partner follow on foot. Eventually, you and your partner corner the man, who is indeed Dylan, in a construction site. Dylan, who is of average height and build, grabs a loose brick and makes threatening motions with it. You pull your gun and, along with your partner, move toward Dylan. You yell, "Drop the brick!" He screams, "You're going to have to kill me!" and rushes at you.

THE LAW The use of force by a law enforcement agent—even deadly force—is based on the concept of reasonableness. In other words, would a reasonable police officer in this officer's shoes have been justified in using force?

YOUR DECISION Does Dylan pose a threat of serious bodily harm to you or your partner? How you answer this question will determine the type of force you use against him. Keep in mind that almost all police officers experience an adrenaline rush in stressful situations, and this may influence your reaction.

[To see how a law enforcement officer in Cincinnati reacted in similar circumstances, go to Example 5.1 in Appendix A.]

Gina Sanders/Shutterstock

purposes, **police corruption** can be defined as the misuse of authority by a law enforcement officer "in a manner designed to produce personal gain." An obvious form of police corruption is *bribery*, in which the police officer accepts money or other forms of payment in exchange for "favors." These favors may include allowing a certain criminal activity to continue or misplacing a key piece of evidence before trial. Related to bribery are *payoffs*, in which an officer demands payment from an individual in return for certain services.

More serious corruption occurs when police engage directly in criminal activity, such as narcotics trafficking. This often leads to further misuse of authority, as the offending officers may resort to brutality and lying in court to protect their illicit activities. Another corruption scenario involves police misconduct that becomes pervasive, infecting a group of officers. In 2012, dozens of Baltimore police officers were implicated in a $1 million kickback scheme. For years, the officers had been diverting autos damaged in traffic accidents to the Majestic Body Shop in return for a payoff of several hundred dollars per car. Sometimes, the officers themselves would cause further damage to the cars to increase the portion of the insurance payout that went into their own pockets. (**CAREER TIP:** Within police departments, *internal affairs officers* are charged with investigating corruption, ethics violations, and other misconduct on the force.)

5-4a
Ethical Dilemmas

Police corruption is intricately connected with the ethics of law enforcement officers. As you saw in Chapter 1, ethics has to do with fundamental questions of the fairness, justice, rightness, or wrongness of any action. Given the significant power that police officers hold, society expects very high standards of ethical behavior from them. Some police actions are obviously unethical, such as the behavior of the police officers who received kickbacks from the Baltimore auto body shop, described above. The majority of ethical dilemmas that a police officer will face are not so clear-cut. Criminologists Joycelyn M. Pollock and Ronald F. Becker define an ethical dilemma as a situation in which law enforcement officers:

- Do not know the right course of action;
- Have difficulty doing what they consider to be right; and/or
- Find the wrong choice very tempting.[77]

Because of the many rules that govern policing—the subject of the next chapter—police officers often find themselves tempted by a phenomenon called **noble cause corruption.** This type of corruption occurs when, in the words of John P. Crank and Michael A. Caldero, "officers do bad things because they believe the outcomes will be good."[78] Examples include planting evidence or lying in court to help convict someone the officer knows to be guilty.

5 LO

5-4b
Elements of Ethics

Pollock and Becker, both of whom have extensive experience as ethics instructors for police departments, further identify four categories of ethical dilemmas, involving discretion, duty, honesty, and loyalty.[79]

- *Discretion.* The law provides rigid guidelines for how police officers must act and how they cannot act, but it does not offer guidelines for how officers *should act* in many circumstances. As mentioned at the beginning of this chapter, police officers often use discretion to determine how they should act, and ethics plays an important role in guiding discretionary actions.
- *Duty.* The concept of discretion is linked with **duty,** or the obligation to act in a certain manner. Society, by passing laws, can make a police officer's duty clearer and, in the process, help eliminate discretion from the decision-making process. But an officer's duty will not always be obvious, and ethical considerations can often supplement "the rules" of being a law enforcement agent.
- *Honesty.* Of course, honesty is a critical attribute for an ethical police officer. A law enforcement agent must make hundreds of decisions in a day, and most of them require him or her to be honest in order to properly do the job.

Police Corruption The abuse of authority by a law enforcement officer for personal gain.

Noble Cause Corruption Knowing misconduct by a police officer with the goal of attaining what the officer believes is a "just" result.

Duty The moral sense of a police officer that she or he should behave in a certain manner.

CJ AND TECHNOLOGY

SELF-SURVEILLANCE

TO lessen police corruption and misconduct, law enforcement agents may soon be under constant surveillance—by their own superiors. At least 1,100 police agencies in the United States are using body-mounted video cameras to document traffic stops, arrests, and other encounters with suspects. These small, self-contained units clip to the officer's uniform, and include tiny radio microphones to record sound.

Some departments are also using head-worn video systems that "look" wherever an officer moves his or her head. Law enforcement agents hope that these devices will help protect them against unfounded charges of misconduct. "In this job we're frequently accused of things we haven't done, or things that [were] kind of embellished," says Bainbridge Island (Washington) police officer Ben Sias. "And the cameras show a pretty unbiased opinion of what actually did happen."

AP Photo/The Topeka Capital Journal, Thad Allton

THINKING ABOUT SELF-SURVEILLANCE

Dennis Kenney, a professor at New York's John Jay College of Criminal Justice, warns that this technology "raises tremendous privacy concerns." What are some of those concerns?

- *Loyalty.* What should a police officer do if he or she witnesses a partner using excessive force on a suspect? The choice often sets loyalty against ethics, especially if the officer does not condone the violence.

Although an individual's ethical makeup is determined by a multitude of personal factors, police departments can create an atmosphere that is conducive to professionalism. Brandon V. Zuidema and H. Wayne Duff, both captains with the Lynchburg (Virginia) Police Department, believe that law enforcement administrators can encourage ethical policing by:

1. Incorporating ethics into the department's mission statement.

2. Conducting internal training sessions in ethics.

3. Accepting "honest mistakes" and helping the officer learn from those mistakes.

4. Adopting a zero-tolerance policy toward unethical decisions when the mistakes are not so honest.[80]

In 2013, Kitsap County (Washington) Deputy Sheriff Krista McDonald received the Public Safety Officer Medal of Valor for rescuing two colleagues during a shootout. What role does the concept of duty play in a law enforcement agent's decision, regardless of her or his own safety, to protect the life of another person?

Mandel Ngan/AFP/Getty Images

REVIEW

✔ **Review what you've read with the quiz below.**

Rip out the Chapter Review card at the back of this book, which includes:
- Chapter Summary and Learning Outcomes
- Key Terms

Or you can go online to CourseMate at www.cengagebrain.com to:
- Complete Practice Quizzes to prepare for tests.
- Review Key Terms Flash Cards (online or print).
- Play games to master concepts.

quiz

1. When a police administration wants to limit officer discretion, it can institute a departmental _____ to guide the officer's decision making in certain situations, such as high-speed chases.

2. One of the primary functions of patrol officers is to _____ crime by maintaining a visible presence in the community.

3. The science of crime investigation is known as _____.

4. The technique of _____ fingerprinting involves crime labs using samples of a person's genetic material to match suspects to crimes.

5. All modern police departments practice _____-driven policing, in which officers respond to calls for service after a crime has occurred.

6. Most patrol officers are assigned to _____ patrols, in which they cover designated areas and react to incidents they encounter.

7. _____ policing is a popular strategy in which officers are encouraged to develop partnerships with citizens to prevent and combat crime.

8. The police subculture is shaped by the physical dangers, such as assault, and the mental dangers, such as high levels of _____, that officers face every day.

9. Police use of nondeadly force is regulated by the concept of _____ force, or the amount of force that a rational person would consider necessary in a given situation.

10. Police _____ is an umbrella term that covers police misconduct from taking bribes to engaging in illegal drug trafficking.

Answers can be found on the Chapter 5 Review card at the end of the book.

AP Photo/Jae C. Hong

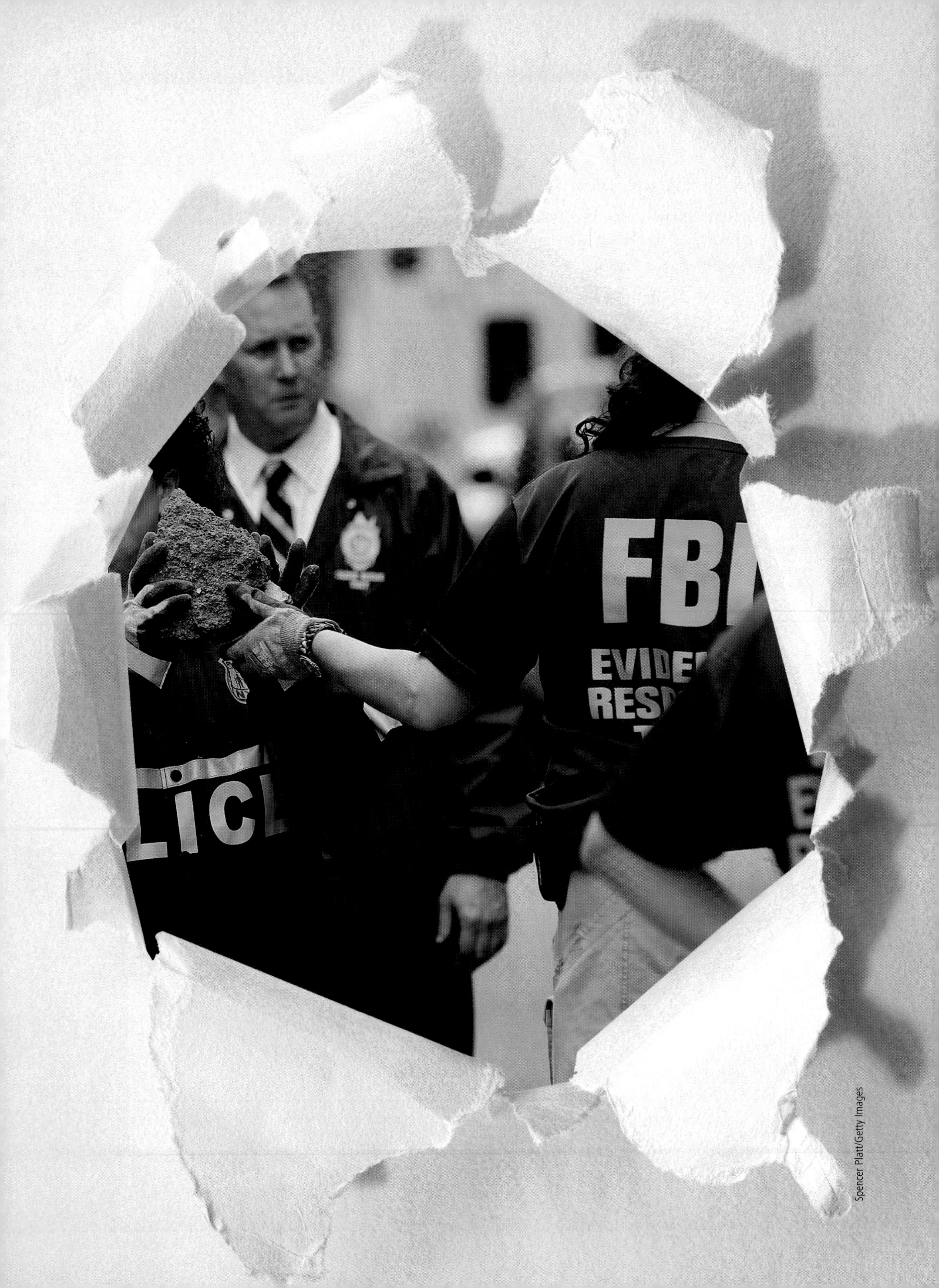

Spencer Platt/Getty Images

Learning **OUTCOMES** | *After studying this chapter, you will be able to...*

1 Outline the four major sources that may provide probable cause.

2 Explain when searches can be made without a warrant.

3 Distinguish between a stop and a frisk, and indicate the importance of the case *Terry v. Ohio.*

4 List the four elements that must be present for an arrest to take place.

5 Indicate situations in which a *Miranda* warning is unnecessary.

POLICE AND THE CONSTITUTION: THE RULES OF LAW ENFORCEMENT

6

What's That Smell?

For the three Lexington-Fayette (Kentucky) narcotics officers, the odds of making the correct decision seemed fifty-fifty. They had just followed a suspected drug dealer into the breezeway of an apartment complex and saw two doors, one on the left and one on the right. They knew the suspect had entered one of the apartments, but they had no way of determining which one. Then the officers smelled marijuana smoke coming from the apartment on the left. They immediately started banging on that door, yelling, "This is the police!" After hearing suspicious movements inside, the officers forced themselves into the apartment.

They did not find their suspect. Instead, the officers discovered Hollis King and two friends sitting on his sofa, smoking marijuana. A quick search of the apartment uncovered a stash of marijuana, powder and crack cocaine, and cash. King was arrested, convicted of several drug-related offenses, and

sentenced to eleven years in prison. He appealed the conviction, claiming that the narcotics officers had improperly burst into and searched his apartment.

Generally, law enforcement agents cannot enter any sort of dwelling without consent from an inhabitant or written permission from a judge, called a *warrant*. As you will learn later in the chapter, however, the warrant requirement does not apply under certain "exigent," or urgent, circumstances. In this case, the narcotics officers believed

that the suspicious noises they heard were made by someone destroying evidence, thus creating an exigent circumstance. Several years ago, the United States Supreme Court ruled in favor of the Lexington-Lafayette officers, holding that their actions were justified even though, as it turned out, the original suspect was not in King's apartment. According to Justice Samuel Alito, the officers' "warrantless entry to prevent the destruction of evidence is reasonable and thus allowed."

Through its decisions, the United States Supreme Court determines the guidelines that law enforcement officers must follow when entering and searching apartments and other dwellings.

Robert Nickelsberg/Getty Images

117

how DOES THE CONSTITUTION LIMIT POLICE BEHAVIOR?

In *Kentucky v. King*, the Supreme Court did not address whether Hollis King was guilty or innocent of the charges against him. That was for the trial court to decide. Rather, the Court ruled that the Lexington-Fayette narcotics officers had not overstepped the boundaries of their authority in entering and searching King's apartment.[1] In the previous chapter, we discussed the importance of discretion for police officers. This discretion, as we noted, is not absolute. A law enforcement agent's actions are greatly determined by the rules for policing set down in the U.S. Constitution and enforced by the courts.

To understand these rules, law enforcement officers must understand the Fourth Amendment, which reads as follows:

> The right of the people to be secure in their persons, houses, papers, and effects, against unreasonable searches and seizures, shall not be violated, and no Warrants shall issue, but upon probable cause, supported by Oath or affirmation, and particularly describing the place to be searched, and the persons or things to be seized.

This amendment contains two critical legal concepts: a prohibition against *unreasonable* **searches and seizures** and the requirement of **probable cause** to issue a warrant.

6-1a
Reasonableness

Law enforcement personnel use searches and seizures to look for and collect the evidence prosecutors need to convict individuals suspected of crimes. As you have just read, when police are conducting a search or seizure, they must be *reasonable*. Though courts have spent innumerable hours scrutinizing the word, no specific meaning for *reasonable* exists. A thesaurus can provide useful synonyms—logical, practical, sensible, intelligent, plausible—but because each case is different, those terms are relative.

In the *King* case, the Supreme Court rejected the argument that the search had been so unreasonable as to violate the Fourth Amendment's prohibition against unreasonable searches and seizures. That does not mean that the police officers' actions would have been reasonable under any circumstances. What if the narcotics officers, after having lost the trail of their suspected drug dealer, had begun randomly kicking down doors in the apartment complex, eventually discovering Hollis King and his illegal drug stash? Under those circumstances, their conduct would almost certainly have been considered unreasonable.

Indeed, one Supreme Court justice, Ruth Bader Ginsburg, did believe that the officers in the *King* case had acted unreasonably. The Court's decision, she warned, "arms the police with a way routinely to dishonor the Fourth Amendment's warrant requirement."[2] For example, she noted, law enforcement agents can now simply roam the hallways of apartment buildings, knock whenever they smell marijuana, and make a forced entry if they think they hear something suspicious.[3]

6-1b
Probable Cause

The concept of reasonableness is linked to probable cause. The Supreme Court has ruled, for example, that any arrest or seizure is unreasonable unless it is supported by probable cause.[4] The burden of probable cause requires more than mere suspicion on a police officer's part. The officer must know of facts and circumstances that would reasonably lead to "the belief that an offense has been or is being committed."[5]

SOURCES OF PROBABLE CAUSE If no probable cause existed when a police officer took a certain action, it cannot be retroactively applied. If, for example, a police officer stops a person for jaywalking and then finds several ounces of marijuana in that person's pocket, the arrest for marijuana possession would probably be disallowed. Remember, suspicion does not equal probable cause. If, however, an informant had tipped the officer off that the person was a drug dealer, probable cause might exist and the arrest

Searches and Seizures
The legal term, as found in the Fourth Amendment to the U.S. Constitution, that generally refers to the searching for and the confiscating of evidence by law enforcement agents.

Probable Cause
Reasonable grounds to believe the existence of facts warranting certain actions, such as the search or arrest of a person.

CAREER**PREP**

ENVIRONMENTAL PROTECTION AGENCY CRIMINAL INVESTIGATION DIVISION SPECIAL AGENT

JOB DESCRIPTION:

- Enforce the nation's environmental laws protecting air, water, and land resources.
- Investigate cases that involve negligent, knowing, or willful violations of federal environmental laws.

WHAT KIND OF TRAINING IS REQUIRED?

- Eight weeks of basic federal law enforcement and criminal investigation training at the Federal Law Enforcement Training Center in Glynco, Georgia.
- An additional eight weeks of training in conducting investigations of the criminal provisions of federal environmental laws.

ANNUAL SALARY RANGE?

- $43,000–$128,000

SOCIAL MEDIA CAREER TIP

For your profile photo, stick with a close-up, business appropriate photo in which you are smiling and wearing something you would wear as a potential employee. Avoid symbols, party photos, long-distance shots, or baby pictures.

Image Source/Corbis

could be valid. Informants are one of several sources that may provide probable cause. Others include:

1. *Personal observation.* Police officers may use their personal training, experience, and expertise to infer probable cause from situations that may not be obviously criminal. If, for example, a police officer observes several people in a car slowly circling a certain building in a high-crime area, that officer may infer that the people are "casing" the building in preparation for a burglary. Probable cause could be established for detaining the suspects.

2. *Information.* Law enforcement officers receive information from victims, eyewitnesses, informants, and official sources such as police bulletins or broadcasts. Such information, as long as it is believed to be reliable, is a basis for probable cause.

3. *Evidence.* In certain circumstances, which will be examined later in this chapter, police have probable cause for a search or seizure based on evidence—such as a shotgun—in plain view.

LO **1**

4. *Association.* In some circumstances, if the police see a person with a known criminal background in a place where criminal activity is openly taking place, they have probable cause to stop that person. Generally, however, association is not adequate to establish probable cause.[6]

In 2013, the Supreme Court confirmed that drug-sniffing dogs are important sources of probable cause. The case involved a "free air sniff" by a German shepherd named Aldo at a traffic stop. The dog's efforts led to the discovery of methamphetamine ingredients in the back of a truck. The defendant claimed that Aldo, who did not have an extensive record of finding illegal drugs, was an unreliable source of probable cause.

The Court disagreed, ruling that the possibility of a dog making a mistake is not enough to overcome probable cause when the animal correctly leads its handler to hidden contraband.[7] (CAREER TIP: Law enforcement dogs provide invaluable services other than sniffing out illegal narcotics, such as detecting bombs, mines, and missing persons. These animals

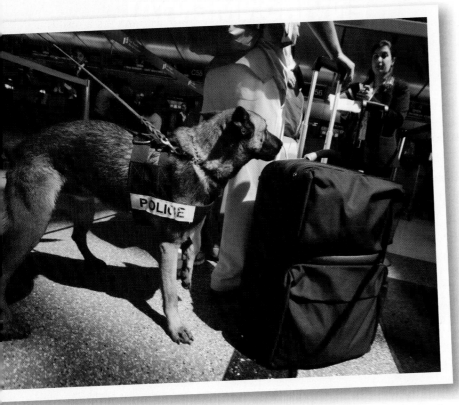

Why are police dogs important sources of probable cause when it comes to contraband hidden in a suitcase at an airport? Why is it reasonable for police to rely on a dog's sense of smell?

AP Photo/Reed Saxon

are prepared for their law enforcement duties by *K-9 [canine] trainers.*)

THE PROBABLE CAUSE FRAMEWORK In a sense, the concept of probable cause allows police officers to do their job effectively. Most arrests are made without a warrant because most arrests are the result of quick police reaction to the commission of a crime. Indeed, it would not be practical to expect a police officer to obtain a warrant before making an arrest on the street. Thus, probable cause provides a framework that limits the situations in which police officers can make arrests, but also gives officers the freedom to act within that framework. In 2003, the Supreme Court reaffirmed this freedom by ruling that Baltimore (Maryland) police officers acted properly when they arrested all three passengers of a car in which cocaine had been hidden in the back seat. "A reasonable officer," wrote Chief Justice William H. Rehnquist, "could conclude that there was probable cause to believe" that the defendant, who had

been sitting in the front seat, was in "possession" of the illicit drug despite his protestations to the contrary.[8]

Once an arrest is made, the arresting officer must prove to a judge that probable cause existed. In *County of Riverside v. McLaughlin* (1991),[9] the Supreme Court ruled that this judicial determination of probable cause must be made within forty-eight hours after the arrest, even if this two-day period includes a weekend or holiday. (**CAREER TIP:** Once a suspect is arrested, he or she is subject to standard booking procedure, which includes providing personal information, being photographed, and being fingerprinted. This process is overseen by a *booking technician,* who may or may not be a sworn police officer.)

6-1c
The Exclusionary Rule

Historically, the courts interpreted the Fourth Amendment for guidance in regulating the activity of law enforcement officers, as the language of the Constitution does not expressly do so. The courts' most potent legal tool in this endeavor is the **exclusionary rule,** which prohibits the use of illegally seized evidence. According to this rule, any evidence obtained by an unreasonable search or seizure is inadmissible (may not be used) against a defendant in a criminal trial.[10] Even highly incriminating evidence, such as a knife stained with the victim's blood, usually cannot be introduced at a trial if illegally obtained. Furthermore, any physical or verbal evidence police are able to acquire by using illegally obtained evidence is known as the **fruit of the poisoned tree** and is also inadmissible. For example, if the police use the existence of the bloodstained knife to get a confession out of a suspect, that confession will be excluded as well.

Exclusionary Rule A rule under which any evidence that is obtained in violation of the accused's rights, as well as any evidence derived from illegally obtained evidence, will not be admissible in criminal court.

Fruit of the Poisoned Tree Evidence that is acquired through the use of illegally obtained evidence and is therefore inadmissible in court.

One of the implications of the exclusionary rule is that it forces police to gather evidence properly. If they follow appropriate procedures, they are more likely to be rewarded with a conviction. If they are careless or abuse the rights of the suspect, they are unlikely to get a conviction. A strict application of the exclusionary rule, therefore, will permit guilty people to go free because of police carelessness or innocent errors. In practice, relatively few apparently guilty suspects benefit from the exclusionary rule. Research shows that about 3 percent of felony arrestees avoid incarceration because of improper police searches and seizures.[11]

THE "INEVITABLE DISCOVERY" EXCEPTION

Critics of the exclusionary rule maintain that, regardless of statistics, the rule hampers the police's ability to gather evidence and causes prosecutors to release numerous suspects before their cases make it to court. Several Supreme Court decisions have mirrored this view and provided exceptions to the exclusionary rule.

The **"inevitable discovery" exception** was established in the wake of the disappearance of ten-year-old Pamela Powers of Des Moines, Iowa, on Christmas Eve, 1968. The primary suspect in the case, a religious fanatic named Robert Williams, was tricked by a detective into leading police to the site where he had buried Powers. The detective convinced Williams that if he did not lead police to the body, he would soon forget where it was buried. This would deny his victim a "Christian burial." Initially, in *Brewer v. Williams* (1977),[12] the Court ruled that the evidence (Powers's body) had been obtained illegally because Williams's attorney had not been present during the interrogation that led to his admission. Several years later, in *Nix v. Williams* (1984),[13] the Court reversed itself, ruling that the evidence was admissible because the body would have eventually ("inevitably") been found by lawful means.

THE "GOOD FAITH" EXCEPTION

The scope of the exclusionary rule has been further diminished by two cases involving faulty warrants. In the first, *United States v. Leon* (1984),[14] the police seized evidence on authority of a search warrant that had been improperly issued by a judge. In the second, *Arizona v. Evans* (1995),[15] due to a computer error, a police officer detained Isaac Evans on the mistaken belief that he was subject to an arrest warrant. As a result, the officer found a marijuana cigarette on Evans's person and, after a search of his car, discovered a bag of marijuana.

In both cases, the Court allowed the evidence to stand under a **"good faith" exception** to the exclusionary rule. Under this exception, evidence acquired by a police officer using a technically invalid warrant is admissible if the officer was unaware of the error. In these two cases, the Court said that the officers acted in "good faith." By the same token, if police officers use a search warrant that they know to be technically incorrect, the good faith exception does not apply, and the evidence can be suppressed.

6-2
what ARE THE RULES FOR SEARCHES AND SEIZURES?

How far can law enforcement agents go in searching and seizing private property? Consider the steps taken by Jenny Stracner, an investigator with the Laguna Beach (California) Police Department. After receiving information that a suspect, Greenwood, was engaged in drug trafficking, Stracner enlisted the aid of the local trash collector in procuring evidence. Instead of taking Greenwood's trash bags to be incinerated, the collector agreed to give them to Stracner. The officer found enough drug paraphernalia in the garbage to obtain a warrant to search the suspect's home. Subsequently, Greenwood was arrested and convicted on narcotics charges.[16]

Remember, the Fourth Amendment is quite specific in forbidding unreasonable searches and seizures. Were Stracner's search of Greenwood's garbage and her seizure of its contents "reasonable"? The Supreme Court thought so, holding that Greenwood's garbage was not protected by the Fourth Amendment.[17]

"Inevitable Discovery" Exception The legal principle that illegally obtained evidence can be admissible in court if police using lawful means would have "inevitably" discovered it.

"Good Faith" Exception The legal principle that evidence obtained with the use of a technically invalid search warrant is admissible during trial if the police acted in good faith when they sought the warrant from a judge.

The Role of Privacy in Searches

A crucial concept in understanding search and seizure law is *privacy*. By definition, a **search** is a governmental intrusion on a citizen's reasonable expectation of privacy. The recognized standard for a "reasonable expectation of privacy" was established in *Katz v. United States* (1967).[18] The case dealt with the question of whether the defendant was justified in his expectation of privacy in the calls he made from a public phone booth. The Supreme Court held that "the Fourth Amendment protects people, not places," and Katz prevailed.

In his concurring opinion, Justice John Harlan, Jr., set a two-pronged test for a person's expectation of privacy:

1. The individual must prove that she or he expected privacy, and

2. Society must recognize that expectation as reasonable.[19]

Accordingly, the Court agreed with Katz's claim that he had a reasonable right to privacy in a public phone booth. Even though the phone booth was a public place, accessible to anyone, Katz had taken clear steps to protect his privacy.

Despite the *Katz* ruling, simply taking steps to protect one's privacy is not enough to protect against law enforcement intrusion. The steps must be reasonably certain to ensure privacy. If a person is unreasonable or mistaken in expecting privacy, he or she may forfeit that expectation. For instance, in *California v. Greenwood* (1988),[20] described above, the Court did not believe that the suspect had a reasonable expectation of privacy when it came to his garbage bags. The Court noted that when we place

our trash on a curb, we expose it to any number of intrusions by "animals, children, scavengers, snoops, and other members of the public."[21] In other words, if Greenwood had truly intended for the contents of his garbage bags to remain private, he would not have left them on the side of the road.

Search The process by which police examine a person or property to find evidence that will be used to prove guilt in a criminal trial.

Search Warrant A written order, based on probable cause and issued by a judge or magistrate, commanding that police officers or criminal investigators search a specific person, place, or property to obtain evidence.

Affidavit A written statement of facts, confirmed by the oath or affirmation of the party making it and made before a person having the authority to administer the oath or affirmation.

CAREER TIP: If you are interested in working abroad, the United Nation posts *international police officers* in countries with weak law enforcement systems or those recovering from national disasters or military conflicts.

Search and Seizure Warrants

To protect against charges that they have unreasonably infringed on privacy rights during a search, law enforcement officers can obtain a **search warrant**. A search warrant is a court order that authorizes police to search a certain area. Before a judge or magistrate will issue a search warrant, law enforcement officers must provide:

- Information showing probable cause that a crime has been or will be committed.
- Specific information on the premises to be searched, the suspects to be found and the illegal activities taking place at those premises, and the items to be seized.

The purpose of a search warrant is to establish, before the search takes place, that a *probable cause to search* justifies infringing on the suspect's reasonable expectation of privacy.

PARTICULARITY OF SEARCH WARRANTS The members of the First Congress specifically did not want law enforcement officers to have the freedom to make "general, exploratory" searches through a person's belongings.[22] Consequently, the Fourth Amendment requires that a warrant describe with "particularity" the place to be searched and the things—either people or objects—to be seized.

This "particularity" requirement places a heavy burden on law enforcement officers. Before going to a judge to ask for a search warrant, they must prepare an **affidavit** in which they provide specific, written information on the property that they wish to search and seize. They must know the specific address of any place they wish to search. General addresses of apartment buildings or office complexes are not sufficient. Furthermore, courts generally frown on vague descriptions of goods to be seized. For example, several years ago, a federal court ruled that a warrant permitting police to search a home for "all handguns, shotguns and rifles" and "evidence showing street gang membership" was too broad. As a result, the seizure of a shotgun was disallowed for lack of a valid search warrant.[23]

A **seizure** is the act of taking possession of a person or property by the government because of a (suspected) violation of the law. In general, four categories of items can be seized by use of a search warrant:

1. Items resulting from the crime, such as stolen goods.
2. Items that are inherently illegal for anybody to possess (with certain exceptions), such as narcotics and counterfeit currency.
3. Items that can be called "evidence" of the crime, such as a bloodstained sneaker or a ski mask.
4. Items used in committing the crime, such as an ice pick or a printing press used to make counterfeit bills.[24]

See Figure 6.1 below for an example of a search warrant.

FIGURE 6.1 Example of a Search Warrant

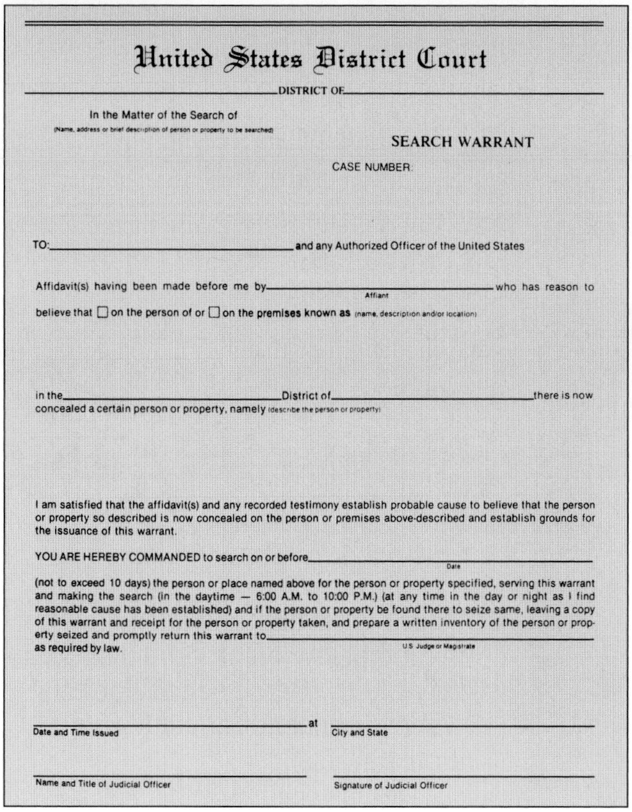
United States District Court

________ DISTRICT OF ________

In the Matter of the Search of
(Name, address or brief description of person or property to be searched)

SEARCH WARRANT

CASE NUMBER:

TO: ________ and any Authorized Officer of the United States

Affidavit(s) having been made before me by ________ (Affiant) who has reason to believe that ☐ on the person of or ☐ on the premises known as (name, description and/or location)

in the ________ District of ________ there is now concealed a certain person or property, namely (describe the person or property)

I am satisfied that the affidavit(s) and any recorded testimony establish probable cause to believe that the person or property so described is now concealed on the person or premises above-described and establish grounds for the issuance of this warrant.

YOU ARE HEREBY COMMANDED to search on or before ________ (Date)

(not to exceed 10 days) the person or place named above for the person or property specified, serving this warrant and making the search (in the daytime — 6:00 A.M. to 10:00 P.M.) (at any time in the day or night as I find reasonable cause has been established) and if the person or property be found there to seize same, leaving a copy of this warrant and receipt for the person or property taken, and prepare a written inventory of the person or property seized and promptly return this warrant to ________ (U.S. Judge or Magistrate) as required by law.

________ Date and Time Issued at ________ City and State

________ Name and Title of Judicial Officer

________ Signature of Judicial Officer

REASONABLENESS DURING A SEARCH AND SEIZURE No matter how "particular" a warrant is, it cannot provide for all the conditions that are bound to come up during its service. Consequently, the law gives law enforcement officers the ability to act "reasonably" during a search and seizure in the event of unforeseeable circumstances. For example, if a police officer is searching an apartment for a stolen MacBook Pro laptop computer and notices a vial of crack cocaine sitting on the suspect's bed, that contraband is considered to be in "plain view" and can be seized.

Note that if law enforcement officers have a search warrant that authorizes them to search for a stolen laptop computer, they would not be justified in opening small drawers. Because a computer could not fit in a small drawer, an officer would not have a basis for reasonably searching one. Hence, officers are restricted in terms of where they can look by the items they are searching for.

6-2c Searches and Seizures without a Warrant

Although the Supreme Court has established the principle that searches conducted without warrants are *per se* (by definition) unreasonable, it has set "specifically established" exceptions to the rule.[25] In fact, most searches take place in the absence of a judicial order. Warrantless searches and seizures can be lawful when police are in "hot pursuit" of a subject or when they search bags of trash left at the curb for regular collection. Because of the magnitude of smuggling activities in "border areas" such as airports, seaports, and international boundaries, a warrant normally is not needed to search property in those places.

Furthermore, in 2006 the Court held unanimously that police officers do not need a warrant to enter a private home in an emergency, such as when they reasonably fear for the safety of the inhabitants.[26] The two most important circumstances in which a warrant is not needed, though, are (1) searches incidental to an arrest and (2) consent searches.

2 LO

Seizure The forcible taking of a person or property in response to a violation of the law.

SEARCHES INCIDENTAL TO AN ARREST The most frequent exception to the warrant requirement involves **searches incidental to arrests,** so called because nearly every time police officers make an arrest (a procedure discussed in detail later in the chapter), they also search the suspect. As long as the original arrest was based on probable cause, these searches are valid for two reasons, established by the Supreme Court in *United States v. Robinson* (1973):

1. The need for a police officer to find and confiscate any weapons a suspect may be carrying.

2. The need to protect any evidence on the suspect's person from being destroyed.[27]

Law enforcement officers are, however, limited in the searches they may make during an arrest. These limits were established by the Supreme Court in *Chimel v. California* (1969).[28] In that case, police arrived at Chimel's home with an arrest warrant but not a search warrant. Even though Chimel refused their request to "look around," the officers searched the entire three-bedroom house for nearly an hour, finding stolen coins in the process. Chimel was convicted of burglary and appealed, arguing that the evidence of the coins should have been suppressed.

The Supreme Court held that the search was unreasonable. In doing so, the Court established guidelines as to the acceptable extent of searches incidental to an arrest. Primarily, the Court ruled that police may search any area within the suspect's "immediate control" to confiscate any weapons or evidence that the suspect could destroy. The Court found, however, that there was no justification

> for routinely searching rooms other than that in which the arrest occurs—or, for that matter, for searching through all desk drawers or other closed or concealed areas in that room itself. Such searches, in the absence of well-recognized exceptions, may be made only under the authority of a search warrant.[29]

The exact interpretation of the "area within immediate control" has been left to individual courts, but in general it has been taken to mean the area within the reach of the arrested person. Thus, the Court is said to have established the "arm's reach doctrine" in its *Chimel* decision.

SEARCHES WITH CONSENT **Consent searches,** the second most common type of warrantless searches, take place when individuals voluntarily give law enforcement officers permission to search their persons, homes, or belongings. The most relevant factors in determining whether consent is voluntary are

1. The age, intelligence, and physical condition of the consenting suspect;

2. Any coercive behavior by the police, such as the language used to request consent; and

3. The length of the questioning and its location.[30]

Searches Incidental to Arrests Searches for weapons and evidence that are conducted on persons who have just been arrested.

Consent Searches Searches by police that are made after the subject of the search has agreed to the action. In these situations, consent, if given of free will, validates a warrantless search.

Under what circumstances do you think that law enforcement should be able to search school lockers without consent from students or their parents?

AP Photo/*The Citizens' Voice*, Kristen Mullen

If a court finds that a person has been physically threatened or otherwise coerced into giving consent, the search is invalid.[31] Furthermore, the search consented to must be reasonable. Several years ago, the North Carolina Supreme Court invalidated a consent search that turned up a packet of cocaine. As part of this search, the police had pulled down the suspect's underwear and shone a flashlight on his groin. The court ruled that a reasonable person in the defendant's position would not consent to such an intrusive examination.[32]

6-2d
Searches of Automobiles

In *Carroll v. United States* (1925),[33] the Supreme Court ruled that the law could distinguish among automobiles, homes, and persons in questions involving police searches. In the years since its *Carroll* decision, the Court has established that the Fourth Amendment does not require police to obtain a warrant to search automobiles or other movable vehicles when they have probable cause to believe that a vehicle contains contraband or evidence of criminal activity.[34]

The reasoning behind such leniency is straightforward: requiring a warrant to search an automobile places too heavy a burden on police officers. By the time the officers could communicate with a judge and obtain the warrant, the suspects could have driven away and destroyed any evidence. Consequently, the Court has consistently held that someone in a vehicle does not have the same reasonable expectation of privacy as someone at home or even in a phone booth.

WARRANTLESS SEARCHES OF AUTOMOBILES
For nearly three decades, police officers believed that if they lawfully arrested the driver of a car, they could legally make a warrantless search of the car's entire front and back compartments. This understanding was based on the Supreme Court's ruling in *New York v. Benton* (1981),[35] which seemed to allow this expansive interpretation of the "area within immediate control" with regard to automobiles.

In *Arizona v. Gant* (2009), however, the Court announced that its *Benton* decision had been misinterpreted. Such warrantless searches are allowed only if (1) the person being arrested is close enough to the car to grab or destroy evidence or a weapon inside the car or (2) the arresting officer reasonably believes that the car contains evidence pertinent to the same crime for which the arrest took place.[36] So, for example, police will no longer be able to search an automobile for contraband if the driver has been arrested for failing to pay previous speeding tickets—unless the officer reasonably believes the suspect has the ability to reach and destroy any such contraband.

SIGNIFICANT POWERS
As you can imagine, the law enforcement community reacted negatively to the new restrictions outlined in the *Gant* decision.[37] Police officers, however, still can conduct a warrantless search of an automobile based on circumstances other than the incidental-to-an-arrest doctrine. These circumstances include probable cause of criminal activity, consent of the driver, and "protective searches" to search for weapons if police officers have a reasonable suspicion that such weapons exist.[38]

In addition, an officer may order passengers as well as the driver out of a car during a traffic stop. The Court has reasoned that the danger to an officer is increased when there is a passenger in the automobile.[39] (**CAREER TIP:** There is some debate as to whether taking blood from a possible drunk driver constitutes a search under the Fourth Amendment. In many jurisdictions, only a licensed *phlebotomist*—not a police officer—is authorized to draw blood from a person suspected of driving under the influence.)

PRETEXTUAL STOPS
Law enforcement agents also have a great deal of leeway regarding automobile stops. Crucially, as long as an officer has probable cause to believe that a traffic law has been broken, her or his "true" motivation for making a stop is irrelevant.[40] So, even if the police officer does not have a legally sufficient reason to search for evidence of a crime such as drug trafficking, the officer can use a minor traffic violation to pull over the car and investigate his or her "hunch." (To learn more about such "pretextual stops," see the feature *You Be the Judge—A Valid Pretext?* on the next page.)

6-2e
The Plain View Doctrine

As we have already seen several times in this chapter, the Constitution, as interpreted by our courts, provides very little protection to evidence in *plain view*.

A VALID PRETEXT?

THE SITUATION Officers Soto and Littlejohn are patrolling a "high drug area" of Washington, D.C., in an unmarked car. They become suspicious of a truck with temporary plates being driven slowly by Michael, a young African American. The officers follow the truck, and when Michael fails to signal while making a right turn, they pull him over for a traffic violation. During the traffic stop, the officers legally notice two large bags of crack cocaine in Michael's possession and arrest him on drug charges. Michael's lawyers claim that the police officers had no probable cause that Michael was carrying drugs, and that the evidence against their client should be suppressed under the exclusionary rule (discussed earlier in the chapter).

THE LAW As far as Fourth Amendment law is concerned, any subjective reasons that a police officer might have for stopping a suspect, including any motives based on racial stereotyping or bias,

Gina Sanders/Shutterstock

are irrelevant. As long as the officer has objective probable cause to believe a traffic violation or other wrongdoing has occurred, the stop is valid.

YOUR DECISION During Michael's trial, Soto is asked whether the "real" reasons for stopping the truck were that it had temporary plates, its driver was African American, and it was moving slowly in an area known for drug dealing. His answer convinces you that, in fact, the traffic violation was a pretext for the police officers' decision to stop Michael's car in the hope that he was carrying illegal drugs. There is no question, however, that Michael did fail to signal while making a right turn. Do you think the evidence against Michael should be allowed in court?

[To see how the United States Supreme Court ruled in a similar situation, go to Example 6.1 in Appendix A.]

For example, suppose a traffic officer pulls over a person for speeding, looks in the driver's side window, and clearly sees what appears to be a bag of heroin resting on the passenger seat. In this instance, under the **plain view doctrine,** the officer would be justified in seizing the drugs without a warrant.

The plain view doctrine was first enunciated by the Supreme Court in *Coolidge v. New Hampshire* (1971).[41] The Court ruled that law enforcement officers may make a warrantless seizure of an item if four criteria are met:

1. The item is positioned so as to be detected easily by an officer's sight or some other sense.

2. The officer is legally in a position to notice the item in question.

3. The discovery of the item is inadvertent. That is, the officer had not intended to find the item.

4. The officer immediately recognizes the illegal nature of the item.

Plain View Doctrine The legal principle that objects in plain view of a law enforcement agent who has the right to be in a position to have that view may be seized without a warrant and introduced as evidence.

Electronic Surveillance The use of electronic equipment by law enforcement agents to record private conversations or observe conduct that is meant to be private.

No interrogation or further investigation is allowed under the plain view doctrine.

6-2f
Electronic Surveillance

During the course of a criminal investigation, law enforcement officers may decide to use **electronic surveillance,** or electronic devices such as wiretaps or hidden microphones ("bugs"), to monitor and record conversations, observe movements, and trace or record telephone calls.

BASIC RULES: CONSENT AND PROBABLE CAUSE Given the invasiveness of electronic surveillance, the Supreme Court has generally held that the practice is prohibited by the Fourth Amendment. In *Burger v. New York* (1967),[42] however, the Court ruled that it was permissible under certain circumstances. That same year, *Katz v. United States* (discussed earlier in the chapter) established that recorded conversations are inadmissible as evidence unless certain procedures are followed.

In general, law enforcement officers can use electronic surveillance only if consent is given by one of the parties to be monitored, or, in the absence of

New York City police officers search a limousine for explosives at a checkpoint set up in response to a credible terrorist threat. If the officers found a stack of counterfeit one hundred dollar bills during this search, would the plain view doctrine allow the seizure of the fake cash? Why or why not?

Justin Sullivan/Getty Images

such consent, with a warrant.[43] For the warrant to be valid, it must:

1. Detail with "particularity" the conversations that are to be overheard.

2. Name the suspects and the places that will be under surveillance.

3. Show probable cause to believe that a specific crime has been or will be committed.[44]

Once the specific information has been gathered, the law enforcement officers must end the electronic surveillance immediately.[45] In any case, the surveillance cannot last more than thirty days without a judicial extension. (**CAREER TIP:** *Electronic surveillance officers carry out court-approved intercepts by hooking up the necessary equipment and listening in on the wiretap. These experts then pass on all pertinent information to the investigating officers.*)

FORCE MULTIPLYING Pervasive forms of electronic surveillance are allowed under the theory that people who are in public places have no reasonable expectation of privacy.[46] For example, many Americans would be surprised to learn how often they are under the watchful eye of law enforcement via closed-circuit television (CCTV) cameras. CCTV surveillance relies on strategically placed video cameras to record and transmit all activity in a targeted area, such as on a public street or in a government building. The images are monitored in real time so that law enforcement personnel can investigate any suspicious or criminal activity captured by the cameras.

CCTV is an example of a *force multiplier*, so called because this form of electronic surveillance allows

laws enforcement agencies to expand their capabilities without a significant increase in personnel. Speaking of CCTV, Brian Harvey, a deputy chief with the Dallas Police Department, says, "One camera operator can cover a lot more area than field officers can."[47]

6-2g

Homeland Security and the Fourth Amendment

Passed in the wake of the September 11, 2001, terrorist attacks, the Patriot Act (discussed in Chapter 1) has generally made it easier for law enforcement agents to conduct searches. For example, to search a suspect's apartment and examine the contents of his or her computer, agents previously needed a warrant based on probable cause that a crime had taken place or was about to take place. The Patriot Act amends the law to allow the Federal Bureau of Investigation (FBI) or other federal agencies to obtain warrants for "terrorism" investigations, "chemical weapons" investigations, or "computer fraud and abuse" investigations as long as agents can prove that such actions have a "significant purpose."[48] In other words, no proof of criminal activity need be provided.

THE PATRIOT ACT AND SURVEILLANCE The Patriot Act also gives law enforcement agents more leeway when conducting surveillance. The Foreign

AN increasingly popular force multiplier involves computerized infrared cameras that take digital photos of license plates. Usually mounted on police cars, these automatic license-plate recognition (ALPR) devices convert the images to text. Then the numbers are instantly checked against databases that contain records of the license plates of stolen cars and automobiles driven by a wide variety of targets, from wanted felons to citizens with unpaid parking tickets. In heavy-traffic areas, ALPR units can check thousands of license plates each hour. After adding ALPR technology to cameras mounted on just two patrol cars, police in Columbia, Missouri, used the system to make fifty arrests in three months. "It allows us to do our job better and more efficiently," says Columbia police lieutenant Brian Richenberger.

Suzanne Kreiter/The Boston Globe via Getty Images

THINKING ABOUT AUTOMATIC LICENSE PLATE RECOGNITION

How might law enforcement use ALPR not only to identify "hot" license plates but also as part of ongoing criminal investigations? For example, how might narcotics officers on a stakeout of a suspected drug dealer's house take advantage of ALPR technology?

Intelligence Surveillance Act of 1978 (FISA) allowed for surveillance of a suspect without a warrant as long as the "primary purpose" of the surveillance was to investigate foreign spying and not to engage in criminal law enforcement.[49] The Patriot Act amends FISA to allow for searches and surveillance if a "significant purpose" of the investigation is intelligence gathering or any other type of anti-terrorist strategy.[50] The statute also provides federal agents with "roving surveillance authority," allowing them to continue monitoring a terrorist suspect on the strength of the original warrant even if the suspect moves to an area outside the control of the court that issued the warrant.[51]

CONGRESS AND WIRETAPPING Following a series of controversies concerning the ability of the National Security Agency (NSA) to wiretap telephone and e-mail communications of terrorism suspects, in 2008 Congress passed an amended version of FISA.[52] The revised law allows the NSA to wiretap for seven days, without a court order, any person "reasonably believed" to be outside the United States, if the surveillance is necessary to protect national security. It also permits the wiretapping of Americans for seven days without a court order, if federal officials have probable cause to believe that the target is linked to terrorism. Supporters of the amendments claim that the average American has nothing to fear from the law "unless you have al Qaeda on your speed dial." Critics, however, see it as a further erosion of Fourth Amendment protections in the name of homeland security.[53]

SOCIAL MEDIA AND CJ

To learn more about online privacy issues, go to the home page of the **Electronic Privacy Information Center (EPIC)** and click on the Facebook icon. You'll see posts by EPIC staff members and other parties interested in the subject.

6-3

when CAN POLICE STOP AND FRISK SUSPECTS?

Several years ago, an Indianapolis (Indiana) police officer was patrolling a high-crime neighborhood when he saw a bicycle sitting next to a car in a gas station parking lot. The officer watched as Michael Woodson got out of the car, put on a backpack, and began to cycle away. After stopping Woodson, the officer searched the backpack, finding more than thirty contraband DVDs. Woodson challenged his eventual conviction on two charges of fraud, claiming that the police officer had no good reason to stop him in the first place.

A three-judge Indiana appeals panel agreed and overturned Woodson's conviction. The panel rejected the argument that, given the setting and Woodson's behavior, the police officer was justified in thinking that a drug deal was taking place. That is, no *reasonable suspicion* existed that a crime had been committed in the gas station parking lot.[54] When such reasonable suspicion does exist, police officers are well within their rights to *stop and frisk* a suspect. In a stop and frisk, law enforcement officers (1) briefly detain a person they reasonably believe to be suspicious, and (2) if they believe the person to be armed, proceed to pat down, or "frisk," that person's outer clothing.[55]

6-3a

The Elusive Definition of Reasonable Suspicion

Like so many elements of police work, the decision of whether to stop a suspect is based on the balancing of conflicting priorities. On the one hand, a police officer feels a sense of urgency to act when he or she believes that criminal activity is occurring or is about to occur. On the other hand, law enforcement agents do not want to harass innocent individuals, especially if doing so runs afoul of the U.S. Constitution. In stop-and-frisk law, this balancing act rests on the fulcrum of reasonable suspicion.

 TERRY V. OHIO The precedent for the ever-elusive definition of a "reasonable" suspicion

in stop-and-frisk situations was established in *Terry v. Ohio* (1968).[56] In that case, a detective named McFadden observed two men (one of whom was Terry) acting strangely in downtown Cleveland. The men would walk past a certain store, peer into the window, and then stop at a street corner and confer. While they were talking, another man joined the conversation and then left quickly. Several minutes later the three men met again at another corner a few blocks away. Detective McFadden believed the trio was planning to break into the store. He approached them, told them who he was, and asked for identification. After receiving a mumbled response, the detective frisked the three men and found handguns on two of them, who were tried and convicted of carrying concealed weapons.

The Supreme Court upheld the conviction, ruling that Detective McFadden had reasonable cause to believe that the men were armed and dangerous and that swift action was necessary to protect himself and other citizens in the area.[57] The Court accepted McFadden's interpretation of the unfolding scene as based on objective facts and practical conclusions. It therefore concluded that his suspicion was reasonable. In contrast, in the case described above, the Indianapolis police officer's grounds for stopping Michael Woodson—activity that looked like an illegal drug deal in a part of town where such activity is common—were not seen by the Indiana appeals court as reasonable.

THE "TOTALITY OF THE CIRCUMSTANCES" TEST For the most part, the judicial system has refrained from placing restrictions on police officers' ability to make stops. In the *Terry* case, the Supreme Court did say that an officer must have "specific and articulable facts" to support the decision to make a stop, but added that the facts may be "taken together with rational inferences."[58] The Court has consistently ruled that because of their practical experience, law enforcement agents are in a unique position to make such inferences and should be given a good deal of freedom in doing so.

In the years since the *Terry* case was decided, the Court has settled on a "totality of the circumstances" test to determine whether a stop is based on reasonable suspicion.[59] In 2002, for example, the

Court ruled that a U.S. Border Patrol agent's stop of a minivan in Arizona was reasonable.[60] On being approached by the Border Patrol car, the driver had stiffened, slowed down his van, and avoided making eye contact with the agent. Furthermore, the children in the van waved at the officer in a mechanical manner, as if ordered to do so. The agent pulled over the van and found 128 pounds of marijuana.

In his opinion, Chief Justice William Rehnquist pointed out that such conduct might have been unremarkable on a busy city highway, but on an unpaved road thirty miles from the Mexican border it was enough to reasonably arouse the agent's suspicion.[61] The justices also made clear that the need to prevent terrorist attacks is part of the "totality of the circumstances" and, therefore, law enforcement agents will have more leeway to make stops near U.S. borders.

6-3b
A Stop

The terms *stop* and *frisk* are often used in concert, but they describe two separate acts. A **stop** takes place when a law enforcement officer has reasonable suspicion that a criminal activity is about to take place.

Stop A brief detention of a person by law enforcement agents for questioning.

Frisk A pat-down or minimal search by police to discover weapons.

Because an investigatory stop is not an arrest, there are limits to the extent police can detain someone who has been stopped. For example, in one situation an airline traveler and his luggage were detained for ninety minutes while the police waited for a drug-sniffing dog to arrive. The Supreme Court ruled that the initial stop of the passenger was constitutional, but that the ninety-minute wait was excessive.[62]

In 2004, the Court held that police officers could require suspects to identify themselves during a stop that is otherwise valid under the *Terry* ruling.[63] The case involved a Nevada rancher who was fined $250 for refusing to give his name to a police officer investigating a possible assault. The defendant argued that such requests force citizens to incriminate themselves against their will, which is prohibited, as we shall see later in the chapter, by the Fifth Amendment. Justice Anthony Kennedy wrote, however, that "asking questions is an essential part of police investigations" that would be made much more difficult if officers could not determine the identity of a suspect.[64] The ruling validated "stop-and-identify" laws in twenty states and numerous cities and towns.

6-3c
A Frisk

The Supreme Court has stated that a **frisk** should be a protective measure. Police officers cannot conduct a frisk as a "fishing expedition" simply to try to find items besides weapons, such as illegal narcotics, on a suspect.[65] A frisk does not necessarily follow a stop and in fact may occur only when the officer is justified in thinking that the safety of police officers or other citizens may be endangered.

Again, the question of reasonable suspicion is at the heart of determining the legality of frisks. In the *Terry* case, the Court accepted that Detective McFadden reasonably believed that the three suspects posed a threat. The suspects' refusal to answer McFadden's questions, though within their rights because they had not been arrested, provided

A police officer frisks a suspect in San Francisco, California. What is the main purpose behind a frisk? When are police justified in frisking someone?

Mark Richards/PhotoEdit

him with sufficient motive for the frisk. In 2009, the Court extended the "stop and frisk" authority by ruling that a police officer could order a passenger in a car that had been pulled over for a traffic violation to submit to a pat-down.[66] To do so, the officer must have a reasonable suspicion that the suspect may be armed and dangerous.

6-4
what IS REQUIRED TO MAKE AN ARREST?

As happened in the *Terry* case discussed above, a stop and frisk may lead to an **arrest.** An arrest is the taking into custody of a citizen for the purpose of detaining him or her on a criminal charge. It is important to understand the difference between a stop and an arrest. In the eyes of the law, a stop is a relatively brief intrusion on a citizen's rights, whereas an arrest—which involves a deprivation of liberty—is deserving of a full range of constitutional protections (see Figure 6.2 below to better understand how a stop differs from an arrest). Consequently, while a stop can be made based on reasonable suspicion, a law enforcement officer needs probable cause, as defined earlier, to make an arrest.[67]

6-4a
Elements of an Arrest

When is somebody under arrest? The easy—and incorrect—answer would be whenever the police officer says so. In fact, the state of being under arrest is dependent not only on the actions of the law enforcement officers but also on the perception of the suspect. Suppose Mr. Smith is stopped by plainclothes detectives, driven to the police station, and detained for three hours for questioning. During this time, the police never tell Mr. Smith he is under arrest, and in fact, he is free to leave at any time. But if Mr. Smith or any other reasonable person *believes* he is not free to leave, then, according to the Supreme Court, that person is in fact under arrest and should receive the necessary constitutional protections.[68]

Criminal justice professor Rolando V. del Carmen of Sam Houston State University has identified four elements that must be present for an arrest to take place:

1. The *intent* to arrest. In a stop, though it may entail slight inconvenience and a short detention period, there is no intent on the part of the law enforcement officer to take the person into custody. Therefore,

4 LO

Arrest To take into custody a person suspected of criminal activity.

FIGURE 6.2 | **The Difference between a Stop and an Arrest**

Both stops and arrests are considered seizures because both police actions involve the restriction of an individual's freedom to "walk away." Both must be justified by a showing of reasonableness as well. You should be aware, however, of the differences between a stop and an arrest. **During a stop,** police can interrogate the person and make a limited search of his or her outer clothing. If anything occurs during the stop, such as the discovery of an illegal weapon, then officers may arrest the person. **If an arrest is made,** the suspect is now in police custody and is protected by the U.S. Constitution in a number of ways that will be discussed later in the chapter.

	STOP	ARREST
Justification	Reasonable suspicion only	Probable cause
Warrant	None	Required in some, but not all, situations
Intent of Officer	To investigate suspicious activity	To make a formal charge against the suspect
Search	May frisk, or "pat down," for weapons	May conduct a full search for weapons or evidence
Scope of Search	Outer clothing only	Area within the suspect's immediate control or "reach"

PhotoDisc

there is no arrest. As intent is a subjective term, it is sometimes difficult to determine whether the police officer intended to arrest. In situations when the intent is unclear, courts often rely—as in our hypothetical case of Mr. Smith—on the perception of the arrestee.[69]

2. The *authority* to arrest. State laws give police officers the authority to place citizens under custodial arrest, or take them into custody. Like other state laws, the authorization to arrest varies among the fifty states. Some states, for example, allow off-duty police officers to make arrests, while others do not.
3. *Seizure or detention.* A necessary part of an arrest is the detention of the subject. Detention is considered to have occurred as soon as the arrested individual submits to the control of the officer, whether peacefully or under the threat or use of force.
4. The *understanding* of the person that she or he has been arrested. Through either words—such as "you are now under arrest"—or actions, the person taken into custody must understand that an arrest has taken place. When a suspect has been forcibly subdued by the police, handcuffed, and placed in a patrol car, he or she is believed to understand that an arrest has been made. This understanding may be lacking if the person is intoxicated, insane, or unconscious.[70]

6-4b

Arrests with a Warrant

When law enforcement officers have established probable cause to arrest an individual who is not in police custody, they obtain an **arrest warrant** for that person. An arrest warrant, similar to a search warrant, contains information such as the name of the person suspected and the crime he or she is suspected of having committed. (See Figure 6.3 on the right for an example of an arrest warrant.) Judges or magistrates issue arrest warrants after first determining that the law enforcement officers have indeed established probable cause.

Arrest Warrant A written order, based on probable cause and issued by a judge or magistrate, commanding that the person named on the warrant be arrested by the police.

Exigent Circumstances Situations that require extralegal or exceptional actions by the police.

ENTERING A DWELLING There is a perception that an arrest warrant gives law enforcement officers the authority to enter a dwelling without first announcing themselves. This is not accurate. In *Wilson v. Arkansas* (1995),[71] the Supreme Court reiterated the common law requirement that police officers must knock and announce their identity and purpose before entering a dwelling. Under certain conditions, known as **exigent circumstances,** law enforcement officers need not announce themselves. As you saw at the beginning of the chapter, these circumstances include situations in which the officers have a reasonable belief of any of the following:

- The suspect is armed and poses a strong threat of violence to the officers or others inside the dwelling.
- Persons inside the dwelling are in the process of destroying evidence or escaping because of the presence of the police.
- A felony is being committed at the time the officers enter.[72]

FIGURE 6.3 Example of an Arrest Warrant

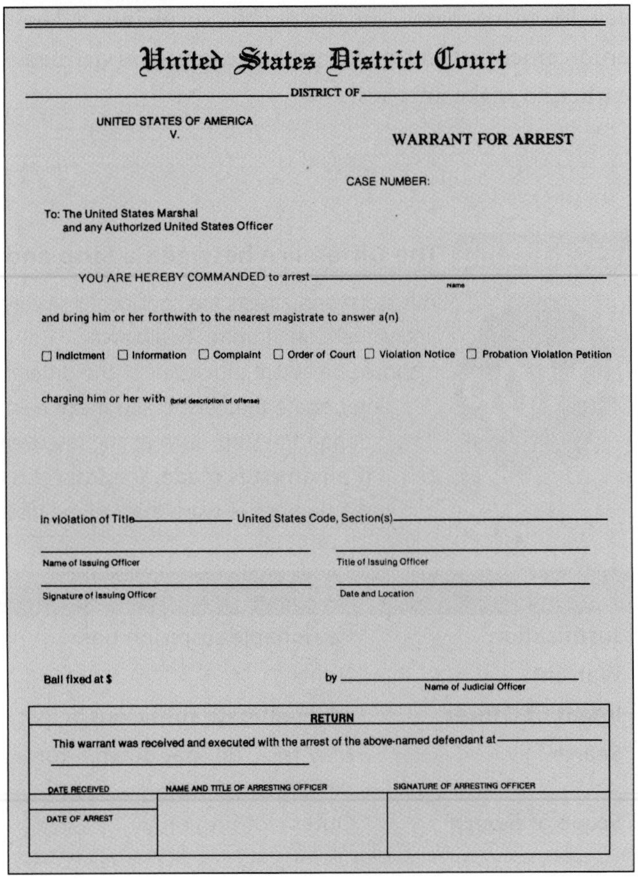
United States District Court

DISTRICT OF

UNITED STATES OF AMERICA
V.

WARRANT FOR ARREST

CASE NUMBER:

To: The United States Marshal
and any Authorized United States Officer

YOU ARE HEREBY COMMANDED to arrest
Name

and bring him or her forthwith to the nearest magistrate to answer a(n)

☐ Indictment ☐ Information ☐ Complaint ☐ Order of Court ☐ Violation Notice ☐ Probation Violation Petition

charging him or her with (brief description of offense)

In violation of Title United States Code, Section(s)

Name of Issuing Officer | Title of Issuing Officer

Signature of Issuing Officer | Date and Location

Bail fixed at $ by
Name of Judicial Officer

RETURN

This warrant was received and executed with the arrest of the above-named defendant at

DATE RECEIVED | NAME AND TITLE OF ARRESTING OFFICER | SIGNATURE OF ARRESTING OFFICER

DATE OF ARREST

THE WAITING PERIOD The Supreme Court severely weakened the practical impact of the "knock and announce" rule with its decision in *Hudson v. Michigan* (2006).[73] In that case, Detroit police did not knock before entering the defendant's home with a warrant. Instead, they announced themselves and then waited only three to five seconds before making their entrance, not the fifteen to twenty seconds suggested by a prior Court ruling.[74] Hudson argued that the drugs found during the subsequent search were inadmissible because the law enforcement agents did not follow proper procedure.

By a 5–4 margin, the Court disagreed. In his majority opinion, Justice Antonin Scalia stated that an improper "knock and announce" is not unreasonable enough to provide defendants with a "get-out-of-jail-free card" by disqualifying evidence uncovered on the basis of a valid search warrant.[75] Thus, the exclusionary rule, discussed earlier in this chapter, would no longer apply under such circumstances. Legal experts still advise, however, that police observe a reasonable waiting period after knocking and announcing to be certain that any evidence found during the subsequent search will stand up in court.[76]

6-4c
Arrests without a Warrant

Arrest warrants are not always required, and in fact, most arrests are made on the scene without a warrant. A law enforcement officer may make a **warrantless arrest** if:

1. The offense is committed in the presence of the officer; or
2. The officer has probable cause to believe that the suspect has committed a particular crime; or
3. The time lost in obtaining a warrant would allow the suspect to escape or destroy evidence, and the officer has probable cause to make an arrest.[77]

The type of crime also comes to bear in questions of arrests without a warrant. As a general rule, officers can make a warrantless arrest for a crime they did not see if they have probable cause to believe that a felony has been committed. For misdemeanors, the crime must have been committed in the presence of the officer for a warrantless arrest to be valid. According to a 2001 Supreme Court ruling, even an arrest for a misdemeanor that involves "gratuitous humiliations" imposed by a police officer "exercising extremely poor judgment" is valid as long as the officer can satisfy probable cause requirements.[78] That case involved a Texas mother who was handcuffed, taken away from her two young children, and placed in jail for failing to wear her seat bet.

what ARE THE MIRANDA RIGHTS?

After the Pledge of Allegiance, there is perhaps no recitation that comes more readily to the American mind than the *Miranda* warning:

> You have the right to remain silent. If you give up that right, anything you say can and will be used against you in a court of law. You have the right to speak with an attorney and to have the attorney present during questioning. If you so desire and cannot afford one, an attorney will be appointed for you without charge before questioning.

The *Miranda* warning is not a mere prop. It strongly affects one of the most important aspects of any criminal investigation—the **interrogation,** or questioning of a suspect from whom the police want to get information concerning a crime and perhaps a confession.

6-5a
The Legal Basis for *Miranda*

The Fifth Amendment guarantees protection against self-incrimination. In other words, as we shall see again in Chapter 8, a defendant cannot be required to provide information about his or her own criminal activity. A defendant's choice *not* to incriminate himself or herself cannot be interpreted as a sign of guilt by a jury in a criminal trial. A confession, or admission of guilt, is by definition a statement of self-incrimination. How, then, to reconcile the Fifth Amendment with the critical need of law enforcement officers to gain confessions? The answer lies in the

Warrantless Arrest An arrest made without first seeking a warrant for the action.

Interrogation The direct questioning of a suspect to gather evidence of criminal activity and to try to gain a confession.

concept of **coercion,** or the use of physical or psychological duress to obtain a confession.

THE *MIRANDA* CASE The Supreme Court first asserted that a confession could not be physically coerced in a 1936 case concerning a defendant who was beaten and whipped until he confessed to a murder.[79] It was not until 1966, however, that the Court handed down its landmark decision in *Miranda v. Arizona.*[80]

The case involved Ernesto Miranda, a produce worker who had been arrested three years earlier in Phoenix and charged with kidnapping and rape. Detectives questioned Miranda for two hours before gaining a confession of guilt. At no time was Miranda informed that he had a right to have a lawyer present. The Court overturned Miranda's conviction, stating that police interrogations are, by their very nature, coercive and therefore deny suspects their constitutional right against self-incrimination by "forcing" them to confess.

MIRANDA RIGHTS The concept of **Miranda rights,** established in this case, is based on what University of Columbia law professor H. Richard Uviller called *inherent coercion*. This terms refers to the assumption that even if a police officer does not lay a hand on a suspect, the general atmosphere of an interrogation is in and of itself coercive.[81]

Though the *Miranda* case is best remembered for the procedural requirement it spurred, at the time the Supreme Court was more concerned about the treatment of suspects during interrogation. The Court found that routine police interrogation strategies, such as leaving suspects alone in a room for several hours before questioning them, were inherently coercive. Therefore, the Court reasoned, every suspect needed protection from coercion, not just those who had been physically abused. The *Miranda* warning is a result of this need. In theory, if the warning is not given to a suspect before an interrogation, the fruits of that interrogation, including a confession, are invalid.

6-5b
When a *Miranda* Warning Is Required

As we shall see, a *Miranda* warning is not necessary under several conditions, such as when no questions are asked of the suspect. Generally, *Miranda* requirements apply only when a suspect is in **custody.** In a series of rulings since *Miranda,* the Supreme Court has defined custody as an arrest or a situation in which a reasonable person would not feel free to leave.[82] Consequently, a **custodial interrogation** occurs when a suspect is under arrest or is deprived of her or his freedom in a significant manner. Remember, a *Miranda* warning is only required before a custodial interrogation takes place. For example, if four police officers enter a suspect's bedroom at 4:00 A.M., wake him, and form a circle around him, then they must give him a *Miranda* warning before questioning. Even though the suspect has not been arrested, he will "not feel free to go where he please[s]."[83]

6-5c
When a *Miranda* Warning Is Not Required

A *Miranda* warning is not necessary in a number of situations:

1. When the police do not ask the suspect any questions that are *testimonial* in nature. Such questions are designed to elicit information that may be used against the suspect in court. Note that "routine booking questions," such as the suspect's name, address, height, and eye color, do not require a *Miranda* warning. Even though answering these questions may provide incriminating evidence (especially if the person answering is a prime suspect), the Supreme Court has held that they are absolutely necessary if the police are to do their jobs.[84] (Imagine the officer not being able to ask a suspect her or his name.)

5 LO

Coercion The use of physical force or mental intimidation to compel a person to do something—such as confess to committing a crime—against her or his will.

Miranda Rights The constitutional rights of accused persons taken into custody by law enforcement officials, such as the right to remain silent and the right to counsel.

Custody The forceful detention of a person, or the perception that a person is not free to leave the immediate vicinity.

Custodial Interrogation The questioning of a suspect after that person has been taken into custody. In this situation, the suspect must be read his or her *Miranda* rights before interrogation can begin.

CAREERPREP

DETECTIVE

JOB DESCRIPTION:

- Collect evidence and obtain facts pertaining to criminal cases.
- Conduct interviews, observe suspects, examine records, and help with raids and busts. Some detectives are assigned to multiagency task forces that deal with specific types of crime, like drug trafficking or gang activity.

WHAT KIND OF TRAINING IS REQUIRED?

- Two to five years of experience as a police officer are required before taking the test to become a detective.
- Larger departments require sixty units of college credit or an associate's degree.

ANNUAL SALARY RANGE?

- $43,920–$76,350

Karen Mower/iStockphoto.com

2. When the police have not focused on a suspect and are questioning witnesses at the scene of a crime.

3. When a person volunteers information before the police have asked a question.

4. When the suspect has given a private statement to a friend or some other acquaintance. *Miranda* does not apply to these statements so long as the government did not orchestrate the situation.

5. During a stop and frisk, when no arrest has been made.

6. During a traffic stop.[85]

In 1984, the Supreme Court also created a "public-safety exception" to the *Miranda* rule. The case involved a police officer who, after feeling an empty shoulder holster on a man he had just arrested, asked the suspect the location of the gun without informing him of his *Miranda* rights. The Court ruled that the gun was admissible as evidence because the police's duty to protect the public is more important than a suspect's *Miranda* rights.[86] In April 2013, federal law enforcement agents relied on this exception to question suspected Boston Marathon bomber Dzhokhar Tsarnaev from a hospital bed without first "Mirandizing" him. Once the agents were satisfied

that Tsarnaev knew of no other active plots or threats to public safety, they read the suspect his *Miranda* rights in the presence of a lawyer.[87]

WAIVING *MIRANDA* Suspects can *waive* their Fifth Amendment rights and speak to a police officer, but only if the waiver is made voluntarily. Silence on the part of a suspect does not mean that his or her *Miranda* protections have been relinquished. To waive their rights, suspects must state—either in writing or orally—that they understand those rights and that they will voluntarily answer questions without the presence of counsel.

To ensure that the suspect's rights are upheld, prosecutors are required to prove by a preponderance of the evidence that the suspect "knowing and intelligently" waived his or her *Miranda* rights.[88] To make the waiver perfectly clear, police will ask suspects two questions in addition to giving the *Miranda* warning:

1. Do you understand your rights as I have read them to you?

2. Knowing your rights, are you willing to talk to another law enforcement officer or me?

If the suspect indicates that she or he does not want to speak to the officer, thereby invoking her or his right to silence, the officer must *immediately* stop

What aspects of the situation shown in this photo indicate that the Aspen (Colorado) police officer is required to "Mirandize" the suspect before asking him any questions, even if the officer never formally places the suspect under arrest?

Photo by Chris Hondros/Getty Images

any questioning.[89] Similarly, if the suspect requests a lawyer, the police can ask no further questions until an attorney is present.[90]

CLEAR INTENT The suspect must be absolutely clear about her or his intention to stop the questioning or have a lawyer present. In *Davis v. United States* (1994),[91] the Supreme Court upheld the interrogation of a suspect after he said, "Maybe I should talk to a lawyer." The Court found that this statement was too ambiguous, saying that it did not want to force police officers to "read the minds" of suspects who make vague declarations. Along these same lines, in *Berghuis v. Thompkins* (2010),[92] the Court upheld the conviction of a suspect who implicated himself in a murder after remaining mostly silent during nearly three hours of police questioning. The defendant claimed that he had invoked his *Miranda* rights by being uncommunicative with the interrogating officers. The Court disagreed, saying that silence is not enough—a suspect must actually state that he or she wishes to cut off questioning for the *Miranda* protections to apply.

RECORDING CONFESSIONS "*Miranda* has become embedded in routine police practice to the point where the warnings have become part of our national culture," wrote Chief Justice William Rehnquist over a decade ago.[93] Nevertheless, the *Miranda* warning may eventually become obsolete. A relatively new trend in law enforcement has been for officers to record interrogations and confessions digitally. Video recording technology has progressed to the point where it is reasonable to ask law enforcement agents to carry a personal video camera with them at all times.[94] Indeed, as we saw in the previous chapter, many police agencies in the United States now use body-mounted video cameras that record all contacts with suspects.

One of the benefits of recording confessions in this manner would be to lessen suspicions that police officers use verbal techniques like accusation and confrontation to elicit false confessions. Such videos contain clear evidence of how an interview is carried out, and whether law enforcement agents have used improper means to gain the confession. In Texas, where false confessions have led at least seven innocent suspects to be wrongfully convicted in recent years, legislators are considering requiring video interrogations in all cases involving violent felonies.[95] Three states—Alaska, Illinois, and Minnesota—and hundreds of municipalities already regularly engage in this practice. Some scholars have suggested that recording all custodial interrogations would satisfy the Fifth Amendment's prohibition against coercion and thus render the *Miranda* warning unnecessary.

REVIEW

✔ **Review what you've read with the quiz below.**

Rip out the Chapter Review card at the back of this book, which includes:
- Chapter Summary and Learning Outcomes
- Key Terms

Or you can go online to CourseMate at www.cengagebrain.com to:
- Complete Practice Quizzes to prepare for tests.
- Review Key Terms Flash Cards (online or print).
- Play games to master concepts.

quiz

1. The Fourth Amendment has been interpreted to require _____ _____ that a crime has been or will be committed before a search warrant can be issued.

2. Judges rely on the _____ rule to keep evidence that has been improperly obtained by the police out of criminal courts.

3. A search is a government intrusion on the _____ of an individual.

4. Law enforcement agents do not need a judge's prior approval to conduct a search if the subject of the search gives her or his _____.

5. A police officer can "stop" a suspect if the officer has a _____ suspicion that a criminal act is taking place or is about to take place.

6. Following a stop, a police officer may _____ the suspect for weapons as a protective measure.

7. An arrest occurs when a law enforcement officer takes a suspect into _____ on a criminal charge.

8. If a police officer has prior knowledge of a suspect's criminal activity, he or she must obtain a _____ from a judge or magistrate before arresting the suspect.

9. In most instances, a *Miranda* warning must be read to a suspect _____ a custodial interrogation takes place.

10. A suspect can _____ her or his *Miranda* rights, but this must be done "knowingly and intentionally."

Answers can be found on the Chapter 6 Review card at the end of the book.

Spencer Platt/Getty Images

Learning **OUTCOMES** | *After studying this chapter, you will be able to . . .*

After you read the chapter, go to the Study Tools at the end of the chapter, page 159.

1 Define *jurisdiction* and contrast geographic and subject-matter jurisdiction.

2 Explain the difference between trial and appellate courts.

3 Explain briefly how a case is brought to the Supreme Court.

4 List the different names given to public prosecutors and indicate the general powers that they have.

5 Explain why defense attorneys must often defend clients they know to be guilty.

COURTS AND THE QUEST FOR JUSTICE

Dark Honeymoon

According to Gabe Watson, his wife Tina's drowning death was a tragic accident. According to Alabama prosecutors, he committed murder. The incident occurred when, eleven days after being married in October 2003, the couple decided to go scuba diving on Australia's Barrier Reef during their honeymoon. In Gabe's version of events, Tina, a novice diver, started to panic underwater. When he tried to save her, she accidentally dislodged his mask and regulator, forcing him to the surface without her. Prosecutors in Alabama countered that Gabe killed Tina to collect on a life insurance policy. He did so, they claimed, by turning off her air supply and holding her in a bear hug until she lost consciousness.

Originally charged with murder by Australian officials, Gabe pleaded guilty to manslaughter for not doing enough to save Tina from drowning. After spending eighteen months in an Australian prison, in 2010 he was sent back to Alabama to face similar charges in his and Tina's home state. If found guilty in an Alabama court, he could have been sentenced to a lifetime in prison. Jefferson County Circuit Judge Tommy Nail, however, was suspicious of the prosecution's arguments from the beginning of trial proceedings. The judge scoffed at Gabe's alleged financial motives, pointing out that the life insurance policy in question was remarkably modest. Furthermore, the only witness who saw Gabe and Tina together underwater testified that he thought Gabe was trying to save her life.

Although a jury had been selected to hear Gabe's murder trial, it never got the chance to find him guilty or innocent. On February 23, 2012, Nail, as was his judicial prerogative, ruled that there was no evidence that Gabe had committed the crime and dismissed the charges against him. "The only way to convict him of intentional murder is to speculate," Nail said. "'Nobody knows exactly what happened in the water." The judge's ruling shocked Tommy Thomas, Tina's father. "It should have gone to the jury for them to decide," he insisted.

Gabe Watson, left, confers with his lawyer in a Birmingham, Alabama, courtroom before Jefferson County Circuit Judge Tommy Nail dismissed charges that Watson had murdered his wife.

AP Photo/Dave Martin

what ROLE DO COURTS PLAY IN SOCIETY?

Following the dismissal of murder charges against Gabe Watson, his attorney said, "It has been a nightmare for Gabe and his family and a nightmare for Tina and her family. We all wanted justice."[1] Did each side get *justice* from the court system? Famed jurist Roscoe Pound once characterized "justice" as society's demand "that serious offenders be convicted and punished," while at the same time "the innocent and unfortunate are not oppressed."[2]

This somewhat idealistic definition obscures the fact that there are two sides to each court proceeding, and Gabe's and Tina's families certainly had different ideas of what would have been a just outcome to the Alabama case. On a more practical level, then, a court is a place where arguments are settled. At best, the court provides a just environment in which the basis of the argument can be decided through the application of the law.

Courts have extensive powers in our criminal justice system: they can bring the authority of the state to seize property and to restrict individual liberty. Given that the rights to own property and to enjoy personal freedom are enshrined in the U.S. Constitution, a court's *legitimacy* in taking such measures must be unquestioned by society. This legitimacy is based on two factors: impartiality and independence.[3] In theory, each party involved in a courtroom dispute must have an equal chance to present its case and must be secure in the belief that no outside factors are going to influence the decision rendered by the court. In reality, as we shall see over the next three chapters, it does not always work that way.

7-1a
Due Process and Crime Control in the Courts

As mentioned in Chapter 1, the criminal justice system has two sets of underlying values: due process and crime control. Due process values focus on protecting the rights of the individual, whereas crime control values stress the punishment and repression of criminal conduct. The competing nature of these two value systems is often evident in the nation's courts.

THE DUE PROCESS FUNCTION The primary concern of early American courts was to protect the rights of the individual against the power of the state. Memories of injustices suffered at the hands of the British monarchy were still strong, and most of the procedural rules that we have discussed in this textbook were created with the express purpose of giving the individual a "fair chance" against the government in any courtroom proceedings. Therefore, the due process function of the courts is to protect individuals from the unfair advantages that the government—with its immense resources—automatically enjoys in legal battles.

Seen in this light, constitutional guarantees

Why is it important that American criminal courtrooms, such as this one in Cape May, New Jersey, are places of impartiality and independence?

AP Photo/*The Press of Atlantic City*, Dale Gerhard

such as the right to counsel, the right to a jury trial, and protection from self-incrimination are equalizers in the "contest" between the state and the individual.

THE CRIME CONTROL FUNCTION Advocates of crime control distinguish between the court's obligation to be fair to the accused and its obligation to be fair to society. The crime control function of the courts emphasizes punishment and retribution—criminals must suffer for the harm done to society, and it is the courts' responsibility to see that they do so. Given this responsibility to protect the public, deter criminal behavior, and "get criminals off the streets," the courts should not be concerned solely with giving the accused a fair chance. Rather than using due process rules as "equalizers," the courts should use them as protection against blatantly unconstitutional acts.

For example, a detective who beats a suspect with a tire iron to get a confession has obviously infringed on the suspect's constitutional rights. If, however, the detective uses trickery to gain a confession, the court should allow the confession to stand because it is not in society's interest that law enforcement agents be deterred from outwitting criminals.

7-1b
The Rehabilitation Function

A third view of the court's responsibility is based on the "medical model" of the criminal justice system. In this model, criminals are analogous to patients, and the courts perform the role of physicians who dispense "treatment."[4] The criminal is seen as sick, not evil, and therefore treatment is morally justified. Of course, treatment varies from case to case, and some criminals require harsh penalties such as incarceration. In other cases, however, it may not be in society's best interest for the criminal to be punished according to the formal rules of the justice system. Perhaps the criminal can be rehabilitated to become a productive member of society and thus save taxpayers the costs of incarceration or other punishment.

7-1c
The Bureaucratic Function

To a certain extent, the crime control, due process, and rehabilitation functions of a court are secondary to its bureaucratic function. In general, a court may have the goal of protecting society or protecting the rights of the individual, but on a day-to-day basis that court has the more pressing task of dealing with the cases brought before it. Like any bureaucracy, a court is concerned with speed and efficiency, and loftier concepts such as justice can be secondary to a judge's need to wrap up a particular case before six o'clock so that administrative deadlines can be met. Indeed, many observers feel that the primary adversarial relationship in the courts is not between the two parties involved but between the ideal of justice and the reality of bureaucratic limitations.[5]

7-2
how DO AMERICAN COURTS OPERATE?

One of the most often cited limitations of the American judicial system is its complex nature. In truth, the United States does not have a single judicial system, but fifty-two different systems—one for each state, the District of Columbia, and the federal government. As each state has its own unique judiciary with its own set of rules, some of which may be in conflict with the federal judiciary, it is helpful at this point to discuss some basics—jurisdiction, trial and appellate courts, and the dual court system.

7-2a
Jurisdiction

In Latin, *juris* means "law," and *diction* means "to speak." Thus, **jurisdiction** literally refers to the power "to speak the law." Before any court can hear a case, it must have jurisdiction over the persons involved in the case or its subject matter. The jurisdiction of every court, even the United States Supreme Court, is limited in some way.

GEOGRAPHIC JURISDICTION One limitation is geographic. Generally, a court can exercise its authority over residents of a certain area. A state trial court, for example, normally has jurisdictional authority over crimes committed in a particular area of the state, such as a county or a

1 LO

> **Jurisdiction** The authority of a court to hear and decide cases within an area of the law or a geographic territory.

How does medical marijuana present a situation of concurrent jurisdiction in which federal law and state law are contradictory?

David Paul Morris/Bloomberg via Getty Images

district. A state's highest court (often called the state supreme court) has jurisdictional authority over the entire state, and the United States Supreme Court has jurisdiction over the entire country.

In the case that opened this chapter, Gabe Watson's attorneys contended that the state of Alabama did not have the power to try their client, as his alleged crime took place in Australia. Prosecutors, however, successfully argued that, since Watson would have planned the alleged murder of his wife in Alabama, that state had geographic jurisdiction over the crime. For the most part, criminal jurisdiction is determined by legislation. The U.S. Congress or a state legislature can determine what acts are illegal within the geographic boundaries it controls, thus giving federal or state courts jurisdiction over those crimes. What happens, however, when more than one court system has jurisdiction over the same criminal act?

Federal versus State Jurisdiction Most criminal laws are state laws, so the majority of all criminal trials are heard in state courts. Many acts that are illegal under state law, however, are also illegal under federal law. As a general rule, when Congress "criminalizes" behavior that is already prohibited under a state criminal code, the federal and state courts both have jurisdiction over

Concurrent Jurisdiction
The situation that occurs when two or more courts have the authority to preside over the same criminal case.

that crime unless Congress states otherwise in the initial legislation. Thus, **concurrent jurisdiction,** which occurs when two different court systems have simultaneous jurisdiction over the same case, is quite common.

Less common is the situation in which federal law and state law contradict each other. As we saw in Chapter 2, Colorado and Washington legalized possession of small amounts of marijuana in 2012. Furthermore, nineteen states and the District of Columbia allow the use of marijuana for medical purposes (see photo above). Federal law, however, continues to treat the possession, sale, or distribution of marijuana as a crime. Consequently, federal law enforcement officials will have to rely on their discretion in deciding whether to prosecute users of the drug in states where such use is "legal."

State versus State Jurisdiction Multiple states can also claim jurisdiction over the same defendant or criminal act, depending on state legislation and the circumstances of the crime. For example, if Billy is standing in State A and shoots Frances, who is standing in State B, the two states could have concurrent jurisdiction to try Billy for murder. Similarly, if a property theft takes places in State A but police recover the stolen goods in State B, concurrent jurisdiction could exist. Some states have also passed laws stating that they have jurisdiction over their own citizens who commit crimes in other states, even if there is no other connection between the home state and the criminal act.[6]

The concept of jurisdiction encourages states to cooperate with each other regarding fugitives from the law. In 2013, for example, Michael Boysen was suspected of killing his grandparents in Renton, Washington. Boysen fled south to Oregon, where local police apprehended him in a Lincoln City hotel room. Oregon officials subsequently *extradited* Boysen back to Washington to stand trial for the double murder. **Extradition** is the formal process by which one legal authority, such as a state or a nation, transfers a fugitive or a suspect to another legal authority that has a valid claim on that person. (**CAREER TIP:** To become a *U.S. Extradition Service agent,* a federal law enforcement officer must complete 120 hours of training in areas such as prisoner transportation, contraband control, and defensive driving.)

INTERNATIONAL JURISDICTION Under international law, each country has the right to create and enact criminal law for its territory. Therefore, the notion that a nation has jurisdiction over any crimes committed within its borders is well established. The situation becomes more delicate when one nation feels the need to go outside its own territory to enforce its criminal law. International precedent does, however, provide several bases for expanding jurisdiction across international borders.

For example, anti-terrorism efforts have been aided by the principle that the United States has jurisdiction over persons who commit crimes against Americans even when the former are citizens of foreign countries and live outside the United States. In October 2012, British authorities extradited Egyptian-born preacher Abu Hamza al-Masri to the United States to face multiple terrorism charges, including conspiring to set up a terrorist training camp in Oregon. Similarly, that same year Thailand extradited Ukrainian citizen Maksym Shynkarenko to New Jersey, where he was to face trial for operating several child pornography Web sites. Even though Shynkarenko had never been to New Jersey before, the fact that at least thirty men in that state accessed his Web sites provided a basis for jurisdiction.

SUBJECT-MATTER JURISDICTION Jurisdiction over subject matter also acts as a limitation on the types of cases a court can hear. State court systems include courts of *general* (unlimited) *jurisdiction* and courts of *limited jurisdiction.* Courts of general jurisdiction have no restrictions on the subject matter they may address, and therefore deal with the most serious felonies and civil cases. Courts of limited jurisdiction, also known as lower courts, handle misdemeanors and civil matters under a certain amount, usually $1,000.

As we will discuss later in the chapter, many states have created special subject-matter courts that only dispose of cases involving a specific crime. For example, a number of jurisdictions have established drug courts to handle an overload of illicit narcotics arrests. Furthermore, under the Uniform Code of Military Justice, the U.S. military has jurisdiction over active personnel who commit crimes, even if those crimes occur outside the course of duty.[7] In such cases, military officials can either attempt to *court-martial* the suspect in military court or allow civilian prosecutors to handle the case in state or federal court.

> **Extradition** The process by which one jurisdiction surrenders a person accused or convicted of violating another jurisdiction's criminal law to the second jurisdiction.

In August 2013, the United States formally requested the extradition of Eric Marques, alleging that the Irish citizen, shown here after being arrested in Dublin, had disseminated "countless" child pornography images to the U.S. via the Internet. Do you think that the American government should have jurisdiction over suspects such as Marques who commit their crimes on foreign soil?

Press Association via AP Images

Trial and Appellate Courts

Another distinction is between courts of original jurisdiction and courts of appellate, or review, jurisdiction. Courts having *original jurisdiction* are courts of the first instance, or **trial courts.** Almost every case begins in a trial court. It is in this court that a trial (or a guilty plea) takes place, and the judge imposes a sentence if the defendant is found guilty. Trial courts are primarily concerned with *questions of fact.* They are designed to determine exactly what events occurred that are relevant to questions of the defendant's guilt or innocence.

LO **2**

Courts having *appellate jurisdiction* act as reviewing courts, or **appellate courts.** In general, cases can be brought before appellate courts only on appeal by one of the parties in the trial court. (Note that because of constitutional protections against being tried twice for the same crime, prosecutors who lose in criminal trial court *cannot* appeal the verdict.) An appellate court does not use juries or witnesses to reach its decision. Instead, its judges make a decision on whether the case should be *reversed* and *remanded,* or sent back to the court of original jurisdiction for a new trial. Appellate judges present written explanations for their decisions, and these **opinions** of the court are the basis for a great deal of the precedent in the criminal justice system.

It is important to understand that appellate courts do not determine the defendant's guilt or innocence—they only make judgments on questions of procedure. In other words, they are concerned with *questions of law* and normally accept the facts as established by the trial court. Only rarely will an appeals court question a jury's decision. Instead, the appellate judges will review the manner in which the facts and evidence were provided to the jury and rule on whether errors were made in the process.

The Dual Court System

As we saw in Chapter 1, America's system of federalism allows the federal government and the governments of the fifty states to hold authority in many areas. As a result, the federal government and each of the fifty states, as well as the District of Columbia, have their own separate court systems. Because of the split between the federal courts and the state courts, this is known as the **dual court system.** (See Figure 7.1 below to get a better idea of how federal and state courts operate as distinct yet parallel entities.)

Trial Courts Courts in which most cases usually begin and in which questions of fact are examined.

Appellate Courts Courts that review decisions made by lower courts, such as trial courts; also known as *courts of appeals.*

Opinions Written statements by the judges expressing the reasons for the court's decision in a case.

Dual Court System The separate but interrelated court system of the United States, made up of the courts on the national level and the courts on the state level.

FIGURE 7.1 The Dual Court System

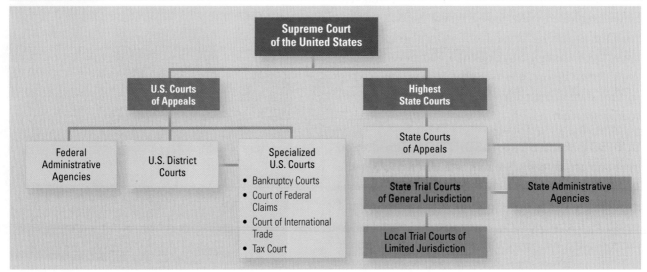

Federal and state courts both have limited jurisdiction. Generally, federal courts preside over cases involving violations of federal law, and state courts preside over cases involving violations of state law. The distinction is not always clear, however. Federal courts have jurisdiction over more than four thousand crimes, many of which also exist in state criminal codes. In 2012, for instance, local and federal law enforcement agents cooperated in apprehending Damon Quick, who had committed a string of armed robberies of stores and restaurants in the Durham, North Carolina, area. Broadly interpreting a federal law outlawing robbery that obstructs commerce between states,[8] the federal government claimed jurisdiction over Quick, as did North Carolina. Following an agreement between the two sides, Quick was prosecuted—and found guilty—in federal court.

7-3

how DO STATES ORGANIZE THEIR COURTS ?

Typically, a state court system includes several levels, or tiers, of courts. State courts may include (1) lower courts, or courts of limited jurisdiction; (2) trial courts of general jurisdiction; (3) appellate courts; and (4) the state's highest court. As previously mentioned, each state has a different judicial structure, in which different courts have different jurisdictions, but there are enough similarities to allow for a general discussion. Figure 7.2 on the following page shows a typical state court system.

7-3a

Courts of Limited Jurisdiction

Most states have local trial courts that are limited to trying cases involving minor criminal matters, such as traffic violations, prostitution, and drunk and disorderly conduct. Although these minor courts usually keep no written record of the trial proceedings and cases are decided by a judge rather than a jury, defendants have the same rights as those in other trial courts. The majority of all minor criminal cases are decided in these lower courts. Courts of limited jurisdiction can also be responsible for the preliminary stages of felony cases. Arraignments, bail hearings, and preliminary hearings often take place in these lower courts.

Magistrates, or, in some states, municipal court judges, preside over courts whose jurisdiction is limited to disputes between private individuals and to crimes punishable by small fines or short jail terms. Magistrate courts have the same limited jurisdiction as do justice courts in rural settings. In most jurisdictions, magistrates are responsible for providing law enforcement agents with search and seizure warrants, discussed in Chapter 6.

As mentioned earlier, many states have created **problem-solving courts** that have jurisdiction over very narrowly defined areas of criminal justice. Not only do these courts remove many cases from the existing court systems, but they also allow court personnel to become experts in a particular subject. Problem-solving courts include:

1. Drug courts, which deal only with illegal substance crimes.

2. Gun courts, which have jurisdiction over crimes that involve the illegal use of firearms.

3. Juvenile courts, which specialize in crimes committed by minors. (We will discuss juvenile courts in more detail in Chapter 13.)

4. Domestic courts, which deal with crimes of domestic violence, such as child and spousal abuse.

5. Mental health courts, which focus primarily on the treatment and rehabilitation of offenders with mental health problems.

As we will see in Chapter 10, many state and local governments are searching for cheaper alternatives to locking up nonviolent offenders in prison or jail. Because problem-solving courts offer a range of treatment options for wrongdoers, these courts are becoming increasingly popular in today's more budget-conscious criminal justice system. For example, at least 2,500 drug courts are now operating in the United States, a number that is expected to increase as the financial benefits of diverting drug law violators

Magistrate A public civil officer or official with limited judicial authority within a particular geographic area, such as the authority to issue an arrest warrant.

Problem-Solving Courts Lower courts that have jurisdiction over one specific area of criminal activity, such as illegal drugs or domestic violence.

FIGURE 7.2 A Typical State Court System

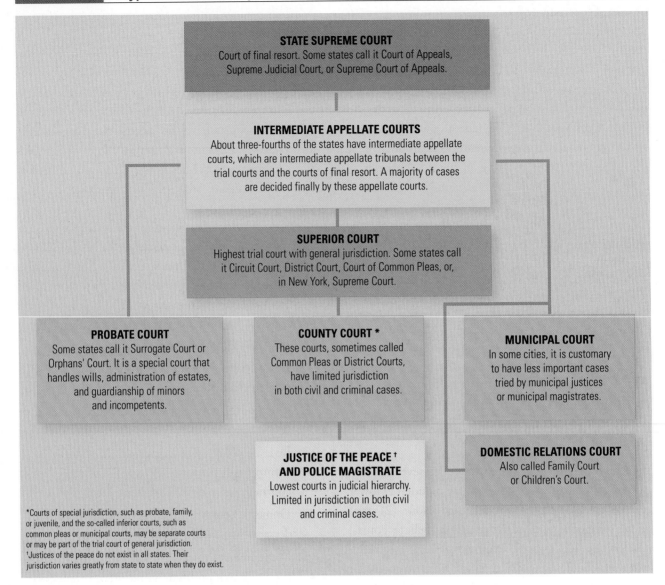

STATE SUPREME COURT
Court of final resort. Some states call it Court of Appeals, Supreme Judicial Court, or Supreme Court of Appeals.

INTERMEDIATE APPELLATE COURTS
About three-fourths of the states have intermediate appellate courts, which are intermediate appellate tribunals between the trial courts and the courts of final resort. A majority of cases are decided finally by these appellate courts.

SUPERIOR COURT
Highest trial court with general jurisdiction. Some states call it Circuit Court, District Court, Court of Common Pleas, or, in New York, Supreme Court.

PROBATE COURT
Some states call it Surrogate Court or Orphans' Court. It is a special court that handles wills, administration of estates, and guardianship of minors and incompetents.

COUNTY COURT *
These courts, sometimes called Common Pleas or District Courts, have limited jurisdiction in both civil and criminal cases.

MUNICIPAL COURT
In some cities, it is customary to have less important cases tried by municipal justices or municipal magistrates.

**JUSTICE OF THE PEACE †
AND POLICE MAGISTRATE**
Lowest courts in judicial hierarchy. Limited in jurisdiction in both civil and criminal cases.

DOMESTIC RELATIONS COURT
Also called Family Court or Children's Court.

*Courts of special jurisdiction, such as probate, family, or juvenile, and the so-called inferior courts, such as common pleas or municipal courts, may be separate courts or may be part of the trial court of general jurisdiction.
†Justices of the peace do not exist in all states. Their jurisdiction varies greatly from state to state when they do exist.

from correctional facilities become more attractive to politicians.

7-3b
Trial Courts of General Jurisdiction

State trial courts that have general jurisdiction may be called county courts, district courts, superior courts, or circuit courts. In Ohio, the name is the court of common pleas and in Massachusetts, the trial court. (The name sometimes does not correspond with the court's functions. For example, in New York the trial court is called the supreme court, whereas in most states the supreme court is the state's highest court.) Courts of general jurisdiction have the authority to hear and decide cases involving many types of subject

matter, and they are the setting for criminal trials (discussed in Chapter 8).

7-3c
State Courts of Appeals

Every state has at least one court of appeals (known as an appellate, or reviewing, court), which may be an intermediate appellate court or the state's highest court. About three-fourths have intermediate appellate courts. The highest appellate court in a state is usually called the supreme court, but in both New York and Maryland, the highest state court is called the court of appeals. The decisions of each state's highest court on all questions of state law are final. Only when issues of federal law or constitutional procedure are involved can the United States Supreme

Judge Sarah Smith, left, talks with an offender at her drug court in downtown Tulsa, Oklahoma. What are some of the benefits of drug courts and other problem-solving courts?

Photo by Adam Wisneski/*Tulsa World*

Court overrule a decision made by a state's highest court.

7-4

how
DOES THE FEDERAL GOVERNMENT ORGANIZE ITS COURTS?

The federal court system is basically a three-tiered model consisting of (1) U.S. district courts (trial courts of general jurisdiction) and various courts of limited jurisdiction, (2) U.S. courts of appeals (intermediate courts of appeals), and (3) the United States Supreme Court.

Unlike state court judges, who are usually elected, federal court judges—including the justices of the Supreme Court—are appointed by the president of the United States, subject to the approval of the Senate. All federal judges receive lifetime appointments (because under Article III of the Constitution they "hold their offices during Good Behavior").

7-4a
U.S. District Courts

On the lowest tier of the federal court system are the U.S. district courts, or federal trial courts. These are the courts in which cases involving federal laws begin, and a judge or jury decides the case (if it is a jury trial). Every state has at least one federal district court, and there is one in the District of Columbia. The number of judicial districts varies over time, primarily owing to population changes and corresponding caseloads. At the present time, there are ninety-four judicial districts. The federal system also includes other trial courts of limited jurisdiction, such as the Tax Court and the Court of International Trade.

7-4b
U.S. Courts of Appeals

In the federal court system, there are thirteen U.S. courts of appeals—also referred to as U.S. circuit courts of appeals. The federal courts of appeals for twelve of the circuits hear appeals from the district courts located within their respective judicial circuits (see Figure 7.3 on the following page). The Court of Appeals for the Thirteenth Circuit, called the Federal Circuit, has national appellate jurisdiction over certain types of cases, such as cases in which the U.S. government is a defendant. The decisions of the circuit courts of appeals are final unless a further appeal is pursued and granted. In that case, the matter is brought before the Supreme Court.

7-4c
The United States Supreme Court

Although it reviews a minuscule percentage of the cases decided in this country each year, the rulings of the United States Supreme Court profoundly

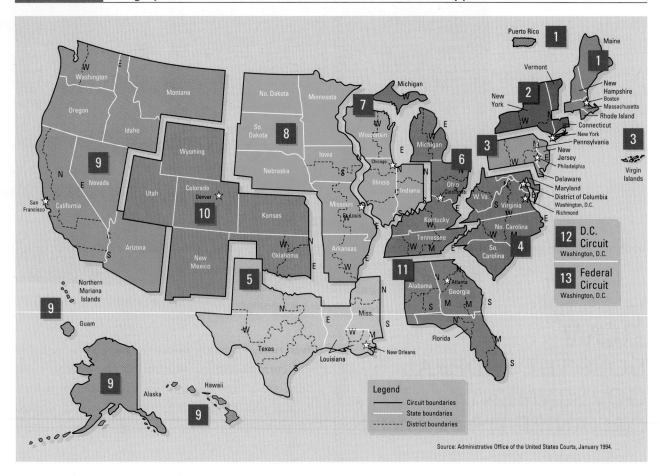

Source: Administrative Office of the United States Courts, January 1994.

affect our lives. The impact of Court decisions on the criminal justice system is equally far reaching: *Gideon v. Wainwright* (1963)[9] established every American's right to be represented by counsel in a criminal trial; *Miranda v. Arizona* (1966)[10] transformed pretrial interrogations; *Furman v. Georgia* (1972)[11] ruled that the death penalty was unconstitutional; and *Gregg v. Georgia* (1976)[12] spelled out the conditions under which it could be allowed. As you have no doubt noticed from references in this textbook, the Court has addressed nearly every important facet of criminal law.

7-4d
Interpreting and Applying the Law

The Supreme Court "makes" criminal justice policy in two important

Judicial Review The power of a court—particularly the United States Supreme Court—to review the actions of the executive and legislative branches and, if necessary, declare those actions unconstitutional.

ways: through *judicial review* and through its authority to interpret the law. **Judicial review** refers to the power of the Court to determine whether a law or action by the other branches of the government is constitutional. For example, in the late 1990s Congress passed a law restricting Internet sales of "crush" videos, which showed women crushing small animals to death with their bare feet or high heels.[13] The wording of the statute prohibited the sale of videos showing any form of graphic violence against animals. Several years after the law's passage, Robert Stevens of Pittsville, Virginia, was sentenced to three years in prison for distributing videos that featured pit bull fights. In 2010, the Supreme Court overturned Stevens's conviction and invalidated the federal law as unconstitutional on the ground that it violated the First Amendment's protections of freedom of expression.[14]

As the final interpreter of the Constitution, the Supreme Court must also determine the mean-

ing of certain statutory provisions when applied to specific situations. In the previous chapter, you learned that a law enforcement officer must immediately stop questioning a suspect who invokes her or his *Miranda* rights. In *Maryland v. Shatzer* (2010),[15] the Court considered a situation in which a sexual abuse suspect invoked his Miranda rights, spent more than two years in prison (for an unrelated crime), and then waived his *Miranda* rights. The Court rejected the suspect's claim that due to his much earlier action, the later waiver, although made willingly, "did not count." Instead, the Court decided on a new rule: a *Miranda* invocation is good for only fourteen days. After that, a suspect must clearly reestablish her or his right to silence.

JURISDICTION OF THE SUPREME COURT The United States Supreme Court consists of nine justices—a chief justice and eight associate justices. The Supreme Court has original, or trial, jurisdiction only in rare instances (set forth in Article III, Section 2, of the Constitution). In other words, only rarely does a case originate at the Supreme Court level. Most of the Court's work is as an appellate court. It has appellate authority over cases decided by the U.S. courts of appeals, as well as over some cases decided in the state courts when federal questions are at issue.

WHICH CASES REACH THE SUPREME COURT?

There is no absolute right to appeal to the United States Supreme Court. Although thousands of cases are filed with the Supreme Court each year, in 2011–2012 the Court heard only seventy-seven. With a **writ of certiorari** (pronounced sur-shee-uh-*rah*-ree), the Supreme Court orders a lower court to send it the record of a case for review. A party can petition the Supreme Court to issue a writ of *certiorari,* but whether the Court will do so is entirely within its discretion. More than 90 percent of the petitions for writs of *certiorari* (or "certs," as they are popularly called) are denied. A denial is not a decision on the merits of a case, nor does it indicate agreement with the lower court's opinion. Therefore, the denial of the writ has no value as a precedent.

3 LO

The Court will not issue a writ unless at least four justices approve of it. This is called the **rule of four.** Although the justices are not required to give their reasons for refusing to hear a case, most often the discretionary decision is based on whether the legal issue involves a "substantial federal question." Often, such questions arise when lower courts split on a particular issue. For example, in recent years different federal and state courts have produced varying opinions on the question of whether police officers can search the contents of cell phones without a search warrant.[16] To clear up confusion on this increasingly important matter, the Court will likely

Writ of *Certiorari* A request from a higher court asking a lower court for the record of a case. In essence, the request signals the higher court's willingness to review the case.

Rule of Four A rule of the United States Supreme Court that the Court will not issue a writ of *certiorari* unless at least four justices approve of the decision to hear the case.

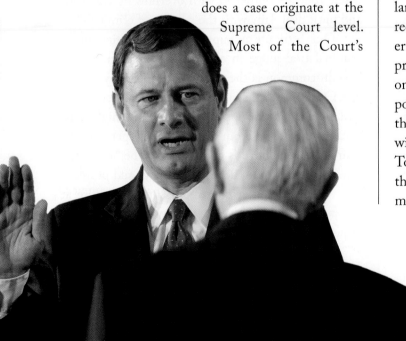

What does it mean to say that Chief Justice John G. Roberts, Jr., pictured here, and the eight associate members of the Supreme Court "make criminal justice policy"?

AP Photo/Lawrence Jackson, File

hear a case involving cell phone searches in the near future. Practical considerations aside, if the justices feel that a case does not address an important federal law or constitutional issue, they will vote to deny the writ of *certiorari*.

SUPREME COURT DECISIONS Like all appellate courts, the Supreme Court normally does not hear any evidence. The Court's decision in a particular case is based on the written record of the case and the written arguments (briefs) that the attorneys submit. The attorneys also present **oral arguments**—arguments presented in person rather than on paper—to the Court, after which the justices discuss the case in *conference*. The conference is strictly private—only the justices are allowed in the room.

Majorities and Pluralities When the Court has reached a decision, the chief justice, if in the majority, assigns the task of writing the Court's opinion to one of the justices. When the chief justice is not in the majority, the most senior justice voting with the majority assigns the writing of the Court's opinion. The opinion outlines the reasons for the Court's decision, the rules of law that apply, and the decision.

From time to time, the justices agree on the outcome of a case, but no single reason for that outcome gains five votes. When this occurs, the rationale that gains the most votes is called the *plurality* opinion. Plurality opinions are problematic, because they do not provide a strong precedent for lower courts to follow. Although still relatively rare, the incidence of plurality opinions has increased over the past fifty years as the Court has become more ideologically fractured.[17]

Concurrence and Dissent Often, one or more justices who agree with the Court's decision may do so for different reasons than those outlined in the majority opinion. These justices may write **concurring opinions** setting forth their own legal reasoning on the issue. Frequently, one or more justices disagree with the Court's conclusion. These justices may write **dissenting opinions** outlining the reasons why they feel the majority erred. Although a dissenting opinion does not affect the outcome of the case before the Court, it may be important later. In a subsequent case concerning the same issue, a justice or attorney may use the legal reasoning in the dissenting opinion as the basis for an argument to reverse the previous decision and establish a new precedent.

7-5

how DO JUDGES FUNCTION IN THE CRIMINAL JUSTICE SYSTEM?

Supreme Court justices are the most visible and best-known American jurists, but in many ways they are unrepresentative of the profession as a whole. Few judges enjoy three-room office suites fitted with a fireplace and a private bath, as do the Supreme Court justices. Few judges have four clerks to assist them. Few judges get a yearly vacation that stretches from July through September. Most judges, in fact, work at the lowest level of the system, in criminal trial courts, where they are burdened with overflowing caseloads and must deal daily with the pettiest of criminals.

One attribute a Supreme Court justice and a criminal trial judge in any small American city do have in common is the expectation that they will be just. Of all the participants in the criminal justice system, no single person is held to the same high standards as the judge. From her or his lofty perch in the courtroom, the judge is counted on to be "above the fray" of the bickering defense attorneys and prosecutors. When the other courtroom contestants rise at the entrance of the judge, they are placing the burden of justice squarely on the judge's shoulders.

7-5a

The Roles and Responsibilities of Trial Judges

One of the reasons that judicial integrity is considered so important is the amount of discretionary

Oral Arguments The verbal arguments presented in person by attorneys to an appellate court. Each attorney presents reasons why the court should rule in his or her client's favor.

Concurring Opinions Separate opinions prepared by judges who support the decision of the majority of the court but who want to make or clarify a particular point or to voice disapproval of the grounds on which the decision was made.

Dissenting Opinions Separate opinions in which judges disagree with the conclusion reached by the majority of the court and expand on their own views about the case.

CAREER TIP: High-level judges enjoy the services of *law clerks,* who prepare reports for the judge on the legal issues of cases and help the judge research and write opinions. Law clerks are often recent law school graduates beginning their legal careers.

power a judge has over the court proceedings. In the opening of this chapter, you saw an example of a judge who ruled that the prosecution's evidence against defendant Gabe Watson was so weak that no trial was necessary. Nearly every stage of the trial process includes a decision or action to be taken by the presiding judge.

BEFORE THE TRIAL A great deal of the work done by a judge takes place before the trial even starts, free from public scrutiny. These duties, some of which you have seen from a different point of view in the section on law enforcement agents, include determining the following:

1. Whether there is sufficient probable cause to issue a search or arrest warrant.

2. Whether there is sufficient probable cause to authorize electronic surveillance of a suspect.

3. Whether enough evidence exists to justify the temporary incarceration of a suspect.

4. Whether a defendant should be released on bail, and if so, the amount of the bail.

5. Whether to accept pretrial motions by prosecutors and defense attorneys.

6. Whether to accept a plea bargain.

During these pretrial activities, the judge takes on the role of the *negotiator.*[18] As most cases are decided through plea bargains rather than through trial proceedings, the judge often offers his or her services as a negotiator to help the prosecution and the defense "make a deal." The amount at which bail is set is often negotiated as well. Throughout the trial process, the judge usually spends a great deal of time in his or her *chambers,* or office, negotiating with the prosecutors and defense attorneys.

DURING THE TRIAL When the trial starts, the judge takes on the role of *referee.* In this role, she or he is responsible for seeing that the trial unfolds according to the dictates of the law and that the participants in the trial do not overstep any legal or ethical bounds. Furthermore, the judge is expected to be neutral, determining the admissibility of testimony and evidence on a completely objective basis. The judge also acts as a *teacher* during the trial, explaining points of law to the jury. If the trial is not a jury trial, then the judge must also make decisions concerning the guilt or innocence of the defendant.

At the close of the trial, if the defendant is found guilty, the judge must decide on the length of the sentence and the type of sentence. (Different types of sentences, such as incarceration, probation, and other forms of community-based corrections, will be discussed in Chapters 9 and 10.)

THE ADMINISTRATIVE ROLE Judges are also *administrators* and are responsible for the day-to-day functioning of their courts. A primary administrative task of a judge is scheduling. Each courtroom has a **docket,** or calendar of cases, and it is the judge's responsibility to keep the docket current. This entails not only scheduling the trial, but also setting pretrial motion dates and deciding whether to grant attorneys' requests for *continuances,* or additional time to prepare for the trial. Judges must

Docket The list of cases entered on a court's calendar and thus scheduled to be heard by the court.

DURING a polygraph test, rubber tubes are placed on a person's chest and abdominal area to record his or her breathing patterns. In addition, two small metal plates are attached to the subject's fingers to measure sweat levels, and a blood pressure cuff indicates her or his heart rate. The examiner asks a series of questions, keeping track of changes in the body's responses to determine if the subject is telling the truth. Law enforcement agents routinely employ polygraphs in the course of criminal investigations, and the technology is widely used by the government to test job applicants and those seeking a security clearance.

In criminal courtrooms, however, polygraph exams are surprisingly absent. The decision to allow evidence of such exams rests primarily with the judge, particularly in federal court. In exercising this discretion, the judge must decide whether the results of the exam are reliable. Even though properly administered polygraphs are, by some measures, accurate about 75 percent of the time, many judges are suspicious of what they believe to be "junk science" and therefore are reluctant to allow it in their courtrooms.

AP Photo/Cecil Whig, Matthew Given

THINKING ABOUT POLYGRAPH EXAMS

In particular, polygraph exams are popular with defendants who want to use the tests to prove their innocence. Assuming that such exams do have 75 percent accuracy rates, are judges justified in keeping the results out of court? Explain your answer.

---

also keep track of the immense paperwork generated by each case and manage the various employees of the court. In some instances, judges are even responsible for the budgets of their courtrooms. In 1939, Congress, recognizing the burden of such tasks, created the Administrative Office of the United States Courts to provide administrative assistance for federal court judges.[19] Most state court judges, however, do not have the luxury of similar aid, though they are supported by a court staff.

Partisan Elections
Elections in which candidates are affiliated with and receive support from political parties.

Nonpartisan Elections
Elections in which candidates are presented on the ballot without any party affiliation.

7-5b
Selection of Judges

In the federal court system, all judges are appointed by the president and con-firmed by the Senate. It is difficult to make a general statement about how judges are selected in state court systems, however, because the procedure varies widely from state to state. In some states, such as New Jersey, all judges are appointed by the governor and confirmed by the upper chamber of the state legislature. In other states, such as Alabama, **partisan elections** are used to choose judges. In these elections, a judicial candidate declares allegiance to a political party, usually the Democrats or the Republicans, before the election. States such as Kentucky that conduct **nonpartisan elections** do not require a candidate to affiliate herself or himself with a political party in this manner.

In 1940, Missouri became the first state to combine appointment and election in a single merit selection. When all jurisdiction levels are counted, nineteen states and the District of Columbia now utilize the **Missouri Plan,** as merit selection has been labeled. The Missouri Plan consists of three basic steps:

- When a vacancy on the bench arises, candidates are nominated by a nonpartisan committee of citizens.
- The names of the three most qualified candidates are sent to the governor or executive of the state judicial system, and that person chooses who will be the judge.
- A year after the new judge has been installed, a "retention election" is held so that voters can decide whether the judge deserves to keep the post.[20]

The goal of the Missouri Plan is to eliminate partisan politics from the selection procedure, while at the same time giving the citizens a voice in the process.

7-5c
Diversity on the Bench

According to a recent report by the Brennan Center for Justice in New York City, "Americans who enter the courtroom often face a predictable presence on the bench: a white male."[21] Overall, about two-thirds of all state appellate judges are white males, and women in particular are notably absent from the highest courts of most states.[22] On both a national and state level, members of minority groups are underrepresented. Arizona's population, for example, is 40 percent nonwhite, but the state has no minority supreme court justices and minorities hold less than 20 percent of other state judgeships.[23]

The federal judiciary shows a similar pattern. Of the nearly 1,800 federal judges in this country, about 10 percent are African American, 6 percent are Hispanic, and less than 2 percent are Asian American. Furthermore, only 19 percent are women.[24] Of the 111 justices who have served on the United States Supreme Court, two have been African American: Thurgood Marshall (1970–1991) and Clarence Thomas (1991–present). In 2009, Sonia Sotomayor became the first Hispanic appointed to the Court and the third woman, following Sandra Day O'Connor (1981–2006) and Ruth Bader Ginsburg (1993–present). A year later, Elena Kagan became the fourth woman appointed to the Court.

what IS THE COURTROOM WORK GROUP?

Television dramas often depict the courtroom as a battlefield, with prosecutors and defense attorneys spitting fire at each other over the loud and insistent protestations of a frustrated judge. Consequently, many people are somewhat disappointed when they witness a real courtroom at work. Rarely does anyone raise his or her voice, and the courtroom professionals appear—to a great extent—to be cooperating with each other. In Chapter 5, we discussed the existence of a police subculture, based on the shared values of law enforcement agents. A courtroom subculture exists as well, centered on the **courtroom work group.**

The most important feature of any work group is that it is a *cooperative* unit, whose members establish shared values and methods that help the group efficiently reach its goals. Though cooperation is not a concept usually associated with criminal courts, it is in fact crucial to the adjudication process.

7-6a
Members of the Courtroom Work Group

The courtroom work group is made up of those individuals who are involved with the defendant from the time she or he is arrested until sentencing. The most prominent members are the judge, the prosecutor, and the defense attorney. Three other court participants complete the work group:

1. The *bailiff of the court* is responsible for maintaining security and order in the judge's chambers and the courtroom. Bailiffs lead the defendant in and out of the courtroom and attend to the needs of the jurors during the trial. A bailiff, often a member of the local sheriff's department but sometimes an employee of the court, also delivers

Missouri Plan A method of selecting judges that combines appointment and election.

Courtroom Work Group The social organization consisting of the judge, prosecutor, defense attorney, and other court workers.

Alina Solovyova-Vincent/iStockphoto.com

summonses in some jurisdictions. (**CAREER TIP:** In some states, such as New York, the court system hires law enforcement agents known as *court officers* to protect judges, court employees, and the public in courthouses.)

2. The *clerk of the court* has an exhausting list of responsibilities. Any plea, motion, or other matter to be acted on by the judge must go through the clerk. The large amount of paperwork generated during a trial, including transcripts, photographs, evidence, and any other records, is maintained by the clerk. The clerk also issues subpoenas for jury duty and coordinates the jury selection process. In the federal court system, judges select clerks, while state clerks are either appointed or, in nearly a third of the states, elected.

3. *Court reporters* record every word that is said during the course of the trial. They also record any *depositions,* or pretrial question-and-answer sessions in which a party or a witness answers an attorney's questions under oath.

7-6b
The Judge in the Courtroom Work Group

The judge is the dominant figure in the courtroom and therefore exerts the most influence over the values and norms of the work group. A judge who runs a "tight ship" follows procedure and restricts the freedom of attorneys to deviate from regulations, while a *"laissez-faire"* judge allows more leeway to members of the work group. A judge's personal philosophy also affects the court proceedings. If a judge has a reputation for being "tough on crime," both prosecutors and defense attorneys will alter their strategies accordingly.

Although preeminent in the work group, a judge must still rely on other members of the group. To a certain extent, the judge is the least informed member of the trio. Like a juror, the judge learns the facts of the case as they are presented by the attorneys. If the attorneys do not properly present the facts, then the judge is hampered in making rulings.

The Prosecution

If, as we suggested earlier in the chapter, the judge is the referee of the courtroom, then the prosecutor and the defense attorney are its two main combatants. On the side of the government, acting in the name of "the people," the **public prosecutor** tries cases against criminal defendants. The public prosecutor in criminal cases is called a U.S. attorney. In cases tried in state or local courts, the public prosecutor may be referred to as a *prosecuting attorney, state attorney, district attorney, county attorney,* or *city attorney*. Given their great autonomy, prosecutors are generally considered the most dominant figures in the American criminal justice system.

LO **4**

In some jurisdictions, the district attorney is the chief law enforcement officer, with broad powers over police operations. Prosecutors have the power to bring the resources of the state against the individual and hold the legal keys to meting out or withholding punishment. Ideally, this power is balanced by a duty of fairness and a recognition that the prosecutor's ultimate goal is not to win cases, but to see that justice is done. In *Berger v. United States* (1935), Justice George Sutherland called the prosecutor

> in a peculiar and very definite sense the servant of the law, the twofold aim of which is that guilt shall not escape or innocence suffer. He may prosecute with earnestness and vigor—indeed, he should do so. But, while he may strike hard blows, he is not at liberty to strike foul ones. It is as much his duty to refrain from improper methods calculated to produce a wrongful conviction as it is to use every legitimate means to bring about a just one.[25]

In part to lessen the opportunity for "foul" behavior by prosecutors, they are not permitted to keep evidence from the defendant that may be useful in showing his or her innocence.[26] For example, in 1995, Juan Smith was convicted of five murders at a party in New Orleans and eventually sentenced to death. The only eyewitness to the crime gave conflicting comments to police, including that he could not "ID anyone because [he] couldn't see faces."[27] Obviously, Smith's defense attorneys could have used such statements to create reasonable doubt about their client's guilt. Because prosecutors never provided them with this evidence, in 2012 the Supreme Court overturned Smith's conviction and ordered a new trial.[28]

THE OFFICE OF THE PROSECUTOR When he or she is acting as an *officer of the law* during a criminal trial, there are limits on the prosecutor's conduct, as we shall see in the next chapter. During the pretrial process, however, prosecutors hold a great deal of discretion in deciding the following:

1. Whether an individual who has been arrested by the police will be charged with a crime.
2. The level of the charges to be brought against the suspect.
3. If and when to stop the prosecution.[29]

There are more than eight thousand prosecutor's offices around the country, serving state, county, and municipal jurisdictions. Even though the **attorney general** is the chief law enforcement officer in any state, she or he has limited (and in some states, no) control over prosecutors within the state's boundaries.

Each jurisdiction has a chief prosecutor, who is sometimes appointed but more often elected. As an elected official, he or she typically serves a four-year term, though in some states, such as Alabama, the term is six years. (**CAREER TIP:** In smaller jurisdictions, the chief prosecutor has several assistants, and they work closely together. In larger ones, the chief prosecutor may have numerous *assistant prosecutors,* many of whom he or she rarely meets. Assistant prosecutors—for the most part, young attorneys recently graduated from law school—may be assigned to particular sections of the organization, such as criminal prosecutions in general or areas of *special prosecution,* such as narcotics or gang crimes.)

THE PROSECUTOR AS ELECTED OFFICIAL The chief prosecutor's autonomy is not absolute. As an elected official, she or he must answer to the voters. (There are exceptions: U.S. attorneys are nominated by the president and approved by the Senate, and chief prosecutors in Alaska, Connecticut, New Jersey, Rhode Island, and the District of Columbia are either appointed or hired as members of the attorney general's office.) The prosecutor may be part of the political machine. In many

Public Prosecutors Individuals, acting as trial lawyers, who initiate and conduct cases in the government's name and on behalf of the people.

Attorney General The chief law officer of a state; also, the chief law officer of the nation.

jurisdictions, the prosecutor must declare a party affiliation and is expected to reward fellow party members with positions in the district attorney's office if elected.

The post of prosecutor is often seen as a "stepping-stone" to higher political office, and many prosecutors have gone on to serve in legislatures or as judges. Sonia Sotomayor (see photo alongside), the first Hispanic member of the United States Supreme Court, started her legal career in 1979 as an assistant district attorney in New York City. While at that job, she first came to public attention by helping to prosecute the "Tarzan Murderer," an athletic criminal responsible for at least twenty burglaries and four killings.

Give several reasons why experience as a prosecutor would make someone such as United States Supreme Court justice Sonia Sotomayor a more effective judge.

AP Photo/Pablo Martinez Monsivais

of instances, the United States Supreme Court has held that defendants are entitled to representation as soon as their rights may be denied, which, in most instances, includes the custodial interrogation and lineup identification procedures.[30] Therefore, an important responsibility of the defense attorney is to represent the defendant at the various stages of the custodial process, such as arrest, interrogation, lineup, and arraignment. Other responsibilities include:

- Investigating the incident for which the defendant has been charged.
- Communicating with the prosecutor, which includes negotiating plea bargains.
- Preparing the case for trial.
- Submitting defense motions, including motions to suppress evidence.
- Representing the defendant at trial.
- Negotiating a sentence, if the client has been convicted.
- Determining whether to appeal a guilty verdict.[31]

7-6d

The Defense Attorney

The media provide most people's perception of defense counsel: the idealistic public defender who nobly serves the poor, the "ambulance chaser," or the celebrity attorney in the $3,000 suit. These stereotypes, though not entirely fictional, tend to obscure the crucial role that the **defense attorney** plays in the criminal justice system. Most persons charged with crimes have little or no knowledge of criminal procedure. Without assistance, they would be helpless in court. By acting as a staunch advocate for her or his client, the defense attorney (ideally) ensures that the government proves every point against that client beyond a reasonable doubt, even for cases that do not go to trial. In sum, the defense attorney provides a counterweight against the state in our criminal justice system.

THE RESPONSIBILITIES OF THE DEFENSE ATTORNEY The Sixth Amendment right to counsel is not limited to the actual criminal trial. In a number

Defense Attorney The lawyer representing the defendant.

DEFENDING THE GUILTY At one time or another in their careers, all defense attorneys will face a difficult question: Must I defend a client whom I know to be guilty? According to the American Bar Association's code of legal ethics, the answer is almost always, "yes."[32] The most important responsibility of the criminal defense attorney is to be an advocate for her or his client. As such, the attorney is obligated to use all ethical and legal means to achieve the client's desired goal, which is usually to avoid or lessen punishment for the charged crime.

5 LO

As Supreme Court justice Byron White once noted, defense counsel has no "obligation to ascertain or present the truth." Rather, our criminal justice system insists that the defense attorney "defend the client whether he is innocent or guilty."[33] Indeed, if

JOB DESCRIPTION:

- Interview low-income applicants for legal services and, if they are eligible, engage in negotiation, trial, and /or appeal of legal issues on their behalf.
- Exercise initiative, sound judgment, and creativity in attempting to solve the legal problems of the poor.

WHAT KIND OF TRAINING IS REQUIRED?

- A law degree and membership in the relevant state bar association.
- Commitment and dedication to the needs of low-income and elderly clients.

ANNUAL SALARY RANGE?

- $44,000–$92,000

Steven Robertson/Getty Images

defense attorneys refused to represent clients whom they believed to be guilty, the Sixth Amendment guarantee of a criminal trial for all accused persons would be rendered meaningless. (**CAREER TIP:** Attorneys who specialize in representing clients in court are called *trial lawyers*. Note, though, that many lawyers rarely or never do trial work, focusing instead on drafting legal documents and doing legal research.)

THE PUBLIC DEFENDER Generally speaking, there are two different types of defense attorneys: (1) private attorneys, who are hired by individuals, and (2) **public defenders,** who work for the government. The distinction is not absolute, as many private attorneys accept employment as public defenders, too. The modern role of the public defender was established by the Supreme Court's interpretation of the Sixth Amendment in *Gideon v. Wainwright* (1963).[34]

In that case, the Court ruled that no defendant can be "assured a fair trial unless counsel is provided for him," and therefore the state must provide a public defender to those who cannot afford to hire one for themselves. Subsequently, the Court extended this protection to juveniles in *In re Gault* (1967)[35]

and those faced with imprisonment for committing misdemeanors in *Argersinger v. Hamlin* (1972).[36] The impact of these decisions has been substantial: about 90 percent of all criminal defendants in the United States are represented by public defenders or other appointed counsel.[37]

Eligibility Issues Although the Supreme Court's *Gideon* decision obligated the government to provide attorneys for poor defendants, it offered no guidance on just how poor the defendant needs to be to qualify for a public defender. In theory, counsel should be provided for those who are unable to hire an attorney themselves without "substantial hardship."[38] In reality, each jurisdiction has its own guidelines, and a defendant refused counsel in one area might be entitled to it in another. A judge in Kittitas County, Washington, to give an extreme example, frequently denies public counsel for college student defendants. This judge believes that any person who chooses to go to school rather than work automatically falls outside the *Gideon* case's definition of indigence.[39]

Public Defenders Court-appointed attorneys who are paid by the state to represent defendants who are unable to hire private counsel.

Effectiveness of Public Defenders Under the U.S. Constitution, a defendant who is paying for her or his defense attorney has a right to choose that attorney without interference from the court. This right of choice does not extend to indigent defendants. According to the United States Supreme Court, "a defendant may not insist on an attorney he cannot afford."[40] In other words, an indigent defendant must accept the public defender provided by the court system. (Note that, unless the presiding judge rules otherwise, a person can waive her or his Sixth Amendment rights and act as her or his own defense attorney.) This lack of control contributes to the widespread belief that public defenders do not provide an acceptable level of defense to indigents. Statistics show, however, that conviction rates of defendants with private counsel and those represented by publicly funded attorneys are generally the same.[41]

ATTORNEY-CLIENT PRIVILEGE To defend a client effectively, a defense attorney must have access to all the facts concerning the case, even those that may be harmful to the defendant. To promote the unrestrained flow of information between the two parties, legislatures and lawyers themselves have constructed rules of **attorney-client privilege.** These rules require that communications between a client and his or her attorney be kept confidential, unless the client consents to the disclosure.

The Privilege and Confessions Attorney-client privilege does not stop short of confessions. Indeed, if, on hearing any statement that points toward guilt, the defense attorney could alert the prosecution or try to resign from the case, attorney-client privilege would be rendered meaningless. Even if the client says, "I have just killed seventeen women. I selected only pregnant women so I could torture them and kill two people at once. I did it. I liked it. I enjoyed it," the defense attorney must continue to do his or her utmost to serve that client.[42]

Without attorney-client privilege, observes legal expert John Kaplan, lawyers would be forced to give their clients the equivalent of the *Miranda*

Defense attorney John Amabile makes a point on behalf of his client in a Woburn, Massachusetts, courtroom. Why are the rules of attorney-client privilege necessary for a defense attorney to properly do his or her job?

ZUMA Press/Newscom

warning before representing them.[43] In other words, lawyers would have to make clear what clients could or could not say in the course of preparing for trial, because any incriminating statement might be used against the client in court. Such a development would have serious ramifications for the criminal justice system.

The Exception to the Privilege The scope of attorney-client privilege is not all encompassing. In *United States v. Zolin* (1989),[44] the Supreme Court ruled that lawyers may disclose the contents of a conversation with a client if the client has provided information concerning a crime that has yet to be committed. This exception applies only to communications involving a crime that is ongoing or will occur in the future. If the client reveals a past crime, the privilege is still in effect, and the attorney may not reveal any details of that particular criminal act.

Attorney-Client Privilege
A rule of evidence requiring that communications between a client and his or her attorney be kept confidential, unless the client consents to disclosure.

REVIEW

✓ **Review what you've read with the quiz below.**

Rip out the Chapter Review card at the back of this book, which includes:
- Chapter Summary and Learning Outcomes
- Key Terms

Or you can go online to CourseMate at www.cengagebrain.com to:
- Complete Practice Quizzes to prepare for tests.
- Review Key Terms Flash Cards (online or print).
- Play games to master concepts.

quiz

1. The due process function of American courts is to protect _____ in light of the various advantages that the prosecution enjoys during legal proceedings.

2. The _____ _____ function of the courts emphasizes punishment and the concept that criminals must suffer for the harm they do to society.

3. Before any court can hear a case, it must have _____ over the persons involved or the subject matter of the dispute.

4. The American court system is a dual court system composed of _____ courts and state courts.

5. When it agrees to hear an appeal of a lower court decision, the United States Supreme Court issues a writ of _____.

6. When a Supreme Court justice agrees with the Court's decision but for different reasons than those outlined in the majority opinion, he or she will write a _____ opinion setting forth his or her legal reasoning.

7. In some states, judges are nominated by the state's _____ and approved by the state legislature.

8. Public _____ initiate and conduct cases on behalf of society against the defendant.

9. The Sixth Amendment states that every person accused of a crime in the United States has a right to the assistance of _____.

10. Those defendants who cannot afford to hire a defense attorney are provided with _____ defenders by the government.

Answers can be found on the Chapter 7 Review card at the end of the book.

AP Photo/Mel Evans

Learning **OUTCOMES** | *After studying this chapter, you will be able to . . .*

end of the chapter, page 184.

1 Identify the steps involved in the pretrial criminal process.

2 Explain the main difference between an indictment and an information.

3 Identify the basic protections enjoyed by criminal defendants in the United States.

4 Contrast challenges for cause and peremptory challenges during *voir dire*.

5 List the standard steps in a criminal jury trial.

PRETRIAL PROCEDURES AND THE CRIMINAL TRIAL 8

The Missing Witness

Prosecutors faced several obstacles in proving that Drew Peterson killed Kathleen Savio, his third wife. To start with, no physical evidence or witnesses linked Peterson to any crime. In addition, when Savio was found dead in her bathtub in 2004, the coroner ruled that she had slipped, hit her head, and accidentally drowned. It was not until Peterson's fourth wife, Stacy, disappeared in 2007 that local police reopened the investigation into Savio's death. In the process, they became convinced that Peterson "took out" Stacy because she knew that he had killed Savio. Though suspicions regarding Peterson's role in Stacy's disappearance were never confirmed, the renewed law enforcement interest did lead to his indictment for murdering Savio.

Peterson and Savio had divorced a year before her death. Prosecutors believed that Peterson killed Savio to avoid splitting his financial assets with her. To succeed in court, they needed

to convince a Will County, Illinois, jury that (1) Savio's death was not an accident, and (2) despite lack of evidence, Peterson was the obvious culprit. The first objective was met with the help of experts who explained that Savio's exhumed body showed signs of fourteen separate injuries—too many to have been caused by a single fall in a relatively small bathtub. The second objective was trickier, because it relied on statements made by an unavailable witness: Stacy Peterson.

Despite protests by the defense, jurors did hear a number of these statements. For

example, Stacy's pastor testified that she told him that Peterson got out of bed and left their house in the middle of the night around the time of Savio's death. Stacy's divorce attorney also spoke in court, recounting a conversation with Stacy in which she "wanted to know if, in my opinion, the fact [that Peterson] killed Kathy could be used against him in the divorce proceeding." This evidence swayed the jury, and it convicted Peterson of murdering Savio. In February 2013, a judge sent him to prison for thirty-eight years.

Drew Peterson, shown here arriving at the Will County Courthouse in Joliet, Illinois, was convicted of murdering Kathleen Savio, his third wife.

AP Photo/M. Spencer Green

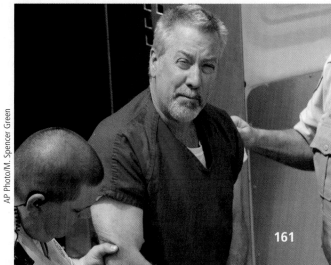

8-1
what HAPPENS AFTER ARREST ?

Not surprisingly, given the sordid nature of Kathleen Savio's death and Stacy Peterson's mysterious disappearance, Drew Peterson's murder trial attracted national attention. Those who followed the proceedings might have gotten a skewed version of how the criminal justice system works. According to the *"wedding cake" model* of our court system, only the top, and smallest, "layer" of trials comes close to meeting constitutional standards of procedural justice.[1] In these celebrity trials, such as Peterson's, committed (and expensive) attorneys argue minute technicalities for days, with numerous (and expensive) expert witnesses taking the stand for both sides.

On the bottom, largest layer of the wedding cake, the vast majority of defendants are dealt with informally, and the end goal seems to be speed rather than justice. Indeed, as you will see in this chapter, trial by jury is quite rare. The fate of most criminal suspects in this country is decided during pretrial procedures, which start almost as soon as the police have identified a suspect.

8-1a
The Initial Appearance

After an arrest has been made, the first step toward determining the suspect's guilt or innocence is the **initial appearance.** During this brief proceeding, a magistrate (see Chapter 7) informs the defendant of the charges that have been brought against him or her and explains his or her constitutional rights—particularly, the right to remain silent (under the Fifth Amendment) and the right to be represented by counsel (under the Sixth Amendment).

At this point, if the defendant cannot afford to hire a private attorney, a public defender may be appointed, or private counsel may be hired by the state to represent the defendant. As the U.S. Constitution does not specify how soon a defendant must be brought before a magistrate after arrest, it has been left to the judicial branch to determine the timing of the initial appearance. The Supreme Court has held that the initial appearance must occur "promptly," which in most cases means within forty-eight hours of booking.[2]

8-1b
Pretrial Detention

In misdemeanor cases, a defendant may decide to plead guilty and be sentenced during the initial appearance. Otherwise, the magistrate will usually release those charged with misdemeanors on their promise to return at a later date for further proceedings. For felony cases, however, the defendant is not permitted to make a plea at the initial appearance because a magistrate's court does not have jurisdiction to decide felonies. Furthermore, in most cases the defendant will be released only if she or he posts **bail**—an amount paid by the defendant to the court and retained by the court until the defendant returns for further proceedings.

Defendants who cannot afford bail are generally kept in a local jail or lockup until the date of their trial, though many jurisdictions are searching for alternatives to this practice because of overcrowded incarceration facilities. Government statisticians estimate that 58 percent of felony defendants are released before their trials.[3]

SETTING BAIL Bail is provided for under the Eighth Amendment. The amendment does not, however, guarantee the right to bail. Instead, it states that "excessive bail shall not be required." This has come to mean that in all cases except those involving a capital crime (where bail is prohibited), the amount of bail required must be reasonable compared with the seriousness of the wrongdoing. It does *not* mean that the amount of bail must be within the defendant's ability to pay.

There is no uniform system for pretrial detention. Each jurisdiction has its own *bail tariffs,* or general guidelines concerning the proper amount of bail. For misdemeanors, the police usually follow a preapproved bail schedule created by local judicial authorities. In felony cases, the primary responsibility to set bail lies with the judge. Figure 8.1 on the facing page shows typical bail amounts for violent offenses.

Initial Appearance An accused's first appearance before a judge or magistrate following arrest.

Bail The dollar amount or conditions set by the court to ensure that an individual accused of a crime will appear for further criminal proceedings.

FIGURE 8.1 Average Bail Amounts for Violent Felonies

These figures represent the mean bail figures for the seventy-five largest counties in the nation.

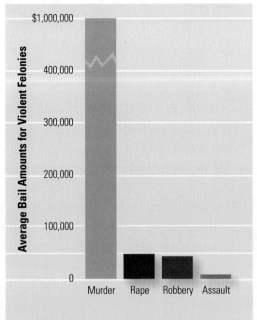

Source: Adapted from Bureau of Justice Statistics, *Felony Defendants in Large Urban Counties, 2006* (Washington, D.C.: U.S. Department of Justice, May 2010), Table 7, page 7.

PREVENTIVE DETENTION The vagueness of the Eighth Amendment has encouraged a second purpose of bail: to protect the community by preventing the defendant from committing another crime before trial. To achieve this purpose, a judge can set bail at a level the suspect cannot possibly afford. In January 2012, for example, a Los Angeles superior court judge set the bail for indigent defendant Harry Burkhart, accused of setting dozens of fires across the city over the New Year's weekend, at $2.85 million.

Alternatively, more than thirty states and the federal government have passed **preventive detention** legislation to the same effect. These laws allow judges to act "in the best interests of the community" by denying bail to arrestees with prior records of violence, thus keeping them in custody prior to trial.

8-1c
Gaining Pretrial Release

One of the most popular alternatives to bail is **release on recognizance (ROR).** This is used when the judge, based on the advice of trained personnel, decides that the defendant is not at risk to "jump" bail and does not pose a threat to the community. The defendant is then released at no cost with the understanding that he or she will return at the time of the trial. The Vera Institute, a nonprofit organization in New York City, introduced the concept of ROR as part of the Manhattan Bail Project in the 1960s, and such programs are now found in nearly every jurisdiction. When properly administered, ROR programs seem to be successful, with less than 5 percent of the participants failing to show for trial.[4]

POSTING BAIL Those suspected of committing a felony, however, are rarely released on recognizance. These defendants may post, or pay, the full amount of the bail in cash to the court. The money will be returned when the suspect appears for trial. Given the large amount of funds required, and the relative lack of wealth of many criminal defendants, a defendant can rarely post bail in cash. Another option is to use real property, such as a house, instead of cash as collateral. These **property bonds** are also rare because most courts require property valued at double the bail amount. Thus, if bail is set at $5,000, the defendant (or the defendant's family and friends) will have to produce property valued at $10,000.

BAIL BOND AGENTS If unable to post bail with cash or property, a defendant may arrange for a **bail bond agent** to post a bail bond on the defendant's behalf. The bond agent, in effect, promises the court that he or she will turn over to the court the full amount of bail if the defendant fails to return for further proceedings. The defendant usually must give the bond agent a certain percentage of the bail (frequently 10 percent) in cash.

This amount, which is often not returned to the defendant later, is considered payment for the bond agent's assistance and

---

Preventive Detention The retention of an accused person in custody due to fears that she or he will commit a crime if released before trial.

Release on Recognizance (ROR) A judge's order that releases an accused from jail with the understanding that he or she will return of his or her own will for further proceedings.

Property Bond An alternative to posting bail in cash, in which the defendant gains pretrial release by providing the court with property valued at the bail amount as assurance that he or she will return for trial.

Bail Bond Agent A businessperson who agrees, for a fee, to pay the bail amount if the accused fails to appear in court as ordered.

assumption of risk. Depending on the amount of the bail bond, the defendant may also be required to sign over to the bond agent rights to certain property (such as a car, a valuable watch, or other asset) as security for the bond. (**CAREER TIP:** Because bail bonds are a form of insurance, most jurisdictions require *bail bond agents* to obtain a license from the state Department of Insurance before starting business.)

8-2

how DOES A PROSECUTOR LINK A DEFENDANT TO A CRIME

Once the initial appearance has been completed and bail has been set, the prosecutor must establish *probable cause.* In other words, the prosecutor must show that a crime was committed and link the defendant to that crime. There are two formal procedures for establishing probable cause at this stage of the pretrial process: preliminary hearings and grand juries.

Preliminary Hearing An initial hearing in which a magistrate decides if there is probable cause to believe that the defendant committed the crime with which he or she is charged.

Discovery Formal investigation by each side prior to trial.

8-2a
The Preliminary Hearing

During the **preliminary hearing,** the defendant appears before a judge or magistrate who decides whether the evidence presented is sufficient for the case to proceed to trial. Normally, every person arrested has a right to this hearing within a reasonable amount of time after his or her initial arrest—usually, no later than ten days if the defendant is in custody or within thirty days if he or she has gained pretrial release.

THE PRELIMINARY HEARING PROCESS The preliminary hearing is conducted in the manner of a mini-trial. Typically, a police report of the arrest is presented by a law enforcement officer, supplemented with evidence provided by the prosecutor. Because the burden of proving probable cause is relatively light (compared with proving guilt beyond a reasonable doubt), prosecutors rarely call witnesses during the preliminary hearing, saving them for the trial.

During this hearing, the defendant has a right to be represented by counsel, who may cross-examine witnesses and challenge any evidence offered by the prosecutor. In most states, defense attorneys can take advantage of the preliminary hearing to begin the process of **discovery,** in which they are entitled to have access to any evidence in the possession of the prosecution relating to the case. Discovery is considered a keystone in the adversary process, as it allows the defense to see the evidence against the defendant prior to making a plea.

WAIVING THE HEARING The preliminary hearing often seems rather perfunctory, although in some jurisdictions it replaces grand jury proceedings. It usually lasts no longer than five minutes, and the judge or magistrate rarely finds that probable cause does not exist. For this reason, defense attorneys commonly advise their clients to waive their right to a preliminary hearing. Once a judge has ruled affirmatively, in many jurisdictions the defendant is bound over to the **grand jury,** a group of citizens called to decide whether probable cause exists. In other jurisdictions, the prosecutor issues an **information,** which replaces the police complaint as the formal charge against the defendant for the purposes of a trial.

8-2b

The Grand Jury

The federal government and about one-third of the states require a grand jury to make the decision as to whether a case should go to trial. Grand juries are *impaneled,* or created, for a period of time usually not exceeding three months. During that time, the grand jury sits in closed (secret) session and hears only evidence presented by the prosecutor—the defendant cannot present evidence at this hearing. The prosecutor presents to the grand jury whatever evidence the state has against the defendant, including photographs, documents, tangible objects, the testimony of witnesses, and other items. If the grand jury finds that probable cause exists, it issues an **indictment** (pronounced in-*dyte*-ment) against the defendant.

LO **2**

Like an information in a preliminary hearing, the indictment becomes the formal charge against the defendant. Some states require a grand jury to indict for certain crimes, while in other states a grand jury indictment is optional. (**CAREER TIP:** If a grand jury needs more evidence, it can issue a document called a subpoena, ordering a person to appear in court and answer its questions. The task of delivering the subpoena is often left to a *process server,* whose career is based on the challenge of finding people who do not want to be found.)

THE "SHIELD" AND THE "SWORD" The grand jury has a long history in the United States, having been brought over from England by the colonists and codified in the Fifth Amendment to the U.S. Constitution. Historically, it has acted as both a "shield" and a "sword" in the criminal justice process. By giving citizens the chance to review government charges of wrongdoing, it "shields" the individual from the power of the state. At the same time, the grand jury offers the government a "sword"—the opportunity to provide evidence against the accused—in its efforts to fight crime and protect society.[5]

A "RUBBER STAMP" Today, the protective function of the grand jury is in doubt—critics say that the "sword" aspect works too well and the "shield" aspect not at all. Statistically, the grand jury is even more prosecutor friendly than the preliminary hearing. Defendants are indicted at a rate of more than 99 percent,[6] leading to the common characterization of the grand jury as little more than a "rubber stamp" for the prosecution.

Certainly, the procedural rules of the grand jury favor prosecutors. The exclusionary rule (see Chapter 7) does not apply in grand jury investigations, so prosecutors can present evidence that would be disallowed at any subsequent trial. Furthermore, because the grand jury is given only one version of the facts—the prosecution's—it is likely to find probable cause. In the words of one observer, a grand jury would indict a "ham sandwich" if the government asked it to do so.[7] As a result of these concerns, a number of jurisdictions have abolished grand juries.

8-2c

Case Attrition

Prosecutorial discretion includes the power *not* to prosecute cases. Generally speaking, of every one hundred felony arrests in the United States, only thirty-five of the arrestees are prosecuted, and only eighteen of these prosecutions lead to incarceration. Consequently, fewer than one in three adults arrested for a felony sees the inside of a prison or jail cell. This phenomenon is known as **case attrition,** and it is explained in part by prosecutorial discretion.

About half of those adult felony cases brought to prosecutors by police are dismissed through a *nolle prosequi* (Latin for "unwilling to pursue"). Why are these cases "nolled," or not

Grand Jury The group of citizens called to decide whether probable cause exists to believe that a suspect committed the crime with which she or he has been charged.

Information The formal charge against the accused issued by the prosecutor after a preliminary hearing has found probable cause.

Indictment A charge or written accusation, issued by a grand jury, that probable cause exists to believe that a named person has committed a crime.

Case Attrition The process through which prosecutors, by deciding whether to prosecute each person arrested, effect an overall reduction in the number of persons prosecuted.

prosecuted by the district attorney? In the section on law enforcement, you learned that the police do not have the resources to arrest every lawbreaker in the nation. Similarly, district attorneys do not have the resources to prosecute every arrest. They must choose how to distribute their scarce resources.

In some cases, the decision is made for prosecutors, such as when police break procedural law and negate important evidence. This happens rarely—less than 1 percent of felony arrests are dropped because of the exclusionary rule, and almost all of these are the result of illegal drug searches.[8]

SCREENING FACTORS Most prosecutors have a *screening* process for deciding when to prosecute and when to "noll." This process varies a bit from jurisdiction to jurisdiction, but most prosecutors consider several factors in making the decision:[9]

- The most important factor in deciding whether to prosecute is not the prosecutor's belief in the guilt of the suspect, but whether there is *sufficient evidence for conviction.* If prosecutors have strong physical evidence and a number of reliable and believable witnesses, they are quite likely to prosecute.
- Prosecutors also rely heavily on *offense seriousness* to guide their priorities, preferring to take on felony offenses rather than misdemeanors. In other words, everything else being equal, a district attorney will prosecute a rapist instead of a jaywalker because the former presents a greater threat to society than does the latter. A prosecutor will also be more likely to prosecute someone with an extensive record of wrongdoing than a first-time offender.
- Sometimes, a case is dropped even when it involves a serious crime and a wealth of evidence exists against the suspect. These situations usually involve *uncooperative victims.* Domestic violence cases are particularly difficult to prosecute because the victims may want to keep the matter private, fear reprisals, or have a strong desire to

Arraignment A court proceeding in which the suspect is formally charged with the criminal offense stated in the indictment.

Nolo Contendere Latin for "I will not contest it." A criminal defendant's plea, in which he or she chooses not to challenge, or contest, the charges brought by the government.

protect their abuser. In some jurisdictions, as many as 80 percent of domestic violence victims refuse to cooperate with the prosecution.[10]

- *Unreliability of victims* can also affect a charging decision. If the victim in a rape case is a crack addict and a prostitute, while the defendant is a decorated military veteran, prosecutors may be hesitant to have a jury decide which one is more trustworthy.
- A prosecutor may be willing to drop a case or reduce the charges against *a defendant who is willing to testify against other offenders.* Federal law encourages this kind of behavior by offering sentencing reductions to defendants who provide "substantial assistance in the investigation or prosecution of another person who has committed an offense."[11]

(To get a better idea of the difficulty of some charging decisions, see the feature *You Be the Prosecutor—A Battered Woman* on the facing page.)

8-3
why DO SO MANY DEFENDANTS PLEAD GUILTY?

3 LO

Based on the information (delivered during the preliminary hearing) or indictment (handed down by the grand jury), the prosecutor submits a motion to the court to order the defendant to appear before the trial court for an **arraignment.** Due process of law, as guaranteed by the Fifth Amendment, requires that a criminal defendant be informed of the charges brought against her or him and be offered an opportunity to respond to those charges. The arraignment is one of the ways in which due process requirements are satisfied by criminal procedure law.

At the arraignment, the defendant is informed of the charges and must respond by pleading not guilty or guilty. In some but not all states, the defendant may also enter a plea of **nolo contendere,** which is Latin for "I will not contest it." The plea of *nolo contendere* is neither an admission nor a denial of guilt. (The consequences for someone who pleads guilty and for someone who pleads *nolo contendere* are the same in a

A BATTERED WOMAN

THE SITUATION For more than twenty years, John regularly beat his wife, Judy. He even put out cigarettes on her skin and slashed her face with glass. John was often unemployed and forced Judy into prostitution to earn a living. He regularly denied her food and threatened to maim or kill her. Judy left home several times, but John always managed to find her, bring her home, and punish her. Finally, Judy took steps to get John put in a psychiatric hospital. He told her that if anybody came for him, he would "see them coming" and cut her throat before they arrived. That night, Judy shot John three times in the back of the head while he was asleep, killing him. You are the prosecutor with authority over Judy.

THE LAW In your jurisdiction, a person can use deadly force in self-defense if it is necessary to kill an unlawful aggressor to save himself or herself from imminent death. (See pages 65–66 for a review of self-defense.) Voluntary manslaughter is the intentional killing of another human being without malice. It covers crimes of passion. First degree murder is premeditated killing, with malice. (See pages 57–58 for a review of the different degrees of murder.)

YOUR DECISION Will you charge Judy with voluntary manslaughter or first degree murder? Alternatively, do you believe she was acting in self-defense, in which case you will not charge her with any crime? Explain your choice.

[To see how a Rutherford County, North Carolina, prosecutor decided a case with similar facts, go to Example 8.1 in Appendix A.]

Gina Sanders/Shutterstock

---

criminal trial, but the latter plea cannot be used in a subsequent civil trial as an admission of guilt.) Most frequently, the defendant pleads guilty to the initial charge or to a lesser charge that has been agreed on through *plea bargaining* between the prosecutor and the defendant. If the defendant pleads guilty, no trial is necessary, and the defendant is sentenced based on the crime he or she has admitted committing.

8-3a

Plea Bargaining in the Criminal Justice System

Plea bargaining most often takes place after the arraignment and before the beginning of the trial. In its simplest terms, it is a process by which the accused, represented by the defense counsel, and the prosecutor work out a mutually satisfactory disposition of the case, subject to court approval.

Usually, plea bargaining involves the defendant's pleading guilty to the charges against her or him in return for a lighter sentence, but other variations are possible as well. The defendant can agree to plead guilty in exchange for having the charge against her or him reduced from, say, felony burglary to the lesser offense of breaking and entering. Or a person charged with multiple counts may agree to plead guilty if the prosecutor agrees to drop one or more of the counts. Whatever the particulars, the results of a plea bargain are generally the same: the prosecutor gets a conviction, and the defendant a lesser punishment.

In *Santobello v. New York* (1971),[12] the Supreme Court held that plea bargaining "is not only an essential part of the process but a highly desirable part for many reasons." Some observers would agree, but with ambivalence. They understand that plea bargaining offers the practical benefit of saving court resources, but question whether it is the best way to achieve justice.[13]

8-3b

Motivations for Plea Bargaining

Given the high rate of plea bargaining—accounting for 97 percent of criminal convictions in state courts[14]—it follows that the prosecutor, defense attorney, and defendant each have strong reasons to engage in the practice.

PROSECUTORS AND PLEA BARGAINING In most cases, a prosecutor has a single goal after charging

> **Plea Bargaining** The process by which the accused and the prosecutor work out a mutually satisfactory conclusion to the case, subject to court approval.

a defendant with a crime: conviction. If a case goes to trial, no matter how certain a prosecutor may be that the defendant is guilty, there is always a chance that a jury or judge will disagree. Plea bargaining removes this risk. Furthermore, the prosecutorial screening process described earlier in the chapter is not infallible. Sometimes, a prosecutor will find that the evidence against the accused is weaker than first thought or will uncover new information that changes the complexion of the case. In these situations, the prosecutor may decide to drop the charges or, if he or she still feels that the defendant is guilty, turn to plea bargaining to "save" a questionable case.

The prosecutor's role as an administrator also comes into play. She or he may be interested in the quickest, most efficient manner to dispose of caseloads, and plea bargains reduce the time and money spent on each case. Personal philosophy can affect the proceedings as well. A prosecutor who feels that a mandatory minimum sentence for a particular crime, such as marijuana possession, is too strict may plea bargain in order to lessen the penalty. Similarly, some prosecutors will consider plea bargaining only in certain instances—for burglary and theft, for example, but not for more serious felonies such as rape and murder.

DEFENSE ATTORNEYS AND PLEA BARGAINING
Political scientist Milton Heumann has said that the most important lesson that a defense attorney learns is that "most of his [or her] clients are guilty."[15]

Given this stark reality, favorable plea bargains are often the best a defense attorney can do for clients, aside from helping them to gain acquittals. Some have suggested that defense attorneys have other, less savory motives for convincing a client to plead guilty, such as a desire to increase profit margins by quickly disposing of cases[16] or a wish to ingratiate themselves with the other members of the courtroom work group by showing their "reasonableness."[17]

DEFENDANTS AND PLEA BARGAINING
The plea bargain allows the defendant a measure of control over his or her fate. In August 2012, for example, Jared Loughner pleaded guilty to killing six people and wounding thirteen others, including Arizona congresswoman Gabrielle Giffords, in Tucson twenty months earlier (see photo below). Had his case gone to trial, Loughner risked being convicted and given the death penalty. Under the terms of the plea agreement, Loughner will spend the rest of his life in prison. Generally speaking, defendants who plea bargain receive significantly lighter sentences on average than those who are found guilty at trial.

VICTIMS AND PLEA BARGAINING
One of the major goals of the victims' rights movement has been to increase the role of victims in the plea bargaining process. In recent years, the movement has had some success in this area. About half of the states now allow for victim participation in plea bargaining. Many have laws similar to North Carolina's statute that requires the district attorney's office to offer victims "the opportunity to consult with the prosecuting attorney" and give their views on "plea possibilities."[18] On the federal level, the Crime Victims' Rights Act grants victims the right to be "reasonably heard" during the process.[19]

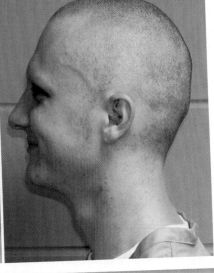

Why did Jared Loughner agree to plead guilty to multiple charges stemming from his shooting rampage in Tucson, Arizona? What incentives might federal prosecutors have had for accepting Loughner's guilty plea and declining to seek his execution?

AP Photo/U.S. Marshal's Office, File

Crime victims often have mixed emotions regarding plea bargains. On the one hand, any form of "negotiated justice" that lessens the offender's penalty may add insult to the victim's emotional and physical injuries. "This is too little, too late," said Suzi Hillman, who had been shot multiple times by Jared Loughner in Tucson.[20] On the other hand, trials can bring up events and emotions that some victims would rather not have to re-experience. In the words of Mark Kelley, Gabrielle Giffords's husband, "Avoiding trial [for Loughner] will allow us, and we hope the whole Southern Arizona community, to continue with our recovery and move forward with our lives."[21]

8-3c
Pleading Not Guilty

Despite the large number of defendants who eventually plead guilty, the plea of not guilty is fairly common at the arraignment. This is true even when the facts of the case seem stacked against the defendant. Generally, a not guilty plea in the face of strong evidence is part of a strategy to (1) gain a more favorable plea bargain, (2) challenge a crucial part of the evidence on constitutional grounds, or (3) submit one of the affirmative defenses discussed in Chapter 3.

Of course, if either side is confident in the strength of its arguments and evidence, it will obviously be less likely to accept a plea bargain. Both prosecutors and defense attorneys may favor a trial to gain publicity, and sometimes public pressure after an extremely violent or high-profile crime will force a chief prosecutor (who is, remember, normally an elected official) to take a weak case to trial. Also, some defendants may insist on their right to a trial, regardless of their attorneys' advice. In the remainder of this chapter, we will examine what happens to the roughly 3 percent of indictments that do lead to the courtroom.

8-4
what ARE THE SPECIAL FEATURES OF CRIMINAL TRIALS?

Criminal trial procedures reflect the need to protect criminal defendants against the power of the state by providing them with a number of rights. Many of the significant rights of the accused are spelled out in the Sixth Amendment, which reads, in part, as follows:

> In all criminal prosecutions, the accused shall enjoy the right to a speedy and public trial, by an impartial jury of the State and the district wherein the crime shall have been committed, . . . and to be informed of the nature and cause of the accusation; to be confronted with the witnesses against him; to have compulsory process for obtaining witnesses in his favor; and to have the Assistance of Counsel for his defense.

In the last chapter, we discussed the Sixth Amendment's guarantee of the right to counsel. In this section, we will examine the other important aspects of the criminal trial, beginning with two protections explicitly stated in the Sixth Amendment: the right to a speedy trial by an impartial jury.

8-4a
A "Speedy" Trial

As you have just read, the Sixth Amendment requires a speedy trial for those accused of a criminal act. The reason for this requirement is obvious: depending on various factors, the defendant may lose his or her right to move freely and may be incarcerated prior to trial. Also, the accusation that a person has committed a crime jeopardizes that person's reputation in the community. If the defendant is innocent, the sooner the trial is held, the sooner his or her innocence can be established in the eyes of the court and the public.

The Sixth Amendment does not specify what is meant by the term *speedy*. The United States Supreme Court has refused to quantify "speedy" as well, ruling instead in *Barker v. Wingo* (1972)[22] that only in situations in which the delay is unwarranted and proved to be prejudicial can the accused claim a violation of Sixth Amendment rights.

Note that the Sixth Amendment's guarantee of a speedy trial does not apply until a person has been accused of a crime. Citizens are protected against unreasonable delays before accusation by **statutes of limitations,** which are legislative time limits that require prosecutors to charge a defendant with a crime within a certain amount of time after the illegal act took place. If the statute of limitations on a particular crime is ten years, and the police do not

Statute of Limitations A law limiting the amount of time prosecutors have to bring criminal charges against a suspect after the crime has occurred.

Despite evidence that he had sexually abused a minor, former Syracuse University assistant basketball coach Bernie Fine, right, was never charged with a crime due to a statute of limitations. What are the arguments for and against statutes of limitations in sexual abuse cases?

Jim McIsaac/Getty Images

identify a suspect until ten years and one day after the criminal act occurred, then that suspect cannot be charged with that particular offense. In general, prosecutions for murder and other offenses that carry the death penalty do not have a statute of limitations.

8-4b
The Role of the Jury

The Sixth Amendment also states that anyone accused of a crime shall be judged by "an impartial jury." In *Duncan v. Louisiana* (1968),[23] the Supreme Court solidified this right by ruling that in all felony cases, the defendant is entitled to a **jury trial.** The Court has, however, left it to the individual states to decide whether juries are required for misdemeanor cases. If the defendant waives her or his right to trial by jury, a **bench trial** takes place in which a judge decides questions of legality and fact, and no jury is involved.

The typical American jury consists of twelve persons. About half the states allow fewer than twelve persons on criminal juries, though rarely for serious felony cases. In federal courts, defendants are entitled to have the case heard by a twelve-member jury unless both parties agree in writing to a smaller jury.

Jury Trial A trial before a judge and a jury.

Bench Trial A trial conducted without a jury, in which a judge makes the determination of the defendant's guilt or innocence.

Acquittal A declaration following a trial that the individual accused of the crime is innocent in the eyes of the law and thus is absolved from the charges.

In most jurisdictions, jury verdicts in criminal cases must be *unanimous* for **acquittal** or conviction. As will be explained in more detail later, if the jury cannot reach unanimous agreement on whether to acquit or convict the defendant, the result is a *hung jury,* and the judge may order a new trial. The Supreme Court has held that unanimity is not a rigid requirement. It declared that jury verdicts must be unanimous in federal criminal trials, but has given states leeway to set their own rules.[24] As a result, Louisiana and Oregon continue to require only ten votes for conviction in criminal cases.

8-4c
The Privilege against Self-Incrimination

In addition to the Sixth Amendment, which specifies the protections we have just discussed, the Fifth Amendment to the Constitution also provides important safeguards for the defendant. The Fifth Amendment states that no person "shall be compelled in any criminal case to be a witness against himself." Therefore, a defendant has the right not to testify at a trial if to do so would implicate him or her in the crime.

It is important to note that not only does the defendant have the right to "take the Fifth," but also that the decision to do so should not prejudice the jury in the prosecution's favor. The Supreme Court came to this controversial decision while reviewing *Adamson v. California* (1947),[25] a case involving the convictions of two defendants who had declined to testify in their own defense against charges of robbery, kidnapping, and murder. The prosecutor in the *Adamson* proceedings frequently and insistently brought this silence to the notice of the jury in his closing argument, insinuating that if the pair had been innocent, they would not have been afraid to testify. The Court ruled that such tactics effectively invalidated the Fifth Amendment by using the defendants' refusal to testify against them. Now judges are required to inform the jury that an accused's decision to remain silent cannot be held against him or her.

8-4d
The Presumption of a Defendant's Innocence

The presumption in criminal law is that a defendant is innocent until proved guilty. The burden of proving guilt falls on the state (the public prosecutor). Even if a defendant did in fact commit the crime, she or he will be "innocent" in the eyes of the law unless the prosecutor can substantiate the charge with sufficient evidence to convince a jury (or judge in a bench trial) of the defendant's guilt.[26]

Sometimes, especially when a case involves a high-profile violent crime, pretrial publicity may have convinced many members of the community—including potential jurors—that a defendant is guilty. In these instances, a judge has the authority to change the venue of the trial to increase the likelihood of an unbiased jury. In 2012, defense attorneys for Thayne Ormsby requested a change of venue for their client's trial for the brutal murders of two men and a ten-year-old boy in Houlton, Maine. Given the size of Houlton—population 6,123—and the case's local notoriety, Ormsby's lawyers successfully argued that the trial should be moved to Caribou, sixty miles to the north.

8-4e
A Strict Standard of Proof

In a criminal trial, the defendant is not required to prove his or her innocence. As mentioned earlier, the burden of proving the defendant's guilt lies entirely with the state. Furthermore, the state must prove the defendant's guilt *beyond a reasonable doubt.* In other words, the prosecution must show that, based on all the evidence, the defendant's guilt is clear and unquestionable. In *In re Winship* (1970),[27] a case involving the due process rights of juveniles, the Supreme Court ruled that the Constitution requires the reasonable doubt standard because it reduces the risk of convicting innocent people and therefore reassures Americans of the law's moral force and legitimacy.

This high standard of proof in criminal cases reflects a fundamental social value—the belief that

it is worse to convict an innocent individual than to let a guilty one go free. The consequences to the life, liberty, and reputation of an accused person from an erroneous conviction for a crime are substantial, and this has been factored into the process. Placing a high standard of proof on the prosecutor reduces the margin of error in criminal cases (at least in one direction).

8-5
how IS THE JURY SELECTED ?

The initial step in a criminal trial involves choosing the jury. The main goal of jury selection is to produce a cross section of the population in the jurisdiction where the crime was committed. Besides having to live in the jurisdiction where the case is being tried, there are very few restrictions on eligibility to serve on a jury. State legislatures generally set the requirements, and they are similar in most states. For the most part, jurors must be

1. Citizens of the United States.
2. Eighteen years of age or over.
3. Free of felony convictions.
4. Healthy enough to function in a jury setting.
5. Sufficiently intelligent to understand the issues of a trial.
6. Able to read, write, and comprehend the English language, with one exception—New Mexico does not allow non-English-speaking citizens to be eliminated from jury lists simply because of their lack of English-language skills. (**CAREER TIP:** In New Mexico, Spanish-speaking jurors require the use of a *court interpreter* to translate the proceedings for them. In all states, court interpreters are often used to help a defendant, witness, or other key trial participant understand what is being said in court.)

The **master jury list,** sometimes called the *jury pool,* is made up of all the eligible jurors in a community. This list is usually drawn from

Master Jury List The list of citizens in a court's district from which a jury can be selected; compiled from voter-registration lists, driver's license lists, and other sources.

A Boston jury waits to be dismissed after finding Christian K. Gerhartsreiter guilty of kidnapping his seven-year-old daughter during a supervised visit. Why is it important for a defendant to be tried by a jury of her or his "peers"?

AP Photo/CJ Gunther, Pool

voter-registration lists or driver's license rolls, which have the benefit of being easily available and timely.

The next step in gathering a jury is to draw together the **venire** (Latin for "to come"). The *venire* is composed of all those people who are notified by the clerk of the court that they have been selected for jury duty. Those selected to be part of the *venire* are ordered to report to the courthouse on the date specified by the notice.

8-5a

Voir Dire

At the courthouse, prospective jurors are gathered, and the process of selecting those who will actually hear the case begins. This selection process is not haphazard. The court ultimately seeks jurors who are free of any biases that may affect their willingness to listen to the facts of the case impartially. To this end, both the prosecutor and the defense attorney have some input into the ultimate makeup of the jury. Each attorney

Venire The group of citizens from which the jury is selected.

Voir Dire The preliminary questions that the trial attorneys ask prospective jurors to determine whether they are biased or have any connection with the defendant or a witness.

Challenge for Cause A *voir dire* challenge for which an attorney states the reason why a prospective juror should not be included on the jury.

questions prospective jurors in a proceeding known as **voir dire** (French for "to speak the truth"). During *voir dire*, jurors are required to provide the court with a significant amount of personal information, including home address, marital status, employment status, arrest record, and life experiences.

QUESTIONING POTENTIAL JURORS The *voir dire* process involves both written and oral questioning of potential jurors. Attorneys fashion their inquiries so as to uncover any biases of prospective jurors and to find persons who might identify with their respective sides. As one attorney noted, though a lawyer will have many chances to talk to a jury as a whole, *voir dire* is his or her only chance to talk with the individual jurors. (To better understand the specific kinds of questions asked, see Figure 8.2 on the facing page.)

CHALLENGING POTENTIAL JURORS During *voir dire*, the attorney for each side may exercise a certain number of challenges to prevent particular persons from serving on the jury. Both sides can exercise two types of challenges: challenges "for cause" and peremptory challenges.

Challenges for Cause If a defense attorney or prosecutor concludes that a prospective juror is unfit to serve, the attorney may exercise a **challenge for cause** and request that that person not be included on the jury. Attorneys must provide the court with a sound, legally justifiable reason for why potential jurors are "unfit" to serve. For example, jurors can be challenged for cause if they are mentally incompetent, do not

FIGURE 8.2 Sample Juror Questionnaire

Drew Peterson, featured in the opening of this chapter, had gone through seemingly endless marital difficulties with Kathleen Savio, his third wife and alleged murder victim. As Peterson's relationship with Savio would play a significant role in the criminal proceedings, both the prosecution and the defense were interested in learning about the personal lives of potential jurors. The lawyers also wanted to determine whether prospective jurors had been exposed to media coverage of Peterson. The following excerpt from the juror questionnaire reflects both of these concerns.

> **7A.** Has your marital status changed since 2010?
>
> **8A.** Have you ever witnessed or been involved in a domestic dispute in which the police were called? If the answer is yes, did it result in an arrest?
>
> **9A.** Do you now or have you ever paid or received child support or maintenance, sometimes called alimony?
>
> **12A.** The *Lifetime* network commissioned and broadcast a made-for-television movie which purported to be about Drew Peterson. Have you seen this movie?

understand English, or are proved to have a prior link—be it personal or financial—with the defendant or victim.

Peremptory Challenges Each attorney may also exercise a limited number of **peremptory challenges.** These challenges are based solely on an attorney's subjective reasoning, and the attorney usually is not required to give any legally justifiable reason for wanting to exclude a particular person from the jury. Because of the rather random nature of peremptory challenges, each state limits the number that an attorney may utilize: between five and ten for felony trials (depending on the state) and between ten and twenty for trials that could possibly result in the death penalty (also depending on the state). Once an attorney's peremptory challenges are used up, he or she must accept forthcoming jurors, unless a challenge for cause can be used.

8-5b

Race and Gender Issues in Jury Selection

For many years, prosecutors used their peremptory challenges as an instrument of segregation in jury selection. Prosecutors were able to keep African Americans off juries in cases in which an African American was the defendant. The argument that African Americans—or members of any other minority group—would be partial toward one of their own was tacitly supported by the Supreme Court. Despite its own assertion, made in *Swain v. Alabama* (1965),[28] that blacks have the same right to appear on a jury as whites, the Court mirrored the apparent racism of society as a whole by protecting the questionable actions of many prosecutors.

THE *BATSON* REVERSAL The Supreme Court reversed this policy in 1986 with *Batson v. Kentucky.*[29] In that case, the Court declared that the Constitution prohibits prosecutors from using peremptory challenges to strike possible jurors on the basis of race. Under the *Batson* ruling, the defendant must prove that the prosecution's use of a peremptory challenge was racially motivated. Doing so requires a number of legal steps:[30]

1. First, the defendant must make a *prima facie* case that there has been discrimination during *venire.* (*Prima facie* is Latin for "at first sight." Legally, it refers to a fact that is presumed to be true unless contradicted by evidence.)

2. To do so, the defendant must show that he or she is a member of a recognizable racial group and that the prosecutor has used peremptory challenges to remove members of this group from the jury pool.

3. Then, the defendant must show that these facts and other relevant circumstances raise the possibility that the prosecutor removed the prospective jurors solely because of their race.

4. If the court accepts the defendant's charges, the burden shifts to the prosecution

Peremptory Challenges *Voir dire* challenges to exclude potential jurors from serving on the jury without any supporting reason or cause.

to prove that its peremptory challenges were race neutral. If the court finds against the prosecution, it rules that a *Batson* violation has occurred.

The Court has revisited the issue of race a number of times in the years since its *Batson* decision. In *Powers v. Ohio* (1991),[31] it ruled that a defendant may contest race-based peremptory challenges even if the defendant is not of the same race as the excluded jurors. In *Georgia v. McCollum* (1992),[32] the Court placed defense attorneys under the same restrictions as prosecutors when making race-based peremptory challenges. Finally, in 2008, the Court, reaffirming its *Batson* decision of twenty-two years earlier, overturned the conviction of an African American death row inmate because a Louisiana prosecutor improperly picked an all-white jury for his murder trial.[33]

WOMEN ON THE JURY In *J.E.B. v. Alabama ex rel. T.B.* (1994),[34] the Supreme Court extended the principles of the *Batson* ruling to cover gender bias in jury selection. The case was a civil suit for paternity and child support brought by the state of Alabama. Prosecutors used nine of their ten challenges to remove men from the jury, while the defense made similar efforts to remove women. When challenged, the state defended its actions by referring to what it called the rational belief that men and women might have different views on the issues of paternity and child support. The Court disagreed and held this approach to be unconstitutional.

8-6 what HAPPENS DURING A CRIMINAL TRIAL?

Once the jury members have been selected, the judge swears them in and the trial itself can begin. (See Figure 8.3 on the facing page for a preview of the stages of a jury trial that will be detailed in this

FIGURE 8.3 The Steps of a Jury Trial

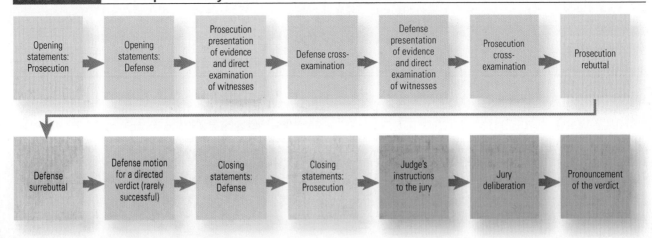

section.) A rather pessimistic truism among attorneys is that every case "has been won or lost when the jury is sworn." This reflects the belief that a juror's values are the major, if not dominant, factor in the decision of guilt or innocence.[35]

In actuality, it is difficult to predict how a jury will go about reaching a decision. Despite a number of studies on the question, researchers have not been able to identify any definitive consistent patterns of jury behavior. Sometimes, jurors in a criminal trial will follow instructions to find a defendant guilty unless there is a reasonable doubt, and sometimes they seem to follow instinct or prejudice and apply the law any way they choose.

8-6a
Opening Statements

Attorneys may choose to open the trial with a statement to the jury, though they are not required to do so. In these **opening statements,** the attorneys give a brief version of the facts and the supporting evidence that they will present during the trial. Because some trials can drag on for weeks or even months, it is extremely helpful for jurors to hear a summary of what will unfold. In short, the opening statement is a kind of "road map" that describes the destination that each attorney hopes to reach and outlines how she or he plans to reach it.

8-6b
The Role of Evidence

Once the opening statements have been made, the prosecutor begins the trial proceedings by presenting the state's evidence against the defendant. Courts have complex rules about what types of evidence may be presented and how the evidence may be brought out during the trial. **Evidence** is anything that is used to prove the existence or nonexistence of a fact. For the most part, evidence can be broken down into two categories: testimony and real evidence. **Testimony** consists of statements by competent witnesses. **Real evidence,** presented to the court in the form of exhibits, includes any physical items—such as the murder weapon or a bloodstained piece of clothing—that affect the case. (**CAREER TIP:** *Evidence technicians help the police and prosecutors gain convictions by identifying, securing, collecting, cataloguing, and storing evidence found at a crime scene.*)

Rules of evidence are designed to ensure that testimony and exhibits presented to the jury are relevant, reliable, and not unfairly prejudicial against the defendant. One of the tasks of the defense attorney is to challenge evidence presented by the prosecution by establishing that the evidence is not reliable. Of course, the prosecutor also tries to demonstrate the irrelevance or unreliability of evidence presented by the defense. The final decision on whether evidence is allowed before the jury rests with the judge, in keeping with his or her role as the "referee" of the criminal trial.

LO **5**

Opening Statements The attorneys' statements to the jury at the beginning of the trial.

Evidence Anything that is used to prove the existence or nonexistence of a fact.

Testimony Verbal evidence given by witnesses under oath.

Real Evidence Evidence that is brought into court and seen by the jury, as opposed to evidence that is described for a jury.

CAREERPREP

JOB DESCRIPTION:

- Pretrial: Research jurors' backgrounds, assist with juror selection, create favorable potential juror profiles, develop *voir dire* questions, and organize mock trials to aid trial attorneys.

- During trial: Carefully watch jurors' body language and behavior to determine if the client trial lawyer is communicating her or his arguments successfully, coach witnesses, and help trial lawyers develop strategies.

WHAT KIND OF TRAINING IS REQUIRED?

- Minimum of a bachelor's degree (although a master's degree or a Ph.D. is ideal) in sociology, political science, criminology, psychology, or behavioral science. Research and data analysis skills are also crucial for this profession.

SOCIAL MEDIA CAREER TIP
You need to differentiate yourself from everyone else online by providing unique, relevant, high-quality content on a regular basis. You should network with a purpose, not just to share fun things.

JURY CONSULTANT

- A strongly developed intuition. Jury consultants are not hired for their expertise in criminal law but for their insight into human behavior, decision making, and motivational patterns.

ANNUAL SALARY RANGE?

- $40,000–$100,000

Alina Solovyova-Vincent/iStockphoto

TESTIMONIAL EVIDENCE A person who is called to testify on factual matters that would be understood by the average citizen is referred to as a **lay witness.** If asked about the condition of a victim of an assault, for example, a lay witness could relate certain facts, such as "she was bleeding from her forehead" or "she was unconscious on the ground for several minutes."

A lay witness could not, however, give information about the medical extent of the victim's injuries, such as whether she suffered from a fractured skull or internal bleeding. Coming from a lay witness, such testimony would be inadmissible.

When the matter in question requires scientific, medical, or technical skill beyond the scope of the average person, prosecutors and defense attorneys may call an **expert witness** to the stand. The expert witness is an individual who has professional training, advanced knowledge, or substantial experience in a specialized area, such as medicine, computer technology, or ballistics.

DIRECT VERSUS CIRCUMSTANTIAL EVIDENCE
Two types of testimonial evidence may be brought into court: direct evidence and circumstantial evidence. **Direct evidence** is evidence that has been witnessed by the person giving testimony. "I saw Bill shoot Chris" is an example of direct evidence. **Circumstantial evidence** is indirect evidence that, even if believed, does not establish the fact in question but only the degree of likelihood of the fact. In other words, circumstantial evidence can create an inference that a fact exists.

Suppose, for example, that the defendant owns a gun that shoots bullets of the type found in the victim's body. This circumstantial evidence, by itself, does not establish that the defendant committed the crime. Combined with other circumstantial evidence, however, it may do just that. For instance, if other circumstantial evidence indicates that the defendant

---

Lay Witness A witness who can truthfully and accurately testify on a fact in question without having specialized training or knowledge.

Expert Witness A witness with professional training or substantial experience qualifying her or him to testify on a certain subject.

Direct Evidence Evidence that establishes the existence of a fact that is in question without relying on inference.

Circumstantial Evidence Indirect evidence that is offered to establish, by inference, the likelihood of a fact that is in question.

had a motive for harming the victim and was at the scene of the crime when the shooting occurred, the jury might conclude that the defendant committed the crime. The prosecutor's successful case against Drew Peterson for the murder of Kathleen Savio, described in the opening of the chapter, was based entirely on circumstantial evidence.

THE "CSI EFFECT" When possible, defense attorneys will almost always make the argument that the state has failed to present any evidence other than circumstantial evidence against their client. Recently, this tactic has been aided by a phenomenon known as the "CSI effect," taking its name from the popular television series *CSI: Crime Scene Investigation* and its spin-offs. According to many prosecutors, these shows have fostered unrealistic notions among jurors as to what high-tech forensic science can accomplish as part of a criminal investigation.

In reality, the kind of physical evidence used to solve crimes on *CSI* is often not available to the prosecution, which must rely instead on witnesses and circumstantial evidence. Several years ago, researchers surveyed more than one thousand jurors in Washtenaw County, Michigan, and found that nearly half "expected the prosecutor to present scientific evidence in every criminal case." This expectation was particularly strong in rape trials and trials lacking direct evidence of a crime.[36]

RELEVANCE Evidence will not be admitted in court unless it is relevant to the case being considered. **Relevant evidence** is evidence that tends to prove or disprove a fact in question. Forensic proof that the bullets found in a victim's body were fired from a gun discovered in the suspect's pocket at the time of arrest, for example, is certainly relevant. The suspect's prior record, showing a conviction for armed robbery ten years earlier, is, as we shall soon see, irrelevant to the case at hand and in most instances will be ruled inadmissible by the judge.

PREJUDICIAL EVIDENCE Evidence may be excluded if it would tend to distract the jury from the main issues of the case, mislead the jury, or cause jurors to decide the issue on an emotional basis. In practice, this rule often precludes prosecutors from using prior purported criminal activities

or actual convictions to show that the defendant has criminal propensities or an "evil character."[37] This concept is codified in the Federal Rules of Evidence, which state that evidence of "other crimes, wrongs, or acts is not admissible to prove the character of a person in order to show action in conformity therewith." Such evidence is allowed only when it does not apply to character construction and focuses instead on "motive, opportunity, intent, preparation, plan, knowledge, identity, or absence of mistake or accident."[38]

Although this legal concept has come under a great deal of criticism, it is consistent with the presumption-of-innocence standards discussed earlier. Arguably, if a prosecutor is allowed to establish that the defendant has shown antisocial or even violent traits in the past, this will prejudice the jury against the defendant in the present trial. Even if the judge instructs jurors that this prior evidence is irrelevant, human nature dictates that it will probably have a "warping influence" on the jurors' perception of the defendant.[39] Therefore, whenever possible, defense attorneys will keep such evidence from the jury.

8-6c
The Prosecution's Case

Because the burden of proof is on the state, the prosecution is generally considered to have a more difficult task than the defense. The prosecutor attempts to establish guilt beyond a reasonable doubt by presenting the *corpus delicti* ("body of the offense" in Latin) of the crime to the jury. The *corpus delicti* is simply a legal term that refers to the substantial facts that show a crime has been committed. By establishing such facts through the presentation of relevant and nonprejudicial evidence, the prosecutor hopes to convince the jury of the defendant's guilt.

DIRECT EXAMINATION OF WITNESSES Witnesses are crucial to establishing the prosecutor's case against the defendant. The prosecutor will call witnesses to the stand and ask them questions pertaining to the sequence of events that the trial is addressing. This form of questioning is

Relevant Evidence
Evidence tending to make a fact in question more or less probable than it would be without the evidence. Only relevant evidence is admissible in court.

Cheri Young is subjected to direct examination during the campaign finance fraud trial of former North Carolina senator John Edwards, her husband's former employer. How do prosecutors use witnesses to establish the *corpus delicti* of an alleged crime?

AP Photo/Sara D. Davis, File

known as **direct examination.** During direct examination, the prosecutor will usually not be allowed to ask *leading questions*—questions that might suggest to the witness a particular desired response.

A leading question might be something like "So, Mrs. Williams, you noticed the defendant threatening the victim with a broken beer bottle?" If Mrs. Williams answers "yes" to this question, she has, in effect, been "led" to the conclusion that the defendant was, in fact, threatening with a broken beer bottle. The fundamental purpose behind testimony is to establish what actually happened, not what the trial attorneys would like the jury to believe happened. (A properly worded query would be, "Mrs. Williams, please describe the defendant's manner toward the victim during the incident.")

COMPETENCE AND RELIABILITY OF WITNESSES The rules of evidence include certain restrictions and qualifications pertaining to witnesses. Witnesses must have sufficient mental competence to understand the significance of testifying under oath. They must also be reliable in the sense that they are able to give a clear and reliable description of the events in question. If not, the prosecutor or defense attorney will make sure that the jury is aware of these shortcomings through *cross-examination.*

Direct Examination The examination of a witness by the attorney who calls the witness to the stand to testify.

Confrontation Clause The part of the Sixth Amendment that guarantees all defendants the right to confront witnesses testifying against them during the criminal trial.

Cross-Examination The questioning of an opposing witness during trial.

Hearsay An oral or written statement made by an out-of-court speaker that is later offered in court by a witness (not the speaker) concerning a matter before the court.

8-6d
Cross-Examination

After the prosecutor has directly examined her or his witnesses, the defense attorney is given the chance to question the same witnesses. The Sixth Amendment states, "In all criminal prosecutions, the accused shall enjoy the right . . . to be confronted with witnesses against him." This **confrontation clause** gives the accused, through his or her attorneys, the right to cross-examine witnesses. **Cross-examination** refers to the questioning of an opposing witness during trial, and both sides of a case are allowed to do so.

Cross-examination allows the attorneys to test the truthfulness of opposing witnesses and usually entails efforts to create doubt in the jurors' minds that the witness is reliable. After the defense has cross-examined a prosecution witness, the prosecutor may want to reestablish any reliability that might have been lost. The prosecutor can do so by again questioning the witness, a process known as *redirect examination.*

Following the redirect examination, the defense attorney will be given the opportunity to ask further questions of prosecution witnesses, or recross-examination. Thus, each side has two opportunities to question a witness. The attorneys need not do so, but only after each side has been offered the opportunity will the trial move on to the next witness or the next stage.

HEARSAY Cross-examination is also linked to problems presented by *hearsay* evidence. **Hearsay** can be defined as any testimony given about a statement made by someone else. Literally, it is what someone heard someone else say. For the most part, hearsay is not admissible as evidence. When a witness offers hearsay, the person making the original remarks is not in court and therefore cannot be cross-examined. If such testimony were allowed, the defendant's Sixth Amendment right to confront witnesses against him or her would be violated.

There are a number of exceptions to the hearsay rule, and as a result a good deal of hearsay evidence finds its way into criminal trials. For example, a hearsay statement is usually admissible if there seems to be little risk of a lie. Therefore, a statement made by someone who believes that his or her death is imminent—a "dying declaration" or a suicide note—is often allowed in court even though it is hearsay.[40] Similarly, the rules of most states allow hearsay when the statement contains an admission of wrongdoing *and* the speaker is not available to testify in court. The logic behind this exception is that a person generally does not make a statement against her or his own best interests unless it is true.[41]

8-6e
The Defendant's Case

After the prosecution has finished presenting its evidence, the defense attorney may offer the defendant's case. Because the burden is on the state to prove the accused's guilt, the defense is not required to offer any case at all. It can simply "rest" without calling any witnesses or producing any real evidence and ask the jury to decide the merits of the case on what it has seen and heard from the prosecution.

CREATING A REASONABLE DOUBT Defense lawyers most commonly defend their clients by attempting to expose weaknesses in the prosecutor's case. Remember that if the defense attorney can create reasonable doubt concerning the client's guilt in the mind of just a single juror, the defendant has a good chance of gaining an acquittal or at least a *hung jury,* a circumstance explained later in the chapter.

Even if the prosecution can present seemingly strong evidence, a defense attorney may succeed by creating reasonable doubt. In an illustrative case, Jason Korey bragged to his friends that he had shot and killed Joseph Brucker in Pittsburgh, Pennsylvania, and

a great deal of circumstantial evidence linked Korey to the killing. The police, however, could find no direct evidence: they could not link Korey to the murder weapon, nor could they match his footprints to those found at the crime scene. Michael Foglia, Korey's defense attorney, explained his client's bragging as an attempt to gain attention, not a true statement. Though this explanation may strike some as unlikely, in the absence of physical evidence it did create doubt in the jurors' minds, and Korey was acquitted. (**CAREER TIP:** By using various methods such as making plaster casts or measuring impressions in the ground, *forensic footprint experts* can match footprints found at a crime scene with a suspect's bare foot or shoe.)

OTHER DEFENSE STRATEGIES The defense can choose among a number of strategies to generate reasonable doubt in the jurors' minds. It can present an *alibi defense,* by submitting evidence that the accused was not at or near the scene of the crime at the time the crime was committed. Another option is to attempt an *affirmative defense,* by presenting additional facts to the ones offered by the prosecution. Possible affirmative defenses, which we discussed in detail in Chapter 3, include the following:

1. Self-defense
2. Insanity
3. Duress
4. Entrapment

With an affirmative defense strategy, the defense attempts to prove that the defendant should be found not guilty because of certain circumstances surrounding the crime. An affirmative strategy can be difficult to carry out because it forces the defense to prove the reliability of its own evidence, not simply disprove the evidence offered by the prosecution.

The defense is often willing to admit that a certain criminal act took place, especially if the defendant has already confessed. In this case, the primary question of the trial becomes not whether the defendant is guilty, but what the defendant is guilty of. In these situations, the defense strategy focuses on obtaining the lightest possible penalty for the defendant. As we saw earlier in the chapter, this strategy is responsible for the high percentage of proceedings that end in plea bargains.

8-6f
Rebuttal and Surrebuttal

After the defense closes its case, the prosecution is permitted to bring new evidence forward that was not used during its initial presentation to the jury. This is called the **rebuttal** stage of the trial. When the rebuttal stage is finished, the defense is given the opportunity to cross-examine the prosecution's new witnesses and introduce new witnesses of its own. This final act is part of the *surrebuttal*. After these stages have been completed, the defense may offer a *motion for a directed verdict*, asking the judge to find in the defendant's favor. If this motion is rejected, and it almost always is, the case is closed, and the opposing sides offer their closing arguments.

8-6g
Closing Arguments

In their **closing arguments,** the attorneys summarize their presentations and argue one final time for their respective cases. In most states, the defense attorney goes first, and then the prosecutor. (In Colorado, Kentucky, and Missouri, the order is reversed.) An effective closing argument includes all of the major points that support the government's or the defense's case. It also emphasizes the shortcomings of the opposing party's case.

8-7
what HAPPENS AT THE END OF A CRIMINAL TRIAL?

Rebuttal Evidence given to counteract or disprove evidence presented by the opposing party.

Closing Arguments Arguments made by each side's attorney after the cases for the plaintiff and defendant have been presented.

Charge The judge's instructions to the jury following the attorneys' closing arguments.

Verdict A formal decision made by the jury.

After closing arguments, the outcome of the trial is in the hands of the jury. Before the jurors begin their deliberations, the judge gives the jury a **charge,** summing up the case and instructing the jurors on the rules of law that apply to the issues in the case. These charges, also called jury instructions, are usually prepared during a special *charging conference* involving the judge and the trial attorneys. In this conference, the attorneys suggest the instructions they would like to see be sent to the jurors, but the judge makes the final decision as to the charges submitted. If the defense attorney disagrees with the charges sent to the jury, he or she can enter an objection, thereby setting the stage for a possible appeal.

8-7a
Jury Deliberation

After receiving the charge, the jury begins its deliberations. Jury deliberation is a somewhat mysterious process, as it takes place in complete seclusion. Most of what is known about how a jury deliberates comes from mock trials or interviews with jurors after the verdict has been reached. A general picture of the deliberation process constructed from this research shows that the romantic notion of jurors with high-minded ideals of justice making eloquent speeches is, for the most part, not the reality. In approximately three out of every ten cases, the initial vote by the jury led to a unanimous decision. In 90 percent of the remaining cases, the majority eventually dictated the decision.[42]

One of the most important instructions that a judge normally gives the jurors is that they should seek no outside information during deliberation. The idea is that jurors should base their verdict *only* on the evidence that the judge has deemed admissible. In extreme cases, the judge will order that the jury be *sequestered,* or isolated from the public, during the trial and deliberation stages of the proceedings. Sequestration is used when deliberations are expected to be lengthy, or the trial is attracting a high amount of interest and the judge wants to keep the jury from being unduly influenced. Juries are usually sequestered in hotels and kept under the watch and guard of officers of the court.

8-7b
The Verdict

Once it has reached a decision, the jury issues a **verdict.** The most common verdicts are guilty and not guilty, though, as we have seen, juries may signify different degrees of guilt if instructed to do so. Following the announcement of a guilty or not guilty verdict, the jurors are discharged, and the jury trial proceedings are finished.

CJ TECHNOLOGY

ONE former juror, fresh from trial, complained that the members of the courtroom work group had not provided the jury with enough information to render a fair verdict. "We felt deeply frustrated at our inability to fill those gaps in our knowledge," he added. Until recently, frustrated jury members have lacked the means to carry out their own investigations in court. Today, however, jurors with smartphones and tablet computers can easily access news stories and online research tools. With these wireless devices, they can look up legal terms, blog and tweet about their experiences, and sometimes even try to contact other participants in the trial through "friend" requests on social media Web sites.

This access can cause serious problems for judges, whose responsibility it is to ensure that no outside information taints the jury's decision. During deliberations at the end of one recent trial in Florida concerning illegal Internet drug sales, the judge found that nine of the twelve jurors had conducted Google research about the case. One jury member even discovered that the defendant had previously prescribed drugs later used in a double suicide—information that the defense had successfully argued should be kept out of court. The judge

Champion Studio/Shutterstock.com

had no choice but to declare a mistrial, requiring that the proceedings start again with a different jury.

THINKING ABOUT WIRELESS DEVICES IN THE COURTROOM

The Sixth Amendment guarantees the accused the right to trial by an "impartial jury." How does the use of wireless devices in the courtroom threaten this right?

When a jury in a criminal trial is unable to agree on a unanimous verdict—or a majority in certain states—it returns with no decision. This is known as a **hung jury.** Following a hung jury, the judge will declare a mistrial, and the case will be tried again in front of a different jury if the prosecution decides to pursue the matter a second time. A judge can do little to reverse a hung jury, considering that "no decision" is just as legitimate a verdict as guilty or not guilty. In some states, if there are only a few dissenters to the majority view, a judge can send the jury back to the jury room under a set of rules set forth more than a century ago by the Supreme Court in *Allen v. United States* (1896).[43] The **Allen Charge,** as this instruction is called, asks the jurors in the minority to recon-

sider the majority opinion. Many jurisdictions do not allow *Allen* Charges on the ground that they improperly coerce jurors with the minority opinion to change their minds.[44]

8-7c
Appeals

Even if a defendant is found guilty, the trial process is not necessarily over. In our criminal justice system, a person convicted of a crime has a right to appeal. An **appeal** is the process

Hung Jury A jury whose members are so irreconcilably divided in their opinions that they cannot reach a verdict.

Allen Charge An instruction by a judge to a deadlocked jury with only a few dissenters that asks the jurors in the minority to reconsider the majority opinion.

Appeal The process of seeking a higher court's review of a lower court's decision for the purpose of correcting or changing this decision.

FIGURE 8.4	The Steps of an Appeal

1. The defendant, or *appellant,* files a **notice of appeal**—a short written statement outlining the basis of the appeal.

2. The appellant transfers the trial court record to the appellate court. This record contains items such as evidence and a transcript of the testimony.

3. Both parties file **briefs.** A brief is a written document that presents the party's legal arguments.

4. Attorneys from both sides present **oral arguments** before the appellate court.

5. Having heard from both sides, the judges of the appellate court retire to deliberate the case and make their decision. As described in Chapter 7, this decision is issued as a **written opinion.** Appellate courts generally do one of the following:
- **Uphold** the decision of the lower court.
- **Modify** the lower court's decision by changing only a part of it.
- **Reverse** the decision of the lower court.
- **Reverse and remand** the case, meaning that the matter is sent back to the lower court for further proceedings.

of seeking a higher court's review of a lower court's decision for the purpose of correcting or changing the lower court's judgment. A defendant who loses a case in a trial court cannot automatically appeal the conviction. The defendant normally must first be able to show that the trial court acted improperly on a question of law. Common reasons for appeals include the introduction of tainted evidence by the prosecution or faulty jury instructions delivered by the trial judge. In federal courts, about 18 percent of criminal convictions are appealed.[45]

DOUBLE JEOPARDY The appeals process is available only to the defense. If a jury finds the accused not guilty, the prosecution cannot appeal to have the decision reversed. To do so would infringe on the defendant's Fifth Amendment rights against multiple trials for the same offense. This guarantee against being tried a second time for the same crime is known as protection from **double jeopardy.** The prohibition against double jeopardy means that once a criminal defendant is found not guilty of a particular crime, the government may not reindict the person and retry him or her for the same crime.

There are several nuances to this rule, however. First, one state's prosecution will not prevent a different state or the federal government from prosecuting the same crime. Second, acquitted defendants can be sued in *civil* court for circumstances arising from the alleged wrongdoing on the theory that they are not being tried for the same *crime* twice. Third, a hung jury is *not* an acquittal for purposes of double jeopardy. So, if a jury is deadlocked, the government is free to seek a new trial.

THE APPEAL PROCESS It is important to understand that once the appeal process begins, the defendant is no longer presumed innocent. The burden of proof has shifted, and the defendant is obligated to prove that her or his conviction should be overturned. The method of filing an appeal differs slightly among the fifty states and the federal government, but the five basic steps are similar enough for summarization in Figure 8.4 above. For the most part, defendants are not required to exercise their right to appeal. The one exception involves the death sentence. Given the seriousness of capital punishment, the defendant is required to appeal the case, regardless of his or her wishes.

HABEAS CORPUS Even after the appeals process is exhausted, a convict many have access to one final procedure, known as **habeas corpus** (Latin for "you have the body"). *Habeas corpus* is a judicial order that commands a corrections official to bring a prisoner before a federal court so that the court can hear the

Double Jeopardy To twice place at risk (jeopardize) a person's life or liberty. Constitutional law prohibits a second prosecution in the same court for the same criminal offense.

Habeas Corpus An order that requires corrections officials to bring an inmate before a court or a judge and explain why he or she is being held in prison.

On January 29, 2013, Doug Prade hugs a supporter in London, Ohio, after DNA evidence exonerated him of his wife's murder. Should prosecutors be disciplined for mistakenly bringing charges against innocent defendants such as Prade, who spent fifteen years in prison? Why or why not?

Phil Masturzo/*Akron Beacon Journal*/MCT/Newscom

how the law was applied in a case, rather than on the facts of the case. But what if a defendant who is factually innocent has been found guilty at trial? For the most part, such **wrongful convictions** can be righted only with the aid of new evidence suggesting the defendant's innocence. When such new evidence is uncovered, a prosecutor's office can choose to reopen the case in order to acquit. Or the defendant's attorneys can use the *habeas corpus* procedure described above to restart court proceedings.

In Chapter 5, we saw how DNA fingerprinting has been a boon for law enforcement. According to the Innocence Project, a New York–based legal group, as of July 2013, the procedure has also led to the exoneration of 310 convicts in the United States.[47] In 1998, for example, Johnny Williams was convicted of sexually assaulting a nine-year-old girl in Oakland, California. Despite the fact that he did not fit the girl's original description of her attacker, Williams was placed in a lineup and identified by the young victim. He told police more than forty times that he was innocent, but eventually confessed after being told that his DNA had been found on the girl's clothing. In 2013, new tests showed that the DNA traces on the clothing did not come from Williams, and his conviction was overturned.

SOCIAL MEDIA AND CJ

The Innocence Project strives to prevent wrongful convictions and reform the criminal justice system. To learn more about the organization, go to its Web site and click on the Facebook icon.

convict's claim that he or she is being held illegally. A writ of *habeas corpus* differs from an appeal in that it can be filed only by someone who is imprisoned. In recent years, defense attorneys have successfully used the *habeas corpus* procedure for a number of their death row clients who have new DNA evidence proving their innocence.[46]

8-7d
Wrongful Convictions

The appeals process is primarily concerned with "legal innocence." That is, appeals courts focus on

Wrongful Conviction The conviction, either by verdict or by guilty plea, of a person who is factually innocent of the charges.

REVIEW

✓ **Review what you've read with the quiz below.**

Rip out the Chapter Review card at the back of this book, which includes:
- Chapter Summary and Learning Outcomes
- Key Terms

Or you can go online to CourseMate at www.cengagebrain.com to:
- Complete Practice Quizzes to prepare for tests.
- Review Key Terms Flash Cards (online or print).
- Play games to master concepts.

quiz

1. Following the initial appearance, in most cases the defendant will be detained until trial unless he or she can post _____.

2. In some states, a group of citizens called a _____ _____ determines whether the prosecution has established probable cause that the defendant committed the crime in question.

3. A _____ _____ occurs when the prosecution and the defense work out an agreement that resolves the case with the defendant admitting guilt.

4. If a defendant waives his or her right to a jury trial, a _____ trial takes place in which the judge decides questions of law and fact.

5. To gain a "guilty" verdict, the prosecution must prove that the defendant is guilty beyond a _____ _____.

6. The process by which the prosecution and defense choose a jury is called _____ _____.

7. Evidence will not be admitted into a criminal trial unless it is relevant and does not unfairly _____ the jury against the defendant.

8. _____ examination takes places when, for example, the prosecution questions those witnesses that it has called to strengthen its case.

9. _____-examination takes place when, for example, defense attorneys question those witnesses that have been called to the stand by the prosecution.

10. If a defendant is convicted, she or he has the option of filing an _____ claiming that the trial court acted improperly on a question of law during the proceedings.

Answers can be found on the Chapter 8 Review card at the end of the book.

AP Photo/Keith Srakocic, Pool

WHY CHOOSE?

Every 4LTR Press solution comes complete with a visually engaging textbook in addition to an interactive eBook. Go to CourseMate for **CJ** to begin using the eBook. Access at **www.cengagebrain.com**

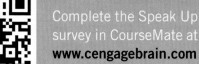

Complete the Speak Up survey in CourseMate at **www.cengagebrain.com**

 Follow us at **www.facebook.com/4ltrpress**

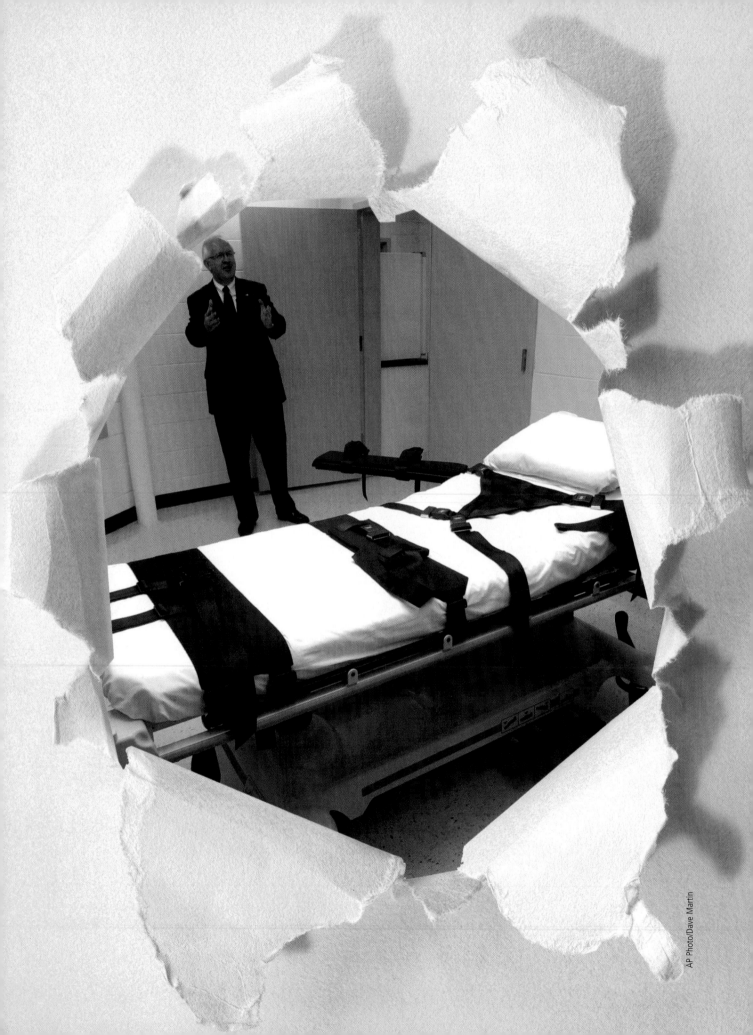

Learning OUTCOMES | *After studying this chapter, you will be able to . . .*

1 List and contrast the four basic philosophical reasons for sentencing criminals.

2 Contrast indeterminate with determinate sentencing.

3 Explain some of the reasons why sentencing reform has occurred.

4 Identify the arguments for and against the use of victim impact statements during sentencing hearings.

5 Identify the two stages that make up the bifurcated process of death penalty sentencing.

PUNISHMENT AND SENTENCING 9

Illegal Viewing

Three weeks into their freshman year at Rutgers University in Piscataway, New Jersey, Dharun Ravi set up a hidden webcam to spy on roommate Tyler Clementi. Ravi then joined another Rutgers student in her room, where the pair briefly watched a live stream of Clementi embracing an older man. "I saw him making out with a dude. Yay," Ravi tweeted soon thereafter. Two days later, Ravi attempted to set up another viewing of his roommate's romantic activities. One day after that, Clementi took a train to nearby New York City and jumped to his death from the George Washington Bridge.

If Clementi had not committed suicide, Ravi's actions would have been, in the words of one observer, "a matter for the Rutgers resident advisers." Instead, the incident touched off a national debate on the evils of "gay bashing," and Ravi was arrested. In March 2012, a jury convicted him of invasion of privacy, tampering with evidence, and bias intimidation. Though these crimes generally carry light punishments, particularly for a first offender, Ravi faced a maximum of ten years in prison because of the bias intimidation charge. (For a review of the penalty enhancement aspects of hate crime laws, see Chapter 3.) Following the verdict, however, Judge Glenn Berman sentenced Ravi to spend thirty days in jail, complete three hundred hours of community service, receive counseling about "alternative lifestyles," and pay an $11,000 fine.

Many observers criticized the sentence as a "slap on the wrist." Ravi's punishment "doesn't feel harsh enough to deter other thoughtless young people from the same callous behavior," wrote columnist Lane Filler in *Newsday*. Judge Berman defended his decision by pointing out that, even though Ravi acted with "colossal insensitivity," nobody could have anticipated Clementi's suicide. "I can't find it in me to remand [Ravi] to state prison that houses people convicted of offenses such as murder, armed robbery, and rape," the judge said.

Dharun Ravi exits Middlesex County Jail in North Brunswick, New Jersey, after serving a short jail term for crimes related to spying on his college roommate with a webcam.

AP Photo/Mel Evans

why DO WE PUNISH CRIMINALS?

Professor Herbert Packer has said that punishing criminals serves two ultimate purposes: the "deserved infliction of suffering on evil doers" and "the prevention of crime."[1] Even this straightforward assessment raises several questions. How does one determine the sort of punishment that is "deserved"? How can we be sure that certain penalties "prevent" crime? Should criminals be punished solely for the good of society, or should their well-being also be taken into consideration? Should Judge Glenn Berman have sent a stronger "message" with a ten-year prison sentence in the Dharun Ravi case, or would such a punishment have unfairly made Ravi a "scapegoat" for a bigoted culture?[2]

Sentencing laws indicate how any given group of people has answered these questions, but do not tell us why they were answered in that manner. To understand why, we must first consider the four basic philosophical reasons for sentencing—retribution, deterrence, incapacitation, and rehabilitation.

9-1a
Retribution

LO 1 The oldest and most common justification for punishing someone is that he or she "deserved it"—as the Old Testament states, "an eye for an eye and a tooth for a tooth." Under a system of justice that favors **retribution,** a wrongdoer who has freely chosen to violate society's rules must be punished for the infraction. Retribution relies on the principle of **just deserts,** which holds that the severity of the punishment must be in proportion to the severity of the crime. Retributive justice is not the same as *revenge.* Whereas revenge implies that the wrongdoer is punished only with the aim of satisfying a victim or victims, retribution is more concerned with the needs of society as a whole.

One problem with retributive ideas of justice lies in proportionality.

Retribution The philosophy that those who commit criminal acts should be punished based on the severity of the crime and that no other factors need be considered.

Just Deserts A sanctioning philosophy based on the assertion that criminals deserve to be punished for breaking society's rules.

Deterrence The strategy of preventing crime through the threat of punishment.

Whether or not one agrees with the death penalty, the principle behind it is easy to fathom: the punishment (death) often fits the crime (murder). But what about the theft of an automobile? How does one fairly determine the amount of time the thief must spend in prison for that crime? Should the type of car or the wealth of the car owner matter? Theories of retribution often have a difficult time providing answers to such questions.[3]

9-1b
Deterrence

The concept of **deterrence** (as well as incapacitation and rehabilitation) takes a different approach than does retribution. That is, rather than seeking only to punish the wrongdoer, the goal of sentencing should be to prevent future crimes. By "setting an example," society is sending a message to potential criminals that certain actions will not be tolerated.

Deterrence can take two forms: general and specific. The basic idea of *general deterrence* is that by punishing one person, others will be discouraged from committing a similar crime. *Specific deterrence* assumes that an individual, after being punished once for a certain act, will be less likely to repeat that act because she or he does not want to be punished again.[4] Those who favored a more severe punishment for Dharun Ravi, whose offenses were covered in the opening of this chapter, often expressed themselves using principles of general deterrence. "You're making an example of Ravi in order to send a message to other people who might be bullying [and] to schools and parents and prosecutors who have not considered this a crime before," explained Marc Poirer of the Seton Hall University School of Law.[5]

Both forms of deterrence have proved problematic in practice. General deterrence assumes that a person commits a crime only after a rational decision-making process, in which he or she implicitly weighs the benefits of the crime against the possible costs of the punishment. This is not necessarily the case, especially for young offenders who tend to value the immediate rewards of crime over the possible future consequences. The argument for specific deterrence is somewhat weakened by the fact that a relatively small number of habitual offenders are responsible for the majority of certain criminal acts.

"OUR society is going through a technological transformation," notes Adam Schwartz, a civil liberties lawyer. "We are at a time where tens of millions of Americans carry around a telephone or other device in their pocket that has an audio-video capacity. Ten years ago, [we] weren't walking around with all these devices." This widespread ability to record interactions with others has increased the possibility that Americans are breaking the law, often without their knowledge. The criminal codes of twelve states require the consent of all parties involved before any conversation can be recorded.

In some cases, the penalties for breaking these laws can be quite harsh. Under the Illinois Eavesdropping Act, audio-recording a civilian without consent is a Class 4 felony, punishable by up to three years in prison. Audio-recording an Illinois law enforcement official who is performing her or his duties without consent is a Class 1 felony, punishable by up to fifteen years in prison.

1000 words/Shutterstock.com

**THINKING ABOUT
ELECTRONIC EAVESDROPPING**
What is the purpose behind making electronic eavesdropping a criminal act deserving of punishment?

9-1c
Incapacitation

"Wicked people exist," said James Q. Wilson. "Nothing avails except to set them apart from innocent people."[6] Wilson's blunt statement summarizes the justification for **incapacitation** as a form of punishment. As a purely practical matter, incarcerating criminals guarantees that they will not be a danger to society, at least for the length of their prison terms. At some level, the death penalty can also be justified in terms of incapacitation, as it prevents the offender from committing any future crimes.

Several studies do support incapacitation's efficacy as a crime-fighting tool. Criminologist Isaac Ehrlich of the University at Buffalo estimated that a 1 percent increase in sentence length will produce a 1 percent decrease in the crime rate.[7] More recently, Avinash Singh Bhati of the Urban Institute in Washington, D.C., found that higher levels of incarceration lead to fewer violent crimes but have little impact on property crime rates.[8]

Incapacitation as a theory of punishment does suffer from several weaknesses. Unlike retribution, it offers no proportionality with regard to a particular crime. Giving a burglar a life sentence would certainly ensure that she or he would not commit another burglary. Does that justify such a severe penalty? Furthermore, incarceration protects society only until the criminal is freed. Many studies have shown that, on release, offenders may actually be more likely to commit crimes than before they were imprisoned.[9] In that case, incapacitation may increase likelihood of crime, rather than diminish it.

9-1d
Rehabilitation

For many, **rehabilitation** is the most "humane" goal of punishment. This line of thinking reflects the view that crime is a "social

Incapacitation A strategy for preventing crime by detaining wrongdoers in prison, thereby separating them from the community and reducing criminal opportunities.

Rehabilitation The philosophy that society is best served when wrongdoers are provided the resources needed to eliminate criminality from their behavioral pattern.

In a Santa Ana, California, courtroom, Andrew Gallo reacts to his sentence of fifty-one years in prison for killing three people in a drunk driving automobile accident. How do theories of deterrence and incapacitation justify Gallo's punishment?

AP Photo/Mark Rightmire, Pool

phenomenon" caused not by the inherent criminality of a person, but by factors in that person's surroundings. By removing wrongdoers from their environment and intervening to change their values and personalities, the rehabilitative model suggests, criminals can be "treated" and possibly even "cured" of their proclivities toward crime. Although studies of the effectiveness of rehabilitation are too varied to be easily summarized, it does appear that, in most instances, criminals who receive treatment are less likely to reoffend than those who do not.[10]

9-1e
Restorative Justice

Despite the emergence of victim impact statements, which we will discuss later in the chapter, victims have historically been restricted from participating in the punishment process. Such restrictions are supported by the general assumption that victims are focused on vengeance rather than justice. According to criminologists Heather Strang of Australia's Center for Restorative Justice and Lawrence W. Sherman of the University of Pennsylvania, however, this is not always the case. After the initial shock of the crime has worn off, Strang and Sherman have found, victims are more interested in three things that have little to do with revenge: (1) an opportunity to participate in the process, (2) financial reparations, and (3) an apology.[11]

Restorative justice strategies focus on these concerns by attempting to repair the damage that a crime does to the victim, the victim's family, and society as a whole. This outlook relies on the efforts of the offender to "undo" the harm caused by the criminal act through an apology and **restitution,** or monetary compensation for losses suffered by the victim(s). Theoretically, the community also participates in the process by providing treatment programs and financial support that allow both offender and victim to reestablish themselves as productive members of society.[12]

One increasingly popular offshoot of the restorative justice movement is *victim-offender dialogue (VOD)*. This practice centers on face-to-face meetings between victims and offenders in a secure setting at the offender's prison. VOD allows the victims to speak directly to offenders about the criminal incident and how it has affected their lives. It also gives the offender a chance to apologize directly to the victim. Today, more than half of state corrections departments support VOD programs within their prisons.[13]

9-2
what IS THE STRUCTURE OF THE SENTENCING PROCESS?

Philosophy not only is integral to explaining *why* we punish criminals, but also influences *how* we do so. The history of criminal sentencing in the United

Restorative Justice An approach to punishment designed to repair the harm done to the victim and the community by the offender's criminal act.

Restitution Monetary compensation for damages done to the victim by the offender's criminal act.

States has been characterized by shifts in institutional power among the three branches of the government. When public opinion moves toward more severe strategies of retribution, deterrence, and incapacitation, legislatures have responded by asserting their power over determining sentencing guidelines. In contrast, periods of rehabilitative justice are marked by a transfer of this power to judges.

9-2a

Legislative Sentencing Authority

Because legislatures are responsible for making laws, these bodies are also initially responsible for passing the criminal codes that determine the length of sentences.

INDETERMINATE SENTENCING Penal codes with **indeterminate sentencing** policies set a minimum and maximum amount of time that a person must spend in prison. For example, the indeterminate sentence for aggravated assault could be three to nine years, or six to twelve years, or twenty years to life. Within these parameters, a judge can prescribe a particular term, after which an administrative body known as the *parole board* decides at what point the offender is to be released. A prisoner is aware that he or she is eligible for *parole* as soon as the minimum time has been served and that good behavior can further shorten the sentence.

Indeterminate Sentencing An indeterminate term of incarceration in which a judge determines the minimum and maximum terms of imprisonment.

DETERMINATE SENTENCING Disillusionment with the somewhat vague nature of indeterminate sentencing often leads politicians to support **determinate sentencing,** or fixed sentencing. As the name implies, in determinate sentencing an offender serves exactly the amount of time to which she or he is sentenced (minus "good time," described below). For example, if the legislature deems that the punishment for a first-time armed robber is ten years, then the judge has no choice but to impose a sentence of ten years, and the criminal will serve ten years minus good time before being freed.

LO 2

"GOOD TIME" AND TRUTH IN SENTENCING

Often, the amount of time prescribed by a judge bears little relation to the amount of time the offender actually spends behind bars. In states with indeterminate sentencing, parole boards have broad powers to release prisoners once they have served the minimum portion of their sentence. Furthermore, all but four states offer prisoners the opportunity to reduce their sentences by doing **"good time"**—or behaving well—as determined by prison administrators. (See Figure 9.1 below for an idea of the effects of good-time regulations and other early-release programs on state prison sentences.)

Sentence-reduction programs promote discipline within a correctional institution and reduce overcrowding, so many prison officials welcome them. The public, however, may react negatively to news that a violent criminal has served a shorter term than ordered by a judge and pressure elected officials to "do something." In Illinois, for example, some inmates were serving less than half their sentences by receiving a one-day reduction in their term for each day of "good time." Under pressure from victims' groups, the state legislature passed a **truth-in-sentencing law** in 1995 that requires murderers and others convicted of serious crimes to complete at least 85 percent of their sentences with no time off for good behavior.[14]

As their name suggests, the primary goal of these laws is to provide the public with more accurate information about the actual amount of time an offender will spend behind bars. The laws also keep convicts incapacitated for longer periods of time. Fifteen years after Illinois passed its truth-in-sentencing law, those murderers subject to the legislation were spending an average of seventeen years more in prison than those not subject to the legislation. For sex offenders in the state, the difference was 3.5 years.[15] Today, forty states have instituted some form of truth-in-sentencing laws, though the future of such statutes is in doubt due to the pressure of overflowing prisons.

Determinate Sentencing
A period of incarceration that is fixed by a sentencing authority and cannot be reduced by judges or other corrections officials.

"Good Time" A reduction in time served by prisoners based on good behavior, conformity to rules, and other positive behavior.

Truth-in-Sentencing Laws
Legislative attempts to ensure that convicts will serve approximately the terms to which they were initially sentenced.

9-2b
Judicial Sentencing Authority

During the pretrial procedures and the trial itself, the judge's role is somewhat passive and reactive.

FIGURE 9.1 Average Sentence Length and Estimated Time to Be Served in State Prison

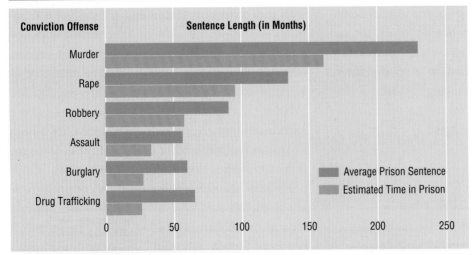

Source: Bureau of Justice Statistics, *National Corrections Reporting Program: Sentence Length of State Prisoners, by Offense, Admission Type, Sex, and Race* (January 20, 2011), "Table 9: First Releases from State Prison, 2008," at **bjs.ojp.usdoj.gov/index.cfm?ty=pbdetail&iid=2056**.

She or he is primarily a "procedural watchdog," ensuring that the rights of the defendant are not infringed while the prosecutor and defense attorney dictate the course of action. At a traditional sentencing hearing, however, the judge is no longer an arbiter between the parties. She or he is now called on to exercise the ultimate authority of the state in determining the defendant's fate.

From the 1930s to the 1970s, when theories of rehabilitation held sway over the criminal justice system, indeterminate sentencing practices were guided by the theory of "individualized justice." Just as a physician gives specific treatment to individual patients depending on their particular health needs, the hypothesis goes, a judge needs to consider the specific circumstances of each individual offender in choosing the best form of punishment. Taking the analogy one step further, just as the diagnosis of a qualified physician should not be questioned, a qualified judge should have absolute discretion in making the sentencing decision. *Judicial discretion* rests on the assumption that a judge should be given ample leeway in determining punishments that fit both the crime and the criminal.[16] As we shall see later in the chapter, the growth of determinate sentencing has severely restricted judicial discretion in many jurisdictions.

JUDICIAL DISPOSITIONS Within whatever legislative restrictions apply, the sentencing judge has a number of options when it comes to choosing the proper form of punishment. These sentences, or *dispositions,* include:

1. *Capital punishment.* Reserved normally for those who commit first degree murder—that is, a premeditated killing—capital punishment is a sentencing option in thirty-two states. It is also an option in federal court, where a defendant can be put to death for murder, as well as for trafficking in a large amount of illegal drugs, *espionage* (spying), and *treason* (betraying the United States).

2. *Imprisonment.* Whether for the purpose of retribution, deterrence, incapacitation, or rehabilitation, a common form of punishment in American history has been imprisonment. In fact, it is used so commonly today that judges—and legislators—are having to take factors such as prison overcrowding into consideration when making sentencing decisions. The issues surrounding imprisonment will be discussed in Chapters 11 and 12.

3. *Probation.* One of the effects of prison overcrowding has been a sharp rise in the use of probation, in which an offender is permitted to live in the community under supervision and is not incarcerated. (Probation is covered in Chapter 10.) *Alternative sanctions* (also discussed in Chapter 10) combine probation with other dispositions such as electronic monitoring, house arrest, boot camps, and shock incarceration.

4. *Fines.* Fines can be levied by judges in addition to incarceration and probation or independently of other forms of punishment. When a fine is the only punishment, it usually reflects the judge's belief that the offender is not a threat to the community and does not need to be imprisoned or supervised. In some instances, mostly involving drug offenders, a judge can order the seizure of an offender's property, such as his or her home.

OTHER FORMS OF PUNISHMENT Whereas fines are payable to the government, restitution and community service are seen as reparations to the injured party or to the community. As noted earlier, restitution is a direct payment to the victim or victims of a crime. Community service consists of "good works"—such as cleaning up highway litter or tutoring disadvantaged youths—that benefit the entire community. Along with restitution, *apologies* play an important role in restorative justice, discussed previously in this chapter. An apology is seen as an effort by the offender to recognize the wrongness of her or his conduct and acknowledge the impact that it has had on the victim and the community.

In some jurisdictions, judges have a great deal of discretionary power and can impose sentences that do not fall into any of these categories. This "creative sentencing," as it is sometimes called, has produced some interesting results. After being convicted of criminal damaging for throwing beer bottles at a car, Jason Householder and John Stockum were ordered

What reasons might a judge have for handing down a "creative" sentence such as the one given to Jason Householder, left, and John Stockum?

AP Photo/Dante Smith/*Coshocton Tribune*

by the judge to walk down Main Street in Coshocton, Ohio, in women's clothing (see the photo above). In Broward County, Florida, a man who shoved his wife was sentenced to "take her to Red Lobster," go bowling with her, and then undergo marriage counseling. A Covington, Kentucky, teenager charged with disorderly conduct for falsely yelling "bingo" in a bingo hall was banned from saying that particular word for six months. Though these types of punishments are often ridiculed, many judges see them as a viable alternative to incarceration for less dangerous offenders.

9-2c
The Sentencing Process

The decision of how to punish a wrongdoer is the end result of what Yale Law School professor Kate Stith and federal appeals court judge José A. Cabranes call the "sentencing ritual."[17] The two main participants in this ritual are the judge and the defendant, but prosecutors, defense attorneys, and probation officers also play a role in the proceedings. Individualized justice requires that the judge consider all the relevant circumstances in making sentencing decisions. Therefore, judicial discretion is often tantamount to *informed* discretion—without the aid of the other members of the courtroom work group, the judge would not have sufficient information to make the proper sentencing choice.

Presentence Investigative Report An investigative report on an offender's background that assists a judge in determining the proper sentence.

THE PRESENTENCE INVESTIGATIVE REPORT For judges operating under various states' indeterminate sentencing guidelines, information in the **presentence investigative report** is a valuable component of the sentencing ritual. Compiled by a probation officer, the report describes the crime in question, notes the suffering of any victims, and lists the defendant's prior offenses (as well as any alleged but uncharged criminal activity). The report also contains a range of personal data such as family background, work history, education, and community activities—information that is not admissible as evidence during trial. In putting together the presentence investigative report, the probation officer is supposed to gain a "feel" for the defendant and communicate these impressions of the offender to the judge.

The report also includes a sentencing recommendation. This aspect has been criticized as giving probation officers too much power in the sentencing process, because less diligent judges would simply rely on the recommendation in determining punishment.[18] For the most part, however, judges do not act as if they were bound by the presentence investigative report. In the case that opened this chapter, for example, Judge Glenn Berman largely disregarded a report recommending that Dharun Ravi not receive any jail time or fine as punishment for his crimes.[19]

SENTENCING AND THE JURY Juries also play an important role in the sentencing process. As we will see later in the chapter, it is the jury, and not the judge, who generally decides whether a convict eligible for the death penalty will in fact be executed. Additionally, six states—Arkansas, Kentucky, Missouri, Oklahoma, Texas, and Virginia—allow juries, rather than judges, to make the sentencing decision even when the death penalty is not an option. In these states, the judge gives the jury instructions on the range of penalties available, and then the jury makes the final decision.[20]

Juries have traditionally been assigned a relatively small role in felony sentencing, largely out of concern that jurors' lack of experience and legal expertise leaves them unprepared for the task. When sentencing by juries is allowed, the practice is popular with prosecutors because jurors are more likely than judges to give harsh sentences, particularly for drug crimes, sexual assault, and theft.[21]

9-2d
Factors of Sentencing

The sentencing ritual strongly lends itself to the concept of individualized justice. With inputs—sometimes conflicting—from the prosecutor, attorney, and probation officer, the judge can be reasonably sure of getting the "full picture" of the crime and the criminal. In making the final decision, however, most judges consider two factors above all others: the seriousness of the crime and any mitigating or aggravating circumstances.

THE SERIOUSNESS OF THE CRIME As would be expected, the seriousness of the crime is the primary factor in a judge's sentencing decision. The more serious the crime, the harsher the punishment, for society demands no less. Each judge has his or her own methods of determining the seriousness of the offense. Many judges simply consider the "conviction offense," basing their sentence on the crime for which the defendant was convicted.

Other judges—some mandated by statute—focus instead on the **"real offense"** in determining the punishment. The "real offense" is based on the actual behavior of the defendant, regardless of the official conviction. For example, through a plea bargain, a defendant may plead guilty to simple assault when in fact he hit his victim in the face with a baseball bat. A judge, after reading the presentence investigative report, could decide to sentence the defendant as if he had committed aggravated assault, which is the "real" offense. Though many prosecutors and defense attorneys are opposed to "real offense" procedures, which can render a plea bargain meaningless, there is a growing belief in criminal justice circles that they bring a measure of fairness to the sentencing decision.[22]

MITIGATING AND AGGRAVATING CIRCUMSTANCES When deciding the severity of punishment, judges and juries are often required to evaluate the *mitigating* and *aggravating circumstances* surrounding the case. **Mitigating circumstances** are those circumstances, such as the fact that the defendant was coerced into committing the crime, that allow a lighter sentence to be handed down. In contrast, **aggravating circumstances,** such as a prior record, blatant disregard for the safety of others, or the use of a weapon, can lead a judge or jury to inflict a harsher penalty than might otherwise be warranted. (**CAREER TIP:** Because they know judges can be swayed in this manner, defense attorneys often rely on *behavioral specialists* to argue against the death penalty for their clients. These health-care experts focus on diagnosing and treating problem behavior.)

Aggravating circumstances play an important role in a prosecutor's decision to charge a suspect with capital murder. The criminal code of every state that employs the death penalty contains a list of aggravating circumstances that make an offender eligible for execution. Most of these codes require that the murder take place during the commission of felony, or create a grave risk of death for multiple victims, or interfere with the duties of law enforcement. (For a comprehensive rundown, go to **www.deathpenalty info.org/aggravating-factors-capital-punishment -state**.) As you will see later in the chapter, mitigating factors such as mental illness and youth can spare an otherwise death-eligible offender from capital punishment.

JUDICIAL PHILOSOPHY Most states and the federal government spell out mitigating and aggravating circumstances in statutes, but there is room for judicial discretion in applying the law to particular cases. Judges are not uniform, or even consistent, in their opinions of which circumstances are mitigating or aggravating. One judge may believe that a fourteen-year-old is not fully responsible for his or her actions, while another may believe that

"Real Offense" The actual offense committed, as opposed to the charge levied by a prosecutor as the result of a plea bargain.

Mitigating Circumstances Any circumstances accompanying the commission of a crime that may justify a lighter sentence.

Aggravating Circumstances Any circumstances accompanying the commission of a crime that may justify a harsher sentence.

teenagers should be treated as adults by criminal courts. A recent study in the journal *Science* found that, faced with a hypothetical situation in which a defendant suffered from brain damage, judges reduced the length of the sentence by about 7 percent.[23]

Often, a judge's personal philosophy will place her or him at odds with prosecutors. In November 2012, for example, three men from the West African country of Mali pleaded guilty in a New York City federal court to trafficking cocaine to raise money for international terrorist organizations. Federal prosecutors requested the maximum punishment of fifteen years in prison for each defendant. Instead, Judge Barbara S. Jones imposed far lesser sentences—about five years each for two of the men, and forty-six months for a third. Judge Jones based these decisions on her belief that the defendants, who had spent most of their lives living in dire poverty, were motivated by financial need rather than anti-American, terrorist ideology.

9-3
what ARE SOME PROBLEMS WITH SENTENCING

Sentencing Disparity A situation in which those convicted of similar crimes do not receive similar sentences.

For some, the natural differences in judicial philosophies, when combined with a lack of institutional con-

trol, raise important questions. Why should a bank robber in South Carolina and a bank robber in Michigan receive different sentences? Even federal indeterminate sentencing guidelines seem overly vague: a bank robber can receive a prison term from one day to twenty years, depending almost entirely on the judge.[24] Furthermore, if judges have freedom to use their discretion, do they not also have the freedom to misuse it?

Purported improper judicial discretion is often the first reason given for two phenomena that plague the criminal justice system: *sentencing disparity* and *sentencing discrimination.* Though the two terms are often used interchangeably, they describe different statistical occurrences—the causes of which are open to debate.

3 LO

9-3a
Sentencing Disparity

Justice would seem to demand that those who commit similar crimes should receive similar punishments. **Sentencing disparity** occurs when this expectation is not met in one of three ways:

1. Criminals receive similar sentences for different crimes of unequal seriousness.

2. Criminals receive different sentences for similar crimes.

3. Mitigating or aggravating circumstances have a disproportionate effect on sentences.

Most of the blame for sentencing disparities is placed at the feet of the judicial profession. Even with the restrictive presence of the sentencing reforms we will discuss shortly, judges have a great deal of influence over the sentencing decision, whether they are making that decision themselves or instructing the jury on how to do so. Like other members of the criminal justice system, judges are individuals, and their discretionary sentencing decisions reflect that individuality.

For offenders, the amount of time spent in prison often depends as much on where the crime was committed as on the crime itself. A comparison of the sentences for drug trafficking reveals that someone convicted of the crime in the Northern District of California faces an average of 78 months in prison, whereas a similar offender in northern Iowa can expect an average of 127 months.[25] The average sentences imposed in the Fourth Circuit, which includes North Carolina, South Carolina, Virginia, and West Virginia, are consistently harsher than those in the Ninth Circuit, comprising most of the western states: 76 months longer for convictions related to kidnapping and 50 months longer for all offenses.[26]

Such disparities can be attributed to a number of different factors, including local attitudes toward crime and available financial resources to cover the expenses of incarceration. Also, because of different sentencing guidelines, which we will discuss later in the chapter, the punishment for the same crime in federal and state courts can be dramatically different. Figure 9.2 on the right shows the sentencing disparities for certain crimes in the two systems.

9-3b

Sentencing Discrimination

Sentencing discrimination occurs when disparities can be attributed to extralegal variables such as the defendant's gender, race, or economic standing.

RACE AND SENTENCING At first glance, racial discrimination would seem to be rampant in sentencing practices. Research by Cassia Spohn of Arizona State University and David Holleran of the College of New Jersey suggests that minorities pay a "punishment penalty" when it comes to sentencing.[27] In Chicago, Spohn and Holleran found that convicted African Americans were 12.1 percent more likely and convicted Hispanics were 15.3 percent more likely to go to prison than convicted whites. Another report released several years ago by the Illinois Disproportionate Justice Impact Study Commission found that African Americans were nearly five times more likely to be sentenced to prison than whites for low-level drug crimes in that state.[28] Nationwide, about 38 percent of all inmates in state and federal prisons are African American,[29] even though members of that minority group make up only about 13 percent of the country's population and represent 28 percent of those arrested.[30]

Interestingly, Spohn and Holleran found that the rate of imprisonment rose significantly for minorities who were young and unemployed. This led them to conclude that the disparities between races were not the result of "conscious" discrimination on the part

Sentencing Discrimination A situation in which the length of a sentence appears to be influenced by a defendant's race, gender, economic status, or other factor not directly related to the crime he or she committed.

FIGURE 9.2 Average Maximum Sentences for Selected Crimes in State and Federal Courts

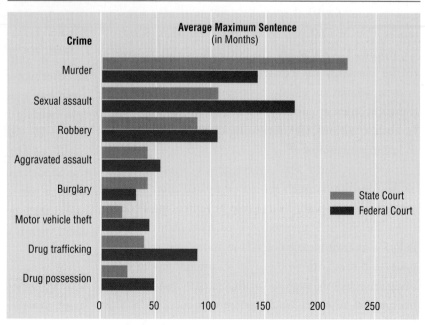

Source: Bureau of Justice Statistics, *Felony Sentences in State Courts, 2006—Statistical Tables* (Washington, D.C.: U.S. Department of Justice, December 2009), Table 1.6, page 9.

of the sentencing judges. Rather, faced with limited time to make decisions and limited information about the offenders, the judges would resort to stereotypes, considering not just race, but age and unemployment as well.[31] Another study, published in 2006, found that older judges and judges who were members of minority groups in Pennsylvania were less likely to send offenders to prison, regardless of their race.[32] Such research findings support the argument in favor of diversity among judges, discussed in Chapter 7.

WOMEN AND SENTENCING Few would argue that race or ethnicity should be a factor in sentencing decisions—the system should be "color-blind." Does the same principle apply to women? In other words, should the system be "gender-blind" as well—at least on a policy level? Congress answered that question in the Sentencing Reform Act of 1984, which emphasized the ideal of gender-neutral sentencing.[33] In practice, however, this has not occurred. Women who are convicted of crimes are less likely to go to prison than men, and those who are incarcerated tend to serve shorter sentences. According to government data, on average, a woman receives a sentence that is twenty-nine months shorter than that of a man for a violent crime and nine months shorter for a property crime.[34] When adjusting for comparable arrest offenses, criminal histories, and other presentencing factors, Sonja B. Starr of the University of Michigan Law School found that male convicts receive sentences that are 60 percent more severe than those for women.[35] One study attributes these differences to the elements of female criminality: in property crimes, women are usually accessories, and in violent crimes, women are usually reacting to physical abuse. In both situations, the mitigating circumstances lead to lesser punishment.[36]

Other evidence also suggests that a *chivalry effect*, or the idea that women should be treated more leniently than men, plays a large role in sentencing decisions. Several self-reported studies have shown that judges may treat female defendants more "gently" than males and that with women, judges are influenced by mitigating factors such as marital status and family background that they would ignore with men.[37]

In certain situations, however, a woman's gender can work against her. In October 2012, Texas prosecutors asked that Elizabeth Escalona receive forty-five years in prison for gluing her two-year-old daughter's hands to the wall and repeatedly beating the child. Instead, district judge Larry Mitchell sentenced Escalona to ninety-nine years in prison, more than double the prosecution's request. According to Keith Crew, a professor of sociology and criminology at the University of Northern Iowa, defendants who are seen as bad mothers often "get the hammer" from judges and juries.[38]

how HAVE POLITICIANS TRIED TO "FIX" SENTENCING?

Judicial discretion, then, appears to be a double-edged sword. Although it allows judges to impose a wide variety of sentences to fit specific criminal situations, it appears to fail to rein in a judge's subjective biases, which can lead to disparity and perhaps discrimination. Critics of judicial discretion believe that its costs (the lack of equality) outweigh its benefits (providing individualized justice). As Columbia law professor John C. Coffee noted:

> If we wish the sentencing judge to treat "like cases alike," a more inappropriate technique for the presentation could hardly be found than one that stresses a novelistic portrayal of each offender and thereby overloads the decision-maker in a welter of detail.[39]

In other words, Professor Coffee feels that judges are given too much information in the sentencing process, making it impossible for them to be consistent in their decisions. It follows that limiting judicial discretion would not only simplify the process but lessen the opportunity for disparity or discrimination. This attitude has spread through state and federal legislatures, causing extensive changes in sentencing procedures within the American criminal justice system.

9-4a
Sentencing Guidelines

In an effort to eliminate the inequities of disparity by removing judicial bias from the sentencing process, many states and the federal government have turned

198 **PART 3** Criminal Courts

to **sentencing guidelines,** which require judges to dispense legislatively determined sentences based on factors such as the seriousness of the crime and the offender's prior record.

STATE SENTENCING GUIDELINES In 1978, Minnesota became the first state to create a Sentencing Guidelines Commission with a mandate to construct and monitor the use of a determinate sentencing structure. The Minnesota Commission left no doubt as to the philosophical justification for the new sentencing statutes, stating unconditionally that retribution was its primary goal.[40] Today, about twenty states employ some form of sentencing guidelines with similar goals.

In general, these guidelines remove discretionary power from state judges by turning sentencing into a mathematical exercise. Members of the courtroom work group are guided by a *grid*, which helps them determine the proper sentence. Figure 9.3 below shows the grid established by the Massachusetts sentencing commission. As in the grids used by most states, one axis ranks the type of crime, while the other refers to the offender's criminal history. In the grid for Massachusetts, the red boxes indicate the "incarceration zone." A prison sentence is required for crimes in this zone. The yellow boxes delineate a "discretionary zone," in which the judge can decide between incarceration or intermediate sanctions, which you will learn about in the next chapter.

FEDERAL SENTENCING GUIDELINES In 1984, Congress passed the Sentencing Reform Act (SRA),[41] paving the way for federal sentencing guidelines that went into effect three years later. Similar in many respects to the state guidelines, the SRA also eliminated parole for federal prisoners and severely limited early release from prison due to good behavior.[42] The impact of the SRA and the state guidelines has been dramatic. Sentences have become harsher—by the mid-2000s, the average federal prison sentence was fifty months, more than twice as long as in 1984.[43]

Furthermore, much of the discretion in sentencing has shifted from the judge to the prosecutor. Because the prosecutor chooses the criminal charge, she or he can, in effect, present the judge with the range of sentences. Defendants and their defense attorneys realize this and are more likely to agree to a plea bargain, which is, after all, a "deal" with the prosecutor.[44]

JUDICIAL DEPARTURES Even in their haste to limit a judge's power, legislators realized that sentencing guidelines could not be

> **Sentencing Guidelines**
> Legislatively determined guidelines that judges are required to follow when sentencing those convicted of specific crimes.

FIGURE 9.3 A Portion of Massachusetts Sentencing Guidelines

Sentencing Guidelines Grid

Level	Illustrative Offenses	Sentence Range				
6	Manslaughter (Involuntary) Armed Robbery (No Gun) A&B DW* (Significant Injury)	40–60 Months	45–67 Months	50–75 Months	60–90 Months	80–120 Months
5	Unarmed Robbery Unarmed Burglary Stalking in Violation of Order Larceny ($50,000 and over)	12–36 Months IS-IV IS-III IS-II	24–36 Months IS-IV IS-III IS-II	36–54 Months	48–72 Months	60–90 Months
	Criminal History Scale	**A** No/Minor Record	**B** Moderate Record	**C** Serious Record	**D** Violent/Repetitive	**E** Serious Violent

Intermediate Sanction Levels

IS-IV	24-Hour Restriction
IS-III	Daily Accountability
IS-II	Standard Supervision

*A&B DW = Assault and Battery, Dangerous Weapon

The numbers in each cell represent the range from which the judge selects the maximum sentence (Not More Than). The minimum sentence (Not Less Than) is two-thirds of the maximum sentence and constitutes the initial parole eligibility date.

www.mass.gov/courts/formsandguidelines/sentencing/grid.html

expected to cover every possible criminal situation. Therefore, both state and federal sentencing guidelines allow an "escape hatch" of limited judicial discretion known as a **departure.** Judges in Massachusetts can "depart" from the grid on the preceding page if a case involves mitigating or aggravating circumstances.[45] In the case of Dharun Ravi that opened this chapter, Judge Glenn Berman made a significant departure from New Jersey guidelines that call for five-to-ten-year prison sentences for hate crimes.

Much to the disappointment of supporters of sentencing reform, a series of Supreme Court decisions handed down midway though the first decade of the 2000s held that federal sentencing guidelines were advisory only.[46] Since then, federal judges have taken advantage of their newfound freedom to depart from these guidelines. A 2012 study by the Transactional Records Access Clearinghouse found widespread sentencing disparities in federal courts, particularly in drug, weapons, and white-collar cases.[47] Furthermore, the U.S. Sentencing Commission reports that racial disparity in federal courts is again on the rise, with African American male defendants receiving sentences of about 20 percent greater lengths than white males who have been convicted of similar offenses.[48]

9-4b
Mandatory Sentencing Guidelines

In an attempt to close even the limited loophole of judicial discretion offered by departures, politicians (often urged on by their constituents) have passed sentencing laws even more contrary to the idea of individualized justice. These **mandatory** (minimum) **sentencing guidelines** further limit a judge's power to deviate from determinate sentencing laws by setting firm standards for certain crimes. Forty-six states have mandatory sentencing laws for crimes such as selling illegal drugs, driving under the influence of alcohol, and committing any crime with a dangerous weapon. In Alabama, for example, any person caught selling illegal drugs must spend at least two years in prison, with five years added to the sentence if the sale takes place within three miles of a school or housing project.[49] Similarly, Congress has set mandatory minimum sentences for more than one hundred crimes, mostly drug offenses.

As might be expected, such laws are often unpopular with judges. After being forced to send a defendant to prison for fifty-five years for selling marijuana and illegally possessing a handgun, U.S. district judge Paul Cassell called the sentence "unjust, cruel, and irrational."[50] Furthermore, mandatory minimum sentences perpetuate many of the inconsistencies previously detailed concerning race, ethnicity, and gender. Nearly 70 percent of all convicts subject to mandatory minimum sentences are African American or Hispanic, and 90 percent of such convicts are men.[51]

"THREE STRIKES" LEGISLATION Habitual offender laws are a common form of mandatory sentencing. Also known as "three-strikes-and-you're-out" laws, these statutes require that any person convicted of a third felony must serve a lengthy prison sentence. In many cases, the crime does not have to be of a violent or dangerous nature. Under Washington's habitual offender law, for example, a "persistent offender" is automatically sentenced to life even if the third felony offense happens to be "vehicular assault" (an automobile accident that causes injury), unarmed robbery, or attempted arson, among other lesser felonies.[52] Today, twenty-six states and the federal government employ "three-strikes" statutes, with varying degrees of severity.

"THREE-STRIKES" IN COURT The United States Supreme Court paved the way for these three-strikes laws when it ruled in *Rummel v. Estelle* (1980)[53] that Texas's habitual offender statute did not constitute "cruel and unusual punishment" under the Eighth Amendment. Basically, the Court gave each state the freedom to legislate such laws in the manner that it deems proper. Twenty-three years later, in *Lockyer v. Andrade* (2003),[54] the Court upheld California's "three-strikes" law. The California statute allows prosecutors to seek penalties up to life imprisonment

Departure A stipulation in many federal and state sentencing guidelines that allows a judge to adjust his or her sentencing decision based on the special circumstances of a particular case.

Mandatory Sentencing Guidelines Statutorily determined punishments that must be applied to those who are convicted of specific crimes.

Habitual Offender Laws Statutes that require lengthy prison sentences for those who are convicted of multiple felonies.

without parole on conviction of any third felony, including for nonviolent crimes. Leandro Andrade received fifty years in prison for stealing $153 worth of videotapes, his fourth felony conviction. A federal appeals court overturned the sentence, agreeing with Andrade's attorneys that it met the definition of cruel and unusual punishment.[55]

In a bitterly divided 5–4 decision, the Supreme Court reversed. Justice Sandra Day O'Connor, writing for the majority, stated that the sentence was not so "objectively" unreasonable that it violated the Constitution.[56] In his dissent, Justice David H. Souter countered that "[i]f Andrade's sentence is not grossly disproportionate, the principle has no meaning."[57] Basically, the justices who upheld the law said that if the California legislature—and by extension the California voters—felt that the law was reasonable, then the judicial branch was in no position to disagree.

Given the Court's *Andrade* decision, it was somewhat ironic when, in 2012, California voters decided that the state's three-strikes law was indeed unreasonable. That year, by a two-thirds vote, Californians passed a ballot initiative revising the law. Now, a life sentence will be imposed only when the third felony conviction is for a serious or violent crime.[58] Furthermore, the measure authorizes judges to resentence those inmates who are serving life prison terms in California prisons because of

a nonviolent "third strike." An estimated 3,000 state inmates—including Leandro Andrade—became eligible for reduced sentences under the revised law.[59] In Chapter 11, we will see that numerous states are similarly rethinking mandatory minimum sentencing in an effort to reduce their large and costly prison populations.

9-4c
Victim Impact Evidence

The final piece of the sentencing puzzle involves victims and victims' families. As was mentioned in the previous chapter, crime victims traditionally were banished to the peripheries of the criminal justice system. This situation has changed dramatically with the emergence of the victims' rights movement over the past few decades. Victims are now given the opportunity to testify—in person or through written testimony—during sentencing hearings about the suffering they experienced as the result of the crime. These **victim impact statements (VISs)** have proved extremely controversial, however, and even the Supreme Court has had a difficult time determining whether they cause more harm than good.

BALANCING THE PROCESS The Crime Victims' Rights Act provides victims the right to be reasonably heard during the sentencing process,[60] and many state victims' rights laws contain similar provisions.[61] In general, these laws allow a victim (or victims) to tell his or her "side

> **Victim Impact Statement (VIS)** A statement to the sentencing body (judge, jury, or parole board) in which the victim is given the opportunity to describe how the crime has affected her or him.

of the story" to the sentencing body, be it a judge, jury, or parole officer. In nonmurder cases, the victim can personally describe the physical, financial, and emotional impact of the crime. When the charge is murder or manslaughter, relatives or friends can give personal details about the victim and describe the effects of her or his death. In almost all instances, the goal of the VIS is to increase the harshness of the sentence.

LO 4

Most of the debate surrounding VISs centers on their use in the sentencing phases of death penalty cases. Supporters point out that the defendant has always been allowed to present character evidence in the hopes of dissuading a judge or jury from capital punishment. According to some, a VIS balances the equation by giving survivors a voice in the process. Presenting a VIS is also said to have psychological benefits for victims, who are no longer forced to sit in silence as decisions that affect their lives are made by others.[62] Finally, on a purely practical level, a VIS may help judges and juries make informed sentencing decisions by providing them with an understanding of all of the consequences of the crime.

THE RISKS OF VICTIM EVIDENCE Opponents of the use of VISs claim that they interject dangerously prejudicial evidence into the sentencing process, which should be governed by reason, not emotion. The inflammatory nature of VISs, they say, may distract judges and juries from the facts of the case, which should be the only basis for a sentence.[63] Furthermore, critics contend that a VIS introduces the idea of "social value" into the courtroom. In other words, judges and juries may feel compelled to base the punishment on the "social value" of the victim (his or her standing in the community, role as a family member, and the like) rather than the circumstances of the crime.

In 1991, the United States Supreme Court gave its approval to the use of VISs, allowing judges to decide whether the statements are admissible on a case-by-case basis just as they do with any other type of evidence.[64] Several years after this decision, Bryan Myers of the University of North Carolina at Wilmington and Jack Arbuthnot of Ohio

Capital Punishment The use of the death penalty to punish wrongdoers for certain crimes.

University decided to test the prejudicial impact of the testimony in question. They ran simulated court proceedings with two groups of mock jurors: one group heard a "family member" give a VIS, while the other group did not. Of those mock jurors who ultimately voted for the death penalty, 67 percent had heard the VIS. In contrast, only 30 percent of those who did not hear it voted to execute the defendant.[65]

9-5

what IS THE STATUS OF CAPITAL PUNISHMENT IN THE UNITED STATES?

"You do not know how hard it is to let a human being die," Abraham Lincoln (1809–1865) once said, "when you feel that a stroke of your pen will save him." Despite these misgivings, during his four years in office Lincoln approved the execution of 267 soldiers, including those who had slept at their posts.[66] Our sixteenth president's ambivalence toward **capital punishment** is reflected in America's continuing struggle to reconcile the penalty of death with the morals and values of society. Capital punishment has played a role in sentencing since the earliest days of the Republic and—having survived a brief period of abolition between 1972 and 1976—continues to enjoy public support.

Still, few topics in the criminal justice system inspire such heated debate. Death penalty opponents such as legal expert Stephen Bright wonder whether "there comes a time when a society gets beyond some of the more primitive forms of punishment."[67] They point out that only twenty-three countries still employ the death penalty and that the United States is the sole Western democracy that continues the practice. Critics also claim that a process whose subjects are chosen by "luck and money and race" cannot serve the interests of justice.[68] Proponents believe that the death penalty serves as the ultimate deterrent for violent criminal behavior and that the criminals who are put to death are the "worst of the worst" and deserve their fate.

Today, about 3,100 convicts are living on "death row" in American prisons, meaning they have been sentenced to death and are awaiting execution. In the 1940s, as many as two hundred people were put to death in the United States in one year. As Figure 9.4 below shows, the most recent high-water mark was ninety-eight in 1999. Despite declines since then, states and the federal government are still regularly executing convicts. Consequently, the questions that surround the death penalty—Is it fair? Is it humane? Does it deter crime?—will continue to mobilize both its supporters and its detractors.

9-5a
Methods of Execution

In its early years, when the United States adopted the practice of capital punishment from England, it also adopted English methods, which included drawing and quartering and boiling the convict alive. By the nineteenth century, these techniques had been deemed "barbaric" and were replaced by hanging. Indeed, the history of capital punishment in America is marked by attempts to make the act more humane. The 1890s saw the introduction of electrocution as a less painful method of execution than hanging, and in 1890 in Auburn Prison, New York, William Kemmler became the first American to die in an electric chair.

The "chair" remained the primary form of execution until 1977, when Oklahoma became the first state to adopt lethal injection. Today, this method dominates executions in all thirty-two states that employ the death penalty. Sixteen states authorize at least two different methods of execution, mean-ing that electrocution (nine states), lethal gas (three states), hanging (three states), and the firing squad (two states) are still used on rare occasions. (**CAREER TIP:** If you want to influence how death penalty legislation and other criminal laws are written in your state, you should consider running for office as a *state legislator* at some point in your career.)

Many states employ a three-drug process to carry out lethal injections. First, the sedative sodium thiopental is administered to deaden pain. Then pancuronium bromide, a paralytic, immobilizes the prisoner. Finally, a dose of potassium chloride stops the heart. Members of the law enforcement and medical communities have long claimed that, if performed correctly, this procedure kills the individual quickly and painlessly. Others, however, contend that the second drug—the paralytic—masks any outward signs of distress and thus keeps observers from knowing whether the inmate suffers extreme pain before death.[69]

9-5b
The Death Penalty and the Supreme Court

The United States Supreme Court's attitude toward the death penalty has been shaped by two decisions made more than a century ago. First, in 1890, the Court established that as long as they are not carried out in an "inhuman" or "barbarous" fashion, executions are not forbidden by the Eighth Amendment.[70] Since that case, the Court has never ruled that any

FIGURE 9.4 Executions in the United States, 1976 to 2012

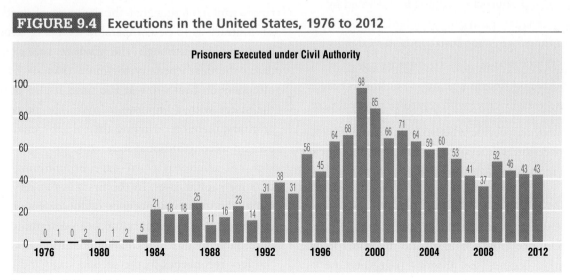

Source: Death Penalty Information Center.

The Virginia Department of Corrections' electric chair is used only at the request of the inmate facing the death sentence. Why has lethal injection replaced the use of the "chair" in most American executions?

AP Photo/Virginia Department of Corrections

method of execution is unconstitutionally "cruel and unusual."

Then, in *Weems v. United States* (1910),[71] the Supreme Court made a ruling that further clarified the meaning of "cruel and unusual" as defined by the Eighth Amendment, though the facts of the case did not involve capital punishment. The defendant had been sentenced to fifteen years of hard labor, a heavy fine, and a number of other penalties for the relatively minor crime of falsifying official records. The Court overturned the sentence, ruling that the penalty was too harsh considering the nature of the offense. Ultimately, in the *Weems* decision, the Court set three important precedents concerning sentencing:

1. Cruel and unusual punishment is defined by the changing norms and standards of society and therefore is not based on historical interpretations.

2. Courts may decide whether a punishment is unnecessarily cruel with regard to physical pain.

3. Courts may decide whether a punishment is unnecessarily cruel with regard to psychological pain.[72]

THE *BAZE* ENDORSEMENT In 2007, two convicted murderers in Kentucky asked the United States Supreme Court to invalidate the state's lethal injection procedure (see previous page) because of the possibility that it inflicted undetectable suffering.

Nearly all of the scheduled executions in the United States were placed on hold while the Court deliberated this issue. In 2008, the Court ruled in *Baze v. Rees* that the mere possibility of pain "does not establish the sort of 'objectively intolerable risk of harm' that qualifies as cruel and unusual" punishment.[73]

Although executions resumed shortly after the *Baze* decision, a number of states changed the ingredients of the drug "cocktails" involved. Today, thirteen states have replaced sodium thiopental in their three-step processes with a similar sedative called pentobarbital, commonly used in this country to euthanize animals. In addition, seven states now use a single, very strong dose of pentobarbital to carry out the death penalty. (**CAREER TIP:** A number of states require a physician known as an *anesthesiologist* to mix the drugs used in the lethal injection process and oversee the execution.)

REFORMING THE DEATH PENALTY In the 1960s, the Supreme Court became increasingly concerned about what it saw as serious flaws in the way the states administered capital punishment. Finally, in 1967, the Court put a moratorium on executions until it could "clean up" the process. The chance to do so came with the *Furman v. Georgia* case, decided in 1972.[74]

The Bifurcated Process In its *Furman* decision, by a 5–4 margin, the Supreme Court essentially held that the death penalty, as administered by the states, violated the Eighth Amendment. Justice Potter Stewart was particularly eloquent in his concurring opinion, stating that the sentence of death was so arbitrary as to be comparable to "being struck by lightning."[75] Although the *Furman* ruling invalidated the death penalty for more than six hundred offenders on death row at the time, it also provided the states with a window to make the process less arbitrary, therefore bringing their death penalty statutes up to constitutional standards.

The result was a two-stage, or *bifurcated*, procedure for capital cases. In the first stage, a jury determines the guilt or innocence of the defendant for a crime that has, by state statute, been determined to be punishable by death. If the defendant is found guilty, the jury reconvenes in the second stage and considers all aggravating and mitigating factors to decide

5 LO

whether the death sentence is in fact warranted. Therefore, even if a jury finds the defendant guilty of a crime, such as first degree murder, that *may be* punishable by death, in the second stage it can decide that the circumstances surrounding the crime justify only a punishment of life in prison.

Court Approval The Supreme Court ruled in favor of Georgia's new bifurcated process in 1976, stating that the process removed the ability of a court to "wantonly and freakishly impose the death penalty."[76] The Court upheld similar procedures in Texas and Florida, establishing a model for all states to follow that would assure them protection from lawsuits based on Eighth Amendment grounds. On January 17, 1977, Gary Gilmore became the first American executed (by Utah) under the new laws, and today thirty-two states and the federal government have capital punishment laws based on the bifurcated process.

The death penalty states do not, however, impose capital punishment at a consistent rate. As Figure 9.5 below shows, a convict's likelihood of being executed is strongly influenced by geography. Five states—Florida, Missouri, Oklahoma, Texas, and Virginia—account for more than two-thirds of all executions. **(CAREER TIP:** Michael Graczyk, an Associated Press reporter, has witnessed more than three hundred executions in Texas. *Journalists* such as Graczyk present important information about the criminal justice system to the public.) Note that state governments are responsible for almost all executions in this country. The federal government has carried out only three death sentences since 1963.

THE JURY'S ROLE The Supreme Court reaffirmed the important role of the jury in death penalties in *Ring v. Arizona* (2002).[77] The case involved Arizona's bifurcated process: after the jury determined a defendant's guilt or innocence, it would be dismissed, and the judge alone would decide whether execution was warranted. The Court found that this procedure violated the defendant's Sixth Amendment right to a jury trial, ruling that juries must be involved in *both* stages of the bifurcated process. The decision invalidated death penalty laws in Arizona, Colorado, Idaho, Montana, and Nebraska, forcing legislatures in those states to hastily revamp their procedures. (To learn how a jury makes this difficult decision, see the feature *You Be the Juror—Life or Death?* on the following page.)

Some states still allow for a measure of judicial discretion in capital punishment decisions. In Alabama, Delaware, and Florida, the jury only recommends a sentence of death or life in prison. If the judge feels that the sentence is unreasonable, he or she can override the jury. In 2012, for example, an Alabama jury voted 9–3 that Gregory Henderson should serve a sentence of life in prison for running over and killing a law enforcement agent during a traffic stop. Nonetheless, Lee County circuit judge Jacob Walker, noting that the defendant showed no remorse for his intentional crime, overruled the jury's recommendation and sentenced Henderson to death.

MITIGATING CIRCUMSTANCES Several mitigating circumstances will prevent a defendant found

FIGURE 9.5 Executions by State, 1976–2012

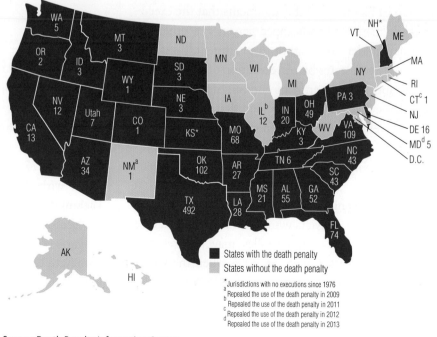

States with the death penalty
States without the death penalty

* Jurisdictions with no executions since 1976
a Repealed the use of the death penalty in 2009
b Repealed the use of the death penalty in 2011
c Repealed the use of the death penalty in 2012
d Repealed the use of the death penalty in 2013

Source: Death Penalty Information Center.

LIFE OR DEATH?

THE SITUATION You are a member of the jury that found Robinson guilty of paying another man to kill his fourteen-year-old girlfriend Chelsea, who was pregnant with Robinson's child. During the trial, you heard evidence that Robinson wanted Chelsea dead so that she could not testify against him in a statutory rape trial. In your state, murder-for-hire is a capital offense, so now you and your fellow jury members must decide whether Robinson deserves the death penalty or, alternatively, life in prison for his crimes.

THE LAW Jurors must weigh aggravating factors against mitigating factors during the death penalty phase of criminal trials. If you believe that the aggravating factors surrounding Robinson's crime outweigh the mitigating factors, you must vote for him to be executed.

Gina Sanders/Shutterstock

YOUR DECISION After presenting testimony from family and friends that Robinson experienced a difficult childhood without parental guidance, the defense attorney asks if there isn't "something in your heart that tells you that death isn't the appropriate punishment?" Indeed, according to state law, "mercy" can be a mitigating factor in this case. The prosecutor counters by saying, "Mercy? You can grant him the same mercy he granted Chelsea." The prosecutor also argues that the heinous nature of the crime is a strong aggravating factor, adding, "If this murder is not worthy of the death penalty, then what is?" After hearing these arguments, do you think that Robinson should receive the death penalty or a life prison sentence? Why?

[To see whether a Kansas jury chose the death sentence in similar circumstances, go to Example 9.1 in Appendix A.]

guilty of first degree murder from receiving the death penalty. In 1986, the United States Supreme Court held that the Constitution prohibits the execution of a person who is insane.[78] Sixteen years later, in *Atkins v. Virginia* (2002),[79] the Court similarly ended the death penalty for mentally handicapped defendants. This later decision underscored the continuing importance of the *Weems* test (see page 204). In 1989, the Court had rejected the arguments that the execution of a mentally handicapped person was "cruel and unusual" under the Eighth Amendment.[80] At the time, only two states barred execution of the mentally handicapped. Thirteen years later, eighteen states had such laws, and the Court decided that this increased number reflected "changing norms and standards of society."

Following the *Atkins* case, many observers, including four Supreme Court justices, hoped that the same reasoning would be applied to the question of whether convicts who committed the relevant crime when they were juveniles may be executed. These hopes were realized in 2005 when the Court issued its *Roper v. Simmons* decision, which effectively ended the execution of those who committed crimes as juveniles.[81] As in the *Atkins* case, the Court relied on the "evolving standards of decency" test, noting

that a majority of the states, as well as every other civilized nation, prohibited the execution of offenders who committed their crimes before the age of eighteen. The *Roper* ruling required that seventy-two convicted murderers in twelve states be resentenced and took the death penalty "off the table" for dozens of pending cases in which prosecutors were seeking capital punishment for juvenile criminal acts.

9-5c
The Immediate Future of the Death Penalty

As noted earlier in the chapter, the number of executions carried out each year in the United States has decreased dramatically since 1999. Other statistics also indicate a decline in death penalty activity. In 2012, only 77 people were sentenced to death, compared with 277 in 1999.[82] According to James S. Liebman, a law professor at Columbia University, prosecutors in 60 percent of the nation's counties no longer seek the death penalty, even with defendants who have been convicted of capital crimes.[83]

REASONS FOR THE DECLINE IN EXECUTIONS We have already addressed some of the reasons for the diminishing presence of executions in the

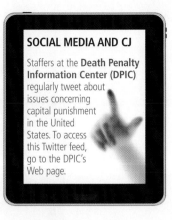

criminal justice system. With its decisions in the *Atkins* (2002) and *Roper* (2005) cases, the United States Supreme Court removed the possibility that hundreds of mentally handicapped and juvenile offenders could be sentenced to death. Furthermore, nearly all of the states that allow for the death penalty now permit juries to impose a sentence of life in prison without parole as an alternative to death. In Texas, the number of death sentences imposed each year dropped by about 50 percent after jurors were given the life-without-parole option, a trend that has been mirrored throughout the United States.[84]

Financial considerations are also starting to color the capital punishment picture. Because of the costs of intensive investigations, extensive *voir dire* (see Chapter 8), and lengthy appellate reviews, pursuing the death penalty can be very expensive. A study by the Urban Institute found that the average death penalty trial costs a state $2 million more than a murder trial in which capital punishment is not sought.[85] Stan Garnett, the district attorney in Boulder County, Colorado, points out that a single death penalty case costs state taxpayers $18 million, while the entire annual budget for his office is $4.6 million.[86] As state budgets come under increased pressure from declining revenues, officials are looking at capital punishment as an area of potential savings.

PUBLIC OPINION AND THE DEATH PENALTY

In March 2013, after the Maryland legislature voted to ban the death penalty, state lieutenant governor Anthony Brown said, "Today is a victory for those who believe that fairness and truth and justice, and not retribution or bias, are fundamental to our core beliefs as Marylanders."[87] Maryland became the sixth state in six years to end capital punishment, along with Connecticut, Illinois, New Jersey, New Mexico, and New York.

Does this mean society's "standards of decency" are changing to the point that the death sentence is in danger of being completely abolished in the United States? Probably not. The Supreme Court has shown no interest in holding that the death penalty itself is unconstitutional. In addition to its *Baze* decision (discussed earlier in this section), in 2007 the Court made it easier for prosecutors to seek the death penalty by allowing them to remove potential jurors who express reservations about the practice.[88]

Although public support for the death penalty has been steadily dropping since the mid-1990s, one poll taken in 2013 showed that 63 percent of Americans still favor the practice.[89] **(CAREER TIP:** *Pollsters,* who conduct surveys of public opinion, have found this percentage drops to about 50 percent when the choice is between execution and a sentence of life in prison without parole.) Another poll found that 58 percent of the respondents favored an official moratorium on executions nationwide to consider the problem of wrongful death sentences.[90] In the 2000s, then, many Americans seem more interested in making the sentence of death fairer than in doing away with it altogether.

REVIEW

✓ **Review what you've read with the quiz below.**

Rip out the Chapter Review card at the back of this book, which includes:
- Chapter Summary and Learning Outcomes
- Key Terms

Or you can go online to CourseMate at www.cengagebrain.com to:
- Complete Practice Quizzes to prepare for tests.
- Review Key Terms Flash Cards (online or print).
- Play games to master concepts.

quiz

1. The goal of the sentencing doctrine called _____ is to prevent future crimes by "setting an example" with punishments for convicted criminals.

2. A sentencing doctrine known as _____ suggests that offenders can be "treated" for their criminal tendencies and possibly "cured" of them.

3. _____ sentences set a minimum and maximum amount of time a convict must spend behind bars, giving corrections officials the discretion to release the inmate within that time period.

4. A determinate sentence indicates the exact length of incapacitation, minus possible reductions for _____ _____.

5. Important factors in sentencing, _____ circumstances can allow for a lighter sentence, while aggravating circumstances can lead to the imposition of a harsher penalty.

6. Sentencing _____ occurs when similar crimes are punished with dissimilar sentences.

7. Sentencing _____ is the result of judicial consideration of extralegal variables such as the defendant's race or gender.

8. With the aim of limiting judicial discretion, many states and the federal government have enacted sentencing _____.

9. By a large margin, _____ _____ is the most widespread method of execution in the United States today.

10. Following the "norms and standards" guidelines it established with the *Weems* decision, in 2005 the United States Supreme Court prohibited the execution of persons who were _____ at the time of their crime.

Answers can be found on the Chapter 9 Review card at the end of the book.

AP Photo/Dave Martin

4LTR Press solutions are designed for today's learners through the continuous feedback of students like you. Tell us what you think about **CJ** and help us improve the learning experience for future students.

YOUR FEEDBACK MATTERS.

 Complete the Speak Up survey in CourseMate at www.cengagebrain.com

 Follow us at www.facebook.com/4ltrpress

1 Explain the justifications for community-based corrections programs.

2 Describe the three general categories of conditions placed on a probationer.

3 Identify the main differences between probation and parole.

4 List the four basic roles of the parole board.

5 List the three levels of home monitoring.

PROBATION, PAROLE, AND INTERMEDIATE SANCTIONS

Lacking Common Sense

In Oklahoma, second degree manslaughter occurs when a person commits a homicide because of "culpable negligence," or the failure to use ordinary care and caution. Eighteen-year-old Krysta Dawson certainly met that standard several years ago by putting her nine-month-old son James in a bathtub and leaving the room. When she returned, James was unresponsive, and the infant died in a hospital the next day. After initially investigating the drowning as an accident, Tulsa police eventually decided that Dawson's actions were criminal, and prosecutors charged her with second degree manslaughter. "A nine-month-old should never be left in that type of situation," said a local authority. "I think that is just common sense."

Dawson pleaded no contest to the charge, leaving her punishment in the hands of District Judge Clancy Smith. Given that Dawson's negligence directly led to the death of a child, one might have expected Smith to be severe.

Judges, however, tend toward leniency in such cases. In 2009, a Morgan County, Colorado, judge sentenced Amanda Holbert to four years of probation for allowing her nine-month-old son to drown in a bathtub while she spoke on the telephone. The next year in Tampa, Florida, Katrina Brooks received five years' probation for similarly neglecting her infant son while on the phone, leading to his drowning death in a bathtub.

It seems that judges often consider the women in these situations as "loving and caring" mothers who

made "a mistake," rather than violent criminals. So, it should have come as no surprise that Judge Smith sentenced Dawson to probation for James's death. As one of the conditions of staying out of prison, Dawson was required to inform local officials if she changed her address. Consequently, when Dawson unwisely moved to Arkansas without notifying the local district attorney's office, she broke the terms of her probation. As a result, in 2013 Dawson was rearrested and, this time, sentenced to spend four years behind bars.

Parents such as Thomas and Emilie Pinski of Edwardsville, Illinois, who accidentally allow their children to drown are often sentenced to probation by judges.

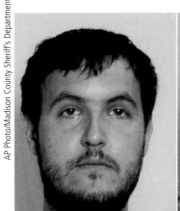

AP Photo/Madison County Sheriff's Department

10-1
why DO WE NEED COMMUNITY CORRECTIONS?

LO **1** Judges who decide not to send criminally negligent mothers such as Krysta Dawson, Amanda Holbert, and Katrina Brooks to prison or jail are hardly breaking new ground. Today, nearly 4 million offenders are serving their sentences in the community on *probation* rather than behind bars. In addition, approximately 850,000 convicts in the United States have been *paroled*, meaning that they are finishing their prison sentences "on the outside" under the supervision of correctional officers.[1]

America, says University of Minnesota law professor Michael Tonry, is preoccupied with the "absolute severity of punishment" and the "widespread view that only imprisonment counts."[2] Consequently, **community corrections** such as probation and parole are often considered a less severe, and therefore a less worthy, alternative to imprisonment. In reality, community corrections are crucially important. One in fifty adults in this country is living under community supervision,[3] and few criminal justice matters are more pressing than the need to successfully reintegrate these offenders into society.

10-1a
Reintegration

A very small percentage of all convicted offenders have committed crimes that warrant life imprisonment or capital punishment. Most, at some point, will return to the community. Consequently, according to one group of experts, the task of the corrections system includes building or rebuilding solid ties between the offender and the community, integrating or reintegrating the offender into community life—restoring family ties, obtaining employment and an education, securing in the larger sense a place for the offender in the routine functioning of society.[4]

Considering that some studies have shown higher recidivism rates for offenders who are subjected to prison culture, a frequent justification of community-based corrections is that they help to reintegrate the offender into society.

Reintegration has a strong theoretical basis in rehabilitative theories of punishment. An offender is generally considered to be "rehabilitated" when he or she no longer represents a threat to other members of the community and therefore is believed to be fit to live in that community.

In the context of this chapter and the two that follow, it will also be helpful to see reintegration as a process through which criminal justice officials such as probation and parole officers provide the offender with incentives to follow the rules of society. These incentives can be positive, such as enrolling the offender in a drug treatment program. They can also be negative—in particular, the threat of return to prison or jail for failure to comply. In all instances, criminal justice professionals must carefully balance the needs of the individual offender against the rights of law-abiding members of the community.

10-1b
Diversion

Another justification for community-based corrections, based on practical considerations, is **diversion**. As you are already aware, many criminal offenses fall into the category of "petty," and it is well-nigh impossible, as well as unnecessary, to imprison every offender for every offense. Community-based corrections are an important means of diverting criminals to alternative modes of punishment so that scarce incarceration resources are consumed by only the most dangerous criminals. In his "strainer" analogy, corrections expert Paul H. Hahn likens this process to the workings of a kitchen strainer. With each "shake" of the corrections "strainer," the less serious offenders are diverted from incarceration. At the end, only the most serious convicts remain in prison.[5] (**CAREER TIP:** In Nevada, judges can sentence problem gamblers to treatment rather than prison. The new legislation has created a demand for *pathological gambling therapists*, who help problem gamblers overcome their addiction.)

Community Corrections The correctional supervision of offenders in the community as an alternative to sending them to prison or jail.

Reintegration A goal of corrections that focuses on preparing the offender for a return to the community unmarred by further criminal behavior.

Diversion In the context of corrections, a strategy to divert those offenders who qualify away from prison and jail and toward community-based and intermediate sanctions.

How might society benefit if offenders such as these Dallas street prostitutes are kept out of jail or prison through diversion programs?

AP Photo/LM Otero, File

The diversionary role of community-based punishments has become more pronounced as prisons and jails have filled up over the past three decades. In fact, probationers and parolees now account for about 70 percent of all adults in the American corrections systems.[6]

10-1c
The "Low-Cost Alternative"

Not all of the recent expansion of community corrections can be attributed to acceptance of its theoretical underpinnings. Many politicians and criminal justice officials who do not look favorably on ideas such as reintegration and diversion have embraced programs to keep nonviolent offenders out of prison. The reason is simple: economics. The cost of constructing and maintaining prisons and jails, as well as housing and caring for inmates, has placed a great deal of pressure on corrections budgets across the country. Indeed, to cut prison operating costs, states are taking such steps as installing windmills and solar panels to save energy and using medical schools to provide less costly health care.[7]

Community corrections offer an enticing financial alternative to imprisonment. Data compiled by the Center for Economic and Policy Research suggest that for each nonviolent offender shifted from incarceration to community supervision, the federal government saves about $22,700, and state governments save about $23,200.[8] Not surprisingly, many

jurisdictions are adopting policies that favor keeping offenders out of prison or jail cells.

By diverting significant numbers of nonviolent criminals from state prisons to probation and parole, for example, New Hampshire estimates that it will save about $190 million, including new prison construction and operating costs, by 2021.[9] Officials can also require community-based criminals to finance their own supervision. In Oklahoma, probationers pay a $40 monthly fee to cover part of the costs of community corrections.[10]

10-2
how DOES PROBATION WORK ?

As Figure 10.1 on the next page shows, **probation** is the most common form of punishment in the United States. Although it is administered differently in various jurisdictions, probation can be generally defined as

> the legal status of an offender who, after being convicted of a crime, has been directed by the sentencing court to remain in the community under the supervision of a probation service for a designated period of time and subject to certain conditions imposed by the court or by law.[11]

The theory behind probation is that certain offenders, having been found guilty of a crime, can be treated more economically and humanely by putting them under controls while still allowing them to live in the community. One of the advantages of probation has been that it provides for the rehabilitation of the offender while

Probation A criminal sanction in which a convict is allowed to remain in the community rather than be imprisoned.

FIGURE 10.1 Probation in American Corrections

As you can see, the majority of convicts under the control of the American corrections system are on probation.

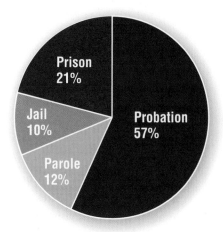

- Prison 21%
- Jail 10%
- Parole 12%
- Probation 57%

Source: Bureau of Justice Statistics, *Correctional Populations in the United States, 2011* (Washington, D.C.: U.S. Department of Justice, November 2012), Table 2, page 3.

saving society the costs of incarceration. Despite probation's widespread use, certain participants in the criminal justice system question its ability to reach its rehabilitative goals. Critics point to the immense number of probationers and the fact that many of them are violent felons as evidence that the system is "out of control." Supporters contend that nothing is wrong with probation in principle, but admit that its execution must be adjusted to meet the goals of modern corrections.[12]

10-2a

Sentencing and Probation

Probation is basically an arrangement between sentencing authorities and the offender. In traditional probation, the offender agrees to comply with certain terms for a specified amount of time in return for serving the sentence in the community. One of the primary benefits for the offender, besides not getting sent to a correctional facility, is that the length of the probationary period is usually considerably shorter than the length of a prison term (see Figure 10.2 on the facing page).

Suspended Sentence A judicially imposed condition in which an offender is sentenced after being convicted of a crime, but is not required to begin serving the sentence immediately.

Split Sentence Probation A sentence that consists of incarceration in a prison or jail, followed by a probationary period in the community.

The traditional form of probation is not the only arrangement that can be made. A judge can hand down a **suspended sentence,** under which a defendant who has been convicted and sentenced to be incarcerated is not required to serve the sentence. Instead, the judge puts the offender on notice, keeping open the option of reinstating the original sentence and sending the offender to prison or jail if he or she reoffends. In practice, suspended sentences are quite similar to probation.

ALTERNATIVE SENTENCING ARRANGEMENTS Judges can also combine probation with incarceration. Such sentencing arrangements include:

- *Split sentences.* In **split sentence probation,** also known as *shock probation,* the offender is sentenced to a specific amount of time in prison or jail, to be followed by a period of probation.
- *Shock incarceration.* In this arrangement, an offender is sentenced to prison or jail with the understanding that after a period of time, she or he may petition the court to be released on probation. Shock incarceration is discussed more fully later in the chapter.
- *Intermittent incarceration.* With intermittent incarceration, the offender spends a certain amount of time each week, usually during the weekend, in a jail, workhouse, or other government institution.

Split sentences are popular with judges, as they combine the "treatment" aspects of probation with the "punishment" aspects of incarceration. According to the U.S. Department of Justice, about a fifth of all probationers are also sentenced to some form of incarceration.[13]

CHOOSING PROBATION Generally, research has shown that offenders are most likely to be denied probation if they:

- Are convicted on multiple charges.
- Were on probation or parole at the time of the arrest.
- Have two or more prior convictions.
- Are addicted to narcotics.
- Seriously injured the victim of the crime.
- Used a weapon during the commission of the crime.[14]

As might be expected, the chances of a felon being sentenced to probation are highly dependent on the seriousness of his or her crime. Only 18 percent of probationers in the United States have committed a violent crime, including domestic violence and sex offenses. The majority of probationers have been convicted of property crimes, drug offenses, or public order crimes such as drunk driving.[15]

As with the child-drowning cases discussed in the opening to this chapter, probation also allows judges to recognize that some offenders are less blameworthy than others. In 2013, for example, a judge in Arizona found himself with the difficult task of punishing eighty-six-year-old George Sanders for fatally shooting Virginia, his eighty-one-year-old wife. Virginia, who was suffering from a painful health condition, had begged George to end her life. In handing down his sentence of two years' probation, Judge John Ditsworth said that his decision tempered "justice with mercy."[16]

10-2b
Conditions of Probation

A judge may decide to impose certain conditions as part of a probation sentence. These conditions repre-sent a "contract" between the judge and the offender, in which the latter agrees that if she or he does not follow certain rules, probation may be revoked. The probation officer usually recommends the conditions of probation, but judges also have the power to set any terms they believe to be necessary. For example, as part of her five-year probationary sentence for drunk driving, actress Lindsay Lohan was required to complete 480 hours of community service and attend psychological counseling sessions four times a month.

PRINCIPLES OF PROBATION A judge's per-sonal philosophy is often reflected in the probation conditions that she or he creates for probationers. In *In re Quirk* (1997),[17] for example, the Louisiana Supreme Court upheld the ability of a trial judge to impose church attendance as a condition of proba-tion. Though judges have a great deal of discretion in setting the conditions of probation, they do operate under several guiding principles. First, the condi-tions must be related to the dual purposes of proba-tion, which most federal and state courts define as (1) the rehabilitation of the probationer and (2) the protection of the community. Second, the condi-tions must not violate the U.S. Constitution, as proba-tioners are generally entitled to the same constitutional rights as other prisoners.[18]

Of course, probationers do give up certain consti-tutional rights when they consent to the terms of pro-bation. Most probationers, for example, agree to spot checks of their homes for contraband such as drugs or weapons, and they therefore have a diminished expecta-tion of privacy.

In *United States v. Knights* (2001),[19] the United States Supreme Court upheld the actions of deputy sheriffs in Napa County, California, who searched a probationer's home without

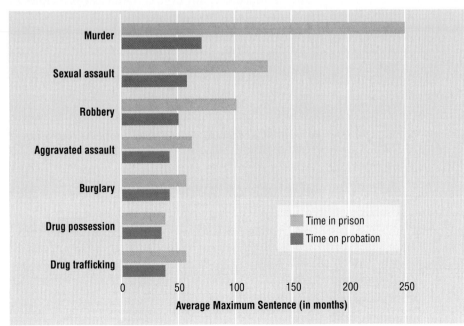

FIGURE 10.2 Average Length of Sentence: Prison versus Probation

As you can see, the average probation sentence is much shorter than the average prison sentence for most crimes.

Source: Bureau of Justice Statistics, *Felony Sentences in State Courts, 2006—Statistical Tables* (Washington, D.C.: U.S. Department of Justice, December 2009), Table 1.3.

a warrant or probable cause. The unanimous decision was based on the premise that because those on probation are more likely to commit crimes, law enforcement agents "may therefore justifiably focus on probationers in a way that [they do] not on the ordinary citizen."[20]

TYPES OF CONDITIONS Obviously, probationers who break the law are very likely to have their probation revoked. Other, less serious infractions may also result in revocation, as we saw with Krysta Dawson at the beginning of this chapter. The conditions placed on a probationer fall into three general categories:

- *Standard conditions*, which are imposed on all probationers. These include reporting regularly to the probation officer, notifying the agency of any change of address, not leaving the jurisdiction without permission, and remaining employed.
- *Punitive conditions*, which usually reflect the seriousness of the offense and are intended to increase the punishment of the offender. Such conditions include fines, community service, restitution, drug testing, and home confinement (discussed later).
- *Treatment conditions*, which are imposed to reverse patterns of self-destructive behavior. Such treatment generally includes counseling for drug and alcohol abuse, anger management, and mental health issues.

LO **2**

SOCIAL MEDIA AND CJ

The world of the probation officer is illuminated through tweets provided by **Probation Officers@ ProbationNews.** You can become a follower by signing on to your Twitter account and searching for "probation officers."

Some observers feel that judges have too much discretion in imposing overly restrictive conditions that no person, much less one who has exhibited antisocial tendencies, could meet. Citing prohibitions on drinking liquor, gambling, and associating with "undesirables," as well as requirements such as meeting early curfews, the late University of Delaware professor Carl B. Klockars claimed that if probation rules were taken seriously, "very few probationers would complete their terms without violation."[21]

As more than six out of ten federal probationers do complete their terms successfully, Klockars's statement suggests that either probation officers are unable to determine that violations are taking place, or many of them are exercising a great deal of discretion in reporting minor probation violations. Perhaps the officers realize that violating probationers for every single "slip-up" is unrealistic and would add to the already significant problem of jail and prison overcrowding.

10-2c

The Supervisory Role of the Probation Officer

The probation officer has two basic roles. The first is investigative and consists of conducting the presentence investigation (PSI), which was discussed in Chapter 9. The second is supervisory and begins as soon as the offender has been sentenced to probation. (**CAREER TIP:** In smaller probation agencies, individual officers perform both tasks. In larger jurisdictions, the trend has been toward separating the responsibilities, with *pretrial services officers* handling the PSI and *line officers* concentrating on supervision.)

Supervisory policies vary and are often a reflection of whether the authority to administer probation services is *decentralized* (under local, judicial control) or *centralized* (under state, administrative control). In any circumstance, however, certain basic principles of supervision apply. Starting with a preliminary interview, the probation officer establishes a relationship with the offender. This relationship is based on the mutual goal of both parties: the successful completion of the probationary period. Just because the line officer and the offender have the same goal, however, does not necessarily mean that cooperation will be a feature of probation.

THE USE OF AUTHORITY The ideal probation officer–offender relationship is based on trust. In reality, this trust often does not exist. Any incentive an offender might have to be completely truthful with a line officer is marred by one simple fact: self-reported wrongdoing can be used to revoke probation. Even probation officers whose primary mission is to rehabilitate are under institutional pressure to punish their clients for violating conditions of proba-

A Washington, D.C., probation officer makes phone curfew checks while her partner watches. Why is trust so often difficult to achieve between probation officers and offenders?

Mark Gail/*The Washington Post*/Getty Images

tion. One officer deals with this situation by telling his clients

> that I'm here to help them, to get them a job, and whatever else I can do. But I tell them too that I have a family to support and that if they get too far off track, I can't afford to put my job on the line for them. I'm going to have to violate them.[22]

In the absence of trust, most probation officers rely on their **authority** to guide an offender successfully through the sentence. An officer's authority, or ability to influence a person's actions without resorting to force, is based partially on her or his power to revoke probation. It also reflects her or his ability to impose a number of lesser sanctions. For example, if a probationer fails to attend a required alcohol treatment program, the officer can send him or her to a "lockup," or detention center, overnight. To be successful, a probation officer must establish this authority early in the relationship because it is the primary tool for persuading the probationer to behave in an acceptable manner.[23]

THE CASELOAD DILEMMA Even the most balanced, "firm but fair" approach to probation can be defeated by the problem of excessive *caseloads*. A **caseload** is the number of clients a probation officer is responsible for at any one time. Heavy probation caseloads seem inevitable: unlike a prison cell, a probation officer can always take "just one more" client.

Furthermore, the ideal caseload size is very difficult to determine because different offenders require different levels of supervision.[24]

The consequences of disproportionate probation officer–probationer ratios are self-evident, however. When burdened with large caseloads, probation officers find it practically impossible to rigorously enforce the conditions imposed on their clients. Lack of surveillance leads to lack of control, which can undermine the very basis of a probationary system. In Sacramento County, California, where probation officers have caseloads of more than 120 each and more than 90 percent of all probationers are unsupervised, these offenders are responsible for 30 percent of the county's total arrests.[25]

10-2d
Revocation of Probation

The probation period can end in one of two ways. Either the probationer successfully fulfills the conditions of the sentence, or the probationer misbehaves and probation is revoked, resulting in a prison or jail term. The decision of whether to revoke after a **technical violation**—such as failing to report a change of address or testing positive for drug use—is often a judgment call by the probation officer and therefore the focus of controversy. (See the feature *You Be the Probation Officer—A Judgment Call* on the following page to learn more about the issues surrounding revocation.)

As we have seen, probationers do not always enjoy

Authority The power designated to an agent of the law over a person who has broken the law.

Caseload The number of individual probationers or parolees under the supervision of a probation or parole officer.

Technical Violation An action taken by a probationer or parolee that, although not criminal, breaks the terms of probation or parole as designated by the court.

YOU BE THE PROBATION OFFICER

A JUDGMENT CALL

THE FACTS Your client, Alain, was convicted of selling drugs and given a split sentence—three years in prison and three years on probation. You meet Alain for the first time two days after his release, and you are immediately concerned about his mental health. His mother confirms your worries, telling you that Alain needs help. You refer him to a psychiatric hospital, but the officials there determine that he "does not require mental health treatment at this time." Several weeks later, Alain's mother tells you that he is staying out late at night and "hanging out with the wrong crowd," both violations of his probation agreement. After he tests positive for marijuana, you warn Alain that, after one more violation, you will revoke his probation and send him back to prison. He tells you that he is "feeling agitated" and "having intermittent rage." You refer him to a substance abuse and mental health treatment facility, where he tests positive for marijuana once again.

THE LAW For any number of reasons, but particularly for the failed drug tests, you can start revocation proceedings against Alain. These proceedings will almost certainly conclude with his return to prison.

YOUR DECISION On the one hand, Alain has violated the terms of his probation agreement numerous times. On the other hand, he has been convicted of only one crime—a drug violation—and you have no evidence that he is behaving violently or poses a danger to himself or others. Furthermore, Alain has strong family support and is willing to enter treatment for his substance abuse problems. Do Alain's technical violations cause you to begin the revocation process? Why or why not?

[To see how a Fairfield County, Connecticut, probation officer dealt with a similar situation, go to Example 10.1 in Appendix A.]

---

the same protections under the U.S. Constitution as other members of society. The United States Supreme Court has not stripped these offenders of all rights, however. In *Mempa v. Rhay* (1967),[26] the Court ruled that probationers were entitled to an attorney during the revocation process. Then, in *Morrissey v. Brewer* (1972) and *Gagnon v. Scarpelli* (1973),[27] the Court established a three-stage procedure by which the "limited" due process rights of probationers must be protected in potential revocation situations:

- *Preliminary hearing.* In this appearance before a "disinterested person" (often a judge), the facts of the violation or arrest are presented, and it is determined whether probable cause for revoking probation exists. This hearing can be waived by the probationer.
- *Revocation hearing.* During this hearing, the probation agency presents evidence to support its claim of violation, and the probationer can attempt to refute this evidence. The probationer has the right to know the charges being brought against him or her. Furthermore, probationers

can testify on their own behalf and present witnesses in their favor, as well as confront and cross-examine adverse witnesses. A "neutral and detached" body must hear the evidence and rule on the validity of the proposed revocation.

- *Revocation sentencing.* If the presiding body rules against the probationer, then the judge must decide whether to impose incarceration and for what length of time. In a revocation hearing dealing with technical violations, the judge will often reimpose probation with stricter terms or intermediate sanctions.

In effect, this is a "bare-bones" approach to due process. Most of the rules of evidence that govern regular trials do not apply to revocation hearings. Probation officers are not, for example, required to read offenders their *Miranda* rights before questioning them about crimes they may have committed during probation. In *Minnesota v. Murphy* (1984),[28] the Supreme Court ruled that a meeting between probation officer and client does not equal custody and, therefore, the Fifth Amendment protection against self-incrimination does not apply, either.

10-2e

Does Probation Work?

On March 28, 2013, Las Cruces, New Mexico, police arrested Cornelius Renteria for murdering his ex-girlfriend in her home. At the time of the murder, Renteria was on probation for kidnapping, child abuse, and aggravated assault charges. Indeed, probationers are responsible for a significant amount of crime. Each year, about 375,000 probationers return to prison or jail, many because of criminal behavior.[29] Such statistics raise a critical question—is probation worthwhile?

PREVENTING RECIDIVISM To measure the effectiveness of probation, one must first establish its purpose. Generally, as we saw earlier, the goal of probation is to reintegrate and divert as many offenders as possible while at the same time protecting the public. Specifically, probation and other community corrections programs are evaluated by their success in preventing **recidivism**—the eventual rearrest of the probationer.[30] Given that most probationers are first-time, nonviolent offenders, the system is not designed to prevent relatively rare outbursts of violence, such as the murder committed by Cornelius Renteria.

RISK FACTORS FOR RECIDIVISM About a quarter of all federal probationers are rearrested within five years of being placed under community

Recidivism The act of committing a new crime after a person has already been punished for a previous crime by being convicted and sent to jail or prison.

CAREER**PREP**

PROBATION OFFICER

JOB DESCRIPTION:

- Work with offenders or clients who have been sentenced to probation and will not go to prison or jail for their offenses. In some departments, investigate offender backgrounds, write presentence reports, and recommend sentences.

- Includes extensive fieldwork to meet with and monitor offenders. May be required to carry a firearm or other weapon for protection.

WHAT KIND OF TRAINING IS REQUIRED?

- A bachelor's degree in criminal justice, social work, psychology, or a related field.

- Must be at least twenty-one years old, have no felony convictions, and have strong writing and interview skills. Experience in multicultural outreach is a plus.

ANNUAL SALARY RANGE?

- $31,500–$51,500

SOCIAL MEDIA CAREER TIP

Manage your online reputation—or someone else will do it for you. Monitor your profile using tools such as iSearch, Pipl, and ZabaSearch. Check BoardTracker, BoardReader, and Omgili for information on what people are saying about you on message boards.

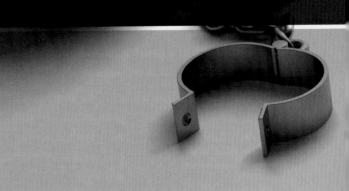

Mark Evans/iStockphoto.com

supervision. There are several risk factors that make a probationer more likely to recidivate, including a criminal history, substance abuse problems, and unemployment.[31] Consequently, probation departments have attempted to focus attention on those probationers with the most risk factors.[32]

In addition, as far as reducing recidivism is concerned, the most effective probation strategy appears to be a mix of supervision (behavior monitoring) and treatment (behavior change). Researchers have labeled this a "hybrid" approach to probation, and numerous studies attest to the benefits of mixing "tough love" and treatment such as drug counseling and continuing education instead of focusing on one or the other.[33] Also, as noted earlier, caseloads matter. A recent study of probation practices in Iowa and Oklahoma found that the lower the caseload for each individual probation officer, the lower the rates of probationers being arrested for new crimes.[34]

10-3
how DOES PAROLE WORK?

At any given time, about 850,000 Americans are living in the community on **parole,** or the *conditional* release of a prisoner after a portion of his or her sentence has been served behind bars. Parole allows the corrections system to continue to supervise an offender who is no longer incarcerated. As long as parolees follow the conditions of their parole, they are allowed to finish their terms outside the prison. If parolees break the terms of their early release, however, they face the risk of being returned to a penal institution.

Parole is based on three concepts:[35]

1. *Grace.* The prisoner has no right to be given an early release, but the government has granted her or him that privilege.

Parole The conditional release of an inmate before his or her sentence has expired.

Parole Contract An agreement between the state and the offender that establishes the conditions of parole.

2. *Contract of consent.* The government and the parolee enter into an arrangement whereby the latter agrees to abide by certain conditions in return for continued freedom.

3. *Custody.* Technically, though no longer incarcerated, the parolee is still the responsibility of the state. Parole is an extension of corrections.

Because of good-time credits and parole, most prisoners do not serve their entire sentence in prison. In fact, the average felon serves only about half of the term handed down by the court.

10-3a
Comparing Probation and Parole

Both probation and parole operate under the basic assumption that the offender serves her or his time in the community rather than in a prison or jail. The main differences between the two concepts—which sound confusingly similar—involve their circumstances. Probation is a sentence handed down by a judge following conviction and usually does not include incarceration. Parole is a conditional release from prison and occurs after an offender has already served some time in a correctional facility. (See Figure 10.3 on the facing page for clarification.)

3 LO

CONDITIONS OF PAROLE In many ways, parole supervision is similar to probation supervision. Like probationers, offenders who are granted parole are placed under the supervision of community corrections officers and required to follow certain conditions. Certain parole conditions mirror probation conditions. All parolees, for example, must comply with the law, and they are generally responsible for reporting to their parole officer at certain intervals.

The frequency of these visits, along with the other terms of parole, is spelled out in the **parole contract,** which sets out the agreement between the state and the paroled offender. Under the terms of the contract, the state agrees to conditionally release the inmate, and the future parolee agrees that her or his conditional release will last only as long as she or he abides by the contract.

PAROLE REVOCATION A large number—about half—of parolees return to prison before the end of

FIGURE 10.3 Probation versus Parole

Probation and parole have many aspects in common. In fact, probation and parole are so similar that many jurisdictions combine them into a single agency. There are, however, some important distinctions between the two systems, as noted below.

	PROBATION	PAROLE
Basic Definition	An **alternative to imprisonment** in which a person who has been convicted of a crime is allowed to serve his or her sentence in the community subject to certain conditions and supervision by a probation officer.	An **early release** from a correctional facility, in which the convicted offender is given the chance to spend the remainder of her or his sentence under supervision in the community.
Timing	The offender is sentenced to a probationary term in place of a prison or jail term. If the offender breaks the conditions of probation, he or she is sent to prison or jail. Therefore, **probation generally occurs *before* imprisonment.**	Parole is a form of early release. Therefore, **parole occurs *after* an offender has spent time behind bars.**
Authority	**Probation is under the domain of the judiciary.** A judge decides whether to sentence a convict to probation, and a judge determines whether a probation violation warrants revocation and incarceration.	**Parole often falls under the domain of the parole board.** This administrative body determines whether the prisoner qualifies for early release and the conditions under which the parole must be served.
Characteristics of Offenders	As a number of studies have shown, probationers are normally less involved in the criminal lifestyle. Most of them are **first-time offenders who have committed nonviolent crimes.**	Many parolees have **spent months or even years in prison** and, besides abiding by conditions of parole, must make the difficult transition to "life on the outside."

their parole period, most because they were convicted of a new offense or had their parole revoked.[36] **Parole revocation** is similar in many aspects to probation revocation. If the parolee commits a new crime, then a return to prison is very likely. If, however, the individual commits a technical violation by breaking a condition of parole, then parole authorities have discretion as to whether revocation proceedings should be initiated. A number of states, including Michigan, Missouri, and New York, have taken steps to avoid reincarcerating parolees for technical violations as part of their continuing efforts to reduce prison populations.[37]

When authorities do attempt to revoke parole for a technical violation, they must provide the parolee with a revocation hearing.[38] Although this hearing does not provide the same due process protections as a criminal trial, the parolee does have the right to be notified of the charges, to present witnesses, to speak in his or her defense, and to question any hostile witnesses (so long as such questioning would not place them in danger). In the first stage of the hearing, the parole authorities determine whether there is probable cause that a violation occurred. Then, they decide whether to return the parolee to prison.

PROBATION AND PAROLE OFFICERS Unlike police officers or sheriffs' deputies, probation and parole officers generally do not wear uniforms. Instead, they have badges that identify their position and agency. The duties of probation officers and parole officers are so similar that many small jurisdictions combine the two posts into a single position.

Given the supervisory nature of their professions, probation and parole officers are ultimately responsible for protecting the community by keeping their clients from committing crimes.

Parole Revocation When a parolee breaks the conditions of parole, the process of withdrawing parole and returning the person to prison.

There is also an element of social work in their duties, and these officers must constantly balance the needs of the community with the needs of the offender.[39] Parole officers in particular are expected to help the parolee readjust to life outside the correctional institution by helping her or him find a place to live and a job, and seeing that she or he receives any treatment that may be necessary.

10-3b
Discretionary Release

As you may recall from Chapter 9, corrections systems are classified by sentencing procedure—indeterminate or determinate. Indeterminate sentencing occurs when the legislature sets a range of punishments for particular crimes, and the judge and the parole board exercise discretion in determining the actual length of the prison term. For that reason, states with indeterminate sentencing are said to have systems of **discretionary release.**

ELIGIBILITY FOR PAROLE Under indeterminate sentencing, parole is not a right but a privilege. This is a crucial point, as it establishes the terms of the relationship between the inmate and the corrections authorities during the parole process. In *Greenholtz v. Inmates of the Nebraska Penal and Correctional Complex* (1979),[40] the Supreme Court ruled that inmates do not have a constitutionally protected right to expect parole, thereby giving states the freedom to set their own standards for determining parole eligibility. In most states that have retained indeterminate sentencing, a prisoner is eligible to be considered for parole release after serving a legislatively determined percentage of the minimum sentence—usually one-half or two-thirds—less any good time or other credits.

Not all convicts are eligible for parole. As we saw in Chapter 9, offenders who have committed the most serious crimes often receive life sentences without the possibility of early release. In general, life without parole is reserved for those who have committed first degree murder or are defined by statute as habitual offenders. Today, about one-third of convicts serving life sentences have no possibility of parole.[41]

PAROLE PROCEDURES A convict does not apply for parole. Rather, different jurisdictions have different procedures for determining discretionary release dates. In many states, the offender is eligible for discretionary release at the end of his or her minimum sentence minus good-time credits (see Chapter 9). For instance, in 2012, Michael Claudy was sentenced to five to ten years in prison for harassing female students at Shippensburg University in Pennsylvania. This means that he will become eligible for parole after serving five years, less good time. In other states, parole eligibility is measured at either one-third or one-half of the maximum sentence, or it is a matter of discretion for the parole authorities.

In most, but not all, states, the responsibility for making the parole decision falls to the **parole board,** whose members are generally appointed by the governor. According to the American Correctional Association, the parole board has four basic roles:

1. To decide which offenders should be placed on parole.
2. To determine the conditions of parole and aid in the continuing supervision of the parolee.
3. To discharge the offender when the conditions of parole have been met.
4. If a violation occurs, to determine whether parole privileges should be revoked.[42]

Most parole boards are small, made up of three to seven members. In many jurisdictions, board members' terms are limited to between four and six years. The requirements for board members vary. Nearly half the states have no prerequisites, while others require a bachelor's degree or some expertise in the field of criminal justice.

THE PAROLE DECISION Parole boards use a number of criteria to determine whether a convict should be given discretionary release. These criteria include the nature of the underlying offense, any prior criminal record, the inmate's behavior behind bars, and the attitude of the victim or the victim's family. In a system that uses discretionary parole,

Discretionary Release The release of an inmate into a community supervision program at the discretion of the parole board within limits set by state or federal law.

Parole Board A body of appointed civilians that decides whether a convict should be granted conditional release before the end of his or her sentence.

In 1975, Michael Skakel, then fifteen years old, beat another teenager to death with a golf club. Should convicted murderers such as Skakel, shown here at his parole grant hearing, be given early release? Why or why not?

Pool photo Jessica Hill/*Hartford Courant*/MCT via Getty Images

the actual release decision is made at a **parole grant hearing.** During this hearing, the entire board or a subcommittee reviews relevant information on the convict. Sometimes, but not always, the offender is interviewed.

Because the board members have only limited knowledge of each offender, key players in the case are often notified in advance of the parole hearing and asked to provide comments and recommendations. These participants include the sentencing judge, the attorneys at the trial, the victims, and any law enforcement officers who may be involved. After these preparations, the typical parole hearing itself is very short—usually lasting just a few minutes.

As parole has become a more important tool for reducing prison populations, corrections authorities are making greater efforts to ensure that the process does not endanger the community. Each of Michigan's approximately 43,000 state prisoners, for example, is subjected to an annual evaluation to determine his or her "risk potential." As this numerical score improves, so do the inmate's chances for parole. State corrections officials are highly motivated to identify potential parolees: parole supervision costs about $2,130 a year, compared with about $34,000 a year for an offender in state prison.[43]

PAROLE DENIAL If parole is denied, the entire process is replayed at the next "action date," which

depends on the nature of the offender's crimes and all relevant laws. In 2012, for example, Mark David Chapman was denied parole for the seventh time. About three decades earlier, Chapman had been convicted of murder for fatally shooting musician John Lennon in New York City and sentenced to twenty years to life in prison.

Although Chapman had not had an infraction behind bars since 1994, the three parole board members told him that his release would "tend to trivialize the tragic loss of life which you caused as a result of this heinous, unprovoked, violent, cold and calculated crime."[44] (See the feature *You Be the Parole Board Member—Cause for Compassion?* on the next page to learn more about the process of discretionary release.)

10-3c
Parole Guidelines

Nearly twenty states have moved away from discretionary release systems to procedures that provide for **mandatory release.** Under mandatory release, offenders leave prison only when their prison terms have expired, minus adjustments for good time. No parole board is involved in this type of release, which is designed to eliminate discretion from the process.

Instead, in mandatory release, corrections officials rely on **parole guidelines** to determine the early release date. Similar to sentencing guidelines (see Chapter 9),

Parole Grant Hearing A hearing in which the entire parole board or a subcommittee reviews information, meets the offender, and hears testimony from relevant witnesses to determine whether to grant parole.

Mandatory Release Release from prison that occurs when an offender has served the full length of his or her sentence, minus any adjustments for good time.

Parole Guidelines Standards that are used in the parole process to measure the risk that a potential parolee will recidivate.

CAUSE FOR COMPASSION?

THE SITUATION Thirty-seven years ago, Susan was convicted of first degree murder and sentenced to life in prison for taking part in a grisly killing spree in Los Angeles. Over the course of two days, Susan and her accomplices killed seven people. Susan stabbed one of the victims—a pregnant woman—sixteen times and wrote the word "PIG" on a door using another victim's blood. During her trial, Susan testified that "I was stoned, man, stoned on acid," at the time of her crimes. Now sixty-one years old, Susan is before your parole board, requesting release from prison. For most of her time behind bars, she has been a model prisoner, and she has apologized numerous times for her wrongdoing. Furthermore, her left leg has been amputated, the left side of her body is paralyzed, and she has been diagnosed with terminal brain cancer.

Gina Sanders/Shutterstock

THE LAW You have a great deal of discretion in determining whether a prisoner should be paroled. Some of the factors you should consider are the threat the prisoner would pose to the community if released, the nature of the offense, and the level of remorse. In addition, California allows for "compassionate release" when an inmate is "terminally ill."

YOUR DECISION Susan obviously poses no threat to the community and is a viable candidate for compassionate release. Should she be set free on parole? Or are some crimes so horrific that the convict should never be given parole, no matter what the circumstances? Explain your vote.

[To see how a California parole board voted in a similar situation, go to Example 10.2 in Appendix A.]

---

parole guidelines determine a potential parolee's risk of recidivism using a mathematical equation. Under this system, inmates and corrections authorities know the *presumptive parole date* soon after the inmate enters prison. So long as the offender does not experience any disciplinary or other problems while incarcerated, he or she can be fairly sure of the time of release.[45]

Note that a number of states and the federal government claim to have officially "abolished" parole through truth-in-sentencing laws. (As described in Chapter 9, this form of legislation requires certain statutorily determined offenders to serve at least 85 percent of their prison terms.) For the most part, however, these laws simply emphasize prison terms that are "truthful," not necessarily "longer." Mechanisms for parole, by whatever name, are crucial to the criminal justice system for several reasons. First, they provide inmates with an incentive to behave properly in the hope of an early release. Second, they reduce the costs related to

Intermediate Sanctions
Sanctions that are more restrictive than probation and less restrictive than imprisonment.

incarceration by keeping down the inmate population, a critical concern for prison administrators.[46]

10-4 what ARE SOME TYPES OF INTERMEDIATE SANCTIONS?

Many observers feel that the most widely used sentencing options—imprisonment and probation—fail to reflect the immense diversity of crimes and criminals. **Intermediate sanctions** provide a number of additional sentencing options for those wrongdoers who require stricter supervision than that supplied by probation, but for whom imprisonment would be unduly harsh and counterproductive.[47] The intermediate sanctions discussed in this section are designed to match the specific punishment and treatment of an individual offender with a corrections program that reflects that offender's situation.

Dozens of different variations of intermediate sanctions are handed down each year. To cover the spectrum succinctly, two general categories of such sanctions will be discussed in this section: those administered primarily by the courts and those administered primarily by corrections departments, including day reporting centers, intensive supervision probation, shock incarceration, and home confinement. Remember that none of these sanctions are exclusive. They are often combined with imprisonment and probation and parole, and with each other.

10-4a
Judicially Administered Sanctions

The lack of sentencing options is most frustrating for the person who, in the majority of cases, does the sentencing—the judge. Consequently, when judges are given the discretion to "color" a punishment with intermediate sanctions, they will often do so. In addition to imprisonment and probation, a judge has five sentencing options:

1. Fines.
2. Community service.
3. Restitution.
4. Pretrial diversion programs.
5. Forfeiture.

Fines, community service, and restitution were discussed in Chapter 9. In the context of intermediate sanctions, it is important to remember that these punishments are generally combined with incarceration or probation. For that reason, some critics feel the retributive or deterrent impact of such punishments is severely limited. Many European countries, in contrast, rely heavily on fines as the sole sanctions for a variety of crimes.

PRETRIAL DIVERSION PROGRAMS Not every criminal violation requires the courtroom process. Consequently, some judges have the discretion to order an offender into a **pretrial diversion program** during the preliminary hearing. (Prosecutors can also offer an offender the opportunity to join such a program in return for reducing or dropping the initial charges.)

These programs represent an "interruption" of the criminal proceedings and are generally reserved for young or first-time offenders who have been arrested on charges of illegal drug use, child or spousal abuse, or sexual misconduct. Pretrial diversion programs usually include extensive counseling, often in a treatment center. If the offender successfully follows the conditions of the program, the criminal charges are dropped.

Several years ago, for example, New York Federal District Judge John Gleeson started offering certain drug-addicted defendants a deal: get clean, and you will not go to prison. The program's first graduate, Emily Leitch, had been arrested at New York City's Kennedy International Airport with about thirty pounds of cocaine in her luggage. For a year, Leitch was subjected to drug tests, took parenting courses, earned her high school equivalency diploma, and got a commercial bus driver's license. In February 2013, a prosecutor agreed to dismiss the drug trafficking charges against Leitch if she did not use drugs or get arrested for eighteen months. "I want to thank the federal government for giving me a chance," Leitch said following the proceedings.[48]

PROBLEM-SOLVING COURTS Many judges have found opportunities to divert low-level offenders by presiding over problem-solving courts. In these comparatively informal courtrooms, judges attempt to address problems such as drug addiction, mental illness, and homelessness that often lead to the eventual rearrest of the offender.[49]

Drug Courts About three thousand problem-solving courts are operating in the United States. Although these specialized courts cover a wide variety of subjects, from domestic violence to juvenile crime to mental illness, the most common problem-solving courts are drug courts.

Drug Court Procedures Although the specific procedures of drug courts vary widely, most follow a general pattern. Either after arrest or on conviction, the offender is given the option of entering a drug court program or continuing through

Pretrial Diversion Program An alternative to trial offered by a judge or prosecutor, in which the offender agrees to participate in a specified counseling or treatment program in return for withdrawal of the charges.

In Pinellas County, Florida, Judge Dee Anna Farnell congratulates graduates of her drug court program. How does society benefit when an offender successfully completes a drug court program rather than being sent to prison or jail?

Scott Keeler/*Tampa Bay Times*/ZUMAPRESS.com

the standard courtroom process. Those who choose the former come under the supervision of a judge who will oversee a mixture of treatment and sanctions designed to cure their addiction. When offenders successfully complete the program, the drug court rewards them by dropping all charges against them. Drug courts operate on the assumption that when a criminal addict's drug use is reduced, his or her drug-fueled criminal activity will also decline.

FORFEITURE In 1970, Congress passed the Racketeer Influenced and Corrupt Organizations Act (RICO) in an attempt to prevent the use of legitimate business enterprises as shields for organized crime.[50] As amended, RICO and other statutes give judges the ability to implement forfeiture proceedings in certain criminal cases. **Forfeiture** is a process by which the government seizes property gained from or used in criminal activity. For example, if a person is convicted for smuggling cocaine into the United States from South America, a judge can order the seizure of not only the narcotics, but also the speedboat the offender used to deliver the drugs to a pickup point off the coast of South Florida. In *Bennis v. Michigan* (1996),[51] the Supreme Court ruled that a person's home or car could be forfeited even though the owner was unaware that the property was connected to illegal activity.

Once property is forfeited, the government has several options. It can sell the property, with the proceeds going to the state and/or federal law enforcement agencies involved in the seizure. Alternatively, the government agency can use the property directly in further crime-fighting efforts or award it to a third party, such as an informant.

Forfeiture can be financially rewarding—the U.S. Marshals Service manages nearly $4 billion worth of contraband and property impounded from criminals and criminal suspects. Each year, the agency shares about $580 million of these funds with state and local law enforcement agencies, with an additional $345 million going to crime victims.[52] (**CAREER TIP:** Local and federal prosecutors often rely on *asset recovery professionals* to coordinate the collection, transportation, and storage of items that have been designated for forfeiture by the government.)

10-4b
Day Reporting Centers

First used in Great Britain, **day reporting centers (DRCs)** are mainly tools to reduce jail and prison overcrowding. Although the offenders are allowed to live in the community rather than jail or prison, they must spend all or part of each day at a reporting center. In general, being sentenced to a DRC is an extreme form of supervision. With offenders under a single roof, they are much more easily monitored and controlled.

DRCs are instruments of rehabilitation as well. They often feature treatment programs for drug and alcohol abusers and provide counseling for a number

Forfeiture The process by which the government seizes private property attached to criminal activity.

Day Reporting Center (DRC) A community-based corrections center to which offenders report on a daily basis for treatment, education, and rehabilitation.

of psychological problems, such as depression and anger management. Many of those found guilty in the Roanoke (Virginia) Drug Court, for example, are ordered to participate in a yearlong day reporting program. At the center, offenders meet with probation officers, submit to urine tests, and attend counseling and education programs, such as parenting and life-skills classes. After the year has passed, if the offender has completed the program to the satisfaction of the judge and has found employment, the charges will be dropped.[53]

10-4c
Intensive Supervision Probation

Over the past several decades, a number of jurisdictions have turned to **intensive supervision probation (ISP)** to solve the problems associated with burdensome caseloads we discussed earlier in the chapter. ISP offers a more restrictive alternative to regular probation, with higher levels of face-to-face contact between offenders and officers and frequent modes of control such as urine tests for drugs.

ISP IN ACTION In New Jersey, for example, ISP officers have caseloads of only 20 offenders (compared with 115 for other probation officers in the state) and are provided with additional resources to help them keep tabs on their charges.[54] Different jurisdictions have different methods of determining who is eligible for ISP, but a majority of states limit ISP to offenders who do not have prior probation violations.

EFFECTIVENESS OF ISP The main goal of ISP is to provide prisonlike control of offenders while keeping them out of prison. Critics of ISP believe that it "causes" high failure rates, as more supervision increases the chances that an offender will be caught breaking conditions of probation.[55]

A recent comparison of ISP with DRCs, however, found the intensive supervision of ISP to be more effective. In the six months following termination of the program, DRC participants were more likely to be convicted for a new offense and to test positive for drugs than their ISP counterparts. The study suggests that when combined with services such as outpatient drug treatment and educational training, ISP can be effective in producing low rates of recidivism.[56]

10-4d
Shock Incarceration

As the name suggests, **shock incarceration** is designed to "shock" criminals into compliance with the law. Following conviction, the offender is first sentenced to a prison or jail term. Then, usually within ninety days, he or she is released and resentenced to probation. The theory behind shock incarceration is that by getting a taste of the brutalities of the daily prison grind, the offender will be shocked into a crime-free existence.

THE VALUE OF SHOCK In the past, shock incarceration was targeted primarily toward youthful, first-time offenders, who were thought to be more likely to be "scared straight" by a short stint behind bars. Recent data show, however, that 20 percent of all adults sentenced to probation spend some time in jail or prison before being released into the community.[57]

Critics of shock incarceration are dismayed by this trend. They argue that the practice needlessly disrupts the lives of low-level offenders who would not otherwise be eligible for incarceration and exposes them to the mental and physical hardships of prison life (which we will discuss in Chapter 12).[58] Furthermore, there is little evidence that shock probationers fare any better than regular probationers when it comes to recidivism rates.[59]

BOOT CAMPS The *boot camp* is a variation on traditional shock incarceration. Instead of spending the "shock" period of incarceration in prison or jail, offenders are sent to a boot camp. Modeled on military basic training, these camps are generally located within prisons and jails, though some can be found in the community. The programs emphasize strict discipline, manual labor, and physical training. They are designed to instill self-responsibility and self-respect in participants, thereby lessening the chances that they will return to a life of crime.

More recently, boot camps have also emphasized rehabilitation, incorporating such components as drug and alcohol treatment programs, anger-management

Intensive Supervision Probation (ISP) A punishment-oriented form of probation in which the offender is placed under stricter and more frequent surveillance and control than in conventional probation.

Shock Incarceration A short period of incarceration that is designed to deter further criminal activity by "shocking" the offender with the hardships of imprisonment.

courses, and vocational training.[60] (**CAREER TIP:** Although boot camps have fallen out of public favor, wilderness therapy programs for teenagers with behavioral problems such as drug or alcohol abuse or antisocial tendencies have flourished. These programs rely on *field guides, outdoor instructors,* and *youth counselors* to succeed.)

10-4e
Home Confinement and Electronic Monitoring

Various forms of **home confinement**—in which offenders serve their sentences not in a government institution but at home—have existed for centuries. It has often served, and continues to do so, as a method of political control, used by totalitarian regimes to isolate and silence dissidents.

For purposes of general law enforcement, home confinement was impracti-

> **Home Confinement** A community-based sanction in which offenders serve their terms of incarceration in their homes.
>
> **Electronic Monitoring** A technique of probation supervision in which the offender's whereabouts are kept under surveillance by an electronic device.

cal until relatively recently. After all, one could not expect offenders to keep their promises to stay at home, and the personnel costs of guarding them were prohibitive. In the 1980s, however, with the advent of **electronic monitoring,** or using technology to guard the prisoner, home confinement became more viable. Today, all fifty states and the federal government have home monitoring programs with about 130,000 offenders, including probationers and parolees, participating at any one time.[61]

THE LEVELS OF HOME MONITORING Home monitoring has three general levels of restriction:

1. *Curfew,* which requires offenders to be in their homes at specific hours each day, usually at night.

2. *Home detention,* which requires that offenders remain home at all times, with exceptions being made for education, employment, counseling, or other specified activities such as the purchase of food or, in some instances, attendance at religious ceremonies.

5 LO

How does an electronic monitoring device such as the one shown here meet many of the goals of intermediate sanctions?

Damon Higgins/ZUMA Press/Newscom

3. *Home incarceration,* which requires the offender to remain home at all times, save for medical emergencies.

Under ideal circumstances, home confinement serves many of the goals of intermediate sanctions. It protects the community. It saves public funds and space in correctional facilities by keeping convicts out of institutional incarceration. It meets public expectations of punishment for criminals. Uniquely, home confinement also recognizes that convicts, despite their crimes, play important roles in the community, and allows them to continue in those roles. An offender, for example, may be given permission to leave confinement to care for elderly parents.

Home confinement is also lauded for giving sentencing officials the freedom to match the punishment with the needs of the offender. In Missouri, for instance, the conditions of detention for a musician required him to remain at home during the day, but allowed him to continue his career at night. In addition, he was obliged to make antidrug statements before each performance, to be verified by the manager at the club where he appeared.

TYPES OF ELECTRONIC MONITORING

According to some reports, the inspiration for electronic monitoring was a *Spider-Man* comic book in which the hero was trailed by the use of an electronic device on his arm. In 1979, a New Mexico judge named Jack Love, having read the comic, convinced an executive at Honeywell, Inc., to begin developing similar technology to supervise convicts.[62]

Two major types of electronic monitoring have grown out of Love's initial concept. The first is a "programmed contact" program, in which the offender is contacted periodically by telephone or beeper to verify his or her whereabouts. Verification is obtained via a computer that uses voice or visual identification techniques or by requiring the offender to enter a code in an electronic box when called.

The second is a "continuously signaling" device, worn around the convict's wrist, ankle, or neck. A transmitter in the device sends out a continuous signal to a "receiver-dialer" device located in the offender's dwelling. If the receiver device does not detect a signal from the transmitter, it informs a central computer, and the police are notified.[63] (**CAREER TIP:** *Electronic monitoring technicians,* usually members of probation departments, are responsible for instructing offenders on the rules and regulations of the monitoring regime, installing the device, and notifying law enforcement when a breach has occurred.)

TECHNOLOGICAL ADVANCES IN ELECTRONIC MONITORING As electronic monitoring technology has evolved, the ability of community corrections officials to target specific forms of risky behavior has greatly increased. A Michigan court, for example, has begun placing black boxes in the automobiles of repeat traffic law violators. Not only do these boxes record information about the offenders' driving habits for review by probation officers, but they also emit a loud beep when the car goes too fast or stops too quickly. Another device—an ankle bracelet—is able to test a person's sweat for alcohol levels and transmit the results over the Internet.

10-4f
Widening the Net

As mentioned above, most of the convicts chosen for intermediate sanctions are low-risk offenders. From the point of view of the corrections official doing the choosing, this makes sense. Such offenders are less likely to commit crimes and attract negative publicity. This selection strategy, however, appears to invalidate

CJ AND TECHNOLOGY

GLOBAL POSITIONING SYSTEM (GPS)

GLOBAL positioning system (GPS) technology is a form of tracking technology that relies on twenty-four military satellites orbiting thousands of miles above the earth. The satellites transmit signals to each other and to a receiver on the ground, allowing a monitoring station to determine the location of a receiving device to within a few feet. GPS provides a much more precise level of supervision than regular electronic monitoring. A probationer wears a transmitter, similar to a traditional electronic monitor, around his or her ankle or wrist. This transmitter communicates with a portable tracking device (PTD), a small box that uses the military satellites to determine the probationer's movements.

GPS technology can be used either "actively" to constantly monitor the subject's whereabouts, or "passively" to ensure that the offender remains within the confines of a limited area determined by a judge or probation officer. Inclusion and exclusion zones are also important to GPS supervision. Inclusion zones are areas such as a home or workplace where the offender is expected to be at certain times. Exclusion zones are areas such as parks, playgrounds, and schools where the offender is not permitted to go. GPS-linked computers can alert officials immediately when an exclusion zone has been breached and create a computerized record

AP Photo/Jeff T. Green

of the probationer's movements for review at a later time. Despite the benefits of this technology, it is rarely implemented. According to the Bureau of Justice Statistics, only about eight thousand probationers are currently being tracked by GPS.

THINKING ABOUT GPS

How might GPS monitoring be used to improve and overhaul the American bail system, covered in Chapter 8?

---

one of the primary reasons intermediate sanctions exist: to reduce prison and jail populations. If most of the offenders in intermediate sanctions programs would otherwise have received probation, then the effect on these populations is nullified. Indeed, studies have shown this to be the case.[64]

At the same time, intermediate sanctions broaden the reach of the corrections system. In other words, they increase rather than decrease the amount of control the state exerts over the individual. Suppose a person is arrested for a misdemeanor such as shoplifting and, under normal circumstances, would receive probation. With access to intermediate sanctions, the judge may add a period of home confinement to the sentence.

Critics contend that such practices **widen the net** of the corrections system by augmenting the number of citizens who are under the control and surveillance of the state and also *strengthen the net* by increasing the government's power to intervene in the lives of its citizens.[65] Technological advances—such as the black boxes in automobiles, sweat-testing ankle bracelets, and GPS devices mentioned in this chapter—will only accelerate the trend.

Widen the Net The criticism that intermediate sanctions designed to divert offenders from prison actually increase the number of citizens who are under the control and surveillance of the American corrections system.

REVIEW

✔️ **Review what you've read with the quiz below.**

Rip out the Chapter Review card at the back of this book, which includes:
- Chapter Summary and Learning Outcomes
- Key Terms

Or you can go online to CourseMate at www.cengagebrain.com to:
- Complete Practice Quizzes to prepare for tests.
- Review Key Terms Flash Cards (online or print).
- Play games to master concepts.

quiz

1. Supporters of community corrections point to the role these programs play in _____ nonviolent offenders from prison and jail.

2. Offenders sentenced to _____ serve their sentence in the community under the supervision of a probation officer.

3. To a large extent, the effectiveness of community corrections programs is measured by _____, or the rate at which participants are rearrested and/or reincarcerated.

4. _____ refers to the conditional release of an inmate before the end of his or her sentence.

5. A _____ violation of the terms of probation or parole makes the offender eligible to be sent, or returned, to prison.

6. In jurisdictions that have systems of discretionary release, a _____ _____ makes the parole decision.

7. In jurisdictions with _____ release, offenders leave prison only when their prison terms have expired, minus adjustments for good time.

8. Judicially administered sanctions include fines, restitution, and _____, a process in which the government seizes property connected to illegal activity.

9. Boot camps, or militaristic programs designed to instill self-responsibility, are a form of _____ incarceration.

10. Home confinement has become more effective in recent years thanks to technology known as _____ _____.

Answers can be found on the Chapter 10 Review card at the end of the book.

AP Photo/Damian Dovarganes

Learning **OUTCOMES** | *After studying this chapter, you will be able to . . .*

1 Contrast the Pennsylvania and the New York penitentiary theories of the 1800s.

2 List and briefly explain the four types of prisons.

3 List the factors that have caused the prison population to grow dramatically in the last several decades.

4 Summarize the distinction between jails and prisons, and indicate the importance of jails in the American corrections system.

5 Indicate some of the consequences of our high rates of incarceration.

PRISONS AND JAILS

11

Cost Cutting in Corrections

The Florida Department of Corrections was facing two major problems. First, it was under orders from the governor to reduce its annual $2.4 billion budget. Second, thanks to dropping crime rates, it had too many prison beds (116,000) for too few prisoners (101,000). Given that, in the words of one state legislator, no "tooth fairy" was likely to come to the rescue with extra funds, Florida corrections officials decided to take a step that would have been unthinkable even five years earlier. In 2012, hoping to alleviate both of its problems, the state announced the closing of seven prisons with the goal of saving $76 million.

Florida has not been alone in taking such drastic steps to reduce corrections costs. Also in 2012, Illinois decided to end operations at two of its prisons, and since 2009 Michigan and New York have shut down eight and seven prisons, respectively. Numerous states have also taken steps to steer nonviolent offenders to community corrections, thereby reserving expensive prison space for riskier criminals. These policy choices reflect a small but significant trend in American corrections: fewer inmates. In 2010, the total U.S. prison population declined for the first time in nearly four decades. Then, in 2011 and 2012, the number of inmates decreased again.

To be sure, the decreases were slight—totaling about 1 percent—and do little to threaten our nation's title as "the globe's leading incarcerator." About 2.3 million Americans are in prison and jail. The United States locks up six times as many of its citizens as Canada does, and seven times as many as most European democracies. Still, the fact that state politicians are willing to accept policies that reduce the number of inmates represents a sea change in the country's corrections strategies. Texas, for example, recently lowered its prison population by more than one thousand by directing eligible inmates into rehabilitation programs that improved their prospects of an early release. According to Jerry Madden, a state representative from Plano, this does not mean that Texans have stopped being "tough on crime." Rather, it shows that "We [are] being smart."

About 2.3 million inmates are incarcerated in the United States, including this group exercising in the main yard at the Pelican Bay State Prison near Crescent City, California.

AP Photo/Rich Pedroncelli, File

11-1

how HAVE AMERICAN PRISONS EVOLVED?

Today's high rates of imprisonment—often referred to as evidence of "mass incarceration" in the United States—are the result of many criminal justice strategies that we have discussed in this textbook. These include truth-in-sentencing guidelines, relatively long sentences for gun and drug crimes, "three-strikes" habitual offender laws, and judicial freedom to incarcerate convicts for relatively minor criminal behavior.

At the base of all these policies is a philosophy that sees prisons primarily as instruments of punishment. The loss of freedom imposed on inmates is the penalty for the crimes they have committed. Punishment has not, however, always been the main reason for incarceration in this country. (**CAREER TIP:** Just as criminologists study crime, *penologists* study the corrections system, often with a focus on prison management and inmate rehabilitation.)

11-1a

English Roots

The prisons of eighteenth-century England, known as "bridewells" after London's Bridewell Palace, had little to do with punishment. These facilities were mainly used to hold debtors or those awaiting trial, execution, or banishment from the community. (In many ways, as will be made clear, these facilities resembled the modern jail.) English courts generally imposed one of two sanctions on convicted felons: they turned them loose, or they executed them.[1] To be sure, most felons were released, pardoned either by the court or the clergy after receiving a whipping or a branding.

The correctional system in the American colonies differed very little from that of their motherland. If anything, colonial administrators were more likely to use corporal punishment than their English counterparts, and the death penalty was not uncommon in early America.

Penitentiary An early form of correctional facility that emphasized separating inmates from society and from each other.

The one dissenter was William Penn, who adopted the "Great Law" in Pennsylvania in 1682. Based on Quaker ideals of humanity and rehabilitation, this criminal code forbade the use of torture and mutilation as forms of punishment. Instead, felons were ordered to pay restitution of property or goods to their victims. If the offenders did not have sufficient property to make restitution, they were placed in a prison, which was primarily a "workhouse."[2] The death penalty was still allowed under the "Great Law," but only in cases of premeditated murder. Penn proved to be an exception, however, and the path to reform was much slower in the colonies than in England.

11-1b

Walnut Street Prison: The First Penitentiary

On William Penn's death in 1718, the "Great Law" was rescinded in favor of a harsher criminal code, similar to those of the other colonies. At the time of the American Revolution, however, the Quakers were instrumental in the first broad swing of the incarceration pendulum from punishment to rehabilitation. In 1776, Pennsylvania passed legislation ordering that offenders be reformed through treatment and discipline rather than simply beaten or executed.[3] Several states, including Massachusetts and New York, quickly followed Pennsylvania's example.

Pennsylvania continued its reformist ways by opening the country's first **penitentiary** in a wing of Philadelphia's Walnut Street Jail in 1790. The penitentiary operated on the assumption that silence and labor provided the best hope of rehabilitating the criminal spirit. Remaining silent would force the prisoners to think about their crimes, and eventually the weight of conscience would lead to repentance. At the same time, enforced labor would attack the problem of idleness—regarded as the main cause of crime by penologists of the time.[4] Consequently, inmates at Walnut Street were isolated from one another in solitary rooms and kept busy with constant menial chores.

Eventually, the penitentiary at Walnut Street succumbed to the same problems that continue to plague institutions of confinement: overcrowding and excessive costs. As an influx of inmates forced more than one person to be housed in a room, maintaining silence became nearly impossible. By the early 1800s, officials could not find work for all of the convicts, so many were left idle.

11-1c

The Great Penitentiary Rivalry: Pennsylvania versus New York

LO 1 The apparent lack of success at Walnut Street did little to dampen enthusiasm for the penitentiary concept. Throughout the first half of the nineteenth century, a number of states reacted to prison overcrowding by constructing new penitentiaries. Each state tended to have its own peculiar twist on the roles of silence and labor, and two such systems—those of Pennsylvania and New York—emerged to shape the debate over the most effective way to run a prison.

THE PENNSYLVANIA SYSTEM After the failure of Walnut Street, Pennsylvania constructed two new prisons: the Western Penitentiary near Pittsburgh (opened in 1826) and the Eastern Penitentiary in Cherry Hill, near Philadelphia (1829). The Pennsylvania system took the concept of silence as a virtue to new extremes. Based on the idea of **separate confinement,** these penitentiaries were constructed with back-to-back cells facing outward from the center. (See Figure 11.1 above for the layout of the original Eastern Penitentiary.) To protect each inmate from the corrupting influence of the others, prisoners worked, slept, and ate alone in their cells. Their only contact with other human beings came in the form of religious instruction from a visiting clergyman or prison official.[5]

THE NEW YORK SYSTEM If Pennsylvania's prisons were designed to transform wrongdoers into honest citizens, those in New York focused on obedience. When New York's Newgate Prison (built in 1791) became overcrowded, the state authorized the construction of Auburn Prison, which opened in 1816. Auburn initially operated under many of the same assumptions that guided the penitentiary at Walnut Street. Solitary confinement, however, seemed to lead to an inordinate amount of sickness, insanity, and even suicide among inmates, and it was abandoned in 1822.

FIGURE 11.1 The Eastern Penitentiary

As you can see, the Eastern Penitentiary was designed in the form of a "wagon wheel," known today as the radial style. The back-to-back cells in each "spoke" of the wheel faced outward from the center to limit contact between inmates. What was the primary goal of this design?

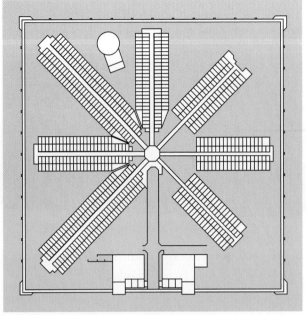

Courtesy Eastern State Penitentiary/www.easternstate.org

Nine years later, Elam Lynds became director at Auburn and instilled the **congregate system,** also known as the Auburn system. Like Pennsylvania's separate confinement system, the congregate system was based on silence and labor. At Auburn, however, inmates worked and ate together, with silence enforced by prison guards.[6]

If either state can be said to have "won" the debate, it was New York. The Auburn system proved more popular, and a majority of the new prisons built during the first half of the nineteenth century followed New York's lead, though mainly for economic reasons rather than philosophical ones. New York's penitentiaries were cheaper to build because they did not require so much space. Furthermore, inmates in New York were employed in workshops, whereas those in Pennsylvania toiled alone in their cells. Consequently, the Auburn system was

Separate Confinement A nineteenth-century penitentiary system developed in Pennsylvania in which inmates were kept separate from each other at all times, with daily activities taking place in individual cells.

Congregate System A nineteenth-century penitentiary system developed in New York in which inmates were kept in separate cells during the night but worked together in the daytime under a code of enforced silence.

Inmates of the Elmira Reformatory in New York attend a presentation at the prison auditorium. To what extent do you believe that treatment should be a part of the incarceration of criminals?

Corbis

better positioned to exploit prison labor in the early years of widespread factory production.

11-1d
The Reformers and the Progressives

The Auburn system did not go unchallenged. In the 1870s, a group of reformers argued that fixed sentences, imposed silence, and isolation did nothing to improve prisoners. These critics proposed that penal institutions should offer the promise of early release as a prime tool for rehabilitation. Echoing the views of the Quakers a century earlier, the reformers presented an ideology that would heavily influence American corrections for the next century.

This "new penology" was put into practice at New York's Elmira Reformatory in 1876 (see the photo above). At Elmira, good behavior was rewarded by early release, and misbehavior was punished with extended time under a three-grade system of classification. On entering the institution, the offender was assigned a grade of 2. If the inmate followed the rules and completed work and school assignments, after six months he was moved up to grade 1, the necessary grade for release. If, however, the inmate broke institutional rules, he was lowered to grade 3. A grade

Medical Model A model of corrections in which the psychological and biological roots of an inmate's criminal behavior are identified and treated.

3 inmate needed to behave properly for three months before he could return to grade 2 and begin to work back toward grade 1 and eventual release.[7]

Although other penal institutions did not adopt the Elmira model, its theories came into prominence in the first two decades of the twentieth century thanks to the Progressive movement in criminal justice. The Progressives believed that criminal behavior was caused by social, economic, and biological factors and, therefore, a corrections system should have a goal of treatment, not punishment. Consequently, they trumpeted a **medical model** for prisons, which held that institutions should offer a variety of programs and therapies to cure inmates of their "ills," whatever the root causes. The Progressives were largely responsible for the spread of indeterminate sentences (Chapter 9), probation (Chapter 10), intermediate sanctions (Chapter 10), and parole (Chapter 10) in the first half of the twentieth century.

11-1e
The Reassertion of Punishment

Even though the Progressives had a great influence on the corrections system as a whole, their theories had little impact on the prisons themselves. Many of these facilities had been constructed in the nineteenth century and were impervious to change. More important, prison administrators usually did not agree with the Progressives and their followers, so the day-to-day lives of most inmates varied little from the congregate system of Auburn Prison.

Academic attitudes began to shift toward the prison administrators in the mid-1960s. Then, in 1974, the publication of Robert Martinson's famous "What Works?" essay provided opponents of the medical model with statistical evidence that rehabilitation efforts did nothing to lower recidivism rates.[8] This is not to say that Martinson's findings went unchallenged. A number of critics argued that rehabilitative programs could be successful.[9] In fact, Martinson himself retracted most of his claims in a little-noticed article published five years after his initial report.[10]

Attempts by Martinson and others to "set the record straight" went largely unnoticed, however, as crime rose sharply in the early 1970s. This trend led many criminologists and politicians to champion "get tough" measures to deal with criminals they now considered "incurable." By the end of the 1980s, the legislative, judicial, and administrative strategies that we have discussed throughout this text had positioned the United States for an explosion in inmate populations and prison construction unparalleled in the nation's history.

11-1f
The Role of Prisons in Modern Society

For reasons that we will explain later in the chapter, the number of federal and state prisoners quadrupled between 1980 and 2010.[11] This increase reflects the varied demands placed on the modern American penal institution. As University of Connecticut sociologist Charles Logan once noted, Americans expect prisons to "correct the incorrigible, rehabilitate the wretched . . . restrain the dangerous, and punish the wicked."[12] Basically, prisons exist to make society a safer place. Whether this is to be achieved through retribution, deterrence, incapacitation, or rehabilitation—the four justifications of corrections introduced in Chapter 9—depends on the operating philosophy of the individual penal institution.

Three general models of prisons have emerged to describe the different schools of thought behind prison organization:

- The *custodial model* is based on the assumption that prisoners are incarcerated for reasons of incapacitation, deterrence, and retribution. All decisions within the prison—such as what form of recreation to provide the inmates—are made with an eye toward security and discipline, and the daily routine of the inmates is highly controlled. The custodial model has dominated the most restrictive prisons in the United States since the 1930s.

- The *rehabilitation model* stresses the ideals of individualized treatment that we discussed in Chapter 9. Security concerns are often secondary to the well-being of the individual inmate, and a number of treatment programs are offered to aid prisoners in changing their criminal and antisocial behavior. The rehabilitation model came into prominence during the 1950s and enjoyed widespread popularity until it began to lose general acceptance in the 1970s and 1980s.

- In the *reintegration model,* the correctional institution serves as a training ground for the inmate to prepare for existence in the community. Prisons that have adopted this model give the prisoners more responsibility during incarceration and offer halfway houses and work programs (both discussed in Chapter 12) to help them reintegrate into society. This model is becoming more influential, as corrections officials react to problems such as prison overcrowding.[13]

Competing views of the prison's role in society are at odds with these three "ideal" perspectives. Professor Alfred Blumstein argues that prisons create new criminals, especially with regard to nonviolent drug offenders. Not only do these nonviolent felons become socialized to the criminal lifestyle while in prison, but the stigma of incarceration makes it more difficult for them to obtain employment on release. Their only means of sustenance "on the outside" is to apply the criminal methods they learned in prison.[14] A study by criminal justice professors Cassia Spohn of Arizona State University and David Holleran of the College of New Jersey found that convicted drug offenders who were sentenced to prison were 2.2 times more likely to be incarcerated for a new offense than those sentenced to probation.[15]

11-2
how ARE PRISONS ORGANIZED AND MANAGED

The United States has a dual prison system that parallels its dual court system, which we discussed in Chapter 7. The Federal Bureau of Prisons (BOP) currently operates about one hundred confinement facilities, ranging from prisons to immigration detention centers to community corrections institutions.[16] In the federal corrections system, a national director, appointed by the president, oversees six regional directors and a staff of over 35,000 employees. All fifty states also operate state prisons, which number over 1,700 and make up more than 90 percent of the country's correctional facilities.[17] Governors are responsible for the organization and operation of state corrections systems, which vary widely based on each state's geography, *demographics* (population characteristics), and political culture.

Generally, those offenders sentenced in federal court for breaking federal law serve their time in federal prisons, and those offenders sentenced in state court for breaking state law serve their time in state prisons. As you can see in Figure 11.2 below, federal prisons hold relatively few violent felons, because relatively few federal laws involve violent crime. At the same time, federal prisons are much more likely to hold public order offenders, a group that includes violators of federal immigration law.

11-2a
Prison Administration

Whether the federal government or a state government operates a prison, its administrators have the same general goals, summarized by Charles Logan as follows:

> The mission of a prison is to keep prisoners—to keep them in, keep them safe, keep them in line, keep them healthy, and keep them busy—and to do it with fairness, without undue suffering and as efficiently as possible.[18]

Considering the environment of a prison—an enclosed world inhabited by people who are generally violent and angry and would rather be anywhere else—Logan's mission statement is somewhat unrealistic. A prison staff must supervise the daily routines of hundreds or thousands of inmates, a duty that includes providing them with meals, education, vocational programs, and different forms of leisure. The smooth operation of this supervision is made more difficult—if not, at times, impossible—by budgetary restrictions, overcrowding, and continual inmate turnover.

FORMAL PRISON MANAGEMENT In some respects, the management structure of a prison is similar to that of a police department, as discussed in Chapter 5. Both systems rely on a hierarchical (top-down) *chain of command* to increase personal responsibility. Both assign different employees to specific tasks, though prison managers have much more direct control over their subordinates than do police managers.

FIGURE 11.2 Types of Offenses of Federal and State Prison Inmates

As the comparison below shows, state prisoners are most likely to have been convicted of violent crimes, while federal prisoners are most likely to have been convicted of drug and public order offenses.

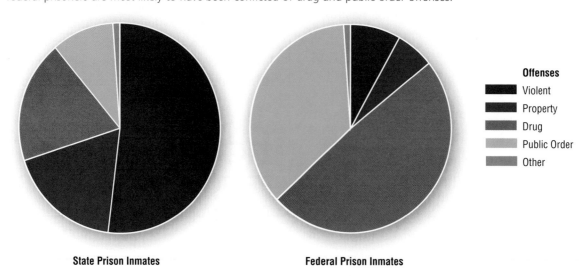

Offenses
- Violent
- Property
- Drug
- Public Order
- Other

State Prison Inmates

Federal Prison Inmates

Source: Bureau of Justice Statistics, *Prisoners in 2011* (Washington, D.C.: U.S. Department of Justice, December 2012), Appendix table 8, page 27; and Appendix table 12, page 29.

The main difference is that police departments have a *continuity of purpose* that is sometimes lacking in prison organizations. All members of a police force are, at least theoretically, working to reduce crime and apprehend criminals. In a prison, this continuity is less evident. An employee in the prison laundry service and one who works in the visiting center have little in common. In some instances, employees may even have cross-purposes: a prison guard may want to punish an inmate, while a counselor in the treatment center may want to rehabilitate her or him.

Consequently, a strong hierarchy is crucial for any prison management team that hopes to meet Charles Logan's expectations. As Figure 11.3 below shows, the **warden** (also known as a superintendent) is ultimately responsible for the operation of a prison. He or she oversees deputy wardens, who in turn manage the various organizational lines of the institution. The custodial employees, who deal directly with the inmates and make up more than half of a prison's staff, operate under a militaristic hierarchy, with a line of command passing from the deputy warden to the captain to the correctional officer. (**CAREER TIP:** With each inmate comes a significant amount of recorded information: criminal background, security designation, special needs, disciplinary restrictions, and the like. The *inmate records coordinator* is responsible for organizing this information and keeping it up to date.)

GOVERNING PRISONS The implications of prison mismanagement can be severe. While study-ing a series of prison riots, sociologists Bert Useem and Peter Kimball found that breakdown in managerial control commonly preceded such acts of mass violence.[19] During the 1970s, for example, conditions at the State Penitentiary in New Mexico deteriorated significantly. Inmates were increasingly the targets of random and harsh treatment at the hands of the prison staff, while at the same time a reduction in structured activities left prison life "painfully boring."[20] The result, in 1980, was one of the most violent prison riots in the nation's history.

What sort of prison management is most suited to avoid such situations? Although there is no single "best" form of prison management, political scientist John DiIulio believes that, in general, the sound governance of correctional facilities is a matter of order, amenities, and services:

- *Order* can be defined as the absence of misconduct such as murder, assault, and rape. Many observers, including DiIulio, believe that, having incarcerated a person, the state has a responsibility to protect that person from disorder in the correctional institution.
- *Amenities* are those comforts that make life "livable," such as clean living conditions, acceptable food, and entertainment. One theory of incarceration holds that inmates should not enjoy a

Warden The prison official who is ultimately responsible for the organization and performance of a correctional facility.

FIGURE 11.3 Organizational Chart for a Typical Correctional Facility

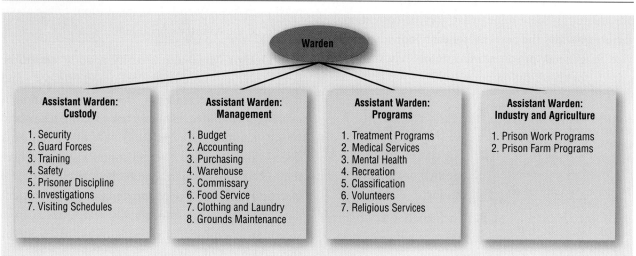

quality of life comparable to life outside prison. Without the basic amenities, however, prison life becomes unbearable, and inmates are more likely to lapse into disorder.

- *Services* include programs designed to improve an inmate's prospects on release, such as vocational training, remedial education, and drug treatment. Again, many feel that a person convicted of a crime does not deserve to participate in these kinds of programs, but they have two clear benefits. First, they keep the inmate occupied and focused during her or his sentence. Second, they reduce the chances that the inmate will go back to a life of crime after she or he returns to the community.[21] (**CAREER TIP:** For spiritual guidance behind bars, inmates of all faiths turn to *prison chaplains,* who coordinate religious services in correctional facilities.)

According to DiIulio, in the absence of order, amenities, and services, inmates will come to see their imprisonment as not only unpleasant but unfair, and they will become much more difficult to control.[22] Furthermore, weak governance encourages inmates to come up with their own methods of regulating their lives. As we shall see in the next chapter, the result is usually high levels of violence and the expansion of prison gangs and other unsanctioned forms of authority.

11-2b
Types of Prisons

One of the most important aspects of prison administration occurs soon after a defendant has been convicted of a crime. In this **classification** process, administrators determine what sort of correctional facility provides the best "fit" for each individual convict. In general, prison administrators rely on three criteria for classification purposes:

Classification The process through which prison officials determine which correctional facility is best suited to the individual offender.

Maximum-Security Prison A correctional institution designed and organized to control and discipline dangerous felons, as well as prevent escape.

1. The seriousness of the crime committed.
2. The risk of future criminal or violent conduct.
3. The need for treatment and rehabilitation programs.[23]

In the federal prison system, this need to classify—and separate—different kinds of offenders has led to six different levels of correctional facilities. Inmates in level 1 facilities are usually nonviolent and require the least amount of security, while inmates in level 6 facilities are the most dangerous and require the harshest security measures. To simplify matters, most observers refer to correctional facilities as being one of three levels—minimum, medium, or maximum. A fourth level—the supermaximum-security prison, known as the "supermax"—is relatively rare and extremely controversial due to its hyperharsh methods of punishing and controlling the most dangerous prisoners.

2 LO

MAXIMUM-SECURITY PRISONS In a certain sense, the classification of prisoners today owes a debt to the three-grade system developed at the Elmira Reformatory, discussed earlier in the chapter. Once wrongdoers enter a corrections facility, they are constantly graded on behavior. Those who serve "good time," as we have seen, are often rewarded with early release. Those who compile extensive misconduct records are usually housed, along with violent and repeat offenders, in **maximum-security prisons.** The names of these institutions—Folsom, San Quentin, Sing Sing, Attica—conjure up foreboding images of concrete and steel jungles, with good reason.

Maximum-security prisons are designed with full attention to security and surveillance. In these institutions, inmates' lives are programmed in a militaristic fashion to keep them from escaping or from harming themselves or the prison staff. About a quarter of the prisons in the United States are classified as maximum security, and these institutions house about a third of the country's prisoners.

The Design Maximum-security prisons tend to be large—holding more than a thousand inmates—and they have similar features. The entire operation is usually surrounded by concrete walls that stand twenty to thirty feet high and have also been sunk deep into the ground to deter tunnel escapes. Fences reinforced with razor-ribbon barbed wire that can be electrically charged may supplement these barriers. The prison walls are studded with watchtowers, from which guards armed with shotguns and rifles survey the movement of prisoners below.

JOB DESCRIPTION:

- As chief managing officer of an adult correctional institution, the warden is responsible for the custody, feeding, clothing, housing, care, treatment, discipline, training, employment, rehabilitation, and well-being of inmates.
- The warden provides institutional staff with effective communications, training, and leadership.

WHAT KIND OF TRAINING IS REQUIRED?

- A bachelor's degree in criminal justice, social work, psychology, or a related field.
- One or more years of work experience in the management of a major division of a correctional institution.

ANNUAL SALARY RANGE?

- $42,000–$95,000 (depending on size of institution and geographic region)

Inmates live in cells, most of them with similar dimensions to those found in the Topeka Correctional Facility, a maximum-security prison in Topeka, Kansas: eight feet by fourteen feet with cinder block walls.[24] The space contains bunks, a toilet, a sink, and possibly a cabinet or closet. Cells are located in rows of *cell blocks,* each of which forms its own security unit, set off by a series of gates and bars.

Most prisons, whether they were built using the radial design (see page 235) or other designs that resemble large courtyards or telephone poles, have cell blocks that open into sprawling prison exercise yards. The "prison of the future," however, rejects this layout. Instead, it relies on a podular design, as evident at the Two Rivers Correctional Institution in Umatilla, Oregon. At Two Rivers, which opened in 2007, fourteen housing pods contain ninety-six inmates each. Each unit has its own yard, so inmates rarely, if ever, interact with members of other pods. This design gives administrators the flexibility to, for example, place violent criminals in pod A and white-collar criminals in pod B without worrying about mixing the two different security levels.[25]

Security Measures Within maximum-security prisons, inmates' lives are dominated by security measures. Whenever they move from one area of the prison to another, they do so in groups and under the watchful eye of armed correctional officers. Television surveillance cameras may be used to monitor their every move, even when sleeping, showering, or using the toilet. They are subject to frequent pat-downs or strip searches at the guards' discretion. Constant "head counts" ensure that every inmate is where he or she should be. Tower guards—many of whom have orders to shoot to kill in the case of a disturbance or escape attempt—constantly look down on the inmates as they move around outdoor areas of the facility.

SUPERMAX PRISONS About thirty states and the Federal Bureau of Prisons (BOP) operate **supermax** (short for supermaximum security) **prisons,** which are supposedly reserved for the "worst of the worst" of America's corrections population. Many of the inmates in these facilities are deemed high risks to commit murder behind

Supermax Prison A correctional facility reserved for those inmates who have extensive records of misconduct.

TECHNOLOGY has added significantly to the overall safety of maximum-security prisons. Walk-through metal detectors and X-ray body scanners, for example, can detect weapons or other contraband hidden on the body of an inmate. The most promising new technology in this field, however, relies on radio frequency identification (RFID). About the size of two grains of rice, an RFID tag consists of a glass capsule that contains a computer chip, a tiny copper antenna, and an electrical device known as a "capacitor" that transmits the data in the chip to an outside scanner. In the prison context, RFID works as a high-tech head count: inmates wear bracelets tagged with the microchips while correctional officers wear small RFID devices resembling pagers.

Guided by a series of radio transmitters and receivers, the system is able to pinpoint the location of inmates and guards within twenty feet. Every two seconds, radio signals "search out" the location of each inmate and guard, and relay this information to a central computer. On a grid of the prison, an inmate shows up as a yellow dot and a correctional officer as a blue dot. Many RFID systems also store all movements in a database for future reference. "[RFID] completely revolutionizes a prison because

Black Creek/TSI PRISM

you know where everyone is—not approximately but exactly where they are," remarked an official at the National Institute of Justice.

THINKING ABOUT RFID TRACKING

Review the discussion of crime mapping and "hot spots" in Chapter 5. Drawing on your knowledge of crime-mapping technology, discuss how RFID technology can reduce violence and other misconduct such as drug sales in prisons.

---

bars—about a quarter of the occupants of the BOP's U.S. Penitentiary Administrative Maximum (ADX) in Florence, Colorado, have killed other prisoners or assaulted correctional officers elsewhere.

Supermax Inmates Supermax prisons are also used as punishment for offenders who commit serious disciplinary infractions in maximum-security prisons, or for those inmates who become involved with prison gangs.[26] In addition, a growing number of supermax occupants are either high-profile individuals who would be at constant risk of attack in a general prison population or convicted terrorists such as Faisal Shahzad, who

> **Lockdown** A disciplinary action taken by prison officials in which all inmates are ordered to their quarters and nonessential prison activities are suspended.

attempted to detonate a bomb in New York City's Times Square in 2010; Ted "the Unabomber" Kaczynski; and Terry Nichols, who was involved in the bombing of a federal office building in Oklahoma City in 1995.

A Controlled Environment The main purpose of a supermax prison is to strictly control the inmates' movement, thereby limiting (or eliminating) situations that could lead to breakdowns in discipline. For the most part, supermax prisons operate in a state of perpetual **lockdown,** in which all inmates are confined to their cells and social activities such as meals, recreational sports, and treatment programs are nonexistent.

The conditions at California's Security Housing Unit (SHU) at Pelican Bay State Prison are representative of most supermax institutions. Prisoners are con-

What security measures can you identify from this photo of a cell block at Arizona State Prison in Florence?

AP Photo/Matt York

fined to their one-person cells for twenty-three hours each day under video camera surveillance. They receive meals through a slot in the door. The cells measure eight by ten feet in size and are windowless. Fluorescent lights are continuously on, day and night, making it difficult for inmates to enjoy any type of privacy or sleep.[27]

MEDIUM-SECURITY PRISONS Medium-security prisons hold about 45 percent of the prison population, and minimum-security prisons 20 percent. Inmates at **medium-security prisons** have for the most part committed less serious crimes than those housed in maximum-security prisons and are not considered high risks for escaping or causing harm. Consequently, medium-security institutions are not designed for control to the same extent as maximum-security prisons and have a more relaxed atmosphere. These facilities also offer more educational and treatment programs and allow for more contact between inmates.

Medium-security prisons are rarely walled, relying instead on high fences. Prisoners have more freedom of movement within the structures, and the levels of surveillance are much lower. Living quarters are less restrictive as well—many of the newer medium-security prisons provide dormitory housing.

MINIMUM-SECURITY PRISONS A **minimum-security prison** seems at first glance to be more like a college campus than an incarceration facility. Most of the inmates at these institutions are first-time offend-

ers who are nonviolent and well behaved. A high percentage are white-collar criminals. Indeed, inmates are often transferred to minimum-security prisons as a reward for good behavior in other facilities. Therefore, security measures are lax compared with even medium-security prisons.

Unlike medium-security institutions, minimum-security prisons do not have armed guards. Prisoners are provided with amenities such as television sets and computers in their rooms. They also enjoy freedom of movement, and are allowed off prison grounds for educational or employment purposes to a much greater extent than those held in more restrictive facilities. (**CAREER TIP:** Many colleges now offer degrees in *recreation management.* Although geared toward corporate fitness/wellness programs, this discipline also has a place in the corrections system. For example, Danbury Women's Prison has a track and a gymnasium that is used for Dancersize, Pilates, and yoga classes.)

11-3 what TRENDS ARE DRIVING THE AMERICAN PRISON POPULATION?

As Figure 11.4 on the next page shows, the number of Americans in prison or jail has increased dramatically in the past three decades. This growth can be attributed to a number of factors, starting with the enhancement and stricter enforcement of the nation's illegal drug laws.

Medium-Security Prison A correctional institution that houses less dangerous inmates and therefore uses less restrictive measures to prevent violence and escapes.

Minimum-Security Prison A correctional institution designed to allow inmates, most of whom pose low security risks, a great deal of freedom of movement and contact with the outside world.

11-3a

Factors in Prison Population Growth

There are more people in prison and jail for drug offenses today than there were for *all* offenses in the early 1970s.[28] In 1980, about 19,000 drug offenders were incarcerated in state prisons, and 4,800 drug offenders were in federal prisons. Thirty-one years later, state prisons held about 258,000 inmates who had been arrested for drug offenses, and the number of drug offenders in federal prisons had risen to almost 95,000 (representing about half of all inmates in federal facilities).[29]

INCREASED PROBABILITY OF INCARCERATION

The growth of America's inmate population also reflects the reality that the chance of someone who is arrested going to prison today is much greater than it was thirty years ago. Most of this growth took place in the 1980s, when the likelihood of incarceration in a state prison after arrest increased fivefold for drug offenses, threefold for weapons offenses, and twofold for crimes such as sexual assault, burglary, auto theft, and larceny.[30] For federal crimes, the proportion of convicted defendants being sent to prison rose from 54 percent in 1988 to 86 percent in 2011.[31]

INMATES SERVING MORE TIME In Chapter 9, we discussed a number of "get tough" sentencing laws passed in reaction to the crime wave of the 1970s and 1980s. These measures, including sentencing guidelines, mandatory minimum sentences, and truth-in-sentencing laws, have significantly increased the length of prison terms in the United States.[32] In California, for example, by 2011 a quarter of the inmate population had been sentenced under the state's "three-strikes" law, and the terms for these inmates were nine years longer because of that legislation.[33]

Overall, inmates released from state prison in 2009 spent an average of nine months—about 36 percent—longer behind bars than those inmates released in 1990.[34] On the federal level, in the fifteen years after the passage of the Sentencing Reform Act of 1984, the average time served in federal prison increased more than 50 percent.[35] Furthermore, about 140,000 state prisoners and 4,000 federal prisoners are serving life prison terms with no chance of release, up from about 34,000 and 400, respectively, in the mid-1980s.[36]

FEDERAL PRISON GROWTH Even though, as noted at the beginning of this chapter, the overall prison population of the United States recently has started to decrease, this is not the case for federal prison populations. In 2011, the number of federal prisoners increased by 3.4 percent.[37] Indeed, between 2000 and 2011, the federal prison population grew 58 percent, from about 125,000 to just over 197,000.[38]

Besides the increase in federal drug offenders already mentioned, this growth can be attributed to increased federal law enforcement attention to weapons crimes and immigration law violations. Between 1998 and 2010, the number of weapons offenders in federal prison almost

---

FIGURE 11.4   **The Inmate Population of the United States**

The total number of inmates in the United States has risen from 744,208 in 1985 to about 2.3 million in 2012.

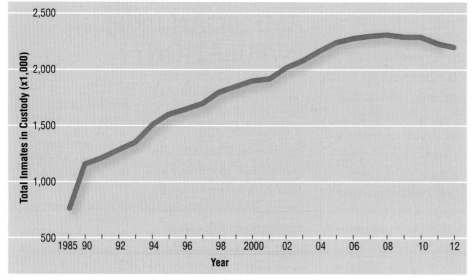

Source: U.S. Department of Justice.

tripled.[39] During that same time period, the number of immigration offenders saw similar increases, as the result of which a third of all federal inmates are now Hispanic.[40] Furthermore, in 2013, approximately 14,200 women were behind bars in federal prison, about double their numbers in 1995.[41] Women still account for only 7 percent of all inmates in the United States, but their rates of imprisonment have been growing more rapidly than those of men for the last decade.[42]

11-3b
The Costs of Incarceration

The escalation in the U.S. prison population has been accompanied by increased costs. Today, the states together spend nearly $40 billion a year to operate their corrections systems—up from $12 billion in 1987. Twelve states allocate in excess of $1 billion a year for corrections-related services, often spending more on prisons than on education or health care.[43] Several years ago, California had a $20 billion budget deficit and was spending $10 billion a year on its prisons.[44] Arizona, which faces a similar problem, has decided to charge $25 for family and friend visits to inmates in its prison system as a fund-raising measure.[45]

11-3c
Decarceration

For most states looking to cut correction costs, the focus has been on *decarceration,* or the reduction of inmate populations. As recently as 2007, one expert lamented the unwillingness of corrections authorities to decarcerate, calling the strategy "practically virgin territory."[46] This is no longer the case, as the high cost of imprisonment has caused policymakers to consider a number of different methods to reduce the number of people in prison. In general, decarceration relies on three strategies:

1. Decreasing the probability that nonviolent offenders will be sentenced to prison.

2. Increasing the rate of release of nonviolent offenders from prison.

3. Decreasing the rate of imprisonment for probation and parole violators.[47]

Many states have adopted one or more of these approaches. Texas, as noted at the beginning of the chapter, now diverts a large number of nonviolent offenders to drug treatment in the community.

Corrections officials in Michigan, Missouri, and New York are making a concerted effort to avoid reincarcerating parolees for technical violations.[48]

11-4
what ARE PRIVATE PRISONS ?

As the prison population soared at the end of the twentieth century, state corrections officials faced a serious problem: too many inmates, not enough prisons. "States couldn't build space fast enough," explains corrections expert Martin Horn. "And so they had to turn to the private sector."[49] With corrections exhibiting all appearance of "a recession-proof industry," American businesses eagerly entered the market.

Today, **private prisons,** or prisons run by private firms to make a profit, are an important part of the criminal justice system. About two dozen private companies operate more than two hundred facilities across the United States. The two largest corrections firms, Corrections Corporation of America (CCA) and the GEO Group, Inc., manage about 130 correctional facilities and generate about $3.3 billion in annual revenue combined.[50] By 2011, private penal institutions housed over 130,000 inmates, representing 8.2 percent of all prisoners in the state and federal corrections systems.[51]

11-4a
Why Privatize?

It would be a mistake to automatically assume that private prisons are less expensive to run than public ones. Nevertheless, the incentive to privatize is primarily financial.

COST EFFICIENCY In the 1980s and 1990s, a number of states and cities reduced operating costs by transferring government-run services such as garbage collection and road maintenance to the private sector. Similarly, private prisons can often be run more cheaply and efficiently than public ones for the following reasons:

- *Labor costs.* The wages of public employees account for nearly two-thirds of a

Private Prisons
Correctional facilities operated by private corporations instead of the government and, therefore, reliant on profits for survival.

prison's operating expenses. Although private corrections firms pay base salaries comparable to those enjoyed by public prison employees, their nonunionized staffs receive lower levels of overtime pay, workers' compensation claims, sick leave, and health-care insurance.

- *Competitive bidding.* Because of the profit motive, private corrections firms have an incentive to buy goods and services at the lowest possible price.

- *Less red tape.* Private corrections firms are not part of the government bureaucracy and therefore do not have to contend with the massive amount of paperwork that can clog government organizations.[52]

In 2005, the National Institute of Justice released the results of a five-year study comparing low-security public and private prisons in California. The government agency found that private facilities cost taxpayers between 6 and 10 percent less than public ones.[53] More recent research conducted at Vanderbilt University found that states saved about $15 million annually when they supplemented their corrections systems with privately managed institutions.[54]

OVERCROWDING AND OUTSOURCING Private prisons are becoming increasingly attractive to state governments faced with the competing pressures of tight budgets and overcrowded corrections facili-ties. Lacking the funds to alleviate overcrowding by building more prisons, state officials are turning to the private institutions for help. Often, the private prison is out of state, which leads to the "outsourcing" of inmates. Hawaii, for example, sends about one-third of its 6,000 inmates to private prisons in Arizona.[55] California has allevi-ated its chronic overcrowding problems by sending more than 10,000 inmates to private institutions in Arizona, Colorado, Michigan, Minnesota, Missouri, Montana, and Oklahoma.[56]

11-4b
The Argument against Private Prisons

The assertion that private prisons offer economic benefits is not universally accepted. A number of studies have found that private prisons are no more cost-effective than public ones.[57] Furthermore, opponents of private prisons worry that, despite the assurances of corporate executives, private cor-rections companies will "cut corners" to save costs, denying inmates important security guarantees in the process.

SAFETY CONCERNS Various studies have uncov-ered disturbing patterns of misbehavior at private prisons. For example, in the year after CCA took over operations of Ohio's Lake Erie Correctional Institution from the state corrections department, the number of assaults against correctional officers and inmates increased by over 40 percent.[58] In addition, research conducted by Curtis R. Blakely of the University of South Alabama and Vic W. Bumphus of the University of Tennessee at Chattanooga found that a prisoner in a private correctional facility was twice as likely to be assaulted by a fellow inmate as a prisoner in a public one.[59]

Why would it make financial sense for private prisons such as the Saguaro Correctional Facility in Eloy, Arizona, shown here, to accept only inmates who are in relatively good health?

Monica Almeida/*New York Times*/Redux Pictures

PHILOSOPHICAL CONCERNS Other critics see private prisons as inherently unjust, even if they do save tax dollars or provide enhanced services. These observers believe that corrections is not simply another industry, like garbage collection or road maintenance, and that only the government has the authority to punish wrongdoers. In the words of John DiIulio:

> It is precisely because corrections involves the deprivation of liberty, precisely because it involves the legally sanctioned exercise of coercion by some citizens over others, that it must remain wholly within public hands.[60]

Furthermore, some observers note, if a private corrections firm receives a fee from the state for each inmate housed in its facility, does that not give management an incentive to increase the amount of time each prisoner serves? Though government parole boards make the final decision on an inmate's release from private prisons, the company could manipulate misconduct and good behavior reports to maximize time served and, by extension, higher profits.[61] "You can put a dollar figure on each inmate that is held at a private prison," says Alex Friedmann of *Prison Legal News*. "They are treated as commodities. And that's very dangerous and troubling when a company sees the people it incarcerates as nothing more than a money stream."[62]

11-4c
The Future of Privatization in the Corrections Industry

In February 2012, Florida's Senate narrowly defeated a bill that would have privatized the state's entire corrections system. The vote seemed to bode ill for what was once considered a recession-proof industry. Indeed, with more states reducing their prison populations, there are signs that the growth of private prisons has stagnated. Between 2010 and 2011, the number of state inmates in private prisons dropped by about 2,000.[63] In an effort to find new avenues of business, CCA recently sent a letter to forty-eight states in which the company offered to purchase unwanted public prisons. So far, only one state has taken this step: Ohio sold the aforementioned Lake Erie Correctional Institution to CCA for nearly $73 million.

Still, most experts see continued profitability for private prisons, for two reasons. First, shrinking budgets may force states to look for less costly alternatives to housing inmates in public prisons. Second, as the number of federal prisoners increases, the Federal Bureau of Prisons has turned to private prisons to expand its capacity. Between 2000 and 2011, the number of federal inmates in private prisons more than doubled, from about 15,500 to about 38,500.[64] The current emphasis on imprisoning violators of immigration law seems likely to ensure that this trend will continue. (**CAREER TIP:** Given the private prison industry's solid prospects, it is no surprise that Corrections Corporation of America is offering positions in all areas of corrections, including security, health care, and administration. For more information, go to the company's career Web page at www.cca.com/careers/available-jobs.)

11-5
why ARE JAILS SO IMPORTANT?

Although prisons and prison issues dominate the public discourse on corrections, there is an argument to be made that jails are the dominant penal institutions in the United States. In general, a prison is a facility designed to house people convicted of felonies for lengthy periods of time, while a **jail** is authorized to hold pretrial detainees and offenders who have committed misdemeanors. On any given day, about 744,000 inmates are in jail in this country, and jails admit almost 12 million persons over the course of an entire year.[65] Nevertheless, jail funding is often the lowest priority for the tight budgets of local governments, leading to severe overcrowding and other dismal conditions.

Many observers see this negligence as having far-reaching consequences for criminal justice. Jail is often the first contact that citizens have with the corrections system. It is at this point that treatment and counseling have the best chance to deter future criminal behavior.[66] By failing to take advantage of this opportunity, says Professor Franklin Zimring of the University of California at Berkeley School of Law, corrections

Jail A facility, usually operated by the county government, used to hold persons awaiting trial or those who have been found guilty of misdemeanors.

officials have created a situation in which "today's jail folk are tomorrow's prisoners."[67]

11-5a

The Jail Population

Like their counterparts in state prisons, jail inmates are overwhelmingly young male adults. About 45 percent of jail inmates are white, 38 percent are African American, and 15 percent are Hispanic.[68] The main difference between state prison and jail inmates involves their criminal activity. As Figure 11.5 below shows, jail inmates are more likely to have been convicted of nonviolent crimes than their counterparts in state prison.

PRETRIAL DETAINEES A significant number of those detained in jails technically are not prisoners. They are **pretrial detainees** who have been arrested by the police and, for a variety of reasons that we discussed in Chapter 8, are unable to post bail. Pretrial detainees are, in many ways, walking legal contradictions. According to the U.S. Constitution, they are innocent until proved guilty. At

Pretrial Detainees Individuals who cannot post bail after arrest and are therefore forced to spend the time prior to their trial incarcerated in jail.

Time Served The period of time a person denied bail (or unable to pay it) has spent in jail prior to his or her trial.

the same time, by being incarcerated while awaiting trial, they are denied a number of personal freedoms and are subjected to the poor conditions of many jails.

In *Bell v. Wolfish* (1979), the Supreme Court rejected the notion that this situation is inherently unfair by refusing to give pretrial detainees greater legal protections than sentenced jail inmates have.[69] In essence, the Court recognized that treating pretrial detainees differently from convicted jail inmates would place too much of a burden on corrections officials and was therefore impractical.[70]

SENTENCED JAIL INMATES According to the U.S. Department of Justice, about 40 percent of those in jail have been convicted of their current charges.[71] In other words, they have been found guilty of a crime, usually a misdemeanor, and sentenced to time in jail. The typical jail term lasts between thirty and ninety days, and rarely does a prisoner spend more than one year in jail for any single crime. Often, a judge will credit the length of time the convict has spent in detention waiting for trial—known as **time served**—toward his or her sentence. This practice acknowledges two realities of jails:

1. Terms are generally too short to allow the prisoner to gain any benefit (that is,

---

FIGURE 11.5 Types of Offenses of Prison and Jail Inmates

As the comparison below shows, jail inmates are more likely than state prisoners to have been convicted of nonviolent crimes. This underscores the main function of jails: to house less serious offenders for a relatively short period of time.

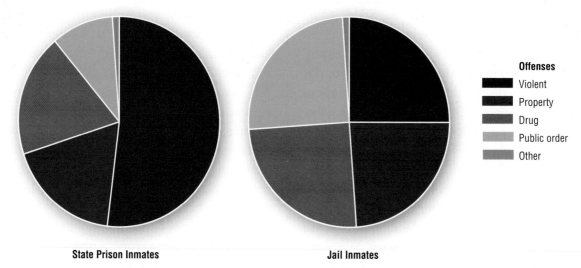

State Prison Inmates   **Jail Inmates**

Offenses
- Violent
- Property
- Drug
- Public order
- Other

Source: Bureau of Justice Statistics, *Prisoners in 2011* (Washington, D.C.: U.S. Department of Justice, December 2011), Appendix table 8, page 27; and Bureau of Justice Statistics, *Profile of Jail Inmates, 2002* (Washington, D.C.: U.S. Department of Justice, July 2004), 1.

rehabilitation) from the jail's often limited or nonexistent treatment facilities. Therefore, the jail term can serve no purpose except to punish the wrongdoer. (Judges who believe jail time can serve purposes of deterrence and incapacitation may not agree with this line of reasoning.)

2. Jails are chronically overcrowded, and judges need to clear space for new offenders.

OTHER JAIL INMATES Pretrial detainees and those convicted of misdemeanors make up the majority of the jail population. Jail inmates also include probation and parole violators, the mentally ill, juveniles awaiting transfer to juvenile authorities, and immigration law violators being held for the federal government. Increasingly, jails are also called on to handle the overflow from state prisons. To comply with a United States Supreme Court order to reduce its prison population, California corrections officials plan to divert an estimated 75,000 inmates from its prisons to its jails by 2015.[72]

11-5b
Jail Administration

Of the nearly 3,370 jails in the United States, more than 2,700 are operated on a county level by an elected sheriff. Most of the remainder are under the control of municipalities, although six state governments (Alaska, Connecticut, Delaware, Hawaii, Rhode Island, and Vermont) manage jails. The capacity of jails varies widely. The Los Angeles County Men's Central Jail holds nearly 7,000 people, but jails that large are the exception rather than the rule. Forty percent of all jails in this country house fewer than 50 inmates.[73]

CAREER**PREP**

DEPUTY SHERIFF/ JAIL DIVISION

JOB DESCRIPTION:
- Be responsible for supervising jail inmates by ensuring that order, discipline, safety, and security are maintained.
- Transport or escort inmates and defendants from jail to courtrooms, attorneys' offices, or medical facilities.

WHAT KIND OF TRAINING IS REQUIRED?
- Depending on the jurisdiction, possession of a high school diploma or bachelor's degree, as well as successful completion of written and physical examinations, training, and a probationary period.
- Some states require completion of a "jail academy" training course of up to sixteen weeks, including field training.

ANNUAL SALARY RANGE?
- $44,000–$55,000

SOCIAL MEDIA CAREER TIP
Regularly reevaluate your social media tools and the methods you use to keep up to date in your fields of interest. If you are still using the same tools as a year ago, you probably aren't keeping up with the latest developments in Internet technology.

Kaupo Kikkas/iStockphoto.com

THE "BURDEN" OF JAIL ADMINISTRATION

Given that the public's opinion of jails ranges from negative to indifferent, some sheriffs neglect their jail management duties. Instead, they focus on high-visibility issues such as putting more law enforcement officers on the streets and improving security in schools. In fact, a jail usually receives publicity only after an escape or an incident in which inmates are abused by jailers.

Nonetheless, with their more complex and diverse populations, jails are often more difficult to manage than prisons. Jails hold people who have never been incarcerated before, people under the influence of drugs or alcohol at the time of their arrival, the mentally ill, and people who exhibit a range of violent behavior—from nonexistent to extreme—that only adds to the unpredictable atmosphere.[74]

THE CHALLENGES OF OVERCROWDING

In many ways, the sheriff is placed in an untenable position when it comes to jail overcrowding. He or she has little control over the number of people who are sent to jail—that power resides with prosecutors and judges. Nevertheless, the jail is expected to find space to hold all comers, regardless of its capacity.

Chronic overcrowding makes the jail experience a miserable one for most inmates. Cells intended to hold one or two people are packed with up to six. Often, inmates are forced to sleep in hallways. In such stressful situations, tempers flare, leading to violent, aggressive behavior. The close proximity and unsanitary living conditions also lead to numerous health problems. In the words of one observer, jail inmates

New-Generation Jail
A type of jail that is distinguished architecturally from its predecessors by a design that encourages interaction between inmates and jailers and that offers greater opportunities for treatment.

share tight space day and night, struggle with human density never before experienced (unless earlier in jail), and search hopelessly for even a moment of solitude. . . . [The congested conditions offer] inmates next to nothing except a stifling idleness that is almost sure to make them worse for the experience. If hard time in prison or jail is time without meaning, there might be no equal to long periods of time in the seriously overcrowded living areas of jails; for above all else (and clearly in comparison to time in prison), jail time is dead time.[75]

Such conditions also raise basic questions of justice: as we noted earlier, many of the inmates in jail have not yet been tried and must be presumed innocent.

11-5c
New-Generation Jails

For most of the nation's history, the architecture of a jail was secondary to its purpose of keeping inmates safely locked away. Consequently, most jails in the United States continue to resemble those from the days of the Walnut Street Jail in Philadelphia. In this *traditional,* or *linear design,* jail cells are located along a corridor. To supervise the inmates while they are in their cells, custodial officers must walk up and down the corridor, so the number of prisoners they can see at any one time is severely limited. With this limited supervision, inmates can more easily break institutional rules.

PODULAR DESIGN In the 1970s, planners at the Federal Bureau of Prisons decided to upgrade the traditional jail design with the goal of improving conditions for both the staff and the inmates. The result was the **new-generation jail,** which differs significantly from its predecessors.[76] The layout of the new facilities makes it easier for the staff to monitor cell-confined inmates. The basic structure of the new-generation jail is based on a podular design. Each "pod" contains "living units" for individual prisoners. These units, instead of lining up along a straight corridor, are often situated in a triangle so that a staff member in the center of the triangle has visual access to nearly all the cells.

Daily activities such as eating and showering take place in the pod, which also has an outdoor exercise area. Treatment facilities are also located in the pod, allowing greater access for the inmates. During the day, inmates stay out in the open and are allowed back in their cells only when given permission. The officer locks the door to the cells from his or her control terminal.

DIRECT SUPERVISION APPROACH The podular design also enables a new-generation jail to be man-

How does the layout of this direct supervision jail differ from that of the maximum-security prison pictured on page 243? What do these differences tell you about the security precautions needed for jail inmates as opposed to prison inmates?

Photo courtesy Bergen County Sheriff's Office, Bergen, NJ

aged using a **direct supervision approach**.[77] One or more jail officers are stationed in the living area of the pod and are therefore in constant interaction with all prisoners in that particular pod. Some new-generation jails even provide a desk in the center of the living area, which sends a very different message to the prisoners than the traditional control booth (see photo above). Theoretically, jail officials who have constant contact with inmates will be able to stem misconduct quickly and efficiently and will also be able to recognize "danger signs" from individual inmates and stop outbursts before they occur. (As noted earlier in the chapter, corrections officials are using aspects of podular design when building new prisons, for many of the same reasons that the trend has been popular in jails.)

11-6
what ARE THE CONSEQUENCES OF OUR HIGH RATES OF INCARCERATION?

For many observers, especially those who support the crime control theory of criminal justice, America's high rate of incarceration has contributed signifi-cantly to the drop in the country's crime rates.[78] At the heart of this belief is the fact, which we discussed in Chapter 2, that most crimes are committed by a relatively small group of repeat offenders. Several studies have tried to corroborate this viewpoint, with varying results—estimates of the number of crimes committed each year by habitual offenders range from 3 to 187.[79] If one accepts the higher estimate, each year a repeat offender spends in prison prevents a significant number of criminal acts.

11-6a
Negative Consequences

Criminologists, however, note the negative consequences of America's immense prison and jail population. For one, incarceration can have severe social consequences for communities and the families that make up those communities. About 2.7 million minors in this country—one in twenty-eight—have a parent in prison.[80] These children are at an increased risk of suffering from poverty, depression, and academic problems, as well as higher levels of juvenile delinquency and eventual incarceration themselves.[81] Studies also link high imprisonment rates to increased incidence of sexually transmitted diseases and teenage pregnancy, as the separation caused by incarceration wreaks havoc on interpersonal relationships.[82]

In addition, incarceration denies one of the basic rights of American democracy—the right to vote—to about 5.9 million Americans with criminal

Direct Supervision Approach A process of prison and jail administration in which correctional officers are in continuous physical contact with inmates during the day.

records.[83] A number of states and the federal government *disenfranchise,* or take away the ability to vote from, those convicted of felonies. This has a disproportionate impact on minority groups, weakening their voice in the democratic debate. Today, African American males are incarcerated at a rate more than six times that of white males and almost three times that of Hispanic males.[84] With more black men behind bars than enrolled in the nation's colleges and universities, Marc Mauer of the Sentencing Project believes that the "ripple effect on their communities and on the next generation of kids, growing up with their fathers in prison, will certainly be with us for at least a generation."[85]

11-6b

The Future of Incarceration

Whether our incarceration situation is "good" or "bad" depends to a large extent on one's personal philosophy. In the end, it is difficult to do a definitive cost-benefit analysis for each person incarcerated, weighing the benefits of preventing crimes that might (or might not) have been committed by an inmate against the costs to the convict's family and society. One thing that can be stated with some certainty is that, even with the growing interest in diversion and rehabilitation described in the previous chapter, the American prison system will remain one of the largest in the world for the foreseeable future.

A mother and child wait outside the Donald W. W. Wyatt Detention Facility in Central Falls, Rhode Island. What are the possible consequences of having a parent behind bars for the affected children and for American society as a whole?

Suzanne DeChillo/*New York Times*/Redux

REVIEW

✔️ **Review what you've read with the quiz below.**

Rip out the Chapter Review card at the back of this book, which includes:
- Chapter Summary and Learning Outcomes
- Key Terms

Or you can go online to CourseMate at www.cengagebrain.com to:
- Complete Practice Quizzes to prepare for tests.
- Review Key Terms Flash Cards (online or print).
- Play games to master concepts.

quiz

1. In the second half of the 1800s, the Progressive movement introduced the _____ model of prison management, which focused on rehabilitation rather than punishment.

2. The _____ (also known as a superintendent) is at the top of a prison's command structure.

3. Using a process called _____, prison administrators determine which correctional facility provides the best "fit" for the offender, based mostly on security concerns.

4. Those offenders who have been convicted of violent crimes and repeat offenders are likely to be sent to _____-security prisons.

5. If a prisoner assaults another inmate or a correctional officer, prison officials may decide to transfer that prisoner to a _____ prison designed to hold the "worst of the worst."

6. Of all the factors in the growth of the prison population in the last several decades, stricter enforcement of the nation's illegal _____ laws has had the greatest impact.

7. Many states are adopting strategies of _____ designed to reduce their inmate populations and the costs associated with their corrections systems.

8. Prison officials often feel pressure to send inmates to private prisons to alleviate _____ of public correctional facilities.

9. Rather than having been convicted of any crime, a significant number of jail inmates are _____ _____ who are unable to post bail.

10. Most jails are operated on a local level by the county _____.

Answers can be found on the Chapter 11 Review card at the end of the book.

AP Photo/Rich Pedroncelli

Learning **OUTCOMES**
After studying this chapter, you will be able to . . .

1 Explain the concept of prison as a total institution.

2 Indicate some of the reasons for violent behavior in prisons.

3 Describe the hands-off doctrine of prisoner law and indicate two standards used to determine if prisoners' rights have been violated.

4 Contrast parole, expiration release, pardon, and furlough.

5 Explain the goal of prisoner reentry programs.

BEHIND BARS: THE LIFE OF AN INMATE

Business as Usual

On June 5, 2012, inmates at the Lee Correctional Institution in Bishopville, South Carolina, ambushed a correctional officer who was escorting a nurse during her evening rounds. The nurse narrowly escaped, and the correctional officer was held hostage for more than six hours before being rescued, relatively unharmed, by local law enforcement. Although state officials promised to review the incident, about three months later inmates wielding homemade knives seized another correctional officer at the same prison. The officer suffered stab wounds and was locked in a broom closet.

"It's part of the business," said South Carolina Corrections Department spokesman Clark Newsom of the two kidnappings. "We're dealing with very dangerous criminals here." Some observers felt, however, that poor management decisions had increased the danger levels at the maximum-security prison. One prison official warned that such

outbursts were a natural consequence of inmates being treated like "wild animals." During the first incident, prisoners demanded improvements in their living conditions, including better medical care, access to reading material, and hot meals. Both kidnappings took place during "off hours," when one correctional officer was responsible for guarding as many as 250 inmates.

In 2013, South Carolina Governor Nikki Haley proposed spending an additional $18 million on state prisons. Part of the funds would go toward hiring more security personnel and buying new ovens for woefully ill-equipped prison kitchens. The proposal was, however,

resisted by legislators who felt the resources should go to other, worthier areas of need. This attitude is in keeping with the "no frills" movement in American corrections, which has succeeded in removing most amenities from inmates' lives. Many state prisons ban weightlifting, televisions, radios, adult magazines, and conjugal visits. All states and the federal government have limited smoking in their correctional facilities, and some institutions spend less than $2 a day per inmate on meals. Consequently, life in today's penal institutions has been described as "grindingly dull routine interrupted by occasional flashes of violence and brutality."

Inmates at the Lee Correctional Institution in Bishopville, South Carolina, seized members of the prison staff on two separate occasions in 2012.

Tim Dominick, TheState.com

how DO INMATES ADJUST TO LIFE IN PRISON ?

In this chapter, we will look at the life of the imprisoned convict, starting with the realities of an existence behind bars and finishing with the challenges of returning to free society. Along the way, we will discuss violence in prison, correctional officers, women's prisons, different types of release, and several other issues that are at the forefront of American corrections today. To start, we must understand the forces that shape prison culture and how those forces affect the overall operation of the correctional facility.

LO **1** Any institution, whether a school, a bank, or a police department, has an organizational culture—a set of values that help the people in the organization understand what actions are acceptable and what actions are unacceptable. According to a theory put forth by the influential sociologist Erving Goffman, prison cultures are unique because prisons are **total institutions** that encompass every aspect of an inmate's life. Unlike a stu-dent or a bank teller, a prisoner cannot leave the institution or have any meaningful interaction with outside communities. Others arrange every aspect of daily life, and all prisoners are required to follow this schedule in the same manner.[1]

Inmates develop their own argot, or language (see Figure 12.1 below). They create their own economy, which, in the absence of currency, is based on the barter of valued items such as food, contraband, and sexual favors. They establish methods of determining power, many of which, as we shall see, involve violence. Isolated and heavily regulated, prisoners create a social existence that is, out of both necessity and design, separate from the outside world.

12-1a
Adapting to Prison Society

On arriving at prison, each convict attends an orientation session and receives a "Resident's Handbook." The handbook provides information such as meal and official count times, disciplinary regulations, and visitation guidelines. The norms and values of the prison society, however, cannot be communicated by the staff or learned from a handbook. As first described by Donald Clemmer in his classic 1940 work, *The Prison Community*, the process of **prisonization**—or adaptation to the prison culture—advances as the inmate gradually understands what constitutes acceptable behavior in the institution, as defined not by the prison officials but by other inmates.[2]

Total Institution An institution, such as a prison, that provides all of the necessities for existence to those who live within its boundaries.

Prisonization The socialization process through which a new inmate learns the accepted norms and values of the prison culture.

FIGURE 12.1 Prison Slang

Ace Another word for "dollar."

Bang A fight to the death, or shoot to kill.

Base head A cocaine addict.

B.G. "Baby gangster," or someone who has never shot another person.

Booty bandit An incarcerated sexual predator who preys on weaker inmates, called "punks."

Bug A correctional staff member, such as a psychiatrist, who is deemed untrustworthy or unreliable.

Bumpin' titties Fighting.

Catch cold To get killed.

Chiva Heroin.

Dancing on the blacktop Getting stabbed.

Diddler Child molester or pedophile.

Green light Prison gang term for a contract killing.

Hacks Correctional officers.

Jug-up Mealtime.

Lugger An inmate who smuggles in and possesses illegal substances.

Punk An inmate subject to rape, usually more submissive than most inmates.

Ride with To perform favors, including sexual favors, for a convict in return for protection or prison-store goods.

Shank Knife.

Tits-up An inmate who has died.

Topped Committed suicide.

Source: www.insideprison.com/glossary.asp.

In studying prisonization, criminologists have focused on two areas: how prisoners change their behavior to adapt to life behind bars, and how life behind bars has changed because of inmate behavior. Sociologist John Irwin has identified several patterns of inmate behavior, each one driven by the inmate's personality and values:

1. Professional criminals adapt to prison by "doing time." In other words, they follow the rules and generally do whatever is necessary to speed up their release and return to freedom.

2. Some convicts, mostly state-raised youths or those frequently incarcerated in juvenile detention centers, are more comfortable inside prison than outside. These inmates serve time by "jailing," or establishing themselves in the power structure of prison culture.

3. Other inmates take advantage of prison resources such as libraries or drug treatment programs by "gleaning," or working to improve themselves to prepare for a return to society.

4. Finally, "disorganized" criminals exist on the fringes of prison society. These inmates may have mental impairments or low levels of intelligence and find it impossible to adapt to prison culture on any level.[3]

The process of categorizing prisoners has a theoretical basis, but it serves a practical purpose as well, allowing administrators to reasonably predict how different inmates will act in certain situations. An inmate who is "doing time" generally does not present the same security risk as one who is "jailing."

12-1b
Who Is in Prison?

The culture of any prison is heavily influenced by its inmates. Their values, beliefs, and experiences will be reflected in the social order that exists behind bars. As we noted in the last chapter, the past three decades have seen incarceration rates of women and minority groups rise sharply. Furthermore, the arrest patterns of inmates have changed over that time period. A prisoner today is much more likely to have been incarcerated on a drug charge or immigration violation than was the case in the 1980s. Today's inmate

is also more likely to behave violently behind bars—a situation that will be addressed shortly.

AN AGING INMATE POPULATION In recent years, the most significant demographic change in the prison population involves age. Though the majority of inmates are still under thirty-four years old, the number of state and federal prisoners over the age of forty has increased dramatically since the mid-1990s. Several factors have contributed to this upsurge, including longer prison terms, mandatory prison terms, recidivism, and higher levels of crimes—particularly violent crimes—committed by older offenders.[4]

Corrections budgets are straining under the financial pressures caused by the health-care needs of aging inmates. According to the American Civil Liberties Union, an elderly inmate is two times more expensive to house than a younger inmate.[5] In Georgia, prisoners sixty-five years or older have average annual medical expenses of about $8,500, compared with an average annual medical expense of $961 for those inmates under sixty-five.[6] Given the burden of inmate medical costs, state corrections officials may be tempted to cut such services whenever possible. As we will see later in the chapter, however, prisoners have a constitutional right to adequate health care. (CAREER TIP: Due to the increase in the number of ailing prison and jail inmates, *registered nurses* are in high demand in the corrections system.)

MENTAL ILLNESS BEHIND BARS Another factor in rising correctional health-care costs is the high incidence of mental illness in American prisons and jails. During the 1950s and 1960s, nearly 600,000 mental patients lived in public hospitals, often against their will. A series of scandals spotlighting the poor medical services and horrendous living conditions in these institutions led to their closure and the elimination of much of the nation's state-run mental health infrastructure.[7] Many mentally ill people now receive no supervision whatsoever, and some inevitably commit deviant or criminal acts.

As a result, in the words of criminal justice experts Katherine Stuart van Wormer and Clemens Bartollas, jails and prison have become "the dumping grounds for people whose bizarre behavior lands them behind bars."[8] Nationwide, 60 percent of jail inmates and 56 percent of state prisoners suffer from some form of mental illness.[9] As with aging and ailing prisoners, correctional facilities are required by law to provide treatment to mentally ill inmates, thus driving the costs associated with their confinement well above the average.[10] For reasons that should become clear over the course of this chapter, correctional facilities are not designed to foster mental well-being, and indeed inmates with mental illnesses often find that their problems are exacerbated by the prison environment.[11]

12-1c
Rehabilitation and Prison Programs

In Chapter 9, we saw that rehabilitation is one of the basic theoretical justifications for punishment. **Prison programs,** which include any organized activities designed to foster rehabilitation, benefit inmates in several ways. On a basic level, these programs get prisoners out of their cells and alleviate the boredom that marks prison and jail life. The programs also help inmates improve their health and skills, giving them a better chance of reintegration into society after release. Consequently, nearly every federal and state prison in the United States offers some form of rehabilitation.[12]

SUBSTANCE ABUSE TREATMENT As we have seen throughout this textbook, there is a strong link between crime and abuse of drugs and alcohol. According to the National Center on Addiction and Substance Abuse (CASA) at New York's Columbia University, 1.5 million prison and jail inmates in the United States meet the medical criteria for substance abuse or addiction. Also according to CASA, only 11 percent of these inmates have received any type of professional treatment behind bars.[13]

The most effective substance abuse programs for prisoners require trained staff, lengthy periods of therapy, expensive medication, and community aftercare, but such programs carry a price tag of nearly $10,000 per inmate. If every eligible prisoner in the United States received

such treatment, the cost would be $12.6 billion. Researchers at CASA contend, however, that "the nation would break even in a year" if just one in ten of these inmates remained substance and crime free and employed for one year after release from prison.[14]

VOCATIONAL AND EDUCATIONAL PROGRAMS
Even if an ex-convict does stay substance free, he or she will have a difficult time finding a steady paycheck. Employers are only about half as likely to hire job applicants with criminal records as they are those with "clean sheets."[15] To overcome this handicap, more than half of all American prisons offer *vocational* training, or prison programs that provide inmates with skills necessary to find a job. The California Institute for Men at Chino, for example,

Why is it beneficial for prisoners such as these two Colorado inmates, seen working on mannequin heads during a cosmetology class, to receive job training while still incarcerated?

AP Photo/*The Daily Record*, Jeff Shane

Prison Programs Organized activities for inmates that are designed to improve their physical and mental health, provide them with vocational skills, or simply keep them busy while incarcerated.

gives certain convicts the chance to complete a program in commercial diving. Nine out of ten prisons also attempt to educate their inmates, offering literacy training, GED (general equivalency degree) programs, and other types of instruction.[16]

Some evidence suggests that such efforts can have a positive effect on rates of reoffending. The Arkansas Department of Corrections figures that GED programs in its jails have cut the state's recidivism rate by 8 percent.[17] Only about 6 percent of the commercial divers from Chino return to prison within three years, compared with California's 70 percent overall recidivism rate.[18]

Proponents of such efforts also point to their potential financial benefits. Researchers at the Washington State Institute for Public Policy estimate that every $1,182 spent for inmate vocational training saves $6,806 in future criminal justice costs and that every $962 spent on inmate education saves $5,306 in future criminal justice costs.[19] (CAREER TIP: Most *prison teachers* are either corrections employees who have obtained the necessary certification or civilians with teaching credentials and previous career experience.)

12-2
how VIOLENT IS LIFE BEHIND BARS?

Prisons and jails are dangerous places to live. Prison culture is predicated on violence—one observer calls the modern institution an "unstable and violent jungle."[20] Prison guards use the threat of violence (and, at times, its reality) to control the inmate population. Sometimes, the inmates strike back. Each year, federal correctional officers are subjected to about eighty assaults and 1,500 less serious attacks such as shoving and pushing.[21]

Among the prisoners, violence is used to establish power and dominance. On occasion, this violence leads to death. About fifty-five inmates in state prisons and twenty inmates in local jails are murdered by fellow inmates each year.[22] (Note, though, that this homicide rate is lower than the national average.) With nothing but time on their hands, prisoners have been known to fashion deadly weapons out of every-

day items such as toothbrushes and mop handles. To carry out their attack on a correctional officer at South Carolina's Lee Correctional Institution, discussed in the chapter opening, inmates fashioned knives out of sawed-off parts of fiberglass shower stalls.

12-2a
Violence in Prison Culture

Until the 1970s, prison culture emphasized "noninterference" and did not support inmate-on-inmate violence. Prison "elders" would themselves punish any of their peers who showed a proclivity toward assaulting fellow inmates. Today, in contrast, violence is used to establish the prisoner hierarchy by separating the powerful from the weak. Humboldt State University's Lee H. Bowker has identified several other reasons for violent behavior:

2 LO

- It provides a deterrent against being victimized, as a reputation for violence may eliminate an inmate as a target of assault.
- It enhances self-image in an environment that does not respect other attributes, such as intelligence.
- In the case of rape, it gives sexual relief.
- It serves as a means of acquiring material goods through extortion or outright robbery.[23]

The **deprivation model** can be used to explain the high level of prison violence. According to this model, the stressful and oppressive conditions of prison life lead to aggressive behavior on the part of inmates. Prison researcher Stephen C. Light found that when conditions such as overcrowding worsen, inmate misconduct often increases.[24] In these circumstances, the violent behavior may not have any express purpose—it may just be a means of relieving tension.

12-2b
Riots

The deprivation model is helpful, though less convincing, in searching for the roots of collective violence. As far back as the 1930s, sociologist Frank Tannenbaum noted that harsh prison conditions can cause tension to build

Deprivation Model A theory that inmate aggression is the result of the frustration inmates feel at being deprived of freedom, consumer goods, sex, and other staples of life outside the institution.

A correctional official displays a set of homemade knives, also known as *shivs*, made by inmates at Attica Correctional Facility in Attica, New York. What are some of the reasons that violence flourishes behind bars?

AP Photo/David Duprey

among inmates until it eventually explodes in the form of mass violence.[25] Living conditions among prisons are fairly constant, however, so how can the seemingly spontaneous outbreak of prison riots be explained?

Researchers have addressed the seeming randomness of prison violence by turning to the concept of **relative deprivation**. These theories focus on the gap between what is expected in a certain situation and what is achieved. Criminologist Peter C. Kratcoski has argued that because prisoners enjoy such meager privileges to begin with, any further deprivation can spark disorder.[26] A number of prison experts have noted that collective violence occurs in response to heightened measures of security at corrections facilities.[27] Thus, the violence is primarily a reaction to additional reductions in freedom for inmates, who enjoy very little freedom to begin with.

Riots, which have been defined as situations in which a number of prisoners are beyond institutional control for a significant amount of time, are relatively rare. These incidents are marked by extreme levels of inmate-on-inmate violence and can often be attributed, at least in part, to poor living conditions and inadequate prison administration. For example, a recent riot at the Adams County Correctional Center in Natchez, Mississippi, that left one correctional officer dead and twenty others injured was sparked by inmate protests over poor food and lack of medical care. Afterwards, a prisoner said, "The guard that died yesterday was a sad tragedy, but the situation is simple: if you treat a human as an animal for over two years, the response will be as an animal."[28]

Relative Deprivation The theory that inmate aggression is caused when freedoms and services that the inmate has come to accept as normal are decreased or eliminated.

12-2c
Issues of Race and Ethnicity

On the morning of March 3, 2013, a huge brawl broke out at the Arizona State Prison Complex in Tucson, with three hundred white and Hispanic inmates battling one hundred African American inmates. Race plays a major role in prison life, and prison violence is often an outlet for racial tension. As prison populations have changed over the past three decades, with African Americans and Hispanics becoming the majority in many penal institutions, issues of race and ethnicity have become increasingly important to prison administrators and researchers.

SEPARATE WORLDS As early as the 1950s, researchers were noticing different group structures in inmate life. At that time, for example, prisoners at California's Soledad Prison informally segregated themselves according to geography as well as race: Tejanos (Mexicans raised in Texas), Chicanos, blacks from California, blacks from the South and Southwest, and the majority whites all formed separate social worlds.[29]

Leo Carroll, professor of sociology at the University of Rhode Island, has written extensively about how today's prisoners are divided into hostile groups, with race determining nearly every aspect of an inmate's life, including friends, job assignments, and cell location.[30] Carroll's research has also shown how minority groups in prison have seized on race to help form their prison identities.[31]

PRISON GANGS In many instances, racial and ethnic identification is the primary focus of the **prison gang**—a clique of inmates who join together in an organizational structure. Gang affiliation is often the cause of inmate-on-inmate violence. For decades, the California prison system has been plagued by feuds involving various gangs such as the Mexican Mafia, composed of U.S.-born inmates of Mexican descent, and their enemies, a spin-off organization called La Nuestra Familia.

In part, the prison gang is a natural result of life in the modern prison. As one expert says of these gangs:

> Their members have done in prison what many people do elsewhere when they feel personally powerless, threatened, and vulnerable. They align themselves with others, organize to fight back, and enhance their own status and control through their connection to a more powerful group.[32]

A member of the Aryan Brotherhood in California's Calipatria State Prison. Why might an inmate join the Aryan Brotherhood or any other prison gang?

Mark Allen Johnson/ZUMA

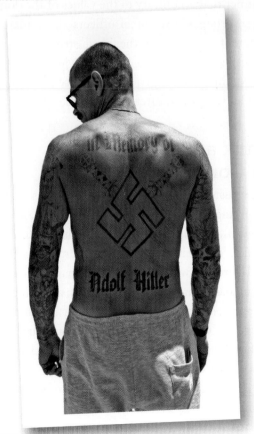

In addition to their important role in the social structure of correctional facilities, prison gangs participate in a wide range of illegal economic activities within these institutions, including prostitution, drug selling, gambling, and loan sharking. A study released in 2011 by Alan J. Drury and Matt DeLisi of Iowa State University found that gang members were more likely to be involved in prison misconduct than those inmates who had been convicted of murder.[33]

The Prevalence of Prison Gangs Recent research places the rate of gang membership at 11.7 percent in federal prisons, 13.4 percent in state prisons, and 15.6 percent in jails.[34] When the National Gang Crime Research Center surveyed prison administrators, however, almost 95 percent said that gang recruitment took place at their institutions, so the overall prevalence of gangs is probably much higher.[35] Los Angeles correctional officials believe that eight out of every ten inmates in their city jails are gang affiliated.

Prison Gang Demographics In many instances, prison gangs are extensions of street gangs. Indeed, investigators believe leaders of the Mexican Mafia put out a contract for (green lighted) a recent outbreak of violence in the Los Angeles jail system discussed earlier in retaliation for an attack that took place on the city streets. Though the stereotypical gang is composed of African Americans or Hispanics, the majority of large prisons also have white, or "Aryan," gangs. One of the largest federal capital prosecutions in U.S. history, involving thirty-two counts of murder, focused on a major prison gang known as the Aryan Brotherhood.

12-2d
Prison Rape

In contrast to riots, the problem of sexual assault in prisons receives very little attention from media sources. This can be partly attributed to the ambiguity of the subject. The occurrence of rape in prisons and jails is undisputed, but determining exactly how widespread the problem is has proved complicated. Prison officials, aware that any sexual contact is prohibited in most penal institutions, are often unwilling to provide realistic figures for fear of negative publicity.

Prison Gang A group of inmates who band together within the corrections system to engage in social and criminal activities.

CONGRESSIONAL ACTION Even when they are willing, they may be unable to do so. Most inmates are ashamed of being rape victims and refuse to report sexual assaults. Consequently, it has been difficult to come up with consistent statistics for sexual assault in prison. To remedy this situation, in 2003 Congress passed the Prison Rape Elimination Act, which mandates that prison officials collect data on the extent of the problem in their facilities.[36] According to a recent survey conducted because of this legislation, about one in ten former state prisoners reports having been sexually victimized by other inmates or prison staff while incarcerated.[37]

HARSH CONSEQUENCES Prison rape, like all rape, is considered primarily an act of violence rather than sex. Inmates subject to rape ("punks") are near the bottom of the prison power structure and, in some instances, may accept rape by one particularly powerful inmate in return for protection from others.[38] Abused inmates often suffer from rape trauma syndrome and a host of other psychological ailments, including suicidal tendencies.

Many prisons do not offer sufficient medical treatment for rape victims, nor does the prison staff take the necessary measures to protect obvious targets of rape—young, slightly built, nonviolent offenders. Furthermore, correctional officials are rarely held responsible for inmate-on-inmate violence. (**CAREER TIP:** According to observers, victims of sexual assault behind bars suffer from a lack of access to *rape crisis counselors* to help them cope with the physical, emotional, and legal consequences of sexual violence.)

12-3

how DO CORRECTIONAL OFFICERS MAINTAIN DISCIPLINE?

Ideally, the presence of correctional officers—the standard term used to describe prison guards—has the effect of lessening violence in American correctional institutions. Practically speaking, this is indeed the case. Without correctional officers, the prison would be a place of anarchy. But in the highly regulated, oppressive environment of the prison, correctional officers must use the threat of violence, if not actual violence, to instill discipline and keep order. Thus, the relationship between prison staff and inmates is marked by mutual distrust. Consider the two following statements, the first made by a correctional officer and the second by a prisoner:

> [My job is to] protect, feed, and try to educate scum who raped and brutalized women and children . . . who, if I turn my back, will go into their cell, wrap a blanket around their cellmate's legs, and threaten to beat or rape him if he doesn't give sex, carry contraband, or fork over radios, money, or other goods willingly. And they'll stick a shank in me tomorrow if they think they can get away with it.[39]

> The pigs in the state and federal prisons . . . treat me so violently, I cannot possibly imagine a time I could ever have anything but the deepest, aching, searing hatred for them. I can't begin to tell you what they do to me. If I were weaker by a hair, they would destroy me.[40]

It may be difficult for an outsider to understand the emotions that fuel such sentiments. French philosopher Michel Foucault points out that discipline, both in prison and in the general community, is a means of social organization as well as punishment.[41] Discipline is imposed when a person behaves in a manner that is contrary to the values of the dominant social group. Correctional officers and inmates have different concepts of the ideal structure of prison society, and, as the two quotations just cited demonstrate, this conflict generates intense feelings of fear and hatred, which often lead to violence.

12-3a

Rank and Duties of Correctional Officers

The custodial staff at most prisons is organized according to four general ranks—captain, lieutenant, sergeant, and officer. In keeping with the militaristic model, captains are primarily administrators who deal directly with the warden on custodial issues. Lieutenants are the disciplinarians of the prison, responsible for policing and transporting the inmates. Sergeants oversee platoons of officers in specific parts of the prison, such as various cell blocks or work spaces.

Lucien X. Lombardo, professor of sociology and criminal justice at Old Dominion University, has

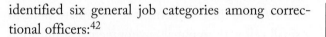
identified six general job categories among correctional officers:[42]

1. *Block officers.* These employees supervise cell blocks containing as many as four hundred inmates, as well as the correctional officers on block guard duty. In general, the block officer is responsible for the well-being of the inmates. He or she tries to ensure that the inmates do not harm themselves or other prisoners and also acts as something of a camp counselor, dispensing advice and seeing that inmates understand and follow the rules of the facility.

2. *Work detail supervisors.* In many penal institutions, the inmates work in the cafeteria, the prison store, the laundry, and other areas. Work detail supervisors oversee small groups of inmates as they perform their tasks.

3. *Industrial shop and school officers.* These officers perform maintenance and security functions in workshop and educational programs. Their primary responsibility is to make sure that inmates are on time for these programs and do not cause any disturbances during the sessions.

4. *Yard officers.* Officers who work the prison yard usually have the least seniority, befitting the assignment's reputation as dangerous and stressful. These officers must be constantly on alert for breaches in prison discipline or regulations in the relatively unstructured environment of the prison yard.

5. *Tower guards.* These officers spend their entire shifts, which usually last eight hours, in isolated, silent posts high above the grounds of the facility. Although their only means of communication are walkie-talkies or cellular devices, the safety benefits of the position can outweigh the loneliness that comes with the job.

6. *Administrative building assignments.* Officers who hold these positions provide security at prison gates, oversee visitation procedures, act as liaisons for civilians, and handle administrative tasks such as processing the paperwork when an inmate is transferred from another institution.

12-3b

Discipline

As Erving Goffman noted in his essay on the "total institution," in the general society adults are rarely placed in a position where they are "punished" as a child would be.[43] Therefore, the strict disciplinary

Inmates at the Deuel Vocational Institution in Tracy, California, walk a lap in the facility's recreation yard. What challenges does this environment pose for correctional officers who must impose discipline in such a setting?

Noah Berger/Bloomberg via Getty Images

measures imposed on prisoners come as something of a shock and can provoke strong defensive reactions. Correctional officers who must deal with these responses often find that disciplining inmates is the most difficult and stressful aspect of their job.

SANCTIONING PRISONERS As mentioned earlier, one of the first things that an inmate receives on entering a correctional facility is a manual that details the rules of the prison or jail, along with the punishment that will result from rule violations. These handbooks can be quite lengthy—running one hundred pages in some instances—and specific. Not only will a prison manual prohibit obvious misconduct such as violent or sexual activity, gambling, and possession of drugs or currency, but it also addresses matters of daily life such as personal hygiene, dress codes, and conduct during meals.

Correctional officers enforce the prison rules in much the same way that a highway patrol officer enforces traffic regulations. For a minor violation, the inmate may be "let off easy" with a verbal warning. More serious infractions will result in a "ticket," or a report forwarded to the institution's disciplinary committee.[44] The disciplinary committee generally includes several correctional officers and, in some instances, outside citizens or even inmates. Although, as we shall see, the United States Supreme Court has ruled that an inmate must be given a "fair hearing" before being disciplined,[45] in reality he or she has very little ability to challenge the committee's decision.

SOLITARY CONFINEMENT Depending on the seriousness of the violation, sanctions can range from a loss of privileges such as visits from family members to the extreme unpleasantness of solitary confinement. Although conditions may vary, in general this term refers to the confinement of an inmate alone in a small cell with minimal environmental stimulation or social interaction. In the past, solitary confinement was primarily a disciplinary tool. Today, however, prison officials use it as a form of preventive detention for inmates, such as gang members, who are deemed a security risk to themselves or others.

Although critics contend that solitary confinement causes severe damage to the mental health of prisoners, no federal laws control its use. Only one state, Washington, places a limit—twenty days—on the length of time an inmate may be kept in isolation. According to estimates, approximately 4.5 percent of the American prison population—about 60,000 inmates—are in solitary confinement at any given time.[46]

USE OF FORCE Most correctional officers prefer to rely on the "you scratch my back and I'll scratch yours" model for controlling inmates. In other words, as long as the prisoner makes a reasonable effort to conform to institutional rules, the correctional officer will refrain from taking disciplinary steps. Of course, the staff-inmate relationship is not always marked by cooperation, and correctional officers often find themselves in situations where they must use force.

Legitimate Security Interests Generally, courts have been unwilling to put too many restrictions on the use of force by correctional officers. As we saw with police officers in Chapter 5, correctional officers are given great leeway to use their experience to determine when force is warranted. In *Whitley v. Albers* (1986),[47] the Supreme Court held that the use of force by prison officials violates an inmate's Eighth Amendment protections only if the force amounts to "the unnecessary and wanton infliction of pain."

Excessive force can be considered "necessary" if the legitimate security interests of the penal institution are at stake. Consequently, an appeals court ruled that when officers at a Maryland prison formed an "extraction team" to remove the leader of a riot from his cell, beating him in the process, the use of force was justified given the situation.[48] (**CAREER TIP:** Most high-security prisons also have *emergency response teams,* or ERTs, made up of specially trained correctional officers who respond to dangerous situations such as riots and other disruptive incidents.)

The "Malicious and Sadistic" Standard The judicial system has not, however, given correctional officers total freedom of discretion to apply force. In *Hudson v. McMillan* (1992),[49] the Supreme Court ruled that minor injuries suffered by a convict at the hands of a correctional officer following an argument did violate the inmate's rights, because there was no security concern at the time of the incident.

In other words, the issue is not *how much* force was used, but whether the officer used the force as part of a good faith effort to restore discipline or acted "maliciously and sadistically" to cause harm. This "malicious and sadistic" standard has been difficult for aggrieved prisoners to meet: in the ten years following the *Hudson* decision, only about 20 percent of excessive force lawsuits against correctional officials were successful.[50]

12-3c
Female Correctional Officers

Security concerns were the main reason that, for many years, prison administrators refused to hire women as correctional officers in men's prisons. The consensus was that women were not physically strong enough to subdue violent male inmates and that their mere presence in the predominantly masculine prison world would cause disciplinary breakdowns. As a result, in the 1970s a number of women brought lawsuits against state corrections systems, claiming that they were being discriminated against on the basis of their gender. For the most part, these legal actions were successful in opening the doors to men's prisons for female correctional officers (and vice versa).[51] Today, more than 150,000 women work in correctional facilities, many of them in constant close contact with male inmates.[52]

As it turns out, female correctional officers have proved just as effective as their male counterparts in maintaining discipline in men's prisons.[53] Furthermore, evidence shows that women prison staff can have a calming influence on male inmates, thus lowering levels of prison violence.[54]

The primary problem caused by women working in male prisons, it seems, involves

About a quarter of the security staff at Sing Sing Correctional Facility in Ossining, New York—shown here—are women. What are some of the challenges that face female correctional officers who work in a men's maximum-security prison?

Susan Farley/*New York Times*/Redux Pictures

sexual misconduct. According to the federal government, nearly 60 percent of prison staff members who engage in sexual misconduct are female, suggesting a disturbing amount of consensual sex with inmates.[55] As we will see in the next section, similar issues exist between male correctional officers and female inmates, though in those cases the sexual contact is much more likely to be coerced.

12-3d

Protecting Prisoners' Rights

LO **3** The general attitude of the law toward inmates is summed up by the Thirteenth Amendment to the U.S. Constitution:

> Neither slavery nor involuntary servitude, except as a punishment for crime whereof the party shall have been duly convicted, shall exist within the United States.

In other words, inmates do not have the same guaranteed rights as other Americans. For most of the nation's history, courts have followed the spirit of this amendment by applying the **"hands-off" doctrine** of prisoner law. This (unwritten) doctrine assumes that the care of inmates should be left to prison officials and that it is not the place of judges to intervene in penal administrative matters.

At the same time, the United States Supreme Court has stated that "[t]here is no iron curtain between the Constitution and the prisons of this country."[56] Consequently, like so many other areas of the criminal justice system, the treatment of prisoners is based on a balancing act—here, between the rights of prisoners and the security needs of the correctional institutions. Of course, as just noted, inmates do not have the same civil rights as do other members of society. In 1984, for example, the Supreme Court ruled that arbitrary searches of prison cells are allowed under the Fourth Amendment because inmates have no reasonable expectation of privacy[57] (see Chapter 6 for a review of this expectation).

"Hands-Off" Doctrine The unwritten judicial policy that favors noninterference by the courts in the administration of prisons and jails.

"Deliberate Indifference" The standard for establishing a violation of an inmate's Eighth Amendment rights, requiring that prison officials were aware of harmful conditions in a correctional institution and failed to take steps to remedy those conditions.

"Identifiable Human Needs" The basic human necessities that correctional facilities are required by the Constitution to provide to inmates.

THE "DELIBERATE INDIFFERENCE" STANDARD

As for those constitutional rights that inmates do retain, in 1976 the Supreme Court established the **"deliberate indifference"** standard. In the case in question, *Estelle v. Gamble*,[58] an inmate had claimed to be the victim of medical malpractice. In his majority opinion, Justice Thurgood Marshall wrote that prison officials violated a convict's Eighth Amendment rights if they "deliberately" failed to provide him or her with necessary medical care.

At the time, the decision was hailed as a victory for prisoners' rights, and it continues to ensure that a certain level of health care is provided. Defining "deliberate" has proved difficult, however. Does it mean that prison officials "should have known" that an inmate was placed in harm's way, or does it mean that officials purposefully placed the inmate in that position?

The Supreme Court seems to have taken the latter position. In *Wilson v. Seiter* (1991),[59] for example, inmate Pearly L. Wilson filed a lawsuit alleging that certain conditions of his confinement—including overcrowding; excessive noise; inadequate heating, cooling, and ventilation; and unsanitary bathroom and dining facilities—were cruel and unusual. The Court ruled against Wilson, stating that he had failed to prove that these conditions, even if they existed, were the result of "deliberate indifference" on the part of prison officials.

"IDENTIFIABLE HUMAN NEEDS" In its *Wilson* decision, the Supreme Court created the **"identifiable human needs"** standard for determining Eighth Amendment violations. The Court asserted that a prisoner must show that the institution has denied her or him a basic need such as food, warmth, or exercise.[60] The Court mentioned only these three needs, however, forcing the lower courts to determine for themselves what other needs, if any, fall into this category.

For example, a number of inmate lawsuits have been filed in response to the use of *nutraloaf*—an unpleasant concoction of nondairy cheese, powdered milk, tomato paste, and dehydrated potato flakes—as prison food (see photo on the facing page). These lawsuits make the argument that nutraloaf is so distasteful as to be cruel and unusual punishment. One

Many prisons punish misbehaving inmates by feeding them nutraloaf. Do you have any concerns about this form of punishment? Explain your answer.

AP Photo/Andy Duback

plaintiff in Milwaukee, Wisconsin, claimed that he became so violently ill after eating nutraloaf that his body weight fell 8 percent due to excessive vomiting. In general, these lawsuits have failed, as courts have been reluctant to create a constitutional right to "decent prison food."[61]

Because of the Supreme Court's *Estelle* decision described above, prisoners do have a well-established right to "adequate" medical care. "Adequate" has been interpreted to mean a level of care comparable to what the inmate would receive if he or she were not behind bars.[62] This concept has not always proved popular with the general public. In 2012, a federal judge in Boston commanded Massachusetts to cover the costs of gender reassignment surgery for a male inmate who had murdered his wife twelve years earlier. After numerous complaints from taxpayers, the judge rescinded his order. Furthermore, several years ago the Supreme Court asserted, controversially, that the overcrowding of California's state prisons was so severe that it denied inmates satisfactory levels of health care.[63]

12-4

are WOMEN'S PRISONS DIFFERENT **?**

When the first women's prison in the United States opened in 1839 on the grounds of New York's Sing Sing institution, the focus was on rehabilitation. Prisoners were prepared for a return to society with classes on reading, knitting, and sewing. Early women's reformatories had few locks or bars, and several included nurseries for the inmates' young children. Today, the situation is dramatically different. "Women's institutions are literally men's institutions, only we pull out the urinals," remarks Meda Chesney-Lind, a criminologist at the University of Hawaii.[64] Given the different circumstances surrounding male and female incarceration, this uniformity can have serious consequences for the women imprisoned in this country.

12-4a
Characteristics of Female Inmates

Male inmates outnumber female inmates by approximately nine to one, and there are only about a hundred women's correctional facilities in the United States. Consequently, most research concerning the American corrections system focuses on male inmates and men's prisons. Enough data exist, however, to provide a useful portrait of women behind bars.

Female inmates are typically low income and undereducated, and have a history of unemployment. Female offenders are much less likely than male offenders to have committed a violent offense. Most are incarcerated for a nonviolent drug or property crime.[65] As Figure 12.2 on the next page shows, the demographics of female prisoners are similar to those of their male counterparts. That is, the majority of female inmates are under the age of forty, and the population is disproportionately African American.

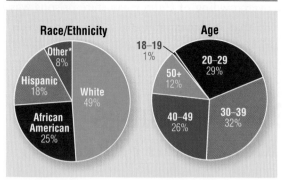

FIGURE 12.2 Female Prisoners in the United States by Race, Ethnicity, and Age

*Includes American Indians, Alaska Natives, Native Hawaiians, other Pacific Islanders, and persons identifying two or more races.

Source: Bureau of Justice Statistics, *Prisoners in 2011* (Washington, D.C.: U.S. Department of Justice, December 2012), Table 7, page 7.

The single factor that most distinguishes female prisoners from their male counterparts is a history of physical or sexual abuse. A self-reported study conducted by the federal government indicates that 55 percent of female jail inmates have been abused at some point in their lives, compared with only 13 percent of male jail inmates.[66]

Fifty-seven percent of women in state prisons and 40 percent of women in federal prisons report some form of past abuse—both figures are significantly higher than those for male prisoners.[67] Health experts believe that these levels of abuse are related to the significant amount of drug and/or alcohol addiction that plagues the female prison population, as well as to the mental illness problems that such addictions can cause or exacerbate.[68]

12-4b

The Motherhood Problem

Drug and alcohol use within a women's prison can be a function of the anger and depression many inmates experience due to being separated from their children. An estimated seven out of every ten female prisoners have at least one minor child. About 1.7 million American children have a mother who is under correctional supervision.[69] Given the scarcity of women's correctional facilities, inmates are often housed at great distances from their children. One study found that almost two-thirds of women in federal prison are more than five hundred miles from their homes.[70]

Further research indicates that an inmate who serves her sentence more than fifty miles from her residence is much less likely to receive phone calls or personal visits from family members. For most inmates and their families, the costs of "staying in touch" are too high.[71]

This kind of separation can have serious consequences for the children of inmates. When a father goes to prison, his children are likely to live with their mother. When a mother is incarcerated, however, her children are likely to live with other relatives or, in about 11 percent of the cases, be sent to foster care.[72] Only six states—California, Indiana, Nebraska, New York, Ohio, and Washington—provide facilities where inmates and their infant children can live together, and even in these facilities nursery privileges generally end once the child is eighteen months old.

12-4c

The Culture of Women's Prisons

After spending five years visiting female inmates in the Massachusetts Correctional Institution (MCI) at Framingham, journalist Cristina Rathbone observed that the medium-security facility seemed "more like a high school than a prison."[73] The prisoners were older and tougher than high school girls, but they still divided into cliques, with the "lifers" at the top of the hierarchy and "untouchables" such as child abusers at the bottom. Unlike in men's prisons, where the underground economy revolves around drugs and weapons, at MCI-Framingham the most treasured contraband items are clothing, food, and makeup.[74]

THE PSEUDO-FAMILY Although both men's and women's prisons are organized with the same goals of control and discipline, the cultures within the two institutions are generally very different. As we have seen, male prison society operates primarily on the basis of power. Deprived of the benefits of freedom, male prisoners tend to create a violent environment that bears little relation to life on the outside.[75]

In contrast, researchers have found that women

SOCIAL MEDIA AND CJ

To learn more about corrections in this country, go to Twitter and locate "correctionsone." You'll see tweets gathered by the staff at **CorrectionsOne .com**, an online resource for news relating to American prisons and jails.

Female inmates at the Women's Eastern Reception, Diagnostic and Correctional Center in Vandalia, Missouri, visit with their daughters and granddaughters. Why is it difficult for many mothers behind bars to see their children?

AP Photo/Whitney Curtis

prisoners prefer to re-create their outside identities by forming social networks that resemble, as noted earlier, high school cliques or, more commonly, the traditional family structure.[76] In these pseudo-families, inmates often play specific roles, with the more experienced convicts acting as "mothers" to younger, inexperienced "daughters." As one observer noted, the younger women rely on their "moms" for emotional support, companionship, loans, and even discipline.[77]

Such a family unit may have a "married" couple at its head, sometimes with a lesbian assuming the role of the father figure. Indeed, homosexuality in women's prisons often manifests itself through the formation of another traditional family model: the monogamous couple.[78] For the most part, sex between inmates plays a different role in women's prisons than in men's prisons. In the latter, rape is an act of aggression and power rather than sex, and "true" homosexuals are relegated to the lowest rungs of the social hierarchy. By contrast, women inmates who engage in sexual activity are not automatically labeled homosexual, and lesbians are not hampered in their social-climbing efforts.[79]

SEXUAL VIOLENCE AND PRISON STAFF

Compared with men's prisons, women's prisons have extremely low levels of race-based, gang-related physical aggression.[80] Furthermore, though rates of sexual victimization can be high, most such episodes involve abusive sexual contacts such as unwanted touching rather than sexual assault or rape.[81]

One form of serious prison violence that does plague women prisoners, however, is sexual misconduct by prison staff. Although no large-scale study on sexual abuse of female inmates by male correctional officers exists, a number of state-level studies suggest that it is widespread.[82] A complaint recently filed with the U.S. Department of Justice claimed that sexual misconduct by male correctional staff toward inmates at Alabama's Tutwiler Prison for Women is "commonplace" and consistently goes unpunished.[83]

12-5
what HAPPENS TO EX-INMATES?

With only a few weeks left to serve on his prison sentence for drug charges, John Cadogan was worried. As he explained in a group therapy session at the men's state prison in Chino, California, his meth-addicted ex-girlfriend wanted to see him "on the outside." Cadogan feared that she was going to tempt him to restart his own drug use. The other inmates agreed that the situation was fraught with difficulty. "It's like playing Russian roulette with a loaded gun," said one.[84]

Each year, about 700,000 inmates are released from American prisons. Many, such as Cadogan, face numerous challenges in their efforts to avoid relapse and reincarceration. More so than in the past, however, ex-convicts are not facing these challenges alone. Given the benefits to society of reducing recidivism, corrections officials and community leaders are making unprecedented efforts to help newly released prisoners establish crime-free lives.

12-5a

Types of Prison Release

The vast majority of all inmates leaving prison—about 80 percent—do so through one of the parole mechanisms discussed in Chapter 10. Of the remaining 20 percent, most are given an **expiration release.**[85] Also known as "maxing out," expiration release occurs when an inmate has served the maximum amount of time on the initial sentence, minus reductions for good-time credits, and is not subjected to community supervision.

Another, quite rare unconditional release is a **pardon,** a form of executive clemency. The president (on the federal level) and the governor (on the state **LO 4** level) can grant a pardon, or forgive a convict's criminal punishment. Most states have a board of pardons—affiliated with the parole board—that makes recommendations to the governor in cases in which it believes a pardon is warranted. Most pardons involve obvious miscarriages of justice, though sometimes a governor will pardon an individual to remove the stain of conviction from her or his criminal record.

Certain temporary releases also exist. Some inmates, who qualify by exhibiting good behavior and generally proving that they do not represent a risk to society, are allowed to leave the prison on **furlough** for a certain amount of time, usually between a day and a week. At times, a furlough is granted because of a family emergency, such as a funeral. Furloughs can be particularly helpful for an inmate who is nearing release and can use them to ease the readjustment period. Finally, *probation release* occurs following a short period of incarceration at the back end of shock probation,

Expiration Release The release of an inmate from prison at the end of his or her sentence without any further correctional supervision.

Pardon An act of executive clemency that overturns a conviction and erases mention of the crime from the person's criminal record.

Furlough Temporary release from a prison for purposes of vocational or educational training, to ease the shock of release, or for personal reasons.

Prisoner Reentry A corrections strategy designed to prepare inmates for a successful return to the community and to reduce their criminal activity after release.

which we discussed in Chapter 10. Generally, however, as you have seen, probationers experience community supervision in place of a prison term.

12-5b

The Challenges of Reentry

What steps can corrections officials take to lessen the possibility that ex-convicts will reoffend following their release? Efforts to answer that question have focused on programs that help inmates make the transition from prison to the outside. In past years, these programs would have come under the general heading of "rehabilitation," but today corrections officials and criminologists refer to them as part of the strategy of **prisoner reentry.**

The concept of reentry has come to mean many things to many people. For our purposes, keep in mind the words of Joan Petersilia of the University of California at Irvine, who defines *reentry* as encompassing "all activities and programming conducted to prepare ex-convicts to return safely to the community and to live as law abiding citizens."[86] In other words, whereas rehab is focused on the individual offender, reentry encompasses the released convict's relationship with society. (**CAREER TIP:** Organizations such as the Fortune Society, which operates out of New York City, provide aid for ex-inmates who may be struggling after release. These entities rely on *reentry counselors* to help ex-convicts deal with issues such as substance abuse, anger management, and joblessness.)

12-5c

Barriers to Reentry

Perhaps the largest obstacle to successful prisoner reentry is the simple truth that life behind bars is very different from life on the outside. As one inmate explains, the "rules" of prison survival are hardly compatible with good citizenship:

> An unexpected smile could mean trouble. A man in uniform was not a friend. Being kind was a weakness. Viciousness and recklessness were to be respected and admired.[87]

The prison environment also insulates inmates. They are not required to make the day-to-day decisions that characterize a normal existence beyond prison bars. Depending on the length of incarceration, a released inmate must adjust to an array of economic, technological, and social changes that took place while she or he was behind bars. Common acts such as using an ATM or a smartphone may be completely alien to someone who has just completed a long prison term.

CHALLENGES OF RELEASE Other obstacles hamper reentry efforts. Housing can be difficult to secure, as many private property owners refuse to rent to someone with a criminal record, and federal and state laws restrict public housing options for ex-convicts. A criminal past also limits the ability to find employment, as does the lack of job skills of someone who has spent a significant portion of his or her life in prison. Felix Mata, who works with ex-convicts in Baltimore, Maryland, estimates that the average male prisoner returning to that city has only $50 in his pocket and owes $8,000 in child support. Furthermore, these men generally have no means of transportation, no place to live, and no ability to gain employment. At best, most ex-prisoners can expect to earn no more than $8,500 annually the first few years after being released.[88]

These economic barriers can be complicated by the physical and mental condition of the freed convict. We have already discussed the high incidence of substance abuse among prisoners and the health-care needs of aging inmates. In addition, one study concluded that as many as one in five Americans leaving jail or prison is seriously mentally ill.[89] (See Figure 12.3 below for a list of the hardships commonly faced by former inmates in their first year out of prison.)

THE THREAT OF RECIDIVISM All of these problems conspire to make successful reentry difficult to achieve. Perhaps it is not surprising that research conducted by the Pew Center on

---

FIGURE 12.3 Prisoner Reentry Issues

Researchers from the Urban Institute in Washington, D.C., asked nearly three hundred former prisoners (all male) in the Cleveland, Ohio, area about the most pressing issues they faced in their first year after release. The answers provide a useful snapshot of the many challenges of reentry.

1. *Housing.* Nearly two-thirds of the men were living with family members, and about half considered their housing situation "temporary." Many were concerned about their living environment: half said that drug dealing was a major problem in their neighborhoods, and almost 25 percent were living with drug and alcohol abusers.

2. *Employment.* After one year, only about one-third of the former inmates had a full-time job, and another 11 percent were working part-time.

3. *Family and friends.* One in four of the men identified family support as the most important thing keeping them from returning to criminality. Another 16 percent said that avoiding certain people and situations was the most crucial factor in their continued good behavior.

4. *Programs and services.* About two-thirds of the former inmates had taken part in programs and services such as drug treatment and continuing education.

5. *Health.* More than half of the men reported suffering from a chronic health condition, and 29 percent showed symptoms of depression.

6. *Substance use.* About half of the men admitted to weekly drug use or alcohol intoxication. Men who had strong family ties and those who were required to maintain telephone contact with their parole officer were less likely to engage in frequent substance use.

7. *Parole violation and recidivism.* More than half of the former inmates reported that they had violated the conditions of their parole, usually by drug use or having contact with other parolees. Fifteen percent of the men returned to prison in the year after release. Four out of five of the returns were the result of a new crime.

Source: Christy A. Visher and Shannon M. E. Courtney, *One Year Out: Experience of Prisoners Returning to Cleveland* (Washington, D.C.: Urban Institute, April 2007), 2.

the States found that 43 percent of ex-prisoners are back in prison or jail within three years of their release dates.[90] These figures highlight the problem of recidivism among those released from incarceration.

12-5d
Promoting Desistance

One ex-inmate compared the experience of being released to entering a "dark room, knowing that there are steps in front of you and waiting to fall."[91] The goal of reentry is to act as a flashlight for convicts by promoting **desistance,** a general term used to describe the continued abstinence from offending and the reintroduction of offenders into society.

Preparation for reentry starts behind bars. In addition to the rehabilitation-oriented prison programs discussed earlier in the chapter, most correctional facilities offer "life skills" classes to inmates. This counseling covers topics such as finding and keeping a job, locating a residence, understanding family responsibilities, and budgeting. After release, however, former inmates often find it difficult to continue with educational programs and counseling as they struggle to readjust to life outside prison. Consequently, parole supervising agencies operate a number of programs to facilitate offenders' desistance efforts while, at the same time, protecting the community to the greatest extent possible.

LO 5

Desistance The process through which criminal activity decreases and reintegration into society increases over a period of time.

Work Release Program Temporary release of convicts from prison for purposes of employment. The offenders may spend their days on the job, but must return to the correctional facility at night and during the weekend.

Halfway House A community-based form of early release that places inmates in residential centers and allows them to reintegrate with society.

WORK RELEASE As is made clear in Figure 12.3 on the previous page, work and lodging are crucial components of desistance. Corrections officials have several options in helping certain parolees—usually low-risk offenders—find employment and a place to live during the supervision period. Nearly a third of correctional facilities offer **work release programs,** in which prisoners nearing the end of their sentences are given permission to work at paid employment in the community.[92]

HALFWAY HOUSES Inmates on work release must either return to the correctional facility in the evening or live in community residential facilities known as **halfway houses.** These facilities, also available to other parolees and those who have finished their sentences, are often remodeled hotels or private homes. They provide a less institutionalized living environment than a prison or jail for a small number of offenders (usually between ten and twenty-five). Halfway houses can be tailored to the needs of the former inmate. Many communities, for example, offer substance-free transitional housing for those whose past criminal behavior was linked to drug or alcohol abuse.

12-5e
The Special Case of Sex Offenders

Despite the beneficial impact of reentry efforts, one group of wrongdoers has consistently been denied access to such programs: those convicted of sex crimes. The eventual return of these offenders to society causes such high levels of community anxiety that the criminal justice system has not yet figured out what to do with them.

FEAR OF SEX OFFENDERS According to one poll, 66 percent of Americans are "very concerned" about child molesters, compared with 52 percent who expressed such concern about violent criminals and 36 percent about terrorists.[93] To a large degree, this attitude reflects the widespread belief that convicted sex offenders cannot be "cured" of their criminality and therefore are destined to continue committing sex offenses after their release from prison.

It is true that the medical health profession has had little success in treating the "urges" that lead to sexually deviant or criminal behavior.[94] This has not, however, translated into rampant recidivism among sex offenders when compared to other types of criminals. According to the U.S. Department of Justice, the rearrest rates of rapists (46 percent) and those convicted of other forms of sexual assault (41 percent) are among the lowest for all offenders.[95]

Furthermore, after analyzing eighty-two recidivism studies, Canadian researchers R. Karl Hanson

HALFWAY HOUSE PROGRAM MANAGER

JOB DESCRIPTION:

- Coordinate recreational, educational, and vocational counseling, and other programs for residents. Also, maintain the security of the house and the residents.
- Serve as a mediator between the residents and the community and as an advocate for the halfway house with community groups.

WHAT KIND OF TRAINING IS REQUIRED?

- A bachelor's degree or master's degree in social work, career counseling, criminal justice, or psychology.
- Also helpful are internships, volunteer work with a halfway house, or community service work through an agency.

ANNUAL SALARY RANGE?

- $29,390–$45,550

Benjamin F. Fink, Jr./Brand X Pictures/Jupiterimages

and Kelly Morton-Bourgon found that only 14 percent of sex offenders were apprehended for another sex crime after release from prison or jail. On average, such offenders were significantly more likely to be rearrested for nonsexual criminal activity, if they were rearrested at all.[96]

CONDITIONS OF RELEASE Whatever their recidivism rates, sex offenders are subject to extensive community supervision after being released from prison. Generally, they are supervised by parole officers and live under the same threat of revocation as other parolees. Specifically, many sex offenders—particularly child molesters—have the following special conditions of release:

- No contact with children under the age of eighteen.
- Psychiatric treatment.
- Must stay a certain distance from schools or parks where children are present.
- Cannot own toys that may be used to lure children.
- Cannot have a job or participate in any activity that involves children.

Recently, states have taken steps to further restrict access of sex offenders to minors over the Internet. In 2012, a federal judge upheld an Indiana law that bans sex offenders from accessing Facebook and other social networking sites used by children. That same year, in New York, providers of online video games such as Xbox Live and PlayStation agreed to close the accounts of more than 3,500 sex offenders. Furthermore, more than half of the states and hundreds of municipalities have passed *residency restrictions* for convicted sex offenders. These laws ban sex offenders from living within a certain distance of places where children naturally congregate.

SEX OFFENDER NOTIFICATION LAWS Perhaps the most dramatic step taken by criminal justice authorities to protect the public from sex crimes involves *sex offender registries*, or databases that contain sex offenders' names, addresses, photographs, and other information. The movement to register sex offenders started about two decades ago, after seven-year-old Megan Kanka of Hamilton Township, New Jersey, was raped and murdered by a twice-convicted pedophile (an adult sexually attracted to children) who had moved into her neighborhood after being released from prison on parole.

The next year, in response to public outrage, the state passed a series of laws known collectively as the New Jersey Sexual Offender Registration Act, or "Megan's Law."[97] Today, all fifty states and the federal government have their own version of Megan's Law, or a **sex offender notification law,** which requires local law authorities to alert the public when a sex offender has been released into the community.

Active and Passive Notification No two sex offender notification laws have exactly the same provisions, but all are designed with the goal of allowing the public to learn the identities of convicted sex offenders living in their midst. In general, the laws demand that a paroled sex offender notify local law enforcement authorities on taking up residence in a state. In Georgia, for example, paroled sex offenders are required to present themselves to both the local sheriff and the superintendent of the public school district where they plan to live. This registration process must be renewed every time the parolee changes address.

The authorities, in turn, notify the community of the sex offender's presence through the use of one of two models. Under the "active" model, the authorities directly notify the community or community representatives. Traditionally, this notification has taken the form of bulletins or posters, distributed and posted within a certain distance from the offender's home. Now, however, a number of states use e-mail alerts to fulfill notification obligations. In the "passive" model, information on sex offenders is made open and available for public scrutiny.

Sex Offender Registries In 2006, Congress passed the Adam Walsh Child Protection and Safety Act, which established a national registry of sex offenders.[98] In addition, all fifty states operate sex offender registries with data on registered sex offenders in their jurisdictions. (For an idea of how this process works, you can visit the Federal Bureau of Investigation's Sex Offender Registry Web site.) The total number of registered sex offenders in the United States is about 740,000.

CIVIL CONFINEMENT To many, any type of freedom, even if encumbered by notification requirements, is too much freedom for a sex offender. "The issue is, what can you do short of putting them all in prison for the rest of their lives?" complained one policymaker.[99] In fact, many jurisdictions have devised a

What are some of the reasons that community members fear the nearby presence of freed sex offenders? Are these fears justified? Why or why not?

Sex Offender Notification Law Legislation that requires law enforcement authorities to notify people when convicted sex offenders are released into their neighborhood or community.

THOSE offenders who have been convicted of motor vehicle theft are rearrested at a rate of nearly 80 percent. Given that this number is nearly twice the recidivism rate for sex offenders, one commentator wonders whether there should be "registry lists that warn the public where they ought to avoid parking or which neighborhoods contain car thieves."

Although no car thief notification laws are on the horizon, local politicians are experimenting with registries for other types of criminals. Suffolk County, New York, has an online registry of animal abusers. Since 2012, convicted murderers released in Illinois have had to register with state authorities, much like sex offenders. Maine and Texas are considering placing registries for drunk drivers on the Internet. "You'd be hard pressed to find a more politically popular movement in recent years," says Wayne Logan, a professor at Florida State University.

State of California Department of Justice/Megan's Law Homepage

State of California Department of Justice — Office of the Attorney General — Kamala D. Harris, Attorney General

California Sex Offender Locator Map

Because maps only reflect sex registrants on whom full address information may be displayed, you are encouraged to utilize the "Name", "City", "ZIP Code", and "County" search functions for access to complete listings of sex registrants available on this Internet site.

THINKING ABOUT CRIME REGISTRIES

One critic has called all crime registries instruments for "public shaming" with few other tangible benefits. Do you agree? Why or why not?

method to keep sex offenders off the streets for, if not their entire lives, then close to it.

A number of states have passed **civil confinement** laws that allow corrections officials to keep sex offenders locked up in noncorrectional facilities such as psychiatric hospitals after the conclusion of their prison terms. Under these laws, corrections officials can keep sexual criminals confined indefinitely, as long as they are deemed a danger to society. Given the recidivism rates of sex offenders, civil confinement laws essentially give the state the power to detain this class of criminal indefinitely—a power upheld by the United States Supreme Court in 2010.[100]

Civil Confinement The practice of confining individuals against their will if they present a danger to the community.

REVIEW

✓ **Review what you've read with the quiz below.**

Rip out the Chapter Review card at the back of this book, which includes:
- Chapter Summary and Learning Outcomes
- Key Terms

Or you can go online to CourseMate at www.cengagebrain.com to:
- Complete Practice Quizzes to prepare for tests.
- Review Key Terms Flash Cards (online or print).
- Play games to master concepts.

quiz

1. Prison culture is different from the cultures of schools or workplaces because prison is a _____ _____ that dominates every aspect of the inmate's life.

2. In recent decades, the prison culture has been affected by the increased average age of inmates, which has led to skyrocketing _____-_____ costs for federal and state corrections systems.

3. The concept of _____ _____, based on the gap between an inmate's expectations and reality, is used to explain the conditions that lead to prison riots.

4. Correctional officers may use force against inmates when a _____ security interest is being served.

5. Courts will not accept any force on the part of correctional officers that is "_____ and sadistic."

6. To prove that prison officials violated constitutional prohibitions against cruel and unusual punishment, the inmate must first show that the officials acted with "_____ indifference" in taking or not taking an action.

7. While levels of physical violence are relatively low in women's prisons, female inmates do face a greater threat of sexual assault from _____ _____ than male inmates do.

8. One way in which the corrections system tries to help inmates prepare for release is by offering _____ programs that include job training and work release opportunities.

9. Corrections officials promote desistance by allowing certain low-risk offenders to live in _____ houses, where they can receive specialized attention and treatment.

10. Sex offender _____ laws mandate that law enforcement officials alert the public when a sex offender has moved into the community.

Answers can be found on the Chapter 12 Review card at the end of the book.

Noah Berger/Bloomberg via Getty Images

USE THE TOOLS.

• Rip out the Review Cards in the back of your book to study.

Or Visit CourseMate to:

• Read, search, highlight, and take notes in the Interactive eBook

• Review Flashcards (Print or Online) to master key terms

• Test yourself with Auto-Graded Quizzes

• Bring concepts to life with Games, Videos, and Animations!

Go to CourseMate for **CJ** to begin using these tools.
Access at **www.cengagebrain.com**

Complete the Speak Up
survey in CourseMate at
www.cengagebrain.com

f Follow us at
www.facebook.com/4ltrpress

Learning **OUTCOMES**

After studying this chapter, you will be able to . . .

1 Describe the child-saving movement and its relationship to the doctrine of *parens patriae*.

2 List the four major differences between juvenile courts and adult courts.

3 Describe the reasoning behind recent U.S. Supreme Court decisions that have lessened the harshness of sentencing outcomes for violent juvenile offenders.

4 Describe the one variable that always correlates highly with juvenile crime rates.

5 Describe the four primary stages of pretrial juvenile justice procedure.

THE JUVENILE JUSTICE SYSTEM

13

Bloody Sunday

Like many teenagers, fifteen-year-old Nehemiah Griego of Albuquerque, New Mexico, was frustrated with his mother. The way that Nehemiah dealt with this frustration was, however, anything but commonplace. Around 1 A.M. on January 19, 2013, Nehemiah sneaked into his parents' upstairs bedroom and, using a family rifle, fatally shot his sleeping mother, Sara. Next, he used the weapon to kill his nine-year-old brother and two sisters, aged five and two. Nehemiah then waited five hours in a downstairs bathroom for his father to return home from work. When Greg Griego walked in the front door, his son shot him as well, resulting in the fifth and final death of that Sunday morning.

According to Bernalillo County law enforcement authorities, Nehemiah had been planning the killings for at least a week, spending much of that time playing violent video games. The teenager had also planned to murder his girl-friend's family and then start shooting random strangers at a local Wal-Mart, with the expectation that he would not survive the expected gunfire exchange with police. Instead, Nehemiah texted a photo of his dead mother to his girl-friend and spent most of the rest of the day with her before being arrested.

Because of the level of premeditation and the horrific nature of the murders, prosecutors decided to charge Nehemiah as an adult rather than a juvenile. If convicted of all the charges against him, including five counts of murder, he faced more than two hundred years in prison. Nehemiah's remaining family members disagreed with this strategy. His uncle, Eric Griego, told reporters that Nehemiah should be given "the fairest chance to turn his life around." Griego also said that his nephew should "not be cast away to an adult prison system where he can never have an opportunity for redemption."

In January 2013, fifteen-year-old Nehemiah Griego of Albuquerque, New Mexico, was arrested for killing five family members.

property bag with all other personal property, sealed and e property room. Money $5.00 and over will be to the Resident Fund bank account and a check will be the child's release. All p___ ___ill be returned from detention.

will conduct a medica___ ___ude ___ry and condition at ti___ ___ts/legal guardian/cus___ ___ild's ___ild's assigned Unit an___ ___e of Unit

showered and pe___ ___d and thing will be launde___ ___d in room until child's relea___ taken to assigned Unit.

279

13-1 **why** DO WE HAVE A SEPARATE JUSTICE SYSTEM FOR JUVENILES ?

A difficult question—asked every time a younger offender such as Nehemiah Griego commits a heinous act of violence—lies at the heart of the juvenile justice debate: Should such acts by youths be given the same weight as those committed by adults, or should they be seen as "mistakes" that can be corrected by care and counseling? From its earliest days, the American juvenile justice system has operated as an uneasy compromise between "rehabilitation and punishment, treatment and custody."[1]

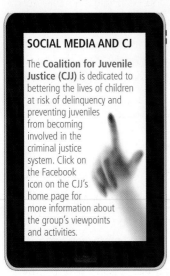

SOCIAL MEDIA AND CJ

The **Coalition for Juvenile Justice (CJJ)** is dedicated to bettering the lives of children at risk of delinquency and preventing juveniles from becoming involved in the criminal justice system. Click on the Facebook icon on the CJJ's home page for more information about the group's viewpoints and activities.

At the beginning of the 1800s, juvenile offenders were treated the same as adult offenders—they were judged by the same courts and sentenced to the same severe penalties. This situation began to change soon after, as urbanization and industrialization created an immigrant underclass that was, at least in the eyes of many reformers, predisposed to deviant activity. Certain members of the Progressive movement, known as the child savers, began to take steps to "save" children from these circumstances, introducing the idea of rehabilitating delinquents in the process.

13-1a The Child-Saving Movement

In general, the child savers favored the doctrine of **parens patriae,** which holds that the state has not only a right but also a duty to care for children who are neglected, delinquent, or in some other way disadvantaged. Juvenile offenders, the child savers believed, required treatment, not punishment,

LO **1**

Parens Patriae A doctrine that holds that the state has a responsibility to look after the well-being of children and to assume the role of parent if necessary.

and they were horrified at the thought of placing children in prisons with hardened adult criminals. In 1967, then Supreme Court justice Abe Fortas said of the child savers:

> They believed that society's role was not to ascertain whether the child was "guilty" or "innocent," but "What is he, how has he become what he is, and what had best be done in his interest and in the interest of the state to save him from a downward career." The child—essentially good, as they saw it—was made "to feel that he is the object of [the government's] care and solicitude," not that he was under arrest or on trial.[2]

Child-saving organizations convinced local legislatures to pass laws that allowed them to take control of children who exhibited criminal tendencies or had been neglected by their parents. To separate these children from the environment in which they were raised, the organizations created a number of institutions, the best known of which was New York's House of Refuge.

Opening in 1825, the House of Refuge implemented many of the same reformist measures popular in the penitentiaries of the time, meaning that its charges were subjected to the healthful influences of hard study and labor. Although the House of Refuge was criticized for its harsh discipline (which caused many boys to run away), similar institutions sprang up throughout the Northeast during the middle of the 1800s.

13-1b The Illinois Juvenile Court

The efforts of the child savers culminated with the passage of the Illinois Juvenile Court Act in 1899. The Illinois legislature created the first court specifically for juveniles, guided by the principles of *parens patriae* and based on the belief that children are not fully responsible for criminal conduct and are capable of being rehabilitated.[3]

The Illinois Juvenile Court and those in other states that followed in its path were (and, in many cases, remain) drastically different from adult courts:

- *No juries.* The matter was decided by judges who wore regular clothes instead of black robes and sat at a table with the other participants rather than behind a bench. Because the primary focus of the court was on the child and not the crime, the judge had wide discretion in disposing of each case.

2 LO

- *Different terminology.* To reduce the stigma of criminal proceedings, "petitions" were issued instead of "warrants." The children were not "defendants," but "respondents," and they were not "found guilty" but "adjudicated delinquent."

- *No adversarial relationship.* Instead of trying to determine guilt or innocence, the parties involved in the juvenile court worked together in the best interests of the child, with the emphasis on rehabilitation rather than punishment.

- *Confidentiality.* To avoid "saddling" the child with a criminal past, juvenile court hearings and records were kept sealed, and the proceedings were closed to the public.

By 1945, every state had a juvenile court system modeled after the first Illinois court. For the most part, these courts were able to operate without interference until the 1960s and the onset of the juvenile rights movement.

13-1c
Juvenile Offending

After the first juvenile court was established in Illinois, the Chicago Bar Association described its purpose as, in part, to "exercise the same tender solicitude and care over its neglected wards that a wise and loving parent would exercise with reference to his [or her] own children under similar circumstances."[4] In other words, the state was given the responsibility of caring for those minors whose behavior seemed to show that they could not be controlled by their parents. As a result, many **status offenders** found themselves in the early houses of refuge and continue to be placed in state-run facilities today.

A status offense is an act that, if committed by a juvenile, is considered illegal and grounds for possible state custody. The same act, if committed by an adult, does not warrant law enforcement action. (See Figure 13.1 above for a list of the most common status offenses.) (**CAREER TIP:** Most states have attendance laws that require students to be in school during school hours. These states employ *truancy officers* to enforce such laws by working with parents and investigating suspicious patterns of absence.)

FIGURE 13.1 Status Offenses

1. Smoking cigarettes	5. Running away from home
2. Drinking alcohol	6. Violating curfew
3. Being truant (skipping school)	7. Participating in sexual activity
4. Disobeying teachers	8. Using profane language

JUVENILE DELINQUENCY More serious than status offending, **juvenile delinquency** refers to conduct that would also be criminal if committed by an adult. According to federal law and the laws of most states, a juvenile delinquent is someone who has not yet reached his or her eighteenth birthday—the age of adult criminal responsibility—at the time of the offense in question. In two states (New York and North Carolina), persons aged sixteen are considered adults, and eleven other states confer adulthood on seventeen-year-olds for purposes of criminal law.

CHARGED AS AN ADULT Under certain circumstances, discussed later in this chapter, children under the age of criminal responsibility can be tried in adult courts and incarcerated in adult prisons and jails. Remember that Nehemiah Griego was fifteen years old when he was charged as an adult for the murders of five family members, described in the opening of the chapter. By contrast, in 2013, high school football players Trent Mays, aged seventeen, and Ma'lik Richmond, aged sixteen, were found to be *delinquent beyond a reasonable doubt* of sexually assaulting an intoxicated sixteen-year-old girl in Steubenville, Ohio (see photo on the next page). Because they were adjudicated as juveniles, Mays and Richmond cannot be incarcerated past their twenty-first birthdays. Griego, charged as an adult, faced the possibility of spending at least two hundred years behind bars.

13-1d
Constitutional Protections and the Juvenile Court

Though the ideal of the juvenile court seemed to offer the "best of both worlds" for

Status Offender A juvenile who has engaged in behavior deemed unacceptable for those under a certain statutorily determined age.

Juvenile Delinquency Behavior that is illegal under federal or state law that has been committed by a person who is under an age limit specified by statute.

Depending on the state, juvenile offenders found to be delinquent such as Trent Mays, left, and Ma'lik Richmond usually will not be incarcerated past their twenty-first birthdays. Is this a just punishment? Why or why not?

AP Photo/Keith Srakocic, Pool

juvenile offenders, in reality the lack of procedural protections led to many children being arbitrarily punished not only for crimes, but for status offenses as well. Juvenile judges were treating all violators similarly, which led to many status offenders being incarcerated in the same institutions as violent delinquents. In response to a wave of lawsuits demanding due process rights for juveniles, the United States Supreme Court issued several rulings in the 1960s and 1970s that significantly changed the juvenile justice system.

KENT V. UNITED STATES The first decision to extend due process rights to children in juvenile courts was *Kent v. United States* (1966).[5] The case concerned sixteen-year-old Morris Kent, who had been arrested for breaking into a woman's house, stealing her purse, and raping her. Because Kent was on juvenile probation, the state sought to transfer his trial for the crime to an adult court (a process to be discussed later in the chapter).

Without giving any reasons for his decision, the juvenile judge consented to this judicial waiver, and Kent was sentenced in the adult court to a thirty- to ninety-year prison term. The Supreme Court overturned the sentence, ruling that juveniles have a right to counsel and a hearing in any instance in which the juvenile judge is considering sending the case to an adult court. The Court stated that, in jurisdiction waiver cases, a child receives "the worst of both worlds," getting neither the

"protections accorded to adults" nor the "solicitous care and regenerative treatment" offered in the juvenile system.[6]

IN RE GAULT The *Kent* decision provided the groundwork for *In re Gault* one year later. Considered by many the single most important case concerning juvenile justice, *In re Gault* involved a fifteen-year-old boy who was arrested for allegedly making a lewd phone call while on probation.[7] In its decision, the Supreme Court held that juveniles facing a loss of liberty were entitled to many of the same basic procedural safeguards granted to adult offenders in this country. These safeguards include notice of charges, the right to counsel, the privilege against self-incrimination, and the right to confront and cross-examine witnesses.

OTHER IMPORTANT COURT DECISIONS Over the next ten years, the Supreme Court handed down three more important rulings on juvenile court procedure. The ruling in *In re Winship* (1970)[8] required the government to prove "beyond a reasonable doubt" that a juvenile had committed an act of delinquency, raising the burden of proof from a "preponderance of the evidence."

In *Breed v. Jones* (1975),[9] the Court held that the Fifth Amendment's double jeopardy clause prevented a juvenile from being tried in an adult court for a crime that had already been adjudicated in juvenile court. In contrast, the decision in *McKeiver v. Pennsylvania* (1971)[10] represented an instance in which the Court did not move the juvenile court further toward the adult model. In that case, the Court ruled that the Constitution did not give juveniles the right to a jury trial.

how IS DELINQUENCY DETERMINED?

In the eyes of many observers, the net effect of the Supreme Court decisions during the 1966–1975 period was to move juvenile justice away from the ideals of the child savers. As a result of these decisions, many young offenders would find themselves in a formalized system that is often indistinguishable from its adult counterpart. But, though the Court has recognized that minors charged with crimes possess certain constitutional rights, it has failed to dictate at what age these rights should be granted. Consequently, the legal status of children in the United States varies depending on where they live, with each state making its own policy decisions on the crucial questions of age and competency.

13-2a
The Age Question

One day several years ago, a twelve-year-old boy was playing with toy trucks and planes in the backyard of his family's Burlington, Colorado, home. Minutes later, he fatally shot his parents, Charles and Marilyn Long, with a .357 Magnum revolver.

In Chapter 3, we saw that early American criminal law recognized infancy as a defense against criminal charges. At that time, on attaining fourteen years of age, a youth was considered an adult and treated accordingly by the criminal justice system. Today, as Figure 13.2 alongside shows, the majority of states, including Colorado (as well as the District of Columbia), allow for the prosecution of juveniles under the age of thirteen as adults. Thus, Colorado officials had the option of prosecuting the Longs' son for murder as an adult, despite his tender years.

Instead, despite the wishes of some Long family members, district attorney Robert E. Watson decided to keep the boy in the state's juvenile justice system. "If you're looking for an adult explanation for why this kid went from playing in dirt to commit murder you'll never get one," said Watson. "This lies in the mind of a very immature twelve-year-old."[11]

As noted earlier, when juveniles who remain in juvenile court are found guilty, they receive "limited" sentences. Under these circumstances, they cannot remain incarcerated in juvenile detention centers past their eighteenth or twenty-first birthday. Consequently, a Colorado juvenile judge eventually sentenced the boy who shot and killed his parents to seven years in juvenile detention.

13-2b
The Culpability Question

Many researchers believe that by the age of fourteen, an adolescent has the same ability as an adult to make a competent decision. Nevertheless, according to some observers, a juvenile's ability to theoretically understand the difference between "right" and "wrong" does not mean that she or he should be held to the same standards of competency as an adult.

FIGURE 13.2 The Minimum Age at Which a Juvenile Can Be Tried as an Adult

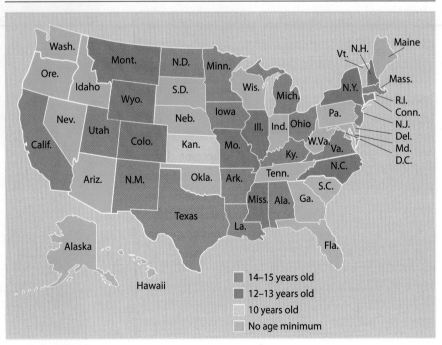

14–15 years old
12–13 years old
10 years old
No age minimum

Source: National Center for Juvenile Justice.

JUVENILE BEHAVIOR A study released in 2003 by the Research Network on Adolescent Development and Juvenile Justice found that 33 percent of juvenile defendants in criminal courts had the same low level of understanding of legal matters as mentally ill adults who had been found incompetent to stand trial.[12] Legal psychologist Richard E. Redding believes that

> adolescents' lack of life experience may limit their real-world decision-making ability. Whether we call it wisdom, judgment, or common sense, adolescents may not have nearly enough.[13]

Juveniles are generally more impulsive, more likely to engage in risky behavior, and less likely to calculate the long-term consequences of any particular action. Furthermore, adolescents are far more likely to respond to peer pressure than are adults. The desire for acceptance and approval may drive them to commit crimes: juveniles are arrested as part of a group at much higher rates than adults.[14] Furthermore, juveniles are less likely than adults to display remorse immediately following a violent act. As a result, they are often penalized by the courts for showing "less grief than the system demands."[15]

DIMINISHED GUILT The "diminished culpability" of juveniles was one of the reasons given by the United States Supreme Court in its landmark decision in *Roper v. Simmons* (2005).[16] As we saw in Chapter 9, that case forbade the execution of offenders who were under the age of eighteen when they committed their crimes. In his majority opinion, Justice Anthony Kennedy wrote that because minors cannot fully comprehend the consequences of their actions, the two main justifications for the death penalty—retribution and deterrence—do not "work" with juvenile wrongdoers.[17]

LO **3**

Parole for Non-Murderers? The Supreme Court applied the same reasoning in two later cases that have dramatically affected the sentencing of violent juvenile offenders. First, in *Graham v. Florida* (2010),[18] the Court held that juveniles who commit crimes that do not involve murder may not be sentenced to life in prison without the possibility of parole. According to Justice Kennedy, who wrote the majority opinion, state officials must give these inmates "some meaningful opportunity to obtain release based on demonstrated maturity and rehabilitation."[19]

Parole for Murderers? Two years later, with *Miller v. Alabama* (2012),[20] the Court banned laws in twenty-eight states that made life-without-parole sentences *mandatory* for juveniles convicted of murder. The case focused on the fate of Evan Miller, who was fourteen years old when he killed a neighbor with a baseball bat. The ruling did not signify that juvenile offenders such as Miller could not, under any circumstances, be sentenced to life without parole. Rather, the Court stated that judges must have the discretion to weigh the mitigating factors in each individual case.

For example, Miller had been abused by his stepfather and neglected by his alcoholic and drug-addicted mother, had spent most of his life in foster care, and had tried to commit suicide four times.[21]

According to the U.S. Supreme Court's *Miller* decision, under what circumstances can juvenile murderers such as T. J. Lane, shown here, receive life-without-parole sentences? In 2013, Lane was convicted for killing three students at Chardon High School in Chardon, Ohio.

AP Photo/Mark Duncan

According to the Court, this type of personal history must be taken into account when determining the proper sentence for a juvenile murderer. Such mitigating factors may indicate that the offender has the potential to be rehabilitated and therefore should be afforded the possibility of parole.

13-3

how MUCH JUVENILE DELINQUENCY IS THERE IN THE UNITED STATES?

When asked, juveniles will admit to a wide range of illegal or dangerous behavior, including carrying weapons, getting involved in physical fights, driving after drinking alcohol, and stealing or deliberately damaging school property.[22] Has the juvenile justice system been effective in controlling and preventing this kind of misbehavior, as well as more serious acts?

To answer this question, many observers turn to the Federal Bureau of Investigation's Uniform Crime Report (UCR), initially covered in Chapter 2. Because the UCR breaks down arrest statistics by age of the arrestee, it has been considered the primary source of information on the presence of juveniles in America's justice system.

This does not mean, however, that the UCR is completely reliable when it comes to measuring juvenile delinquency. The process measures only those juveniles who were caught and therefore does not accurately reflect all delinquent acts in any given year. Furthermore, it measures the number of arrests but not the number of arrestees, meaning that—due to repeat offenders—the number of juveniles actually in the system could be below the number of juvenile arrests.

13-3a
Delinquency by the Numbers

With these cautions in mind, UCR findings are quite clear as to the extent of juvenile delinquency in the United States today. In 2011, juveniles accounted for 12.7 percent of violent crime arrests and 11.8 percent of criminal activity arrests in general.[23] According to the 2011 UCR, juveniles were responsible for

- 8 percent of all murder arrests.
- 19 percent of all aggravated assault arrests.
- 14 percent of all forcible rapes.
- 18 percent of all weapons arrests.
- 22 percent of all robbery arrests.
- 20 percent of all Part I property crimes.
- 19 percent of all drug offenses.

13-3b
The Rise and Fall of Juvenile Crime

As Figure 13.3 on the next page shows, juvenile arrest rates for violent crimes have fluctuated dramatically over the past three decades. In the 2000s, with a few exceptions, juvenile crime in the United States has decreased at a rate similar to that of adult crime, as discussed earlier in this textbook. From 1997 to 2009, juvenile court delinquency caseloads declined by 20 percent.[24] Not surprisingly, the drop in juvenile arrests and court appearances has led to fewer juveniles behind bars. The national population of juvenile inmates decreased 12 percent between 2006 and 2008, allowing officials in some states, including California, Ohio, and Texas, to close juvenile detention facilities.[25]

A number of theories have been put forth to explain this downturn in juvenile offending. Some observers point to the increase in police action against "quality-of-life" crimes such as loitering, which they believe stops juveniles before they have a chance to commit more serious crimes. Similarly, about 80 percent of American municipalities enforce juvenile curfews, which restrict the movement of minors during certain hours, usually after dark.[26] In 2011, law enforcement made nearly 60,000 arrests for curfew and loitering law violations.[27]

Furthermore, hundreds of local programs designed to educate children about the dangers of drugs and crime operate across the country. Though the results of such community-based efforts are difficult, if not impossible, to measure—it cannot be assumed that children would have become delinquent if they had not participated—these programs are generally considered a crucial element of keeping youth crime under control.

FIGURE 13.3 Arrest Rates of Juveniles

After rising dramatically in the mid-1990s, juvenile arrest rates for violent crimes have—with a few exceptions—continued to drop steadily in the 2000s.

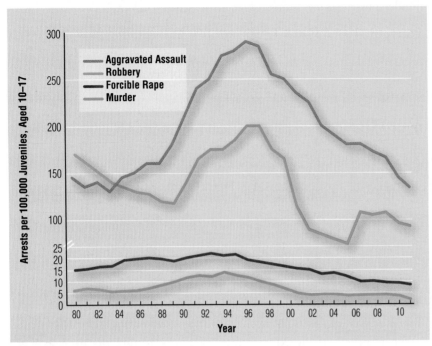

Source: Office of Juvenile Justice and Delinquency Prevention, *Statistical Briefing Book,* at **www.ojjdp.ncjrs.org/ojstatbb/crime/JAR.asp**.

13-3c

Girls in the Juvenile Justice System

Although overall rates of juvenile offending have been dropping, arrest rates for girls are declining more slowly than those for boys. Between 1997 and 2009, the number of cases involving males in delinquency courts declined 24 percent, while the female caseload in such courts declined by only 1 percent.[28] Self-reported studies show, however, that there has been little change in girls' violent behavior over the past few decades.[29] Why, then, is the presence of girls in the juvenile and criminal justice system increasing relative to their male counterparts?

A GROWING PRESENCE Although girls have for the most part been treated more harshly than boys for status offenses,[30] a "chivalry effect" (see Chapter 9) has traditionally existed in other areas of the juvenile justice system. In the past, police were likely to arrest offending boys while allowing girls to go home to the care of their families for similar behavior. This is no longer the case. According to the Office of Juvenile Justice and Delinquency Prevention, juvenile courts handled twice as many cases involving girls in 2009 as they did in 1985.[31] A particular problem area for girls appears to be the crime of assault. In 2011, females accounted for 24 percent of all juvenile arrests for aggravated assault and 36 percent of those arrests for simple assault, higher percentages than for other violent crimes.[32]

FAMILY-BASED DELINQUENCY Criminologists disagree on whether rising arrest rates for female juveniles reflect a change in behavior or a change in law enforcement practices. A significant amount of data supports the latter proposal, especially research showing that police are much more likely to make arrests in situations involving domestic violence than they were even a decade ago. Experts have found that girls are four times more apt to fight with parents or siblings than are boys, who usually engage in violent encounters with strangers. Consequently, a large percentage of female juvenile arrests for assault arise out of family disputes—arrests that until relatively recently would not have been made.[33]

Evidence also shows that law enforcement agents continue to treat girls more harshly for some status offenses. More girls than boys are arrested for the status offense of running away from home,[34] for example, even though studies show that male and female juveniles run away from home with equal frequency.[35] Criminologists who focus on issues of gender hypothesize that such behavior is considered normal for boys, but is seen as deviant for girls and therefore more deserving of punishment.[36]

13-3d

School Violence and Bullying

One Thursday morning in January 2013, sixteen-year-old Bryan Oliver walked into a science class at Taft

A police officer interviews two teenage girls who were involved in a fight in Tucson, Arizona. What are some of the reasons that the arrest rate for female juveniles has increased over the past few decades?

Photo by Scott Olson/Getty Images

a teacher at Columbine High School near Littleton, Colorado, in 1999, many schools have improved security measures. From 1999 to 2011, the percentage of American schools using security cameras to monitor their campuses increased from 19 to 61 percent. Today, 92 percent of public schools control access to school buildings by locking or monitoring their doors.[40]

Union High School in Kern County, California, with a shotgun. Oliver opened fire, wounding one student, and was later charged with premeditated attempted murder. The incident was every student's (and teacher's and parent's) worst nightmare. Like other episodes of school violence, it received heavy media coverage, fanning fears that our schools are unsafe.

SAFE SCHOOLS Research does show that juvenile victimization and delinquency rates increase during the school day, and the most common juvenile crimes, such as simple assaults, are most likely to take place on school grounds.[37] In spite of well-publicized mass shootings such as the one that took place at Sandy Hook Elementary School in Newtown, Connecticut, in December 2012, however, violent crime is not commonplace in American schools. In fact, school-age youths are more than fifty times more likely to be murdered away from school than on a campus.[38] Furthermore, between 1995 and 2011, victimization rates of students for nonfatal crimes at school declined significantly, meaning that, in general, schools are safer today than they were in the recent past.[39]

For the most part, these statistics mirror the downward trend of all criminal activity in the United States since the mid-1990s. In addition, since the fatal shootings of fourteen students and

ZERO TOLERANCE The Columbine shootings also led many schools to adopt "zero tolerance" policies when it comes to student behavior. These policies require strict punitive measures, such as suspension, expulsion, or referral to the police, for *any* breach of the school's disciplinary code. On January 2, 2013, for instance, a first-grader at Roscoe Nix Elementary School in Silver Spring, Maryland, was suspended for pointing his fingers in the shape of a gun. Finally, the increasing number of high-profile shootings on school grounds has spurred students themselves to take preventive action. Such was the case in December 2012 when students at Laurel High School in Laurel, Maryland, warned authorities about a classmate's increasingly disturbing behavior. School security searched the young man's locker, finding graphs, charts, and diagrams suggesting a future attack.

BULLIED STUDENTS According to Kern County law enforcement officials, Bryan Oliver, mentioned at the beginning of this section, did not choose his targets in the science class at random. Oliver was specifically trying to harm two students who had *bullied* him for his social awkwardness and bookishness. Broadly defined as repeated, aggressive behavior with physical (hitting, punching, and spitting) and verbal (teasing, name calling, and spreading false rumors) components, **bullying** has traditionally been seen more as an inevitable rite of passage than as deviant behavior.

In recent years, however, society has become more aware of the negative consequences of bullying, underscored by a number of high-profile "bullycides." In April 2012, for example, fourteen-year-old Kenneth Weishuhn hanged himself in the garage of his home in Primghar, Iowa, after being subjected to anti-gay slurs at South O'Brien High School. Weishuhn was at least the fifth American teenage boy to commit suicide after being bullied about his sexuality since 2009.

Bullying Overt acts taken by students with the goal of intimidating, harassing, or humiliating other students.

ANTI-BULLYING LAWS According to data gathered by the federal government, 28 percent of students aged twelve to eighteen have been victims of bullying.[41] In particular, gay students are targeted—nine out of ten report being bullied each year.[42] As a response to this problem, every state but Montana has passed anti-bullying legislation. These laws focus mostly on "soft" measures, such as training school personnel how to recognize and respond to bullying.[43] As yet, state legislatures have been reluctant to take "harder" measures such as specifically defining bullying as a crime. For instance, no criminal charges were filed against the students who repeatedly harassed Kenneth Weishuhn before his death.

CJ AND TECHNOLOGY — CYBERBULLYING

ALTHOUGH it is not clear whether bullying in general is more prevalent now than in the past, one form of bullying is definitely on the rise. As the Internet, texting, and social networking sites such as Facebook have become integral parts of youth culture, so, it seems, has cyberbullying. Studies have shown that between one-fifth and one-third of American teenagers are targets of cyberbullying, which occurs when a person uses computers, smartphones, or other electronic devices to inflict willful and repeated emotional harm.

Cyberbullying returned to the national spotlight in September 2012 when fifteen-year-old Audrie Pott of Saratoga, California, committed suicide after photos of a sexual assault in which she was the victim were disseminated via smartphone. Pott was the fourth young woman in the United States and Canada since 2009 to take her life as a result of this sort of humiliation. To many, cyberbullying can be even more devastating than "old school" bullying. Not only does the anonymity of cyberspace seem to embolden perpetrators, causing them to be more vicious than they might be in person, but, as one expert points out, when bullying occurs online, "you can't get away from it."

THINKING ABOUT CYBERBULLYING
How should the criminal justice system respond to cyberbullying, if at all?

13-4 why DO JUVENILES COMMIT CRIMES?

An influential study conducted by Professor Marvin Wolfgang and several colleagues in the early 1970s introduced the "chronic 6 percent" to criminology. The researchers found that out of one hundred boys, six will become chronic offenders, meaning that they are arrested five or more times before their eighteenth birthdays. Furthermore, Wolfgang and his colleagues determined that these chronic offenders are responsible for half of all crimes and two-thirds of all violent crimes within any given cohort (a group of persons who have similar characteristics).[44]

Does this "6 percent rule" mean that no matter what steps society takes, six out of every hundred juveniles are "bad seeds" and will act delinquently? Or does it point to a situation in which a small percentage of children may be more likely to commit crimes under certain circumstances?

Most criminologists favor the second interpretation. In this section, we will examine the four factors that have traditionally been used to explain juvenile criminal behavior and violent crime rates: age, substance abuse, family problems, and gangs. Keep in mind, however, that the factors influencing delinquency are not limited to these topics. Researchers are constantly interpreting and reinterpreting statistical evidence to provide fresh perspectives on this very important issue.

13-4a The Age-Crime Relationship

Crime statistics are fairly conclusive on one point: the older a person is, the less likely he or she will exhibit criminal behavior. Self-reported studies confirm that most people are involved in some form of criminal behavior—however "harmless"—during their early years. In fact, Terrie Moffitt of Duke University has said that "it is statistically aberrant to refrain from crime during adolescence."[45] So, why do the vast majority of us not become chronic offenders?

LO 4

AGING OUT According to many criminologists, particularly Travis Hirschi and Michael Gottfredson, any group of at-risk persons—regardless of gender, race, intelligence, or class—will commit fewer crimes as they grow older.[46] This process is known as **aging out** (or, sometimes, *desistance*, a term we first encountered in the previous chapter). Professor Robert J. Sampson and his colleague John H. Laub believe that this phenomenon is explained by certain events, such as marriage, employment, and military service, which force delinquents to "grow up" and forgo criminal acts.[47]

AGE OF ONSET Another view sees the **age of onset,** or the age at which the youth begins delinquent behavior, as a consistent predictor of future criminal behavior. One study compared recidivism rates between juveniles first judged to be delinquent before the age of fifteen and those first adjudicated delinquent after the age of fifteen. Of the seventy-one subjects who made up the first group, 32 percent became chronic offenders. Of the sixty-five who made up the second group, none became chronic offenders.[48]

Furthermore, according to the Office of Juvenile Justice and Delinquency Prevention, the earlier a youth enters the juvenile justice system, the more likely he or she will become a violent offender.[49] This research suggests that juvenile justice resources should be concentrated on the youngest offenders, with the goal of preventing crime and reducing the long-term risks for society.

13-4b Substance Abuse

As we have seen throughout this textbook, substance abuse plays a strong role in criminal behavior for adults. The same can certainly be said for juveniles. According to the University of Michigan's Institute for Social Research, 27 percent of American tenth-graders and 40 percent of American twelfth-graders are regular alcohol drinkers, increasing their risks for violent behavior, delinquency, academic problems, and unsafe sexual behavior.[50] Furthermore, regular marijuana use among high school seniors reached a thirty-year high in 2011.[51] (See Figure 13.4 on the next page for an overview of juvenile drug use in the United States.)

Aging Out A term used to explain the fact that criminal activity declines with age.

Age of Onset The age at which a juvenile first exhibits delinquent behavior.

FIGURE 13.4 Drug Use among Juveniles

Among Americans aged twelve to seventeen, the percentage who admit to using illegal drugs in the past month dropped each year from 2002 to 2008 before rising in 2009 and holding steady in the two years that followed.

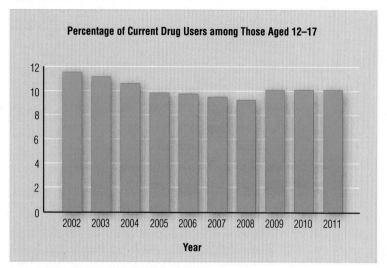

Percentage of Current Drug Users among Those Aged 12–17

Source: National Survey on Drug Use and Health, 2003–2012.

A STRONG CORRELATION As with adults, substance abuse among juveniles seems to play a major role in offending. Drug use is associated with a wide range of antisocial and illegal behaviors by juveniles, from school suspensions to large-scale theft.[52] Nearly all young offenders (94 percent) entering juvenile detention self-report drug use at some point in their lives, and 85 percent have used drugs in the previous six months.[53]

According to the Arrestee Drug Abuse Monitoring Program, nearly 60 percent of male juvenile detainees and 46 percent of female juvenile detainees test positive for drug use at the time of their offense.[54] Drug use is a particularly strong risk factor for girls: 75 percent of young women incarcerated in juvenile facilities report regular drug and alcohol use—starting at the age of fourteen—and one study found that 87 percent of female teenage offenders need substance abuse treatment.[55]

STRONG CAUSATION?
The correlation between substance abuse and offending for juveniles seems

obvious. Does this mean that substance abuse *causes* juvenile offending? Researchers make the point that most youths who become involved in antisocial behavior do so before their first experience with alcohol or drugs. Therefore, it would appear that substance abuse is a form of delinquent behavior rather than its cause.[56] Still, a recent study of adolescent offenders did find that substance abuse treatment reduces criminal behavior in the short term, suggesting that, at the least, the use of illegal drugs is an integral component of the juvenile delinquent lifestyle.[57]

13-4c
Child Abuse and Neglect

Abuse by parents also plays a substantial role in juvenile delinquency. **Child abuse** can be broadly defined as the infliction of physical or emotional damage on a child. Similar though not the same, **child neglect** refers to deprivations—of love, shelter, food, and proper care—children undergo by their parents. According to the National Survey of Children's Exposure to Violence, one in ten children in the United States experiences mistreatment at the hands of a close family member.[58]

Children in homes characterized by violence or neglect suffer from a variety of physical, emotional, and mental health problems at a much greater rate than their peers.[59] This, in turn, increases their chances of engaging in delinquent behavior. One survey of violent juveniles showed that 75 percent had been subjected to severe abuse by a family member and 80 percent had witnessed violence in their homes.[60] Nearly half of all juveniles—and 80 percent of girls—sentenced to life in prison suffered high rates of abuse.[61]

Cathy Spatz Widom, currently a professor of psychology at John Jay College of Criminal Justice, compared the arrest records of two groups of subjects—one made up of 908 cases of substantiated parental abuse and neglect and the other made up of 667 children who had not been abused or neglected. Widom found that those who had been abused or neglected were 53 percent more likely to

Child Abuse Mistreatment of children by causing physical, emotional, or sexual damage without any plausible explanation, such as an accident.

Child Neglect A form of child abuse in which the child is denied certain necessities such as shelter, food, care, and love.

be arrested as juveniles than those who had not.[62] Simply put, according to researchers Janet Currie of Columbia University and Erdal Tekin of Georgia State University, "child maltreatment roughly doubles the probability that an individual engages in many types of crime."[63]

13-4d
Gangs

When youths cannot find the stability and support they require in the family structure, they will often turn to their peers. This is just one explanation for why juveniles join **youth gangs.** Although jurisdictions may have varying definitions, for general purposes a youth gang is viewed as a group of three or more persons who (1) self-identify as an entity separate from the community by special clothing, vocabulary, hand signals, and names and (2) engage in criminal activity. According to an exhaustive survey of law enforcement agencies, there are probably around 33,000 gangs with approximately 1.4 million members in the United States.[64]

Juveniles who have experienced the risk factors discussed in this section are more likely to join a gang, and once they have done so, they are more likely to engage in delinquent and violent behavior than non-gang members.[65] Statistics show high levels of gang involvement in most violent criminal activities in the United States.[66] One-half of all murders in Chicago and one-third of all murders in Los Angeles are gang related.[67] Furthermore, a study of criminal behavior among juveniles in Seattle found that gang members were considerably more likely to commit crimes than at-risk youths who shared many characteristics with gang members but were not affiliated with any gang.

WHO JOINS GANGS? The average gang member is seventeen to eighteen years old,

though members tend to be older in cities with long traditions of gang activity such as Chicago and Los Angeles. Although it is difficult to determine with any certainty the makeup of gangs as a whole, one recent survey found that 49 percent of all gang members in the United States are Hispanic, 35 percent are African American, and 9 percent are white, with the remaining 7 percent belonging to other racial or ethnic backgrounds.[68]

Though gangs tend to have racial or ethnic characteristics—that is, one group predominates in each gang—many researchers do not believe that race or ethnicity is the dominant factor in gang membership. Instead, gang members seem to come from lower-class or working-class communities, mostly in urban areas but with an increasing number from the suburbs and rural counties. In addition, researchers are finding that adolescents who will eventually join a gang display significantly higher levels of delinquent behavior than those who will never become involved in gang activity.[69]

WHY DO YOUTHS JOIN GANGS? Gang membership often appears to be linked with status in the community. This tends to be true of both males and females. Many teenagers,

> **Youth Gang** A self-formed group of youths with several identifiable characteristics, including a gang name and other recognizable symbols, a geographic territory, and participation in illegal activities.

In Los Angeles, a gang member signifies his allegiance to the "Street Villains" through a series of elaborate tattoos. What role does identity play in a juvenile's decision to join a gang?

Kevork Djansezian/Getty Images

feeling alienated from their families and communities, join gangs for the social relationships and the sense of identity a gang can provide.

A number of youths, especially those who live in high-crime neighborhoods, see gang membership as a necessity—joining a gang is a form of protection against violence from other gangs. For example, Mara Salvatrucha (MS-13) was formed by the children of immigrants who fled the civil war of El Salvador for Los Angeles in the 1980s. Finding themselves easy prey for the established local gangs, these young Salvadorans started MS-13 as a protective measure.

Excitement is another attraction of the gang life, as is the economic incentive of enjoying the profits from illegal gang activities such as dealing drugs or robbery. Finally, some teenagers are forced to join gangs by the threat of violence from gang members.

13-5
what HAPPENS AFTER A JUVENILE IS ARRESTED ?

As part of the Juvenile Robbery Intervention Program, New York City detectives spend hours monitoring the Facebook pages and Twitter accounts of teenagers at risk for gang involvement and violent crime. Most commonly, however, contact between juvenile offenders and law enforcement takes place on the streets, initiated by a police officer on patrol who either apprehends the juvenile while he or she is committing a crime or answers a call for service. (See Figure 13.5 below for an overview of the juvenile justice process.) The youth is then passed on to an officer of the juvenile court, who must decide how to handle the case.

13-5a
Police Discretion and Juvenile Crime

Police arrest about 1.1 million youths under the age of eighteen each year. In most states, police officers must have probable cause to believe that the minor has committed an offense, just as they would if the suspect was an adult. Police power with regard to juveniles is greater than with adults, however, because police can take youths into custody for status offenses, such as possession of alcohol or truancy. In these cases, the officer is acting *in loco parentis*, or in the place of the parent. The officer's role is not necessarily to punish the youths, but to protect them from harmful behavior.

Police officers also have a great deal of discretion in deciding what to do with juveniles who have

---

FIGURE 13.5 The Juvenile Justice Process

This diagram shows the possible tracks that a young person may take after her or his first contact with the juvenile justice system (usually a police officer).

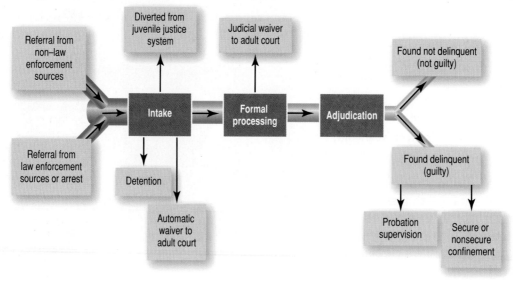

Source: Office of Juvenile Justice and Delinquency Prevention.

committed crimes or status offenses. Juvenile justice expert Joseph Goldstein labels this discretionary power **low-visibility decision making** because it relies on factors that the public is not generally in a position to understand or criticize. When a grave offense has taken place, a police officer may decide to formally arrest the juvenile, send him or her to juvenile court, or place the youth under the care of a social-service organization. In less serious situations, the officer may simply issue a warning or take the offender to the police station and release the child into the custody of her or his parents.

In making these discretionary decisions, police generally consider the following factors:

- The nature of the child's offense.
- The offender's past history of involvement with the juvenile justice system.
- The setting in which the offense took place.
- The ability and willingness of the child's parents to take disciplinary action.
- The attitude of the offender.
- The offender's race and gender.

Law enforcement officers notify the juvenile court system that a particular young person requires its attention through a process known as a **referral.** Anyone with a valid reason, including parents, relatives, welfare agencies, and school officials, can refer a juvenile to the juvenile court. The vast majority of cases in juvenile courts, however, are referred by the police.[70]

13-5b
Intake

As noted earlier, if, following arrest, a police officer feels the offender warrants the attention of the juvenile justice process, the officer will refer the youth to juvenile court. Once this step has been taken, a complaint is filed with a special division of the juvenile court, and the **intake** process begins. Intake may be followed by diversion to a community-based program, transfer to an adult court, or detention to await trial in juvenile court. Thus, intake, diversion, transfer, and detention are the four primary stages of pretrial juvenile justice procedure.

During intake, an official of the juvenile court— usually a probation officer, but sometimes a judge— must decide, in effect, what to do with the offender. The intake officer has several options during intake.

1. Simply dismiss the case, releasing the offender without taking any further action. This occurs in about one in five cases, usually because the judge cannot determine a sufficient reason to continue.[71]

2. Divert the offender to a social-services program, such as drug rehabilitation or anger management.

3. File a **petition** for a formal court hearing. The petition is the formal document outlining the charges against the juvenile.

4. Transfer the case to an adult court, where the offender will be tried as an adult.

With regard to status offenses, judges have sole discretion to decide whether to process the case or *divert* the youth to another juvenile service agency.

13-5c
Pretrial Diversion

In the early 1970s, Congress passed the first Juvenile Justice and Delinquency Prevention (JJDP) Act, which ordered the development of methods "to divert juveniles from the traditional juvenile justice system."[72] Within a few years, hundreds of diversion programs had been put into effect. Today, diversion refers to the process of removing low-risk offenders from the formal juvenile justice system by placing them in community-based rehabilitation programs.

Diversion programs vary widely, but fall into three general categories:

1. *Probation.* In this program, the juvenile is returned to the community, but placed under the supervision of a juvenile probation officer. If the youth breaks the conditions of probation, he or she can be returned to the formal juvenile system.

2. *Treatment and aid.* Many juveniles have

Low-Visibility Decision Making A term used to describe the discretionary power police have in determining what to do with misbehaving juveniles.

Referral The notification process through which a law enforcement officer or other concerned citizen makes the juvenile court aware of a juvenile's unlawful or unruly conduct.

Intake The process by which an official of the court must decide whether to file a petition, release the juvenile, or place the juvenile under some other form of supervision.

Petition The document filed with a juvenile court alleging that the juvenile is a delinquent or a status offender and requesting that the court either hear the case or transfer it to an adult court.

behavioral or medical conditions that contribute to their delinquent behavior, and many diversion programs offer remedial education, drug and alcohol treatment, and other forms of counseling to alleviate these problems.

3. *Restitution.* In these programs, the offender "repays" her or his victim, either directly or symbolically through community service.[73]

Proponents of diversion programs include many criminologists who believe that contact with the formal juvenile justice system "labels" the youth a delinquent, which leads to further delinquent behavior. (**CAREER TIP:** Increasingly, juvenile justice practitioners are relying on principles of restorative justice [see Chapter 9] to divert adolescents from formal institutions. For example, *victim-offender dialogue specialists* give juvenile offenders the opportunity to apologize directly to their victims rather than engage with the juvenile court.)

13-5d
Transfer to Adult Court

One side effect of diversionary programs is that the youths who remain in the juvenile courts are more likely to be seen as "hardened" and thus less amenable to rehabilitation. This, in turn, increases the likelihood that the offender will be transferred to an adult court, a process in which the juvenile court waives jurisdiction over the youth. As the American juvenile justice system has shifted away from ideals of treatment and toward punishment, transfer to adult court has been one of the most popular means of "getting tough" on delinquents.

Judicial Waiver The process in which the juvenile judge, based on the facts of the case at hand, decides that the alleged offender should be transferred to adult court.

Automatic Transfer The process by which a juvenile is transferred to adult court as a matter of state law.

Prosecutorial Waiver A procedure used in situations where the prosecutor has discretion to decide whether a case will be heard by a juvenile court or an adult court.

Detention The temporary custody of a juvenile in a secure facility after a petition has been filed and before the adjudicatory process begins.

TYPES OF TRANSFERS There are three types of transfer laws, and most states use more than one of them depending on the jurisdiction. Juveniles are most commonly transferred to adult courts through **judicial waiver,** in which the juvenile judge is given the power to determine whether a young offender's case will be waived to adult court. The judge makes this decision based on the offender's age, the nature of the offense, and any criminal history. All but five states employ judicial waiver.

Twenty-nine states have taken the waiver responsibility out of judicial hands through **automatic transfer,** also known as *legislative waiver.* In these states, the legislatures have designated certain conditions—usually involving serious crimes such as murder and rape—under which a juvenile case is automatically "kicked up" to adult court. In Rhode Island, for example, a juvenile aged sixteen or older with two prior felony adjudications will automatically be transferred on being accused of a third felony.[74]

Fifteen states also allow for **prosecutorial waiver,** in which prosecutors are allowed to choose whether to initiate proceedings in juvenile or criminal court when certain age and offense conditions are met.

INCIDENCE OF TRANSFER Each year, about 8,000 delinquency cases are waived to adult criminal court—less than 0.5 percent of all cases that reach juvenile court.[75] As we saw earlier in the chapter, those juveniles who commit the most violent felonies are the most likely to be transferred. For example, when she was thirteen years old, Tyasia Jackson was arrested for killing her two-year-old stepsister Sasha Ray in Waldrop Trail, Georgia. Under state law, prosecutors have the discretion to charge thirteen-year-olds who have committed capital crimes either as juveniles or as adults.[76] In this case, given that Jackson stabbed Ray seven times and then left her in the backyard of their family home, prosecutors decided that the defendant warranted transfer to adult court.

13-5e
Detention

Once the decision has been made that the offender will face adjudication in a juvenile court, the intake official must decide what to do with him or her until the start of the trial. Generally, the juvenile is released into the custody of parents or a guardian—most jurisdictions favor this practice in lieu of setting money bail for youths. The intake officer may also place the offender in **detention,** or temporary custody in a secure facility, until the disposition

JOB DESCRIPTION:

- Provide safety, security, custodial care, discipline, and guidance for youths held in juvenile correctional facilities.

- Play a critical role in the rehabilitation of youthful offenders and, as a result, have a potentially great impact on their success during and after incarceration.

WHAT KIND OF TRAINING IS REQUIRED?

- A bachelor's degree in human services, behavioral science, or a related field.

- Professional and respectful communication skills and a commitment and dedication to the needs of adolescent offenders and their families.

ANNUAL SALARY RANGE?

- $33,000–$52,000

SOCIAL MEDIA CAREER TIP

Potential employers want information about you, but they do not want your life story. To capitalize on two primary benefits of social media, personalize your message and be concise.

Lisa F. Young/iStockphoto

process begins. Once a juvenile has been detained, most jurisdictions require that a **detention hearing** be held within twenty-four hours. During this hearing, the offender has several due process safeguards, including the right to counsel, the right against self-incrimination, and the right to cross-examine and confront witnesses.

In justifying its decision to detain, the court will usually address one of three issues:

1. Whether the child poses a danger to the community.

2. Whether the child will return for the adjudication process.

3. Whether detention will provide protection for the child.

The Supreme Court upheld the practice of preventive detention (see Chapter 8) for juveniles in *Schall v. Martin* (1984)[77] by ruling that youths can be detained if they are deemed a "risk" to the safety of the community or to their own welfare. Partly as a

result, the number of detained juveniles increased by 29 percent between 1985 and 2009.[78]

13-6

how ARE JUVENILES TRIED AND PUNISHED?

In just over half of all referred cases, the juvenile is eventually subject to formal proceedings in juvenile court.[79] As noted earlier, changes in the juvenile justice system since *In re Gault* (1967) have led many to contend that juvenile courts have become indistinguishable, both theoretically and practically, from adult courts.[80] Just over half of the states, for example, permit juveniles to request a jury trial under certain circumstances. Juvenile justice proceedings may still be distinguished from the

> **Detention Hearing** A hearing to determine whether a juvenile should be detained, or remain detained, while waiting for the adjudicatory process to begin.

adult system of criminal justice, however, and these differences are evident in the adjudication and disposition of the juvenile trial.

13-6a
Adjudication

During the adjudication stage of the juvenile justice process, a hearing is held to determine whether the offender is delinquent or in need of some form of court supervision. Most state juvenile codes dictate a specific set of procedures that must be followed during the **adjudicatory hearing,** with the goal of providing the respondent with "the essentials of due process and fair treatment." Consequently, the respondent in an adjudicatory hearing has the right to notice of charges, counsel, and confrontation and cross-examination, and the privilege against self-incrimination. Furthermore, "proof beyond a reasonable doubt" must be

Adjudicatory Hearing The process through which a juvenile court determines whether there is sufficient evidence to support the initial petition.

established to find the child delinquent. When the child admits guilt—that is, admits to the charges of the initial petition—the judge must ensure that the admission was voluntary.

At the close of the adjudicatory hearing, the judge is generally required to rule on the legal issues and evidence that have been presented. Based on this ruling, the judge determines whether the respondent is delinquent or in need of court supervision. Alternatively, the judge can dismiss the case based on a lack of evidence. It is important to remember that finding a child delinquent is *not* the same as convicting an adult of a crime. A delinquent does not face the same restrictions imposed on adult convicts in some states, such as limits on the right to vote and to run for political office (discussed in Chapter 11).

13-6b
Disposition

Once a juvenile has been adjudicated delinquent, the judge must decide what steps will be taken

CAREERPREP
JUVENILE DETENTION OFFICER

JOB DESCRIPTION:

- Oversee the detention of juvenile offenders being held in temporary custody before the adjudicatory process begins. Observe the behavior of and, when necessary, counsel the juvenile offenders to ensure their safety during the detention period.

- Maintain personal relationships with the juvenile offenders so as to supervise their progress in educational, recreational, and therapeutic activities while housed at the detention center.

WHAT KIND OF TRAINING IS REQUIRED?

- A high school diploma plus at least three years of work experience involving children of school age (seven to seventeen years) or one year of college education for each year of experience lacking.

- Physical agility and strength, as well as a firm manner in dealing with juveniles who may present severe disciplinary problems.

ANNUAL SALARY RANGE?

- $29,000 to $62,000

PhotoDisc

toward treatment and/or punishment. Most states provide for a *bifurcated* process in which a separate **disposition hearing** follows the adjudicatory hearing. Depending on state law, the juvenile may be entitled to counsel at the disposition hearing.

SENTENCING JUVENILES In an adult trial, the sentencing phase is primarily concerned with the needs of the community to be protected from the convict. In contrast, a juvenile judge uses the disposition hearing to determine a sentence that will serve the needs of the child. For assistance in this crucial process, the judge will order the probation department to gather information on the juvenile and present it in the form of a **predisposition report.** The report usually contains information concerning the respondent's family background, the facts surrounding the delinquent act, and interviews with social workers, teachers, and other important figures in the child's life.

JUDICIAL DISCRETION In keeping with the rehabilitative tradition of the juvenile justice system, juvenile judges generally have a great deal of discretion in choosing one of several disposition possibilities. A judge can tend toward leniency, delivering only a stern reprimand or warning before releasing the juvenile into the custody of parents or other legal guardians. Otherwise, the choice is among incarceration in a juvenile correctional facility, probation, or community treatment.

In most cases, the seriousness of the offense is the primary factor used in determining whether to incarcerate a juvenile, though history of delinquency, family situation, and the offender's attitude are all relevant. (**CAREER TIP:** Many *juvenile court judges* are elected to their posts, meaning that, like their counterparts in the adult criminal justice system, these judges face the pressures of public opinion in dealing with juvenile offenders.)

13-6c
Juvenile Corrections

In general, juvenile corrections are based on the concept of **graduated sanctions**—that is, the severity of the punishment should fit the crime. Consequently, status and first-time offenders are diverted or placed on probation, repeat offenders find themselves in intensive community supervision or treatment programs, and serious and violent offenders are placed in correctional facilities.

As society's expectations of the juvenile justice system have changed, so have the characteristics of its corrections programs. In some cities, for example, juvenile probation officers join police officers on the beat. Because the former are not bound by the same search and seizure restrictions as other law enforcement officials, this interdepartmental teamwork provides more opportunities to fight youth crime aggressively. Juvenile correctional facilities are also changing their operations to reflect public mandates that they should both reform and punish. Also, note that about 6,000 juveniles are in adult jails and another 25,000 are serving time in adult prisons.[81]

JUVENILE PROBATION The most common form of juvenile corrections is probation—33 percent of all delinquency cases disposed of by juvenile courts result in conditional diversion. The majority of all adjudicated delinquents (60 percent) will never receive a disposition more severe than being placed on probation.[82] These statistics reflect a general understanding among juvenile court judges and other officials that a child should normally be removed from her or his home only as a last resort.

The organization of juvenile probation is very similar to adult probation (see Chapter 10), and juvenile probationers are increasingly subjected to electronic monitoring and other supervisory tactics. The main difference between the two programs lies in the attitude toward the offender. Adult probation officers have an overriding responsibility to protect the community from the probationer, while juvenile probation officers are expected to take the role of a mentor or a concerned relative in looking after the needs of the child. (**CAREER TIP:** *Juvenile probation officers* earn an

Disposition Hearing Similar to the sentencing hearing for adults, a hearing in which the juvenile judge or officer decides the appropriate punishment for a youth found to be delinquent or a status offender.

Predisposition Report A report prepared during the disposition process that provides the judge with relevant background material to aid in the disposition decision.

Graduated Sanctions The practical theory in juvenile corrections that a delinquent or status offender should receive a punishment that matches in seriousness the severity of the wrongdoing.

Juvenile inmates prepare to enter a dormitory at Texas's Marlin Orientation and Assessment Unit. What might be some of the reasons that juvenile correctional facilities often operate similarly to adult prisons and jails?

Michael Ainsworth/*Dallas Morning News*/Corbis

average salary of $45,000 and usually have caseloads of about 50 young clients.)

CONFINING JUVENILES About 70,000 American youths (down from approximately 107,000 in 1995) are incarcerated in public and private juvenile correctional facilities in the United States.[83] Most of these juveniles have committed crimes against people or property, but a significant number (about 15 percent) have been incarcerated for technical violations of their probation or parole agreements.[84] After deciding that a juvenile needs to be confined, the judge has two sentencing options: nonsecure juvenile institutions and secure juvenile institutions.

Residential Treatment Program A government-run facility for juveniles whose offenses are not deemed serious enough to warrant incarceration in a training school.

Boot Camp A variation on traditional shock incarceration in which juveniles (and some adults) are sent to secure confinement facilities modeled on military basic training camps instead of prison or jail.

Nonsecure Confinement Some juvenile delinquents do not require high levels of control and can be placed in **residential treatment programs.** These programs, run by either probation departments or social-services departments, allow their subjects freedom of move-

ment in the community. Generally, this freedom is predicated on the juveniles following certain rules, such as avoiding alcoholic beverages and returning to the facility for curfew. Residential treatment programs can be divided into four categories:

1. *Foster care programs,* in which the juveniles live with a couple who act as surrogate parents.

2. *Group homes,* which generally house between twelve and fifteen youths and provide treatment, counseling, and education services by a professional staff.

3. *Family group homes,* which combine aspects of foster care and group homes, meaning that a single family, rather than a group of professionals, looks after the needs of the young offenders.

4. *Rural programs,* which include wilderness camps, farms, and ranches where between thirty and fifty children are placed in an environment that provides recreational activities and treatment programs.

Secure Confinement Secure facilities are comparable to the adult prisons and jails we discussed in Chapters 11 and 12. These institutions go by a confusing array of names depending on the state in which they are located, but the two best known are boot camps and training schools. A **boot camp** is the juvenile variation of shock probation.

As we noted in Chapter 10, boot camps are modeled after military training for new recruits. Boot camp programs are based on the theory that by giving wayward youths a taste of the "hard life" of military-like training for short periods of time, usually no longer than 180 days, they will be "shocked" out of a life of crime. New York's Camp Monterey Shock Incarceration Facility is typical of the boot camp experience. Inmates are grouped in platoons and live in dormitories. They spend eight hours a day training, drilling, and doing hard labor, and also participate in programs such as basic adult education and job skills training.[85]

TRAINING SCHOOLS No juvenile correctional facility is called a "prison." This does not mean they lack a strong resemblance to prisons. The facilities that most closely mimic the atmosphere at an adult correctional facility are **training schools,** alternatively known as youth camps, youth development centers, industrial schools, and several other similar titles. Whatever the name, these institutions claim to differ from their adult countparts by offering a variety of programs to treat and rehabilitate the young offenders. In reality, training schools are plagued by many of the same problems as adult prisons and jails, including high levels of inmate-on-inmate violence, substance abuse, gang wars, and overcrowding.

AFTERCARE Juveniles leave correctional facilities through an early release program or because they have served the length of their sentences. Juvenile corrections officials recognize that many of these children, like adults, need assistance readjusting to the outside world. Consequently, released juveniles are often placed in **aftercare** programs.

Based on the same philosophy that drives the prisoner reentry movement (discussed in the previous chapter), aftercare programs are designed to offer services for the juveniles, while at the same time supervising them to reduce the chances of recidivism. The ideal aftercare program includes community support groups, aid in finding and keeping employment, and continued monitoring to ensure that the juvenile is able to deal with the demands of freedom. (**CAREER TIP:** *Aftercare coordinators help juvenile offenders during the critical transitional period immediately after discharge from a youth correctional facility, when old temptations, acquaintances, and stresses pose the greatest threat to rehabilitation.*)

Training School A correctional institution for juveniles found to be delinquent or status offenders.

Aftercare The variety of therapeutic, educational, and counseling programs made available to juvenile delinquents (and some adults) after they have been released from a correctional facility.

Two young inmates learn how to make wooden children's chairs during a woodworking class at a state Juvenile Justice Department lockup in Mart, Texas. Why is it crucial that juvenile delinquents receive job skills training while incarcerated?

AP Photo/*Waco Tribune Herald,* Jerry Larson

REVIEW

✔ **Review what you've read with the quiz below.**

Rip out the Chapter Review card at the back of this book, which includes:
- Chapter Summary and Learning Outcomes
- Key Terms

Or you can go online to CourseMate at www.cengagebrain.com to:
- Complete Practice Quizzes to prepare for tests.
- Review Key Terms Flash Cards (online or print).
- Play games to master concepts.

quiz

1. At its inception, the American juvenile justice system was guided by the principles of *parens patriae,* which holds that the _____ has a responsibility to look after children when their parents cannot do so.

2. When a juvenile engages in wrongdoing that would not be a crime if done by an adult, she or he has committed a _____ _____.

3. The U.S. Supreme Court relied on the concept of "diminished culpability" when, in 2005, it prohibited the _____ _____ for offenders who were juveniles when they committed their crimes.

4. Experts rely on the concept of _____ _____ to explain why young people commit fewer offenses as they grow older.

5. Youth who become involved in _____ are more likely to engage in criminal activity than those who do not.

6. If the circumstances are serious enough, a police officer can formally _____ an offending juvenile.

7. In less serious circumstances, a police officer can _____ the juvenile to the juvenile court system.

8. If a juvenile court judge believes that the seriousness of the offense so warrants, he or she can transfer the juvenile into the adult court system through a process called judicial _____.

9. A juvenile offender's delinquency is determined during the _____ hearing, which is similar in many ways to an adult trial.

10. If the juvenile is found to be delinquent, her or his sentence is determined during the _____ hearing.

Answers can be found on the Chapter 13 Review card at the end of the book.

Carline Jean/*Sun Sentinel*/MCT via Getty Images

WHY CHOOSE?

Every 4LTR Press solution comes complete with a visually engaging textbook in addition to an interactive eBook. Go to CourseMate for **CJ** to begin using the eBook. Access at **www.cengagebrain.com**

Complete the Speak Up
survey in CourseMate at
www.cengagebrain.com

 Follow us at
www.facebook.com/4ltrpress

©iStockphoto.com/A-Digit | © Cengage Learning 2011

Learning **OUTCOMES** | *After studying this chapter, you will be able to . . .*

1 Explain how the U.S. Supreme Court has interpreted the Second Amendment's right to "bear arms."

2 Identify three important trends in international terrorism.

3 Distinguish cyber crime from "traditional" crime.

4 Outline the three major reasons why the Internet is conducive to the dissemination of child pornography.

5 Indicate some of the ways that white-collar crime is different from violent or property crime.

TODAY'S CHALLENGES IN CRIMINAL JUSTICE 14

Bad Day at Sandy Hook

As a student at Newtown High School in Newtown, Connecticut, Adam Lanza was under constant watch by teachers, counselors, and security officers. "At that point in his life, he posed no threat to anyone else," remembers one staff member. "We were worried about him being the victim [of bullying] or that he could hurt himself." Classmates also noticed Lanza's odd behavior, which included carrying a black briefcase to school and wearing a "uniform" of khakis and a shirt buttoned to the neck. Lanza "was always very nervous and socially awkward" and "it appeared physically difficult for him to speak," remarked a fellow student.

By late 2012, Lanza's behavior had become so erratic that his mother Nancy was reportedly preparing to commit him to a psychiatric institution. She never got the chance. On the morning of December 14, 2012, Lanza—now twenty years old—fatally shot Nancy at their home. Dressed in black combat gear, he then drove her car to Sandy Hook Elementary School. Armed with a .223 Bushmaster semiautomatic rifle and two automatic pistols, Lanza broke into Sandy Hook and, in a matter of minutes, shot and killed six adults and twenty schoolchildren between the ages of five and ten. He then ended his own life with a bullet to his head.

Afterwards, many wondered how Lanza could have gotten his hands on such weaponry. Under federal law, it is illegal to sell or transfer a firearm to a person who has been officially designated as "mentally defective." Despite widespread concerns about his behavior, however, Lanza had never been "red-flagged" by a mental health care professional. Furthermore, Nancy Lanza had legally purchased all the guns used by her son to commit his murders. Under existing law, then, it seems little could have been done to prevent the tragedy. "Adam Lanza has been a weird kid since we were five years old," wrote a neighbor on Twitter afterwards. "As horrible as this was, I can't say I'm surprised."

Connecticut State police officers lead shocked residents away from the scene of Adam Lanza's shooting spree at Sandy Hook Elementary School in Newtown, Connecticut, on December 14, 2012.

Don Emmert/AFP/Getty Images

14-1
what IS THE DEBATE OVER GUN CONTROL?

After Adam Lanza's shooting spree in Newtown, Connecticut, the debate over **gun control,** or the policies that the government implements to regulate firearm ownership, revived along predictable lines. Advocates of more restrictive gun control argued that fewer guns available to fewer people would reduce the likelihood of such massacres. Advocates of gun rights argued the opposite, claiming that more guns were needed to defend citizens against deranged criminals such as Lanza.

According to the Congressional Research Service, there are about 310 million firearms in the United States, not counting weapons on military bases.[1] Legal ownership of guns is widespread in this country, with almost one-third of American households possessing at least one gun.[2] The vast majority of gun owners are law-abiding citizens who use firearms for self-protection or recreational activities.

At the same time, about 31,000 people are killed by gunfire in the United States each year, and firearms are used in 68 percent of the nation's murders and 41 percent of its robberies.[3] Furthermore, illegally obtained firearms are a constant concern for law enforcement officials and, apparently, many citizens. One national poll conducted several weeks after Lanza's violent outburst found that about two of every three Americans favored measures to limit gun sales.[4]

14-1a
Regulating Gun Ownership

The Second Amendment to the U.S. Constitution states, "A well regulated Militia, being necessary to the security of a free State, the right of the people to keep and bear Arms, shall not be infringed." The United States Supreme Court has tried to clarify this somewhat unclear language. Over the course of two separate rulings, the Court has stated that the Second Amendment provides individuals with a constitutional right to bear arms and that this right must be recognized at all levels of government—federal, state, and local.[5]

1 LO

BACKGROUND CHECKS In both cases, the Supreme Court emphasized that, to promote public safety, the government could continue to prohibit certain individuals—such as criminals and the mentally ill—from legally purchasing firearms. The primary method for doing so in the United States involves **background checks** of individuals who purchase firearms from licensed gun dealers.

The mechanics of background checks are regulated by the Brady Handgun Violence Prevention Act.[6] Known as the Brady Bill, the legislation requires a person wishing to purchase a gun from a licensed firearms dealer to *apply* for the privilege of doing so. This application process includes a background check by a law enforcement agency, usually the Federal Bureau of Investigation (FBI). The applicant can be prohibited from purchasing a firearm if his or her record contains, for example, a previous felony conviction, or evidence of illegal drug addiction, or designation as a "mental defective."[7]

PROGRAM EFFECTIVENESS Annually, the FBI conducts about 6 million background checks for potential firearms purchasers and rejects about 70,000 applications (a denial rate of approximately 1 percent).[8] Critics of the process believe that far too many ineligible consumers are able to buy guns. The problem, they point out, is that the database of criminal and mental health records used by the FBI is woefully inadequate, and therefore does not effectively screen out ex-convicts and "mental defectives."[9]

To cite one well-known example, in 2005 a Virginia state judge declared Virginia Tech student Seung-Hui Cho mentally ill. The state did not, however, submit Cho's name to the FBI, as required by federal law. Consequently, Cho was able to pass a background check and purchase several handguns. On April 16, 2007, Cho used the weapons to kill thirty-two people and injure seventeen others on the Virginia Tech campus in Blacksburg.

LEGISLATIVE EFFORTS The Brady Bill has also been criticized for requiring background checks only for those consumers who purchase guns from federally

---

Gun Control Efforts by a government to regulate or control the sale of firearms.

Background Checks An investigation of a person's history to determine whether that person should be allowed a certain privilege, such as the ability to possess a firearm.

A customer examines the merchandise at the National Armory gun store in Pompano Beach, Florida. Do you think potential gun buyers should be required to pass a firearms safety test as a condition of their purchase? Why or why not?

Joe Raedle/Getty Images

licensed firearms dealers. It does not cover purchases made at gun shows or from private citizens, which cover between 30 and 40 percent of the market.

In the aftermath of the massacre at Sandy Hook Elementary School, the U.S. Senate considered a bill to expand background checks for gun buyers. The proposed legislation would also have banned certain semiautomatic weapons, which can rapidly fire multiple rounds, and the high-capacity ammunition clips that allow them to do so. In April 2013, the Senate defeated these measures.[10]

Thus, it has been left to the individual states to pass strict gun control measures, if their residents and politicians choose to do so. Seven states, for example, have banned new sales of military-style assault weapons. In Maryland, potential handgun buyers must pass a background check, submit their fingerprints to the state government, and undergo firearms training in a classroom and on a target range.[11] **(CAREER TIP:** In states like Maryland, experts called *certified handgun instructors* administer firearms training to those individuals who want a gun permit.)

14-1b
Debating Gun Control

Critics of our nation's gun laws have been disappointed that high-profile shooting such as those carried out by Adam Lanza, James Holmes (see Chapter 2), and Jared Loughner (see Chapter 8) have not led to greater gun control. These critics reject the notion that guns are needed for self-protection. Less than 1 percent of all gun deaths involve self-defense, with the rest being accidents, suicides, and homicides.[12] Furthermore, if fully automatic weapons such as machines guns are illegal, why should individuals be allowed to use semiautomatic weapons? According to one editorial, the .223 Bushmaster used by Lanza is designed only for mass slaughter and "does not belong in private hands."[13]

Opponents of stricter gun control laws reject the notion that firearms themselves are to blame for violent crime. Said one gun seller, "That's like pointing a finger at Ford and blaming them for car deaths."[14] Opponents also contend that gun control laws do not decrease crime, for the simple reason that someone who is going to commit a crime with a gun is probably going to obtain that firearm illegally. Consequently, stricter gun control would "prevent only law-abiding citizens from owning handguns."[15] Furthermore, as discussed in Chapter 2, violent crime is at historically low levels in the United States, leading many to reject the argument that the country needs to change its gun laws.[16]

14-2
what THREATS ARE POSED BY INTERNATIONAL TERRORISM?

In the first chapter of this textbook, we defined terrorism as the use of violence in furtherance of political or social objectives. Today, the dominant

On April 16, 2013, a suicide bombing at a campaign rally in Peshawar, Pakistan, claimed nine lives. The attack was intended to disrupt the country's political process. Explain why such acts of violence are considered "terrorism."

A. Majeed/AFP/Getty Images

strain of terrorism mixes political goals with very strong religious affiliations. Modern terrorism is also characterized by extreme levels of violence. The January 24, 2011, suicide bombing at Russia's busiest airport in Moscow killed at least 35 people and injured 150 more. The three-day November 2008 raid on the financial district of Mumbai, India, left 173 dead and more than 300 wounded. And, of course, the September 11, 2001, attacks on New York and Washington, D.C., claimed nearly 3,000 lives. Indeed, the power of terrorism is a direct result of the fear caused by this violence—not only the fear that such atrocities will be repeated, but also that next time, they will be much worse.

14-2a
The Global Context of Terrorism

Generally, terrorist acts are not the acts of nations or legally appointed governments. Rather, terror is the realm of **nonstate actors,** free of control by or allegiance to any nation, who use violence to further their own goals. At the same time, as David A. Westbrook of the University at Buffalo (New York) points out, the large scale and financial resources of some modern terrorist organizations make them as powerful as many nations, if not more so.[17]

Nonstate Actor An entity that plays a role in international affairs but does not represent any established state or nation.

In addition, the high body counts associated with the worst terrorist acts seem better described in terms of war than of crime, which in most cases involves two people—the criminal and the victim. Thus, perhaps the most satisfying description of terrorism is as a "supercrime" that incorporates many of the characteristics of international warfare.[18] Indeed, it often seems that the United States is "at war" with al Qaeda, the organization responsible for the September 11, 2001, attacks against this country.

AL QAEDA VERSUS THE UNITED STATES On May 1, 2011, a team of U.S. Navy Seals in helicopters descended on a three-story house in Abbottabad, a town located about thirty miles northeast of Islamabad, the capital of Pakistan. Forty minutes later, they left with the body of Osama bin Laden, whom they had killed after a shootout with his bodyguards. "Justice has been done," said President Obama, echoing the sentiments of many Americans for whom the event marked a symbolic triumph in the struggle against international terrorism.[19]

The Issue of *Jihad* Osama bin Laden's al Qaeda organization grew out of a network of volunteers who migrated to Afghanistan in the 1980s to rid that country of foreign occupiers. (Ironically, in light of later events, bin Laden and his comrades received significant American financial aid.) For bin Laden, these efforts took the form of *jihad*, a controversial term that also has been the subject of much confusion.

Contrary to what many think, *jihad* does not mean "holy war." Rather, it refers to three kinds of struggle, or exertion, required of the Muslim faithful: (1) the struggle against the evil in oneself, (2) the struggle against the evil outside oneself, and (3) the struggle against nonbelievers.[20] Many Muslims believe that this struggle can be achieved without violence and denounce the form of *jihad* practiced by al Qaeda. Clearly, however, bin Laden and his followers rejected the notion that *jihad* can be accomplished through peaceable efforts.

Osama bin Laden and al Qaeda In the 1990s, bin Laden began to turn his attention to the United States, and al Qaeda set its sights on American interests abroad. In 1998, for example, the organization bombed two U.S. embassies in Africa, killing 231 people. Two years later, al Qaeda agents launched a suicide attack on the U.S.S. *Cole*, a Navy destroyer docked in Aden, a port in the small Middle Eastern country of Yemen, during which seventeen U.S. sailors died.

About a year after the September 11, 2001, attacks, bin Laden wrote a letter to the American people outlining the reasons behind al Qaeda's opposition to the U.S. government. These included American support for Israel, which is widely seen as an enemy to Muslims, and U.S. exploitation of Islamic countries for their oil. Furthermore, bin Laden criticized the presence of U.S. military forces in the Middle East, "spreading your ideology and thereby polluting the hearts of our people."[21]

A Continuing Threat Two years before his death, Osama bin Laden boasted that his disciples would "continue *jihad* for another seven years, seven years after that, and even seven years more after."[22] A year after bin Laden's death, however, Matthew Olsen, the director of the National Counterterrorism Center, said that the "core al Qaeda," which operates out of Pakistan, "was at its weakest point in the last ten years."[23] More than half of the group's leaders had been killed by American military raids and drone strikes, and its members were focused more on survival than on planning large-scale terrorist operations.[24]

Weakened as it may be, al Qaeda is still a formidable organization. It now relies on a loose affiliation of franchises that operate in Iraq, Yemen, Somalia,

Nigeria, and other nations—"more of a McDonald's . . . than a General Motors," in the words of one expert.[25] For example, an al Qaeda spinoff operating out of Algeria has been linked with the killings of four Americans in Benghazi, Libya, on September 11, 2012. In April 2013, Canadian authorities foiled an alleged plot to bomb a passenger train supported by al Qaeda elements in Iran. Overall, al Qaeda affiliates conducted more operations in the year after bin Laden's death than they did in the final year of his life.[26] (See Figure 14.1 on the next page for a description of some of al Qaeda's "franchises.")

Self-Radicalization Despite heavy activity by al Qaeda splinter groups near their home bases in the Middle East, one U.S. official says that is it "really hard to imagine" one of them "gathering together the resources, the talent, and the money to mount another 9/11-type of attack."[27] As an alternative, al Qaeda propagandists use the Internet to try to recruit "lonely people who are looking for a cause."[28]

Such was certainly the case with Major Nidal Hasan, a U.S. Army psychiatrist who fatally shot thirteen people in Fort Hood, Texas, in 2009. Hasan was influenced by the online writings of Anwar al-Awlaki, a radical U.S.-born cleric affiliated with al Qaeda in the Arabian Peninsula. (Al-Awlaki was killed by an American drone strike in Yemen several years ago.) In turn, Hasan is held up as a positive example in a video produced by the "core" al Qaeda in Pakistan called "You Are Only Responsible for Yourself." This video urges Muslims in the United States and Europe to stage terrorist attacks without orders from foreign operatives.[29]

"Self-radicalized" terrorists such as Nidal Hasan have the ability to operate under law enforcement's radar up until the moment they strike. This ability is often used as justification for preventive policing, described in Chapter 5, which relies on informants and undercover agents to stop homegrown terrorist plots before they develop. Such tactics can be effective on the international level as well. Several years ago, for example, a double agent posing as a suicide bomber managed to infiltrate al Qaeda in the Arabian Peninsula. When, in 2012, this agent was given a mission to destroy a U.S.-bound airplane with a bomb to be hidden in his clothing, he delivered the explosive device to American intelligence agents instead.[30]

TERRORISM TRENDS FOR THE FUTURE Smaller operations involving American-born terrorists influenced by international sources reflect several trends identified by homeland security expert Brian M. Jenkins. Each of these trends de-emphasizes the importance of any single, dominant organization such as al Qaeda:[31]

LO 2

1. *Terrorists have developed more efficient methods of financing their operations* through avenues such as Internet fund-raising, drug trafficking, and money laundering schemes.

2. *Terrorists have developed more efficient organizations* based on the small-business model, in which individuals are responsible for different tasks including recruiting, planning, propaganda, and social services such as supporting the families of suicide bombers. These "employees" do not answer to a single leader but rather function as a network that is quick to adjust and difficult to infiltrate.

3. *Terrorists have exploited new communications technology to mount global campaigns,* relying on the Internet for immediate, direct communication among operatives and as a crucial recruiting tool. Furthermore, large numbers of "jihobbyists" are operating online, disseminating extremist writings and videos and using social media to spread the terrorist message in cyberspace.

As you may have noted, each of these trends favors the global terrorism movement. Indeed, Jenkins finds that today's *jihadists* are dangerous, resilient survivors who have achieved some strategic results and are determined to continue attacking their enemies. "Destroying their terrorist enterprise," he concludes, "will take years."[32] (**CAREER TIP:** Federal law enforcement agencies are in dire need of *Middle East specialists* to gather intelligence about terrorist activities abroad and, more generally, to help government officials better understand the political and religious complexities of the region.)

FIGURE 14.1 Al Qaeda's Global Partners

The Islamist groups described in this figure are loosely affiliated with the "original" al Qaeda. They have a number of different goals, showing the diversity of international terrorist groups that base themselves in the Middle East.

GROUP	GOALS	HIGH-PROFILE ACTIVITY
A. Al Qaeda in Islamic Maghreb (AQIM)	Remove Algeria's government, attack U.S.	In 2007, detonated car bombs outside the Algerian prime minister's office and several police stations—the blasts killed more than 30 and wounded more than 150.
B. Al Qaeda in Iraq (AQI)	Harass American military in Iraq; oust elected Iraqi government.	Destabilizes Iraqi society with numerous suicide bombing attacks on U.S. military personnel and local civilians.
C. Al Qaeda in the Arabian Peninsula (AQAP)	Establish safe haven for like-minded terrorists in Yemen.	Trained underwear suicide bomber, who attempted to destroy a Northwest Airlines flight to Detroit in 2009, shipped packages containing bombs to Jewish religious centers in Chicago in 2010.
D. Al Shabaab	Establish Islamic law in Somalia.	In 2010, set off bombs in two Ugandan bars that were screening soccer's World Cup tournament, killing at least 70 people.
E. Lashkar-e-Taiba	Establish Islamic rule in India; unite Muslims in region.	Launched three days of coordinated attacks in Mumbai, India, in 2008, killing 164 and wounding 308.

ON December 25, 2009, Umar Abdulmutallab boarded Northwest Flight 253 from Amsterdam to Detroit with a bomb hidden in his underwear. Abdulmutallab's suicide mission failed largely thanks to the bomb's failure to detonate. The explosive device did not trigger the airport metal detector he passed through because it was not made of metal. Instead, it was fashioned out of plastic, the apparent creation of a bomb maker associated with al Qaeda in the Arabian Peninsula (AQAP) named Ibrahim al-Asiri. In response, the Transportation Security Administration (TSA) has installed full-body scanners at nearly two hundred airports in the United States. These scanners, at least theoretically, are better able to detect nonmetallic explosives.

There are indications, however, that the body scanners have not dissuaded AQAP's efforts to get explosives onto American airliners. Two years after Abdulmutallab's failed attempt, federal agents uncovered a more sophisticated version of the original underwear bomb, thanks to the undercover agent mentioned previously who had infiltrated AQAP in Yemen. Furthermore, some U.S. intelligence agents believe that al-Asiri is working on a bomb that would be surgically implanted in the body of a suicidal subject. "The idea is to insert the device in the terrorist's love handle," said one government source. Though seemingly far-fetched, such reports raise the uncomfortable specter of explosive devices that the TSA is unable to detect.

Photo by David L. Ryan/*The Boston Globe* via Getty Images

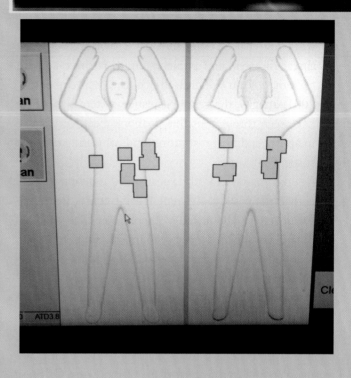

THINKING ABOUT THE "BODY BOMB"
Recognizing the possibility that potential suicide bombers may be able to get dangerous devices on airplanes without being detected, the TSA has trained some security screeners in the art of the "chat down." These screeners should be able to spot passengers who are security risks by their facial expressions, body language, and speech patterns. What are some of the potential benefits and drawbacks of this form of airport security?

14-2b

Terrorists in Court

On the morning of September 12, 2001, al Qaeda spokesman Sulaiman Abu Ghaith stood by the side of his father-in-law, Osama bin Laden, and celebrated the previous day's attacks against the United States. Almost twelve years later, in February 2013, American agents arrested Abu Ghaith in the Middle Eastern country of Jordan. Abu Ghaith was immediately brought to a federal court in New York City, where he pleaded not guilty to charges of conspiring to kill Americans.

A number of politicians disagreed with this strategy, arguing that Abu Ghaith should be treated as a military prisoner and, in the words of Kentucky Republican Senator Mitch McConnell, "interrogated without having to overcome the objections of his civilian lawyers."[33] The debate over "what to do" with suspected terrorists has divided American lawmakers for more than a decade and appears set to continue well into the future.

THE CRIMINAL JUSTICE MODEL Under the *criminal justice model* of homeland security, terrorism is treated like any other crime. That is, the law enforcement, court, and corrections systems work together to deter terrorist activity through the threat of arrest and punishment, as is the case with Sulaiman Abu Ghaith. Since the September 11, 2001, attacks, the criminal justice system has, as we have seen throughout this textbook, been very active in apprehending, prosecuting, and convicting terrorist suspects.

From 2001 to 2011, nearly 500 individuals were convicted in sixty different federal courts in thirty-seven states. About 220 of these defendants violated federal laws related directly to international terrorism such as the use of *weapons of mass destruction* and conspiracy to murder Americans in foreign countries.[34] (**Weapon of mass destruction** is an umbrella term used to cover deadly instruments that represent a significant threat to persons or property.) At the end of 2012, the Federal Bureau of Prisons was holding 362 people convicted in terrorism-related cases. Of these inmates, 269 were found guilty in connection with international terrorism.[35]

THE MILITARY MODEL From 2001 to 2009, the administration of President George W. Bush made it clear that, besides the criminal justice model, there was a parallel response to the terrorist threat: the *military model*. Although the scope of this textbook does not include U.S. military actions in Afghanistan, Iraq, and other global "hot spots," the militarization of the fight against terrorists did lead to several developments with repercussions for the criminal justice system.

Under President Bush, the U.S. Department of Defense was authorized to designate certain terrorist suspects detained during the course of military operations as **enemy combatants.** According to the policy at the time, this designation allowed a suspect to be "held indefinitely until the end of America's war on terrorism or until the military determines on a case-by-case basis that the particular detainee no longer poses a threat to the United States or its allies."[36] As a result, about eight hundred enemy combatants were transferred to the U.S. Naval Base at Guantánamo Bay, Cuba (GTMO).

At the time, American officials insisted that, because these al Qaeda and Afghanistan-based operatives had been captured during military operations, they could be held indefinitely without being charged with any wrongdoing.[37] The detainees were denied access to legal representation or family members and were subjected to harsh interrogation tactics such as simulated drowning, sleep and food deprivation, physical stress positions, and isolation.[38] As a result of the conditions at GTMO, the U.S. government has come under a great deal of international criticism, particularly from Arab and Muslim countries and from those non-Muslim nations, such as Australia and Great Britain, whose citizens have been held at the detention center.

Political Issues By 2013, only about 170 detainees remained at GTMO, with the rest having been released or repatriated to their home countries. The Obama administration has indicated a strong desire to close down the facility, and no new prisoners have been sent to GTMO since President Obama took office in 2009. Indeed, that year the president proposed moving all GTMO detainees to a supermax prison in Illinois. As a response, the U.S. Congress passed legislation that barred the transfer of any detained enemy combatants onto domestic soil.[39] (See the feature *You Be the President—The Enemy Within?* on the facing page to learn how this issue resurfaced following the capture of one of the alleged Boston Marathon bombers following the April 2013 attacks that left three dead and more than 260 injured, as described in the first chapter of this tetxtbook.)

Security Issues Regardless of congressional opposition, the president does have the option of using an executive waiver to transfer GTMO detainees to the mainland United States. Despite his misgivings about "keeping individuals in no man's land in perpetuity,"[40] as of the summer of 2013 President Obama had not taken advantage of this waiver. The reason: many homeland security officials believe that these detainees still pose a threat. About one in seven

Weapon of Mass Destruction A weapon that has the capacity to cause large number of casualties or significant property damage.

Enemy Combatant An individual who has supported foreign terrorist organizations such as al Qaeda that are engaged in hostilities against the military operations of the United States.

YOU BE THE PRESIDENT

THE ENEMY WITHIN?

THE FACTS As Dzhokhar Tsarnaev recovered from life-threatening injuries in a Boston hospital bed, a number of lawmakers insisted that he be treated as a war criminal rather than a common criminal. Certainly, the carnage that resulted from two pressure-cooker bombs detonated during the Boston Marathon by Dzhokhar and his brother Tamerlan resembled a battlefield more than a crime scene. Furthermore, if designated an enemy combatant, Dzokhar could be interrogated by federal agents without the protections afforded to criminal suspects in this country. "We're at war," said South Carolina Republican Senator Lindsey Graham. "The idea that the only way we can question [Dzhokhar] about national security matters is to go through his lawyer—that is absolutely crazy."

THE LAW According to federal statute, an enemy combatant must be a foreign national associated with al Qaeda in some capacity. Dzhokhar is a U.S. citizen, and although he and his brother seem to have been influenced by al Qaeda propaganda,

there is no evidence that either had any direct contact with the terrorist organization. In 2004, however, the U.S. Supreme Court suggested that, in "narrow circumstances," there is "no bar to this nation's holding one of its own citizens as an enemy combatant."

YOUR DECISION Senator Graham of South Carolina does not suggest that Dzhokhar be transferred directly from his hospital bed to a military prison. Rather, Graham wants him to be interrogated for thirty days as an enemy combatant to determine whether he and his brother have more substantial ties to al Qaeda. As president, you have a great deal of discretion to determine when "narrow circumstances" exist. Should Dzhokhar be designated an enemy combatant for purposes of interrogation, or should he be arrested and provided the protections of the criminal justice system?

To see how the administration of President Barack Obama dealt with this situation, go to Example 14.1 in Appendix A.

released from GTMO has returned, or is suspected of having returned, to terrorist activities.[41] One former prisoner, Said Ali al-Shihri, became the deputy leader of al Qaeda operations in Yemen.

In 2008, the United States Supreme Court ruled that GTMO detainees should have a "meaningful opportunity" to challenge their incarceration in court.[42] Four years later, however, even though the federal government had provided no such opportunity, the Court refused to revisit the issue.[43] Furthermore, at least fifty GTMO inmates are considered too dangerous for release. Federal officials will review their status periodically, but in theory they could be held indefinitely. In the spring of 2013, frustration over the possibility of indefinite detention led to hunger strikes involving nearly one hundred GTMO detainees.

MILITARY JUSTICE Besides indefinite detention, the other possibility for those who remain incarcerated at GTMO involves **military tribunals,** which are carried out at the naval base. Such tribunals—also known as *military commissions*—offer more limited protections than those afforded to defendants in

civilian courts, as described in Chapter 8. In a tribunal, the accused does not have the right to a trial by jury, as guaranteed by the Sixth Amendment. Instead, a panel of at least five military commissioners acts in place of the judge and jury and decides questions of both "fact and law."

Only two-thirds of the panel members need to agree for a conviction, in contrast to the unanimous jury required by criminal trials. Furthermore, evidence that would be inadmissible in criminal court, such as some forms of hearsay testimony (discussed in Chapter 8) and "fruit of the poisoned tree" from unreasonable searches and seizures (discussed in Chapter 6), is allowed before these tribunals.[44]

By May 2013, only seven of the 779 prisoners housed at GTMO had been convicted by military tribunals. To improve these odds, federal officials have decided, when possible, to offer plea bargains—particularly to "low-value" detainees who have not committed violence against Americans.[45] The pace of such efforts has been slow, however, and tribunals

Military Tribunal A court that is operated by the military rather than the criminal justice system and is presided over by military officers rather than judges.

Detainees in orange jumpsuits sit in a holding area at the U.S. Naval Base at Guantánamo Bay, Cuba. Do you think non-U.S. citizens who are in the custody of the U.S. military should be protected by our Constitution? Why or why not?

of "high-value" detainees such as Khalid Sheikh Mohammed are expected to take years to complete. As a result, it will take an act of formidable political will from the Obama administration to close down GTMO in the foreseeable future.

14-2c
Cyberattacks— The Future of Terrorism?

On the morning of August 15, 2012, employees of the Saudi Arabian oil company Saudi Aramco who turned on their computer screens at work were in for a surprise. Instead of accessing documents, spreadsheets, or e-mails, they saw an image of a burning American flag. Though it caused the oil company significant cost and inconvenience, this **cyberattack** was probably designed to make a political statement protesting the company's ties with the United States.[46] Such unlawful attempts to disrupt computer systems have the potential to do much greater damage, and are considered by many homeland security experts to be the next great challenge of international terrorism.

INFRASTRUCTURE SECURITY In the context of homeland security, concern about cyberattacks focuses on the ability of outside parties to attack our infrastructure. As you may recall from Chapter 4, a nation's infrastructure

Cyberattack An attempt to damage or disrupt computer systems or electronic networks operated by computers.

includes large-scale operations that control supplies of energy, transportation, food, and public health. According to the Department of Homeland Security, America's infrastructure suffered two hundred cyberattacks in 2012, though none caused widespread disruption of services.[47]

In general, cyberattacks are carried out by the use of malicious computer programs known as *malware*—discussed later in the chapter—that damage computer systems. In particular, malware can be designed to create *denial-of-service*, a situation in which the targeted operation can no longer function. In 2009, for example, malware known as Stuxnet effectively sabotaged the operation of Iran's nuclear facilities. The worst-case scenario involving cyberattacks would, in the words of one American homeland security official, make "9/11 look like a tea party."[48] Among the possible catastrophes: gas pipelines destroyed, national bank records wiped clean, 911 call centers jammed, air traffic control centers shut down, and hospitals rendered inoperable.

STATE ACTORS As much as international terrorist organizations such as al Qaeda might desire these types of results, cyberattacks remain beyond their abilities for the time being. Creating malware such as Stuxnet requires the work of numerous well-trained computer experts and costs upwards of $1 million.[49] In fact, most large-scale cyberattacks today involve nations rather than individuals. Stuxnet was probably created with the support of the governments of the United States and Israel. Iran, in turn, is believed to be behind the cyberattack on Saudi Aramco described previously. In September 2012, Chinese operatives apparently gained access to the computer

system of Telvent, a company that monitors half the oil and gas pipelines in North America.

Consequently, large-scale cyberattacks are treated as a military problem. Still, the possibility that nonstate actors will, at some point, have the technical ability to launch a widespread computer attack is a growing concern for anti-terrorism law enforcement agencies. Private companies, which may not have the funds or expertise to protect against cyberattacks, control about 90 percent of the infrastructure in the United States.

Several years ago, a computer expert showed that it would be relatively easy to manipulate the equipment that chemically treats California's drinking water.[50] According to James Lewis of the Center for Strategic and International Studies, America suffers from a "misplaced sense of invulnerability" when it comes to cyberattacks, just as it did regarding international terrorism prior to September 11, 2001.[51]

14-3 what IS CYBER CRIME?

"No one expected the Internet to become a critical global infrastructure," an international security expert told lawmakers in Washington, D.C., several years ago. "The Internet is incredibly valuable, but it's easy to attack."[52]

The expert was speaking about cyberattacks, but he easily could have been describing many other areas where the World Wide Web and the criminal justice system intersect. In May 2013, for example, federal prosecutors brought charges against seven men who were part of a global crime ring that stole $45 million from automated teller machines (ATMs). The "ingenious" scheme started when its ringleaders used the Internet to break into the computer system of an Indian company that handles prepaid debit-card transactions for Visa and MasterCard. The cyber criminals then raised the withdrawal limits on numerous debit accounts, and provided operatives in twenty-seven countries with the account numbers and passwords. These accomplices then made about 4,500 fraudulent ATM transactions over the course of several hours. The seven Americans, working in New York City, stole about $2.8 million.

"In the place of guns and masks, this cyber crime organization used laptops and the Internet," said one of the federal prosecutors involved in the case.[53] In fact, guns and masks are no longer the preferred tools of bank robbers. From 2001 to 2011, the rate of bank robberies in the United States dropped by half, a trend industry insiders explain by pointing to the rise in criminal operations such as the ATM scheme. "Clearly, as more and more transactions become electronic, more bank crimes become electronic," says Doug Johnson of the American Bankers Association.[54]

"You know, you can do this just as easily online."

P.C. Vey/Conde Nast Publications/www.cartoonbank.com

14-3a
Computer Crime and the Internet

Nearly every business in today's economy, banks included, relies on computers to conduct its daily affairs and to provide consumers with easy access to its products and services. Furthermore, more than 500 million American household devices are now connected to the Internet, and the proliferation of handheld Internet devices has made it possible to be online at almost any time or place. In short, the Internet has become a place where large numbers of people interact socially and commercially. In any such environment, wrongdoing has an opportunity to flourish.

In this chapter, we will be using a broad term, **cyber crime,** to describe any criminal activity occur-

Cyber Crime A crime that occurs online, in the virtual community of the Internet, as opposed to in the physical world.

ring via a computer in the virtual community of the Internet. It is very difficult, if not impossible, to determine how much cyber crime actually takes place. Often, people never know that they have been the victims of this type of criminal activity. Furthermore, businesses sometimes fail to report such crimes for fear of losing customer confidence. Nonetheless, in 2012, the Internet Crime Complaint Center (IC3), operated as a partnership between the FBI and the National White Collar Crime Center, received about 290,000 complaints representing just over $525 million in victim losses.[55] According to the Norton Cybercrime Report, nearly 70 percent of all adults who use the Internet have been victimized by cyber crime, with annual global losses exceeding $380 billion.[56]

14-3b
Cyber Crimes against Persons and Property

Most cyber crimes are not "new" crimes. Rather, they are existing crimes in which the Internet is the instrument of wrongdoing. The challenge for law enforcement is to apply traditional laws, which were designed to protect persons from physical harm or to safeguard their physical property, to crimes committed in cyberspace. This challenge is

3 LO

made all the greater by two aspects of the Internet that may aid the perpetrators of cyber crimes—the anonymity it provides and the ease with which large amounts of information may be transferred quickly. Here, we look at several types of activity that constitute "updated" crimes against persons and property—online consumer fraud, cyber theft, and cyberstalking.

CYBER CONSUMER FRAUD

The expanding world of e-commerce has created many benefits for consumers. It has also led to some challenging problems, including fraud conducted via the Internet. In general, fraud is any misrepresentation knowingly made with the intention of deceiving another person. Furthermore, the victim must reasonably rely on the fraudulent information to her or his detriment. **Cyber fraud,** then, is fraud committed over the Internet.

A New Venue for Fraud Scams that were once conducted solely by mail or phone can now be found online, and new technology has led to increasingly more creative ways to commit fraud. Online dating scams, for example, have increased dramatically in recent years, with fraudsters creating fake profiles to deceive unwitting romantic partners. According to the IC3, in 2012 online romance scam artists defrauded victims out of more than $55 million.[57] In one case, a fictitious American solider in Iraq convinced his online "sweetheart" that he had been kidnapped and needed $250,000 from her to buy his freedom.

Common Online Frauds Overall, fraud accounts for the largest percentage of losses related to consumer cyber crime. Two widely reported forms of cyber crime are *advance fee fraud* and *online auction fraud.* In the simplest form of advance fee fraud, consumers order and pay for items such as automobiles or antiques that are never delivered.

Online auction fraud is also fairly straightforward. A person lists an item for auction, on either a legitimate or a fake auction site, and then refuses to send the product after receiving payment. In 2012, for example, the FBI uncovered a scheme in which an Oregon couple took photos of items on store shelves, offered them for auction on the Internet, and collected more than $300,000 from unsuspecting bidders. (**CAREER TIP:** Online auction companies hire *Internet fraud investigators* to ensure the authenticity

of their services. In some instances, investigators must travel to countries with a reputation for harboring cyber criminals, such as Romania, Russia, and Ukraine. "The fraudsters need to know we're coming after them," says the head of eBay's Trust and Safety Division.)

CYBER THEFT

In cyberspace, thieves are not subject to the physical limitations of the "real" world. A thief can steal data stored in a networked computer with network access from anywhere on the globe. Only the speed of the connection and the thief's computer equipment limit the quantity of data that can be stolen.

Identity Theft This freedom from physical limitations has led to a marked increase in **identity theft,** which occurs when the wrongdoer steals a form of identification—such as a name, date of birth, or Social Security number—and uses the information to access the victim's financial resources. According to the federal government, about 7 percent of American households have at least one member who has been the victim of identity theft.[58]

More than half of identity theft involves the misappropriation of an existing credit-card account.[59] In the "real world," this is generally accomplished by stealing an actual credit card. Online, an identity thief can steal financial information by fooling Web sites into thinking that he or she is the actual account holder. For example, important personal information such as one's birthday, hometown, or employer that is available on social media sites such as Facebook can be used to convince a third party to reveal the victim's Social Security or bank account number.

Password Protection The more personal information a cyber criminal obtains, the easier it is for him or her to find a victim's online user name. Once the online user name has been compromised, the easier it is to steal a victim's password, which is often the last line of defense to financial information. Numerous software programs aid identity thieves in illegally obtaining passwords. A technique called *keystroke logging,* for example, relies on software that embeds itself in

Cyber Fraud Any misrepresentation knowingly made over the Internet with the intention of deceiving another and on which a reasonable person would and does rely to his or her detriment.

Identity Theft The theft of personal information, such as a person's name, driver's license number, or Social Security number.

a victim's computer and records every keystroke made on that computer. User names and passwords are then recorded and sold to the highest bidder.

Internet users should also be wary of any links contained within e-mails sent from an unknown source, as these links can sometimes be used to illegally obtain personal information. (See Figure 14.2 alongside for some hints on how to protect your online passwords.)

FIGURE 14.2 Protecting Online Passwords

Once an online password has been compromised, the information on the protected Web site is fair game for identity thieves. By following these simple rules, you can strengthen the protection provided by your online passwords.

1. **Don't** use existing words such as your pet's name or your hometown. Such words are easy for computer identity theft programs to decode.

2. **Do** use at least eight characters in your passwords, with a nonsensical combination of upper- and lower-case letters, numbers, and symbols. A weak password is "scout1312." A strong password is "4X$dQ%3Z9j."

3. **Don't** use the same username and password for different Web accounts. If you do, then each account is in danger if one account is compromised.

4. **Do** use a different password for each Web account. If necessary, write down the various passwords and keep the list in a safe place.

5. **Don't** use information that can be easily found online or guessed at in choosing the questions that Web sites use to verify your password. That is, don't select questions such as "What is your birthday?" or "What is your city of birth?" Instead, choose questions with obscure answers that you are certain to remember or can easily look up.

6. **Don't** log on to any Web site if you are connected to the Internet via a wireless network (Wi-Fi) that is not itself password protected.

Phishing A distinct form of identity theft known as **phishing** adds a different wrinkle to this particular form of cyber crime. In a phishing attack, the perpetrators "fish" for financial data and passwords from consumers by posing as a legitimate business such as a bank or credit-card company. The "phisher" sends an e-mail asking the recipient to "update" or "confirm" vital information, often with the threat that an account or some other service will be discontinued if the information is not provided. Once the unsuspecting target enters the information, the phisher can use it to masquerade as the person or to drain his or her bank or credit account.

In 2012, thousands of unwitting users were fooled by e-mails allegedly sent by local utility companies offering federal aid—apparently authorized by President Barack Obama—in paying their electrical bills. Victims were required to provide their Social Security number to ensure that they qualified for the help. Over the past several years, dozens of companies, including Amazon.com, Zappos.com, and LinkedIn, have been forced to warn consumers that fraudulent e-mails asking for personal and financial information had been sent in the companies' names.

Phishing scams have also spread to other areas,

Phishing Sending an unsolicited e-mail that falsely claims to be from a legitimate organization in an attempt to acquire sensitive information from the recipient.

such as text messaging and social-networking sites. Nearly 13 percent of all phishing, for example, takes place using Facebook alerts.[60] A new form of this fraud, called spear phishing, is much more difficult to detect because the messages seem to have come from co-workers, friends, or family workers. "It's a really nasty tactic because it's so personalized," explains security expert Bruce Schneier. "It's an e-mail from your mother saying she needs your Social Security number for the will she's doing."[61]

CYBER AGGRESSION AND THE NEW MEDIA

The growing use of mobile devices such as smartphones and tablets has added another outlet for online criminal activity. About 10 percent of cyber crime now targets such devices.[62] In particular, widespread smartphone use seems to have exacerbated cyberbullying, which we discussed in the context of school crime in the previous chapter. According to a recent survey, American teenagers who consider themselves "heavy users" of their cell phones are much more likely to experience cyberbullying than those who consider themselves "normal users" of the devices.[63]

In 2009, the U.S. Department of Justice released a landmark study that shed light on the high incidence of stalking in the United States. Defined as a "credible threat" that puts a person in reasonable

COMPUTER FORENSIC SPECIALIST

JOB DESCRIPTION:

- Investigate misbehavior on computer systems by collecting and analyzing computer-related evidence. Retrieve data that have been encrypted or electronically stored on a commercial or personal computer.

- Work for a law enforcement or homeland security agency to investigate crimes or terrorists' activities, or for a private company to protect commercial data and defend against worms, viruses, and other malware.

WHAT KIND OF TRAINING IS REQUIRED?

- An extensive knowledge of computers, computer programming, and data retrieval is essential. A number of colleges, universities, and online educational organizations offer computer forensic courses that provide the skills necessary for this career.

- A complete understanding of the rules of evidence in criminal courts and the ability to establish a proper chain of custody for all evidence retrieved from targeted computer databases.

ANNUAL SALARY RANGE?

- $50,000–$85,000

ryasick/iStockphoto.com

fear for her or his safety or the safety of the person's immediate family, stalking, according to the study, affects approximately 3.4 million Americans each year.[64] About one in four of these victims experiences a form of **cyberstalking,** in which the perpetrator uses e-mail, text messages, or some other form of electronic communication to carry out his or her harassment.[65]

Nearly every state and the federal government have passed legislation to combat this criminal behavior. For instance, in January 2012, Patrick Macchione was sentenced to four years in state prison for cyberstalking fellow University of Central Florida student Kristen Pratt. Macchione sent death threats to Pratt using Twitter, posted lewd messages to her Facebook account, and directed nearly thirty threatening videos at her on YouTube.

14-3c
Cyber Crimes in the Business World

Just as cyberspace can be a dangerous place for consumers, it presents a number of hazards for businesses that wish to offer their services on the Internet. In the ATM "bank robbery" case described earlier in the section, the victims were not individual bank account holders but rather two banks—both located in the Middle East—that supplied funds for the debit cards involved. The same circumstances that enable companies to reach a large number of consumers also leave them vulnerable to cyber crime. For example, in 2012 federal law enforcement agents arrested Dutch

> **Cyberstalking** The crime of stalking, committed in cyberspace through the use of e-mail, text messages, or another form of electronic communication.

citizen David Schrooten for infecting the online sales systems of several Seattle businesses with spyware programs. This spyware collected at least 44,000 credit-card numbers, subsequently sold by Schrooten to third parties for fraudulent use.

HACKERS David Schrooten is a particular type of cyber criminal known as a *hacker*. **Hackers** are people who use one computer to illegally access another. The danger posed by hackers has increased significantly because of **botnets,** or networks of computers that have been appropriated by hackers without the knowledge of their owners. A hacker will secretly install a program on thousands, if not millions, of personal computer "robots," or "bots," that allows him or her to forward transmissions to an even larger number of systems. The program attaches itself to the host computer when someone operating the computer opens a fraudulent e-mail.

Malware Programs that create botnets are one of the latest forms of *malware,* a term that refers to any program that is harmful to a computer or, by extension, a computer user. A **worm,** for example, is a software program that is capable of reproducing itself as it spreads from one computer to the next. A **virus,** another form of malware, is also able to reproduce itself, but must be attached to an "infested" host file to travel from one computer network to another. Worms and viruses can be programmed to perform a number of functions, such as prompting host computers to continually "crash" and reboot, or otherwise infect the system.

Malware is increasingly being used to target specific companies or organizations. In 2011, for example, hackers used malware to carry out a targeted attack on Sony's PlayStation network, thus gaining access to personal information and, possibly, the credit-card numbers of 77 million online gamers worldwide. Sony, a Japanese company, was forced to shut down the network for twenty-four days, costing the company $170 million. The Ponemon Institute, a private research organization, estimates that individual American businesses lose an average of $8.9 million a year because of malware and other cyber crime.[66]

The Spread of Spam Businesses and individuals alike are targets of **spam,** or unsolicited "junk e-mails" that flood virtual mailboxes with advertisements, solicitations, and other messages. Considered relatively harmless in the early days of the Internet, in 2012, an average of 87 billion spam messages were being sent each day. Nearly 2 billion of these spam messages contained some form of malware.[67] To rectify this situation, in 2003 Congress passed the Controlling the Assault of Non-Solicited Pornography and Marketing Act (CAN-SPAM), which requires all unsolicited e-mails to be labeled and to include opt-out provisions and the sender's physical address.[68]

Spam is also the preferred method of phishing, the identity theft scam described earlier. By sending millions or even billions of these fraudulent e-mails, phishers need only entice a few users to "take the bait" to ensure a successful and lucrative operation.

Finally, "social" spam is becoming more common on social-networking sites such as Facebook. This form of hacking relies on fake messages, such as "hey, check out this free iPad," that appear to be from a friend rather than an unknown company. The message includes a link to download a coupon for the free product. In reality, however, by clicking on the link, the unsuspecting user has allowed malware to infect his or her computer. (**CAREER TIP:** *Computer programmers* create software to protect consumers and businesses from the negative effects of spam and other malware.)

PIRATING INTELLECTUAL PROPERTY ONLINE Most people think of wealth in terms of houses, land, cars, stocks, and bonds. Wealth, however, also includes **intellectual property,** which consists of the products that result from intellectual, creative pro-

Hacker A person who uses one computer to break into another.

Botnet A network of computers that have been appropriated without the knowledge of their owners and used to spread harmful programs via the Internet; short for *robot network.*

Worm A computer program that can automatically replicate itself and interfere with the normal use of a computer. A worm does not need to be attached to an existing file to move from one network to another.

Virus A computer program that can replicate itself and interfere with the normal use of a computer. A virus cannot exist as a separate entity and must attach itself to another program to move through a network.

Spam Bulk e-mails, particularly of commercial advertising, sent in large quantities without the consent of the recipient.

Intellectual Property Property resulting from intellectual, creative processes.

cesses. The government provides various forms of protection for intellectual property, such as copyrights and patents. These protections ensure that a person who writes a book or a song or creates a software program is financially rewarded if that product is sold in the marketplace.

Intellectual property such as books, films, music, and software is vulnerable to "piracy"—the unauthorized copying and use of the property. In the past, copying intellectual products was time consuming, and the quality of the pirated copies was clearly inferior. In today's online world, however, things have changed. Simply clicking a mouse can now reproduce millions of unauthorized copies, and pirated duplicates of copyrighted works obtained via the Internet are often exactly the same as the original, or close to it. The Business Software Alliance estimates that 42 percent of all business software is pirated, costing software makers more than $63.4 billion in 2012.[69]

14-3d
Cyber Crimes against the Community

One of the greatest challenges cyberspace presents for law enforcement is how to enforce laws governing activities that are prohibited under certain circumstances but are not always illegal. Such laws generally reflect the will of the community, which recognizes behavior as acceptable under some circumstances and unacceptable under others. Thus, while it is legal in many areas to sell a pornographic video to a fifty-year-old, it is never legal to sell the same item to a fifteen-year-old. Similarly, placing a bet on a football game with a bookmaker in Las Vegas, Nevada, is legal, but doing the same thing with a bookmaker in Cleveland, Ohio, is not. Of course, in cyberspace it is often impossible to know whether the customer buying porn is age fifty or fifteen, or if the person placing the bet is in Las Vegas or Cleveland.

ONLINE PORNOGRAPHY The Internet has been a boon to the pornography industry. Twelve percent of all Web sites have pornographic content, and these sites generate $4.2 billion in revenue a year.[70] Though no general figures are available, the Internet has undoubtedly also been a boon to those who illegally produce and sell material depicting sexually explicit conduct involving a child—child pornography. As we have seen with other cyber crimes, the Internet is conducive to child pornography for a number of reasons:

- *Speed.* The Internet is the fastest means of sending visual material over long distances. Child pornographers can deliver their material faster and more securely online than through regular mail.
- *Security.* Any illegal material that passes through the hands of a mail carrier is inherently in danger of being discovered. This risk is significantly reduced with e-mail. Furthermore, Internet sites that offer child pornography can protect their customers with passwords, which keep random Web surfers (or law enforcement agents) from stumbling on the site of chat rooms.
- *Anonymity.* Obviously, anonymity is the most important protection offered by the Internet for sellers and buyers of child pornography, as it is for any person engaged in illegal behavior in cyberspace.[71]

4 LO

Because of these three factors, courts and lawmakers have had a difficult time controlling the dissemination of illegal sexual content via the Internet. In 2008, however, the United States Supreme Court upheld a federal law known as the Protect Act. This legislation makes it a crime to exchange "any material or purported material" online that would cause "another to believe" it depicted a minor engaged in sex, whether "actual or simulated."[72] Essentially, this law gives prosecutors the power they need to arrest purveyors of virtual child pornography, which uses computer images—not real children—to depict sexual acts.

GAMBLING IN CYBERSPACE In general, gambling is illegal. All states have statutes that regulate gambling—defined as any scheme that involves the distribution of property by chance among persons who have risked something of value for the opportunity to receive the property. In some states, certain

such as credit-card transactions, at those sites.[73]

Legalizing Online Poker The environment for online gambling changed dramatically in 2011. That year, the U.S. Department of Justice released a memo essentially allowing states to operate gambling Web sites as long as the bets do not involve a "sporting event or contest."[74] In April 2013, this led to the United States' first legal online poker site, operating out of Nevada. Other states, including Delaware and New Jersey, are expected to follow suit.

The challenge is that, according to federal law, these sites must be *intrastate*. In other words, someone using the Nevada poker Web site must be in the state of Nevada. Given the difficulty of determining an Internet user's physical location, states will undoubtedly struggle to keep their new online gambling Web sites within the parameters of the law.[75]

forms of gambling, such as casino gambling or horse racing, are legal. Many states also have legalized state-operated lotteries, as well as lotteries, such as Bingo, conducted for charitable purposes. A number of states also allow gambling on Native American reservations.

A Problem of Jurisdiction In the past, this mixed bag of gambling laws has presented a legal quandary: Can citizens in a state that does not allow gambling place bets to a Web site located in a state that does? After all, states have no constitutional authority over activities that take place in other states. Complicating the problem was the fact that many Internet gambling sites are located outside the United States in countries where Internet gambling is legal, and no state government has authority over activities that take place in other countries.

In 2006, Congress, concerned about money laundering stemming from online gambling, the problem of addiction, and underage gambling, passed legislation that greatly strengthened efforts to reduce online gaming. The Unlawful Internet Gambling Enforcement Act of 2006 cuts off the money flow to Internet gambling sites by barring the use of electronic payments,

14-4
what IS WHITE-COLLAR CRIME?

A woman in Huntsville, Alabama, squanders $60,000 in student loans on house bills and "entertainment." The owners of the Glory Pharmacy in Hernando County, Florida, knowingly accept 1,400 fake prescriptions for the painkiller oxycodone. A New Jersey defense contractor sells the U.S. Army faulty helicopter parts. A former Massachusetts state treasurer is indicted for using lottery funds to finance an unsuccessful campaign to become governor.

These court cases represent a variety of criminal behavior with different motives, different methods, and different victims. Yet they all fall into the category of *white-collar crime,* an umbrella term for wrongdoing marked by deceit and scandal rather than violence. As we mentioned in Chapter 1, white-collar crime has a broad impact on the global economy, causing American businesses alone approximately $300 billion in losses each year.[76] Despite its global and national importance, however, white-collar crime has consistently challenged a criminal justice system that struggles to define the problem, much less effectively combat it.

14-4a
Defining White-Collar Crime

White-collar crime is not an official category of criminal behavior measured by the federal government in the Uniform Crime Report. Rather, it covers a broad range of illegal acts involving "lying,

LO 5

cheating, and stealing," according to the FBI's Web site on the subject.[77] To give a more technical definition, white-collar crimes are financial activities characterized by deceit and concealment that do not involve physical force or violence. Figure 14.3 below lists and describes some common types of white-collar crime.

DIFFERENT TECHNIQUES To differentiate white-collar crime from "regular" crime, criminologists Michael L. Benson of the University of Cincinnati and Sally S. Simpson of the University of Maryland focus on technique. For example, in an ordinary burglary, a criminal uses physical means, such as picking a lock, to get somewhere he or she should not be—someone else's home—to do something that is clearly illegal. Furthermore, the victim is a specific identifiable individual—the homeowner. In contrast, white-collar criminals usually (1) have legal access to the place where the crime occurs; (2) are spatially separated from the victim, who is often unknown; and (3) behave in a manner that is, at least superficially, legitimate.[78]

FIGURE 14.3 **White-Collar Crimes**

Embezzlement
Embezzlement is a form of employee fraud in which an individual uses his or her position within an organization to *embezzle,* or steal, the employer's funds, property, or other assets. Pilferage is a less serious form of employee fraud in which the individual steals items from the workplace.

Digital Vision CD

Tax Evasion
Tax evasion occurs when taxpayers underreport (or do not report) their taxable income or otherwise purposely attempt to evade a tax liability.

PhotoDisc/Getty Images

Credit-Card and Check Fraud
Credit-card fraud involves obtaining credit-card numbers through a variety of schemes (such as stealing them from the Internet) and using the numbers for personal gain. Check fraud includes writing checks that are not covered by bank funds, forging checks, and stealing traveler's checks.

Mail and Wire Fraud
This umbrella term covers all schemes that involve the use of mail, radio, television, the Internet, or a telephone to intentionally deceive in a business environment.

Securities Fraud
Securities fraud covers illegal activity in the stock market. Stockbrokers who steal funds from their clients are guilty of securities fraud, as are those who engage in *insider trading,* which involves buying or selling securities on the basis of information that has not been made available to the public.

Bribery
Also known as *influence peddling,* bribery occurs in the business world when somebody within a company or government sells influence, power, or information to a person outside the company or government who can benefit. A county official, for example, could give a construction company a lucrative county contract to build a new jail. In return, the construction company would give some

of the proceeds, known as a *kickback,* to the official.

Consumer Fraud
This term covers a wide variety of activities designed to defraud consumers, from selling counterfeit art to offering "free" items, such as electronic devices or vacations, that include a number of hidden charges.

Insurance Fraud
Insurance fraud involves making false claims in order to collect insurance payments. Faking an injury in order to receive payments from a workers' compensation program, for example, is a form of insurance fraud.

Digital Vision CD

Several years ago, Rita Crundwell was convicted of stealing more than $54 million from the city of Dixon, Illinois, for which she had been working as a financial officer. Why does Crundwell's wrongdoing fall into the category of white-collar crime?

AP Photo/Sauk Valley Media, Alex T. Paschal, File

for example, an automobile dealership "rolls back" the odometers of used cars so that a higher price can be charged for the vehicles. As soon as the fraud is discovered, the scheme can no longer succeed.

Benson and Simpson also identify three main techniques used by white-collar criminals to carry out their crimes:[79]

1. *Deception.* White-collar crime almost always involves a party who deceives and a party who is deceived. The nation's federal Medicare system, which provides health insurance for those sixty-five years of age and older, is a frequent target of deceptive practices. For example, in 2013, the FBI arrested six Detroit-area in-home health-care providers who recruited dishonest Medicare beneficiaries to request costly and unnecessary nursing services. When the federal government reimbursed these health-care providers for the home care—which was never actually performed—the white-collar criminals kept the funds for themselves.

2. *Abuse of trust.* A white-collar criminal often operates in a position of trust and misuses that trust for personal benefit. In 2013, for example, the FBI arrested three men for stealing about $6.7 million from a victim by convincing him that they invested the funds in large blocks of Facebook, Inc., stock.

3. *Concealment and conspiracy.* To continue their illegal activities, white-collar criminals need to conceal those activities. In *odometer fraud,*

VICTIMS OF WHITE-COLLAR CRIME As the above examples show, sometimes the victim of a white-collar crime is obvious. A fraudulent stockbroker is stealing directly from his or her clients, and odometer fraud denies consumers the actual value of their purchased automobiles. But who was victimized in the fraudulent Medicare benefits scheme? In that instance, the "victims" were the U.S. taxpayers, who collectively had to cover the cost of the unwarranted benefits. Often, white-collar crime does not target individuals but rather large groups or even abstract concepts such as "society" or "the environment."

CORPORATE WHITE-COLLAR CRIME For legal purposes, a corporation can be treated as a person capable of forming the intent necessary to commit a crime. For instance, the Deepwater Horizon oil spill off the coast of Louisiana in April 2010 caused a great deal of obvious harm. Eleven workers were killed in the oil rig explosion that caused the spill, and the Louisiana coastline suffered immense ecological damage, threatening the livelihoods of thousands of seafood suppliers. In November 2012, BP, the corporation that operated Deepwater Horizon, pleaded guilty to fourteen different criminal charges relating to the incident. The company agreed to pay $4.5 billion in fines and submit to four years of government monitoring of its safety practices and ethics. (Three BP officers aboard the oil rig at the time of the accident were also individually charged with one count of manslaughter for each of the workers who died in the explosion.)

14-4b
Regulating and Policing White-Collar Crime

In 2012, Genwal Resources, Inc., which operates the Crandall Canyon coal mine in central Utah, pleaded guilty to two misdemeanor charges of violating health and safety standards and paid a $500,000 fine. The charges stemmed from a collapse at the mine that ultimately killed six miners, two rescuers, and a government inspector. The deaths of nine people because of Genwal Resources' failure to enforce safety measures at its coal mine are an example of *corporate violence*. In contrast to assaults committed by individual people, **corporate violence** is a result of policies or actions undertaken by a corporation. In the United States, parallel regulatory and criminal systems have evolved to prevent corporate violence and other forms of white-collar crime.

THE REGULATORY JUSTICE SYSTEM Although most white-collar crimes cause harm, these harms are not necessarily covered by criminal statutes. Indeed, more often they are covered by *administrative* laws, which we first encountered in Chapter 3. Such laws make up the backbone of the U.S. regulatory system, through which the government attempts to control the actions of individuals, corporations, and other institutions. The goal of **regulation** is not prevention or punishment as much as **compliance,** or the following of regulatory guidelines. For example, as part of their efforts to clean up the massive oil spill of 2010, BP and government agencies used dispersants, which cause oil to disintegrate in water. Agents from the Environmental Protection Agency (EPA) monitored levels of these chemicals to ensure that further damage was not done to the Gulf of Mexico (see the photo above).

The EPA—which regulates practices relating to air quality, water quality, and toxic waste—is one of the federal administrative agencies whose compliance oversight brings them into contact with white-collar crime. Another, the Occupational Safety and Health Administration (OSHA), enforces workplace health and safety standards.

What role did the Environmental Protection Agency (EPA) play in monitoring efforts to clean up the oil slick from the Deepwater Horizon oil spill? Why is the EPA considered a regulatory agency and not a law enforcement agency?

Ted Jackson/*The Times-Picayune*/Landov

In addition, the Federal Trade Commission regulates business interactions, and the Securities and Exchange Commission (SEC) ensures that financial markets such as the New York Stock Exchange operate in a fair manner. (**CAREER TIP:** Federal, state, and local government agencies employ *occupational health and safety inspectors* to ensure that working environments such as offices, factories, and restaurants are safe for employees and the public.)

Corporate Violence Physical harm to individuals or the environment that occurs as the result of corporate policies or decision making.

Regulation Governmental control of society through rules and laws that is generally carried out by administrative agencies.

Compliance The state of operating in accordance with governmental standards.

LAW ENFORCEMENT AND WHITE-COLLAR CRIME In general, when officials at a regulatory agency find that criminal prosecution is needed to punish a particular violation, they will refer the matter to the U.S. Department of Justice. Either through such referrals or at their own discretion, federal officials prosecute white-collar crime using the investigatory powers of several different federal law enforcement agencies. The FBI has become the lead agency when it comes to white-collar crime, particularly in response to the recent financial scandals, as we shall soon see. The U.S. Postal Inspection Service is also quite active in such investigations, as fraudulent activities often involve the U.S. mail. In addition, the Internal Revenue Service's Criminal Investigative Division has jurisdiction over a wide variety of white-collar crimes, including tax fraud, and operates perhaps the most effective white-collar crime lab in the country.[80]

Local and state agencies also investigate white-collar crimes, but because of the complexity and costs of such investigations, most are handled by the federal government. Federal prosecutors are also in a unique position to enforce the federal Racketeer Influenced and Corrupt Organizations Act (RICO), which we discussed briefly in Chapter 10. Originally designed to combat organized crime, RICO makes it illegal to receive income through a pattern of *racketeering*.[81] The definition of **racketeering** is so inclusive—basically covering any attempt to earn illegal income involving more than one person—that it can be used against a broad range of white-collar wrongdoing. Several years ago, for example, federal prosecutors used RICO to convict eleven tobacco companies for misleading the American public about the addictive qualities of cigarettes.

Racketeering The criminal action of being involved in an organized effort to engage in illegal business transactions.

14-4c
White-Collar Crime in the 2000s

The decade that ended in 2010 was marked by two periods of financial scandal. First, in 2001 and 2002, fraudulent accounting practices led to the demise of giant corporations such as Enron and Worldcom, costing investors tens of billions of dollars. Then, near the end of the decade, the collapse of the subprime mortgage market caused millions of Americans to lose their homes to foreclosure and led to the collapse of major financial institutions such as Lehman Brothers and Washington Mutual. In the latter period, headlines focused on widespread *mortgage fraud*, or dishonest practices relating to home loans, along with the misdeeds of Bernard Madoff. Before his 2008 arrest, Madoff managed to defraud thousands of investors out of approximately $65 billion.

As has often occurred in U.S. history, these scandals and the concurrent economic downturns led to greater regulation and criminalization of white-collar crime. In 1934, for example, in the wake of the Great Depression, Congress established the SEC to watch over the American economy. Similarly, in 2002 Congress passed legislation which, among other things, enhanced the penalties for those convicted of white-collar crimes.[82]

In response to the "Great Recession" of 2008 and 2009, the FBI created the National Mortgage Fraud Team and began to crack down on a variety of white-collar crimes. Indeed, FBI agents are increasingly using aggressive tactics such as going undercover, planting wiretaps, and raiding offices—tactics previously reserved for drug dealers, mobsters, and terrorists—against white-collar criminals.

REVIEW

✔️ **Review what you've read with the quiz below.**

Rip out the Chapter Review card at the back of this book, which includes:
- Chapter Summary and Learning Outcomes
- Key Terms

Or you can go online to CourseMate at www.cengagebrain.com to:
- Complete Practice Quizzes to prepare for tests.
- Review Key Terms Flash Cards (online or print).
- Play games to master concepts.

quiz

1. The Brady Bill requires a person who wants to purchase a firearm from a licensed dealer to undergo a _____ _____ to determine whether he or she is eligible for gun ownership.

2. The U.S. Supreme Court has ruled that a government body can prohibit gun ownership for those with a criminal record or a history of _____ _____.

3. Generally speaking, terrorists are _____ actors, meaning that they are not affiliated with any established nation.

4. Under the criminal justice model of homeland security, terrorist acts are treated as _____, and terrorists are prosecuted in civilian courts.

5. Under the military model of homeland security, suspected terrorists are designated _____ _____ and tried by military tribunals.

6. Web thieves have opportunities to practice _____ theft because of the large amount of personal financial information that is stored on the Internet.

7. Hackers sometimes employ _____, or networks of hijacked computers, to carry out various improper online activities.

8. _____ _____ such as films and music is vulnerable to being "pirated" by unauthorized users on the Internet.

9. White-collar criminals often use deception, concealment, and the abuse of _____ to perpetrate theft without violence.

10. Regulatory agencies require _____ with various guidelines to protect individuals from corporate violence.

Answers can be found on the Chapter 14 Review card at the end of the book.

CHAPTER 1

1. Quoted in Tim Rohan, "War Zone at Mile 26: 'So Many People without Legs,'" *New York Times* (April 16, 2013), A1.
2. Kelly Ayotte, Lindsey Graham, and John McCain, "Failure to Call Tsarnaev Enemy Combatant Hampers Probe," *Boston Globe* (May 1, 2013), A13.
3. Herman Bianchi, *Justice as Sanctuary: Toward a New System of Crime Control* (Bloomington: Indiana University Press, 1994), 72.
4. *Health Poll: Physician Assisted Suicide* (Ann Arbor, MI: Truven Health Analytics, December 2012), at **healthcare.thomsonreuters.com/npr/assets/NPR_reports _PhysicianAssisted Suicide_1212.pdf**.
5. *2012 Report to the Nations: Occupational Fraud and Abuse* (Austin, TX: Association of Certified Fraud Examiners, 2012), 2.
6. Megan Kurlychek, "What Is My Left Hand Doing? The Need for Unifying Purpose and Policy in the Criminal Justice System," *Criminology & Public Policy* (November 2011), 909.
7. *Gonzales v. Oregon*, 546 U.S. 243 (2006). Many United States Supreme Court cases will be cited in this book, and it is important to understand these citations. *Gonzales v. Oregon* refers to the parties in the case that the Court is reviewing. "U.S." is the abbreviation for *United States Reports*, the official publication of United States Supreme Court decisions. "546" refers to the volume of the *United States Reports* in which the case appears, and "243" is the page number. The citation ends with the year the case was decided, in parentheses. Most, though not all, Supreme Court case citations in this book will follow this formula.
8. President's Commission on Law Enforcement and Administration of Justice, *The Challenge of Crime in a Free Society* (Washington, D.C.: Government Printing Office, 1967), 7.
9. John Heinz and Peter Manikas, "Networks among Elites in a Local Criminal Justice System," *Law and Society Review* 26 (1992), 831–861.
10. James Q. Wilson, "What to Do about Crime: Blaming Crime on Root Causes," *Vital Speeches* (April 1, 1995), 373.
11. Herbert Packer, *The Limits of the Criminal Sanction* (Stanford, CA: Stanford University Press, 1968), 154–173.
12. *Ibid.*
13. Daniel Givelber, "Meaningless Acquittals, Meaningful Convictions: Do We Reliably Acquit the Innocent?" *Rutgers Law Review* 49 (Summer 1997), 1317.
14. Andrea Simmons, "Texting While Driving Laws Rarely Enforced," *Atlanta-Journal-Constitution* (October 30, 2012), A1.
15. "Texting While Driving Ban Is Hard to Enforce, Police Officers Say," *Associated Press* (November 12, 2012).
16. Simmons.
17. George P. Fletcher, "Some Unwise Reflections about Discretion," *Law & Contemporary Problems* (Autumn 1984), 279.
18. David Royce, "Texting and Driving Ban Bill Filed—Again—in Tallahassee," *Miami Herald* (November 22, 2012), at **www.miamiherald.com/2012/11/22 /3109627/texting-and-driving-ban-bill-filed.html**.
19. Antonin Scalia, "The Rule of Law as a Law of Rules," *University of Chicago Law Review* 56 (1989), 1178–1180.
20. John Kleinig, *Ethics and Criminal Justice: An Introduction* (New York: Cambridge University Press, 2008), 33–35.
21. Elizabeth Banks, *Criminal Justice Ethics: Theory and Practice* (Los Angeles: Sage Publications, 2008), 13.
22. Packer, 154–173.
23. Givelber, 1317.
24. "Most Americans Believe Crime in U.S. Is Worsening," *Gallup.com* (October 31, 2011), at **www.gallup.com/poll/150464/americans-believe-crime-worsening .aspx**.
25. Matt Pearce, "Crime Declines, Fear Remains," *Sun Sentinel* (Ft. Lauderdale, FL) (June 19, 2012), 9A.
26. Quoted in Richard Oppel, Jr., "Steady Decline in Major Crime Baffles Experts," *New York Times* (May 24, 2011), A1.
27. Uniting and Strengthening America by Providing Appropriate Tools Required to Intercept and Obstruct Terrorism (USA PATRIOT) Act of 2001, Pub. L. No. 107-56, 115 Stat. 272 (2001).
28. Pew Research Center for the People and the Press, "Public Remains Divided over the Patriot Act" (February 15, 2011), at **pewresearch.org/pubs/1893 /poll-patriot-actrenewal**.
29. Bureau of Justice Statistics, *Correctional Populations in the United States, 2011* (Washington, D.C.: U.S. Department of Justice, November 2012), Table 2, page 3.
30. Quoted in "U.S. Prison Population Rises despite a Drop in 20 States" *Associated Press* (December 9, 2009).
31. Zain Shauk, "Will They Post on Facebook Their Guilt in Heist?" *Houston Chronicle* (August 19, 2011), B2.
32. Joe Mozingo, "'They Saw This as Jihad,'" *Los Angeles Times* (November 21, 2012), 1.
33. Quoted in Patrik Jonsson, "'Flash Robs': How Twitter Is Being Twisted for Criminal Gain," *Christian Science Monitor* (August 3, 2011), at **www. csmonitor.com/USA/2011/0803/Flash-robs-How-Twitter-is-being-twisted -for-criminal-gain-VIDEO**.

CHAPTER 2

1. Michael L. Sulkowski and Philip J. Lazarus, "Contemporary Responses to Violent Attacks on College Campuses," *Journal of School Violence* (October 2011), 343.
2. Ethan Bronner, "Other States, and Other Times, Would Have Posed Obstacles for Gunman," *New York Times* (July 25, 2012), A12.
3. James Q. Wilson and Richard J. Hernstein, *Crime and Human Nature: The Definitive Study of the Causes of Crime* (New York: Simon & Schuster, 1985), 44.
4. Jack Katz, *Seductions of Crime: Moral and Sensual Attractions of Doing Evil* (New York: Basic Books, 1988).
5. National Coalition for the Homeless, "Hate Crimes and Violence against People Experiencing Homelessness," at **www.nationalhomeless.org/factsheets /hatecrimes.html**.
6. David C. Rowe, *Biology and Crime* (Los Angeles: Roxbury, 2002), 2.
7. L. E. Kreuz and R. M. Rose, "Assessment of Aggressive Behavior and Plasma Testosterone in Young Criminal Population," *Psychosomatic Medicine* 34 (1972), 321–332.
8. H. Persky, K. Smith, and G. Basu, "Relation of Psychological Measures of Aggression and Hostility to Testosterone Production in Men," *Psychosomatic Medicine* 33 (1971), 265, 276.
9. Benjamin J. Sadock, Harold I. Kaplan, and Virginia A. Sadock, *Kaplan & Sadock's Synopsis of Psychiatry* (Philadelphia: Lippincott Williams & Wilkins, 2007), 865.
10. Robert J. Meadows and Julie Kuehnel, *Evil Minds: Understanding and Responding to Violent Predators* (Upper Saddle River, NJ: Pearson Prentice Hall, 2005), 156–157.
11. *Ibid.*, 157, 169.
12. Bureau of Justice Statistics, *Health Problems of Prison and Jail Inmates* (Washington, D.C.: U.S. Department of Justice, September 2006), 1.
13. Quoted in Eileen Sullivan, "Loners Like Tucson Gunman 'Fly below the Radar,'" *Associated Press* (January 17, 2011).
14. Herman Bianchi, *Justice as Sanctuary: Toward a New System of Crime Control* (Bloomington: Indiana University Press, 1994), 72.
15. Philip Zimbardo, "Pathology of Imprisonment," *Society* (April 1972), 4–8.
16. David Canter and Laurence Alison, "The Social Psychology of Crime: Groups, Teams, and Networks," in *The Social Psychology of Crime: Groups, Teams, and Networks,* ed. David Canter and Laurence Alison (Hanover, NH: Dartmouth, 2000), 3–4.
17. Monica Davey, "In a Soaring Homicide Rate, a Divide in Chicago," *New York Times* (January 3, 2013), A1.
18. Clifford R. Shaw and Henry D. McKay, *Report on the Causes of Crime*, vol. 2: *Social Factors in Juvenile Delinquency* (Washington, D.C.: National Commission on Law Observance and Enforcement, 1931).
19. Emile Durkheim, *The Rules of Sociological Method*, trans. Sarah A. Solovay and John H. Mueller (New York: Free Press, 1964).
20. Robert K. Merton, *Social Theory and Social Structure* (New York: Free Press, 1957). See the chapter on "Social Structure and Anomie."
21. Robert Meier, "The New Criminology: Continuity in Criminology Theory," *Journal of Criminal Law and Criminology* 67 (1977), 461–469.
22. Philip G. Zimbardo, "The Human Choice: Individuation, Reason, and Order versus Deindividuation, Impulse, and Chaos," in *Nebraska Symposium on Motivation,* ed. William J. Arnold and David Levie (Lincoln, NE: University of Nebraska Press, 1969), 287–293.
23. Edwin H. Sutherland, *Criminology*, 4th ed. (Philadelphia: Lippincott, 1947).
24. L. Rowell Huesmann, Jessica Moise-Titus, Cheryl-Lynn Podolski, and Leonard D. Eron, "Longitudinal Relations between Children's Exposure to TV Violence and Their Aggressive and Violent Behavior in Young Adulthood: 1977–1992," *Developmental Psychology* (March 2003), 201.
25. Telecommunications Act of 1996, 47 U.S.C. Section 303 (1999).

26. Travis Hirschi, *Causes of Delinquency* (Berkeley: University of California Press, 1969).

27. James Q. Wilson and George L. Kelling, "Broken Windows," *Atlantic Monthly* (March 1982), 29.

28. Francis T. Cullen and Robert Agnew, *Criminological Theory, Past to Present: Essential Readings,* 2d ed. (Los Angeles: Roxbury Publishing Co., 2003), 443.

29. Michael R. Gottfredson and Travis Hirschi, *A General Theory of Crime* (Stanford, CA: Stanford University Press, 1990).

30. *Ibid.,* 90.

31. *Ibid.*

32. Terrie Moffitt, "Adolescent-Limited and Life-Course-Persistent Antisocial Behavior: A Developmental Taxonomy," *Psychological Review* 100 (1993), 679–680.

33. *Ibid.,* 674.

34. Howard S. Becker, *Outsiders: Studies in the Sociology of Deviance* (New York: Free Press, 1963).

35. David G. Myers, *Psychology,* 7th ed. (New York: Worth Publishers, 2004), 75–76.

36. Peter B. Kraska, "The Unmentionable Alternative: The Need for and Argument against the Decriminalization of Drug Laws," in *Drugs, Crime, and the Criminal Justice System,* ed. Ralph Weisheit (Cincinnati, OH: Anderson Publishing, 1990).

37. Bureau of Justice Statistics, "Alcohol and Crime: Data from 2002 to 2008," at **bjs.ojp.usdoj.gov/content/acf/29_prisoners_and_alcoholuse.cfm and bjs.ojp .usdoj.gov/content/acf/30_jails_and_alcoholuse .cfm**.

38. *ADAM II: 2011 Annual Report* (Washington, D.C.: Office of National Drug Policy, May 2012), vii.

39. James A. Inciardi, *The War on Drugs: Heroin, Cocaine, and Public Policy* (Palo Alto, CA: Mayfield, 1986), 148.

40. *Ibid.,* 106.

41. "Briefing: How America's Views of Marijuana Are Changing," *Christian Science Monitor Weekly* (June 18, 2012), 13.

42. Federal Bureau of Investigation, *Uniform Crime Reporting Handbook* (Washington, D.C.: U.S. Department of Justice, 2004), 74.

43. Federal Bureau of Investigation, *Crime in the United States, 2011* (Washington, D.C.: U.S. Department of Justice, 2012), at **www.fbi.gov/about-us/cjis/ucr /crime-in-the-u.s/2011/crime-in-the-u.s.-2011/about-cius**.

44. *Ibid.*

45. Federal Bureau of Investigation, *Crime in the United States, 2010* (Washington, D.C.: U.S. Department of Justice, 2011), at **www.fbi.gov/about-us/cjis/ucr /crime-in-the-u.s/2010/crime-in-the-u.s.-2010/tables/10tbl01.xls**.

46. Jeffrey Reiman, *The Rich Get Richer and the Poor Get Prison,* 4th ed. (Boston: Allyn & Bacon, 1995), 59–60.

47. *Crime in the United States, 2011,* at **www.fbi.gov/about-us/cjis/ucr/crime-in -the-u.s/2011/crime-in-the-u.s.-2011/tables/expanded-homicide-data -table-10**.

48. *Ibid.,* at **www.fbi.gov/about-us/cjis/ucr/crime-in-the-u.s/2011/crime-in-the -u.s.-2011/tables/table-1**.

49. *Ibid.,* at **www.fbi.gov/about-us/cjis/ucr/crime-in-the-u.s/2011/crime-in-the -u.s.-2011/tables/table-29** and **www.fbi.gov/about-us/cjis/ucr/crime-in -the-u.s/2011/crime-in-the-u.s.-2011/offense-definitions**.

50. *Ibid.,* at **www.fbi.gov/about-us/cjis/ucr/crime-in-the-u.s/2011/crime-in-the -u.s.-2011/tables/table-29**.

51. Marcus Felson, *Crime in Everyday Life* (Thousand Oaks, CA: Pine Forge Press, 1994), 3.

52. *Crime in the United States, 2011,* at **wwwfbi.gov/about-us/cjis/ucr/crime-in-the -u.s/2011/crime-in-the-u.s.-2011/about-cius**.

53. David Hirschel, "Expanding Police Ability to Report Crime: The National Incident-Based Reporting System," *In Short: Toward Criminal Justice Solutions* (Washington, D.C.: National Institute of Justice, July 2009), 1–2.

54. Peter B. Wood, Walter R. Grove, James A. Wilson, and John K. Cochran, "Nonsocial Reinforcement and Criminal Conduct: An Extension of Learning Theory," 35 *Criminology* (May 1997), 335–366.

55. Lynne N. Henderson, "The Wrongs of Victims' Rights," 37 *Stanford Law Review* (1985), 947–948.

56. Lois H. Harrington et al., *President's Task Force on Victims of Crime: Final Report* (Washington, D.C.: U.S. Department of Justice, December 1982), viii.

57. 18 U.S.C. Section 3771 (2006).

58. Susan Herman, *Parallel Justice for Victims of Crime* (Washington, D.C.: The National Center for Victims of Crime, 2010), 45–48.

59. Emily Bazelon, "Money Is No Cure," *New York Times Magazine* (January 27, 2013), 28.

60. Herman, 17–21.

61. Lynn Langton, *Use of Victim Service Agencies by Victims of Serious Violent Crime, 1993–2009* (Washington, D.C.: U.S. Department of Justice, August 2011), 1.

62. Chris E. Kubrin, et al., "Does Fringe Banking Exacerbate Neighborhood Crime Rates?" *Criminology and Public Policy* (May 2011), 437–464.

63. Larry Cohen and Marcus Felson, "Social Change and Crime Rate Trends: A Routine Activity Approach," *American Sociological Review* (1979), 588–608.

64. Kubrin, et al., 441.

65. Cohen and Felson.

66. Herman, 13–16.

67. Katy Reckdahl, "NOPD Release of Murder Victims Criminal Records Is Challenged," *New Orleans Times–Picayune* (January 1, 2012), 1.

68. Quoted in Kevin Johnson, "Criminals Target Each Other, Trend Shows," *USA Today* (August 31, 2007), 1A.

69. Franklin E. Zimring, *The Great American Crime Decline* (New York: Oxford University Press, 2007), 45–72.

70. James Q. Wilson, "Concluding Essay in Crime," in James Q. Wilson and Joan Petersilia, eds., *Crime* (San Francisco: Institute for Contemporary Studies Press, 1995), 507.

71. Zimring, 6.

72. *Ibid.,* 197–198.

73. Quoted in Andrew Mach, "Violent Crime Rates in the U.S. Drop, Approach Historical Lows," msnbc.com (June 11, 2012), at **usnews.nbcnews.com/_news /2012/06/11/12170947-fbi-violent-crime-rates-in-the-us-drop-approach -historic-lows?lite**.

74. *Ibid.*

75. Alexia Cooper and Erica L. Smith, *Homicide Trends in the United States, 1980– 2008* (Washington, D.C.: Bureau of Justice Statistics, November 2011), 16.

76. Cameron McWhirter and Gary Fields, "Communities Struggle to Break a Grim Cycle of Killing," *Wall Street Journal* (August 18–19, 2012), A1.

77. Cooper and Smith, 13.

78. *Crime in the United States, 2011,* at **www.fbi.gov/about-us/cjis/ucr/crime-in-the -u.s/2011/crime-in-the-u.s.-2011/tables/table-43**.

79. *Targeting Blacks: Drug Law Enforcement and Race in the United States* (New York: Human Rights Watch, May 2008), 3.

80. Charles Puzzanchera, Benjamin Adams, and Melissa Sickmund, *Juvenile Court Statistics, 2008* (Washington, D.C.: National Center for Juvenile Justice, July 2011), 20.

81. Ruth D. Peterson, "The Central Place of Race in Crime and Justice—The American Society of Criminology's 2011 Sutherland Address," *Criminology* (May 2012), 303–327.

82. Patricia Y. Warren, "Inequality by Design: The Connection between Race, Crime, Victimization, and Social Policy," *Criminology & Public Policy* (November 2010), 715.

83. William Alex Pridemore, "A Methodological Addition to the Cross-National Empirical Literature on Social Structure and Homicide: A First Test of the Poverty-Homicide Thesis," *Criminology* (February 2008), 133.

84. Caroline Wolf Harlow, *Education and Correctional Populations* (Washington, D.C.: Bureau of Justice Statistics, January 2003), 1.

85. Cooper and Smith, Table 4, page 9.

86. Bureau of Justice Statistics, *Jail Inmates at Midyear 2011—Statistical Tables* (Washington, D.C.: U.S. Department of Justice, April 2012), Table 6, page 6; Bureau of Justice Statistics, *Prisoners in 2011* (Washington, D.C.: U.S. Department of Justice, December 2012), Table 1, page 2; and *Crime in the United States, 2011* at **www.fbi.gov/about-us/cjis/ucr/crime-in-the-u.s.-2011/persons-arrested/persons-arrested**.

87. Federal Bureau of Justice, *Crime in the United States, 2000* (Washington, D.C.: U.S. Department of Justice, 2001), Table 33, page 221; and *Crime in the United States, 2011* at **www.fbi.gov/about-us/cjis/ucr/crime-in-the-u.s/2011 /crime-in-the-u.s.-2011/tables/table-33**.

88. *Prisoners in 2011,* Table 1, page 2.

89. Jennifer Schwartz and Bryan D. Rookey, "The Narrowing Gender Gap in Arrests: Assessing Competing Explanations Using Self-Report, Traffic Fatality, and Official Data on Drunk Driving, 1980–2004," *Criminology* (August 2008), 637–638.

90. Quoted in Barry Yeoman, "Violent Tendencies: Crime by Women Has Skyrocketed in Recent Years," *Chicago Tribune* (March 15, 2000), 3.

91. *Crime in the United States, 2011,* at **www.fbi.gov/about-us/cjis/ucr/crime-in-the -u.s/2011/crime-in-the-u.s.-2011/tables/table-42**.

92. Schwarz and Rookey, 637–671.

93. Meda Chesney-Lind, "Patriarchy, Prisons, and Jails: A Critical Look at Trends in Women's Incarceration," *Prison Journal* (Spring/Summer 1991), 57.

94. Doris J. James and Lauren E. Glaze, *Mental Heath Problems of Prison and Jail Inmates* (Washington, D.C.: U.S. Department of Justice, September 2006), 3.

95. The Gun Control Act of 1968, 18 U.S.C. Section 922(g).

96. Richard A. Friedman, "In Gun Debate, a Misguided Focus on Mental Illness," *New York Times* (December 18, 2012), D5.

97. Seena Fazel and Martin Grann, "The Population Impact of Severe Mental Illness on Violent Crime," *American Journal of Psychiatry* (August 2006), 1397–1403.

98. Jeffrey W. Swanson et al., "Violence and Psychiatric Disorder in the Community: Evidence from the Epidemiologic Catchment Area Surveys," *Hospital & Community Psychiatry* (July 1990), 761–770.

99. James and Glaze, 6.

CHAPTER 3

1. John S. Baker, Jr., *Measuring the Explosive Growth of Federal Crime Legislation* (Washington, D.C.: The Federalist Society for Law and Public Policy Studies, 2008), 1.

2. Quoted in "Judge: Federal Law Trumps Montana's Medical Pot Law," *Associated Press* (January 23, 2012).
3. *Texas v. Johnson,* 491 U.S. 397 (1989).
4. Clean Water Act Section 309, 33 U.S.C.A. Section 1319 (1987).
5. Joel Feinberg, *The Moral Limits of the Criminal Law: Harm to Others* (New York: Oxford University Press, 1984), 221–232.
6. Henry M. Hart, Jr., "The Aims of the Criminal Law," *Law & Contemporary Problems* 23 (1958), 405–406.
7. John L. Diamond, "The Myth of Morality and Fault in Criminal Law Doctrine," *American Criminal Law Review* 34 (Fall 1996), 111.
8. The Humane Society of the United States, "Ranking of State Cockfighting Laws," June 2010, at **www.humanesociety.org/assets/pdfs/animal_fighting /cockfighting_statelaws.pdf**; and Animal Welfare Act Amendments of 2007, Pub. L. No. 110-246, 122 Statute 223 (2007).
9. John Monk, "Cockfighters Take Fight to Federal Appeals Court,") *The State (Columbia, SC)* (December 4, 2011), A1.
10. Lawrence M. Friedman, *Crime and Punishments in American History* (New York: Basic Books, 1993), 10.
11. *Federal Criminal Rules Handbook,* Section 2.1 (West 2008).
12. 625 Illinois Compiled Statutes Annotated Section 5/16-104 (West 2002).
13. Johannes Andenaes, "The Moral or Educative Influence of Criminal Law," *Journal of Social Issues* 27 (Spring 1971), 17, 26.
14. Thomas A. Mullen, "Rule without Reason: Requiring Independent Proof of the *Corpus Delicti* as a Condition of Admitting Extrajudicial Confession," *University of San Francisco Law Review* 27 (1993), 385.
15. *Hawkins v. State,* 219 Ind. 116, 129, 37 N.E.2d 79 (1941).
16. David C. Biggs, "'The Good Samaritan Is Packing': An Overview of the Broadened Duty to Aid Your Fellowman, with the Modern Desire to Possess Concealed Weapons," *University of Dayton Law Review* 22 (Winter 1997), 225.
17. Terry Halbert and Elaine Ingulli, *Law and Ethics in the Business Environment,* 6th ed. (Mason, OH: South-Western Cengage Learning, 2009), 8.
18. Model Penal Code Section 2.02(c).
19. *United States v. Dotterweich,* 320 U.S. 277 (1943).
20. *State v. Stiffler,* 763 P.2d 308, 311 (Idaho Ct.App. 1988).
21. *State v. Harrison,* 425 A.2d 111 (1979).
22. Richard G. Singer and John Q. LaFond, *Criminal Law: Examples and Explanations* (New York: Aspen Law & Business, 1997), 322.
23. *State v. Linscott,* 520 A.2d 1067 (1987).
24. Adam Liptak, "Serving Life for Providing Car to Killers," *New York Times* (December 4, 2007), A1.
25. *Morissette v. United States,* 342 U.S. 246, 251–252 (1952).
26. Federal Bank Robbery Act, 18 U.S.C.A. Section 2113.
27. Quoted in Marc Santora, "Women Is Charged with Murder as a Hate Crime in a Fatal Subway Push," *New York Times* (December 30, 2012), A15.
28. *United States v. Jiminez Recio,* 537 U.S. 270 (2003).
29. Paul H. Robinson, *Criminal Law Defenses* (St. Paul, MN: West, 2008), Section 173, Ch. 5Bl.
30. *M'Naghten's* Case, 10 Cl.&F. 200, Eng.Rep. 718 (1843). Note that the name is also spelled M'Naughten and McNaughten.
31. Model Penal Code Section 401 (1952).
32. Joshua Dressler, *Cases and Materials on Criminal Law,* 2d ed. (St. Paul, MN: West Group, 1999), 599.
33. Stephen Lally, "Making Sense of the Insanity Plea," *Washington Post Weekly Edition* (December 1, 1997), 23.
34. Lawrence P. Tiffany and Mary Tiffany, "Nosologic Objections to the Criminal Defense of Pathological Intoxication: What Do the Doubters Doubt?" *International Journal of Law and Psychiatry* 13 (1990), 49.
35. 518 U.S. 37 (1996).
36. Kenneth W. Simons, "Mistake and Impossibility, Law and Fact, and Culpability: A Speculative Essay," *Journal of Criminal Law and Criminology* 81 (1990), 447.
37. Quoted in Gary Fields and John R. Emshwiller, "As Criminal Laws Proliferate, More Are Ensnared," *Wall Street Journal* (July 23, 2011), at **online.wsj.com /article/SB10001424052748703749504576172714184601654.html**.
38. *Lambert v. California,* 335 U.S. 225 (1957).
39. Federal Bureau of Investigation, *Crime in the United States, 2011* (Washington, D.C.: U.S. Department of Justice, 2012), at **www.fbi.gov/about-us/cjis/ucr/crime -in-the-u.s/2011/crime-in-the-u.s.-2011/tables/expanded-homicide-data -table-14**; and **www.fbi.gov/about-us/cjis/ucr/crime-in-the-u.s/2011 /crime-in-the-u.s.-2011/tables/expanded-homicide-data-table-15**.
40. Craig L. Carr, "Duress and Criminal Responsibility," *Law and Philosophy* 10 (1990), 161.
41. Arnold N. Enker, "In Supporting the Distinction between Justification and Excuse," *Texas Tech Law Review* 42 (2009), 277.
42. *People v. Murillo,* 587 N.E.2d 1199, 1204 (Ill.App.Ct. 1992).
43. Florida Statutes Section 776.03 (2005).
44. *Ibid.*
45. Michael Bloomberg, quoted in "A Lethal Right to Self-Defense," *The Week* (May 4, 2012), 13.

46. Jeff Weiner, "Court Motions Offer Preview of Zimmerman Case," *Sun Sentinel (Fort Lauderdale, FL)* (May 29, 2012), 6B.
47. 287 U.S. 435 (1932).
48. *Jacobson v. United States,* 503 U.S. 540 (1992).
49. Henry J. Abraham, *Freedom and the Court: Civil Liberties in the United States,* 7th ed. (New York: Oxford University Press, 1998), 38–41.
50. Arthur L. Alarcon and Paula M. Mitchell, "Executing the Will of the Voters? A Legislature's Multi-Billion Dollar Death Penalty Debacle," *Loyola of Los Angeles Law Review* 44 (2011), S109.
51. *Skinner v. Oklahoma,* 316 U.S. 535, 546–547 (1942).

CHAPTER 4

1. Kirk Johnson, "Hey, @SeattlePD: What's the Latest?" *New York Times* (October 2, 2012), A16.
2. Egon Bittner, *The Functions of Police in a Modern Society,* Public Health Service Publication No. 2059 (Chevy Chase, MD: National Institute of Mental Health, 1970), 38–44.
3. Carl Klockars, "The Rhetoric of Community Policing," in *Community Policing: Rhetoric or Reality,* ed. Jack Greene and Stephen Mastrofski (New York: Praeger Publishers, 1991), 244.
4. Jack R. Greene and Carl B. Klockars, "What Do Police Do?" in *Thinking about Police,* 2d ed., ed. Carl B. Klockars and Stephen D. Mastrofski (New York: McGraw-Hill, 1991), 273–284.
5. John S. Dempsey and Linda S. Forst, *An Introduction to Policing,* 6th ed. (Clifton Park, NY: Delmar Cengage Learning, 2012), 380–381.
6. Federal Bureau of Investigation, *Crime in the United States, 2011* (Washington, D.C.: U.S. Department of Justice, 2011), at **www.fbi.gov/about-us/cjis/ucr /crime-in-the-u.s/2011/crime-in-the-u.s.-2011/tables/table-29**.
7. Reprinted in *The Police Chief* (January 1990), 18.
8. Robert J. Kaminski, Clete DiGiovanni, and Raymond Downs, "The Use of Force between the Police and Persons with Impaired Judgment," *Police Quarterly* (September 2004), 311–338.
9. Jerome H. Skolnick, "Police: The New Professionals," *New Society* (September 5, 1986), 9–11.
10. Quoted in Nancy Ritter, ed., "LAPD Chief Bratton Speaks Out: What's Wrong with Criminal Justice Research—and How to Make It Right," *National Institute of Justice Journal* 257 (2007), 29.
11. Klockars, 250.
12. James Q. Wilson, *Varieties of Police Behavior: The Management of Law and Order in Eight Communities* (Cambridge, MA: Harvard University Press, 1968).
13. Quoted in Ronnie Garrett, "Predict and Serve," *Law Enforcement Technology* (January 2013), 19.
14. *Ibid.*
15. Charlie Beck and Colleen McCue, "Predictive Policing: What Can We Learn from Wal-Mart and Amazon about Fighting Crime in a Recession?" *The Police Chief* (November 2009), 19.
16. Quoted in "Spies among Us," *U.S. News & World Report* (May 8, 2006), 43.
17. *Ibid.,* 41–43.
18. Raymond W. Kelly, "Homeland Security Preparedness in New York City," pre-pared statement before the U.S. House of Representatives, 2005.
19. Dana Priest and William M. Arkin, "Monitoring America," *Washington Post* (December 20, 2010), A1; and Lois M. Davis et al., *Law Enforcement's Post-9/11 Focus on Counterterrorism and Homeland Security* (Santa Monica, CA: RAND Corporation, 2010), 8.
20. Sara Schreiber, "Social Media and the Mob," *Law Enforcement Technology* (September 2012), 38–39.
21. Quoted in Joel Rubin, "Stopping Crime before It Starts," *Los Angeles Times* (August 21, 2010), A17.
22. James H. Chenoweth, "Situational Tests: A New Attempt at Assessing Police Candidates," *Journal of Criminal Law, Criminology and Police Science* 52 (1961), 232.
23. Yossef S. Ben-Porath et al., "Assessing the Psychological Suitability of Candidates for Law Enforcement Positions," *The Police Chief* (August 2011), 64-70.
24. D. P. Hinkle, "College Degree: An Impractical Prerequisite for Police Work," *Law and Order* (July 1991), 105.
25. Bureau of Justice Statistics, *Local Police Departments, 2007* (Washington, D.C.: U.S. Department of Justice, December 2010), Table 5, page 11.
26. Kevin Johnson, "Police Agencies Find It Hard to Require Degrees," *USA Today* (September 18, 2006), 3A.
27. D. P. Hinkle, "College Degree: An Impractical Prerequisite for Police Work," *Law and Order* (July 1991), 105.
28. *Local Police Departments, 2007,* 12.
29. Bureau of Justice Statistics, *State and Local Law Enforcement Training Academies, 2006* (Washington, D.C.: U.S. Department of Justice, February 2009), 7.
30. National Advisory Commission on Civil Disorder, *Report* (Washington, D.C.: U.S. Government Printing Office, 1968), Chapter 11.
31. *Local Police Departments, 2007,* 14.

32. National Center for Women and Policing, *Equality Denied: The Status of Women in Policing: 2001* (Washington, D.C.: U.S. Government Printing Office, 2002), 4.

33. Jacqueline Mroz, "Female Police Chiefs: A Novelty No More," *New York Times* (April 6, 2008), 3.

34. Gene L. Scaramella, Steven M. Cox, and William P. McCamey, *Introduction to Policing* (Thousand Oaks, CA: Sage Publications, 2011), 318.

35. Quoted in Teresa Lynn Wertsch, "Walking the Thin Blue Line: Policewomen and Tokenism Today," *Women and Criminal Justice* (1998), 35–36.

36. Katherine Stuart van Wormer and Clemens Bartollas, *Women and the Criminal Justice System*, 3d ed. (Upper Saddle River, NJ: Pearson Education, 2011), 318–319.

37. Susan L. Webb, *The Global Impact of Sexual Harassment* (New York: Master Media Limited, 1994), 26.

38. The Cato Institute, "National Police Misconduct Statistics and Reporting Project: 2010 Quarterly Q3 Report," at **www.policemisconduct.net/statistics /2010-quarterly-q3-report**.

39. Joseph L. Gustafson, "Tokenism in Policing: An Empirical Test of Kanter's Hypothesis," *Journal of Criminal Justice* 36 (2008), 5–7.

40. *Local Police Departments, 2007*, 14.

41. David Alan Sklansky, "Not Your Father's Police Department: Making Sense of the New Demographics of Law Enforcement," *Journal of Criminal Law and Criminology* (Spring 2006), 1209–1243.

42. Peter C. Moskos, "Two Shades of Blue: Black and White in the Blue Brotherhood," *Law Enforcement Executive Forum* (2008), 57.

43. Scaramella, Cox, and McCamey, 324.

44. Dempsey and Forst, 183.

45. *Wygant v. Jackson Board of Education*, 476 U.S. 314 (1986).

46. Bureau of Justice Statistics, *Census of State and Local Law Enforcement Agencies, 2008* (Washington, D.C.: U.S. Department of Justice, July 2011), 1; and Bureau of Justice Statistics, *Federal Law Enforcement Officers, 2008* (Washington, D.C.: U.S. Department of Justice, June 2012), 1.

47. *Census of State and Local Law Enforcement Agencies, 2008*, 3.

48. *Local Police Departments, 2007*, Table 3, page 9.

49. *Census of State and Local Law Enforcement Agencies, 2008*, 4.

50. *Ibid.*, Table 4, page 5.

51. Bureau of Justice Statistics, *Sheriffs' Offices, 2003* (Washington, D.C.: U.S. Department of Justice, May 2006), 15–18.

52. Bureau of Justice Statistics, *Sheriffs' Departments, 1997* (Washington, D.C.: U.S. Department of Justice, February 2000), 14.

53. Doris Meissner et al., *Immigration Enforcement in the United States: The Rise of a Formidable Machinery* (Washington, D.C.: Migration Policy Institute, January 2013), 2.

54. Marc Lacey, "At the Border, on the Night Watch," *New York Times* (October 13, 2011), A17.

55. "CBP's 2011 Fiscal Year in Review," at **www.cbp.gov/xp/cgov/newsroom/news _releases/national/2011_news _archive/12122011.xml**.

56. Charlie Savage, "F.B.I. Focusing on Security Over Ordinary Crime," *New York Times* (August 24, 2011), A15.

57. United States Marshals Service, "Fact Sheet," at **www.justice.gov/marshals /duties/factsheets/general-1209.html**.

58. *Private Security Services to 2014* (Cleveland, OH: Freedonia Group, November 2010), 15.

59. John B. Owens, "Westec Story: Gated Communities and the Fourth Amendment," *American Criminal Law Review* (Spring 1997), 1138.

60. National Retail Federation, "Retail Fraud, Shoplifting Rates Decrease, According to National Retail Security Survey," at **www.nrf.com/modules .php?name=News&op=viewlive&sp_id=945**.

61. William C. Cunningham, John J. Strauchs, and Clifford W. Van Meter, *The Hallcrest Report II: Private Security Trends, 1970 to 2000* (Boston: Butterworth-Heinemann, 1990), 236.

CHAPTER 5

1. Kenneth Culp David, *Police Discretion* (St. Paul, MN: West Publishing Co., 1975).

2. C. E. Pratt, "Police Discretion," *Law and Order* (March 1992), 99–100.

3. "More than a Hunch," *Law Enforcement News* (September 2004), 1.

4. Herbert Jacob, *Urban Justice* (Boston: Little, Brown, 1973), 27.

5. Larry Copeland, "Chases by Police Yield High Fatalities," *USA Today* (April 23, 2010), 3A.

6. Bureau of Justice Statistics, *Local Police Departments, 2003* (Washington, D.C.: U.S. Department of Justice, May 2006), 24.

7. Jack Richter, "Number of Police Pursuits Drop Dramatically in Los Angeles," *Los Angeles Police Department Press Release* (August 20, 2003).

8. L. Craig Parker, Robert D. Meier, and Lynn Hunt Monahan, *Interpersonal Psychology for Criminal Justice* (St. Paul, MN: West Publishing Co., 1989), 113.

9. National Institute of Justice, "Table 1. States with Mandatory Arrest Provisions," at **www.nij.gov/publications/dv-dual-arrest-222679/exhibits/table1.htm**.

10. David Hirschel, Eve Buzawa, April Pattavina, and Don Faggiani, "Domestic Violence and Mandatory Arrest Laws: To What Extent Do They Influence Police Arrest Decisions?" *Journal of Criminal Law and Criminology* (Fall 2007), 255–298.

11. Peter K. Manning, *Police Work: The Social Organization of Policing*, 2d ed. (Prospect Heights, IL: Waveland Press, 1997), 96.

12. Samuel Walker, *The Police in America: An Introduction*, 2d ed. (New York: McGraw-Hill, 1992), 16.

13. George L. Kelling and Mark H. Moore, "From Political to Reform to Community: The Evolving Strategy of Police," in *Community Policing: Rhetoric or Reality*, ed. Jack Greene and Stephen Mastrofski (New York: Praeger Publishers, 1988), 13.

14. Michael White, *Controlling Officer Behavior in the Field* (New York: John Jay College of Criminal Justice, 2011), 19.

15. Henry M. Wrobleski and Karen M. Hess, *Introduction to Law Enforcement and Criminal Justice*, 7th ed. (Belmont, CA: Wadsworth/Thomson Learning, 2003), 119.

16. Bureau of Justice Statistics, *Local Police Departments, 2007* (Washington, D.C.: U.S. Department of Justice, December 2010), 6.

17. Connie Fletcher, "What Cops Know," *On Patrol* (Summer 1996), 44–45.

18. David H. Bayley, *Police for the Future* (New York: Oxford University Press, 1994), 20.

19. Walker, 103.

20. Eric J. Scott, *Calls for Service: Citizens Demand an Initial Police Response* (Washington, D.C.: National Institute of Justice, 1981), 28–30.

21. William G. Gay, Theodore H. Schell, and Stephen Schack, *Routine Patrol: Improving Patrol Productivity*, vol. 1 (Washington, D.C.: National Institute of Justice, 1977), 3–6.

22. Gary W. Cordner, "The Police on Patrol," in *Police and Policing: Contemporary Issues*, ed. Dennis Jay Kenney (New York: Praeger Publishers, 1989), 60–71.

23. Anthony V. Bouza, *The Police Mystique: An Insider's Look at Cops, Crime, and the Criminal Justice System* (New York: Plenum Press, 1990), 27.

24. Quoted in Sarah Stillman, "The Throwaways," *New Yorker* (September 3, 2012), 38–39.

25. Center on Law and Security, *Terrorist Trial Report Card: September 11, 2001– September 11, 2009* (New York: New York University School of Law, January 2010), 42–44.

26. Richard A. Serrano, "D.C. Bomb Plot Foiled," *Baltimore Sun* (February 18, 2012), 10A.

27. Debbie Siegelbaum, "Authorities Foil Planned Suicide Bombing Attack on Capitol Building," *The Hill* (February 17, 2012), at **thehill.com/homenews /news/211447-authoritiesfoil-planned-suicide-bombing-attack-on-capitol -building**.

28. Federal Bureau of Investigation, *Crime in the United States, 2011* (Washington, D.C.: U.S. Department of Justice, 2012), at **www.fbi.gov/about-us/cjis/ucr /crime-in-the.u.s/2011/crime-in-the-u.s.-2011/tables/table_25**.

29. James M. Cronin, Gerard R. Murphy, Lisa L. Spahr, Jessica I. Toliver, and Richard E. Weger, *Promoting Effective Homicide Investigations* (Washington, D.C.: Police Executive Research Forum, August 2007), 102–103.

30. Robert C. Davis, Carl Jenses, and Karin E. Kitchens, *Cold Case Investigations: An Analysis of Current Practices and Factors Associated with Successful Outcomes* (Santa Monica, CA: RAND Corporation, 2011), xii.

31. Ronald F. Becker, *Criminal Investigations*, 2d ed. (Sudbury, MA: Jones & Bartlett, 2004), 7.

32. Bureau of Justice Statistics, *Census of Publicly Funded Forensic Crime Laboratories, 2009* (Washington, D.C.: U.S. Department of Justice, August 2012), 1.

33. Joseph Peterson, Ira Sommers, Deborah Baskin, and Donald Johnson, *The Role and Impact of Forensic Evidence in the Criminal Justice Process* (Washington, D.C.: National Institute of Justice, September 2010), 8–9.

34. Simon A. Cole, "More Than Zero: Accounting for Error in Latent Fingerprinting Identification," *Journal of Criminal Law and Criminology* (Spring 2005), 985–1078.

35. Quoted in "New DNA Database Helps Crack 1979 N.Y. Murder Case," *Miami Herald* (March 14, 2000), 18A.

36. Judith E. Lewter, "The Use of Forensic DNA in Criminal Cases in Kentucky as Compared with Other Selected States," *Kentucky Law Journal* (1997–1998), 223.

37. "CODIS—NDIS Statistics," at **www.fbi.gov/about-us/lab/biometric-analysis /codis/ndis-statistics**.

38. *Maryland v. King*, 569 U.S. __ (2013).

39. Wrobleski and Hess, 173.

40. Eddie Reyes, "Next Generation 9-1-1: What It Is—and Why Police Chiefs Should Care," *The Police Chief* (December 2012), 86–87.

41. *Local Police Departments, 2007*, Table 12, page 15.

42. Jerry H. Ratcliffe, et al., "The Philadelphia Foot Patrol Experiment: A Randomized Controlled Trial of Police Patrol Effectiveness in Violent Crime Hotspots," *Criminology* (August 2011), 795–830.

43. David Weisburd and Cynthia Lum, "The Diffusion of Computerized Crime Mapping in Policing: Linking Research and Practice," *Police Practice and Research* 6 (2005), 419–434.

44. Quoted in "New Model Police," *Economist* (June 9, 2007), 29.

45. Lawrence W. Sherman, "Policing for Crime Prevention," in *Contemporary Policing: Controversies, Challenges, and Solutions*, ed. Quint C. Thurman and Jihong Zhao (Los Angeles: Roxbury Publishing Co., 2004), 63–66.

46. *Ibid.*, 65.

47. Brigitte Gassaway, Steven Armon, and Dana Perez, "Engaging the Community: Operation Heat Wave," *Geography and Public Safety* (October 2011), 8–9.

48. Wesley K. Skogan and Megan Alderden, *Police and the Community* (Washington, D.C.: National Police Research Platform, February 2011), 4.

49. *Ibid.*, 5–6.

50. Robert C. Trojanowicz and David Carter, "The Philosophy and Role of Community Policing," at **www.cj.msu.edu/~people/cp/cpphil.html**.

51. Herman Goldstein, "Improving Policing: A Problem-Oriented Approach," *Crime and Delinquency* 25 (1979), 236–258.

52. Bureau of Justice Assistance, *Problem-Oriented Drug Enforcement: A Community-Based Approach for Effective Policing* (Washington, D.C.: Office of Justice Programs, 1993), 5.

53. J. Pete Blair, et al., "Reasonableness and Reaction Time," *Police Quarterly* (December 2011), 324.

54. William A. Geller and Michael S. Scott, *Deadly Force: What We Know* (Washington, D.C.: Police Executive Research Forum, 1992).

55. Blair, et al., 327.

56. Harry J. Mullins, "Myth, Tradition, and Ritual," *Law and Order* (September 1995), 197.

57. William Westly, *Violence and the Police: A Sociological Study of Law, Custom, and Morality* (Cambridge, MA: MIT Press, 1970).

58. Officer Down Memorial Page, at **www.odmp.org/search/year/2013?ref=sidebar and www.odmp.org/search/year?year=2012**.

59. Federal Bureau of Investigation, *Law Enforcement Officers Killed and Assaulted, 2011* (Washington, D.C.: U.S. Department of Justice, 2012), at **www.fbi.gov /about-us/cjis/ucr/leoka/2011/officers-assaulted-1/officers-assaulted**.

60. John S. Dempsey and Linda S. Forst, *An Introduction to Policing*, 6th ed. (Clifton Park, NY: Delmar Cengage Learning, 2011), 170.

61. Steven G. Brandl and Meghan S. Stroshine, "The Physical Hazards of Police Work Revisited," *Police Quarterly* (September 2012), 263.

62. The Officer Down Memorial Page; and Craig W. Floyd and Kevin P. Morrison, "Officer Safety on Our Roadways: What the Numbers Say about Saving Lives," *The Police Chief* (July 2010), 28.

63. National Highway Traffic Safety Administration, *Characteristics of Law Enforcement Officers' Fatalities in Motor Vehicle Crashes* (Washington, D.C.: U.S. Department of Transportation, January 2011), Figure 15, page 25.

64. Gail A. Goolsakian, et al., *Coping with Police Stress* (Washington, D.C.: National Institute of Justice, 1985).

65. J. L. O'Neil and M. A. Cushing, *The Impact of Shift Work on Police Officers* (Washington, D.C.: Police Executive Research Forum, 1991), 1.

66. University at Buffalo, "Impact of Stress on Police Officers' Physical and Mental Health," *Science Daily* (September 29, 2008), at **www.sciencedaily.com /releases/2008/09/080926105029.htm**.

67. James Hibberd, "Police Psychology," *On Patrol* (Fall 1996), 26.

68. Daniel W. Clark, Elizabeth K. White, and John M. Violanti, "Law Enforcement Suicide: Current Knowledge and Future Directions," *The Police Chief* (May 2012), 48.

69. Bureau of Justice Statistics, *Contacts between Police and the Public, 2008* (Washington, D.C.: U.S. Department of Justice, October 2011), 1.

70. Bureau of Justice Statistics, *Arrest-Related Deaths, 2003–2009, Statistical Tables* (Washington, D.C.: U.S. Department of Justice, November 2011), 1.

71. David J. Spotts, "Reviewing Use-of-Force Practices," *The Police Chief* (August 2012), 12.

72. H. Range Hutson, Deirdre Anglin, Phillip Rice, Demetrious N. Kyriacou, Michael Guirguis, and Jared Strote, "Excessive Use of Force by Police: A Survey of Academic Emergency Physicians," *Emergency Medicine Journal* (January 2009), 20–22.

73. 471 U.S. 1 (1985).

74. 471 U.S. 1, 11 (1985).

75. 490 U.S. 386 (1989).

76. *Brosseau v. Haugen*, 543 U.S. 194 (2004).

77. Jocelyn M. Pollock and Ronald F. Becker, "Ethics Training Using Officers' Dilemmas," *FBI Law Enforcement Bulletin* (November 1996), 20–28.

78. Quoted in Thomas J. Martinelli, "Dodging the Pitfalls of Noble Cause Corruption and the Intelligence Unit," *The Police Chief* (October 2009), 124.

79. Pollock and Becker, 20–28.

80. Brandon V. Zuidema and H. Wayne Duff, "Organizational Ethics through Effective Leadership," *Law Enforcement Bulletin* (March 2009), 8–9.

CHAPTER 6

1. *Kentucky v. King*, 131 S.Ct. 1849 (2011).

2. *Ibid.*, 1858.

3. *Ibid.*, 1869.

4. *Michigan v. Summers*, 452 U.S. 692 (1981).

5. *Brinegar v. United States*, 338 U.S. 160 (1949).

6. Rolando V. del Carmen, *Criminal Procedure for Law Enforcement Personnel* (Monterey, CA: Brooks/Cole Publishing Co., 1987), 63–64.

7. *Florida v. Harris*, ____ U.S. ____ (2013).

8. *Maryland v. Pringle*, 540 U.S. 366 (2003).

9. 500 U.S. 44 (1991).

10. *United States v. Leon*, 468 U.S. 897 (1984).

11. Thomas Y. Davis, "A Hard Look at What We Know (and Still Need to Learn) about the 'Costs' of the Exclusionary Rule: The NIJ Study and Other Studies of 'Lost' Arrests," *A.B.F. Research Journal* (1983), 680.

12. 430 U.S. 387 (1977).

13. 467 U.S. 431 (1984).

14. 468 U.S. 897 (1984).

15. 514 U.S. 1 (1995).

16. *California v. Greenwood*, 486 U.S. 35 (1988).

17. *Ibid.*

18. 389 U.S. 347 (1967).

19. *Ibid.*, 361.

20. 486 U.S. 35 (1988).

21. *Ibid.*

22. *Coolidge v. New Hampshire*, 403 U.S. 443, 467 (1971).

23. *Millender v. Messerschmidt*, 620 F.3d 1016 (9th Cir. 2010).

24. del Carmen, 158.

25. *Katz v. United States*, 389 U.S. 347, 357 (1967).

26. *Brigham City v. Stuart*, 547 U.S. 398 (2006).

27. 414 U.S. 234–235 (1973).

28. 395 U.S. 752 (1969).

29. *Ibid.*, 763.

30. Carl A. Benoit, "Questioning 'Authority': Fourth Amendment Consent Searches," *FBI Law Enforcement Bulletin* (July 2008), 24.

31. *Bumper v. North Carolina*, 391 U.S. 543 (1968).

32. *State v. Stone*, 362 N.C. 50, 653 S.E.2d 414 (2007).

33. 267 U.S. 132 (1925).

34. *United States v. Ross*, 456 U.S. 798, 804–809 (1982); and *Chambers v. Maroney*, 399 U.S. 42, 44, 52 (1970).

35. 453 U.S. 454 (1981).

36. *Arizona v. Gant*, 556 U.S. 332 (2009).

37. Adam Liptak, "Justices Significantly Cut Back Officers' Searches of Cars of People They Arrest," *New York Times* (April 22, 2009), A12.

38. Dale Anderson and Dave Cole, "Search and Seizure after *Arizona v. Gant*," *Arizona Attorney* (October 2009), 15.

39. *Maryland v. Wilson*, 519 U.S. 408 (1997).

40. *Whren v. United States*, 517 U.S. 806 (1996).

41. 403 U.S. 443 (1971).

42. 388 U.S. 42 (1967).

43. 18 U.S.C. Sections 2510(7), 2518(1)(a), 2516 (1994).

44. Christopher K. Murphy, "Electronic Surveillance," in "Twenty-Sixth Annual Review of Criminal Procedure," *Georgetown Law Journal* (April 1997), 920.

45. *United States v. Nguyen*, 46 F.3d 781, 783 (8th Cir. 1995).

46. Joseph Siprut, "Privacy through Anonymity: An Economic Argument for Expanding the Right of Privacy in Public Places," *Pepperdine Law Review* 33 (2006), 311, 320.

47. Quoted in Rebecca Kanable, "Dallas' First Year with CCTV," *Law Enforcement Technology* (February 2008), 35.

48. Pub. L. No. 107-56, Section 201-2-2, 115 Stat. 272, 278 (2001).

49. 50 U.S.C. Section 1803 (2000).

50. Patriot Act, Section 203(d)(1), 115 Stat. 272, 280 (2001).

51. Patriot Act, Section 206, amending Section 105(c)(2)(B) of the Foreign Intelligence Surveillance Act.

52. FISA Amendments Act of 2008, Pub. L. No. 110-261, 122 Stat. 2436 (2008).

53. Eric Lichtblau, "Senate Approves Bill to Broaden Wiretap Powers," *New York Times* (July 10, 2008), A1.

54. *Woodson v. Indiana*, No. 49A05-1106-CR-306 (2011).

55. Karen M. Hess and Henry M. Wrobleski, *Police Operation: Theory and Practice* (St. Paul, MN: West Publishing Co., 1997), 122.

56. 392 U.S. 1 (1968).

57. *Ibid.*, 20.

58. *Ibid.*, 21.

59. See *United States v. Cortez*, 449 U.S. 411 (1981); and *United States v. Sokolow*, 490 U.S. 1 (1989).

60. *United States v. Arvizu*, 534 U.S. 266 (2002).

61. *Ibid.*, 270.

62. *United States v. Place*, 462 U.S. 696 (1983).

63. *Hibel v. Sixth Judicial District Court*, 542 U.S. 177 (2004).

64. *Ibid.*, 182.

65. *Minnesota v. Dickerson*, 508 U.S. 366 (1993).

66. *Arizona v. Johnson*, 555 U.S. 328 (2009).

67. Rolando V. del Carmen and Jeffrey T. Walker, *Briefs of Leading Cases in Law Enforcement,* 2d ed. (Cincinnati, OH: Anderson, 1995), 38–40.
68. *Florida v. Royer,* 460 U.S. 491 (1983).
69. See also *United States v. Mendenhall,* 446 U.S. 544 (1980).
70. del Carmen, 97–98.
71. 514 U.S. 927 (1995).
72. Linda J. Collier and Deborah D. Rosenbloom, *American Jurisprudence,* 2d ed. (Rochester, NY: Lawyers Cooperative Publishing, 1995), 122.
73. 547 U.S. 586 (2006).
74. *United States v. Banks,* 540 U.S. 31, 41 (2003).
75. *Hudson v. Michigan,* 547 U.S. 586, 593 (2006).
76. Tom Van Dorn, "Violation of Knock-and-Announce Rule Does Not Require Suppression of All Evidence Found in Search," *The Police Chief* (October 2006), 10.
77. "Warrantless Searches and Seizures" in *Georgetown Law Journal Annual Review of Criminal Procedure, 2011* (Washington, D.C.: Georgetown Law Journal, 2011), 955.
78. *Atwater v. City of Lago Vista,* 532 U.S. 318, 346–347 (2001).
79. *Brown v. Mississippi,* 297 U.S. 278 (1936).
80. 384 U.S. 436 (1966).
81. H. Richard Uviller, *Tempered Zeal* (Chicago: Contemporary Books, 1988), 188–198.
82. *Orozco v. Texas,* 394 U.S. 324 (1969); *Oregon v. Mathiason,* 429 U.S. 492 (1977); and *California v. Beheler,* 463 U.S. 1121 (1983).
83. *Orozco,* 325.
84. *Pennsylvania v. Muniz,* 496 U.S. 582 (1990).
85. del Carmen, 267–268.
86. *New York v. Quarles,* 467 U.S. 649 (1984).
87. Ethan Bonner and Michael S. Schmidt, "In Questions at First, No *Miranda* for Suspect," *New York Times* (April 23, 2013), A13.
88. *Moran v. Burbine,* 475 U.S. 412 (1986).
89. *Michigan v. Mosley,* 423 U.S. 96 (1975).
90. *Fare v. Michael C.,* 442 U.S. 707, 723–724 (1979).
91. 512 U.S. 452 (1994).
92. 560 U.S. ___ (2010).
93. *Dickerson v. United States,* 530 U.S. 428 (2000).
94. James Schnabl, "Are Video Police Reports the Answer?" *The Police Chief* (September 2012), 32.
95. Maurice Chammah, "80 Murder Confession Raises Calls to Require Police to Record Interrogations," *New York Times* (December 28, 2012), A19.

CHAPTER 7

1. Quoted in Eric Velasco, "Watson Acquitted of Wife's Murder," *Birmingham News* (February 24, 2012), 1.
2. Roscoe Pound, "The Administration of Justice in American Cities," *Harvard Law Review* 12 (1912).
3. Russell Wheeler and Howard Whitcomb, *Judicial Administration: Text and Readings* (Englewood Cliffs, NJ: Prentice Hall, 1977), 3.
4. Larry J. Siegel, *Criminology: Instructor's Manual,* 6th ed. (Belmont, CA: West/Wadsworth Publishing Co., 1998), 440.
5. Gerald F. Velman, "Federal Sentencing Guidelines: A Cure Worse Than the Disease," *American Criminal Law Review* 29 (Spring 1992), 904.
6. Wayne R. LaFave, "Section 4.6. Multiple Jurisdiction and Multiple Prosecution," *Substantive Criminal Law,* 2d ed. (C.J.S. Criminal Section 254), 2007.
7. 18 U.S.C. Section 3231; and *Solorio v. United States,* 483 U.S. 435 (1987).
8. 18 U.S.C.A. Section 1951.
9. 372 U.S. 335 (1963).
10. 384 U.S. 436 (1966).
11. 408 U.S. 238 (1972).
12. 428 U.S. 153 (1976).
13. 18 U.S.C. Section 48 (1999).
14. *United States v. Stevens,* 559 U.S. ____ (2010).
15. 559 U.S. _____ (2010).
16. Somini Sengupta, "Courts Divided Over Searches of Cellphones," *New York Times* (November 26, 2012), A1.
17. David R. Stras and James F. Spriggs II, "Explaining Plurality Opinions," *Georgetown Law Journal* 99 (March 2010), 519.
18. Barry R. Schaller, *A Vision of American Law: Judging Law, Literature, and the Stories We Tell* (Westport, CT: Praeger, 1997).
19. Pub. L. No. 76-299, 53 Stat. 1223, codified as amended at 28 U.S.C. Sections 601–610 (1988 & Supp. V 1993).
20. James E. Lozier, "The Missouri Plan a.k.a. Merit Selection Is the Best Solution for Selecting Michigan's Judges," *Michigan Bar Journal* 75 (September 1996), 918.
21. Ciara Torres-Spelliscy, Monique Chase, and Emma Greenman, *Improving Judicial Diversity,* 2d ed. (New York: Brennan Center for Justice, 2010), 1.
22. *Ibid.*
23. *Ibid.*

24. Federal Judicial Center, "Diversity on the Bench," at **www.fjc.gov/history /home.nsf/page/judges_diversity.html**.
25. 295 U.S. 78 (1935).
26. *Brady v. Maryland,* 373 U.S. 83 (1963).
27. *Smith v. Cain,* 132 S.Ct. 627 (2012).
28. *Ibid.*
29. Celesta Albonetti, "Prosecutorial Discretion: The Effects of Uncertainty," *Law and Society Review* 21 (1987), 291–313.
30. *Gideon v. Wainwright,* 372 U.S. 335 (1963); *Massiah v. United States,* 377 U.S. 201 (1964); *United States v. Wade,* 388 U.S. 218 (1967); *Argersinger v. Hamlin,* 407 U.S. 25 (1972); and *Brewer v. Williams,* 430 U.S. 387 (1977).
31. Larry Siegel, *Criminology,* 6th ed. (Belmont, CA: West/Wadsworth Publishing Co., 1998), 487–488.
32. Center for Professional Responsibility, *Model Rules of Professional Conduct* (Washington, D.C.: American Bar Association, 2003), Rules 1.6 and 3.1.
33. *United States v. Wade,* 388 U.S. 218, 256–258 (1967).
34. 372 U.S. 335 (1963).
35. 387 U.S. 1 (1967).
36. 407 U.S. 25 (1972).
37. Laurence A. Benner, "Eliminating Excessive Public Defender Workloads," *Criminal Justice* (Summer 2011), 25.
38. American Bar Association, "Providing Defense Services," Standard 5-7.1, at **www.abanet.org/crimjust/standards/defsvcs_blk.html#7.1**.
39. Robert C. Boruchowitz, "The Right to Counsel: Every Accused Person's Right," *Washington State Bar Association Bar News* (January 2004), at **www.wsba.org /media/publications/barnews/2004/jan-04-boruchowitz.htm**.
40. *Wheat v. United States,* 486 U.S. 153, 159 (1988).
41. Bureau of Justice Statistics, *Defense Counsel in Criminal Cases* (Washington, D.C.: U.S. Department of Justice, 2000), 3.
42. Randolph Braccialarghe, "Why Were Perry Mason's Clients Always Innocent?" *Valparaiso University Law Review* (Fall 2004), 65.
43. John Kaplan, "Defending Guilty People," *University of Bridgeport Law Review* (1986), 223.
44. 491 U.S. 554 (1989).

CHAPTER 8

1. Lawrence M. Friedman and Robert V. Percival, *The Roots of Justice* (Chapel Hill, NC: University of North Carolina Press, 1981).
2. *Riverside County, California v. McLaughlin,* 500 U.S. 44 (1991).
3. Thomas H. Cohen, *Pretrial Release and Misconduct in Federal District Courts, 2008–2010* (Washington, D.C.: U.S. Department of Justice, November 2012), Table 2, page 4.
4. Wayne H. Thomas, Jr., *Bail Reform in America* (Berkeley, CA: University of California Press, 1976), 4.
5. Andrew D. Leipold, "Why Grand Juries Do Not (and Cannot) Protect the Accused," *Cornell Law Review* 80 (January 1995), 260.
6. Sam Skolnick, "Grand Juries: Power Shift?" *The Legal Times* (April 12, 1999), 1.
7. New York Court of Appeals Judge Sol Wachtler, quoted in David Margolik, "Law Professor to Administer Courts in State," *New York Times* (February 1, 1985), B2.
8. Milton Hirsh and David Oscar Markus, "Fourth Amendment Forum," *Champion* (December 2002), 42.
9. Bruce Frederick and Don Stemen, *The Anatomy of Discretion: An Analysis of Prosecutorial Decision Making—Summary Report* (New York: Vera Institute of Justice, December 2012), 4–16.
10. Tom Lininger, "Evidentiary Issues in Federal Prosecutions of Violence against Women," *Indiana Law Review* 36 (2003), 709.
11. 18 U.S.C. Section 3553(e) (2006).
12. 404 U.S. 257 (1971).
13. Fred C. Zacharias, "Justice in Plea Bargaining," *William and Mary Law Review* 39 (March 1998), 1121.
14. Bureau of Justice Statistics, *Prosecutors in State Courts, 2007—Statistical Tables* (Washington, D.C.: U.S. Department of Justice, December 2011), 2.
15. Milton Heumann, *Plea Bargaining: The Experiences of Prosecutors, Judges, and Defense Attorneys* (Chicago: University of Chicago Press, 1978), 58.
16. Albert W. Alschuler, "The Defense Attorney's Role in Plea Bargaining," *Yale Law Journal* 84 (1975), 1200.
17. Stephen J. Schulhofer, "Plea Bargaining as Disaster," *Yale Law Journal* 101 (1992), 1987.
18. North Carolina General Statutes Section 15A-832(f) (2003).
19. 18 U.S.C. Section 3771 (2004).
20. Quoted in Fernanda Santos, "Life Term for Gunman after Guilty Plea in Tucson Killings," *New York Times* (August 8, 2012), A9.
21. Quoted in *ibid.*
22. 407 U.S. 514 (1972).
23. 391 U.S. 145 (1968).
24. *Apodaca v. Oregon,* 406 U.S. 404 (1972); and *Lee v. Louisiana,* No. 07-1523 (2008).

25. 332 U.S. 46 (1947).
26. Barton L. Ingraham, "The Right of Silence, the Presumption of Innocence, the Burden of Proof, and a Modest Proposal," *Journal of Criminal Law and Criminology* 85 (1994), 559–595.
27. 397 U.S. 358 (1970).
28. 380 U.S. 224 (1965).
29. 476 U.S. 79 (1986).
30. Eric L. Muller, "Solving the *Batson* Paradox: Harmless Error, Jury Representation, and the Sixth Amendment," *Yale Law Journal* 106 (October 1996), 93.
31. 499 U.S. 400 (1991).
32. 502 U.S. 1056 (1992).
33. *Snyder v. Louisiana*, 552 U.S. 472 (2008).
34. 511 U.S. 127 (1994).
35. Harry Kalven and Hans Zeisel, *The American Jury* (Boston: Little, Brown, 1966), 163–167.
36. Donald E. Shelton, "Juror Expectations for Scientific Evidence in Criminal Cases: Perceptions and Reality about the 'CSI Effect' Myth," *Thomas M. Cooley Law Review* 27 (2010), at **lawreview.tmc.cooley.edu/Resources/Documents /1_27-1%20Shelton%20Article.pdf**.
37. Thomas J. Reed, "Trial by Propensity: Admission of Other Criminal Acts Evidenced in Federal Criminal Trials," *University of Cincinnati Law Review* 50 (1981), 713.
38. *Ibid.*
39. *People v. Zackowitz*, 254 N.Y. 192 (1930).
40. Federal Rules of Procedure, Rule 804(b)(2).
41. Arthur Best, *Evidence: Examples and Explanations*, 4th ed. (New York: Aspen Law & Business, 2001), 89–90.
42. David W. Broeder, "The University of Chicago Jury Project," *Nebraska Law Review* 38 (1959), 744–760.
43. 164 U.S. 492 (1896).
44. *United States v. Fioravanti*, 412 F.2d 407 (3d Cir. 1969).
45. Bureau of Justice Statistics, *Federal Justice Statistics, 2009* (Washington, D.C.: U.S. Department of Justice, December 2011), 13, 18.
46. William J. Morgan, Jr., "Justice in Foresight: Past Problems with Eyewitness Identification and Exoneration by DNA Technology," *Southern Regional Black Law Students Association Law Journal* (Spring 2009), 87.
47. The Innocence Project, "Innocence Project Case Files," at **www.innocenceproject .org/know**.

CHAPTER 9

1. Herbert L. Packer, "Justification for Criminal Punishment," in *The Limits of Criminal Sanction* (Palo Alto, CA: Stanford University Press, 1968), 36–37.
2. Jay Michaelson, "Can Suicide Be a Hate Crime?" *Newsweek* (March 19, 2012), 17.
3. Harold Pepinsky and Paul Jesilow, *Myths That Cause Crime* (Cabin John, MD: Seven Locks Press, 1984).
4. Brian Forst, "Prosecution and Sentencing," in *Crime*, ed. James Q. Wilson and Joan Petersilia (San Francisco: ICS Press, 1995), 376.
5. Quoted in Kate Zernike, "In Rutgers Spying Case, Voices for Gay Rights Urge Leniency," *New York Times* (May 21, 2012), A1.
6. James Q. Wilson, *Thinking about Crime* (New York: Basic Books, 1975), 235.
7. Isaac Ehrlich, "Participation in Illegitimate Activities: A Theoretical and Empirical Investigation," *Journal of Political Economy* 81 (May/June 1973), 521–564.
8. Avinash Singh Bhati, *An Information Theoretic Method for Estimating the Number of Crimes Averted by Incapacitation* (Washington, D.C.: Urban Institute, July 2007), 18–33.
9. Todd Clear, *Harm in Punishment* (Boston: Northeastern University Press, 1980).
10. Patricia M. Clark, "An Evidence-Based Intervention for Offenders," *Corrections Today* (February/March 2011), 62–64.
11. Heather Strang and Lawrence W. Sherman, "Repairing the Harm: Victims and Restorative Justice," *Utah Law Review* (2003), 15, 18, 20–25.
12. Todd R. Clear, George F. Cole, and Michael D. Reisig, *American Corrections*, 7th ed. (Belmont, CA: Thomson Wadsworth, 2006), 68–69.
13. Josh Allen, "Jon Wilson Helps Crime Victims Talk with Their Offenders," *The Christian Science Monitor Weekly* (April 9, 2012), 45.
14. Gregory W. O'Reilly, "Truth-in-Sentencing: Illinois Adds Yet Another Layer of 'Reform' to Its Complicated Code of Corrections," *Loyola University of Chicago Law Journal* (Summer 1996), 986, 999–1000.
15. David E. Olson, et al., *Final Report: The Impact of Illinois' Truth-in-Sentencing Law on Sentence Lengths, Time to Serve and Disciplinary Incidents of Convicted Murderers and Sex Offenders* (Chicago: Illinois Criminal Justice Information Authority, June 2009), 4–5.
16. Paul W. Keve, *Crime Control and Justice in America: Searching for Facts and Answers* (Chicago: American Library Association, 1995), 77.
17. Kate Stith and José A. Cabranes, "Judging under the Federal Sentencing Guidelines," *Northwestern University Law Review* 91 (Summer 1997), 1247.
18. Mark M. Lanier and Claud H. Miller III, "Attitudes and Practices of Federal Probation Officers towards Pre-Plea/Trial Investigative Report Policy," *Crime & Delinquency* 41 (July 1995), 365–366.
19. Kate Zernike, "Judge Defends Penalty in Rutgers Spying Case, Saying It Fits Crime," *New York Times* (May 31, 2012), A22.
20. Nancy J. King and Rosevelt L. Noble, "Felony Jury Sentencing in Practice: A Three-State Study," *Vanderbilt Law Review* (2004), 1986.
21. Jena Iontcheva, "Jury Sentencing as Democratic Practice," *Virginia Law Review* (April 2003), 325.
22. Julie R. O'Sullivan, "In Defense of the U.S. Sentencing Guidelines Modified Real-Offense System," *Northwestern University Law Review* 91 (1997), 1342.
23. Lisa G. Aspinwall, Teneille R. Brown, and James Tabery, "The Double-Edged Sword: Does Biomechanism Increase or Decrease Judges' Sentencing of Psychopaths?" *Science* (August 2012), 846–849.
24. 18 U.S.C. Section 2113(a) (1994).
25. United States Sentencing Commission, "Statistical Information Packet, Fiscal Year 2011, Northern District of California," Table 7, at **www.ussc.gov/Data _and_Statistics/Federal_Sentencing_Statistics/State_District_Circuit /can11.pdf**; and "Statistical Information Packet, Fiscal Year 2011, Northern District of Iowa," Table 7, at **www.ussc.gov/Data_and_Statistics/Federal _Sentencing_Statistics/State_District_Circuit/2011/ian11.pdf**.
26. United States Sentencing Commission, "Statistical Information Packet, Fiscal Year 2011, Fourth Circuit," Table 7, at **www.ussc.gov/Data_and_Statistics /Federal_Sentencing_Statistics/State_District_Circuit/2011/4c11.pdf**; and "Statistical Information Packet, Fiscal Year 2011, Ninth Circuit," Table 7, at **www.ussc.gov/Data_and_Statistics/Federal_Sentencing_Statistics/State _District_Circuit/2011/9c11.pdf**.
27. Cassia Spohn and David Holleran, "The Imprisonment Penalty Paid by Young, Unemployed Black and Hispanic Male Offenders," *Criminology* 35 (2000), 281.
28. Illinois Disproportionate Justice Impact Study Commission, "Key Findings and Recommendations" (2011), at **www.senatedem.ilga.gov/phocadownload /PDF/Attachments/2011/djisfactsheet.pdf**.
29. Bureau of Justice Statistics, *Prisoners in 2011* (Washington, D.C.: U.S. Department of Justice, December 2012), Table 7, page 7.
30. Federal Bureau of Investigation, *Crime in the United States, 2011*, at **www.fbi.gov /aboutus/cjis/ucr/crime-in-the-u.s/2011/crime-in-the-u.s.-2011/tables/table-43**.
31. Spohn and Holleran, 301.
32. Brian Johnson, "The Multilevel Context of Criminal Sentencing: Integrating Judge- and County-Level Influences," *Criminology* (May 2006), 259–298.
33. 28 U.S.C. Section 991 (1994).
34. Bureau of Justice Statistics, *Felony Sentences in State Courts, 2006—Statistical Tables* (Washington, D.C.: U.S. Department of Justice, December 2009), Table 3.5, page 20.
35. Sonja B. Starr, "Estimating Gender Disparities in Federal Criminal Cases," *University of Michigan Law and Economics Research Paper* (August 29, 2012), at **papers.ssrn.com/sol3/papers.cfm?abstract_id=2144002**.
36. Clarice Feinman, *Women in the Criminal Justice System*, 3d ed. (Westport, CT: Praeger, 1994), 35.
37. Darrell Steffensmeier, John Kramer, and Cathy Streifel, "Gender and Imprisonment Decisions," *Criminology* 31 (1993), 411.
38. Quoted in Kareem Fahim and Karen Zraick, "Seeing Failure of Mother as Factor in Sentencing," *New York Times* (November 17, 2008), A24.
39. John C. Coffee, "Repressed Issues of Sentencing," *Georgetown Law Journal* 66 (1978), 987.
40. J. S. Bainbridge, Jr., "The Return of Retribution," *ABA Journal* (May 1985), 63.
41. Pub. L. No. 98-473, 98 Stat. 1987, codified as amended at 18 U.S.C. Sections 3551–3742 and 28 U.S.C. Sections 991–998 (1988).
42. Julia L. Black, "The Constitutionality of Federal Sentences Imposed under the Sentencing Reform Act of 1984 after *Mistretta v. United States*," *Iowa Law Review* 75 (March 1990), 767.
43. *Fifteen Years of Guidelines Sentencing: An Assessment of How Well the Federal Criminal Justice System Is Achieving the Goals of Sentencing Reform* (Washington, D.C.: U.S. Sentencing Commission, November 2004), 46.
44. Clear, Cole, and Reisig, 86.
45. Neal B. Kauder and Brian J. Ostrom, *State Sentencing Guidelines: Profiles and Continuum* (Williamsburg, VA: National Center for State Courts, 2008), 15.
46. *Blakely v. Washington*, 542 U.S. 296 (2004); *United States v. Booker*, 543 U.S. 220 (2005); and *Gall v. United States*, 552 U.S. 38 (2007).
47. Transactional Records Access Clearinghouse, "Wide Variations Seen in Federal Sentencing" (March 5, 2012), at **trac.syr.edu/whatsnew/email.120305.html**.
48. *Demographic Differences in Federal Sentencing Practices: An Update of the Booker Report's Multivariate Regression Analysis* (Washington, D.C.: U.S. Sentencing Commission, March 2010), C-3.
49. Alabama Code 1975 Section 20-2-79.
50. Quoted in Melinda Rogers, "Reluctant Utah Judge Orders Man to 57 Years in Prison for Gang Robberies," *Salt Lake Tribune* (December 15, 2011), at **www.sltrib.com/sltrib/mobile/53124012-90/maumauprison-angelos -court.html.csp**.

51. United States Sentencing Commission, *Report to Congress: Mandatory Minimum Penalties in the Federal Criminal Justice System* (Washington, D.C.: United States Sentencing Commission, October 2011), xxviii.

52. Washington Revised Code Annotated Section 9.94A.030.

53. 445 U.S. 263 (1980).

54. 538 U.S. 63 (2003).

55. *Lockyer v. Andrade,* 270 F.3d 743 (9th Cir. 2001).

56. *Lockyer v. Andrade,* 538 U.S. 63, 76 (2003).

57. *Ibid.,* 83.

58. Marisa Lagos and Ellen Huet, " 'Three Strikes' Law Changes Approved by Wide Margin," *San Francisco Chronicle* (November 7, 2012), A14.

59. Nicole D. Porter, *The State of Sentencing 2012* (Washington, D.C.: The Sentencing Project, January 2013), 4.

60. Justice for All Act of 2004, Pub. L. No. 108-405, 118 Stat. 2260.

61. Paul G. Cassell, "In Defense of Victim Impact Statements," *Ohio State Journal of Criminal Law* (Spring 2009), 614.

62. Edna Erez, "Victim Voice, Impact Statements, and Sentencing: Integrating Restorative Justice and Therapeutic Jurisprudence Principles in Adversarial Proceedings," *Criminal Law Bulletin* (September/October 2004), 495.

63. Bryan Myers and Edith Greene, "Prejudicial Nature of Impact Statements," *Psychology, Public Policy, and Law* (December 2004), 493.

64. *Payne v. Tennessee,* 501 U.S. 808 (1991).

65. Bryan Myers and Jack Arbuthnot, "The Effects of Victim Impact Evidence on the Verdicts and Sentencing Judgments of Mock Jurors," *Journal of Offender Rehabilitation* (1999), 95–112.

66. Walter Berns, "Abraham Lincoln (Book Review)," *Commentary* (January 1, 1996), 70.

67. Comments made at the Georgetown Law Center, "The Modern View of Capital Punishment," *American Criminal Law Review* 34 (Summer 1997), 1353.

68. David Bruck, quoted in Bill Rankin, "Fairness of the Death Penalty Is Still on Trial," *Atlanta Constitution-Journal* (July 29, 1997), A13.

69. *Baze v. Rees,* 217 S.W.3d 207 (Ky. 2006).

70. *In re Kemmler,* 136 U.S. 447 (1890).

71. 217 U.S. 349 (1910).

72. Pamela S. Nagy, "Hang by the Neck until Dead: The Resurgence of Cruel and Unusual Punishment in the 1990s," *Pacific Law Journal* 26 (October 1994), 85.

73. 553 U.S. 35 (2008).

74. 408 U.S. 238 (1972).

75. 408 U.S. 309 (1972) (Stewart, concurring).

76. *Gregg v. Georgia,* 428 U.S. 153 (1976).

77. 536 U.S. 584 (2002).

78. *Ford v. Wainwright,* 477 U.S. 399, 422 (1986).

79. 536 U.S. 304 (2002).

80. *Penry v. Lynaugh,* 492 U.S. 302 (1989).

81. 543 U.S. 551 (2005).

82. *The Death Penalty in 2012: Year End Report* (Washington, D.C.: Death Penalty Information Center, December 2012), 1.

83. Quoted in Ethan Bronner, "Use of Death Sentences Continues to Fall in U.S.," *New York Times* (December 21, 2012), A24.

84. David McCord, "What's Messing with Texas Death Sentences?" *Texas Tech Law Review* (Winter 2011), 601–608.

85. Cited in "Saving Lives and Money," *The Economist* (March 14, 2009), 32.

86. Quoted in Bronner.

87. Quoted in Mark Morgenstein, "Maryland Legislature Votes to End Death Penalty," *CNN Justice* (March 15, 2013), at **www.cnn.com/2013/03/15/justice/maryland-death-penalty-ban**.

88. *Uttecht v. Brown,* 551 U.S. 1 (2007).

89. Gallup, "U.S. Death Penalty Support Stable at 63%" (January 9, 2013), at **www.gallup.com/poll/159770/death-penalty-support-stable.aspx**.

90. Richard C. Dieter, *A Crisis of Confidence: Americans' Doubts about the Death Penalty* (Washington, D.C.: Death Penalty Information Center, June 2007), 5, 9.

CHAPTER 10

1. Bureau of Justice Statistics, *Probation and Parole in the United States, 2011* (Washington, D.C.: U.S. Department of Justice, November 2012), 1–2.

2. Michael Tonry, *Sentencing Matters* (New York: Oxford Press, 1996), 28.

3. *Probation and Parole in the United States, 2011,* 2.

4. Corrections Task Force of the President's Commission on Law Enforcement and Administration of Justice (1967).

5. Paul H. Hahn, *Emerging Criminal Justice: Three Pillars for a Proactive Justice System* (Thousand Oaks, CA: Sage Publications, 1998), 106–108.

6. Bureau of Justice Statistics, *Correctional Populations in the United States, 2011* (Washington, D.C.: U.S. Department of Justice, November 2012), Table 2, page 3.

7. "Cutting Costs: How States Are Addressing Corrections Budget Shortfalls," *Corrections Directions* (December 2008), 6.

8. John Schmitt, Kris Warner, and Sarika Gupta, *The High Budgetary Cost of Incarceration* (Washington, D.C.: Center for Economic and Policy Research, June 2010), Table 4, page 11.

9. Donna Lyons, "States Are Reshaping Policies to Save Money and Maintain Public Safety with 'Justice Reinvestment' Reforms," *State Legislature Magazine* (January 2013), at **www.ncsl.org/issues-research/justice/high-yield-corrections.aspx**.

10. Nathan Koppel, "Probation Pays Bills for Prosecutors," *Wall Street Journal* (February 12, 2012), A2.

11. Paul W. Keve, *Crime Control and Justice in America* (Chicago: American Library Association, 1995), 183.

12. Gerald Bayens and John Ortiz Smykla, *Probation, Parole, & Community-Based Corrections* (New York: McGraw-Hill, 2013), 186–217.

13. Bureau of Justice Statistics, *Probation and Parole in the United States, 2010* (Washington, D.C.: U.S. Department of Justice, December 2011), Appendix table 3, page 31.

14. Joan Petersilia and Susan Turner, *Prison versus Probation in California: Implications for Crime and Offender Recidivism* (Santa Monica, CA: RAND Corporation, 1986).

15. *Probation and Parole in the United States, 2011,* Appendix table 3, page 17.

16. Brian Skoloff, "George Sanders Gets Probation in Mercy Killing," *Associated Press* (March 29, 2013).

17. 705 So.2d 172 (La. 1997).

18. Neil P. Cohen and James J. Gobert, *The Law of Probation and Parole* (Colorado Springs, CO: Shepard's/McGraw-Hill, 1983), Section 5.01, 183–184; Section 5.03, 191–192.

19. 534 U.S. 112 (2001).

20. *Ibid.,* 113.

21. Carl B. Klockars, Jr., "A Theory of Probation Supervision," *Journal of Criminal Law, Criminology, and Police Science* 63 (1972), 550–557.

22. *Ibid.,* 551.

23. Hahn, 116–118.

24. Matthew T. DeMichele, *Probation and Parole's Growing Caseloads and Workload Allocation: Strategies for Managerial Decision Making* (Lexington, KY: American Probation and Parole Association, May 2007).

25. Brad Branna, "Sacramento County Probation Officers Have Highest Caseload in State," *Sacramento Bee* (April 10, 2013), at **www.sacbee.com/2013/04/10/5329755/sacramento-county-probation-officers.html**.

26. 389 U.S. 128 (1967).

27. *Morrissey v. Brewer,* 408 U.S. 471 (1972); and *Gagnon v. Scarpelli,* 411 U.S. 778 (1973).

28. 465 U.S. 420 (1984).

29. *Probation and Parole in the United States, 2011,* table 4, page 6.

30. Jennifer L. Skeem and Sarah Manchak, "Back to the Future: From Klockars' Model of Effective Supervision to Evidence-Based Practice in Probation," *Journal of Offender Rehabilitation* 47 (2008), 231.

31. William Rhodes, et al., *Recidivism of Offenders on Federal Community Supervision* (Cambridge, MA: Abt Associates, December 2012), 8, 12–13.

32. Elizabeth K. Drake, Steve Aos, and Robert Barnoski, *Washington's Offender Accountability Act: Final Report on Recidivism Outcomes* (Olympia, WA: Washington State Institute for Public Policy, January 2010).

33. Skeem and Manchak, 226–229.

34. Sarah K. Jalbert, et al., *A Multi-Site Evaluation of Reduced Probation Caseload Size in an Evidence-Based Setting* (Cambridge, MA: Abt Associates, March 2011), 8–10.

35. Todd R. Clear, George F. Cole, and Michael D. Reisig, *American Corrections,* 9th ed. (Belmont, CA: Wadsworth Cengage Learning, 2011), 408.

36. *Probation and Parole in the United States, 2011,* table 6, page 8.

37. Joseph Walker, "Rules May Help Parolees Avoid Jail for Small Errors," *New York Times* (January 5, 2012), at **cityroom.blogs.nytimes.com/2012/01/05/rating-a-parolees-risk-before-a-return-to-prison**.

38. *Morrissey v. Brewer,* 408 U.S. 471 (1972).

39. Todd R. Clear and Edward Latessa, "Probation Officer Roles in Intensive Supervision: Surveillance versus Treatment," *Justice Quarterly* 10 (1993), 441–462.

40. 442 U.S. 1 (1979).

41. Marie Gottschalk, "Days without End: Life Sentences and Penal Reform," *Prison Legal News* (April 11, 2013), at **www.prisonlegalnews.org/24102_displayArticle.aspx**.

42. William Parker, *Parole: Origins, Development, Current Practices, and Statutes* (College Park, MD: American Correctional Association, 1972), 26.

43. "Michigan Lets Prisoners Go—and Saves a Bundle," *Bloomberg Businessweek* (December 11, 2011), 16.

44. Quoted in Michael Virtanen, "Chapman Denied Parole a Seventh Time," *Associated Press* (August 24, 2012).

45. Clear, Cole, and Reisig, 420–421.

46. Mark P. Rankin, Mark H. Allenbaugh, and Carlton Fields, "Parole's Essential Role in Bailing Out Our Nation's Criminal Justice Systems," *Champion* (January 2009), 47–48.

47. Norval Morris and Michael Tonry, *Between Prison and Probation: Intermediate Punishments in a Rational Sentencing System* (Oxford: Oxford University Press, 1990).

48. Quoted in Mosi Secret, "Outside Box, Federal Judges Offer Addicts a Free Path," *New York Times* (March 2, 2013), A1.

49. West Huddleston and Douglas B. Marlowe, *Painting the Current Picture: A National Report on Drug Courts and Other Problem-Solving Programs in the United States* (Alexandria, VA: National Drug Court Institute, July 2011).

50. 18 U.S.C. Sections 1961–1968.

51. 516 U.S. 442 (1996).

52. David Ashenfelter, "Police Gain Millions from Forfeited Assets," *Detroit Free Press* (February 27, 2012), A3.

53. Model State Drug Court Legislation Committee, *Model State Drug Court Legislation: Model Drug Offender Accountability and Treatment Act* (Alexandria, VA: National Drug Court Institute, May 2004), 42.

54. New Jersey Courts, "ISP Fact Sheet," at **www.judiciary.state.nj.us/probsup /11556_overviewfactsheet.pdf**.

55. Joan Petersilia and Susan Turner, "Intensive Probation and Parole," *Crime and Justice* 17 (1993), 281–335.

56. Douglas J. Boyle, et al., *Outcomes of a Randomized Trial of an Intensive Community Corrections Program—Day Reporting Center— for Parolees, Final Report for the National Institute of Justice* (October 2011), 3–4.

57. *Probation and Parole in the United States, 2010,* Appendix table 3, page 31.

58. Clear, Cole, and Reisig, 125.

59. Paul Stageberg and Bonnie Wilson, *Recidivism Among Iowa Probationers* (Des Moines, IA: The Iowa Division of Criminal and Juvenile Justice Planning, July 2005); and Paul Koniceck, *Five Year Recidivism Follow-Up Offender Releases* (Columbus, OH: Ohio Department of Rehabilitation and Correction, August 1996).

60. Dale Parent, *Correctional Boot Camps: Lessons from a Decade of Research* (Washington, D.C.: U.S. Department of Justice, June 2003), 6.

61. Robert S. Gable, "Left to Their Own Devices: Should Manufacturers of Offender Monitoring Equipment Be Liable for Design Defect?" *University of Illinois Journal of Law, Technology, and Policy* (Fall 2009), 334.

62. Josh Kurtz, "New Growth in a Captive Market," *New York Times* (December 31, 1989), 12.

63. Edna Erez, Peter R. Ibarra, and Norman A. Lurie, "Electronic Monitoring of Domestic Violence Cases—A Study of Two Bilateral Programs," *Federal Probation* (June 2004), 15–20.

64. Michael Tonry and Mary Lynch, "Intermediate Sanctions," in *Crime and Justice,* vol. 20, ed. Michael Tonry (Chicago: University of Chicago Press, 1996), 99.

65. Dennis Palumbo, Mary Clifford, and Zoann K. Snyder-Joy, "From Net Widening to Intermediate Sanctions: The Transformation of Alternatives to Incarceration from Benevolence to Malevolence," in *Smart Sentencing: The Emergence of Intermediate Sanctions,* ed. James M. Byrne, Arthur Lurigio, and Joan Petersilia (Newbury Park, CA: Sage, 1992), 231.

CHAPTER 11

1. James M. Beattie, *Crime and the Courts in England, 1660–1800* (Princeton, NJ: Princeton University Press, 1986), 506–507.

2. Samuel Walker, *Popular Justice* (New York: Oxford University Press, 1980), 11.

3. Michael Meranze, *Laboratories of Virtue: Punishment, Revolution, and Authority in Philadelphia, 1760–1835* (Chapel Hill, NC: University of North Carolina Press, 1996), 55.

4. Negley K. Teeters, *The Cradle of the Penitentiary: The Walnut Street Jail at Philadelphia, 1773–1835* (Philadelphia: Pennsylvania Prison Society, 1955), 30.

5. Negley K. Teeters and John D. Shearer, *The Prison at Philadelphia's Cherry Hill* (New York: Columbia University Press, 1957), 142–143.

6. Henry Calvin Mohler, "Convict Labor Policies," *Journal of the American Institute of Criminal Law and Criminology* 15 (1925), 556–557.

7. Zebulon Brockway, *Fifty Years of Prison Service* (Montclair, NJ: Patterson Smith, 1969), 400–401.

8. Robert Martinson, "What Works? Questions and Answers about Prison Reform," *Public Interest* 35 (Spring 1974), 22.

9. See Ted Palmer, "Martinson Revisited," *Journal of Research on Crime and Delinquency* (1975), 133; and Paul Gendreau and Bob Ross, "Effective Correctional Treatment: Bibliotherapy for Cynics," *Crime & Delinquency* 25 (1979), 499.

10. Robert Martinson, "New Findings, New Views: A Note of Caution Regarding Sentencing Reform," *Hofstra Law Review* 7 (1979), 243.

11. Byron Eugene Price and John Charles Morris, eds., *Prison Privatization: The Many Facets of a Controversial Industry, Volume 1* (Santa Barbara: Praeger, 2012), 58.

12. Charles H. Logan, *Criminal Justice Performance Measures in Prisons* (Washington, D.C.: U.S. Department of Justice, 1993), 5.

13. Todd R. Clear and George F. Cole, *American Corrections,* 4th ed. (Belmont, CA: Wadsworth Publishing Co., 1997), 245–246.

14. Alfred Blumstein, "Prisons," in *Crime,* ed. James Q. Wilson and Joan Petersilia (San Francisco: ICS Press, 1995), 392.

15. Cassia Spohn and David Holleran, "The Effect of Imprisonment on Recidivism Rates of Felony Offenders: A Focus on Drug Offenders," *Criminology* (May 1, 2002), 329–357.

16. Bureau of Justice Statistics, *Census of State and Federal Correctional Facilities, 2005* (Washington, D.C.: U.S. Department of Justice, October 2008), 2.

17. *Ibid.*

18. Charles H. Logan, "Well Kept: Comparing Quality of Confinement in a Public and Private Prison," *Journal of Criminal Law and Criminology* 83 (1992), 580.

19. Bert Useem and Peter Kimball, *Stages of Siege: U.S. Prison Riots, 1971–1986* (New York: Oxford University Press, 1989).

20. Bert Useem, "Disorganization and the New Mexico Prison Riot of 1980," *American Sociology Review* 50 (1985), 685.

21. John J. DiIulio, *Governing Prisons* (New York: Free Press, 1987), 12.

22. *Ibid.*

23. Todd R. Clear, George F. Cole, and Michael D. Reisig, *American Corrections,* 9th ed. (Belmont, CA: Wadsworth Cengage Learning, 2010), 162.

24. Heather Stokes, "The Design to Aging Foundations" (November 13, 2012), at **prezi.com/l3mrp0gvomor/the-design-to-aging-foundations**.

25. Douglas Page, "The Prison of the Future," *Law Enforcement Technology* (January 2012), 11–13.

26. *Madrid v. Gomez,* 889 F.Supp. 1146 (N.D. Cal. 1995).

27. Keramet Reiter, *Parole, Snitch, or Die: California's Supermax Prisons and Prisoners, 1987–2007* (Berkeley, CA: University of California Institute for the Study of Social Change, 2010), 1.

28. Steven D. Levitt, "Understanding Why Crime Fell in the 1990s: Four Factors That Explain the Decline and Six That Do Not," *Journal of Economic Perspectives* (Winter 2004), 177.

29. Bureau of Justice Statistics, *Prisoners in 2011* (Washington, D.C.: U.S. Department of Justice, December 2012), Appendix table 7, page 26, and appendix table 12, page 29.

30. Allen J. Beck, "Growth, Change, and Stability in the U.S. Prison Population, 1980–1995," *Corrections Management Quarterly* (Spring 1997), 9–10.

31. U.S. District Courts, "Criminal Defendants Sentenced after Conviction, by Offense, during the 12-Month Period Ending September 30, 2011" at **www.uscourts.gov /uscourts/Statistics/JudicialBusiness/2011/appendices/D05Sep11.pdf**.

32. Joan Petersilia, "Beyond the Prison Bubble," *Wilson Quarterly* (Winter 2011), 27.

33. California State Auditor, *Inmates Sentenced under the Three Strikes Law and a Small Number of Inmates Receiving Specialty Care Represent Significant Costs* (Sacramento, CA: Bureau of State Audits, May 2011), 1.

34. *Time Served: The High Cost, Low Return of Longer Prison Terms* (Washington, D.C.: The Pew Center on the States, June 2012), 2.

35. *Fifteen Years of Guidelines Sentencing: An Assessment of How Well the Federal Criminal Justice System Is Achieving the Goals of Sentencing Reform* (Washington, D.C.: U.S. Sentencing Commission, November 2004), 46.

36. *Old Behind Bars: The Aging Prison Population of the United States* (New York: Human Rights Watch, January 2012), 33–34.

37. *Prisoners in 2011,* 1.

38. *Ibid.,* Table 5, page 6.

39. Kamala Mallik-Kane, Barbara Parthasarathy, and William Adams, *Examining Growth in the Federal Prison Population, 1998 to 2010* (Washington, D.C.: Urban Institute, September 2012), 4.

40. Mark Motivans, *Immigration Offenders in the Federal Justice System, 2010* (Washington, D.C.: U.S. Department of Justice, July 2012), 1; and Federal Bureau of Prisons, "Quick Facts about the Bureau of Prisons" (March 30, 2013), at **www.bop.gov/news/quick.jsp**.

41. "Quick Facts about the Bureau of Prisons"; and Bureau of Justice Statistics, *Prison and Jail Inmates, 1995* (Washington, D.C.: U.S. Department of Justice, August 1996), Table 6, page 6.

42. *Prisoners in 2011,* Table 1, page 2.

43. Christian Henrichson and Ruth Delaney, *The Price of Prisons: What Incarceration Costs Taxpayers* (New York: Center for Sentencing and Corrections, January 2012), 6, 8.

44. Rosemary Gartner, Anthony N. Doob, and Franklin E. Zimring, "The Past as Prologue? Decarceration in California Then and Now," *Criminology & Public Policy* (May 2011), 292.

45. Erica Goode, "Inmate Visits Now Carry Added Cost in Arizona," *New York Times* (September 5, 2011), A10.

46. James B. Jacobs, "Finding Alternatives to the Carceral State," *Social Research* (Summer 2007), 695.

47. Gartner, Doob, and Zimring, 294–296.

48. Joseph Walker, "Rules May Help Parolees Avoid Jail for Small Errors," *New York Times* (January 5, 2012), at **cityroom.blogs.nytimes.com/2012/01/05 /rating-a-parolees-risk-before-a-return-to-prison**.

49. Quoted in Scott Cohn, "Private Prison Industry Grows Despite Critics," *cnbc. com* (October 18, 2011), at **www.nbcnews.com/id/44936562/ns/business-cnbc _tv/t/private-prison-industry-grows-despite-critics/#.UW6vC7_zdzU**.

50. Suevon Lee, "By the Numbers: The U.S.'s Growing For-Profit Detention Industry," *ProPublica* (June 20, 2012), at **www.propublica.org/article/by-the -numbers-the-u.s.s-growing-for-profit-detention-industry**.

51. *Prisoners in 2011,* Appendix table 15, page 32.

52. "A Tale of Two Systems: Cost, Quality, and Accountability in Private Prisons," *Harvard Law Review* (May 2002), 1872.

53. Douglas C. McDonald and Kenneth Carlson, *Contracting for Imprisonment in the Federal Prison System: Cost and Performance of the Privately Operated Taft Correctional Institution* (Cambridge, MA: Abt Associates, Inc., October 2005), vii.

54. Vanderbilt University Law School, "New Study Shows Benefits of Having Privately and Publicly Managed Prisons in the Same State" (November 25, 2008), at **law.vanderbilt.edu/article-search/article-detail/index.aspx?nid=213**.

55. Nelson Daranciang, "Isle Inmates Brought Home," *Honolulu Star-Advertiser* (January 28, 2011), A3.

56. John Tunison, "Baldwin Prisoners Will Be Classified Medium Security," *Grand Rapids* (MI) *Press* (December 11, 2010), A4.

57. "Behind the Bars: Experts Question Benefits of Private Prisons," *Kentucky Courier Journal* (July 5, 2010), at **www.courier-journal.com/article/20100705 /NEWS01/7050312/Behind-Bars-Experts-question-benefitsprivate-prisons**.

58. Gregory Geisler, *CIIC: Lake Erie Correctional Institution* (Columbus, OH: Correctional Institution Inspection Committee, January 2013), 16.

59. Curtis R. Blakely and Vic W. Bumphus, "Private and Public Sector Prisons," *Federal Probation* (June 2004), 27.

60. John DiIulio, "Prisons, Profits, and the Public Good: The Privatization of Corrections," in *Criminal Justice Center Bulletin* (Huntsville, TX: Sam Houston State University, 1986).

61. Richard L. Lippke, "Thinking about Private Prisons," *Criminal Justice Ethics* (Winter/Spring 1997), 32.

62. Quoted in Cohn.

63. *Prisoners in 2011,* Appendix table 15, page 32.

64. *Ibid.*

65. Bureau of Justice Statistics, *Jail Inmates at Midyear 2012—Statistical Tables* (Washington, D.C.: U.S. Department of Justice, May 2013), 1, 4.

66. Arthur Wallenstein, "Jail Crowding: Bringing the Issue to the Corrections Center Stage," *Corrections Today* (December 1996), 76–81.

67. Quoted in Fox Butterfield, "'Defying Gravity,' Inmate Population Climbs," *New York Times* (January 19, 1998), A10.

68. *Jail Inmates at Midyear 2011—Statistical Tables,* Table 6, page 6.

69. 441 U.S. 520 (1979).

70. *Ibid.*, at 546.

71. *Jail Inmates at Midyear 2011—Statistical Tables,* Table 12, page 10.

72. Vauhini Vara and Bobby White, "County Jails Prepare for Extra Guests," *Wall Street Journal* (August 10, 2011), A4.

73. Bureau of Justice Statistics, *Census of Jail Facilities, 2006* (Washington, D.C.: U.S. Department of Justice, December 2011), 14.

74. Philip L. Reichel, *Corrections: Philosophies, Practices, and Procedures,* 2d ed. (Boston: Allyn & Bacon, 2001), 283.

75. Robert G. Lawson, "Turning Jails into Prisons—Collateral Damage from Kentucky's 'War on Crime,'" *Kentucky Law Journal* (2006–2007), 1.

76. R. L. Miller, "New Generation Justice Facilities: The Case for Direct Supervision," *Architectural Technology* 12 (1985), 6–7.

77. David Bogard, Virginia A. Hutchinson, and Vicci Persons, *Direct Supervision Jails: The Role of the Administrator* (Washington, D.C.: National Institute of Corrections, February 2010), 1–2.

78. Dan Seligman, "Lock 'Em Up," *Forbes* (May 23, 2005), 216–217.

79. Franklin E. Zimring and Gordon Hawkins, *Incapacitation: Penal Confinement and the Restraint of Crime* (New York: Oxford University Press, 1995), 38, 40, 145.

80. Bruce Western and Becky Pettit, *Collateral Costs: Incarceration's Effect on Economic Mobility* (Washington, D.C.: The Pew Charitable Trusts, 2010), 4.

81. John Tierney, "Prison and the Poverty Trap," *New York Times* (February 19, 2013), D1.

82. *Ibid.*

83. Christopher Uggen, Sarah Shannon, and Jeff Manza, *State-Level Estimates of Felon Disenfranchisement in the United States, 2010* (Washington, D.C.: The Sentencing Project, July 2012), 1.

84. Bureau of Justice Statistics, *Prisoners in 2010* (Washington, D.C.: U.S. Department of Justice, December 2011), Appendix table 14, page 27.

85. Quoted in Fox Butterfield, "Study Finds 2.6% Increase in U.S. Prison Population," *New York Times* (July 28, 2003), A8.

CHAPTER 12

1. Erving Goffman, "On the Characteristics of Total Institutions," in *Asylums: Essays on the Social Situation of Mental Patients and Other Inmates* (New York: Doubleday, 1961), 6.

2. Donald Clemmer, *The Prison Community* (Boston: Christopher, 1940).

3. John Irwin, *Prisons in Turmoil* (Boston: Little, Brown, 1980), 67.

4. *Old Behind Bars: The Aging Prison Population in the United States* (Human Rights Watch, 2012), 24–42.

5. *At America's Expense: The Mass Incarceration of the Elderly* (New York: American Civil Liberties Union, June 2012), vii.

6. *Old Behind Bars: The Aging Prison Population in the United States,* 76.

7. Michael Vitiello, "Addressing the Special Problems of Mentally Ill Prisoners: A Small Piece of the Solution to Our Nation's Prison Crisis," *Denver University Law Review* (Fall 2010), 57–62.

8. Katherine Stuart van Wormer and Clemens Bartollas, *Women and the Criminal Justice System,* 3d ed. (Upper Saddle River, NJ: Pearson Education, 2011), 143.

9. Bureau of Justice Statistics, *Mental Health Problems of Prison and Jail Inmates* (Washington, D.C.: U.S. Department of Justice, September 2006), 1.

10. Fred Osher, et al., *Adults with Behavioral Health Needs Under Correctional Supervision: A Shared Framework for Reducing Recidivism and Promoting Recovery* (New York: Council of State Governments Justice Center, 2012), 8.

11. William Kanapaux, "Guilty of Mental Illness," *Psychiatric Times* (January 1, 2004), at **www.psychiatrictimes.com/forensic-psych/content/article/10168/ 47631**.

12. Bureau of Justice Statistics, *Census of State and Federal Correctional Facilities, 2005* (Washington, D.C.: U.S. Department of Justice, October 2008), 6.

13. *Behind Bars II: Substance Abuse and America's Prison Population* (New York: The National Center on Addiction and Substance Abuse at Columbia University, February 2010), 4.

14. *Ibid.,* 83–84.

15. Devah Pager and Bruce Western, *Investigating Prisoner Reentry: The Impact of Conviction Status on the Employment Prospects of Young Men* (Washington, D.C.: National Institute of Justice, October 2009), 6.

16. *Census of State and Federal Correctional Facilities, 2005,* 6.

17. Ron Barnett, "Incarcerated Getting Educated," *USA Today* (September 26, 2008), 2A.

18. Kevin Johnson, "Prison Diving Program Anchors Former Inmates," *USA Today* (July 14, 2008), 4A.

19. Steve Aos, Marna Miller, and Elizabeth Drake, *Evidence-Based Public Policy Options to Reduce Future Prison Construction, Criminal Justice Costs, and Crime Rates* (Olympia, WA: Washington State Institute for Public Policy, 2006), Exhibit 4, page 9.

20. Robert Johnson, *Hard Time: Understanding and Reforming the Prison,* 2d ed. (Belmont, CA: Wadsworth, 1996), 133.

21. Federal Bureau of Prisons report, cited in Kevin Johnson, "Report Points to Prison Security Failures," *USA Today* (June 8, 2009), 3A.

22. *Mortality in Local Jails and State Prisons, 2000–2010—Statistical Tables,* Table 1, page 5; and Table 12, page 13.

23. Lee H. Bowker, *Prison Victimization* (New York: Elsevier, 1981), 31–33.

24. Stephen C. Light, "The Severity of Assaults on Prison Officers: A Contextual Analysis," *Social Science Quarterly* 71 (1990), 267–284.

25. Frank Tannenbaum, *Crime and Community* (Boston: Ginn & Co., 1938).

26. Randy Martin and Sherwood Zimmerman, "A Typology of the Causes of Prison Riots and an Analytical Extension to the 1986 Virginia Riot," *Justice Quarterly* 7 (1990), 711–737.

27. Bert Useem, "Disorganization and the New Mexico Prison Riot of 1980," *American Sociological Review* 50 (1985), 677–688.

28. Quoted in R. L. Nave, "Private Prisons, Public Problems," *Jackson (MS) Free Press* (June 6, 2012), at **www.jacksonfreepress.com/news/2012/jun/06 /private-prisons-public-problems**.

29. Irwin, 47.

30. Leo Carroll, "Race, Ethnicity, and the Social Order of the Prison," in *The Pains of Imprisonment,* ed. R. Johnson and H. Toch (Beverly Hills, CA: Sage, 1982).

31. Leo Carroll, *Hacks, Blacks, and Cons: Race Relations in a Maximum-Security Prison* (Lexington, MA: Lexington Books, 1988), 78.

32. Craig Haney, "Psychology and the Limits of Prison Pain," *Psychology, Public Policy, and Law* (December 1977), 499.

33. Alan J. Drury and Matt DeLisi, "Gangkill: An Exploratory Empirical Assessment of Gang Membership, Homicide Offending, and Prison Misconduct," *Crime & Delinquency* (January 2011), 130–146.

34. *A Study of Gangs and Security Threat Groups in America's Adult Prisons and Jails* (Indianapolis: National Major Gang Task Force, 2002).

35. George W. Knox, *The Problem of Gangs and Security Threat Groups (STGs) in American Prisons Today: Recent Research Findings from the 2004 Prison Gang Survey,* available at **www.ngcrc.com/corr2006.html**.

36. 42 U.S.C. Sections 15601–15609 (2006).

37. Bureau of Justice Statistics, *Sexual Victimization Reported by Former State Prisoners, 2008* (Washington, D.C.: U.S. Department of Justice, May 2012), 5.

38. James E. Robertson, "The Prison Rape Elimination Act of 2003: A Primer," *Criminal Law Bulletin* (May/June 2004), 270–273.

39. Quoted in John J. DiIulio, Jr., *No Escape: The Future of American Corrections* (New York: Basic Books, 1991), 268.

40. Jack Henry Abbott, *In the Belly of the Beast* (New York: Vintage Books, 1991), 54.

41. Michel Foucault, *Discipline and Punish: The Birth of the Prison* (New York: Pantheon Books, 1977), 128.

42. Lucien X. Lombardo, *Guards Imprisoned: Correctional Officers at Work* (Cincinnati, OH: Anderson Publishing Co., 1989), 51–71.

43. Goffman, 7.

44. Todd R. Clear, George F. Cole, and Michael D. Reisig, *American Corrections*, 9th ed. (Belmont, CA: Wadsworth Cengage Learning, 2011), 333.

45. *Wolff v. McDonnell*, 418 U.S. 539 (1974).

46. Camille Graham Camp and George M. Camp, eds., *The Corrections Yearbook, 2000* (New York: Criminal Justice Yearbook, 2000), 26.

47. 475 U.S. 312 (1986).

48. *Stanley v. Hejirika*, 134 F.3d 629 (4th Cir. 1998).

49. 503 U.S. 1 (1992).

50. Darrell L. Ross, "Assessing *Hudson v. McMillan* Ten Years Later," *Criminal Law Bulletin* (September/October 2004), 508.

51. Cristina Rathbone, *A World Apart: Women, Prison, and a Life behind Bars* (New York: Random House, 2006), 46.

52. Carl Nink et al., *Women Professionals in Corrections: A Growing Asset* (Centerville, UT: MTC Institute, August 2008), 1.

53. Denise L. Jenne and Robert C. Kersting, "Aggression and Women Correctional Officers in Male Prisons," *Prison Journal* (1996), 442–460.

54. Nink et al., 8–9.

55. Matt Gouras, "Female Prison Guards Often behind Sex Misconduct," *Associated Press* (March 14, 2010).

56. *Wolff v. McDonnell*, 539.

57. *Hudson v. Palmer*, 468 U.S. 517 (1984).

58. 429 U.S. 97 (1976).

59. 501 U.S. 294 (1991).

60. *Wilson v. Seiter*, 501 U.S. 294, 304 (1991).

61. Adam Cohen, "Can Food Be Cruel and Unusual Punishment?" *Time* (August 2, 2012), at **ideas.time.com/2012/04/02can-food-be-cruel-and-unusual-punishment**.

62. *Woodall v. Foti*, 648 F.2d, 268, 272 (5th Cir. 1981).

63. *Brown v. Plata*, 563 U.S. ____ (2011).

64. Quoted in Alexandra Marks, "Martha Checks in Today," *Seattle Times* (October 8, 2004), A8.

65. Bureau of Justice Statistics, *Sourcebook of Criminal Justice*, 3d ed. (Washington, D.C.: U.S. Department of Justice, 2003), Table 6.56, page 519; and Bureau of Justice Statistics, *Prisoners in 2011* (Washington, D.C.: U.S. Department of Justice, December 2012), Table 9, page 9.

66. Bureau of Justice Statistics, *Profile of Jail Inmates, 2002* (Washington, D.C.: U.S. Department of Justice, July 2004), 10.

67. Bureau of Justice Statistics, *Prior Abuse Reported by Inmates and Probationers* (Washington, D.C.: U.S. Department of Justice, April 1999), 2.

68. *Caught in the Net: The Impact of Drug Policies on Women and Families* (Washington, D.C.: American Civil Liberties Union, 2004), 18–19.

69. Sarah Schirmer, Ashley Nellis, and Marc Mauer, *Incarcerated Parents and Their Children: Trends 1991–2007* (Washington, D.C.: The Sentencing Project, February 2009), 2.

70. Kelly Bedard and Eric Helland, "Location of Women's Prisons and the Deterrent Effect of 'Harder' Time," *International Review of Law and Economics* (June 2004), 152.

71. *Ibid.*

72. Schirmer, Nellis, and Mauer, 5.

73. Rathbone, 4.

74. *Ibid.*, 158.

75. Van Wormer and Bartollas, 137–138.

76. Barbara Bloom and Meda Chesney-Lind, "Women in Prison," in Roslyn Muraskin, ed., *It's a Crime: Women and Justice*, 4th ed. (Upper Saddle River, NJ: Prentice Hall, 2007), 542–563.

77. Piper Kerman, *Orange Is the New Black: My Year in a Women's Prison* (New York: Spiegal and Grau, 2011), 131.

78. Esther Heffernan, *Making It in Prison: The Square, the Cool, and the Life* (New York: Wiley, 1972), 91.

79. Leanne F. Alarid, "Female Inmate Subcultures," in *Corrections Contexts: Contemporary and Classical Readings*, ed. James W. Marquart and Jonathan R. Sorenson (Los Angeles: Roxbury Publishing Co., 1997), 136–137.

80. Barbara Owen et al., *Gendered Violence and Safety: A Contextual Approach to Improving Security in Women's Facilities*, December 2008, 12–14, at **www.ncjrs .gov/pdffiles1/nij/grants/225340.pdf**.

81. Nancy Wolff, Cynthia Blitz, Jing Shi, Jane Siegel, and Ronet Bachman, "Physical Violence inside Prisons: Rates of Victimization," *Criminal Justice and Behavior* 34 (2007), 588–604.

82. Van Wormer and Bartollas, 146–148.

83. Equal Justice Initiative, "Investigation into Sexual Violence at Tutwiler Prison for Women" (May 2012), at **www.eji.org/files/EJI%20Findings_from _Tutwiler_Investigation.pdf**.

84. Quoted in Sean J. Miller, "When Prison Doors Swing Open," *Christian Science Monitor Weekly* (May 21, 2012), 29.

85. Bureau of Justice Statistics, "Reentry Trends in the United States," at **www.bjs .gov/content/reentry/reentry.cfm**.

86. Joan Petersilia, *When Prisoners Come Home: Parole and Prisoner Reentry* (New York: Oxford University Press, 2003), 39.

87. Victor Hassine, *Life without Parole: Living in Prison Today*, ed. Thomas J. Bernard and Richard McCleary (Los Angeles: Roxbury Publishing Co., 1996), 12.

88. Christy A. Visher, Sara A. Debus-Sherrill, and Jennifer Yahner, "Employment after Prison: A Longitudinal Study of Former Prisoners," *Justice Quarterly* 28 (2011), 713.

89. *Ill Equipped: U.S. Prisons and Offenders with Mental Illness* (New York: Human Rights Watch, 2003).

90. Pew Center on the States, *State of Recidivism: The Revolving Door of America's Prisons* (Washington, D.C.: The Pew Charitable Trusts, April 2011), 2.

91. Quoted in Kevin Johnson, "After Years of Solitary, Freedom Is Hard to Grasp," *USA Today* (June 9, 2005), 2A.

92. *Census of State and Federal Correctional Facilities, 2005,* Table 6, page 5.

93. "The Greatest Fear," *The Economist* (August 26, 2006), 25.

94. Belinda Brooks Gordon and Charlotte Bilby, "Psychological Interventions for Treatment of Adult Sex Offenders," *British Medical Journal* (July 2006), 5–6.

95. Bureau of Justice Statistics, *Recidivism of Prisoners Released in 1994* (Washington, D.C.: U.S. Department of Justice, June 2002), Table 9, page 8.

96. R. Karl Hanson and Kelly Morton-Bourgon, "The Characteristics of Persistent Sexual Offenders: A Meta-Analysis of Recidivism Studies," *Journal of Consulting and Clinical Psychology* 73 (2005), 1154–1163.

97. New Jersey Revised Statute Section 2C:7-8(c) (1995).

98. Public Law Number 109-248, Section 116, 120 Statute 595 (2006).

99. Abby Goodnough, "After Two Cases in Florida, Crackdown on Molesters," *Law Enforcement News* (May 2004), 12.

100. *United States v. Comstock,* 560 U.S. 126 (2010).

CHAPTER 13

1. Jennifer M. O'Connor and Lucinda K. Treat, "Getting Smart about Getting Tough: Juvenile Justice and the Possibility of Progressive Reform," *American Criminal Law Review* 33 (Summer 1996), 1299.

2. *In re Gault*, 387 U.S. 1, at 15 (1967).

3. Samuel Davis, *The Rights of Juveniles: The Juvenile Justice System*, 2d ed. (New York: C. Boardman Co., 1995), Section 1.2.

4. Quoted in Anthony Platt, *The Child Savers* (Chicago: University of Chicago Press, 1969), 119.

5. 383 U.S. 541 (1966).

6. *Ibid.*, 556.

7. 387 U.S. 1 (1967).

8. 397 U.S. 358 (1970).

9. 421 U.S. 519 (1975).

10. 403 U.S. 528 (1971).

11. Quoted in "Colo. Boy Pleads Guilty to Killing Parents," *Associated Press* (September 29, 2011).

12. Research Network on Adolescent Development and Juvenile Justice, *Youth on Trial: A Developmental Perspective on Juvenile Justice* (Chicago: John D. & Catherine T. MacArthur Foundation, 2003), 1.

13. Richard E. Redding, "Juveniles Transferred to Criminal Court: Legal Reform Proposals Based on Social Science Research," *Utah Law Review* (1997), 709.

14. Howard N. Snyder and Melissa Sickmund, *Juvenile Offenders and Victims: A National Report* (Washington, D.C.: U.S. Department of Justice, 1995), 47.

15. Martha Grace Duncan, "'So Young and So Untender': Remorseless Children and the Expectations of the Law," *Columbia Law Review* (October 2002), 1469.

16. 543 U.S. 551 (2005).

17. *Ibid.*, 567.

18. 130 S.Ct. 2011 (2010).

19. *Ibid.*, at 2030.

20. 132 S.Ct. 2455 (2012).

21. *Ibid.*, at 2463.

22. *Surveillance Summaries: Youth Risk Behavior Surveillance—United States, 2011* (Washington, D.C.: Centers for Disease Control and Prevention, June 8, 2012).

23. Federal Bureau of Investigation, *Crime in the United States, 2011* (Washington, D.C.: U.S. Department of Justice, 2012), at **www.fbi.gov/about-us/cjis/ucr /crime-in-the-u.s/2011/crime-in-the-u.s.-2011/tables/table-38**.

24. Charles Puzzanchera, Benjamin Adams, and Sarah Hockenberry, *Juvenile Court Statistics 2009* (Washington, D.C.: National Center for Juvenile Justice, May 2012), 7.

25. Office of Juvenile Justice and Delinquency Prevention, *Juvenile Residential Facility Census, 2008: Selected Findings* (Washington, D.C.: U.S. Department of Justice, July 2011), 1; and Todd Richmond, "Fewer Young Criminals Push States to Close Prisons," *Associated Press* (June 7, 2010).

26. David McDowell, "Juvenile Curfew Laws and Their Influence on Crime," *Federal Probation* (December 2006), 58.

27. *Crime in the United States, 2011,* at **www.fbi.gov/about-us/cjis/ucr/crime -in-the-u.s/2011/crime-in-the-u.s.-2011/tables/table-38**.

28. Puzzanchera, Adams, and Hockenberry, 12.
29. Sara Goodkind et al., "Are Girls Really Becoming More Delinquent? Testing the Gender Convergence Hypothesis by Race and Ethnicity, 1976–2005," *Children and Youth Services Review* (August 2009), 885–889.
30. Kimberly Kempf-Leonard and Lisa Sample, "Disparity Based on Sex: Is Gender-Specific Treatment Warranted?" *Justice Quarterly* 17 (2000), 89–128.
31. Crystal Knoll and Melissa Sickmund, *Delinquency Cases in Juvenile Court, 2009* (Washington, D.C.: Office of Juvenile Justice and Delinquency Prevention, October 2012), 2.
32. *Crime in the United States, 2011,* at **www.fbi.gov/about-us/cjis/ucr/crime -in-the-u.s/2011/crime-in-the-u.s.-2011/tables/table-33**.
33. Margaret A. Zahn et al., "The Girls Study Group—Charting the Way to Delinquency Prevention for Girls," *Girls Study Group: Understanding and Responding to Girls' Delinquency* (Washington, D.C.: Office of Juvenile Justice and Delinquency Prevention, October 2008), 3.
34. Puzzanchera, Adams, and Hockenberry, 77.
35. Melissa Sickmund and Howard N. Snyder, *Juvenile Offenders and Victims: 1999 National Report* (Washington, D.C.: Office of Juvenile Justice and Delinquency Prevention, 1999), 58.
36. Meda Chesney-Lind, *The Female Offender: Girls, Women, and Crime* (Thousand Oaks, CA: Sage Publications, 1997).
37. Denise C. Gottfredson and David A. Soulé, "The Timing of Property Crime, Violent Crime, and Substance Abuse among Juveniles," *Journal of Research in Crime and Delinquency* (February 2005), 110–120.
38. National Center for Education Statistics and Bureau of Justice Statistics, *Indicators of School Crime and Safety: 2011* (Washington, D.C.: U.S. Department of Justice, February 2012), 6.
39. *Ibid.,* 10–15.
40. *Ibid.,* 82–83.
41. *Ibid.,* 44.
42. Jessica Bennett, "From Lockers to Lockup," *Newsweek* (October 11, 2010), 39.
43. Adam J. Speraw, "No Bullying Allowed: A Call for a National Anti-Bullying Statute to Promote a Safer Learning Environment in American Public Schools," *Valparaiso University Law Review* (Summer 2010), 1151–1198.
44. Marvin E. Wolfgang, *From Boy to Man, from Delinquency to Crime* (Chicago: University of Chicago Press, 1987).
45. Quoted in John H. Laub and Robert J. Sampson, "Understanding Desistance from Crime," in *Crime and Justice: A Review of Research* (Chicago: University of Chicago Press, 2001), 6.
46. Travis Hirschi and Michael Gottfredson, "Age and the Explanation of Crime," *American Journal of Sociology* 89 (1982), 552–584.
47. Robert J. Sampson and John H. Laub, "A Life-Course View on the Development of Crime," *Annals of the American Academy of Political and Social Science* (November 2005), 12.
48. David P. Farrington, "Offending from 10 to 25 Years of Age," in *Prospective Studies of Crime and Delinquency,* ed. Katherine Teilmann Van Dusen and Sarnoff A. Mednick (Boston: Kluwer-Nijhoff Publishers, 1983), 17.
49. Office of Juvenile Justice and Delinquency Prevention, *Juveniles in Court* (Washington, D.C.: U.S. Department of Justice, June 2003), 29.
50. Lloyd D. Johnston et al., *Monitoring the Future: National Results on Adolescent Drug Use—Overview of Key Findings, 2011* (Ann Arbor, MI: Institute for Social Research, February 2012), 36.
51. Anahad O'Connor, "Regular Marijuana Use by High School Students Hits New Peak, Report Finds," *New York Times* (December 15, 2011), A16.
52. Carl McCurley and Howard Snyder, *Co-occurrence of Substance Abuse Behaviors in Youth* (Washington, D.C.: Office of Juvenile Justice and Delinquency Prevention, 2008).
53. Gary McClelland, Linda Teplin, and Karen Abram, "Detection and Prevalence of Substance Abuse among Juvenile Detainees," *Juvenile Justice Bulletin* (Washington, D.C.: Office of Juvenile Justice and Delinquency Prevention, June 2004), 10.
54. Arrestee Drug Abuse Monitoring Program, *Preliminary Data on Drug Use and Related Matters among Adult Arrestees and Juvenile Detainees* (Washington, D.C.: National Institute of Justice, 2003).
55. National Mental Health Association, "Mental Health and Adolescent Girls in the Justice System," at **www.nmha.org/children/justjuv/girlsjj.cfm**.
56. Larry J. Siegel and Brandon C. Welsh, *Juvenile Delinquency: The Core,* 4th ed. (Belmont, CA: Wadsworth Cengage Learning, 2011), 268.
57. Edward P. Mulvey, *Highlights from Pathways to Desistance: A Longitudinal Study of Serious Adolescent Offenders* (Washington, D.C.: Office of Juvenile Justice and Delinquency Prevention, March 2011), 1–3.
58. Sherry Hamby et al., *Juvenile Justice Bulletin: Children's Exposure to Intimate Partner Violence and Other Family Violence* (Washington, D.C.: Office of Juvenile Justice and Delinquency Prevention, October 2011), 1.57.
59. Kimberly A. Tyler and Katherine A. Johnson, "A Longitudinal Study of the Effects of Early Abuse on Later Victimization among High-Risk Adolescents," *Violence and Victims* (June 2006), 287–291.
60. Grover Trask, "Defusing the Teenage Time Bombs," *Prosecutor* (March/April 1997), 29.

61. Ashley Nellis, *The Lives of Juvenile Lifers: Findings from a National Survey* (Washington, D.C.: The Sentencing Project, March 2012), 2.
62. Cathy Spatz Widom, *The Cycle of Violence* (Washington, D.C.: National Institute of Justice, October 1992).
63. Janet Currie and Erdal Tekin, *Does Child Abuse Cause Crime?* (Atlanta: Andrew Young School of Policy Studies, April 2006), 27–28.
64. *2011 National Gang Threat Assessment—Emerging Trends* (Washington, D.C.: National Gang Intelligence Center, 2012), 9.
65. Chris Melde and Finn-Aage Esbensen, "Gang Membership as a Turning Point in the Life Course," *Criminology* (August 2011), 513–546.
66. *2011 National Gang Threat Assessment—Emerging Trends,* 15–17.
67. James C. Howell et al., "U.S. Gang Problems Trends and Seriousness, 1996–2009," *National Gang Center Bulletin Number 6* (May 2011), 10.
68. "Race/Ethnicity of Gang Members," *National Youth Gang Survey Analysis* (Institute for Intergovernmental Research/National Youth Gang Center, 2009), at **www.iir.com/nygc/nygsa**.
69. Rachel A. Gordon, Benjamin B. Lahey, Eriko Kawai, Rolf Loeber, and Magda Stouthamer-Loeber, "Antisocial Behavior and Youth Gang Membership: Selection and Socialization," *Criminology* (February 2004), 55–89.
70. Puzzanchera, Adams, and Hockenberry, 31.
71. Knoll and Sickmund, 3.
72. 42 U.S.C. Sections 5601–5778 (1974).
73. S'Lee Arthur Hinshaw II, "Juvenile Diversion: An Alternative to Juvenile Court," *Journal of Dispute Resolution* (1993), 305.
74. Rhode Island General Laws Section 14-1-7.1 (1994 and Supp. 1996).
75. Knoll and Sickmund, 3.
76. Code of Georgia, Section 15-11-39.
77. 467 U.S. 253 (1984).
78. Puzzanchera, Adams, and Hockenberry, 32.
79. Knoll and Sickmund, 3.
80. Barry C. Feld, "Criminalizing the American Juvenile Court," *Crime and Justice* 17 (1993), 227–254.
81. Bureau of Justice Statistics, *Jail Inmates at Midyear 2011—Statistical Tables* (Washington, D.C.: U.S. Department of Justice, April 2012), 1; and Bureau of Justice Statistics, *Prisoners in 2009* (Washington, D.C.: U.S. Department of Justice, December 2010), Appendix table 13, page 27.
82. Knoll and Sickmund, 3.
83. *Reducing Youth Incarceration in the United States* (Baltimore, MD: The Annie E. Casey Foundation, February 2013), 1.
84. Howard N. Snyder and Melissa Sickmund, *Juvenile Offenders and Victims: 2006 National Report* (Washington, D.C.: National Center for Juvenile Justice, March 2006), 98.
85. Dean John Champion, *The Juvenile Justice System: Delinquency, Processing, and the Law,* 5th ed. (Upper Saddle River, NJ: Pearson Prentice Hall, 2007), 581–582.

CHAPTER 14

1. Bureau of Alcohol, Tobacco, Firearms and Explosives, *Firearms Commerce in the United States 2011* (Washington, D.C.: U.S. Department of Justice, August 2011), 15.
2. James Lindgren, "Fall from Grace: Arming America and the Bellesiles Scandal," *Yale Law Journal* 111 (2002), 2203.
3. Federal Bureau of Investigation, *Crime in the United States, 2011* (Washington, D.C.: U.S. Department of Justice, 2012), at **www.fbi.gov/about-us/cjis/ucr /crime-in-the-u.s/2011/crime-in-the-u.s.-2011/tables/expanded-homicide -data-table-7** and **www.fbi.gov/about-us/cjis/ucr/crime-in-the-u.s/2011/crime -in-the-u.s.-2011/tables/10tbl15.xls**.
4. Cited in Jonathan Weisman, "Democrats Quietly Renew Push for Gun Measures," *New York Times* (June 14, 2013), A17.
5. *District of Columbia v. Heller* (2008); and *McDonald v. Chicago,* 561 U.S. 3025 (2010).
6. 18 U.S.C. 922(t).
7. Ronald J. Frandsen, *Enforcement of the Brady Act, 2010* (St. Louis, MO: Regional Justice Information Service, August 2012), 4.
8. *Ibid.*
9. Michael S. Schmidt and Charlie Savage, "Gaps in F.B.I. Data Undercut Background Checks for Guns," *New York Times* (December 21, 2012), A1.
10. Jonathan Weisman, "Senate Blocks Drive for Gun Control," *New York Times* (April 18, 2013), A1.
11. Trip Gabriel, "New Gun Restrictions Pass the Legislature in Maryland," *New York Times* (April 5, 2013), A12.
12. Michael Grunwald, "The Tucson Tragedy: Fire Away," *Time* (January 24, 2011), 38.
13. "We Can Do Better," *Washington Post* (December 18, 2012), A20.
14. Quoted in Adam Magourney, "In an Ocean of Firearms, Tucson Is Far Away," *New York Times* (January 20, 2011), A15.
15. Quoted in David Nakamura and Robert Barnes, "Appeals Court Rules D.C. Handgun Ban Unconstitutional," *Washington Post* (March 10, 2007), A1.

16. Harry Wilson, quoted in David Espo and Nancy Benac, "Gun Control Agenda Seems Futile Despite Tragedies," *Arizona Daily Star* (July 22, 2012), A10.
17. David A. Westbrook, "Bin Laden's War," *Buffalo Law Review* (December 2006), 981–1012.
18. George P. Fletcher, "The Indefinable Concept of Terrorism," *Journal of International Criminal Justice* (November 2006), 894–911.
19. Quoted in Kimberly Dozier and David Espo, "U.S. Kills Osama bin Laden Decade after 9/11 Attacks," *Associated Press* (May 2, 2011).
20. Ahmed S. Hashim, "Al-Qaida: Origins, Goals, and Grand Strategy," in *The McGraw-Hill Homeland Security Handbook,* ed. David G. Kamien (New York: McGraw-Hill, 2006), 24.
21. Quoted in *ibid.,* 9.
22. Quoted in "The Growing, and Mysterious, Irrelevance of al Qaeda," *The Economist* (January 24, 2009), 64.
23. Quoted in Steve Coll, "Name Calling," *New Yorker* (March 4, 2013), 17.
24. Brian Michael Jenkins, *New Challenges to U.S. Counterterrorism Efforts: An Assessment of the Current Terrorist Threat* (Santa Monica, CA: RAND Corporation, July 2012), 2.
25. Quoted in Josh Meyer, "Small Groups Seen as Biggest Threat in U.S.," *Los Angeles Times* (August 16, 2007), 1.
26. "Al Qaida: No Longer a Real Threat?" *The Week* (May 11, 2012), 18.
27. Quoted in Siobhan Gorman, "Terror Risk Falls, U.S. Officials Say," *Wall Street Journal* (April 28–29, 2012), A4.
28. Quoted in Scott Shane, "A Homemade Style of Terror: Jihadists Push New Tactics," *New York Times* (May 6, 2013), A1.
29. *Ibid.*
30. Daniel Klaidman and Christopher Dickey, "The Body Bomb," *Newsweek* (May 21, 2012), 20.
31. Brian Michael Jenkins, "The New Age of Terrorism," in *The McGraw-Hill Homeland Security Handbook,* ed. David G. Kamien (New York: McGraw-Hill, 2006), 117–129.
32. *Ibid.,* 128.
33. Quoted in Marc Santora and William K. Rashbaum, "Bin Laden Relative Pleads Not Guilty in Terrorism Case," *New York Times* (March 9, 2013), A14.
34. "Nearly 500 Convicted on Terror-Related Charges since 9/11: Report," *Reuters* (July 12, 2012).
35. Scott Shane, "Beyond Guantánamo, a Web of Prisons for Terrorism Inmates," *New York Times* (December 11, 2011), A1.
36. *In re Guantánamo Detainee Cases,* 535 F.Supp.2d 443, 447 (D.D.C. 2005).
37. Richard M. Pious, *The War on Terrorism and the Rule of Law* (Los Angeles: Roxbury Publishing Co., 2006), 165–166.
38. Michael Greenberger, "You Ain't Seen Nothin' Yet: The Inevitable Post-Hamdan Conflict between the Supreme Court and the Political Branches," *Maryland Law Review* 66 (2007), 805, 807.
39. Public Law Number 111-383 (January 7, 2011).
40. Quoted in Charlie Savage, "Obama Renews Push to Close Cuba Prison," *New York Times* (May 1, 2013), A1.
41. "One in 7 Who Leave Guantanamo Involved in Terrorism," *Reuters* (May 26, 2009).
42. *Boumediene v. Bush,* 553 U.S. 723 (2008).
43. Adam Liptak, "Justices Reject Detainees' Appeal, Leaving Cloud over Earlier Guantánamo Ruling," *New York Times* (June 12, 2012), A14.
44. Military Commission Act of 2009, Pub. L. No. 111-84, Sections 1801–1807, 123 Stat. 2190 (2009).
45. Charlie Savage, "Delays Keep Former Qaeda Child Soldier at Guantánamo, Despite Plea Deal," *New York Times* (March 25, 2012), 18.
46. Nicole Perloth, "Cyberattack on Saudi Firm Disquiets U.S.," *New York Times* (October 24, 2012), A1.
47. Nicole Perloth, David E. Sanger, and Michael S. Schmidt, "As Hacking Against U.S. Rises, Experts Try to Pin Down Motive," *New York Times* (March 4, 2013), A1.
48. Quoted in "Hype and Fear," *The Economist* (December 8, 2012), 62.
49. Ben Flanagan, "Former CIA Chief Speaks Out on Iran Stuxnet Attack," *The National* (December 15, 2011), at **www.thenational.ae/thenationalconversation/industry-insights/technology/former-cia-chief-speaks-out-on-iran-stuxnet-attack**.
50. Ken Dilanian, "Beware the Coming Cyber Attack," *The Week* (April 8, 2011), 14.
51. James Lewis, "Examining the Cyber Threat to Critical Infrastructure and the American Economy," *Hearing before the Subcommittee on Cybersecurity, Infrastructure Protection, and Security Technologies* (Washington, D.C.: U.S. Government Printing Office, 2012), 41.
52. *Ibid.*
53. Quoted in Marc Santora, "In Hours, Thieves Took $45 Million in A.T.M. Scheme," *New York Times* (May 10, 2013), A1.
54. Jack Nicas, "Crime That No Longer Pays," *Wall Street Journal* (February 5, 2013), A3.
55. Internet Crime Complaint Center, *IC3 2012 Internet Crime Report* (Glen Allen, VA: National White Collar Crime Center, 2013), 4.
56. Symantec, press release, "Norton Study Calculates Cost of Global Cybercrime" (September 7, 2011), at ww.symantec.com/about/news/release/article.jsp?prid=20110907_02.
57. Internet Crime Complaint Center, 16.
58. Bureau of Justice Statistics, *Identity Theft Reported by Households, 2005–2010* (Washington, D.C.: U.S. Department of Justice, November 2011), 1.
59. *Ibid.,* Table 4, page 5.
60. Benny Evangelista Alejandro Martinez-Cabrera, "Big Jump in Number of People on Twitter," *San Francisco Chronicle* (September 4, 2010), D2.
61. Quoted in Matt Richtel and Verne G. Kopytoff, "E-Mail Fraud Hides behind Friendly Face," *New York Times* (June 3, 2011), A1.
62. Ben Rooney, "Cybercrime Exacts a Daily Toll," *Wall Street Journal* (September 12, 2011), 29.
63. Openet, press release, "Openet-Sponsored Study Reveals 41 Percent of Teenagers Experience Cyber-bullying" (January 18, 2012), at **www.openet.com/company/news-events/pressreleases?id=482**.
64. Bureau of Justice Statistics, *Stalking Victimization in the United States* (Washington, D.C.: U.S. Department of Justice, January 2009), 1.
65. *Ibid.*
66. *2012 Cost of Cyber Crime Study: United States* (Traverse City, MI: Ponemon Institute, October 2012), 1.
67. Eduard Kovacs, "87 Billion Spam Emails Sent Out Each Day in Q3 of 2012, Commtouch Reports," *Softpedia* (October 25, 2012), at **news.softpedia.com/news/87-Billion-Spam-Emails-Sent-Out-Each-Day-in-Q3-of-2012-Commtouch-Reports-302232.shtml**.
68. 15 U.S.C. Sections 7701–7713 (2003).
69. *Shadow Market: 2011 BSA Global Software Piracy Study* (Washington, D.C.: Business Software Alliance, May 2012), 1.
70. "The Internet Porn 'Epidemic': By the Numbers," *The Week* (June 17, 2010), at **theweek.com/article/index/204156/theinternet-porn-epidemic-by-the-numbers**.
71. William R. Graham, Jr., "Uncovering and Eliminating Child Pornography Rings on the Internet," *Law Review of Michigan State University Detroit College of Law* (Summer 2000), 466.
72. *United States v. Williams,* 533 U.S. 285 (2008).
73. 31 U.S.C. Sections 5361 *et seq.* (2006).
74. Memorandum Opinion for the Assistant Attorney General, Criminal Division, "Whether Proposals by Illinois and New York to Use the Internet and Out-of-State Transaction Processors to Sell Lottery Tickets to In-State Adults Violate the Wire Act" (September 20, 2011), at **www.justice.gov/olc/2011/state-lotteries-opinion.pdf**.
75. Cyrus Farivar, "State-by-State, America Keeps Betting on Online Poker and Gambling," *Arstechnica.com* (May 19, 2013), at **arstechnica.com/business/2013/05/state-by-state-america-keeps-betting-on-online-poker-and-gambling**.
76. Legal Information Institute, "White Collar Crime," at **www.law.cornell.edu/wex/white-collar_crime**.
77. Federal Bureau of Investigation, "White-Collar Crime" at **www.fbi.gov/about-us/investigate/white_collar/whitecollarcrime**.
78. Michael L. Benson and Sally S. Simpson, *White-Collar Crime: An Opportunity Perspective* (New York: Routledge, 2009), 79–80.
79. *Ibid.,* 81–87.
80. David O. Friedrichs, *Trusted Criminals: White Collar Crime in Contemporary Society,* 4th ed. (Belmont, CA: Wadsworth Cengage Learning, 2010), 278–283.
81. Lawrence Salinger, *Encyclopedia of White-Collar and Corporate Crime,* 2d ed. (Thousand Oaks, CA: Sage, 2004), 361.
82. White-Collar Crime Penalty Enhancement Act of 2002, 18 U.S.C. Sections 1341, 1343, 1349–1350.

1.1 In general, state legislators reject the idea of banning distracted walking as unwarranted government interference. Over the past several years, distracted walking bills have failed in Arkansas, Illinois, and New York. Recently, the Utah Transit Authority did adopt a rule that subjects anyone who crosses the light rail tracks on the streets of Salt Lake City while distracted by an electronic device to a $50 fine. The state legislature refused, however, to implement the rule statewide. "Look, I get distracted all the time," said one Utah lawmaker who opposed the proposal. "Walking on sidewalks, in stores and malls, and maybe in a crosswalk sometimes I'm using my cellphone. But I try to stay connected to my environment. I never thought the government needed to cite me for using my cellphone in a reasonable manner."

3.1 The appellate court refused to throw out the charges. Although Emil was unconscious at the time his car struck the schoolgirls, he had made the initial decision to get behind the wheel despite the knowledge that he suffered from epileptic seizures. In other words, the *actus reus* in this crime was not Emil's driving into the girls, but his decision to drive in the first place. That decision was certainly voluntary and therefore satisfies the requirements of *actus reus*. Note that if Emil had never had an epileptic seizure before and had no idea that he suffered from that malady, the court's decision would probably have been different.

5.1 As these events actually played out, fifteen Cincinnati law enforcement officers had surrounded a suspect named Lorenzo Collins when he brandished the brick, and the two officers closest to Collins fatally shot him. The two officers were cleared of any wrongdoing, given that a reasonable officer in their position could have seen the brick as an instrument that could cause death or serious bodily harm. The court of public opinion, however, was against the police officers, who were accused by members of the community of needlessly killing a mentally unstable man who was carrying a brick, not a knife or a gun.

6.1 The United States Supreme Court upheld Michael's conviction, ruling that as long as police officers have probable cause to believe that a traffic violation has occurred, the "real" reason for making the stop is irrelevant. As Justice Antonin Scalia put it, "Subjective intentions play no role in ordinary, probable-cause, Fourth Amendment analysis." In practical terms, this ruling gives law enforcement agents the ability to confirm "hunches" about serious illegal behavior as long as the target of these hunches commits even the most minor traffic violation. Such violations could include failing to properly signal during a turn, or making a rolling stop at a stop sign, or driving five miles over the posted speed limit.

8.1 The North Carolina prosecutor in this case charged Judy Norman with first degree murder, reasoning that self-defense did not apply because Judy did not face any *imminent* danger from her husband, John. Despite his threats and the years of abuse, John was, at the time of his murder, asleep and thus incapable of harming her. A jury in the case, however, found Judy guilty of voluntary manslaughter only, and she was sentenced to six years in prison. This case gained national attention because the trial court refused to allow evidence of *battered woman syndrome (BWS)* to be presented to the jury. The term describes the psychological state a person descends into following a lengthy period of physical abuse. In a courtroom, an expert might argue that anyone suffering from this syndrome is in a constant, and reasonable, fear for her or his life. Some states do allow evidence of BWS to support the defendant's claim of self-defense in these sorts of cases, and it has been effective. A New York woman who shot her abusive husband as he slept, for example, was acquitted after a jury accepted her self-defense claims, bolstered by expert testimony on BWS.

9.1 Before the sentencing phase of this trial began, Sedgwick County (Kansas) District Judge Ben Burgess allowed the prosecution to tell the jury that Elgin Robinson's murder-for-hire plot was "heinous, atrocious, and cruel." The defense had argued unsuccessfully that, as Robinson did not commit the murder himself, the crime's heinousness should not be an aggravating factor. Despite this ruling, after four hours of deliberation, the jury could not reach a unanimous verdict for the death penalty, with jurors voting 9–3 in favor of execution. By Kansas law, therefore, Robinson was sentenced to life in prison. Alabama and Florida are the only states that do not require a unanimous verdict for a jury to sentence a convict to be executed. Alabama requires ten votes, and Florida requires seven votes to impose the death penalty.

10.1 Alain LeConte's probation officer did not take any steps to revoke his probation. The issue became moot, however, when LeConte was arrested for killing a gas station attendant during an armed robbery in Norwalk, Connecticut. The crime took place between his first and second failed drug tests. LeConte's probation officer came under a great deal of criticism for failing to revoke his probation, but she received support from her supervisor. "We can only do so much," he said. "[LeConte's] probation officer went out of her way to assist this young man, but unfortunately it wasn't successful." The supervisor also pointed out that LeConte had no known history of violent behavior and had been a generally cooperative probationer when it came to getting treatment. This case underscores the difficult aspects of a probation officer's job. A misjudgment, even if it was based on a reasonable evaluation of the situation, can end in tragedy.

10.2 Susan Atkins was a disciple of cult leader Charles Manson and, in the summer of 1969, participated in one of the most sensationalized mass murders in American history. The woman Atkins stabbed sixteen times was Sharon Tate, an actress and the wife of film director Roman Polanski. On September 2, 2009, the California Board of Parole unanimously denied compassionate release for Atkins, marking the eighteenth time she had been refused parole. Three months later, Atkins died of brain cancer. Her case highlights the extent to which parole boards are often swayed by the nature of the crime above all other considerations.

14.1 On April 22, 2013, federal authorities charged Dzhokhar Tsarnaev with one count of using and conspiring to use a weapon of mass destruction resulting in death and one count of malicious destruction of property by means of an explosive device resulting in death. White House spokesman Jay Carney said that because Dzhokhar is a U.S. citizen, it would not have been appropriate to designate him an enemy combatant. In general, the Obama administration has indicated its preference for trying all terrorist suspects apprehended in the United States through the criminal justice system.

malware, 318
pirating intellectual property online, 318–319
spam, 318
vs. community
gambling, 319–320
online pornography, 319
cyberattacks as future of terrorism, 312–313
defined, 7, 313–314
gambling, 319–320
incidence of, 314
opportunity and anonymity of, 315
vs. persons and property
advanced fee fraud, 315
cyberbullying, 316–317
cyber fraud, 315
cyberstalking, 317
identity theft, 315
keystroke logging, 315–316
online auction fraud, 315
online dating fraud, 315
phishing, 316
trends in, 313–314
Cyber fraud, 315
Cyberstalking, 317

D

Dark figure of crime, 37
Dawson, Krysta, 211–212
Day reporting centers, 226–227
Deadly force, 111–112
justifiable use of force, 65–66
Death penalty, 202–207
age and, 206
arbitrariness of, 204
bifurcated process, 204–205
in colonies, 234
decline in executions, 206–207
defined, 202
Eighth Amendment, 204, 205, 206
executions by state, 205
as form of punishment, 193
future of, 206–207
historical perspective on, 202–203
incapacitation argument, 189
insanity, 206
jury and, 194–195, 204–205
juveniles and, 206, 284
legal cost of, 207
mentally handicapped and, 206
methods of execution, 203
mitigating circumstances, 205–206
number of executions 1976 to 2009, 202, 203
number of prisoners on death row, 202–203
public opinion of, 207
rational choice theory and, 25
Sixth Amendment, 205
Supreme Court rulings and, 203–206
victim impact statement, 202

Death row, number of prisoners on, 202–203
Decarceration, 245
Deception, white-collar crime and, 322
Decker, Scott, 20
Deepwater Horizon oil spill, 322–323
Defendants
appeals, 181–183
arraignment, 166
attorney-client privilege and, 158
in civil cases, 52–53
defined, 52
federal sentencing guidelines, 199
Fifth Amendment, 170–171
plea bargaining and, 167–169, 168
presumption of innocence, 171
self-incrimination, 170–171
Defense(s)
affirmative defense, 179
alibi, 61, 179
creating reasonable doubt, 179
duress, 65, 179
entrapment, 66–67, 179
infancy, 62
insanity, 62–63, 179
intoxication, 63–64
justifiable use of force, 65–66
mistake, 64
necessity, 66
self-defense, 65, 179
Defense attorney
attorney-client privilege and, 158
charging conference, 180
closing arguments, 180
in courtroom work group, 156–158
creating reasonable doubt, 179
cross-examination, 178–179
defending the guilty, 156–157
defense strategies, 179
evidence and, 175
federal sentencing guidelines, 199
hearsay, 178–179
jury selection and, 172–173
opening statements, 175
plea bargaining and, 168
preliminary hearing and, 164–165
private attorney, 157
public defenders, 157–158
responsibilities of, 156
surrebuttal, 180
del Carmen, Rolando V., 131
Delegation of authority, 99
Deliberate indifference standard, 266
DeLisi, Matt, 261
Dempsey, John S., 109
Denial-of-service, 312
Department of Homeland Security (DHS). See Homeland Security, Department of (DHS)
Departure, 200
Depositions, 154

Deprivation model, 259
Deputy sheriff/jail division, 249
Desistance, 272, 289
Detective, 101, 135
Detention
as element of arrest, 132
of juveniles, 294–295
preventive, 295
Detention hearing, 295
Determinate sentencing, 192
Deterrence
general, 188
patrol officers, 100
as purpose of sentencing, 188
specific, 188
Deviance, 5–6
DHS. See Homeland Security, Department of (DHS)
Diamond, John L., 51–52
Diaz, John, 73
Differential association, theory of, 31
Dilulio, John, 239, 240
Directed patrol, 106
Direct evidence, 176–177
Direct examination, 177–178
Direct supervision approach in jails, 250–251
Discovery, 164
Discretion
in criminal justice system, 13–14
defined, 13
elements of, 96
ethical dilemmas of, 113
high-speed pursuits and, 96–97
of judges, 150–151
judicial, 193–194, 198, 297
juvenile crime and, 292–293
limiting, 96–97
low-visibility decision making, 293
mandatory arrest policies and, 97
of patrol officers, 96–97
pitfalls of, 15
probation officers, 216
prosecutors, 155, 165–166
sixth sense and, 96
Discretionary release, 222–223
Discrimination, in sentencing, 197–198
Disorderly conduct, 54
Disorganized zones, 29
Disposition hearing, 297
Dispositions, 193
Dissenting opinions, 150
District attorney, 155
District courts, U.S., 12, 147
Ditsworth, John, 215
Diversion
community corrections as, 212–213
pretrial diversion programs, 225, 293–294
probation, 293
restitution, 294
treatment and aid, 293–294

Diversity
benefits of, in police force, 83
judges and, 153
DNA data
CODIS and, 105
collections and arrests, 105
databases and cold hits, 105
DNA fingerprinting and, 103–104
Docket, 151
Domestic courts, 145
Domestic terrorism
defined, 102
future trends, 308
preventive policing, 102
Domestic violence, 97
mandatory arrest policies, 97
uncooperative victims, 166
Domestic violence counselors, 97
Dopamine, 27
Dorner, Christopher, 83
Double jeopardy, 68
civil suits and, 182
defined, 182
hung jury and, 182
juveniles and, 282
Double marginality, 82–83
Downing, Michael, 78
Drug(s)
decriminalization of marijuana, 34
defined, 32
mandatory sentencing guidelines, 200
psychoactive, 32
Drug abuse
addiction models, 34
defined, 33
juvenile delinquency and, 289–290
Drug courts, 145, 225–226
Drug Enforcement Administration (DEA), 11
responsibilities of, 89–90
Drug offenses
average length of sentence, 215
growth in prison population and, 243–244
increased probability of incarceration and, 244
by juveniles, 285
sentencing disparity, 197
Drug trafficking
average length of sentence, 215
sentencing disparity, 197
Drug use
crime and, 32–34, 33–34
drug abuse and, 33
schizophrenia and, 28
theories of, 32–33
in United States, 32, 33
Drug Use Forecasting Program, 37
Drury, Alan J., 261
Dual court system, 144–145
Due process
constitutional guarantee of, 67

boot camp, 298–299
confinement, 298–299
graduated sanctions, 297
probation, 297–298
residential treatment
programs, 298
training school, 299
training schools, 299
rise and fall of juvenile crime,
285–286
school violence, 287
status offenders, 281
on trial, 295–297
tried as adults, 281, 283, 294

K

Kaczynski, Ted, 242
Kagan, Elena, 153
Kaplan, John, 158
Katz, Jack, 25
Kelley, Mark, 169
Kelling, George L., 31, 107
Kelly, Raymond, 76
Kemmler, William, 203
Kennedy, Anthony, 130, 284
Kennedy, David, 41
Kennedy, Robert, 88
Kent, Morris, 282
Keystroke logging, 315
Khan, Samir, 3
Kimball, Peter, 239
King, Hollis, 117
Klockars, Carl B., 74, 75, 216
K-9 trainers, 120
Knock and announce rule, 133
Korey, Jason, 179
Kratcoski, Peter C., 260
Kurlychek, Megan, 8
Kwaska, Leo, 62

L

LaFree, Gary, 42
La Neustra Familia, 261
Lanza, Adam, 44, 90, 303–304,
305
Lanza, Nancy, 303
Larceny, 6, 36
Laub, John H., 289
Law clerk, 151
Law enforcement
in criminal justice system,
10–11
federal, 11
intelligence-led policing, 76,
77–78
local, 10–11
as responsibility of police, 74–76
state, 11
Law enforcement agencies,
83–92
benefits of diversity, 83
chain of command, 98–99
federal agencies, 85–91
municipal agencies, 83
number of, 83
sheriffs and county agencies,
84–85

social media used by, 73,
77–78
state police and highway
patrol, 85
Law Enforcement Code of Ethics,
74
Law enforcement officers. *See
also* Police
academy training, 80
authority and, 111–112
broken windows theory, 107
career overview, 10
community policing, 107–108
community services provided,
74–75, 100
corruption by, 112–113
crime prevention and, 75
danger of police work,
109–110
deaths of, 109–110
discretion and, 15, 96–97
educational requirements, 79
enforcing laws, 74
entry-level, average salary for, 78
field services, 99–101
field training, 80
high-speed chases and
discretion, 96–97
investigations, 101–105
juveniles and discretion of,
292–293
minorities as, 82–83
patrol, 99–101
peacekeeping role, 75–76
probationary period, 80
problem-oriented policing, 108
recruitment for, 78
requirements for, 78–80
salary, 78
stress and mental dangers of,
110
subculture of, 109
undercover officers, 101–102
use of force, 111–112
women as, 81–82
Laws. *See also* Criminal law
administrative, 50
case law, 50
civil, 52–53
common, 48
constitutional, 48
ethics and, 16
legal function of, 51
legal supremacy, 49
police enforcing, 74
social function of, 51–52
statutory, 48–50
uncodified, 48
Lay witness, 176
Lazarus, Philip J., 24
Leading questions, 178
Learning theory, 31
violence in media and, 31
Lecky, Raymar, 73
Legal assistant, 58
Legal duty, 56
Legislative sentencing authority,
191–192
Legislative waiver, 294

Legitimate security interests, 265
Lehman Brothers, 324
Leitch, Emily, 225
Lennon, John, 223
Lethal injection, 203
Lewis, James, 313
Liability, 53
Liable, 53
Liebman, James S., 206
Lie detector, 152
Life course theory of crime, 31–32
continuity theory of crime, 32
Light, Stephen C., 259
Limited jurisdiction, 143, 145–146
Lincoln, Abraham, 202
Line officers, 216
Line services, 99
Loan sharking, 7
Local government, law
enforcement, 10–11
Local law enforcement. *See*
Municipal law enforcement
agencies
Lockdown, 242
Logan, Charles, 237, 238, 239
Logan, Wayne, 275
Lohan, Lindsay, 215
Lombardo, Lucien X., 262–263
Los Angeles County Sheriff's
Department, 84
Los Angeles Police Department,
high-speed chase policy,
96–97
Loughner, Jared, 27, 168, 169,
305
Love, Jack, 229
Lower courts, 143
Low-visibility decision making,
293
Loyalty, ethical dilemmas of,
114
Lynds, Elam, 235

M

Macchione, Patrick, 317
Madden, Jerry, 233
Madoff, Bernard, 324
Magistrates, 145
Mail and wire fraud, 321
Mala in se crimes, 55
Mala prohibita crimes, 55
Malice aforethought, 57
Malicious and sadistic standard,
265
Malware, 312, 318
Mandatory arrest policies, 97
Mandatory release, 223–224
Mandatory sentencing
guidelines, 200–201
increase in time served and,
244
Manhattan Bail Project, 163
Manslaughter
involuntary, 58
voluntary, 58
Mara Salvatrucha (MS-13), 292
Marijuana
decriminalization of, 34

legalization of, 49–50
Marshall, Thurgood, 153, 266
Martin, Trayvon, 19, 65–66
Martinson, Robert, 236–237
Master jury list, 171–172
Mata, Felix, 271
Mauer, Marc, 252
Maximum-security prisons,
240–241
Maxing out, 270
Mays, Trent, 281, 282
McConnell, Mitch, 309
McDonald, Krista, 114
McDonald, Ricky, 57–58
McKay, Henry, 29
Media, violence and learning
theory, 31
Mediation specialist, 191
Medical examiner, 85
Medical model, 236
of addiction, 34
of criminal justice system, 141
Medicare fraud, 322
Medium-security prisons, 243
Meeks, Shirley, 62
Megan's Law, 274
Mendez, Erika, 60–61
Mens rea
accomplice liability, 59–60
categories of, 56–57
defined, 56
degree of crime, 57–58
duress and, 65
felony-murder legislation, 59–60
strict liability, 58–59
Mental handicap, death penalty
and, 206
Mental health courts, 145
Mental illness
crime and, 44
prisoners and, 257–258
Merton, Robert K., 30
Mexican Mafia, 261
Middle East specialists, 308
Military commissions, 311
Military tribunal, 311–312
Miller, Charles E., 96
Miller, Evan, 284
Minimum-security prisons, 243
Minorities
consequences of high
incarceration rate, 251–252
as judges, 153
jury selection and, 173–174
as law enforcement officers,
82–83
sentencing discrimination,
197–198
Miranda, Ernesto, 134
Miranda warning, 133–136, 149
legal basis for, 133–134
public-safety exception, 135
recording confessions, 136
waiving rights of, 135–136
when not required, 134–136
when required, 134
wording of, 133
Misdemeanor
bail for, 162

STEPS OF THE CRIMINAL JUSTICE SYSTEM

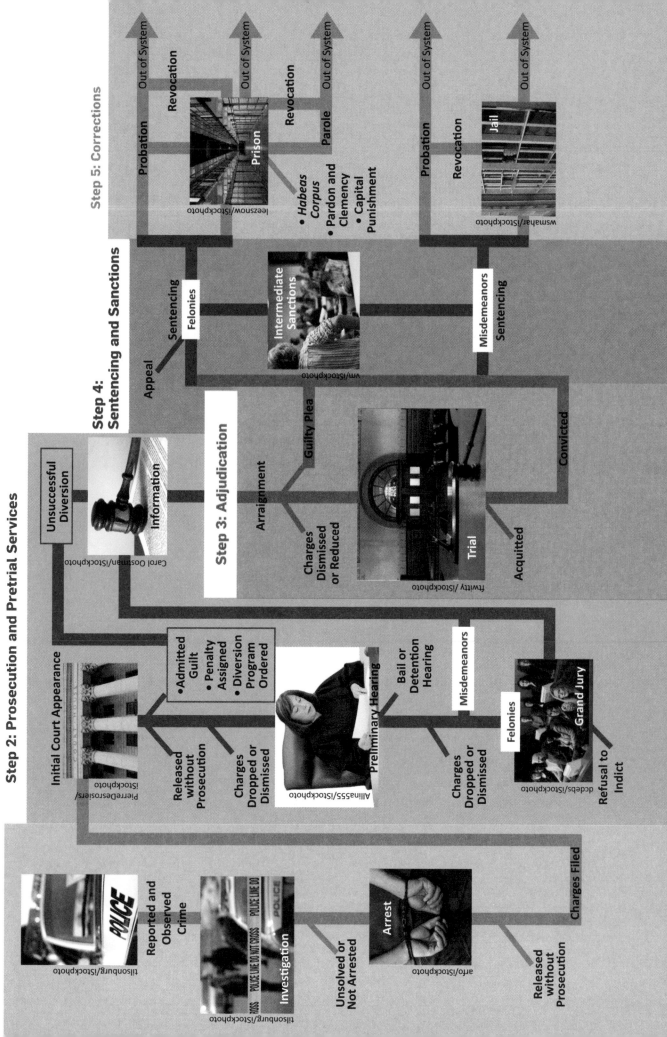

Step 1:
Entry into the System

Step 2: Prosecution and Pretrial Services

Step 3: Adjudication

Step 4:
Sentencing and Sanctions

Step 5: Corrections

Reported and Observed Crime

Investigation

Unsolved or Not Arrested

Arrest

Charges Filed

Released without Prosecution

Initial Court Appearance

- Admitted Guilt
- Penalty Assigned
- Diversion Program Ordered

Released without Prosecution

Charges Dropped or Dismissed

Preliminary Hearing

Bail or Detention Hearing

Misdemeanors

Charges Dropped or Dismissed

Felonies

Grand Jury

Refusal to Indict

Unsuccessful Diversion

Information

Arraignment

Guilty Plea

Charges Dismissed or Reduced

Trial

Acquitted

Convicted

Appeal

Felonies
Sentencing

Intermediate Sanctions

Misdemeanors
Sentencing

Probation   Out of System

Revocation

Prison

Revocation

Parole   Out of System

- *Habeas Corpus*
- Pardon and Clemency
- Capital Punishment

Probation   Out of System

Revocation

Jail

Out of System

tilsonburg/iStockphoto

tilsonburg/iStockphoto

arfo/iStockphoto

PierreDesrosiers/iStockphoto

Allin555/iStockphoto

dcdebs/iStockphoto

Carol Oostman/iStockphoto

ftwitty/iStockphoto

vm/iStockphoto

leezsnow/iStockphoto

wsmahar/iStockphoto

STEPS OF THE CRIMINAL JUSTICE SYSTEM

Step 1: Entry into the System

- Once a law enforcement agency has established that a crime has been committed, a suspect must be identified and apprehended for the case to proceed through the system.

- Sometimes a suspect is apprehended at the scene of the crime; at other times, however, identification of a suspect requires an extensive investigation.

- Often, no one is identified or apprehended. In some instances, a suspect is arrested, and later the police determine that no crime was committed and the suspect is released.

Step 2: Prosecution and Pretrial Services

- After an arrest, law enforcement agencies present information about the case and about the accused to the prosecutor, who will decide if formal charges will be filed with the court.

- A suspect charged with a crime must be taken before a judge without unnecessary delay.

- At the initial appearance, the judge informs the accused of the charges and decides whether there is probable cause to detain the accused person.

- If the offense is not serious, the determination of guilt and an assessment of a penalty may also occur at this stage.

- Often, the defense counsel is assigned at the initial appearance. All suspects charged with serious crimes have a right to be represented by an attorney. If the suspect cannot afford a defense attorney, the court will provide one for him or her at the public's expense.

- A pretrial release decision may also be made at the initial appearance. The court may decide that the suspect poses a threat to society and place him or her in jail until the trial.

- The court may decide to release the suspect with the understanding that he or she will return for the trial, or release the suspect on bail (meaning he or she must provide the court with monetary payment [bail], which will be returned when the suspect appears for the trial).

- In many jurisdictions, the initial appearance may be followed by a preliminary hearing. The main function of this hearing is to discover if there is probable cause to believe that the accused committed a known crime within the jurisdiction of the court. If the judge does find probable cause or the accused waives his or her right to the preliminary hearing, the case may be sent to a grand jury.

- A grand jury hears evidence against the accused presented by the prosecutor and decides if there is sufficient evidence to cause the accused to be brought to trial. If the grand jury finds sufficient evidence, it submits to the court an indictment, a written statement of the essential facts of the offense charged against the accused.

- Misdemeanor cases and some felony cases proceed by the issuance of an information, a formal, written accusation submitted to the court by a prosecutor.

- In some jurisdictions, defendants—often those without prior criminal records—may be eligible for diversion programs. In these programs, the suspect does not go to trial and instead must complete a rehabilitation program, such as drug treatment. If he or she is successful, the charges may be dropped, and his or her criminal record may remain clear.

Step 3: Adjudication

- Once an indictment or information has been filed with the trial court, the accused is scheduled for an arraignment.

- At the arraignment, the accused is informed of the charges, advised of his or her rights, and asked to enter a plea to the charges.

- Sometimes a plea of guilty is the result of negotiations between the prosecutor and the defendant. If the defendant pleads guilty and this plea is accepted by the judge, no trial is held and the defendant is sentenced.

- If the accused pleads not guilty, a date is set for the trial. A person accused of a serious crime is guaranteed a trial by jury.

- During the trial, the prosecution and defense present evidence, and the judge decides issues of law. The jury then decides whether the defendant will be acquitted (found not guilty) or convicted (found guilty of the initial charges or of other offenses).

- If the defendant is found guilty, he or she may request that the trial be reviewed by a higher court to assure that the rules of trial procedure were followed.

Step 4: Sentencing and Sanctions

- After a conviction, a sentence is imposed. In most cases, the judge decides the sentence, though sometimes the jury makes this decision.

- Some of the sentencing choices available to judges and juries include: the death penalty, incarceration in prison or jail, probation (allowing the convicted person to remain in the community as long as he or she follows certain rules), and fines. In many jurisdictions, persons convicted of certain types of offenses must serve a prison term.

Step 5: Corrections

- Offenders sentenced to incarceration usually serve time in a local jail or a prison. Offenders sentenced to less than one year usually go to jail, while those sentenced to more than one year go to prison.

- A prisoner may become eligible for parole after serving part of his or her sentence. Parole is the release of a prisoner before the full sentence has been served. If released under parole, the convict will be supervised in the community for the balance of his or her sentence.

CRIMINAL JUSTICE TIMELINE

		Supreme Court Criminal Justice Decisions		Legal Events
1900s	1903	Lottery ticket ban upheld		
1910s	1914	*Weeks v. U.S.:* Exclusionary rule adopted for federal courts	1914	Harrison Narcotics Act passed
	1919	*Schenck v. U.S.:* Socialist found guilty of obstructing war effort	1919	Prohibition begins
1920s	1923	*Frye v. U.S.:* Scientific evidence admissible if it has gained general acceptance	1921	William Taft becomes Chief Justice
	1927	*Tumey v. Ohio:* Paying a judge only if defendant is found guilty is unconstitutional	1925	Federal Probation Act
	1928	*Olmstead v. U.S.:* Wiretaps legal if no trespass		
1930s	1932	*Powell v. Alabama:* Limited right to counsel in capital cases established	1930	Charles Evans Hughes becomes Chief Justice
	1939	*U.S. v. Miller:* Right to bear arms limited to militia	1931	National Commission on Law Observance and Enforcement—Wickersham Commission
			1933	Prohibition ends
			1935	199 executions in U.S.; highest rate in 20th century
			1937	FDR's court packing plan defeated
			1939	Administrative Office of U.S. Courts created
1940s			1941	Harlan Stone becomes Chief Justice
			1946	Fred Vinson becomes Chief Justice
1950s	1956	*Griffin v. Illinois:* Indigents entitled to court-appointed attorney for first appeal	1953	Earl Warren becomes Chief Justice
1960s	1961	*Mapp v. Ohio:* Exclusionary rule required in state courts	1966	Bail Reform Act favors pretrial release
	1963	*Fay v. Noia:* Right to *habeas corpus* expanded	1967	President's Commission on Law Enforcement and Administration of Justice
		Brady v. Maryland: Prosecutors must turn over evidence favorable to defense	1969	Warren Burger becomes Chief Justice
		Gideon v. Wainwright: Indigents have right to counsel		
	1966	*Sheppard v. Maxwell:* Conviction reversed based on prejudicial pretrial publicity		
		Miranda v. Arizona: Suspects must be advised of rights before interrogation		
	1967	*In re Gault:* Requires counsel for juveniles		
1970s	1972	*Furman v. Georgia:* Declares state death penalty laws unconstitutional	1970	Organized Crime Control Act
		Barker v. Wingo: Adopts flexible approach to speedy trial	1971	Prison riot in Attica, New York
	1975	*Gerstein v. Pugh:* Arrestee entitled to a prompt hearing	1972	Break-in at Watergate
	1976	*Gregg v. Georgia:* Upholds death penalty	1973	National Advisory Commission on Criminal Justice Standards and Goals
		North v. Russell: Non-lawyer judges are upheld	1973	Nixon declares war on drugs
	1979	*Burch v. Louisiana:* Six-member juries must be unanimous	1977	Determinate sentencing enacted in 4 states
1980s	1986	*Batson v. Kentucky:* Jurors cannot be excluded because of race	1982	Victim and Witness Protection Act
	1987	*U.S. v. Salerno:* Preventive detention upheld	1984	Bail Reform Act: judge may consider if defendant is a danger to the community
	1989	*Mistretta v. U.S.:* U.S. sentencing guidelines upheld	1985	DNA first used in criminal case
			1986	William Rehnquist becomes Chief Justice
			1987	U.S. Sentencing Guidelines begin
1990s	1991	*Payne v. Tennessee:* Victim impact statements admissible during sentencing	1993	Three-strikes laws gain currency
		Burns v. Reed: Prosecutors have qualified immunity in civil lawsuits	1994	New Jersey passes Megan's Law
		Chisom v. Roemer: Voting Rights Act applies to elected judges	1995	U.S. prison population tops one million
	1995	*U.S. v. Lopez:* Federal law barring guns in school unconstitutional	1996	Antiterrorism and Effective Death Penalty Act limits *habeas* petitions in federal court
2000s	2004	*Hamdi v. Rumsfeld:* U.S. citizens seized overseas during anti-terror military operations must be given access to U.S. courts	2002	The Patriot Act enacted into law; Department of Homeland Security established
	2005	*Roper v. Simmons:* Capital punishment for crimes committed when the offender was under eighteen years of age is unconstitutional	2005	John Roberts, Jr., becomes Chief Justice
			2012	California voters modify the state's "three-strikes" law to allow for a life sentence only when the new felony conviction is "serious or violent"
	2013	*Maryland v. King:* As part of the normal booking process, law enforcement officers may take DNA samples of those suspects arrested for serious crimes	2013	The U.S. prison and jail population levels off at approximately 2.3 million

	Famous Trials		Leading Crimes
1900s		1901	President McKinley assassinated by anarchist
		1908	Butch Cassidy and the Sundance Kid killed in Bolivia
1910s		1915	Anti-Semitic lynching of Leo Frank in Atlanta
		1919	Black Sox scandal in baseball
1920s	1921 Sacco and Vanzetti sentenced to death for murder	1921	Charles Ponzi sentenced to prison for pyramid scheme
	1925 Scopes "Monkey Trial"	1924	Leopold and Loeb plead guilty to thrill murder
	1927 Teapot Dome trials become symbol of government corruption	1929	St. Valentine's Day massacre, ordered by Al Capone in Chicago
1930s	1931 Chicago mobster Al Capone found guilty of income tax evasion	1934	Bonnie and Clyde killed
	1935 Bruno Hauptman convicted of kidnapping Charles Lindbergh's young son		"Baby Face" Nelson and "Pretty Boy" Floyd killed
	1939 Crime boss "Lucky" Luciano found guilty of compulsory prostitution		
1940s	1941 Murder, Inc. trials	1945	Bank robber Willie Sutton escapes from prison
	1948 Caryl Chessman sentenced to death for kidnapping and robbery	1947	Hollywood hopeful Black Dahlia's mutilated body found
	1949 Alger Hiss found guilty of perjury in the onset of the Cold War		
1950s	1951 Julius and Ethel Rosenberg sentenced to death for espionage	1950	Brinks armored car robbery in Boston
	1954 Dr. Samuel Sheppard convicted of murder	1957	George Metesky confesses to a string of New York City bombings
	1958 Daughter of movie actress Lana Turner found not guilty of killing mom's hoodlum lover	1959	Murder of Kansas farm couple becomes basis of *In Cold Blood*
1960s	1964 Teamster President Jimmy Hoffa found guilty	1962	French Connection drug bust
	1966 Dr. Sam Sheppard acquitted in second trial	1963	President Kennedy assassinated
	1968 Black Panther Huey Newton found guilty of voluntary manslaughter	1964	Boston Strangler arrested
	1969 Chicago 7 found guilty of incitement to riot and conspiracy	1966	Richard Speck kills eight Chicago nurses
		1968	Martin Luther King, Jr., and Robert Kennedy assassinated
		1969	Manson family commits Helter Skelter murders
1970s	1971 Lt. William Calley found guilty of murder in My Lai massacre	1971	Skyjacker D.B. Cooper disappears
	1976 Heiress Patty Hearst found guilty of bank robbery	1974	Heiress Patty Hearst kidnapped by terrorists
	1977 Maryland governor Marvin Mandel found guilty of mail fraud	1975	Jimmy Hoffa disappears
		1977	Serial murderer Son of Sam arrested in New York
		1978	Jonestown massacre
1980s	1980 John Wayne Gacy convicted of killing 33 boys	1980	Headmistress Jean Harris kills Scarsdale Diet Doctor
	1982 Automaker John DeLorean acquitted of cocaine trafficking	1981	President Ronald Reagan survives assassination attempt by John Hinckley
	1984 Mayflower Madam pleads guilty to misdemeanor of promoting prostitution	1984	21 killed at San Diego McDonald's
	1987 Subway vigilante Bernhard Goetz acquitted of attempted murder	1987	Savings and loan mogul Charles Keating accused of millions in fraud
	1989 Televangelist Jim Baker found guilty of fraud	1989	Junk bond king Michael Milken pays $600 million fine
1990s	1993 L.A. police officers found guilty in federal court of civil rights violations against Rodney King	1992	Boxer Mike Tyson charged with rape
	1995 O. J. Simpson found not guilty of murdering his ex-wife Nicole and her friend, Ronald Goldman	1994	Fire in Waco kills Branch Davidians
	1996 During second trial, Menendez brothers found guilty of killing wealthy parents	1995	Oklahoma City bombing
	1997 Timothy McVeigh sentenced to death for Oklahoma City bombing	1997	Nanny in Boston charged with child murder
2000s	2000 NYPD officers acquitted for killing Amadou Diallo	2001	Terrorists strike targets in New York City and the Washington, D.C.-area
	2003 Washington State's Gary Ridgway sentenced as worst serial killer in U.S. history	2007	Student Cho Seung Hui murders five faculty members and twenty-seven students on the campus of Virginia Tech in Blacksburg, Virginia
	2006 Zacarias Moussaoui convicted for conspiring to kill U.S. citizens as part of the September 11, 2001, terrorist attacks	2009	Bernard Madoff pleads guilty to running a $65 billion Ponzi scheme
	2013 George Zimmerman found not guilty of second degree murder by reason of self-defense for killing teenager Trayvon Martin during an altercation in Sanford, Florida	2012	Adam Lanza kills twenty children and six adult staff members during a shooting spree at Sandy Hook Elementary School in Newtown, Connecticut

CRIMINAL JUSTICE TODAY

CHAPTER SUMMARY & LEARNING OUTCOMES

1 **Define *crime* and identify the different types of crime.**
Crime is any action punishable under criminal statutes and is considered an offense against society. Types of crime include (a) violent crime, (b) property crime, (c) public order crime, (d) white-collar crime, (e) organized crime, and (f) high-tech crime.

2 **Outline the three levels of law enforcement.**
Because we have a federal system of government, law enforcement occurs at the (a) national, or federal, level and the (b) state level and within the states at (c) local levels. Because crime is mostly a local concern, most employees in the criminal justice system work for local governments. Agencies at the federal level include the FBI, the DEA, and the U.S. Secret Service, among others.

3 **List the essential elements of the corrections system.**
Criminal offenders are placed on probation, incarcerated in a jail or prison, transferred to community-based corrections facilities, or released on parole.

4 **Define ethics, and describe the role that it plays in discretionary decision making.**
Ethics consist of the moral principles that guide a person's perception of right and wrong. Most criminal justice professionals have a great deal of discretionary leeway in their day-to-day decision making, and their ethical beliefs can help ensure that they make such decisions in keeping with society's established values.

5 **Contrast the crime control and due process models.**
The crime control model assumes that the criminal justice system is designed to protect the public from criminals. Thus, its most important function is to punish and repress criminal conduct. The due process model presumes that the accused are innocent and provides them with the most complete safeguards, usually within the court system.

CHAPTER 1 QUIZ ANSWERS

1. Violent
2. Property
3. Federalism
4. State
5. Discretion

6. Ethics
7. Crime control
8. Due process
9. Decreased
10. Terrorism

Photo by Joshua Lott/Getty Images

KEY TERMS

Assault A threat or an attempt to do violence to another person that causes that person to fear immediate physical harm. 6

Battery The act of physically contacting another person with the intent to do harm, even if the resulting injury is insubstantial. 6

Burglary The act of breaking into or entering a structure (such as a home or office) without permission for the purpose of committing a felony. 6

Civil Liberties The basic rights and freedoms for American citizens guaranteed by the U.S. Constitution, particularly in the Bill of Rights. 18

Conflict Model A criminal justice model in which the content of criminal law is determined by the groups that hold economic, political, and social power in a community. 4

Consensus Model A criminal justice model in which the majority of citizens in a society share the same values and beliefs. Criminal acts are acts that conflict with these values and beliefs and that are deemed harmful to society. 4

Crime An act that violates criminal law and is punishable by criminal sanctions. 4

Crime Control Model A criminal justice model that places primary emphasis on the right of society to be protected from crime and violent criminals. 16

Criminal Justice System The interlocking network of law enforcement agencies, courts, and corrections institutions designed to enforce criminal laws and protect society from criminal behavior. 8

Deviance Behavior that is considered to go against the norms established by society. 5

Discretion The ability of individuals in the criminal justice system to make operational decisions based on personal judgment instead of formal rules or official information. 13

Due Process Model A criminal justice model that places primacy on the right of the individual to be protected from the power of the government. 16

Ethics The moral principles that govern a person's perception of right and wrong. 16

Federalism A form of government in which a written constitution provides for a division of powers between a central government and several regional governments. 9

Formal Criminal Justice Process The model of the criminal justice process in which participants follow formal rules to create a smoothly functioning disposition of cases from arrest to punishment. 13

Homeland Security A concerted national effort to prevent terrorist attacks within the United States and reduce the country's vulnerability to terrorism. 17

Informal Criminal Justice Process A model of the criminal justice system that recognizes the informal authority exercised by individuals at each step of the criminal justice process. 14

Justice The quality of fairness that must exist in the processes designed to determine whether individuals are guilty of criminal wrongdoing. 8

Larceny The act of taking property from another person without the use of force with the intent of keeping that property. 6

Morals Principles of right and wrong behavior, as practiced by individuals or by society. 4

Murder The unlawful killing of one human being by another. 6

Organized Crime Illegal acts carried out by illegal organizations engaged in the market for illegal goods or services, such as illicit drugs or firearms. 7

Public Order Crime Behavior that has been labeled criminal because it is contrary to shared social values, customs, and norms. 7

Robbery The act of taking property from another person through force, threat of force, or intimidation. 6

Sexual Assault Forced or coerced sexual intercourse (or other sexual acts). 6

System A set of interacting parts that, when functioning properly, achieve a desired result. 13

Terrorism The use or threat of violence to achieve political objectives. 17

White-Collar Crime Nonviolent crimes committed by business entities or individuals to gain a personal or business advantage. 7

THE CRIME PICTURE: THEORIES AND TRENDS

CHAPTER SUMMARY & LEARNING OUTCOMES

1 Discuss the difference between a hypothesis and a theory in the context of criminology. A hypothesis is a proposition, usually presented in an "If . . . , then . . ." format, that can be tested by researchers. If enough different authorities are able to test and verify a hypothesis, it will usually be accepted as a theory. Because theories can offer explanations for behavior, criminologists often rely on them when trying to determine the causes of criminal behavior.

2 Contrast the medical model of addiction with the criminal model of addiction. Those who support the former believe that addicts are not criminals, but mentally or physically ill individuals who are forced into acts of petty crime to "feed their habit." Those in favor of the criminal model of addiction believe that abusers and addicts endanger society with their behavior and should be treated like any other criminals.

3 Distinguish between the National Crime Victimization Survey (NCVS) and self-reported surveys. The NCVS involves an annual survey of more than 40,000 households conducted by the Bureau of the Census along with the Bureau of Justice Statistics. The survey queries citizens on crimes that have been committed against them. As such, the NCVS includes crimes not necessarily reported to police. Self-reported surveys, in contrast, involve asking individuals about criminal activity to which they may have been a party.

4 Describe the three ways that victims' rights legislation increases the ability of crime victims to participate in the criminal justice system. (a) The right to be informed of victims' rights in general and of specific information relating to the relevant criminal case; (b) the right to be present at court proceedings involving the victim; and (c) the right to be heard on matters involving the prosecution, punishment, and release of the offender.

5 Identify the three factors most often used by criminologists to explain changes in the nation's crime rate. (a) Levels of incarceration, because an offender behind bars cannot commit any additional crimes and the threat of imprisonment acts as a deterrent to criminal behavior; (b) the size of the youth population, because those under the age of twenty-four commit the majority of crimes in the United States; and (c) the health of the economy, because when income and employment levels fall, those most directly affected may turn to crime for financial gain.

Robert Nickelsberg/Getty Images

CHAPTER 2 QUIZ ANSWERS

1. Criminologists
2. Theory
3. Rational choice
4. Psychology
5. Disorganization
6. Learning
7. Abuse
8. Uniform Crime Report
9. Victim
10. Self-reported

KEY TERMS

Anomie A condition in which the individual feels a disconnect from society due to the breakdown or absence of social norms. 30

Biology The science of living organisms, including their structure, function, growth, and origin. 26

Causation The relationship in which a change in one measurement or behavior creates a recognizable change in another measurement or behavior. 24

Control Theory A series of theories that assume that all individuals have the potential for criminal behavior, but are restrained by the damage that such actions would do to their relationships with family, friends, and members of the community. 31

Correlation The relationship between two measurements or behaviors that tend to move in the same direction. 24

Crime Victim Any person who suffers physical, emotional, or financial harm as the result of a criminal act. 38

Criminal Model of Addiction An approach to drug abuse that holds that drug offenders harm society by their actions to the same extent as other criminals and should face the same punitive sanctions. 34

Criminology The scientific study of crime and the causes of criminal behavior. 24

Dark Figure of Crime A term used to describe the actual amount of crime that takes place. The "figure" is "dark," or impossible to detect, because a great number of crimes are never reported to the police. 37

Drug Any substance that modifies biological, psychological, or social behavior; in particular, an illegal substance with those properties. 32

Drug Abuse The use of drugs that results in physical or psychological problems for the user, as well as disruption of personal relationships and employment. 33

Hormone A chemical substance, produced in tissue and conveyed in the bloodstream, that controls certain cellular and body functions such as growth and reproduction. 26

Hypothesis A possible explanation for an observed occurrence that can be tested by further investigation. 24

Learning Theory The hypothesis that delinquents and criminals must be taught both the practical and the emotional skills necessary to participate in illegal activity. 31

Life Course Criminology The study of crime based on the belief that behavioral patterns developed in childhood can predict delinquent and criminal behavior later in life. 31

Medical Model of Addiction An approach to drug addiction that treats drug abuse as a mental illness and focuses on treating and rehabilitating offenders rather than punishing them. 34

Neurotransmitter A chemical that transmits nerve impulses between nerve cells and from nerve cells to the brain. 27

Part I Offenses Crimes reported annually by the FBI in its Uniform Crime Report. Part I offenses include murder, rape, robbery, aggravated assault, burglary, larceny, and motor vehicle theft. 35

Part II Offenses All crimes recorded by the FBI that do not fall into the category of Part I offenses. These crimes include both misdemeanors and felonies. 36

Psychoactive Drug A chemical that affects the brain, causing changes in emotions, perceptions, and behavior. 32

Psychology The scientific study of mental processes and behavior. 26

Rational Choice Theory A school of criminology that holds that wrongdoers act as if they weigh the possible benefits of criminal or delinquent activity against the expected costs of being apprehended. 25

Repeat Victimization The theory that certain people and places are more likely to be subject to repeated criminal activity and that past victimization is a strong indicator of future victimization. 41

Self-Reported Survey A method of gathering crime data that relies on participants to reveal and detail their own criminal or delinquent behavior. 37

Social Conflict Theories A school of criminology that views criminal behavior as the result of class conflict. 30

Social Disorganization Theory The theory that deviant behavior is more likely in communities where social institutions such as the family, schools, and the criminal justice system fail to exert control over the population. 29

Social Process Theories A school of criminology that considers criminal behavior to be the predictable result of a person's interaction with his or her environment. 31

Sociology The study of the development and functioning of groups of people who live together within a society. 29

Strain Theory The assumption that crime is the result of frustration felt by individuals who cannot reach their financial and personal goals through legitimate means. 30

Testosterone The hormone primarily responsible for the production of sperm and the development of male secondary sex characteristics such as the growth of facial and pubic hair and the change of voice pitch. 26

Theory An explanation of a happening or circumstance that is based on observation, experimentation, and reasoning. 24

Uniform Crime Report (UCR) An annual report compiled by the FBI to give an indication of criminal activity in the United States. 35

Victim Surveys A method of gathering crime data that directly surveys participants to determine their experiences as victims of crime. 37

INSIDE CRIMINAL LAW

3

CHAPTER SUMMARY & LEARNING OUTCOMES

1 **List the four written sources of American criminal law.**
(a) The U.S. Constitution and state constitutions; (b) statutes passed by Congress and state legislatures (plus local ordinances); (c) administrative agency regulations; and (d) case law.

2 **Explain the differences between crimes *mala in se* and *mala prohibita*.**
A criminal act is *mala in se* if it is inherently wrong, while a criminal act *mala prohibita* is illegal only because it is prohibited by the laws of a particular society. It is sometimes difficult to distinguish between these two sorts of crimes because it is difficult to define a "pure" *mala in se* crime—that is, it is difficult to separate a crime from the culture that has deemed it a crime.

3 **List and briefly define the most important excuse defenses for crimes.**
Insanity—different tests of insanity can be used, including (a) the *M'Naghten* rule (right-wrong test); (b) the ALI/MPC test, also known as the substantial-capacity test; and (c) the irresistible-impulse test. **Intoxication**—voluntary and involuntary, the latter being a possible criminal defense. **Mistake**—sometimes valid if the law was not published or reasonably known or if the alleged offender relied on an official statement of the law that was erroneous. Also, a mistake of fact may negate the mental state necessary to commit a crime.

4 **Describe the four most important justification criminal defenses.**
Duress—requires that (a) the threat is of serious bodily harm or death, (b) the harm is greater than that caused by the crime; (c) the threat is immediate and inescapable; and (d) the defendant became involved in the situation through no fault of his or her own. **Justifiable use of force**—the defense of one's person, dwelling, or property, or the prevention of a crime. **Necessity**—justifiable if the harm sought to be avoided is greater than that sought to be prevented by the law defining the offense charged. **Entrapment**—that the criminal action was induced by certain governmental persuasion or trickery.

5 **Distinguish between substantive and procedural criminal law.**
The former concerns questions about what acts are actually criminal. The latter concerns procedures designed to protect the constitutional rights of individuals and to prevent the arbitrary use of power by the government.

CHAPTER 3 QUIZ ANSWERS

1. Constitution
2. Case
3. Civil
4. Felony
5. Misdemeanor
6. Intent
7. Insanity
8. Self-defense
9. Entrapment
10. Supreme Court

Wilfred Y. Wong/Getty Images

KEY TERMS

Actus Reus (pronounced *ak*-tus *ray*-uhs). A guilty (prohibited) act. 55

Administrative Law The body of law created by administrative agencies (in the form of rules, regulations, orders, and decisions) in order to carry out their duties and responsibilities. 50

Alibi A defense offered by a person accused of a crime showing that she or he was elsewhere at the time the crime took place. 61

Attempt The act of taking substantial steps toward committing a crime while having the ability and the intent to commit the crime, even if the crime never takes place. 56

Attendant Circumstances The facts surrounding a criminal event that must be proved to convict the defendant of the underlying crime. 60

Ballot Initiative A procedure in which the citizens of a state, by collecting enough signatures, can force a public vote on a proposed change to state law. 49

Beyond a Reasonable Doubt The degree of proof required to find the defendant in a criminal trial guilty of committing the crime. The defendant's guilt must be the only reasonable explanation for the criminal act before the court. 53

Bill of Rights The first ten amendments to the U.S. Constitution. 67

Case Law The rules of law announced in court decisions. 50

Civil Law The branch of law dealing with the definition and enforcement of all private or public rights, as opposed to criminal matters. 52

Competency Hearing A court proceeding to determine whether the defendant is mentally well enough to understand the charges filed against him or her and cooperate with a lawyer in presenting a defense. 63

Conspiracy A plot by two or more people to carry out an illegal or harmful act. 61

Constitutional Law Law based on the U.S. Constitution and the constitutions of the various states. 48

Corpus Delicti The body of circumstances that must exist for a criminal act to have occurred. 55

Defendant In a civil court, the person or institution against whom an action is brought. In a criminal court, the person or entity who has been formally accused of violating a criminal law. 52

Due Process Clause The provisions of the Fifth and Fourteenth Amendments to the Constitution that guarantee that no person shall be deprived of life, liberty, or property without due process of law. 69

Duress Unlawful pressure brought to bear on a person, causing the person to perform an act that he or she would not otherwise perform. 65

Duty to Retreat The requirement that a person claiming self-defense prove that she or he first took reasonable steps to avoid the conflict that resulted in the use of deadly force. 65

Entrapment A defense in which the defendant claims that he or she was induced by a public official—usually an undercover agent or police officer—to commit a crime that he or she would otherwise not have committed. 66

Felony A serious crime, usually punishable by death or imprisonment for a year or longer. 54

Felony-Murder An unlawful homicide that occurs during the attempted commission of a felony. 59

Hate Crime Law A statute that provides for greater sanctions against those who commit crimes motivated by bias against an individual or a group based on race, ethnicity, religion, gender, sexual orientation, disability, or age. 60

Inchoate Offenses Conduct deemed criminal without actual harm being done, provided that the harm that would have occurred is one the law tries to prevent. 61

Infancy A condition that, under early American law, excused young wrongdoers of criminal behavior because presumably they could not understand the consequences of their actions. 62

Infraction In most jurisdictions, a noncriminal offense for which the penalty is a fine rather than incarceration. 54

Insanity A defense for criminal liability that asserts a lack of criminal responsibility due to mental instability. 62

Intoxication A defense for criminal liability in which the defendant claims that the taking of intoxicants rendered him or her unable to form the requisite intent to commit a criminal act. 63

Involuntary Manslaughter A homicide in which the offender had no intent to kill her or his victim. 58

Irresistible-Impulse Test A test for the insanity defense under which a defendant who knew his or her action was wrong may still be found insane if he or she was unable, as a result of a mental deficiency, to control the urge to complete the act. 63

Liability In a civil court, legal responsibility for one's own or another's actions. 53

Mala in Se A descriptive term for acts that are inherently wrong, regardless of whether they are prohibited by law. 55

Mala Prohibita A descriptive term for acts that are made illegal by criminal statute and are not necessarily wrong in and of themselves. 55

Mens Rea (pronounced mehns *ray*-uh). Mental state, or intent. A wrongful mental state is usually as necessary as a wrongful act to establish criminal liability. 56

Misdemeanor A criminal offense that is not a felony; usually punishable by a fine and/or a jail term of less than one year. 54

M'Naghten Rule A common law test of criminal responsibility, derived from *M'Naghten's* Case in 1843, that relies on the defendant's inability to distinguish right from wrong. 62

Necessity A defense against criminal liability in which the defendant asserts that circumstances required her or him to commit an illegal act. 66

Negligence A failure to exercise the standard of care that a reasonable person would exercise in similar circumstances. 57

Plaintiff The person or institution that initiates a lawsuit in civil court proceedings by filing a complaint. 52

Precedent A court decision that furnishes an example of authority for deciding subsequent cases involving similar facts. 50

Preponderance of the Evidence The degree of proof required to decide in favor of one side or the other in a civil case. In general, this requirement is met when a plaintiff proves that a fact more likely than not is true. 53

Procedural Criminal Law Rules that define the manner in which the rights and duties of individuals may be enforced. 67

Procedural Due Process A provision in the Constitution that states that the law must be carried out in a fair and orderly manner. 69

Recklessness The state of being aware that a risk does or will exist and nevertheless acting in a way that consciously disregards this risk. 57

Self-Defense The legally recognized privilege to protect one's self or property from injury by another. 65

Statutory Law The body of law enacted by legislative bodies. 48

Statutory Rape A strict liability crime in which an adult engages in a sexual act with a minor. 59

Strict Liability Crimes Certain crimes, such as traffic violations, in which the defendant is guilty regardless of her or his state of mind at the time of the act. 58

Substantial-Capacity Test (ALI/MPC Test) A test for the insanity defense that states that a person is not responsible for criminal behavior when he or she "lacks substantial capacity" to understand that the behavior is wrong or to know how to behave properly. 62

Substantive Criminal Law Law that defines the rights and duties of individuals with respect to one another. 67

Substantive Due Process The constitutional requirement that laws used in accusing and convicting persons of crimes must be fair. 69

Supremacy Clause A clause in the U.S. Constitution establishing that federal law is the "supreme law of the land" and shall prevail when in conflict with state constitutions or statutes. 49

Voluntary Manslaughter A homicide in which the intent to kill was present in the mind of the offender, but malice was lacking. 58

LAW ENFORCEMENT TODAY

CHAPTER SUMMARY & LEARNING OUTCOMES

1 List the four basic responsibilities of the police.

(a) To enforce laws, (b) to provide services, (c) to prevent crime, and (d) to preserve the peace.

2 Identify the differences between the police academy and field training as learning tools for recruits.

The police academy is a controlled environment where police recruits learn the basics of policing from instructors in classrooms. In contrast, field training takes place in the "real world": the recruit goes on patrol with an experienced police officer.

3 Describe the challenges facing women who choose law enforcement as a career.

Many male officers believe that their female counterparts are not physically or mentally strong enough for police work, which puts pressure on women officers to continually prove themselves. Female officers must also deal with tokenism, or the stigma that they were hired only to fulfill diversity requirements, and sexual harassment in the form of unwanted advances or obscene remarks.

4 Indicate some of the most important law enforcement agencies under the control of the Department of Homeland Security.

(a) U.S. Customs and Border Protection, which polices the flow of goods and people across the United States' international borders and oversees the U.S. Border Patrol; (b) U.S. Immigration and Customs Enforcement, which investigates and enforces our nation's immigration and customs laws; and (c) the U.S. Secret Service, which protects high-ranking federal government officials and federal property.

5 Analyze the importance of private security today.

In the United States, businesses and citizens spend billions of dollars each year on private security. Heightened fear of crime and increased crime in the workplace have fueled the growth in spending on private security.

CHAPTER 4 QUIZ ANSWERS

1. Enforce
2. Services
3. Intelligence
4. Probationary
5. Double
6. Sheriffs'
7. Highway
8. FBI (Federal Bureau of Investigation)
9. ATF (Bureau of Alcohol, Tobacco, Firearms and Explosives)
10. Deter

Jared Wickerham/Getty Images

KEY TERMS

Coroner The medical examiner of a county, usually elected by popular vote. 85

Double Marginality The double suspicion that minority law enforcement officers face from their white colleagues and from members of the minority community to which they belong. 82

Drug Enforcement Administration (DEA) The federal agency responsible for enforcing the nation's laws and regulations regarding narcotics and other controlled substances. 89

Federal Bureau of Investigation (FBI) The branch of the Department of Justice responsible for investigating violations of federal law. 88

Field Training The segment of a police recruit's training in which he or she is removed from the classroom and placed on the beat, under the supervision of a senior officer. 80

Infrastructure The services and facilities that support the day-to-day needs of modern life, such as electricity, food, transportation, and water. 88

Intelligence-Led Policing An approach that measures the risk of criminal behavior associated with certain individuals or locations so as to predict when and where such criminal behavior is most likely to occur in the future. 76

Private Security The practice of private corporations or individuals offering services traditionally performed by police officers. 92

Probationary Period A period of time at the beginning of a police officer's career during which she or he may be fired without cause. 80

Recruitment The process by which law enforcement agencies develop a pool of qualified applicants from which to select new members. 78

Sexual Harassment A repeated pattern of unwelcome sexual advances and/or obscene remarks in the workplace. Under certain circumstances, sexual harassment is illegal and can be the basis for a civil lawsuit. 81

Sheriff The primary law enforcement officer in a county, usually elected to the post by a popular vote. 84

U.S. Customs and Border Protection (CBP) The federal agency responsible for protecting U.S. borders and facilitating legal trade and travel across those borders. 86

U.S. Immigration and Customs Enforcement (ICE) The federal agency that enforces the nation's immigration and customs laws. 87

U.S. Secret Service A federal law enforcement organization with the primary responsibility of protecting the president, the president's family, the vice president, and other important political figures. 88

PROBLEMS AND SOLUTIONS IN MODERN POLICING

CHAPTER SUMMARY & LEARNING OUTCOMES

1 Explain why police officers are allowed discretionary powers.

Police officers are considered trustworthy and able to make honest decisions. They have experience and training. They are knowledgeable in criminal behavior. Finally, they must have the discretion to take reasonable steps to protect themselves.

2 List the three primary purposes of police patrol.

(a) The deterrence of crime, (b) the maintenance of public order, and (c) the provision of services that are not related to crime.

3 Describe how forensic experts use DNA fingerprinting to solve crimes.

Law enforcement agents gather trace evidence such as blood, semen, skin, or hair from the crime scene. Because these items are rich in DNA, which provides a unique genetic blueprint for every living organism, crime labs can create a DNA profile of the suspect and test it against other such profiles stored in databases. If the profiles match, then law enforcement agents have found a strong suspect for the crime.

4 Determine when police officers are justified in using deadly force.

Police officers must make a reasonable judgment in determining when to use force that will place the suspect in threat of injury or death. That is, given the circumstances, the officer must reasonably assume that the use of such force is necessary to avoid serious injury or death to the officer or someone else.

5 Explain what an ethical dilemma is and name four categories of ethical dilemmas that a police officer typically may face.

An ethical dilemma is a situation in which police officers (a) do not know the right course of action, (b) have difficulty doing what they consider to be right, and/or (c) find the wrong choice very tempting. The four types of ethical dilemmas involve (a) discretion, (b) duty, (c) honesty, and (d) loyalty.

AP Photo/Jae C. Hong

CHAPTER 5 QUIZ ANSWERS

1. Policy
2. Deter/prevent
3. Forensics
4. DNA
5. Incident

6. Random
7. Community
8. Stress
9. Reasonable
10. Corruption

KEY TERMS

Ballistics The study of firearms, including the firing of the weapon and the flight of the bullet. 103

Blue Curtain A metaphorical term used to refer to the value placed on secrecy and the general mistrust of the outside world shared by many police officers. 109

Broken Windows Theory Wilson and Kelling's theory that law enforcement should crack down on quality-of-life crimes to reduce overall crime. 107

Bureaucracy A hierarchically structured administrative organization that carries out specific functions. 98

Burnout A mental state that occurs when a person suffers from exhaustion and has difficulty functioning normally as a result of overwork and stress. 110

Clearance Rate A comparison of the number of crimes cleared by arrest and prosecution with the number of crimes reported during any given time period. 102

Cold Case A criminal investigation that has not been solved after a certain amount of time. 103

Cold Hit The establishment of a connection between a suspect and a crime, often through the use of DNA evidence, in the absence of an ongoing criminal investigation. 105

Community Policing A policing philosophy that emphasizes community support for and cooperation with the police in preventing crime. 107

Confidential Informant (CI) A human source for police who provides information concerning illegal activity in which he or she is involved. 102

Crime Mapping Technology that allows crime analysts to identify trends and patterns of criminal behavior within a given area. 106

Deadly Force Force applied by a police officer that is likely or intended to cause death. 111

Delegation of Authority The principles of command on which most police departments are based, in which personnel take orders from and are responsible to those in positions of power directly above them. 99

Detective The primary police investigator of crimes. 101

Directed Patrol A patrol strategy that is designed to focus on a specific type of criminal activity at a specific time. 106

DNA Fingerprinting The identification of a person based on a sample of her or his DNA, the genetic material found in the cells of all living things. 103

Domestic Terrorism Acts of terrorism that take place within the territorial jurisdiction of the United States without direct foreign involvement. 102

Domestic Violence The act of willful neglect or physical violence that occurs within a familial or other intimate relationship. 97

Duty The moral sense of a police officer that she or he should behave in a certain manner. 113

Forensics The application of science to establish facts and evidence during the investigation of crimes. 103

Hot Spots Concentrated areas of high criminal activity that draw a directed police response. 106

Incident-Driven Policing A reactive approach to policing that emphasizes a speedy response to calls for service. 105

Mandatory Arrest Law Requires a police officer to detain a person for committing a certain type of crime as long as there is probable cause that he or she committed the crime. 97

Noble Cause Corruption Knowing misconduct by a police officer with the goal of attaining what the officer believes is a "just" result. 113

Police Corruption The abuse of authority by a law enforcement officer for personal gain. 113

Police Subculture The values and perceptions that are shared by law enforcement agents. 109

Policy A set of guiding principles designed to influence the behavior and decision making of police officers. 96

Proactive Arrests Arrests that occur because of concerted efforts by law enforcement agencies to respond to a particular type of criminal or criminal behavior. 107

Problem-Oriented Policing A policing philosophy that requires police to identify potential criminal activity and develop strategies to prevent or respond to that activity. 108

Random Patrol A patrol strategy that relies on police officers monitoring a certain area with the goal of detecting crimes in progress or preventing crime due to their presence. Also known as general or preventive patrol. 106

Reactive Arrests Arrests that come about as part of the ordinary routine of police patrol and responses to calls for service. 106

Reasonable Force The degree of force that is appropriate to protect the police officer or other citizens and is not excessive. 111

Socialization The process through which a police officer is taught the values and expected behavior of the police subculture. 109

Stressors The aspects of police work and life that lead to feelings of stress. 110

Trace Evidence Evidence such as a fingerprint, blood, or hair found in small amounts at a crime scene. 103

STUDY ONLINE WITH COURSEMATE www.cengagebrain.com

To help you refresh your understanding of each major chapter section **go online to access the relevant Self-Assessment quiz.** You'll know right away whether you need to go back and read that section again to cement your understanding of major concepts!

CHAPTER REVIEW

POLICE AND THE CONSTITUTION: THE RULES OF LAW ENFORCEMENT

CHAPTER SUMMARY & LEARNING OUTCOMES

1 **Outline the four major sources that may provide probable cause.**

(a) Personal observation, usually due to an officer's personal training, experience, and expertise; (b) information, gathered from informants, eyewitnesses, victims, police bulletins, and other sources; (c) evidence, which often has to be in plain view; and (d) association, which generally must involve a person with a known criminal background who is seen in a place where criminal activity is openly taking place.

2 **Explain when searches can be made without a warrant.**

Searches and seizures can be made without a warrant if they are incidental to an arrest (but they must be reasonable); when they are made with voluntary consent; when they involve the "movable vehicle" exception; when property has been abandoned; and when items are in plain view, under certain restricted circumstances (see *Coolidge v. New Hampshire*).

3 **Distinguish between a stop and a frisk, and indicate the importance of the case *Terry v. Ohio.***

Though the terms *stop* and *frisk* are often used in concert, a stop is the separate act of detaining a suspect when an officer reasonably believes that a criminal activity is about to take place. A frisk is the physical "pat-down" of a suspect. In *Terry v. Ohio*, the Supreme Court ruled that an officer must have "specific and articulable facts" before making a stop, but those facts may be "taken together with rational inferences."

4 **List the four elements that must be present for an arrest to take place.**

(a) Intent, (b) authority, (c) seizure or detention, and (d) the understanding of the person that he or she has been arrested.

5 **Indicate situations in which a *Miranda* warning is unnecessary.**

(a) When no questions that are testimonial in nature are asked of the suspect; (b) when there is no suspect and witnesses in general are being questioned at the scene of a crime; (c) when a person volunteers information before the police ask anything; (d) when a suspect has given a private statement to a friend without the government orchestrating it; (e) during a stop and frisk when no arrests have been made; (f) during a traffic stop; and (g) when a threat to public safety exists.

Spencer Platt/Getty Images

CHAPTER 6 QUIZ ANSWERS

1. Probable cause
2. Exclusionary
3. Privacy
4. Consent
5. Reasonable

6. Frisk
7. Custody
8. Warrant
9. Before
10. Waive

KEY TERMS

Affidavit A written statement of facts, confirmed by the oath or affirmation of the party making it and made before a person having the authority to administer the oath or affirmation. 122

Arrest To take into custody a person suspected of criminal activity. 131

Arrest Warrant A written order, based on probable cause and issued by a judge or magistrate, commanding that the person named on the warrant be arrested by the police. 132

Coercion The use of physical force or mental intimidation to compel a person to do something—such as confess to committing a crime—against her or his will. 134

Consent Searches Searches by police that are made after the subject of the search has agreed to the action. In these situations, consent, if given of free will, validates a warrantless search. 124

Custodial Interrogation The questioning of a suspect after that person has been taken into custody. In this situation, the suspect must be read his or her *Miranda* rights before interrogation can begin. 134

Custody The forceful detention of a person, or the perception that a person is not free to leave the immediate vicinity. 134

Electronic Surveillance The use of electronic equipment by law enforcement agents to record private conversations or observe conduct that is meant to be private. 126

Exclusionary Rule A rule under which any evidence that is obtained in violation of the accused's rights, as well as any evidence derived from illegally obtained evidence, will not be admissible in criminal court. 120

Exigent Circumstances Situations that require extralegal or exceptional actions by the police. 132

Frisk A pat-down or minimal search by police to discover weapons. 130

Fruit of the Poisoned Tree Evidence that is acquired through the use of illegally obtained evidence and is therefore inadmissible in court. 120

"Good Faith" Exception The legal principle that evidence obtained with the use of a technically invalid search warrant is admissible during trial if the police acted in good faith when they sought the warrant from a judge. 121

"Inevitable Discovery" Exception The legal principle that illegally obtained evidence can be admissible in court if police using lawful means would have "inevitably" discovered it. 121

Interrogation The direct questioning of a suspect to gather evidence of criminal activity and to try to gain a confession. 133

Miranda Rights The constitutional rights of accused persons taken into custody by law enforcement officials, such as the right to remain silent and the right to counsel. 134

Plain View Doctrine The legal principle that objects in plain view of a law enforcement agent

who has the right to be in a position to have that view may be seized without a warrant and introduced as evidence. 126

Probable Cause Reasonable grounds to believe the existence of facts warranting certain actions, such as the search or arrest of a person. 118

Search The process by which police examine a person or property to find evidence that will be used to prove guilt in a criminal trial. 122

Search Warrant A written order, based on probable cause and issued by a judge or magistrate, commanding that police officers or criminal investigators search a specific person, place, or property to obtain evidence. 122

Searches and Seizures The legal term, as found in the Fourth Amendment to the U.S. Constitution, that generally refers to the searching for and the confiscating of evidence by law enforcement agents. 118

Searches Incidental to Arrests Searches for weapons and evidence that are conducted on persons who have just been arrested. 124

Seizure The forcible taking of a person or property in response to a violation of the law. 123

Stop A brief detention of a person by law enforcement agents for questioning. 130

Warrantless Arrest An arrest made without first seeking a warrant for the action. 133

COURTS AND THE QUEST FOR JUSTICE

CHAPTER SUMMARY & LEARNING OUTCOMES

1 Define *jurisdiction* and contrast geographic and subject-matter jurisdiction.
Jurisdiction relates to the power of a court to hear a particular case. Courts are typically limited in geographic jurisdiction—for example, to a particular state. Some courts are restricted in subject matter, such as a small claims court, which can hear only cases involving civil matters under a certain monetary limit.

2 Explain the difference between trial and appellate courts.
Trial courts are courts of the first instance, where a case is first heard. Appellate courts review the proceedings of a lower court. Appellate courts do not have juries.

3 Explain briefly how a case is brought to the Supreme Court.
Cases decided in U.S. courts of appeals, as well as cases decided in the highest state courts (when federal questions arise), can be appealed to the Supreme Court. If at least four justices approve of a case filed with the Supreme Court, the Court will issue a writ of *certiorari,* ordering the lower court to send the Supreme Court the record of the case for review.

4 List the different names given to public prosecutors and indicate the general powers that they have.
At the federal level, the prosecutor is called the U.S. attorney. In state and local courts, the prosecutor may be referred to as the prosecuting attorney, state attorney, district attorney, county attorney, or city attorney. Prosecutors in general have the power to decide when and how the state will pursue an individual suspected of criminal wrongdoing. In some jurisdictions, the district attorney is also the chief law enforcement officer, holding broad powers over police operations.

5 Explain why defense attorneys must often defend clients they know to be guilty.
In our criminal justice system, the most important responsibility of a defense attorney is to be an advocate for her or his client. This means ensuring that the client's constitutional rights are protected during criminal justice proceedings, regardless of whether the client is guilty or innocent.

CHAPTER 7 QUIZ ANSWERS

1. Defendants
2. Crime control
3. Jurisdiction
4. Federal
5. *Certiorari*
6. Concurring
7. Governor
8. Prosecutors
9. Counsel
10. Public

KEY TERMS

Appellate Courts Courts that review decisions made by lower courts, such as trial courts; also known as *courts of appeals*. 144

Attorney-Client Privilege A rule of evidence requiring that communications between a client and his or her attorney be kept confidential, unless the client consents to disclosure. 158

Attorney General The chief law officer of a state; also, the chief law officer of the nation. 155

Concurrent Jurisdiction The situation that occurs when two or more courts have the authority to preside over the same criminal case. 142

Concurring Opinions Separate opinions prepared by judges who support the decision of the majority of the court but who want to make or clarify a particular point or to voice disapproval of the grounds on which the decision was made. 150

Courtroom Work Group The social organization consisting of the judge, prosecutor, defense attorney, and other court workers. 153

Defense Attorney The lawyer representing the defendant. 156

Dissenting Opinions Separate opinions in which judges disagree with the conclusion reached by the majority of the court and expand on their own views about the case. 150

Docket The list of cases entered on a court's calendar and thus scheduled to be heard by the court. 151

Dual Court System The separate but interrelated court system of the United States, made up of the courts on the national level and the courts on the state level. 144

Extradition The process by which one jurisdiction surrenders a person accused or convicted of violating another jurisdiction's criminal law to the second jurisdiction. 143

Judicial Review The power of a court—particularly the United States Supreme Court—to review the actions of the executive and legislative branches and, if necessary, declare those actions unconstitutional. 148

Jurisdiction The authority of a court to hear and decide cases within an area of the law or a geographic territory. 141

Magistrate A public civil officer or official with limited judicial authority within a particular geographic area, such as the authority to issue an arrest warrant. 145

Missouri Plan A method of selecting judges that combines appointment and election. 153

Nonpartisan Elections Elections in which candidates are presented on the ballot without any party affiliation. 152

Opinions Written statements by the judges expressing the reasons for the court's decision in a case. 144

Oral Arguments The verbal arguments presented in person by attorneys to an appellate court. Each attorney presents reasons why the court should rule in his or her client's favor. 150

Partisan Elections Elections in which candidates are affiliated with and receive support from political parties. 152

Problem-Solving Courts Lower courts that have jurisdiction over one specific area of criminal activity, such as illegal drugs or domestic violence. 145

Public Defenders Court-appointed attorneys who are paid by the state to represent defendants who are unable to hire private counsel. 157

Public Prosecutors Individuals, acting as trial lawyers, who initiate and conduct cases in the government's name and on behalf of the people. 155

Rule of Four A rule of the United States Supreme Court that the Court will not issue a writ of *certiorari* unless at least four justices approve of the decision to hear the case. 149

Trial Courts Courts in which most cases usually begin and in which questions of fact are examined. 144

Writ of *Certiorari* A request from a higher court asking a lower court for the record of a case. In essence, the request signals the higher court's willingness to review the case. 149

PRETRIAL PROCEDURES AND THE CRIMINAL TRIAL **8**

CHAPTER SUMMARY & LEARNING OUTCOMES

1 **Identify the steps involved in the pretrial criminal process.**
(a) Suspect taken into custody or arrested; (b) initial appearance before a magistrate; (c) the posting of bail or release on recognizance; (d) preventive detention, if deemed necessary to ensure the safety of other persons or the community, or regular detention, if the defendant is unable to post bail; (e) preliminary arraignment; (f) grand jury hearings, after which an indictment is issued against the defendant if the grand jury finds probable cause; (g) arraignment; and (h) plea bargaining.

2 **Identify the main difference between an indictment and an information.**
An indictment is the grand jury's declaration that probable cause exists to charge a defendant with a specific crime. In jurisdictions that do not use grand juries, the prosecution issues an information as the formal charge of a crime.

3 **Identify the basic protections enjoyed by criminal defendants in the United States.**
According to the Sixth Amendment, a criminal defendant has the right to a speedy and public trial by an impartial jury in the physical location where the crime was committed. Additionally, a person accused of a crime must be informed of the nature of the crime and be confronted with the witnesses against him or her. Further, the accused must be able to summon witnesses in her or his favor and have the assistance of counsel.

4 **Contrast challenges for cause and peremptory challenges during** *voir dire.*
A challenge for cause occurs when an attorney provides the court with a legally justifiable reason why a potential juror should be excluded. In contrast, peremptory challenges do not require any justification by the attorney and are usually limited to a small number. They cannot, however, be based, even implicitly, on race or gender.

5 **List the standard steps in a criminal jury trial.**
(a) Opening statements by the prosecutor and the defense attorney; (b) presentation of evidence; (c) cross-examination by the defense attorney of the same witnesses; (d) presentation of the defendant's case; (e) cross-examination by the prosecutor; (f) after the defense closes its case, rebuttal by the prosecution; (g) cross-examination of the prosecution's new witnesses by the defense and introduction of new witnesses of its own, called the surrebuttal; (i) closing arguments by both the defense and the prosecution; (j) the charging of the jury by the judge; (k) jury deliberations; and (l) presentation of the verdict.

CHAPTER 8 QUIZ ANSWERS

1. Bail
2. Grand jury
3. Plea bargain
4. Bench
5. Reasonable doubt
6. *Voir dire*
7. Prejudice
8. Direct
9. Cross
10. Appeal

KEY TERMS

Acquittal A declaration following a trial that the individual accused of the crime is innocent in the eyes of the law and thus is absolved from the charges. 170

Allen Charge An instruction by a judge to a deadlocked jury with only a few dissenters that asks the jurors in the minority to reconsider the majority opinion. 181

Appeal The process of seeking a higher court's review of a lower court's decision for the purpose of correcting or changing this decision. 181

Arraignment A court proceeding in which the suspect is formally charged with the criminal offense stated in the indictment. 166

Bail The dollar amount or conditions set by the court to ensure that an individual accused of a crime will appear for further criminal proceedings. 166

Bail Bond Agent A businessperson who agrees, for a fee, to pay the bail amount if the accused fails to appear in court as ordered. 163

Bench Trial A trial conducted without a jury, in which a judge makes the determination of the defendant's guilt or innocence. 170

Case Attrition The process through which prosecutors, by deciding whether to prosecute each person arrested, effect an overall reduction in the number of persons prosecuted. 165

Challenge for Cause A *voir dire* challenge for which an attorney states the reason why a prospective juror should not be included on the jury. 172

Charge The judge's instructions to the jury following the attorneys' closing arguments. 180

Circumstantial Evidence Indirect evidence that is offered to establish, by inference, the likelihood of a fact that is in question. 176

Closing Arguments Arguments made by each side's attorney after the cases for the plaintiff and defendant have been presented. 180

Confrontation Clause The part of the Sixth Amendment that guarantees all defendants the right to confront witnesses testifying against them during the criminal trial. 178

Cross-Examination The questioning of an opposing witness during trial. 178

Direct Evidence Evidence that establishes the existence of a fact that is in question without relying on inference. 176

Direct Examination The examination of a witness by the attorney who calls the witness to the stand to testify. 178

Discovery Formal investigation by each side prior to trial. 164

Double Jeopardy To twice place at risk (jeopardize) a person's life or liberty. Constitutional law prohibits a second prosecution in the same court for the same criminal offense. 182

Evidence Anything that is used to prove the existence or nonexistence of a fact. 175

Expert Witness A witness with professional training or substantial experience qualifying her or him to testify on a certain subject. 176

Grand Jury The group of citizens called to decide whether probable cause exists to believe that a suspect committed the crime with which she or he has been charged. 165

Habeas Corpus An order that requires corrections officials to bring an inmate before a court or a judge and explain why he or she is being held in prison. 182

Hearsay An oral or written statement made by an out-of-court speaker that is later offered in court by a witness (not the speaker) concerning a matter before the court. 178

Hung Jury A jury whose members are so irreconcilably divided in their opinions that they cannot reach a verdict. 181

Indictment A charge or written accusation, issued by a grand jury, that probable cause exists to believe that a named person has committed a crime. 165

Information The formal charge against the accused issued by the prosecutor after a preliminary hearing has found probable cause. 165

Initial Appearance An accused's first appearance before a judge or magistrate following arrest. 162

Jury Trial A trial before a judge and a jury. 170

Lay Witness A witness who can truthfully and accurately testify on a fact in question without having specialized training or knowledge. 176

Master Jury List The list of citizens in a court's district from which a jury can be selected; compiled from voter-registration lists, driver's license lists, and other sources. 171

Nolo Contendere Latin for "I will not contest it." A criminal defendant's plea, in which he or she chooses not to challenge, or contest, the charges brought by the government. 166

Opening Statements The attorneys' statements to the jury at the beginning of the trial. 175

Peremptory Challenges *Voir dire* challenges to exclude potential jurors from serving on the jury without any supporting reason or cause. 173

Plea Bargaining The process by which the accused and the prosecutor work out a mutually satisfactory conclusion to the case, subject to court approval. 167

Preliminary Hearing An initial hearing in which a magistrate decides if there is probable cause to believe that the defendant committed the crime with which he or she is charged. 164

Preventive Detention The retention of an accused person in custody due to fears that she or he will commit a crime if released before trial. 163

Property Bond An alternative to posting bail in cash, in which the defendant gains pretrial release by providing the court with property valued at the bail amount as assurance that he or she will return for trial. 163

Real Evidence Evidence that is brought into court and seen by the jury, as opposed to evidence that is described for a jury. 175

Rebuttal Evidence given to counteract or disprove evidence presented by the opposing party. 180

Release on Recognizance (ROR) A judge's order that releases an accused from jail with the understanding that he or she will return of his or her own will for further proceedings. 163

Relevant Evidence Evidence tending to make a fact in question more or less probable than it would be without the evidence. Only relevant evidence is admissible in court. 177

Statute of Limitations A law limiting the amount of time prosecutors have to bring criminal charges against a suspect after the crime has occurred. 169

Testimony Verbal evidence given by witnesses under oath. 175

Venire The group of citizens from which the jury is selected. 172

Verdict A formal decision made by the jury. 180

Voir Dire The preliminary questions that the trial attorneys ask prospective jurors to determine whether they are biased or have any connection with the defendant or a witness. 172

Wrongful Conviction The conviction, either by verdict or by guilty plea, of a person who is factually innocent of the charges. 183

PUNISHMENT AND SENTENCING

CHAPTER SUMMARY & LEARNING OUTCOMES

1 **List and contrast the four basic philosophical reasons for sentencing criminals.**
(a) Retribution, (b) deterrence, (c) incapacitation, and (d) rehabilitation. Under the principle of retributive justice, the severity of the punishment is in proportion to the severity of the crime. Punishment is an end in itself. In contrast, the deterrence approach seeks to prevent future crimes by setting an example. Such punishment is based on its deterrent value and not necessarily on the severity of the crime. The incapacitation theory of punishment simply argues that a criminal in prison cannot inflict further harm on society. In contrast, the rehabilitation theory asserts that criminals can be rehabilitated in the appropriate prison environment.

2 **Contrast indeterminate with determinate sentencing.**
Indeterminate sentencing follows from legislative penal codes that set minimum and maximum amounts of incarceration time. Determinate sentencing carries a fixed amount of time, although this may be reduced for "good time."

3 **Explain some of the reasons why sentencing reform has occurred.**
One reason is sentencing disparity, which is indicative of a situation in which those convicted of similar crimes receive dissimilar sentences (often due to a particular judge's sentencing philosophy). Sentencing discrimination has also occurred on the basis of defendants' gender, race, or economic standing. An additional reason for sentencing reform has been a general desire to "get tough on crime."

4 **Identify the arguments for and against the use of victim impact statements during sentencing hearings.**
Proponents of victim impact statements believe that they allow victims to provide character evidence in the same manner as defendants have always been allowed to do and that they give victims a therapeutic "voice" in the sentencing process. Opponents argue that the statements bring unacceptable levels of emotion into the courtroom and encourage judges and juries to make sentencing decisions based on the "social value" of the victim rather than the facts of the case.

5 **Identify the two stages that make up the bifurcated process of death penalty sentencing.**
The first stage of the bifurcated process requires a jury to find the defendant guilty or not guilty of a crime that is punishable by execution. If the defendant is found guilty, then, in the second stage, the jury reconvenes to decide whether the death sentence is warranted.

CHAPTER 9 QUIZ ANSWERS

1. Deterrence

2. Rehabilitation

3. Indeterminate

4. Good time

5. Mitigating

6. Disparity

7. Discrimination

8. Guidelines

9. Lethal injection

10. Juveniles

KEY TERMS

Aggravating Circumstances Any circumstances accompanying the commission of a crime that may justify a harsher sentence. 195

Capital Punishment The use of the death penalty to punish wrongdoers for certain crimes. 202

Departure A stipulation in many federal and state sentencing guidelines that allows a judge to adjust his or her sentencing decision based on the special circumstances of a particular case. 200

Determinate Sentencing A period of incarceration that is fixed by a sentencing authority and cannot be reduced by judges or other corrections officials. 192

Deterrence The strategy of preventing crime through the threat of punishment. 188

"Good Time" A reduction in time served by prisoners based on good behavior, conformity to rules, and other positive behavior. 192

Habitual Offender Laws Statutes that require lengthy prison sentences for those who are convicted of multiple felonies. 200

Incapacitation A strategy for preventing crime by detaining wrongdoers in prison, thereby separating them from the community and reducing criminal opportunities. 189

Indeterminate Sentencing An indeterminate term of incarceration in which a judge determines the minimum and maximum terms of imprisonment. 191

Just Deserts A sanctioning philosophy based on the assertion that criminals deserve to be punished for breaking society's rules. 188

Mandatory Sentencing Guidelines Statutorily determined punishments that must be applied to those who are convicted of specific crimes. 200

Mitigating Circumstances Any circumstances accompanying the commission of a crime that may justify a lighter sentence. 195

Presentence Investigative Report An investigative report on an offender's background that assists a judge in determining the proper sentence. 194

"Real Offense" The actual offense committed, as opposed to the charge levied by a prosecutor as the result of a plea bargain. 195

Rehabilitation The philosophy that society is best served when wrongdoers are provided the resources needed to eliminate criminality from their behavioral pattern. 189

Restitution Monetary compensation for damages done to the victim by the offender's criminal act. 190

Restorative Justice An approach to punishment designed to repair the harm done to the victim and the community by the offender's criminal act. 190

Retribution The philosophy that those who commit criminal acts should be punished based on the severity of the crime and that no other factors need be considered. 188

Sentencing Discrimination A situation in which the length of a sentence appears to be influenced by a defendant's race, gender, economic status, or other factor not directly related to the crime he or she committed. 197

Sentencing Disparity A situation in which those convicted of similar crimes do not receive similar sentences. 196

Sentencing Guidelines Legislatively determined guidelines that judges are required to follow when sentencing those convicted of specific crimes. 199

Truth-in-Sentencing Laws Legislative attempts to ensure that convicts will serve approximately the terms to which they were initially sentenced. 192

Victim Impact Statement (VIS) A statement to the sentencing body (judge, jury, or parole board) in which the victim is given the opportunity to describe how the crime has affected her or him. 201

STUDY ONLINE WITH COURSEMATE www.cengagebrain.com

To help you refresh your understanding of each major chapter section go online to access the relevant Self-Assessment quiz. You'll

CHAPTER REVIEW

PROBATION, PAROLE, AND INTERMEDIATE SANCTIONS

CHAPTER SUMMARY & LEARNING OUTCOMES

1 **Explain the justifications for community-based corrections programs.**

One justification involves reintegration of the offender into society. Reintegration restores family ties, encourages employment and education, and secures a place for the offender in the routine functioning of society. Other justifications involve diversion and cost savings. By diverting criminals to alternative modes of punishment, further overcrowding of jail and prison facilities can be avoided, as can the costs of incarcerating the offenders.

2 **Describe the three general categories of conditions placed on a probationer.**

(a) Standard conditions, such as requiring that the probationer notify the agency of a change of address, not leave the jurisdiction without permission, and remain employed; (b) punitive conditions, such as restitution, community service, and home confinement; and (c) treatment conditions, such as required drug or alcohol treatment.

3 **Identify the main differences between probation and parole.**

Probation is a sentence handed down by a judge that generally acts as an alternative to incarceration. Parole is a form of early release from prison determined by a parole authority, often a parole board. Probationers are usually first-time offenders who have committed nonviolent crimes, while parolees have often spent significant time in prison.

4 **List the four basic roles of the parole board.**

Parole boards (a) decide which inmates should be granted parole, (b) determine the conditions of parole, (c) resolve when an offender has satisfied his or her parole requirements, and (d) determine whether parole privileges should be revoked if a violation has occurred.

5 **List the three levels of home monitoring.**

(a) Curfew, which requires that the offender be at home during specified hours; (b) home detention, which requires that the offender be at home except for education, employment, and counseling; and (c) home incarceration, which requires that the offender be at home at all times except for medical emergencies.

AP Photo/Damian Dovarganes

CHAPTER 10 QUIZ ANSWERS

1. Diverting
2. Probation
3. Recidivism
4. Parole
5. Technical

6. Parole board
7. Mandatory
8. Forfeiture
9. Shock
10. Electronic monitoring

KEY TERMS

Authority The power designated to an agent of the law over a person who has broken the law. 217

Caseload The number of individual probationers or parolees under the supervision of a probation or parole officer. 217

Community Corrections The correctional supervision of offenders in the community as an alternative to sending them to prison or jail. 212

Day Reporting Center (DRC) A community-based corrections center to which offenders report on a daily basis for treatment, education, and rehabilitation. 226

Discretionary Release The release of an inmate into a community supervision program at the discretion of the parole board within limits set by state or federal law. 222

Diversion In the context of corrections, a strategy to divert those offenders who qualify away from prison and jail and toward community-based and intermediate sanctions. 212

Electronic Monitoring A technique of probation supervision in which the offender's whereabouts are kept under surveillance by an electronic device. 228

Forfeiture The process by which the government seizes private property attached to criminal activity. 226

Home Confinement A community-based sanction in which offenders serve their terms of incarceration in their homes. 228

Intensive Supervision Probation (ISP) A punishment-oriented form of probation in which the offender is placed under stricter and more frequent surveillance and control than in conventional probation. 227

Intermediate Sanctions Sanctions that are more restrictive than probation and less restrictive than imprisonment. 224

Mandatory Release Release from prison that occurs when an offender has served the full length of his or her sentence, minus any adjustments for good time. 223

Parole The conditional release of an inmate before his or her sentence has expired. 220

Parole Board A body of appointed civilians that decides whether a convict should be granted conditional release before the end of his or her sentence. 222

Parole Contract An agreement between the state and the offender that establishes the conditions of parole. 220

Parole Grant Hearing A hearing in which the entire parole board or a subcommittee reviews information, meets the offender, and hears testimony from relevant witnesses to determine whether to grant parole. 223

Parole Guidelines Standards that are used in the parole process to measure the risk that a potential parolee will recidivate. 223

Parole Revocation When a parolee breaks the conditions of parole, the process of withdrawing parole and returning the person to prison. 221

Pretrial Diversion Program An alternative to trial offered by a judge or prosecutor, in which the offender agrees to participate in a specified counseling or treatment program in return for withdrawal of the charges. 225

Probation A criminal sanction in which a convict is allowed to remain in the community rather than be imprisoned. 213

Recidivism The act of committing a new crime after a person has already been punished for a previous crime by being convicted and sent to jail or prison. 219

Reintegration A goal of corrections that focuses on preparing the offender for a return to the community unmarred by further criminal behavior. 212

Shock Incarceration A short period of incarceration that is designed to deter further criminal activity by "shocking" the offender with the hardships of imprisonment. 227

Split Sentence Probation A sentence that consists of incarceration in a prison or jail, followed by a probationary period in the community. 214

Suspended Sentence A judicially imposed condition in which an offender is sentenced after being convicted of a crime, but is not required to begin serving the sentence immediately. 214

Technical Violation An action taken by a probationer or parolee that, although not criminal, breaks the terms of probation or parole as designated by the court. 217

Widen the Net The criticism that intermediate sanctions designed to divert offenders from prison actually increase the number of citizens who are under the control and surveillance of the American corrections system. 230

STUDY ONLINE WITH COURSEMATE www.cengagebrain.com

To help you refresh your understanding of each major chapter section **go online to access the relevant Self-Assessment quiz.** You'll know right away whether you need to go back and read that section again to cement your understanding of major concepts.

CHAPTER REVIEW

PRISONS AND JAILS

CHAPTER SUMMARY & LEARNING OUTCOMES

1 Contrast the Pennsylvania and the New York penitentiary theories of the 1800s.
Basically, the Pennsylvania system imposed total silence on its prisoners. Based on the concept of separate confinement, penitentiaries were constructed with back-to-back cells facing both outward and inward. Prisoners worked, slept, and ate alone in their cells. In contrast, New York used the congregate system: silence was imposed, but inmates worked and ate together.

2 List and briefly explain the four types of prisons.
(a) Maximum-security prisons, which are designed mainly with security and surveillance in mind. Such prisons are usually large and consist of cell blocks, each of which is set off by a series of gates and bars. (b) Medium-security prisons, which offer considerably more educational and treatment programs and allow more contact between inmates. Such prisons are usually surrounded by high fences rather than by walls. (c) Minimum-security prisons, which permit prisoners to have television sets and computers and often allow them to leave the grounds for educational and employment purposes. (d) Supermaximum-security (supermax) prisons, in which prisoners are confined to one-person cells for up to twenty-three hours per day under constant video camera surveillance.

3 List the factors that have caused the prison population to grow dramatically in the last several decades.
(a) The enhancement and stricter enforcement of the nation's drug laws; (b) increased probability of incarceration; (c) inmates serving more time for each crime; (d) federal prison growth; and (e) rising incarceration rates for women.

4 Summarize the distinction between jails and prisons, and indicate the importance of jails in the American corrections system.
Generally, a prison is for those convicted of felonies who will serve lengthy periods of incarceration, whereas a jail is for those who have been convicted of misdemeanors and will serve less than a year of incarceration. Jails also hold individuals awaiting trial, juveniles awaiting transfer to juvenile authorities, probation and parole violators, and the mentally ill. In any given year, approximately 12 million people are admitted to jails, and therefore jails often provide the best chance for treatment or counseling that may deter future criminal behavior by these low-level offenders.

5 Indicate some of the consequences of our high rates of incarceration.
Some people believe that the reduction in the country's crime rate is a direct result of increased incarceration rates. Others believe that high incarceration rates are having increasingly negative social consequences, such as financial hardships, reduced supervision and discipline of children, and a general deterioration of the family structure when one parent is in prison.

AP Photo/Rich Pedroncelli

CHAPTER 11 QUIZ ANSWERS

1. Medical
2. Warden
3. Classification
4. Maximum
5. Supermax

6. Drug
7. Decarceration
8. Overcrowding
9. Pretrial detainees
10. Sheriff

KEY TERMS

Classification The process through which prison officials determine which correctional facility is best suited to the individual offender. 240

Congregate System A nineteenth-century penitentiary system developed in New York in which inmates were kept in separate cells during the night but worked together in the daytime under a code of enforced silence. 235

Direct Supervision Approach A process of prison and jail administration in which correctional officers are in continuous physical contact with inmates during the day. 251

Jail A facility, usually operated by the county government, used to hold persons awaiting trial or those who have been found guilty of misdemeanors. 247

Lockdown A disciplinary action taken by prison officials in which all inmates are ordered to their quarters and nonessential prison activities are suspended. 242

Maximum-Security Prison A correctional institution designed and organized to control and discipline dangerous felons, as well as prevent escape. 240

Medical Model A model of corrections in which the psychological and biological roots of an inmate's criminal behavior are identified and treated. 236

Medium-Security Prison A correctional institution that houses less dangerous inmates and therefore uses less restrictive measures to prevent violence and escapes. 243

Minimum-Security Prison A correctional institution designed to allow inmates, most of whom pose low security risks, a great deal of freedom of movement and contact with the outside world. 243

New-Generation Jail A type of jail that is distinguished architecturally from its predecessors by a design that encourages interaction between inmates and jailers and that offers greater opportunities for treatment. 250

Penitentiary An early form of correctional facility that emphasized separating inmates from society and from each other. 234

Pretrial Detainees Individuals who cannot post bail after arrest and are therefore forced to spend the time prior to their trial incarcerated in jail. 248

Private Prisons Correctional facilities operated by private corporations instead of the government and, therefore, reliant on profits for survival. 245

Separate Confinement A nineteenth-century penitentiary system developed in Pennsylvania in which inmates were kept separate from each other at all times, with daily activities taking place in individual cells. 235

Supermax Prison A correctional facility reserved for those inmates who have extensive records of misconduct. 241

Time Served The period of time a person denied bail (or unable to pay it) has spent in jail prior to his or her trial. 248

Warden The prison official who is ultimately responsible for the organization and performance of a correctional facility. 239

STUDY ONLINE WITH COURSEMATE www.cengagebrain.com

To help you refresh your understanding of each major chapter section **go online to access the relevant Self-Assessment quiz.** You'll know right away whether you need to go back and read that section again to cement your understanding of major concepts!

BEHIND BARS: THE LIFE OF AN INMATE

CHAPTER SUMMARY & LEARNING OUTCOMES

1 **Explain the concept of prison as a total institution.**

Though many people spend time in partial institutions—schools, companies where they work, and religious organizations—only in prison is every aspect of an inmate's life controlled, and that is why prisons are called total institutions. Every detail for every prisoner is fully prescribed and managed.

2 **Indicate some of the reasons for violent behavior in prisons.**

(a) To separate the powerful from the weak and establish a prisoner hierarchy; (b) to minimize one's own probability of being a target of assault; (c) to enhance one's self-image; (d) to obtain sexual relief; and (e) to obtain material goods through extortion or robbery.

3 **Describe the hands-off doctrine of prisoner law and indicate two standards used to determine if prisoners' rights have been violated.**

The hands-off doctrine assumes that the care of prisoners should be left to prison officials and that it is not the place of judges to intervene. Nonetheless, the Supreme Court has created two standards to be used by the courts in determining whether a prisoner's Eighth Amendment protections against cruel and unusual punishment have been violated. Under the "deliberate indifference" standard, prisoners must show that prison officials were aware of harmful conditions at the facility but failed to remedy them. Under the "identifiable human needs" standard, prisoners must show that they were denied a basic need such as food, warmth, or exercise.

4 **Contrast parole, expiration release, pardon, and furlough.**

Parole is an early release program for those incarcerated. Expiration release occurs when the inmate has served the maximum time for her or his initial sentence minus good-time credits. A pardon can be given only by the president or one of the fifty governors. Furlough is a temporary release while in jail or prison.

5 **Explain the goal of prisoner reentry programs.**

Based on the ideals of promoting desistance, these programs have two main objectives: (a) to prepare a prisoner for a successful return to the community, and (b) to protect the community by reducing the chances that the ex-convict will continue her or his criminal activity after release from prison.

Noah Berger/Bloomberg via Getty Images

CHAPTER 12 QUIZ ANSWERS

1. Total institution
2. Health-care
3. Relative deprivation
4. Legitimate
5. Malicious

6. Deliberate
7. Correctional officers
8. Reentry
9. Halfway
10. Notification

KEY TERMS

Civil Confinement The practice of confining individuals against their will if they present a danger to the community. 275

"Deliberate Indifference" The standard for establishing a violation of an inmate's Eighth Amendment rights, requiring that prison officials were aware of harmful conditions in a correctional institution and failed to take steps to remedy those conditions. 266

Deprivation Model A theory that inmate aggression is the result of the frustration inmates feel at being deprived of freedom, consumer goods, sex, and other staples of life outside the institution. 259

Desistance The process through which criminal activity decreases and reintegration into society increases over a period of time. 272

Expiration Release The release of an inmate from prison at the end of his or her sentence without any further correctional supervision. 270

Furlough Temporary release from a prison for purposes of vocational or educational training, to ease the shock of release, or for personal reasons. 270

Halfway House A community-based form of early release that places inmates in residential centers and allows them to reintegrate with society. 272

"Hands-Off" Doctrine The unwritten judicial policy that favors noninterference by the courts in the administration of prisons and jails. 266

"Identifiable Human Needs" The basic human necessities that correctional facilities are required by the Constitution to provide to inmates. 266

Pardon An act of executive clemency that overturns a conviction and erases mention of the crime from the person's criminal record. 270

Prison Gang A group of inmates who band together within the corrections system to engage in social and criminal activities. 261

Prison Programs Organized activities for inmates that are designed to improve their physical and mental health, provide them with vocational skills, or simply keep them busy while incarcerated. 258

Prisoner Reentry A corrections strategy designed to prepare inmates for a successful return to the community and to reduce their criminal activity after release. 270

Prisonization The socialization process through which a new inmate learns the accepted norms and values of the prison culture. 256

Relative Deprivation The theory that inmate aggression is caused when freedoms and services that the inmate has come to accept as normal are decreased or eliminated. 260

Sex Offender Notification Law Legislation that requires law enforcement authorities to notify people when convicted sex offenders are released into their neighborhood or community. 274

Total Institution An institution, such as a prison, that provides all of the necessities for existence to those who live within its boundaries. 256

Work Release Program Temporary release of convicts from prison for purposes of employment. The offenders may spend their days on the job, but must return to the correctional facility at night and during the weekend. 272

THE JUVENILE JUSTICE SYSTEM

13

CHAPTER SUMMARY & LEARNING OUTCOMES

1 Describe the child-saving movement and its relationship to the doctrine of *parens patriae*.

Under the doctrine of *parens patriae*, the state has a right and a duty to care for neglected, delinquent, or disadvantaged children. The child-saving movement, based on the doctrine of *parens patriae*, started in the 1800s. Its followers believed that juvenile offenders require treatment rather than punishment.

2 List the four major differences between juvenile courts and adult courts.

(a) No juries, (b) different terminology, (c) limited adversarial relationship, and (d) confidentiality.

3 Describe the reasoning behind recent U.S. Supreme Court decisions that have lessened the harshness of sentencing outcomes for violent juvenile offenders.

In banning capital punishment and limiting the availability of life sentences without parole for offenders who committed their crimes as juveniles, the Supreme Court has focused on the concept of "diminished capacity." This concept is based on the notion that violent juvenile offenders cannot fully comprehend the consequences of their actions and are more deserving of the opportunity for rehabilitation than adult violent offenders.

4 Describe the one variable that always correlates highly with juvenile crime rates.

The older a person is, the less likely he or she will exhibit criminal behavior. This process is known as aging out. Thus, persons in any at-risk group will commit fewer crimes as they get older.

5 Describe the four primary stages of pretrial juvenile justice procedure.

(a) Intake, in which an official of the juvenile court engages in a screening process to determine what to do with the youthful offender; (b) pretrial diversion, which may consist of probation, treatment and aid, and/or restitution; (c) jurisdictional waiver to an adult court, in which case the youth leaves the juvenile justice system; and (d) some type of detention, in which the youth is held until the disposition process begins.

CHAPTER 13 QUIZ ANSWERS

1. Government/state
2. Status offense
3. Death penalty
4. Aging out
5. Gangs

6. Arrest
7. Refer
8. Waiver
9. Adjudicatory
10. Disposition

Carline Jean/*Sun Sentinel*/MCT via Getty Images

KEY TERMS

Adjudicatory Hearing The process through which a juvenile court determines whether there is sufficient evidence to support the initial petition. 296

Aftercare The variety of therapeutic, educational, and counseling programs made available to juvenile delinquents (and some adults) after they have been released from a correctional facility. 299

Age of Onset The age at which a juvenile first exhibits delinquent behavior. 289

Aging Out A term used to explain the fact that criminal activity declines with age. 289

Automatic Transfer The process by which a juvenile is transferred to adult court as a matter of state law. 294

Boot Camp A variation on traditional shock incarceration in which juveniles (and some adults) are sent to secure confinement facilities modeled on military basic training camps instead of prison or jail. 298

Bullying Overt acts taken by students with the goal of intimidating, harassing, or humiliating other students. 288

Child Abuse Mistreatment of children by causing physical, emotional, or sexual damage without any plausible explanation, such as an accident. 290

Child Neglect A form of child abuse in which the child is denied certain necessities such as shelter, food, care, and love. 290

Detention The temporary custody of a juvenile in a secure facility after a petition has been filed and before the adjudicatory process begins. 294

Detention Hearing A hearing to determine whether a juvenile should be detained, or remain detained, while waiting for the adjudicatory process to begin. 295

Disposition Hearing Similar to the sentencing hearing for adults, a hearing in which the juvenile judge or officer decides the appropriate punishment for a youth found to be delinquent or a status offender. 297

Graduated Sanctions The practical theory in juvenile corrections that a delinquent or status offender should receive a punishment that matches in seriousness the severity of the wrongdoing. 297

Intake The process by which an official of the court must decide whether to file a petition, release the juvenile, or place the juvenile under some other form of supervision. 293

Judicial Waiver The process in which the juvenile judge, based on the facts of the case at hand, decides that the alleged offender should be transferred to adult court. 294

Juvenile Delinquency Behavior that is illegal under federal or state law that has been committed by a person who is under an age limit specified by statute. 281

Low-Visibility Decision Making A term used to describe the discretionary power police have in determining what to do with misbehaving juveniles. 293

Parens Patriae A doctrine that holds that the state has a responsibility to look after the well-being of children and to assume the role of parent if necessary. 280

Petition The document filed with a juvenile court alleging that the juvenile is a delinquent or a status offender and requesting that the court either hear the case or transfer it to an adult court. 293

Predisposition Report A report prepared during the disposition process that provides the judge with relevant background material to aid in the disposition decision. 297

Prosecutorial Waiver A procedure used in situations where the prosecutor has discretion to decide whether a case will be heard by a juvenile court or an adult court. 294

Referral The notification process through which a law enforcement officer or other concerned citizen makes the juvenile court aware of a juvenile's unlawful or unruly conduct. 293

Residential Treatment Program A government-run facility for juveniles whose offenses are not deemed serious enough to warrant incarceration in a training school. 298

Status Offender A juvenile who has engaged in behavior deemed unacceptable for those under a certain statutorily determined age. 281

Training School A correctional institution for juveniles found to be delinquent or status offenders. 299

Youth Gang A self-formed group of youths with several identifiable characteristics, including a gang name and other recognizable symbols, a geographic territory, and participation in illegal activities. 291

TODAY'S CHALLENGES IN CRIMINAL JUSTICE

14

CHAPTER SUMMARY & LEARNING OUTCOMES

1 Explain how the U.S. Supreme Court has interpreted the Second Amendment's right to "bear arms."

The Supreme Court has ruled that most individuals do have a constitutional right to purchase and own firearms. The Court has made clear, however, that the government can restrict this right to promote public safety, thus allowing for laws that prohibit criminals and the mentally ill from owning guns.

2 Identify three important trends in international terrorism.

(a) Terrorists have developed more efficient methods of financing their operations. (b) Terrorists have developed more efficient organizations based on the small-business model. (c) Terrorists have exploited new communications technology to mount global campaigns.

3 Distinguish cyber crime from "traditional" crime.

Most cyber crimes are not "new" types of crimes. Rather, they are traditional crimes committed in cyberspace. Perpetrators of cyber crimes are often aided by certain aspects of the Internet, such as its ability to cloak the user's identity and its effectiveness as a conduit for transferring—or stealing—large amounts of information very quickly.

4 Outline the three major reasons why the Internet is conducive to the dissemination of child pornography.

The Internet provides (a) a quick way to transmit child pornography from providers to consumers; (b) security such as untraceable e-mails and password-protected Web sites and chat rooms; and (c) anonymity for buyers and sellers of child pornography.

5 Indicate some of the ways that white-collar crime is different from violent or property crime.

A wrongdoer committing a standard crime usually uses physical means to get somewhere he or she legally should not be in order to do something clearly illegal. Also, the victims of violent and property crimes are usually easily identifiable. In contrast, a white-collar criminal usually has legal access to the crime scene where he or she is doing something seemingly legitimate. Furthermore, victims of white-collar crimes are often unknown or unidentifiable.

Reuters/Jim Urquhart

CHAPTER 14 QUIZ ANSWERS

1. Background check
2. Mental illness
3. Nonstate
4. Crimes
5. Enemy combatants
6. Identity
7. Botnets
8. Intellectual property
9. Trust
10. Compliance

KEY TERMS

Background Checks An investigation of a person's history to determine whether that person should be allowed a certain privilege, such as the ability to possess a firearm. 304

Botnet A network of computers that have been appropriated without the knowledge of their owners and used to spread harmful programs via the Internet; short for *robot network*. 318

Compliance The state of operating in accordance with governmental standards. 323

Corporate Violence Physical harm to individuals or the environment that occurs as the result of corporate policies or decision making. 323

Cyberattack An attempt to damage or disrupt computer systems or electronic networks operated by computers. 312

Cyber Crime A crime that occurs online, in the virtual community of the Internet, as opposed to in the physical world. 314

Cyber Fraud Any misrepresentation knowingly made over the Internet with the intention of deceiving another and on which a reasonable person would and does rely to his or her detriment. 315

Cyberstalking The crime of stalking, committed in cyberspace through the use of e-mail, text messages, or another form of electronic communication. 317

Enemy Combatant An individual who has supported foreign terrorist organizations such as al Qaeda that are engaged in hostilities against the military operations of the United States. 310

Gun Control Efforts by a government to regulate or control the sale of firearms. 304

Hacker A person who uses one computer to break into another. 318

Identity Theft The theft of personal information, such as a person's name, driver's license number, or Social Security number. 315

Intellectual Property Property resulting from intellectual, creative processes. 318

Military Tribunal A court that is operated by the military rather than the criminal justice system and is presided over by military officers rather than judges. 311

Nonstate Actor An entity that plays a role in international affairs but does not represent any established state or nation. 306

Phishing Sending an unsolicited e-mail that falsely claims to be from a legitimate organization in an attempt to acquire sensitive information from the recipient. 316

Racketeering The criminal action of being involved in an organized effort to engage in illegal business transactions. 324

Regulation Governmental control of society through rules and laws that is generally carried out by administrative agencies. 323

Spam Bulk e-mails, particularly of commercial advertising, sent in large quantities without the consent of the recipient. 318

Virus A computer program that can replicate itself and interfere with the normal use of a computer. A virus cannot exist as a separate entity and must attach itself to another program to move through a network. 318

Weapon of Mass Destruction A weapon that has the capacity to cause large number of casualties or significant property damage. 310

Worm A computer program that can automatically replicate itself and interfere with the normal use of a computer. A worm does not need to be attached to an existing file to move from one network to another. 318

STUDY ONLINE WITH COURSEMATE www.cengagebrain.com

To help you refresh your understanding of each major chapter section **go online to access the relevant Self-Assessment quiz.** You'll know right away whether you need to go back and read that section again to cement your understanding of major concepts!